Ecuador Handbook

South American Handbook, the longest running
guidebook in the English language, has provided
generations of travellers with comprehensive coverage
of the entire continent. This Handbook is in
Footprint's series of new guides to the individual
countries of Latin America. The first to be published
are Handbooks to Peru, Chile and Ecuador &
Galápagos. These will be followed by guides to Brazil,
Colombia, Bolivia, Argentina and Venezuela.

You won't find a country with more natural wonders than Ecuador.

You won't find an airline with more flights to Latin America than the Iberia Group.

With its equatorial climate and towering volcano cones reaching heights of over 5,000 metres – not to mention the spectacular wildlife of the Galapagos Islands – few countries have more to offer the adventurer than Ecuador.

And of course, with our Circular Fares which give you the freedom to travel throughout Latin America as you please, no one proves a better travelling companion than the Iberia Group.

To book, call Iberia Group Reservations on **0171-830 0011** or contact your specialist travel agent.

Leading the way to Latin America.

Ecuador
& Galápagos
Handbook

Alan Murphy

Latin America series editor:Ben Box

Footprint Handbooks

*They passed the snow-covered peak of Chimborazo,
cold in the moonlight and the constant wind of the
high Andes. The view from the high mountain pass
seemed from another, larger planet than Earth.*

William Burroughs *Queer* (1985)

Footprint Handbooks

6 Riverside Court, Lower Bristol Road
Bath BA2 3DZ England
T 01225 469141 F 01225 469461
E mail handbooks@footprint.cix.co.uk
www.fooprint-handbooks.co.uk

ISBN 0 900751 83 5 ISSN 1363-7398
CIP DATA: A catalogue record for this book is
available from the British Library

In North America, published by

🛇 **PASSPORT BOOKS**

a division of *NTC/Contemporary Publishing Company*
Lincolnwood, Illinois USA

4255 West Touhy Avenue, Lincolnwood
(Chicago), Illinois 60646-1975, USA
T 847 679 5500 F 847 679 24941
E mail NTCPUB2@AOL.COM

ISBN 0-8442-4915-7
Library of Congress Catalog Card
Number: 96-72523
Passport Books and colophon are registered
trademarks of NTC Publishing group

©Footprint Handbooks Limited
1st Edition
February 1997

**Every effort has been made to ensure that
the facts in this Handbook are accurate.
However travellers should still obtain
advice from consulates, airlines etc about
current travel and visa requirements and
conditions before travelling. The authors
and publishers cannot accept responsibility
for any loss, injury or inconvenience,
however caused.**

Cover design by Newell and Sorrell; cover
photography by Life File/C Klein, Tony Morrison/
South American Pictures and Life File/Nigel
Sitwell

Production: Design by Mytton Williams;
Typesetting by Jo Morgan, Ann Griffiths and
Melanie Mason-Fayon; Maps by Sebastian
Ballard, Alasdair Dawson and Kevin Feeney;
Charts by Ann Griffiths; Original line drawings
by Andrew Newton and Katy Box; Proofread
by Rod Gray and David Cotterell.

Printed and bound in Great Britain by
Clays Ltd., Bungay, Suffolk

Contents

The Editors

Alan Murphy

Like Scott of the Antarctic 100 years before, Alan Murphy's 'Voyage of Discovery' originated in the Scottish city of Dundee. Having ended a career in journalism with local publishing giant, DC Thomson in order to put some letters after his name, Alan then left his native Scotland for the steamy jungles of South America, informing family and friends that he "might be gone for some time".

He travelled extensively throughout the continent, particularly in Ecuador where he developed a deep and lasting affection for the country and its people, finally leaving to take up residence in La Paz and a job writing for the fledgling Bolivian Times newspaper.

Now living in London, Alan's growing involvement with Footprint Handbooks means that he can continue his relationship with this most fascinating of countries.

Ben Box

A doctorate in medieval Spanish and Portugese studies provided very few job prospects for Ben Box, but a fascination for all things Latin. While studying for his degree, Ben travelled extensively in Spain and Portugal. He turned his attention to contemporary Iberian and Latin American affairs in 1980, beginning a career as a freelance writer at that time. He contributed regularly to national newspapers and learned tomes, and after increasing involvement with the *South American Handbook*, became its editor in 1989. Although he has travelled from the

US/Mexico border to southern Chile (not all in one go) and in the Caribbean, Ben recognizes that there are always more places to explore. He also edits the *Mexico and Central American Handbook* and is series editor for Footprint Handbook's Latin American titles. To seek diversion from a household immersed in Latin America, he plays village cricket in summer and cycles the lanes of Suffolk.

Jean Brown

Jean Brown came to Ecuador 20 years ago and is a founder member of the South American Explorers Club in Quito. She taught for many years at the American School in Quito and also worked with Presley Norton at the Salango Museum. Now a part owner of Safari tours, Jean boasts an encyclopaedic knowledge of Ecuador and is currently writing a guide to Hot Springs. Jean researched the Southern Sierra, Oriente, Central Sierra, Pacific Coast and Quito; she wrote the articles on Birdwatching and Hot Springs. She also supplied many maps and provided much general guidance.

Specialist contributors

Peter Pollard for geography; Dr Nigel Dunstone (University of Durham) for flora and fauna; Dr Jonathan D Kent (Metropolitan State College of Denver) for archaeology; Charlie Nurse for history; Ben Box for literature; Dr Valerie Fraser (University of Essex) for fine art and sculpture; Nigel Gallop for music and dance; Sarah Cameron for the economy section; Mark Duffy and Simon Harvey for adventure tourism; Ashley

8

Rawlings for motorcycling; Hallam Murray for cycling; Richard Robinson for world wide radio information; Dr David Snashall for health; Deidre Platt for her contribution on the Pacific coastal landscape.

For specific contributions to the text: Daisy and Robert Kunstaetter hail from Ecuador and Canada, respectively. Having lived and travelled throughout Latin America since 1983, they currently make their home in Quito where they edit *The Latin American Travel Advisor* and produce a travel programme for short-wave radio. They are regional correspondents for the *South American Handbook* and authors of the *Pocket Guide to Ecuador*. Daisy and Robert can be reached on the Internet at LATA@pi.pro.ec. They researched and helped to write the Central Sierra, Guayaquil and the Southern Lowlands, and provided many maps. Information on the Galápagos Islands was provided by David Horwell, tour guide and author of *Galápagos: the enchanted isles*, and David Gayton of Safari Tours, Quito. David lived on the Galápagos for 6 years where he maintained boats for one of the major tour companies. He has his captain's papers and has sailed around the Atlantic and Caribbean, as well as the Galápagos. Information on Quito, Northern Ecuador, the Central Sierra, the Southern Sierra and the Oriente was contributed by the South American Explorers Club, in particular Melanie Ebertz and Damaris Carlisle. Lucy Davies and Mo Fini (Tumi) for permission to use material from *Arts and Crafts of South America*. Simon Harvey and Mark Duffy who helped in researching Northern Ecuador.

Writing to the editor

Many people write to us - with corrections, new information, or simply comments. If you want to let us know something, we would be delighted to hear from you. Please give us as precise information as possible, quoting the edition and page number of the Handbook you are using and send as early in the year as you can. Your help will be greatly appreciated, especially by other travellers. In return we will send you details about our special guidebook offer.

For hotels and restaurants, please let us know:

- each establishment's name, address, phone and fax number
- number of rooms, whether a/c or air-cooled, attached (clean?) bathroom
- location - how far from the station or bus stand, or distance (walking time) from a prominent landmark
- if it's not already on one of our maps, can you place it?
- your comments - either good or bad - as to why it is distinctive
- tariff cards
- local transport used

For places of interest:

- location
- entry, camera charge
- access - by whatever means of transport is most approriate, eg time of main buses or trains to and from the site, journey time, fare
- facilities - nearby drinks stalls, restaurants, for the disabled
- any problems, eg steep climb, wildlife, unofficial guides
- opening hours
- site guides

Introduction and hints

ASK MOST PEOPLE what they know of Ecuador and they will probably mention a group of islands lying due west which inspired a humble Englishman to change the face of modern biology. The Galápagos now attract more than the occasional passing scientist. Tourists flock here in droves to marvel at the islands' unique wildlife.

Tourism is no stranger to other parts of this country, one of the smallest in South America. Its compact and manageable size is, in fact, one of its attractions. Here you can watch dawn break over the jungle canopy, have lunch high in the Andean mountains in the capital, Quito, then watch the sun slip into the Pacific Ocean while dining on the finest of seafood. All in the same day!

Given a few weeks, even the most unhurried of visitors can enjoy Ecuador's most popular attractions: the many volcanoes, its traditional Andean markets, colonial architecture, Inca ruins, jungle and, of course, those famous islands.

Now a new form of tourism is beginning to sweep the country. Ecotourism is designed to protect Ecuador's precious natural assets from the demands of modern industrial society and to preserve the rich cultural heritage.

In the northern jungle province of Napo, for example, the native Huaorani are beginning to assert their rights, thanks to the work of more enlightened tour operators. Environmentally and culturally sensitive tourists can now visit remote indigenous communities happy in the knowledge that their money is helping to defend Huaorani interests in the face of the oil and timber industries.

On the Manabí coast tour agencies are working to protect the few remaining areas of fragile mangroves from the thriving shrimp industry while successful local conservation schemes have ensured miles of pristine beaches. Ecuador's coastline offers other diversions: boat trips to watch mating humpback whales in its warm waters and, in the hot and steamy province of Esmeraldas, a canoe can be taken up river deep into primary rainforest for the nature trip of a lifetime.

This small, yet diverse country may be best known for its 'Enchanted Islands', as the invading Spaniards named them, but visitors will find the rest of Ecuador just as enchanting and equal to the demands of the most adventurous or conscientious of people.

Ecuador

Where to go

Weather permitting, travelling around Ecuador is easy. Air services are quite extensive and flight tickets do not cost a great deal. The road network is generally good, running down the Andean spine connecting all major cities and towns. Paved roads link the highlands and the Pacific Lowlands, with several alternatives between Quito and Guayaquil, the two principal commercial centres. From Guayaquil, the coastal route S to Peru is a major artery. From Guayaquil N, the route does not run unbroken to San Lorenzo near the Colombian border. Two stretches (Cojimíes-Muisne, La Tola-Limones-San Lorenzo) have to be done by boat. A new road from San Lorenzo to Ibarra, although still subject to washouts, will eventually replace the adventurous railway journey on the same route. On the eastern side of the Andes, the roads are less good in the Oriente (Amazonian Lowlands). In addition, one of the main access routes, Baños-Puyo, is currently being rebuilt and disruption can be expected for quite some time. Beyond the roads' end, at Coca, Lago Agrio or Misahuallí, transport is by boat on the tributaries of the Amazon.

One of the most spectacular railway lines in the world is Guayaquil to Quito, rising from the fertile flatlands to the corridor of volcanoes that stand above the Andean plateau. Renowned for its engineering and views, this line should be travelled, if only in part, as a highlight of any visit to Ecuador.

PLACES TO VISIT

As the introduction above indicates, Ecuador is small enough to allow you to traverse the country E to W (or vice versa) in a day. Such a whistle-stop itinerary would only be for those with an overloaded agenda and is not for those wishing to learn about the place. However, the possibility of doing this underlines the difficulty of suggesting itineraries for the visitor. There are just too many alternatives. Much better is to point out some of the highlights in each region and let the reader mix-and-match the options according to the time available and his/her interests. The following list should only be treated as the basis from which to embark on a great variety of excursions and activities. The main body of the text that follows enlarges upon these suggestions to the full.

QUITO

The capital has two distinct cities: the colonial, with most of the renowned churches and historic buildings, and the new city. There is a wide range of museums and it is the language course capital of South America. Just about any type of holiday or activity can be arranged here. Excursions include a range of day trips, including to nature reserves and climbing. If not on a language course, a week could be spent in Quito without exhausting the possibilities.

NORTH OF QUITO

Most visitors head for Otavalo, either just for its famous market (1½ hrs from Quito by road), or to explore handicraft centres nearby, and natural sites such as Lake Cuicocha. Alternatively, you can stay in Ibarra, a bit further N; this is the starting point for the trip to San Lorenzo on the coast. There are several nature reserves in this area. 3-4 days can easily be spent in Otavalo and surroundings. There are also several hiking possibilities.

SOUTH OF QUITO

As you travel S of the capital down the Andes, you will encounter: Cotopaxi National Park (minimum 1 day, or longer if you wish to climb the volcano); the town

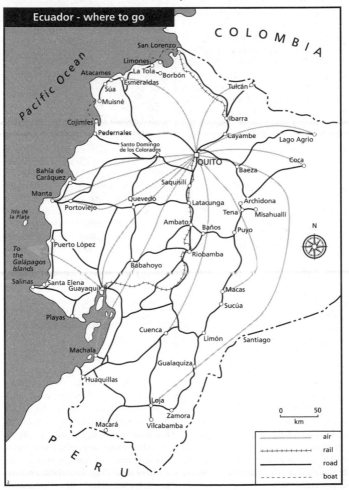

Ecuador - where to go

of Latacunga (2 hrs from Quito) and the
Quilotoa circuit for small villages and a
trip to a volcanic crater (1 day with a car,
longer without); Saquisilí market (Thur
– 2½ hrs from Quito, 1 day); Baños, a very
popular spa with hiking and climbing
nearby (3½ hrs from Quito, 1 day in town,
1 day round about, or more if climbing);
the provincial capital of Riobamba (3½
hrs from Quito), trains run from here to
Guayaquil and, twice a week, to Quito;
close by is the mountain of Chimborazo
for climbing. Ingapirca, Ecuador's principal Inca ruin is between Riobamba and
Cuenca (2 hrs from Cuenca); allow a day
for a visit by public transport. Cuenca
itself is the heart of the southern Sierra
(10 hrs from Quito by bus, 45 mins by
air); 1-2 days can be spent here, visiting
its churches and museums. Nearby is the
national park of El Cajas National Recreational Area. Routes S of Cuenca go to
the provincial capital of Loja (4½ hrs
from Cuenca) and Vilcabamba, a further
1½ hrs. From Loja the Podocarpus National Park can be reached. 2-3 days can
be spent in the area. **NB** The suggested
visiting times are minimums and can be
extended, either in the places mentioned
or in the many towns and villages in
between.

GUAYAQUIL

Guayaquil is 45 mins by air from Quito;
by bus 8 hrs, or 5½ hrs from Cuenca, 5
from Riobamba (or 12 hrs by train). Not
itself favoured by many tourists, but it
does have its attractions. To Peru is 4 hrs
by road from Guayaquil via Machala. The
Manglares-Churute ecological reserve is on this route.

THE PACIFIC COAST

From Guayaquil it is 2 hrs W to resorts
like Playas and 2½ to Salinas. In the
extreme W is the Santa Elena peninsula.
Northwards the coast has a variety of
places: the Valdivia area with precolumbian associations; Puerto López and the

Machalilla National Park (about 4½ hrs
from Guayaquil). The Park has lots of
different attractions (including the Isla
La Plata) and in the vicinity is the famous
Alandaluz ecologically-based tourist
complex. The next town is Manta (Quito
9 hrs by bus, also air; Guayaquil 6 hrs). 3
hrs N of Manta is Bahía de Caráquez, a
resort on the estuary of the Río Chone
with some interesting natural attractions
(Isla de Fragatas – frigate birds) and evidence of the clash between mangroves
and shrimp farms. As you continue N
there are little towns and banana ports,
then the northern beaches of Same, Súa
and Atacames, the last named 40 mins by
road before Esmeraldas (Quito 5-6 hrs,
or air 30 mins; Guayaquil 7 hrs). North
of Esmeraldas are La Tola, Limones and
Borbón, with access into the coastal river
jungles and the Cotacachi-Cayapas National Park. Suggested lengths of stay in
any one place on the coast are not easy to
quantify as it depends how much time
you want to spend lazing on the beach,
how many stop-offs you wish to make and
how much time you want to dedicate to
the natural and cultural sites of interest.
A week should be sufficient for a general
impression, but again there is ample
scope for further exploration.

THE ORIENTE

There are three main access routes: 1)
Quito-Baeza-Lago Agrio (10-11 hrs from
Quito by road, also flights), or Coca
(Quito 10 hrs, or flights); from either
place there are jungle tours. From Baeza
a road also goes to Archidona and Tena
(jungle tours), thence to Misahuallí (6
hrs from Baeza, 8 from Quito), jungle
tours from here too. 2) Baños-Puyo (when
the road is in use), for jungle tours, or
access to Misahuallí. Also from Puyo you
can continue S to Macas, which can also
be reached from Cuenca (11 hrs). 3) Loja-
Zamora (2½ hrs), then head N via
Gualaquiza to Macas. The southern Oriente is less developed, but tourist interest

in the region is growing. Each of these routes descends from the highlands to the lowland jungle, passing through fine scenery. There is some scope for lingering on the descent. Once in the lowlands, the more wildlife you wish to see, the further you have to go by boat from the end of the road. Trips to jungle lodges, which offer the best opportunities to see the jungle, should be of at least two nights because the boat ride into and out of any lodge's vicinity is time-consuming.

THE GALAPAGOS

This is the final area of the country; there is no need to detail its attractions here. It is 2½ hrs by air from Guayaquil. Trips to the Islands are a minimum of 3 days/4 nights; 7 days allows time to see more islands.

ADVENTURE TOURISM

Ecuador's size and varied topography make it an ideal destination in which to sample several different adventure activities within a 3 or 4 week holiday. A reliable and efficient transport system ensures easy access to all areas of the country. In comparison to other South American destinations, it is still relatively cheap to hire the equipment needed for outdoor activities. Adventure tourism appears to be fairly established owing mainly to Ecuador's popularity with foreign tourists. Mountaineering and trekking still remain the most popular outdoor pursuits and rafting is gaining in popularity throughout the country.

MOUNTAINEERING

Ecuador's mountains are one of its greatest attractions. There are 10 summits over 5,000m, and **Chimborazo** at 6,310m, is one of the highest peaks in the Andes. (For access, see page 196).

The 'Avenue of the Volcanoes' runs through the Central Sierra south of Quito and offers climbs of varying

degrees of difficulty. **Cotopaxi** (5,897m), the world's highest active volcano, and Chimborazo are two of the most promoted mountains on itineraries offered by tourist agencies in Quito and overseas. Cotopaxi (see page 164) is on most travellers' list of trekking peaks and though it is not a technical climb, it is strenuous nonetheless and it is advisable to take a qualified guide. For many, Cotopaxi is their first experience of high altitude trekking and it is vital to have spent at least a few days acclimatizing before attempting the climb.

Of the more technical climbs (for professional mountaineers only) **Antisana** (5,705m) is considered one of the most difficult climbs in the country, especially the N-W and S summits (see page 297).

Cayambe (5,790m) is becoming more popular thanks to the completion of a better access road to the *refugio*. It is heavily crevassed and good ice climbing experience is necessary (see page 138). **Illiniza Sur** (5,305m) is also a top grade ice climb and should not be attempted by those without proper experience (see page 164). Another difficult technical climb is **El Altar** (5,315m) (see page 197). An easier technical climb is **Carihuairazo** (5,020m), which is near Chimborazo (see page 188).

There are many possibilities for experienced climbers to explore new routes but good advice should be sought from the Mountain Guide Association or the better adventure tour operators.

For those who find the thought of crampons, ice axe and harness a daunting prospect, there are several mountains and extinct volcanoes within a 2-hour drive S of Quito. In Cotopaxi National Park, **Rumiñahui** (4,722m) and **Sincholagua** (4,919m) are two ideal peaks for those who wish to experience the Ecuadorian *páramo*. (For access to Rumiñahui see page 165). Both can be climbed easily on day excursions from the capital and offer wonderful views across the Sierra to the surrounding snow-capped cones. They are excellent 'warm-up' climbs and anyone considering the more ambitious heights of Cotopaxi, Cayambe or Chimborazo would do well to acclimatize here first.

Other acclimatization climbs are: Fuya Fuya, near Lagunas de Mojanda; Imbabura, near Otavalo; Atacazo, S of Quito; Pasochoa, the Pichinchas and the Puntas. Also good for acclimatization is the trek from Papallacta to Sincholagua (which reaches 4,500m) and from Cangahua to Oyacachi (with cloudforest and thermal baths en route).

ASEGUIM

The Ecuadorian Association of Mountain Guides (ASEGUIM), was formed in 1993 in response to the growing demand from local and international climbers to regulate climbing in the country. A highly professional organization, made up of Ecuadorian and foreign climbers, many of whom have climbed internationally, the association aims to give the best possible advice about climbing Ecuador's peaks.

Rock and ice climbing courses on Cayambe, Cotopaxi and Chimborazo are also offered. A basic course in ice climbing costs US$110. There is usually only one per year, but ASEGUIM might organize others if there is sufficient interest; ie if a reasonable number of tourists organize themselves into a group.

Members of the association who wish to become guides undergo training to meet strict international standards. There is a 2-year course to become an assistant guide, the 'Diploma de Aspirante a Guía', which entitles the guide to accompany a fully-fledged ASEGUIM guide. To become a full guide requires a further 2 years. Apart from climbing techniques, this covers flora and fauna, archaeology, tourism, ecology, avalanche training and rescue techniques. Thus far, there are around 40 ASEGUIM guides and 60 assistant guides.

A rescue service is available which is free for groups or individuals who have contracted a guide from the association. The usual cost is around US$1,500 per rescue. All guides carry 2-way radio and keep in contact with the centres in Quito, Riobamba, Ambato, Latacunga and Baños in order to coordinate rescue. There is no helicopter rescue and, as yet, little cooperation from the army, police or government, though ASEGUIM is trying to work with the state tourism department, CETUR, to disseminate information on the mountains and recommend guides for tourists and mountaineers.

Despite the obstacles, this is an excellent service in a country where relying on the state for assistance in an emergency can be a slow and extremely costly experience. Eight ASEGUIM guides have been trained in ice and rescue techniques at Chamonix. There is a magazine, *Informativo ASEGUIM*, which comes out twice a year, usually Feb/March and Sept/Oct. It has course dates, a calendar of events and articles on climbs, rescue etc.

NB Many of the guides in Baños have refused to join the ASEGUIM guiding programme, with the result that there is no regulation and many 'cowboy' operators exist. Some guides who haven't joined are, however, very experienced, but ask advice.

ASEGUIM is at Calle Juan Larrea 657 y Rio de Janeiro, near Escuela Espejo, just off Parque El Ejido, open 0830-1230, or PO Box 17-03-357, Quito, F 568-664. The President is Rafael Martínez and he is in the office most mornings for advice.

Equipment

Several agencies and outdoor equipment shops in Quito rent gear. Although prices per item are roughly similar, it is worth shopping around to check quality. Many climbing parties leave behind rope, harnesses etc, but these should be checked for obvious flaws. Seek advice from the more established tour agencies.

Mountain refuges (refugios)

These are mainly of international standard with many improvements in recent years. Most provide the basic services: electric light; running water; and cooking facilities. They usually have a warden throughout the main climbing season. Nightly tariffs are usually US$10 (mid-1996).

Climate and seasons

East facing slopes are generally colder and wetter. Glaciers start at 4,700m on the eastern flanks of mountains, except Cayambe, Chimborazo and Carihuairazo, where they start lower down. On the other flanks they start at 5,000m, except Cayambe and Chimborazo. The snow state is unpredictable in the tropical zones and does not change clearly by season.

The best times are: Nov-Jan, when the climate is stable and there is little rain; July-Aug, there is some rain and sometimes high winds from the Amazon; also May-June, which is not too wet and windy.

Reading

Mountaineering journals include: *Campo Abierto* (not produced by the Travel Agency of the same name), an annual magazine on expeditions, access to mountains etc, US$1; *Montaña* is the annual magazine of the *Colegio San Gabriel* mountaineering club, US$1.50.

Recommended books are: *Montañas del Sol*, by Marcos Serrano, Iván Rojar and Freddy Landazuri, Ediciones Campo Abierto, 1994; it covers 20 main mountains and is an excellent introduction, it costs US$5; *Cotopaxi: Mountain of Light*, by Freddy Landazuri, Ediciones Campo Abierto, 1994, in English and Spanish, is a thorough history of the mountain. *The High Andes, A Guide for climbers*, by John Biggar (Castle Douglas, Kirkcudbrightshire, Scotland: Andes, 1996), has a chapter on Ecuador.

TREKKING

There is sometimes a very fine line between climbing and trekking. Some of the more popular volcanoes, such as Cotopaxi and Tungurahua, are strenuous but not technical, despite needing rope and proper equipment. Many travellers who have never climbed before are tempted by these high altitude 'treks' and, as long as the person is in good physical condition and properly acclimatized, there is no reason why any keen enthusiast should not attempt them. However, a guide is strongly recommended.

The opportunities for trekking are plentiful. Cotopaxi National Park is very popular, camping is possible and trips of several days' duration can easily be organized.

The Oriente is also a very popular area, particularly for those looking for the authentic jungle experience, and trips can be arranged with relative ease from Quito, Misahuallí or Tena. If arranging tours from any of these centres, it is worth visiting different agencies to see what's on offer, check the quality of the guides and, most importantly, try to find out whether or not the tour operator places an emphasis on 'responsible' tourism. All too often agencies spring up whose sole interest is financial gain. As always, in a popular destination like Ecuador it is worth checking with other travellers about routes, guides and agencies. Some of the bigger tour operators offer 'combination' trips which include mountain biking, rafting and trekking.

DIVING

The coast of Ecuador is a paradise for divers, combining both cool and warm water dive destinations in one of the most biologically diverse marine environments on earth.

The Galápagos Islands are undoubtedly the most popular destination, but diving in lesser known waters such as those off the central coast of Ecuador has been gaining in popularity in recent years. The secluded coves of Isla La Plata, 45 km off the coast of Machalilla National Park, contain an abundance of multicoloured tropical fish which make diving and snorkelling a great experience. Colonies of sea lions can be seen, as well as migrating humpback whales, from late June to Oct, and many species of marine birds.

The Galápagos Islands are well known for their distinctive marine environments and offer more than 20 dive sites including opportunities for night diving – especially Tagus cove on the island of Isabela (Albemarle). Each island contains its own unique environment and many are home to underwater life forms endemic to this part of the world; seahorses, rare coral and the Galápagos marine iguana to name but a few.

Diving is becoming more popular with tourists since the cost of doing a PADI course in Ecuador is relatively low (or elsewhere in South America). There are several agencies in Quito which feature diving and full instruction on their programmes. Equipment can be hired easily from most of the adventure tour operators, but it is advisable to check everything thoroughly. The larger bookshops also stock diving books and identification guides for fish and other marine life.

Among the agencies specializing in diving are *Metropolitan Touring* (see page 117 for address), and *Tropic Ecological Adventures* (see page 118). See also the Galápagos chapter for diving agencies in Puerto Ayora.

RAFTING

Rafting has been high on the agenda of adventure tour operators in Ecuador for quite a few years now. The geography of the country could not be more suitable for this exciting, action-packed experi-

ence. Rivers born high in the western Andes flow to the Pacific Ocean, offering all classes of rafting from grades I to V, and the opportunity to see the gradual changes in vegetation from cloudforest to tropical jungle in descents of up to 2,000m.

In the north, the rivers Blanco and Toachi are within easy reach of Quito and are the most popular with Quito-based agencies. They offer rapids of varying degrees of difficulty, according to season. They are suitable for the novice keen to experience rafting for the first time, to the experienced professional looking for all the excitement of a grade V run.

The Oriente, particularly the province of Napo, offers some of the best rafting in the country, with grades III to V on the Río Quijos, one of the most spectacular rivers in the country. Warm waters in the Oriente are an added advantage. The Río Pastaza also offers top grade runs according to season. Tena is the base for many rafting trips in the province of Napo. Many rivers in Napo offer different grades from I to V. The rivers Napo and Anzu are appropriate for beginners with rapids ranging from grades I to III. The Misahuallí and Alto Napo (also known as the Río Jatunyacu) have rapids ranging from grades III to V.

The best season is from the end of Dec to the end of May when waters are highest, thereby ensuring more secure descents. Outside this period, waters can be much lower and rocks present problems for boats.

There is no shortage of agencies in Quito featuring rafting on their itineraries. *Sierra Nevada* (see page 117) is one of the most professional; their guides are French-trained and their equipment of top quality European standard. In Tena, Gynner Coronel runs *Ríos Ecuador* and has several years experience of operating in Ecuador. *Row Expediciones*, a North American rafting company, has been offering rafting tours in the country since 1979. Prices are fairly constant; expect to pay US$60-70 per day, which includes transport, guides and usually breakfast before departure. Most boats have a guide and between four and six crew members. As with most adventure activities, there are many outfits offering rafting and it is worth checking with other travellers and spending some time shopping around.

Note that, despite the fun and experience, rafting is not considered the most environmentally-friendly of adventure sports. Boats with crews of screaming enthusiasts racing their way down river cause a lot of noise pollution, scaring wildlife on the way, particularly through jungle areas. Though most of the guides are highly professional and responsible, do make sure that, if you picnic along the way, you take all your rubbish with you. Remember that many of the rivers run through pristine highland or jungle territory.

MOUNTAIN BIKING

Needless to say, in a mountainous country like Ecuador there is ample opportunity to practice this increasingly popular activity. Most specialist tour operators can advise on the best areas. If they don't offer mountain biking themselves, they can put you in touch with those who know. It is worth contacting ASEGUIM, the mountain guide association (see above), as they can advise on strenuous rides which can be combined with high altitude treks as part of an acclimatization programme before attempting the higher peaks.

Trips lasting 1 day to 1 week or more can easily be arranged and there are a number of outdoor equipment shops that hire equipment. The more adventurous can make up their own itineraries following advice from locals.

Most popular routes near Quito
1. Calderón-Guallabamba-Quinche-

Tumbaco: this is difficult because of its 80 km length. The best stretch is the 46 km between Quinche and Tumbaco along old railway lines and through tunnels.
2. The 40 km descent from Refugio Machachi on Cotopaxi through the National Park is a popular trip.
3. The Circuito El Burro, from Quito to Mitad del Mundo, goes through rough terrain in a dry, harsh landscape.
4. The Pululahua Volcano is 40 km from Quito; a 3-3½-hr circuit which can be muddy.
5. Valle Tumbaco/Hilalo is 4 hrs up and down. It is steep and difficult with many holes on the trail.
6. Lagunas de Mojanda, from Tolas to the Pirámides Cochasqui archaeological site, is very scenic; 9 km one way, return on the same track.
7. Other routes are: Paschoa/Sangolquí, 35 km up and down; and to the Antenna de Pichincha, though it's advisable to go in a group of three or more to deter robbers.

Competitions
There are two every month from Quito. The most used courses are: Calderón to Guallabamba along the old route; Antennas de Cerro Monjas; and Pululahua.

Agencies
Bike Tech, Andagoya 498 y Ruiz de Castilla, owners Santiago and Regis have informal 'meets' every Sun; anyone is welcome; no charge. They ride 20 or more routes around Quito, including the above mentioned. They also have a good repair shop and cheap parts. They are friendly and glad to advise on routes.
Biking Dutchman, Mountain Bike Tours, Foch 714 y Juan León Mera, T 542-806, T/F 449-568, run 1-day and 2-day tours: eg Lagunas Mojanda to Ibarra; Cotopaxi to Quilatoa crater; Papallacta to San Rafael falls; Antisana volcano.
Pedal Andes, T 220-674, E-mail: explorer@saec.org.ec, run back-road mountain bike tours, cultural as well as

physical, highly rec, can combine with whitewater rafting.

See Quito section, page 117, for bike shops.

SKIING

Skiing is not yet an organized activity in Ecuador, although there are plans to build a ski lift on Carihuairazo (5,116m). A few interested Europeans resident in Quito have skied some of the glaciers. Until such time as a ski lift is built, interested groups will have to contend with spending hours trudging up the mountains with full gear in order to enjoy a 20-30-min descent. For those who wish to find out more about skiing, it is best to contact ASEGUIM or one of the specialist tour operators.

PARAPENTING

This is a relatively new addition to Ecuador's list of activities. *Escuela Pichincha* have an office at Carlos Endara 160, near the airport, T 256-592, 455-076, F 444-594. They offer 8-day courses for US$350, which includes 70 flights near Quito (though no tandem flights as it is too dangerous for landing), minimum of three people; or every Sat over 3 months for the same price. They also sell equipment, which is cheaper than in Europe.

FISHING

Though not everyone's idea of an adventure sport, fishing is possible in the lakes of the central Sierra, N and S of Quito, and in the rivers of the Oriente. This is more popular with locals than with tourists, but excursions can, nevertheless, be organized. The lakes near Papallacta offer excellent trout fishing, but recent work by the state water company means the area is out of bounds at present (until mid-1997).

Recommended lakes and rivers N of Quito are Lagunas del Voladero, near El Angel, and Lagunas San Marcos, Mojanda and Cojos, all near Imbabura. S of Quito are Lagunas de Secos and Lagunas de Mica or Micacocha, both near Pintag, and Río Chalupas, at Cotopaxi. In the Oriente is the Río Quijos (W of Lago Agrio and E of El Chaco beyond Baeza), Río Casanga (W of Casanga) and Laguna Pañacocha, E of Coca.

How to go

WHEN TO GO

In the northern and central Sierra, the best time is May to Sept; in the southern Sierra Aug to Jan. The Pacific coast is best visited between Dec and June; even though this is the hottest, wettest time on the coastal plain, the beach is usually dry. From June to Sept, a sea mist (*garúa*) hangs over the coast, so this is not a good time to visit this part of the country. In the Oriente rain can fall at any time, but it is wettest from April to September. The Galápagos are hot from Jan to April, when heavy showers are likely; from May to Sept is the cooler *garúa* season.

HOW TO GET THERE

International flights into the country arrive either at Quito or Guayaquil. Unless going immediately to the Galápagos from Guayaquil, it is advisable to start your visit in Quito. This is where you will find all the tourist information, travel agencies, language schools and the widest range of hotels and eating houses. If your flight only goes to Guayaquil (eg on some Latin American flights), there are frequent shuttle flights up to the capital if you do not want to go overland. Paris, Madrid, Amsterdam and Frankfurt are the European gateways for direct access to Ecuador. In the USA, Miami, New York and Houston are the main departure points. The country is also served from all points of Latin America.

The number of nationalities requiring a consular **visa** to visit Ecuador is very small (a major exception being the French). A tourist card has to be obtained on entry. 90 days (multiple entry) in any 365-day period is the maximum stay allowed in the country. Business visitors and students requiring more than 90 days should apply for a visa in their home country.

PRACTICALITIES

MONEY

The currency is the sucre and Ecuador has one of the most relaxed exchange rate regimes in Latin America. Changing US dollars (cash, travellers' cheques, or with a credit card) presents no problems, but it is wise to shop around for optimum rates. Only take dollars, though.

COMMUNICATIONS

Communications into and out of Ecuador are good by phone, fax, e-mail and courier and reasonably good by post. The official language is Spanish. In Quito there are many people who speak English and quite a few speak other European languages, but outside the capital, travelling without some knowledge of the local language would be a hindrance (see elsewhere in the text on language courses in Quito).

ONCE YOU ARE THERE

Ecuador is generally a **safe** country, although there are certain places in which you should take care: markets and bus stations everywhere, but also in Quito and Guayaquil. Away from crowded areas, however, visitors should find a warm welcome. There are **hotels** to suit every budget and in many places there are establishments which offer excellent value, particularly where foreign tourists go and foreigners have opened facilities (eg Otavalo, Baños). The same applies with restaurants. Away from the major cities, high-class hotels are few and far between, but this does not mean that only basic conditions are to be expected. In the jungle lowlands there are some first-class lodges to stay in, built in rustic style, but offering good standards of service, food and guiding. There are also nature reserves, some of which have lodging, which can be an interesting alternative to other types of places to stay.

In Quito you can find every style of **restaurant** since it has become such a cosmopolitan city. Seafood is very good, especially on the coast. Andean dishes tend to be based around maize and meat and are 'warming' to suit the altitude. To hot it up, add chili sauce.

MOVING AROUND

Because the country is not large and travelling times in many parts are not excessive, getting around is not difficult by public transport. **Motorists** may not be as accustomed to local conditions as the bus drivers, so a little care should be taken while getting used to the state of the roads and the traffic. Do not drive at night unless you absolutely have to. Saying that distances are not great should not imply that you can dash about, see plenty and then fly home. Many of the most interesting places require some effort to get to, either because they are not on paved roads, or because they are remote. This is especially true of the nature reserves. Their inaccessibility or unsuitability for agriculture is the prime reason for their becoming reserves (they are indicated in the text that follows) and they will only remain havens for bird, animal and plant life if they are not overrun by tourists.

Ecuador is a good country for **adventure tourism** and the options are detailed in the relevant section below. In this, as in other areas, obtaining information is straightforward and it is advisable to get it in advance, for prior planning will ensure that the season and accessibility match your interests and the time of your visit.

There is little point in giving indicators here on travel in the **Galápagos Islands**. Being a unique destination in every way, all the relevant facts and hints are given in the chapter dedicated to the islands themselves. It is worth noting, though, that if your itinerary is taking in both the Galápagos and Ecuador proper, you should prepare in such a way that non-essentials for your boat cruise can be left in safe keeping on the mainland, rather than cluttering up the restricted cabin space.

HEALTH

For anyone travelling overseas health is a key consideration. With sensible precautions the visitor to Ecuador should remain as healthy as at home. There are general rules to follow which should keep you in good health when travelling in Latin America. These are dealt with in detail in the full health section on pages 389.

KEEPING HEALTHY IN ECUADOR

Before you travel make sure the medical insurance you take out is adequate. Have a check-up with your doctor, if necessary and arrange your immunisations well in advance. Try ringing a specialist travel clinic if your own doctor is unfamiliar with health in Latin America. You would do well to be protected by immunisation against typhoid, polio, tetanus and hepatitis A. Yellow fever vaccination with a certificate is only required if you are coming from infected areas of the world or, for your own protection, you are visiting the Oriente.

Check malaria prophylaxis for lowlands rural areas to be visited, especially the Oriente and the Costa. Vaccination against cholera is not necessary, but occasionally immigration officials might ask to see a certificate.

WHILE YOU ARE TRAVELLING

The commonest affliction of visitors to Ecuador is probably traveller's diarrhoea. Shellfish are always a risk and so in Ecuador is *ceviche* (raw fish marinated in lime). They are all delicious, however, and should be safe in well run hygienic establishments. Fruit is plentiful and excellent, but ensure it is washed or peel it yourself. Avoid raw food, undercooked food (including eggs) and reheated food. Food that is cooked in front of you and offered hot all through is generally safe.

Tap water in Ecuador is unsafe to drink. The better hotels have their own water purification systems and in many restaurants you can get boiled water, water that has been filtered or, more popular these days, commercially bottled water. There are good doctors and reasonable hospitals in the major Ecuadorean cities, but don't expect good facilities away from the major centres.

Hospitals on the Galápagos Islands are rudimentary.

ALTITUDE AND CLIMATE

In Ecuador you can travel within a few hours by road or rail from sea level to 3,600m plus – enough to give you soroche if you have travelled directly from the coast. Quito stands at 2,850m which is enough to make you a bit breathless at first. If you are climbing higher, respect the altitude and follow the advice in the main health section. There are various local remedies such as *mate de coca* – particularly popular in the Highlands, helpful and perfectly legal.

You will not be surprised to hear that Ecuador, considering its latitude, can be extremely hot, almost entirely dependent on altitude. Keep up your fluid intake. It is also extremely cold at high altitude, so take appropriate clothing and do not forget about sun protection at altitude, where the ultraviolet rays are particularly strong.

RETURNING HOME

Report any symptoms to your doctor and say exactly where you have been. Keep taking anti-malarial tablets for 6 weeks after leaving the malarial area.

Horizons

THE LAND

GEOLOGY AND LANDSCAPE

Ecuador, named for its position on the equator, is the smallest country of South America after Uruguay and the Guianas. It is bounded by Colombia in the N, by Peru to the E and S, and by the Pacific Ocean to the W. Its population of 11.5 million is also small, but is larger than Bolivia and Paraguay as well as Uruguay and the Guianas. It has the highest density of any of the South American republics: 42 per square kilometre in 1995.

The border has been a source of conflict with its neighbours, and Ecuador lost a significant part of its former territory towards the Amazon to Peru in 1941-2. This border is still not stable and has not been satisfactorily defined. The latest armed conflict, though on a small scale, was around the headwaters of the Ríos Cenepa and Zamora in the SE of the country in early 1995.

The Galápagos Islands were annexed by Ecuador in 1832. They lie in the Pacific, 970 km W of the mainland, on the equator, and consist of six principal islands and numerous smaller islands and rocks totalling about 8,000 sq km and scattered over 60,000 sq km of ocean. They are the most significant island group in the eastern Pacific Ocean.

Structure

Geologically, Ecuador is the creation of the Andean mountain-building process, caused in turn by the South American Plate moving W, meeting the Nasca plate which is moving E and sinking beneath the continent. This process began in the late Cretaceous Period around 80 million years ago and has continued to the present day. Before this, and until as late as perhaps 25 million years ago, the Amazon basin tilted W and the river drained into the Pacific through what is now southern Ecuador.

The Andes between Peru and Colom-

bia are at their narrowest (apart from their extremities in Venezuela and southern Chile), ranging from 100-200 km in width. Nevertheless, they are comparatively high with one point, Chimborazo, over 6,000m and several others not much lower. Unlike Peru to the S, most of the peaks in Ecuador are volcanoes, and Cotopaxi is the highest active volcano in the world, at 5,897m. This suggests a fractured and unstable area beneath the surface. A dramatic example of this was an eruption of Cotopaxi in 1877 which was followed by a *nuée ardente* (literally, a burning cloud) which flowed down the side of the volcano engulfing many settlements. Snow and ice at the summit melted to create another volcanic phenomenon called a *lahar*, or mud flow, which almost reached Latacunga, 29 km from the cone.

The eastern third of the country is part of the Amazon basin filled with sedimentary deposits from the E, since the formation of the Andes, from the mountains to the W. The coastlands rise up to 1,000m and are mainly remnants of Tertiary basalts, similar to the base rocks of the Amazon basin on the other side of the Andes.

The Galápagos are not structurally connected to the mainland and, so far as is known, were never part of the South American Plate. They lie near the boundary between the Nasca Plate and the Cocos Plate to the N. A line of weakness, evidenced by a ridge of undersea lava flows, stretches SW from the coast of Panama. This meets another undersea ridge running along the equator from Ecuador but separated from the continental shelf by a deep trench. At this conjuncture appear the Galápagos. Volcanic activity here has been particularly intense and the islands are the peaks of structures that rise from 7,000m to 10,000m from the ocean floor. Fossil evidence suggests that Santa Cruz and Baltra are around 6 million years old and

lavas on Española have been dated at 2 million years old. In geological terms therefore, these islands have only recently appeared from the ocean and volcanic activity continues on at least five of the islands.

The Andes

The Andes form the backbone of the country. In Colombia to the N, three distinct ranges come together near Pasto and become orogenically active, with three volcanoes overlooking the border near Tulcán. Although it is essentially one range through Ecuador, there is a trough of between 1,800m and 3,000m above sea level running S for over 400 km with volcanoes, many active on either side. The snowline is at about 5,000m, and with at least 15 peaks over that height, this makes for a dramatic landscape. The climate in this trough is comfortable and it is a principal area of settlement, including Quito, the capital. Overlooking Quito to the W is Pichincha which was climbed in 1802 by Alexander Von Humboldt, the Prussian explorer and geologist, who, on his return to the city, was accused of causing an eruption of the volcano by throwing gunpowder into the crater. He climbed many other Ecuadorean volcanoes including Chimborazo where he reached over 6,000m (though not the top); the first recorded climb to this height. He suffered badly from altitude sickness, but correctly deduced that this was caused by a lack of oxygen. Incidentally, at that time, Chimborazo was believed to be the highest mountain in the world.

Further S, near Cuenca, is Volcán Sangay, 5,230m, which today is the most violently active of Ecuador's volcanoes. There are fewer volcanoes towards the Peruvian border and the scenery is less dramatic. The mountains rarely exceed 4,000m and the passes are as low as 2,200m. Although active volcanoes are concentrated in the northern half of the country, there are many places where there are sulphur baths or hot springs and the whole Andean area is seismically active with severe earthquakes from time to time.

The central trough is crossed by several transversal ranges of extruded volcanic material, creating separate basins. Due in the main to rain shadow effects, there is a wide range of climate in central Ecuador. In the N, the basins are higher and temperatures warm by day and cool at night. It rains mostly between Oct and May, Quito has an average of 1,300 mm per year. S of Quito, the basins are lower, the climate hotter and drier with semi-desert stretches. The lack of surface water is aggravated by large quantities of volcanic dust which is easily eroded by wind and water and can produce dry 'badland' topography. Landslides in this unstable and precipitous terrain are common. A serious example was in the Paute valley near Cuenca in 1993 when a hillside which had been intensively cultivated gave way in unusually heavy rains. An earth dam was formed which later collapsed causing further damage downstream. Near the border with Peru, the mountain climate can be very pleasant. Vilcabamba in Loja province is reputed to have a most favourable climate for a long and healthy life.

The Coast

West of the Andes, there is from 100-200 km of lowlands with some hilly ground up to 1,000m. The greater part is drained by the Daule, Vinces and Babahoyo rivers that run north to south to form the Guayas, which meets the sea at Guayaquil. There are several shorter rivers in the N including the Esmeraldas whose headwaters include the Río Machángara which rises near Quito. Another system reaches the ocean at La Tola. All of these rivers have created fertile lowlands which are used for banana, cacao and rice production, and there are good cattle lands in the Guayas basin.

The climate along the Pacific coast is a transition area between the heavy tropical rainfall of Colombia and the deserts of Peru. Mangrove swamps thrive on coastal mudflats in tropical rainforest zones and are typical of parts of Esmeraldas, Manabí and Guayas provinces. These are now having to compete with shrimp fisheries, a growing export product. Attempts are being made to restrict the destruction of mangroves in the Guayas estuary.

The rainfall is progressively less S of Guayaquil, the mangroves disappear, and by the border with Peru, it is semi-arid. This change of climate is due to the offshore Humboldt current which flows N along the South American Pacific coast from Chile to Ecuador. This relatively cold water inhibits rain producing clouds from 27° S northwards, but just S of the equator, the current is turned W and the climate is dramatically changed.

Amazonia

The eastern foothills of the Andes are mainly older granite (Mezozoic) rocks, more typical of Brazil than the Pacific coast countries. As with most of the western Amazon basin, it has a heavy rainfall coming in from the E and much is covered with tropical forest along a dozen or so significant tributaries of the Amazon. Partly as a result of the territory being opened up by oil-field exploitation, land is being cleared for crops at a high rate. However, certain areas are being developed for ecotourism and it remains to be seen if this will help to arrest the destruction of the environment.

With good water flow and easy gradients, many of the rivers of this region are navigable at least to small craft. The Napo in particular is a significant communications route to Iquitos in Peru and the Amazon, though this is not a connection permitted to tourists.

CLIMATE

In spite of its small size, the range of tropical climates in Ecuador is large. The meeting of the north flowing Humboldt current with the warm Pacific equatorial water takes place normally off Ecuador, giving the contrast between high rainfall to the N and desert conditions further S in Peru. Changes in the balance between these huge bodies of water, known as the *El Niño* phenomenon, can lead to heavy rains to the S, and this anomaly has affected the region during each of the years 1990-95 to a varying degree. There is much speculation that this may indicate a change in world climate.

Significant but not excessive rainfall in the coastal region, together with the well-distributed volcanic soils and good N-S communications along the Guayas river system have favoured crop production and make this one of the best agricultural areas of South America. Inland, however, the size of the Andean peaks and volcanoes creates many different mini-climates, from the permanent snows over 5,000m to the semi-desert hollows in the central trough. In the Oriente, however, the climate is indistinguishable from the hot, very humid lands of the western Amazon basin.

The Galápagos are also affected by the cool water from the SE Pacific which turns W near the equator. Surface water temperatures can fall to 16°C in July-Sept, causing low cloud and cool air conditions. Rain normally falls only on the highest terrain, with occasional drizzle on the lower ground. As with its geology and remoteness, the climate is another facet in the uniqueness of the islands.

FLORA AND FAUNA

As the **Geology** section above shows, Ecuador contains the most varied and extreme habitats, despite its small area. These range from awesome mountains to lush green forest.

High altitude and páramo

The diversity of life is markedly reduced above 3,200m. The characteristic cold moorlands experience daily temperatures between 6°C and 12°C with common night time frosts. Lakes and marshes are also a common feature since the ground is generally level. The moorland vegetation is grasses with fruit-bearing shrubs and blueberry. Interspersed amongst the grasses are clumps of clubmoss and *chuquiraguas*. In the zone of the high *páramo* there are many lakes. Birds frequently seen in this area include the Andean teal, Andean coot and a variety of hummingbird species. Andean Condor (Vultur gryphus) the largest land bird, weighing 12 kg and with a wingspan of 3m, may be seen effortlessly gliding on the updraught from the warmer valleys below.

From about 3,200m to 4,800m the high Andes are covered by *páramo* named after the grass (Stipa-ichu) or *Pajanol* which grows here. Some protection from the severe climate and the icy winds that can blast this harsh environment may be provided in the deeply incised gorges. Here there may be a lush growth of shrubs, orchids, reeds and dwarf trees providing a marked visual contrast to the superficially drier *páramo*. On the often steep open plains, plant growth is considerably stunted by the harsh environment, but the vegetation can be very rich, particularly in the favourable sheltered micro-climatic conditions provided in the gaps between the tall clumps of grass where nestle compact colonies of gentians, lupins and prostrate mosses.

There is little evidence of mammal life here, the occasional paw print of the Andean fox, or the skull of its most common prey, the *Sacha cuy*, wild ancestor of the domestic guinea pig. White-tailed deer, once common, have now been hunted out, their lands overrun by cattle. These cloud forest areas are designated as sub-tropical, and the zone where they meet the higher colder *páramos* tend to be foggy due to the condensation of the moisture-laden upwelling air from the warm humid jungles to the E. Consequently the inter-Andean valleys tend to be dry because the moisture has been deposited on the eastern slopes.

This almost constant drenching by mist, fog and rain leads to a profusion of plants with intense competition for space, such that the trees and shrubs are all covered with a great variety of epiphytes: orchids, mosses, lichens and bromeliads. Both giant and dwarf tree ferns are characteristic *páramo* species. These are highly resistant to fire, the traditional manner of maintaining grazing lands. Pollination is effected by a variety of agents. Fragrant odours and bright colours are used by some orchids to attract nectivorous birds including some species of humming birds and insects. Others exude putrid smells to attract flies to carry out the same process. Tangled stands of bamboo intermingled with the Polylepis forest are the dominant vegetation feature. A desolate zone of volcanic ash and bare rock marks the end of the moorland zones. Here there is little vegetation apart from the valiant colonization attempts of lichens which grow well even at 6,000m in the bright sunlight and unpolluted atmosphere. Glaciers descend to about 4,700m above sea level.

At 4,000m Polylepis forest clothes the deeply incised canyons and sides of the valleys, a tangled, lichen and fern bedecked world, dripping water from the moisture-laden air, onto a mid-storey of tangled bamboo and lush tree ferns. A plentiful supply of bromeliads provide food for spectacled bears and the abundant, chewed remains, testify to the good populations of this endangered species.

Rivers originate from the streams that cascade from the mountain ridges; secluded pools and rapids provide foraging opportunities for the whiteheaded dipper and the rare torrent duck. Many of these upland rivers are, surprisingly, devoid of fish. Not even the introduced rainbow trout can survive in the acidic waters running off the volcanic slopes. The steep slopes of the gullies are clothed in a dense blanked of giant cabbage-like *paraguillas*, or umbrella plant.

Tracks of mountain tapir are commonly found along the sandy beaches, and the prints of the diminutive *pudu*, a small Andean deer, are also occasionally found. Mammals are rarely seen on the *páramo* during the day since most seek refuge in the fringing cloud forest, only venturing onto the open moors at night or under the protection of the swirling mists.

Birds of the *páramo* include the mountain caracara and a variety of other raptors such as the red-backed hawk. Andean swifts, tapaculos, hummingbirds, fringillids and thrushes are common.

Masked trogons are also common in the *aliso* (birch) forests, evidence of recent colonization of areas devastated by the frequent landslides. Colourful tanagers and tiny hummingbirds are frequently encountered flitting between the flowers. At night the hills reverberate with the incessant croak of frogs and toads.

The lower slopes

Low montane rain forest extends from 1,800m to 2,100m. These steep slopes experience somewhat lower temperatures and are slightly less moist than those below. Above this zone, from 2,800m to 3,200m, marks the transition from montane forest to grassland, with lesser gradients. Trees and shrubs still dominate the habitat and bamboo is abundant.

Gradually the forest grades into riverine forest. Here torrent duck forage for insect larvae in the secluded tumbling rivers and river otter fish the pools for trout. In this sub-tropical zone insect life is plentiful, with clouds of sweat bees and mosquitos.

Lowland forest

In the lowland forests, many of the trees

are buttress rooted, with flanges extending 3-4m up the trunk of the tree. Among the smaller trees stilt-like prop roots are also common. Frequently flowers are not well developed, and some emerge directly from the branches and even the trunk. This is possibly an adaptation for pollination by the many bats, giving easier access than if they were obscured by leaves.

Lianas are plentiful, especially where there are natural clearings resulting from the death of old trees. These woody vines reach the tops of all but the tallest trees, tying them together and competing with them for space and light. Included here are strangling figs. These start life as epiphytes, their seeds germinating after deposition by birds. Aerial roots develop which quickly grow down to the ground. These later envelop the trunk, killing the host and leaving the hollow 'trunk' of the strangler.

In the canopy epiphytes are also common and include bromeliads, orchids, ferns, mosses and lichens. Their nutrition is derived from mineral nutrients in the water and organic debris they collect often in specialised pitcher-like structures. Animals of the canopy have developed striking adaptations to enable them to exist in this green wilderness, for example, the prehensile tails of the opossums and many of the monkeys, and the peculiar development of the claws of the sloth.

Many of the birds species which creep around in the understorey are drab, eg tinamou and cotingas, but have loud, clear calls. Scuttling around in the understorey are armadillos. Rarely seen, their presence is demonstrated by burrows. Pock-marked areas may be indicative of the foraging activities of pacas or peccaries, where their populations have not been exploited by over-hunting.

The forest is at its densest along the river margins; here the diffused light reduces the density of the understorey plant community. The variety of trees is amazing, there are no pure stands. The forest giants are the kapok and the para nut or *castanheiro*.

The river corridors are often the best places to observe wildlife. Caiman and turtles are commonly seen basking on the river banks. Neotropical cormorants, Roseate spoonbills and Jabiru storks are commonly observed fishing in the shallow waters. The swollen rivers of the lowland forest are home to perhaps 2,000 species of fish including piranha, sting ray and electric eel. Many species provide an important source of protein for the native communities, for example giant catfish. River dolphins also frequent these torpid waters, whereas the very rare Amazonian manatee favours areas of dense vegetation.

NATIONAL PARKS

Ecuador has over 20 national parks and ecological reserves. They are managed by **Inefan**, the Instituto Ecuatoriano Forestal y de Areas Naturales y Vida Silvestre.

Mountain parks
Reserva Ecológica Antisana, 120,000 ha, Pichincha and Napo provinces: varied altitude; Antisana volcano; Andean condors; landscapes.

Parque Nacional Sangay, 517,725 ha, Chimborazo, Tungurahua and Santiago-Morona provinces: 800m to 5,319m; Altar, Sangay and Tungurahua volcanoes; rain forest; contains several threatened mammals, eg spectacled bear, tigrillo, mountain tapir.

Parque Nacional Cotopaxi, 33,939 ha, Cotopaxi, Pichincha and Napo provinces: high altitude park.

Reserva Ecológica Cayambe-Coca, 403,103 ha, Imbabura, Pichincha and Sucumbíos provinces; varied altitude with diversity of flora and fauna; Cayambe volcano (dormant); lakes, waterfalls.

Reserva de Producción Faunística Chimborazo, 58,560 ha, Chimborazo, Bolívar and Tungurahua provinces: centre for the preservation of llama, alpaca

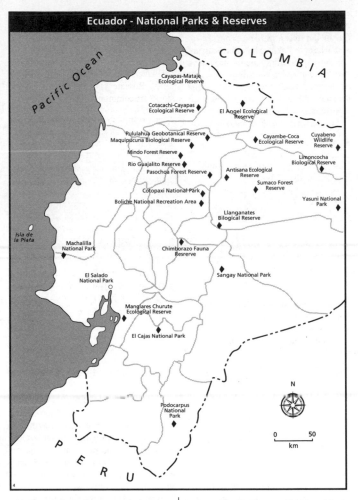

Ecuador - National Parks & Reserves

Pacific Ocean

COLOMBIA

Cayapas-Mataje
Ecological Reserve

Cotacachi-Cayapas
Ecological Reserve

El Angel Ecological
Reserve

Pululahua Geobotanical Reserve
Maquipucuna Biological Reserve

Cayambe-Coca
Ecological Reserve

Cuyabeno
Wildlife
Reserve

Mindo Forest Reserve

Limoncocha
Biological Reserve

Rio Guajalito Reserve

Pasochoa Forest Reserve

Antisana Ecological
Reserve

Cotopaxi National Park

Sumaco Forest
Reserve

Boliche National Recreation Area

Yasuni National
Park

Llanganates
Bilogical Reserve

Isla de
la Plata

Machalilla
National Park

Chimborazo Fauna
Reserve

Sangay National Park

El Salado
National Park

Manglares Churute
Ecological Reserve

El Cajas National Park

N

PERU

Podocarpus
National
Park

0   50
km

---

and vicuña; Chimborazo and Carihuairazo mountains.

Reserva Geobotánica Pululahua, 3,383 ha, 13 km NW of Quito: extinct crater of Pululahua volcano.

Highland parks

Area de Recreación El Cajas, 28,800 ha, 30 km from Cuenca: lakes and scenery.

Area de Recreación El Boliche, 1,077 ha, inside Cotopaxi National Park.

Reserva Ecológica El Angel, 15,715 ha, Carchi province: *frailejones* plants, Chiles volcano; lakes and rivers.

Parque Nacional Llanganates, 219,707 ha, newly created: Andean forest.

Mixed habitats

Reserva Ecológica Cotacachi-Cayapas, 204,420 ha, Imbabura and Esmeraldas provinces: western slopes of the Andes to beaches; tropical forests, lakes (inc Cuicocha) and rivers, scenery.

Parque Nacional Podocarpus, 146,200 ha, Loja and Zamora provinces: cloud forest; rivers; birdlife.

Parque Nacional Sumaco-Napo-Galeras, 205,249 ha, Napo province: Andean and sub-tropical forests; rivers; river otters, jaguar, spectacled bear.

Amazonian parks

Parque Nacional Yasuni, 982,006 ha, Napo province: Amazonian rainforest; lakes, animals and birdlife.

Reserva de Producción Faunística Cuyabeno, 655,781 ha, Sucumbíos province: tropical forests; lakes; endemic fauna.

Reserva Biológica Limoncocha, 4,613 ha, Sucumbíos province: Lake Limoncocha and surroundings; black caiman; birdlife.

Coastal parks

Parque Nacional Machalilla, 55,000 ha, Manabí province: dry coastal forest; beaches; archaeology.

Reserva Ecológica Manglares-Churute, 49,383 ha, Guayas province: mangroves; dry tropical forest.

Reserva Ecológica Cayapas-Mataje, 51,300 ha, Esmeraldas province, newly created.

The Galápagos Islands

693,700 ha: unique fauna; marine reserve. A separate chapter describes these islands.

Wildlife

All under increasing threat from human encroachment of their habitat, including the jaguar, puma, tapir, several kinds of monkey, the armadillo, spectacled bear, squirrel, porcupine, peccary, various kinds of deer, and many rodents, including the guinea pig. There are also tortoises, lizards and iguanas. Among the birds are condors, falcons, kites, macaws, owls, flamingoes, parrots, ibises, cranes, and storks. Unhappily,

every type of insect is found in the coastal towns and the Oriente. The Galápagos Islands have their own selection of nearly tame wildlife.

Access

All foreigners have to pay to enter each national park; the charge for the Galápagos is now US$80. For lowland parks (the coast, the Oriente and the lowland portions that overlap lowlands and highlands) the charge is US$14 in sucres; for highland parks (all sierra parks and highland portions of overlapping parks), US$7 in sucres. No student discounts are available in these two categories. There is no separate National Parks office, Parks fall under Inefan. Their office in Quito can provide some tourist information but it is best to contact the Inefan office in the city nearest the Park you wish to visit, eg the Cuenca office for Cajas, Loja for Podocarpus, etc.

Fundación Natura, Av América 5653 y Voz Andes, Quito, T 447-343/4, 459-013, is a private charitable organization concerned with nature reserves. They have some limited tourist information, notably on Pasochoa, which they manage; there is a resource library and knowledgeable staff who can give technical information on parks and reserves.

BIRDWATCHING

Of the 32 World Life Zones, 26 are found in Ecuador. Only slightly larger than Oregon, Ecuador occupies approximately 0.02% of the world's land surface, but contains easily 10% of all species, many endemic to very tiny microclimates found between sea level and 4,500m. There are still many undescribed species and even some undescribed genera of plants and trees. Many are pollinated exclusively by one species of bird or insect. Danish expert Niels Krabbe estimates that, including migrants and seabirds, 1,600 bird species can be found in Ecuador and the Galápagos Islands, from the smallest of the hummingbirds

A condor

to the Andean condor.

There is as yet no single illustrated guide book which covers the entire country; however, Paul Greenfield has been working for many years on the plates for such a book, which should be published soon. Meanwhile, the coverage can be obtained from *Birds of the High Andes*, *Birds of Colombia*, *Landbirds of South America*; *The Birds of Ecuador Checklist* is an unillustrated but useful listing. Tom Heijnen's self-published book of 75 good birding sites in Ecuador is a useful guide for planning specialist trips, despite a few errors in place names.

The areas of greatest diversity are found where different life zones intersect and birds from more than one zone can be seen. The cloud forests are noted particularly for their abundance of Hummingbirds, Tanagers, Mountain Toucans, Cock of the Rock, Cotingas and Manakins. Below are a selection of accessible sites which give a good overview of the diversity.

West Flank Cloud Forests (above 1,000m)

Santo Tomas de Intag is 2 hrs W of Otavalo and a short walk from the Apuela road. There are cabins close to the forest which require reservations only for large groups. Buses leave Otavalo three times a day.

Intag Cloud Forest is also 2 hrs W of Otavalo and then a 1-hr walk from Santa Rosa. Facilities are simple and excellent, but reservations are essential. A 2-day minimum stay is required and groups of less than four are discouraged. There are no other nearby facilities. Write for reservations: Casilla 18, Otavalo, Imbabura, Ecuador.

Maquipucuna Reserve is about 2 hrs W of Quito and N of Nanegalito. Direct buses to Nanegal will drop one at the Marianitas turning for a 1-hr walk to the reserve, alternatively take one of the many buses to Nanegalito and rent a truck. Make reservations at their Quito offices (T 507-200); see also page 132.

Bellavista Cloud Forest Reserve, 2 hrs W of Quito and then S of Nanegalito, has five double rooms and a dormitory for another 10. It offers packages including transportation from Quito, or bus to Nanegalito and rent a truck. If you enjoy a good stiff walk, get off at the Río Tandayapa Bridge and hike 3 hrs uphill on the road for good birding en route. Reservations through *Safari* in Quito (T 552-505).

Los Cedros Reserve is about 6 hrs by bus from Quito and then 6 more on foot or mule. Transportes Minas have a daily bus to Saguangal which is the nearest village, departure times vary. Either stay in the village at Moises Quito's rustic hotel or walk an hour to Don Pepe's where horses leave for the reserve. Reservations are through the Centro de Investigaciones de Bosques Tropicales (T 221-324).

Mindo is one of the more famous birding locations in northern Ecuador (see page 132). There are several private reserves and several places to stay in the village. A daily bus leaves Quito at 1500. Thur to Sun there is also an 0800 bus. There are several buses a week from Santo Domingo de los Colorados. Numerous westbound buses pass the entrance on the new road to the northern coast from which there is a downhill walk of 7 km.

Nono Road, Inca Ditch and **Yanacocha** are all found on a transect beginning in northern Quito, passing the village of

Nono and dropping down to Tandayapa, continuing past Bellavista to Pueblo Nuevo. This road is now little used and public transport does not pass this way unless landslides block the new road. Purchase a day tour or rent a car, preferably 4WD, or ride an early morning truck from Cotocollao to Nono.

Chiriboga Road from S Quito, which has no signs, no gas stations, and almost no traffic, follows the pipeline and for maintenance purposes is always kept open. Although often birded in one day, there are so many ecological zones on this road from 3,500m down to 800m, that it really warrants 2 days. There are, however, no tourist facilities and few places to camp. Rent a 4WD vehicle or join an organized tour. To hike or bike it, take an early morning truck from Calzado or Chillogallo to San Juan de Chillogallo.

Chilla, **Guanazán**, **Manu** and **Selva Alegre** are all in the S of the country on a minor road which connects Saraguro with the coastal lowlands. Although passable most of the year, driving conditions can become extreme between Dec and May (the rainy season), especially between Manu and Chilla. All through this section are remnants, both large and small, of the original cloud forest. Many humming birds, monkeys and bears are still seen. Only Chilla has formal accommodation at a house for religious pilgrims on the main plaza; during the first weeks of Sept it is often full.

Daucay Reserve and **Piñas Forest** are on the S side of the Cordillera de Arcos close to the roads from Machala to Piñas. Daucay is off the road to Buenavista and Paccha. For visitor information contact the Red de Bosques Privados at **Fundación Natura** (T 447-341). Piñas Forest is on the N side of the road between Saracay and Piñas. Leave the paved road at the large blue and white tent-shaped shelter for the Virgin Mary, then it's a short walk to the forest.

Guachanama Ridge is crossed by the

road between Alamor and Catacocha. From the village of Celica turn N and follow the dirt road past the military base. Celica has two small hotels on the main plaza. Many people here talk about the 'pájaros de colores', or colourful birds. Unfortunately, the forests are diminishing and fewer species are found each year.

The **Sozoranga to Nueva Fátima** road passes remnants of the original forest and many Tumbes Basin Endemics may be seen. The small hotel above the *Farmacia Ideal* hosts an immense number of swift nests on the back wall.

East Flank Cloud Forests

Laguna San Marcos is NE of Cayambe. Access is through Olmedo and Chimbo, beyond which there is no public transport. Camping gear is essential, as is a 4WD vehicle, unless you plan to hike.

Oyacachi offers a very similar climatic region and access is from the S side of Cayambe through Canguahua; again 4WD and camping gear are needed.

San Rafael Falls just beside the Baeza to Lago Agrio road offers accommodation and some lovely observation spots. Take a bus bound for Lago Agrio and ask to be let off at the falls. It's a short walk to the bungalows owned by *Hotel Quito*. Most buses on this route run at night so check timetables.

Papallacta to Baeza is a popular transect covering many forest zones. There are many short walks off the road which are very rewarding to the birdwatcher. There are only hotels in Papallacta and Baeza.

Baeza to Tena transect, beginning in Baeza, has many trails up into the forests. Some of the best leave town up the hill towards the antennae. Shortly before Cosanga, *Cabañas San Isidro* (book in Quito, T 446-404) have several good forest trails. *Guacamayos* is the cloud forest between Cosanga and Jondachi. It is difficult to get far off the road. There

are few trails, but it's a good area for birds and orchids. Between Jondachi and Archidona a few forest patches survive, but they're going fast.

Loreto Road is the new road to Coca and Lago Agrio. To the S is the Galeras Protected Forest so there is some control on colonization. This road is best done either on a tour or in a rental car as there is no accommodation on the route and a plethora of birding sites. One of the favourites is the quarry about 20 mins from the beginning of the road where there are several good trails.

Llanganates is the name given to one of Ecuador's more mysterious regions. Famous for its tales of lost treasures and lost treasure hunters, this is the newest National Park. Dropping from 4,500m on Cerro Hermoso to 1,000m up river from Tena, the area has until now been protected only by its inaccessibility and heavy rainfall. Entering the area without a local guide would be foolish.

Guamote to Macas Road is a newly-opened transect. At the time of writing it is passable only on foot. Sangay National Park was recently extended southwards to encompass this road, which may give it some protection for a while. There are many birdwatching delights as much of the forest is still pristine. Problems with the indigenous population, however, make it unsafe to enter.

Macas Pass is the name given to the road from Cuenca to Limón-Indanza. Above Gualaceo the road climbs up onto the *páramos* and then begins its slow and tortuous descent through the stunted forests. This cold, misty, windy and apparently inhospitable area is home to many mountain tanagers and spectacular hummingbirds. Descending through many levels of forests this is an excellent road for birds. Most buses run through here at night.

On the **Loja-Zamora Road** the forests begin on the E side of the nearby pass descending to the jungles at Zamora. The road hugs the sides of a narrow valley and is subject to landslides, causing considerable delays. Zamora has the best access to the lower parts of the Podocarpus National Park.

Lowland Forests below 1,000m

Tinalandia has been a hotel for 40 years, it was run by the indomitable Tina Garzón, who died in 1996. The running of this graceful establishment has passed to her heir, Sergio Platanov. This is the best known birdwatchers' hotel in Ecuador. *Safari Tours* in Quito has an agreement with them for low season prices and special offers for pre-paid inclusive packages. Forest trails are well maintained and access from the Santo Domingo-Quito road couldn't be simpler. If you don't want the friendly dogs to follow you on the trails ask that they be tied up as they disturb the birds.

La Hesperie is a privately-owned reserve with accommodation for about 15 people. Although bordering the Santo Domingo-Alóag road, it is a long hike up to the house. Reservations are made direct to Dr Mario Jativa, T 241-887 or 464-800 in Quito.

Bisa reserve, about 20 km NW of Quininde, has simple accommodation. Access is by truck from Quininde to Herrera or La Y in the dry season (Aug-Dec), then a 1-3 hr walk, or in the rainy season a slog in the mud for 6-8 hrs. Reservations through Fundación Jatun Sacha in Quito, T 441-592.

Río Palenque Reserve, 47 km S of Santo Domingo, is accessible from the road just S of the village of Patricia Pilar. It is administered from Quito by Dr Calaway Dodson; reservations in Quito, T 561-646.

On the **Latacunga to Quevedo road** the best parts of the transect are from above Pilaló to La Maná (see page 263). Stay at *Carmita's* in La Esperanza del Tingo (there's no sign on the wooden house beside the road) to visit El Copal and other nearby forest remnants. Close to La Maná is *Hostería Rancho Inmisahu*

for the lower end of the road.

Machalilla National Park has several micro-climates. Prinicpal sites include the cloud forest at San Sebastián, accessible from the village of Agua Blanca. Horses and local guides and limited accommodation are available. The Río Ayampe, which can be entered from the village of the same name, offers good birding. Hike the road S of the river or, in the dry season, walk beside the river. The park office in Puerto López and entrance tickets (5-day validity) should be purchased there. Boats to **Isla de la Plata** also leave from Puerto López (see page 273).

Salt Ponds, favourite resting and nesting area of many seabirds, are found at Pacoa to the S of Manglaralto and to the SE of Salinas. Both are accessible on foot although a bicycle might make the approaches easier.

Cerro Blanco, just W of Guayaquil, is easily accessible from the main Guayaquil-Salinas road; there are signs. The trails are well maintained and excellent guides are available. Reservations are needed for groups and on national holidays, otherwise it's open Wed to Sun, T 871-900 (see page 237).

Access to **Manta Real** is a turning just before the village of Cochancay, 11 km E of La Troncal. There are two or three trucks a day, all in the morning, which will take you part of the way into the reserve. There are no formal places to stay, but arrangements can be made in the village, or with Juan Pozo who lives just beyond the village and closer to the forests. Bring sleeping bags and thermal vests.

Manglares-Churute to the SE of Guayaquil are part of the Ecological reserve system to be administered through the Ministry of Agriculture. There is a park office beside the road between Km 26 and Puerto Inca, or make arrangements for a tour at the MAG offices in Guayaquil (see page 237).

Puyango petrified forest 61 km S of

Arenillas on the road to Alamor is home to many Tumbesian Endemics. Hike in and camp. For more information T 930-021 in Machala (see page 251).

Interandean Valleys

These areas are found in the rainshadow of both the western and eastern cordilleras. There are few accessible forests remnants and high plain areas where the habitat is relatively undisturbed.

The northern parts of the **Páramos de El Angel** can be visited from Tulcán. On Calle Sierra take the midday bus bound for Maldonado and Chical. Camping gear is essential as there is nowhere to stay between Tulcán and Maldonado. Southern *Páramo* access is from the town of El Angel which has one small *hostal* on the plaza, or the Alvarez family has rooms. The traverse from El Angel in the S to Las Juntas near Tulcán in the N no longer has public transport and is only passable with 4WD vehicles.

Pasochoa Reserve, about 40 mins drive SE of Quito is accessible by bus to Amaguaña. The lower forest is secondary, but hike to the upper part and the crater rim for frequent sightings of condors (see page 133).

El Cajas Recreational Area lies to the W of Cuenca and bus access from the city is easy early in the morning from San Sebastián. Pay the entrance fee at the roadside office, you'll be given a map. There are numerous areas for birdwatching, excellent trails and good camping (see page 216).

The **Oña-Saraguro-Santiago road** crosses the *páramos* between Cuenca and Loja passing many areas of polylepis and scrub forest. The birding within 100m of the road is excellent in many areas.

Podocarpus National Park has its highland access at Cajanuma, only 30 mins S of Loja on the road to Vilcabamba. From the entrance to the refuge and park office it's an 8-km hike. There are excellent trails and information is available at the MAG offices in Loja. There is also roadside access S of Yangana on the road to Zumba (see page 223).

The Amazon Basin

Most people wishing to bird in the areas accessed from Lago Agrio and Coca go to one of the lodges and take a tour. The operators supply good guides and lists. Logistics in this part of the Amazon are not easy and tend to be time-consuming. There is good information in Tom Heijnen's book for those who wish to go it alone.

The Galápagos

Only the inhabited islands may be visited without taking an organized and guided tour. To visit the uninhabited ones independently, you have to obtain scientific permission, which is difficult. See the Galápagos chapter.

Bibliography

Dunning, JS *South American Land Birds – A photographic aid to identification* Harrowood Books, USA, 1982; Fjeldsa, J and Krabbe, N *Birds of the High Andes*, Apollow Books, Svendborg, Denmark, 1990; Heijnen, T *Birdwatching in Mainland Ecuador*, A guide to 75 Birding Sites, Eersel, The Netherlands, 1995; Hilty, S and Brown, W *A guide to the Birds of Colombia*, Princetown University Press, USA, 1986; Ortiz Crespo, F, Greenfield, PJ and Matheus JC *Birds of Ecuador*, locational checklist with English and Spanish common names, FEPROTUR, Quito, Ecuador, 1990; Taylor, K *A Birders Guide to Ecuador*, Victoria, B.C. Canada, 1995.

HOT SPRINGS

Ecuador is located on the 'Ring of Fire' and has many volcanoes, active, dormant, and non-active (dead). The hot springs are associated with all three, although they are mostly found with the older volcanoes where sufficient time has elapsed since the last eruptions for water systems to become established. There are several areas where one can look for hot springs:

1. On the coastal lowlands, pressure from the collision of the continental and oceanic plates causes friction and heat is dissipated into the water system. Many of the these springs have a high mineral content and these sulphurous waters are frequently praised for their curative properties. Very few are large enough to warrant development. Temperatures range from 20°C to 30°C.

2. At the foot of the Andes, water temperatures are elevated by pressure caused by plate tectonics. South of Guayaquil there are several springs with minimal or no development, all in temperature ranges from 40°C to 55°C. To the N of Guayaquil there are fewer springs and the temperatures are much lower.

3. In the Andes above 1,500m most of the springs are directly associated with older volcanic action. The vast majority of Ecuadorean hot springs are found in the Andes N of Chimborazo and up to Colombia. To the S of Riobamba the only major hot springs are associated with a mineralized rock outcrop a few kilometres S of Cuenca.

4. The few springs at the foot of the Andes in the upper Amazon are mostly associated with secondary ridges of mountains and the heat source seems to be pressure caused by uplifting and folding mountains. None of these has been developed and access to all is difficult.

5. In the craters of Alcedo Volcano, in the Galápagos Islands, and Guagua Pichincha direct contact with heat sources causes rainwater to boil. In the Galápagos this produces an intermittent geyser, and on Pichincha a small hot stream with minimal mineral content flows down from the active crater.

A selection of Ecuador's best springs, from N to S:

Aguas Hediondas are about 1½ hrs W of Tulcán. Unsuccessful attempts have been made to develop this area and the remains of a proposed thermal bath centre is at the end of road. Several buses a day leave Tulcán for Tufiño, but only the midday one goes up the hill to the turning for the walk into Aguas Hediondas (stinking waters). From the turning it's 8 km and unless you have a car you will need to take camping gear for the night. At the end of the road you'll find a small stream with numerous little pools; a small irrigation channel can be diverted into the stream to cool the water to acceptable temperatures. Do not go alone and be very careful of the sulphurous gases; many people have passed out and drowned in this spring, so take turns and watch each other.

Chachimbiro At weekends there are direct buses from Ibarra to this resort; during the week take buses to Pablo Arenas or Cahuasqui (about five a day) and get off at Tumbabiro. From here take a pickup (camioneta) or walk, mostly uphill, 8 km through San Francisco (attractive hotel here) to Chachimbiro. There are cabins and some larger rooms for rent at the restaurant before the entrance. Weekends can be quite crowded. There is one exceedingly hot pool for therapy and several of mixed water for soaking and playing.

Nangulvi From Otavalo two buses a day and several trucks pass right by these springs, a third bus passes within 20 mins walk. All depart from one of the corners where Calle Colón and 31 de Octubre intersect. The nearby village of Apuela has accommodation if the cabins beside the pools are full. Again, as with most developed springs in the country they tend to be busy and full at weekends. There are four hot pools here and one large cold one for plunging.

Oyacachi This village was isolated until 1995 when a road was cut through the mountains from Canguahua near Cayambe. Before that time this was possibly the best semi-developed spring in the country. Unfortunately foreign aid money was provided to develop the springs. There was little or no care taken in overseeing the development and the same agency which provided the money is now warning people not to bathe in the spring as it is polluted. No attempt has yet been made to try to correct the damage. There is public transport from Cayambe to Canguahua hourly, beyond there, only infrequent, rental trucks are available. Alternatively, hire a horse or walk about 25 km. Several families in the village will provide floors to sleep on, or you can ask to sleep in one of the churches or in the school.

Papallacta This is now probably the most attractively developed set of springs in Ecuador. In 1995 this spring changed ownership and major improvements are ongoing. Ecuadorean architect Juan Alfonso Peña and his wife Cynthia specialize in tasteful buildings using traditional materials where possible. They have spent considerable time rehabilitating many of the structures and pools, adding new ones and removing ugly ones. The hot water is channelled into three pools large enough for swimming, three smaller shallow pools and two tiny family-size pools. There is also a steam room, six hot showers and two cold plunge pools as well as access to the river. Within the complex there are two cabins for up to eight people each and a good restaurant. A newly constructed hostel has seven double rooms, a hot tub and its own separate swimming facilities. From the hot pools on clear days one can look down the valley directly at the snow-capped Antisana. The small stream beside the road is also hot, and more springs in this area provide the village of Papallacta with abundant hot water and fill a couple of simple pools in the village. Many buses a day pass the village on their way to and from the jungle; it is then a short half hour walk up the hill to the complex.

Guagua Pichincha Access to this spring involves a long and potentially dangerous hike. 2 years ago vulcanology students conducting studies in the crater were killed by an explosion. The only known access to this hot river is down into the crater past the active fumeroles and the explosion crater, and then down further below the lower lip of the crater. As the activity continues the Ecuadorean Civil Defence has put out repeated warnings against entering the crater. The National Geophysical Institute has constant monitoring devices in place.

El Tingo and **La Merced** These thermal pools are among the easiest to get to (all within 30-40 mins of Quito). There are numerous complexes all with comfortably warm water for swimming. Buses leave the La Marín area of Quito about every 30 mins throughout the day.

Baños de Tungurahua These are positively the best known springs in Ecuador. The town of Baños has more than 100 hotels, *residencias, pensiones* and guest houses, all of which can be full during national holidays, especially Carnival. There are four major complexes of pools run by the Municipalidad. Two complexes are open from 0400 till 1700 daily: Salado which is just outside town on the hill beside the Río Bascún, and Águas del Virgen below the waterfall in town. The Piscinas Modernas are open only at weekends and are pleasant for swimming. Santa Clara has a gym and sauna open everyday. Neither Modernas nor Santa Clara is as hot as the first two. Out of town on the way to the jungle are two more complexes which take their water from the same source. Comfortably warm and less visited because of their location are Baños Nuevo and the renovated Santa Ana.

Palitagüe About 1 hr S of Baños on the flanks of Tungurahua, these springs are a couple of hours walk up from the village of Puela. Tucked into a narrow mountain valley, surrounded by forest and below a cold waterfall are three water sources, the two hotter ones are contained in small cement tanks.

El Placer Access to this spring takes a couple of days, but it's well worth the effort. It is located in Sangay National Park by the headwaters of the Río Palora. There is on average one truck or colectivo daily from Riobamba to Alao, where you can camp at the park ranger's office and pay your park fees. There may soon be some tourist cabins, but plans move slowly here. From Alao horses can be found to take you past Laguna Negra to Magdalena; we are told that in some seasons it is possible to take them right down to the refuge by the spring; or you can hike. The trail is clear and easy to follow. The pool has been enlarged and deepened and a new refuge built to shelter about 15 people. Take sleeping bags and mats. The foot trails continue down through the ruins of Huamboya to Macas. A local guide is essential for this one week hike.

Baños de Cuenca These are the hottest commercial springs in the country and only 10 mins by city bus from Cuenca. There are four complexes: Rodas, Marchan, Familiar and Durán. The last are by far the largest and best maintained and although associated with the hotel of the same name are open to the public. There are numerous hot pools and tubs and steam baths open from dawn till 2100 or 2200.

Baños San Vicente These springs are close to Salinas and Libertad on the coast; they are famed for the curative properties of the warm mud lake which people slide into before baking themselves dry. There are also several indoor pools of different temperatures, some steam rooms and massage facilities. Take a bus running between Guayaquil and Libertad and get off about 15 km E of Santa Elena; a large sign suggests that it is only 4 mins drive to San Vicente, it obviously should say 14 mins. Small trucks and cars pick up passengers at this junction. There are a couple of small hotels in the village.

Yanayacu 2 hrs E of Guayaquil on the road to Cuenca is the village of Cochancay. About 1 km up the hill from the village there is a small turning on the left; this is the old unpaved road to the mountains. 1 km along the road there is a turning to the left which leads down to the Baños of Yanayacu. There are numerous small and medium-sized hot pools on a rock outcrop beside the Río Bulu Bulu. The small *residencia* here has a few rooms and food on the weekend.

History

Introduction

During the approximately 10,000 years of occupation of what is now politically Ecuador, humans developed various forms of social, economic and political integration. There also arose a complex web of exchange relationships, not only between coast, sierra (highlands) and jungle, but also along the coast, via maritime trade, with places as far away as Central America and Chile. Ecuadorean artisans were the equals of any in the Americas and were unrivaled in certain crafts such as platinum metallurgy and shell work.

One difficulty that confronts the archaeologist is the sometimes poor preservation of organic remains in the tropical climate. The wooden artefacts, the thatched roofs, the clothing people wore, the balsa rafts they used to dominate the seas, and many of their ornaments of bone and feathers are often missing, and we frequently have little direct evidence about the use of these materials. In Ecuador, an occasionally occurring impression of a woven cloth on a pottery fragment (made when the clay was soft) is considered a lucky find. Nevertheless, the archaeology of Ecuador is abundant in its clues about the lives of the ancient inhabitants of the area.

Chronological framework

In the summary that follows, a widely-accepted chronological framework is presented first. Using this as our organizational scheme, we then discuss different regions' outstanding archaeological developments and, where appropriate, specific sites. The pre-European archaeological sequence of Ecuador has traditionally been divided into four distinct periods: Preceramic, 8000 (or earlier?)-3300 BC; Formative, 3300-500 BC; Regional Development, 500 BC-AD 800; Integration, AD 800-European Contact. The following discussions will be presented region by region, beginning in the Preceramic Period and ending with European contact at the end of the Integration Period. As a cross-reference, the following outline is arranged chronologically:

I PRECERAMIC PERIOD
(8000 BC [or earlier?] to 3300 BC)
A **Northern Sierra**
  El Inga Site
B **Southern Sierra**
  Chobshi Cave Site
C **Guayas Coast**
  Las Vegas Culture
    OGSE-80 Site

II FORMATIVE PERIOD
(3300-500 BC)
A **Guayas and Manabí Coasts**
  Valdivia Culture
    Loma Alta Site
    Real Alto Site
    Río Chico Site
    Isla La Plata Sites
  Jama-Coaque Culture
  Machalilla Culture
    Salango Factory Site
  Chorrera and Engoroy Cultures
    Salango Factory Site
B **Southern Sierra**
  Cerro Narrio Site
  Putushio Site
  Pirincay Site
C **Northern Sierra**
  Cotacollao Site
D **Northern Esmeraldas**
  La Tolita Site

III REGIONAL DEVELOPMENT PERIOD
(500 BC TO AD 800)
A **Guayas and Southern-Central Manabí Coasts**
 Guangala Culture
 Bahía Culture
B **Northern Manabí and Esmeraldas Coasts**
 Jama-Coaque Culture
 La Tolita Culture
C **Northern Sierra**
 La Florida Site
 Jardín del Este Site

IV INTEGRATION PERIOD
(AD 800 TO EUROPEAN CONTACT)
A **Guayas and Manabí Coasts**
 Manteño/Huancavilca Culture
 Agua Blanca Site
 Salango Site
 Los Frailes Site
 Milagro/Quevedo Culture
B **Northern Sierra**
 Cochasquí Site
 Inca Culture
 Rumicucho Site
 Quitaloma Site
C **Southern Sierra**
 Cañari Culture
 Inca Culture
 Tomebamba Site
 Ingapirca Site

Northern Sierra
A secure chronology for the earliest human remains in Ecuador, which occur in the Northern Sierra, has yet to be accomplished. A few sites have assumed great importance, however, and facilitate our understanding of the first Ecuadoreans.

El Inga is a cave site of the northern sierra, in Pichincha province some 22 km SE of Quito on the shore of the Río Inga and on the flanks of the extinct volcano Ilaló. It is situated near some of Ecuador's largest outcrops of obsidian, a black volcanic glass highly valued by natives for its ready manufacture into various stone tools. When thin flakes of obsidian are produced, the result is an edge that is sharper than a razor or a surgical scalpel. Indeed, obsidian blades are still used for soft tissue surgery in modern hospitals. It was one of the most abundant and apparently preferred materials (along with basalt) used at early sites like El Inga, and throughout subsequent periods it was traded to southern sierra, coast and jungle. At El Inga, fluted spear points are found, but in deposits that are somewhat difficult to interpret because of disturbance of the soils. These points may be contemporary with similar styles from the Paleo-Indian Period of North America. They occur at El Inga together with points having stems and concave bases (also called 'fish-tail' points). Bones from

Figure from the Integration period
Source: Ecuador Ediciones Libri Mundi Quito, 1980

now-extinct species of mammoth, horse and camel are also found in the lower deposits at the site, although not in direct association with the artefacts. The available radiocarbon (C-14) determinations may not serve to date the human occupation of the site directly because they were derived from carbon flecks distributed through various soil layers. Nevertheless, the point styles, especially the 'fish tail' stemmed type, have very similar counterparts from well-dated contexts elsewhere in the Andes and are possibly the earliest artefacts in Ecuador.

The best known site of the Formative Period of this region is **Cotocollao**, lying now beneath a housing development in northern Quito. Its occupation began at about 1500 BC, and it was abandoned by 500 BC, a date coinciding with a series of volcanic eruptions in the area. It started as a small village of rectangular houses and apparently never grew much beyond that. Its ceramics were similar to those of the Machalilla Culture on the coast, including the stirrup-spout vessel form so characteristic of the latter (see below). The fact that sophisticated pottery appeared suddenly here in a series of styles that mimicked those of the coast, and had no local antecedents, has lead some archaeologists to suggest a coastal origin for the Formative people of the Quito Basin. The probable close relationship between coast and sierra continued throughout the Formative Period. One motive for coastal peoples to continue the relationship may have been to ensure access to the deposits of obsidian from the Mullumica source located E of Quito.

La Florida site has produced the largest array of material culture relating to the Regional Development Period. The site has been dated from about AD 300 to just before AD 500. Located in north-central, urban Quito on the edge of the Pichincha Volcano, it is spread over three spurs of land known as the Barrio San Vicente de La Florida, the Barrio San Lorenzo and the Barrio Osorio, separated from one another by deep quebradas. Two spurs may have the remains of living quarters and tombs of the lower and middle classes of this stratified society while the third spur is exclusively a cemetery. Most notable are incredibly deep, shaft tombs, varying from 12-16m. A round, 2-3m deep central pit forms the base of the tomb, and a raised bench-like stone collar surrounds the top of the central pit. The sides of the shaft are wider than the central pit at its base, thus giving the tomb a profile that resembles an upside down, short-necked wine bottle. The interior walls of the shaft are coated in coloured clay, either red, orange or yellow. The shaft tomb concept is widespread all along the Ecuadorean coast in Late Formative times and subsequently. Those of the Quito Basin are distinct in form, but similar to all the others in concept. As in shaft tombs elsewhere in the Americas, these contain the remains of an important individual with elaborate grave goods in the deepest central pit. Several other individuals were placed on the bench above, but interred with fewer sumptuary funeral goods, suggesting that the central person had a higher social rank. Interments of younger individuals had fewer offerings than those of adults. Deer bones and spear-thrower hooks were included among the offerings in the central pits, implying that hunting was perhaps restricted to the upper tier of society at this time, much like in ancient Egypt. Also among the offerings in these tombs is a variety of foodstuffs and manufactured goods from different ecological zones. Included are items such as gold and copper ornaments (possibly from either the southern sierra or Esmeraldas coast), *Spondylus* and mother-of-pearl shell beads (from the coast), and a variety of pottery vessels including bottles, pedestaled and tripod-footed plates, cups, jars, figurines, and both decorated and undecorated bowls.

The **Jardín del Este** site is located on the right shore of the Río Machángara, 5 km due E of Quito in the Tumbaco Valley at 2,400m. The site consists of mostly shallow, oval tombs with single burials. It dates to about 100 BC. What is significant are the grave offerings. These include figurines, tripod-footed plates, cups and decorated and undecorated bowls and jars. Also found are copper and gold (14-16.6 carats!) ornaments. Some figurines resemble those of the Classic La Tolita culture of coastal Esmeraldas, while others have traits better associated with Jama-Coaque of northern Manabí (see below).

In the Quito area, the number of Integration Period sites and probably politically distinct cultures is large prior to the arrival of Europeans. One of this period's most distinctive characteristics is the construction of monumental architecture, such as 'tolas' (artificial earth mounds) and truncated pyramids, along with artificial modifications of the landscape to increase agricultural productivity. Among the most notable of the latter are the extensive areas of ridged field systems and terracing, easily observed today from the air. These are found in the Caranquí and Tumbaco Valley regions N of Quito, at sites such as **Cochasquí**, located about half-way between Quito and Otavalo. They are also found in the areas around Cayambe, San José de Minas, Atahualpa, and on the southern slopes of the Nudo de Mojanda.

In the decades just prior to the arrival of the Spaniards, local populations of the sierra felt the impact of the Incas' northward expansion. The Incas certainly left their mark on Ecuador and constructed several administrative centres. The Inca practice of relocating portions of distinct tribes from all over their conquered territory resulted in the importation of speakers of Quechua, the *lingua franca* of the Incas, and even of native Aymara-speaking peoples from around Lake Titicaca into Ecuador. Conversely, peoples from Ecuador ended up in Cusco, Copacabana (Lake Titicaca) and Jauja (E of Lima in the highlands of Peru).

The Incas' partial conquest of the northern sierra undoubtedly helped pave the way for the subsequent Spanish invasion. A number of sites characterized by stone fortresses (or *pukaras*), situated on hilltops and other defensible locations, were built by local people at about the time of the Inca invasion (late 1400s). **Rumicucho**, just S of Quito, is one such site. Other fortress-like sites were probably built by the Incas, such as the site of **Quitaloma**, on the Inca road leading northward from Quito into the Tumbaco Valley. Finally, in Quito itself, there were buildings contructed by the Incas for their nobility, such as those called the 'pleasure houses' of the Inca ruler Huayna Cápac near the present-day Convento de la Merced.

The Coast

Broad-spectrum foraging and incipient agriculture characterize the earliest Preceramic Period culture of the coast, the **Las Vegas Culture**. It is dated from about 7500-4500 BC, and is defined by a series of 16 sites on the Santa Elena Peninsula between the Guayas Basin and the modern town of Salinas. The first real houses in Ecuador probably belong to this culture. Evidence from phytoliths (fossilized, silicated plant cells) of maize suggest this plant's presence and possible use sometime prior to 5000 BC. In similarly dated contexts were found remains of bottle gourds and squash (*zapallo*). This evidence for an early appearance of maize in Ecuador has altered thinking about this plant's domestication. It was once believed to have originated solely in Mexico at about 5000 BC and to have spread from there. Given the new data from coastal Ecuador and other early dates on maize from Panama, maize is now seen to have had multiple centres of origin. The Las Vegas sites that have been studied demonstrate a very diversified economy, with incipient agriculture and hunting. The exploitation of the mangroves was equally important. They provided abundant resources, especially wood and estuarine molluscs such as oysters.

Excavations at a large cemetery at one of the Las Vegas sites, designated **OGSE-80**, revealed that at least 192 individuals were buried sometime between 6000-4000 BC. Many were in a flexed (knees to chest) position, lying on their sides. It is believed that most were secondary burials (ie exhumed after initial burial and then reburied) and were wrapped with a twined mat blanket that was tied closed. An interesting aspect of the cemetery is that burials were either single or double. One double burial of two adults lying on their sides closely facing one another as if locked in an eternal embrace was dubbed locally the 'Amantes de Sumpa'. A museum dedicated in April, 1996, near Santa Elena, the Museo de los Amantes de Sumpa, eloquently tells the story of the inhabitants of the site and the Las Vegas culture in general.

In the Santa Elena Peninsula, there seems to be an unexplained gap in the occupation between the end of the Preceramic Period, marked by the Las Vegas Culture, and the start of the Formative Period, marked by the Valdivia Culture. The Formative Period in this area has been the subject of the most intensive archaeological research and consequently the most prolific body of literature.

The Formative Period is signalled by the earliest appearance of pottery. Ceramics appear on the Guayas coast of Ecuador and on Caribbean coasts of Colombia and Venezuela at about the same time. Earliest Ecuadorean ceramics date to around 3300 BC and belong to the **Valdivia Culture**, named after a fishing village to the north of the Santa Elena Peninsula on the way to Manabí (see box in **The Pacific Lowlands** section). Valdivia villages inland have very little evidence for contact with coastal ones. One inland site, **Loma Alta**, has produced plant remains that demonstrate heavy dependence on cultivation of maize and *canavalia* beans. This was supplemented by riverine fishing, shellfish gathering and hunting and collecting wild game such as reptiles, rodents, birds, armadillos, anteaters and other mammals. At the same time, refuse from coastal sites reflects the procurement of marine shell fish, crustaceans and fish with very little evidence of the use of agriculture or game. Whether there was an exchange of food stuffs between the coastal and inland communities is not proven, even though the pottery from the two zones is similar.

Some Valdivia villages at the start of the Formative Period were large, U-shaped or circular in layout, and the houses surrounded open plazas. By 2300 BC, the first traces of mound-building appeared: a few villages have a pair of mounds placed in the open plazas as if they were a focal point. One of the best studied of these is the site of **Real Alto**, on the Santa Elena Peninsula near Chanduy. Real Alto was the largest site in the area at the time and probably functioned as a civic and ceremonial centre. By 1500 BC, these large villages were no longer the focus of settlement, and a more evenly spaced pattern of small hamlets strung up and down the inland river valleys and along the coast emerges.

Before 2000 BC, the majority of settlements were coastal and near the mouths of rivers. Only a handful of inland sites are known. In the earlier Valdivia coastal sites, there would have been available a diversity of protein-rich food (fish, molluscs, crustaceans and shore birds). There would also have been easy access to good agricultural lands and an abundance of wood in nearby forests. **Río Chico**, 1 km S of Salango in southern Manabí, has provided such data for Early and Middle Valdivia times (ie before 2000 BC). The excavation units may be viewed and a site museum with excellent explanations was opened in June 1996.

Before the very end of the Valdivia Period, however, settlements increased greatly in number and extended over a much wider geographical range. The coastal zone does not seem to have been an exclusive focal point of settlement any longer. This may be related to a more diversified, agriculturally-based economy. Evidence for social stratification and an increase in ritual activities exists.

Perhaps not coincidentally, at the same time, we find the first evidence of navigation on the high seas, probably involving rafts with sails. On the **Isla La Plata**, 30-40 km from the closest mainland ports, are sites with late Valdivia ceramics. Strong cross-winds and crosscurrents would make the use of rafts without sails to traverse this distance difficult. Some sites have permanent structures, but food and water are scarce, suggesting that contact with the mainland was constant. It is conjectured that the Valdivia rafts may have been of balsa, but there is no direct evidence of this.

One of the principal activities of the Valdivians who came to **Isla La Plata** was the exploitation of *Spondylus*, the thorny oyster whose brilliant red or purple rim was made into a variety of ornaments. According to Spanish chroniclers, *Spondylus* ornaments were more highly valued than gold or silver by western South American peoples. Artefacts made of *Spondylus* and even the unmodified shells were traded widely, from Mesoamerica to Chile.

The subsequent culture of the Manabí and Guayas coast is the **Machalilla Culture** (1500-1100 BC). What mainly distinguishes Machalilla from Late Valdivia are changes in ceramics and figurines, the design of houses and the pattern of life in the community, and the kinds of food consumed and the tools used to obtain them. On ceramics, design details change, and a new vessel form appears: the globular pot with a spout connected to the body by a pair of tubes forming an arch or 'stirrup' below the mouth of the vessel. These stirrup-spouted pots seem to have been invented in the central Manabí area, but soon spread to the Upper Amazon Basin and eventually to Perú to cultures such as Chavín, Vicús and Moche. They are found as well in the northern sierra at sites such as Cotocollao. Machalilla figurines are males, not females as in Valdivia times. This may reflect changes in religious and/or social forms. Houses were rectangular, not ovoid as in Valdivia times. They were also set up on wooden stilts, as they are in many coastal areas today. The layout of the villages also changed. The open plaza disappeared. Waste accumulated underneath the houses, instead of being disposed of at the perimeter of the community. Evidence from fish remains, largely from excavations at the **Salango Factory Site** in the town of Salango, show that the fish were often larger than those of Valdivia times, and in many cases, the fish skeletons were either partly or wholly articulated. It appears that the fishhooks used by Machalilla people were more robust than those used by their predecessors; a high percentage of fish bones belong to open-sea species like tuna, rather than the catfish found in estuaries; while Valdivians cooked their fish in pots and boiled them, the Machalillans grilled them directly on the open hearth. The high frequency of pelagic fish suggests much more raft-with-sail travel than employed by the Valdivians. Further, some archaeologists suspect that fish might have been prepared for trading after being smoke-cured. Obvious destinations would be into the highlands and

S toward what is Peru today.

Such forays would represent much more extensive cultural contacts than in Valdivia times. The spread of Machalilla vessel forms also provides evidence for broader networks of interaction. It is likely that people of the eastern Andes and those of highland Ecuador were in contact with coastal Machalillans as materials from the Amazon part of Ecuador (turquoise and chrysocolla), from the northern highlands of Ecuador (obsidian) and from as far away as the Atacama desert of Chile (lapis lazuli) have been found.

Following Machalilla in this region is the **Chorrera/Engoroy Culture** (1100 BC-0 AD/BC). This culture begins in the Formative Period and continues into the Regional Development Period. It is contemporary with the Chavín Culture in Peru and with the Olmec of Mexico. Indeed, several naturalistic icons are shared among these three regions, including the harpy eagle, feline, cayman and fer-de-lance serpent; these animals all appear on Chorrera ceramics. *Spondylus* and the conch *Strombus* were also sacred throughout the regions mentioned. In Chorrera sites these marine shells were manufactured into a variety of items and traded widely. The pottery of this culture is distinct from that of earlier periods in that it is polychrome.

The **Engoroy Culture** (a term not used by some archaeologists who prefer 'Chorreroid' to refer to the later portion of this period) is thought to begin about 650 BC. Engoroy subsistence was maritime-based. In some areas, urban centres developed, with streets, open plazas, drainage systems, specialized production districts (including shell workshops), public buildings and cemeteries for the élites. This seems to have been the first appearance of urban life in Ecuador. Unfortunately, few aboveground remains of these communities can be seen today.

Engoroy pottery is easily recognized by its predominantly irridescent pigment. It appeared as far away as the Isla La Plata and even the Galápagos Islands. These ceramics are found northward along the Manabí coast as far as the Río Chone, beyond which the materials of the Jama-Coaque Culture (discussed below) began to predominate. Such regional differences in material culture are what give the subsequent period (the Regional Development Period) its name, but they clearly began in the Formative.

In general, the Regional Development Period was a time of increasing sociopolitical complexity, with the emergence of chiefdoms in many areas, temple mounds, growing populations, and greater interactions among regions. At the same time, in different regions strong political control over a well-defined territory emerged, partly as a result of competition over long distance trade networks.

At this point, three major regions developed on the coast: (1) Guayas/S and central Manabí; (2) Jama-Coaque in far northern Manabí; and (3) northern Esmeraldas near the Colombian border. Furthermore, several strong political groups developed within each of these three regions.

The **Guangala Culture** (circa 100 BC-AD 800) of Guayas and S and central Manabí showed marked population increases in urban centres, rigid social hierarchies and intense craft specialization. This included the production of sumptuary pottery, shell working, stone working, metallurgy, textile production, fishing and fish processing, shell diving, navigation on the high seas, and long-distance and local commerce. Data from inland sites indicate that maize agriculture was more intensive than earlier and most sites show evidence of storage facilities and the redistribution of food surpluses under centralized leadership. Obsidian for stone tools was being obtained from the northern highlands in whole nodules, rather than in partly finished form as was the case previously, suggesting that the people of the coastal chiefdoms had direct access to the source. Mould-made figurines, first observed in Chorrera times, were frequent in Guangala sites. They became predominant in the later Integration Period.

Bahía is the name given to coastal chiefdoms of Guayas during this period and the following Integration Period. More than any other people of the Ecuadorian coast, they were navigators. The sites are found in almost every sheltered bay, inlet and river mouth from the Bahía de Caráquez to La Libertad. The Bahía people dominated the maritime trade networks that stretched from Central America to southern Peru or beyond. This development had its roots in late Valdivia times and is well illustrated in the Salango Museum. Owing to the enormous economic and political power accruing to these Bahía merchants, urbanism and the differentiation of élites to an elevated status reached its peak.

At around 1600 BC (in the Late Formative Period), and continuing into Spanish Colonial times, the people of the **Jama-Coaque Culture** began to build settlements along the mangrove-rich estuaries and rivers of northern Manabí, reaching inland to the area known today as Santo Domingo de los Colorados. At several junctures in their long development, these people seem to have been heavily influenced by the neighbouring La Tolita Culture of northern Esmeraldas. Known for many years only for its quite elaborate ceramics that portray houses, élites, local and mythical animals and plants, and various daily activities and rituals, this culture is now the subject of a long-term archaeological research project.

La Tolita Culture (called Tumaco in Colombia because it extends over the current border) is named after a site on an estuary-surrounded island at the mouth of the Río Santiago. Because of the quality and quantity of remains found there, it is thought that this site was the primary centre of the society. There are, however, hundreds of sites along a broad coastal and inland band some 500 km long, from the Bahía de San Mateo in Esmeraldas to the Río San Juan in Colombia. During its peak, the culture extended inland up the Río Santiago to what is now the territory of the Cayapas people.

The initial occupations date to around 600 BC (Formative Period) and were small hamlets and isolated households never very far from the shore. Subsistence was oriented primarily towards marine foods. Ceramics show strong Chorrera influences from Manabí (see above). Face masks, probably for the dead, are incised with designs resembling both contemporary Chavín and Olmec icons. Feminine figurines recall those of Valdivia and there are also realistic representations of felines, birds, reptiles and fish.

By 300 BC, the occupants of La Tolita had begun to transform the landscape by filling in the swamps with imported clay and cutting the mangrove trees to reclaim the water's edge. These efforts suggest that there was a need for additional settlement and agricultural area, probably due to (and permitting) increasing population. The result was an extensive area that could produce several agricultural harvests each year. The first evidence for gold metallurgical production appeared at this time.

The La Tolita Classic Phase (300 BC–AD 100) was the time of greatest population density and of the culture's maximum extent. Numerous 'tolas' (which give the site its name), flat-topped, conical, artificially-filled mounds, were constructed in the centre of the site, many of which can still be seen. A complex social organization had emerged, along with specialized craftspeople. A regionally distinctive art style had also emerged, characterized by mould-made ceramics, metal ornaments, stone tools, and sculpture in bone and wood. The La Tolita artisans dominated a variety of metallurgical techniques, including the lamination of several metals, repoussée, filigree, soldering and gilding. This site is also the only place in the Americas where we see the alloying of gold and platinum. La Tolita metallurgical expertise was widely appreciated: a gold figurine of a human male in the La Tolita style was found at El Angel in Carchi province on the border with Colombia and a virtually identical one at Lambayeque in northern Peru.

During the subsequent 250 years, the population appears to have expanded beyond the ability of the society to support it. Perhaps the society was becoming top-heavy, with too many demands placed on the populace by their chiefs. By AD 400, all of the Tolita Culture sites had been abandoned. When the Spanish arrived in the 16th century, they reported the area to be uninhabited.

In 1526, a Spanish captain, Bartolomé Ruiz, was sent by Francisco Pizarro to explore the Ecuadorean coast for the first time in search of the fabulous empire Pizarro had heard about from the natives of Panama. Ruiz was most surprised to see a cotton sail on the horizon. He captured the balsa wood raft and made a detailed description of it and its cargo to the chronicler Sámano-Jerex. It was the first raft the Spaniards had seen of what archaeologists now call the **Manteño/Huancavilca Culture**, belonging to the Integration Period. With their urban centres just inland from the shore, the Manteño/Huancavilca people extended their political rule from the Gulf of Guayaquil and Isla Puná northward to Manta, beginning just before AD 1000. They had probably learned much about maritime trade from their Bahía predecessors. Sámano-Jerex reported that the raft belonged to the 'lord' (Señor) of a chiefdom called Salangome, which comprised four contiguous towns with a sacred island in front. It has been determined that he was referring to the area in and around the modern town of Agua Blanca in south-central Manabí. Agua Blanca should be visited as the ruins are quite visible and have been cared for by the current inhabitants of the town. The site is now part of the Parque Nacional Machalilla. A small communal museum tells the story of the site and has an excellent three-dimensional model of the ruins in their natural settings.

Large, ceramic blackware figures of the lord and other nobles have been recovered which are distinctive of this Manteño/Huancavilca Culture. They often depict the individual on a U-shaped seat. These seats (thrones?) which have actually been found in one of the buildings at Agua Blanca, are about two feet high and made of granitic stone. Another of the four towns of the Salangome chiefdom is located beneath the modern fishing village of Salango. The island mentioned by Sámano-Jerex is the Isla Salango, a short boat ride from the village. The dominion of the Salangome lord extended northward to the Río Chone, but not to the South. S of

Stone sculpture dated 1000 AD from Manabí area

Source: Osborne, H (1968) *South American Mythology* Hamlyn: London

Salango, the rule of the Punaes of the Isla Puná (Gulf of Guayaquil), the chief (cacique) of Olón (northern coastal Guayas), and others maintained their political independence from the Salangome. They, too, controlled the maritime trade in their respective regions, yet they share with the Manteños so much of their material culture that many archaeologists group them together. It is significant, too, that groups like the Punaes maintained their political independence from the Salangome, for the Punaes also managed to retain their political independence when the Incas attempted, unsuccessfully, to conquer them.

To the S and E of the area dominated by the Manteño/Huancavilca culture, a similar Integration Period political entity emerged along the shores of the middle and upper Río Guayas and the Río Daule, the **Milagro/Quevedo Culture**. It appears that the principal trading orientation of the Milagro/Quevedo was inland rather than coastal and their primary trading partners were the chiefdoms of the highlands of southern Ecuador. Like the Manteño/Huancavilcans, the people of the Milagro/Quevedo Culture were excellent metallurgists, with extremely close similarities between the metal items of the Río Daule sites and those of the Cañari sites of the southern sierra (see below). The Milagro/Quevedo sites also contain T-shaped copper axes and flattened copper plaques called 'axe-money'. These latter were in use throughout the northwestern part of South America and are thought to have been a medium of exchange.

Both of these Integration Period cultures excelled in transforming the landscape. Vast tracts of land were terraced, irrigated and/or modified by the creation of raised field systems in order to increase agricultural productivity. The Museo Antropológico del Banco Central in Guayaquil has a highly recommended exhibit on the pre-European cultures of Ecuador, including a life-size balsa raft, fully equipped and carrying the same cargo described by the Spanish chroniclers. It is a striking reconstruction and occupies almost half of the exhibit hall on the first floor.

Southern Sierra

The earliest well-documented Pre-ceramic Period site in the southern sierra is **Chobshi Cave**. It has produced radiocarbon dates from tools of between 8000-6000 BC. Located in the province of Azuay at 2,400m, the site appears to have been used as a hunter-gatherer base camp. In the cave have been found laurel-leaf shaped spear points for hunting and tools for animal and/or plant processing. Rare obsidian artefacts may have been traded in from the N.

Sites of the Formative Period are being found with increasing frequency in this area, and our picture of this region's contributions to Ecuadorean life will undoubtedly change as this trend continues. One of the most important sites is **Cerro Narrio**, near the town of Cañar and almost due W of Ingapirca (see below). Clear evidence of trade with the coast is the presence of only the red/purple rims of the *Spondylus* shell and none of the white core. A similar pattern is observed in highland sites of northern Peru, suggests some sort of exchange between highlanders and coastal peoples, probably by about 2000 BC. Cerro Narrio also contains some of the earliest maize in the sierra of Ecuador.

Another important site is **Putushio**. Situated strategically in a pass connecting the Ecuadorean jungle with the coast at 1,750m, its occupants may well have participated in the burgeoning trade networks of the second millenium BC (see Machalilla, above). The site is in a zone of outcrops of workable stone and rich mineral deposits, especially of nugget gold. The site has dense architecture and extensive terracing, together with a communal, small-scale gold industry (there were several small furnaces and areas where gold was made into ornaments). The analysis of animal bone remains from Formative Period deposits indicates, for the first time, the presence of llamas in the Ecuadorean Andes. First domesticated earlier in the Peruvian Andes, these animals may have been used at Putushio for the transport of both gold ore and foodstuffs. The architecture and even the greenish tailings from gold-copper alloying can still be seen at the site, only 1 hr's walk from the modern town of Oña.

The site of **Pirincay**, NE of Cuenca in the Paute Valley, also provides evidence for the use of domesticated camelids in the Formative, albeit later than at Putushio. Pirincay had its own craft emphasis, namely the production of crystal beads. Putushio reached its maximum extent in the Regional Development Period and the presence of non-local ceramics in levels dated to this time suggest contacts with other sierra and coastal areas. In the Cuenca area, a pre-Incan chiefdom called **Cañari** had emerged by the Integration Period, combining local traditions with influences from further S in the Andes. Some day it may be possible to document the presence of the Cañari in the preceding period. At both the site of **Tomebamba**, in the modern city of Cuenca itself, and at the site of Ingapirca (see below), pre-Inca levels with Cañari-style materials contain evidence of a distinctive local pottery and also of metallurgy that was derived, at least in part, from the gold-workers of the Andes further S. A Cañari woman's burial showed she had attained considerable status within the society as she was buried with both male and female attendants. The Cañari maintained strong exchange relationships with the riverine Guayas peoples of the Milagro/Quevedo Culture (see above). The Cañari people were one of the southern sierra groups that clashed with the Incas on their expansion into Ecuador from Peru in the third quarter of the 15th Century.

At both Tomebamba and Ingapirca, the Incas took over the use of the buildings and constructed some of their own. At **Ingapirca**, 5.5 km E of Cañar between the Río Silante and the Río Huayrapungo, typical imperial Cusco-style architecture can be seen, such as the tightly fitting stonework and trapezoidal doorways of the 'castillo' and the 'governor's house'. These sites became admistrative cogs in the Inca state machinery. The Museo del Banco Central in Cuenca has an excellent series of exhibits on these southern sierra sites.

CONQUEST AND COLONIAL RULE

The Incas of Peru began to conquer the Sierra of Ecuador, already densely populated, towards the middle of the 15th century. A road was built between Cusco and Quito, and the empire was ruled after the death of the Inca Huayna Capac by his two sons, Huáscar at Cusco and Atahualpa at Quito. Pizarro's main Peruvian expedition took place in 1532, when there was civil war between the two brothers. Atahualpa, who had won the war, was put to death by Pizarro in 1533, and the Inca Empire collapsed.

Pizarro claimed the N kingdom of Quito, and his lieutenants Sebastián de Benalcázar (also Belalcázar) and Diego de Almagro took the city in 1534. Pizarro founded Lima in 1535 as capital of the whole region, and 4 years later replaced Benalcázar at Quito for Gonzalo, his brother. Gonzalo later set out on the exploration of the Oriente. He moved down the Napo River, and sent Francisco de Orellana to prospect. Orellana did not return. He drifted down the river finally to reach the mouth of the Amazon: the first white man to cross the continent in this way.

Quito became an *audiencia* under the Viceroy of Peru. For the next 280 years

Ecuador reluctantly accepted the new ways brought by the conqueror. Gonzalo had already introduced pigs and cattle; wheat was now added. The Indians were Christianized, colonial laws, customs and ideas introduced. The marriage of the arts of Spain to those of the Incas led to a remarkable efflorescence of painting, sculpting and building at Quito. In the 18th century black slave labour was brought in to work the plantations near the coast.

INDEPENDENCE AND AFTER

Ecuadorean independence came about in several stages. In 1809, taking advantage of the chaos produced in Spain by Napoleon's invasion and the forced abdication of the Spanish king, some members of the Quito elite formed a junta and declared independence: this lasted only 3 months before being put down by royalist troops. Fearing further trouble, the royalists executed the leaders of the junta the following year, provoking an uprising and the establishment of another junta which governed in Quito until it was crushed by a royalist army two years later. The defeat of these early moves for independence discouraged any further opposition to Spanish rule in Quito, though members of the coastal elites led a rising in 1820. Independence therefore had to wait until royalist forces were defeated by Antonio José de Sucre in the Battle of Pichincha in 1822. For the next 8 years Ecuador was a province of Gran Colombia under the leadership of Simon Bolívar. As Gran Colombia collapsed in 1830 Ecuador became an independent state.

After independence Ecuadorean politics were dominated by the small elite, divided between a coastal faction, based in Guayaquil, and a faction from the Sierra, based in Quito. Separated by different landholding systems, distinct economic patterns and interests and widely divergent social attitudes, these

Simon Bolívar

two factions struggled for control of Ecuador through the nineteenth century. Although there were several presidents from the coast, all governments until 1895 represented the interests of the conservative landowners of the Sierra against the commercial interests of the agro-exporting landowners and traders of Guayaquil and the coast whom they disdainfully called *monos* (monkeys).

After 1830 Ecuador became a chronic example of the political chaos and instability which affected much of Spanish America in the 19th century. Of the 21 individuals and juntas who occupied the presidency for a total of 34 times between 1830 and 1895 only six completed their constitutional terms of office. Four men stand out as the most notorious of the *caudillos* (political strongmen) who dominated politics, either as Presidents or from behind the scene: Gen Juan José Flores (president 1830-4, 1839-45), a Venezuelan who led the struggle for independence from Gran Colombia; José

María Urbina (1851-1856) who abolished slavery but imposed stern military rule; Gabriel García Moreno (1860-5 and 1869-75) renowned for his attempt to force Catholicism on the population; and Ignacio Veintimilla (1876-83) who was so unpopular that he united all the factions in the country against his dictatorship.

The 20th Century
The seizure of power in 1895 by the coastal elite led by the Radical Liberal *caudillo* Eloy Alfaro (president 1895-1901 and 1906-11), was followed by important changes as the Radical Liberals began to implement a programme which they saw as bringing Ecuador into the modern world. A key part of this was reducing the power of the church: secular education, civil marriage and divorce were introduced and church lands were confiscated. Capital punishment was also abolished.

The overthrow of the Radical Liberals by a group of military officers led to the restoration to power of the Quito elite. Between 1925 and 1931 the military-backed government of Isidro Ayora carried out some of the reforms suggested by a team of economic advisors from the United States, including the establishment of a Central Bank. The onset of the Great Depression, however, led to severe economic problems as demand for Ecuador's exports collapsed and prices fell. In the following years the country experienced its worst period of political instability: between 1931 and 1948 there were 21 governments, none of which succeeded in completing its term of office. "There were ministers who lasted hours, presidents who lasted for days, and dictators who lasted for week." (G Abad, *El proceso de lucha por el poder en el Ecuador*, Mexico 1970).

Political stability was only restored after 1948 when Ecuador entered another period of economic expansion, this time based on the production of bananas on coastal plantations. Banana exports grew from 18,000 tons in 1945 to 900,000 tons in 1960 by which time they accounted for two-thirds of exports; with cocoa and coffee prices also improving, there was a shift in population from the Sierra to the coast and Guayaquil grew rapidly. Between 1948 and 1960 three successive presidents managed to complete their terms of office. However, conflict between Velasco Ibarra and Congress in 1961 brought a return to instability: Velasco was succeeded by his Vice-President, Carlos Julio Arosemena, a *costeño* who was attacked by the Quito elite who saw him as favourable to the Cuban Revolution. Arosemena scandalised the Quito elite and the military with his indecorous behaviour. He was incapably drunk at a formal reception for the Chilean President, once received a visiting mission dressed in his bathrobe and enjoyed visiting sleazy bars and shooting at the waiters. Insulting the United States ambassador at a banquet provided the military with an excuse to overthrown him.

Between 1963 and 1979 Ecuador experienced two periods of military rule. The first, from 1963 to 1966, took strong measures against what it saw as a threat of Communism; an Agrarian Reform Law introduced in 1964, though inadequate to challenge many of the country's outdated landholding practices, was enough to upset the elite and the junta was forced from office. During the brief interlude of civilian rule which followed, new elections in 1968 led to the return of Velasco Ibarra. His overthrow by the armed forces in 1972 coincided with the increase in oil revenues from the Oriente and was followed by 7 years of military rule. Between 1972 and 1976 Gen Rodríguez Lara led a 'revolutionary and nationalist' government of which the aim was to use the oil revenues to build up the country's infrastructure and to finance agricultural, industrial and social projects. In fact, the

Give me a balcony and I will govern

José María Velasco Ibarra, who dominated Ecuadorean politics from the 1930s until 1972, was born in Quito in 1893. After qualifying as a lawyer and writing a weekly column for *El Comercio* in the 1920s, he studied at the Sorbonne before being elected to Congress in 1932. 2 years later he led moves in Congress to depose Martínez Mera and succeeded him as President. His attempt in 1935 to abolish Congress and rule as dictator was cut short by a military coup. Undeterred he contested the Presidential election of 1939 as a Socialist, losing an election which was widely regarded as corrupt. Elected President in 1944 on promises of radical reform, he declared himself dictator 2 years later but was soon overthrown by his Minister of the Interior.

Elected President for the third time in 1952, he managed to serve out his four year term, this time with conservative support. Elected yet again in 1960, he clashed with Congress and his Vice President, who overthrew him . His final term of office began in 1968; this time he governed with the support of the Liberal Radical Party, his historic enemy. In 1970 he assumed dictatorial powers, only to be overthrown by the armed forces in 1972. Most of his period out of office was spent in exile, most frequently in Argentina, the native land of his wife, where he lived austerely as a university teacher. In the late 1970s his offers to return again to lead Ecuador's transition from military rule were met with a loud silence from the country's leaders. He returned to Ecuador in February 1979 to bury his wife and he himself died a month later.

Five times elected President, four times overthrown, Velasco Ibarra's political allegiance shifted with the wind, though he was essentially a conservative who attracted strong support from shanty-town dwellers with extravagant promises. Once in office his supporters soon became disillusioned and Velasco himself was

Rodríguez Lara government lacked clear objectives, while disagreements within the armed forces and the opposition of many of the powerful sections of Ecuadorean society, eventually led to the president's replacement by a junta which promised to return the country to civilian rule.

Return to democracy

Since 1979 Ecuador has enjoyed its longest period of civilian constitutional government since independence. In 1978 Jaime Roldós was elected president after campaigning on a 21 point programme, which proposed using the oil revenues to promote national agricultural and industrial production, with hydroelectric power, transport and rural education among its priorities. By the time of Roldós's death in a plane crash in May 1981 his plans had been frustrated by the decline in oil prices in 1980 and the opposition of Congress. Roldós's successor, his Vice President Oswaldo Hurtado, was threatened by a series of political and economic crises which might have led to military intervention; Hurtado held on by forming an unstable alliance with left and centre parties in Congress. Unpopular measures taken to curb spending and increase taxes were forced on the government by the need to deal with its increased foreign debt. These cost the government much of its leftist support and the centre-left candidate in the 1984 elections, Rodrigo Borja Cevallos was narrowly defeated by the right wing León Febres Cordero. Febres Cordero suffered the disadvantage of facing a Congress controlled by the centre left parties. His attempt to introduce a neoliberal economic programme failed to control infla-

temperamentally unsuited to the frustrations and compromises of democracy. Famous for his – often contradictory – comments on Ecuadorean politics, he was described *Velasquism* as 'a liberal doctrine, a Christian doctrine, a socialist doctrine'.

Central to Velasco's style of politics was his appearance and public performance. 'Tall, spare, quixotesque; with a high forehead which premature baldness progressively enlarged and over which he wore a lumpy felt hat in the town or a straw hat in the countryside; quick bright eyes which glinted behind his spectacles as he jerked his head brusquely to and fro; a moustache like García Moreno's, which turned white early; cheeks as sunken as a fasting hermit; extended neck; the long supple hands of a conjuror, made for hypnotic gestures and the flourishes of thrilling oratory, extended in the air above him, the right index finger shaking in permanent prophetic denunciation; his erect figure standing out from those around him...elegantly turned out, even in moments of extreme poverty; the dominant speaker in conversation or in debate...the unmistakeable modulations of his voice, now soothing, now inflaming, crackling with steely nuances, sometimes shrill and strident, with strange inflexions running the whole length of the scale, full of yells, repetitions, outbursts, quivers, reiterated syllables, pauses and above all, taunts and insults – thunderous taunts and insults that leave an indelible impression, pouring out in a tidal wave that sweeps all before it, personal in the extreme... a style that has had many imitators, though none have succeded in capturing that same quality of electrifying momentousness. Such is Velasco Ibarra.' Jorge Salvador Lara, *Escorzos de historia patria*, quoted in D Corkill and D Cubitt, *Ecuador: Fragile Democracy*, Latin America Bureau, 1988.

tion or end recession, but sparked an upsurge in political violence and confrontation including coup attempts and clashes with students and workers. When Rodrigo Borja won the 1988 election, he at least enjoyed the advantage of the support of a majority in Congress. His inheritance from Febres Cordero was, however, difficult: high inflation, high unemployment and a large public spending deficit. His measures to deal with this situation, which included increases in taxes and electricity and fuel prices, made him unpopular with the left, while right wing parties argued this was insufficient. The latter half of Borja's presidency was marked by conflict with Congress and labour unrest.

1992 to the present day

The elections of 1992 were won by Sixto Durán Ballén of the Partido de Unidad Republicana in coalition with Alberto Dahik of the Partido Conservador (who became vice-president). The popularity of President Durán Ballén's government declined steadily with the implementation of an economic modernization programme aimed at reducing inflation and replenishing foreign reserves by cutting public spending (and public sector jobs) and by privatizing state enterprises. Strikes, protests and an overwhelming victory for opposition parties in mid-term congressional elections (May 1994) indicated the depth of popular feeling, while the PSC, led by presidential hopeful Jaime Nebot Saadi, scored major gains.

The country's political situation changed dramatically when Ecuadoreans responded to the Jan-Feb 1995 border conflict with Peru (see below) with

Political parties and conflict in modern Ecuador

Although Ecuadorean political parties reflect the regionalism of the country, this alone does not explain the myriad of parties which exist. The country's oldest parties, the *Partido Conservador* and the *Partido Liberal Radical*, were formed to represent the elites of the *sierra* and the *costa* respectively. Marxist parties have never enjoyed much support, both the Socialist party (founded in 1926) and the Communist party (established in 1931) remaining small organisations. Most other parties have tended to be based around personalities, rising and falling with their leaders' fortunes: Velasco Ibarra who claimed to dislike political parties, ran for election supported by a variety of parties, but *Velasquismo* died with its founder. By contrast the *Concentración de Fuerzas Populares*, a party which draws its main support from the shantytowns of Guayaquil, has managed to survive the death of its charismatic leader Asaad Bucaram to win the Presidency in 1996.

Since the return to constitutional rule in 1979 the most important parties have included two centre left parties *Democracia Popular* (the party of Osvaldo Hurtado) and *Izquierda Democrática* (the party of Rodrigo Borja). The main right wing parties include the *Partido Social Cristiano* (the party of León Febres Cordero) and the traditional Conservative and Radical Liberal parties. The proliferation of parties has contributed to the problems of governing since 1979. To win the presidency candidates need to form electoral alliances with other parties: these often disintegrate shortly afterwards leaving the President facing a hostile majority in Congress.

a massive display of national unity, backing their government and armed forces to an extent not seen in recent years and sending the President's popularity ratings well above 90%. This backing was short-lived as a combination of the financial cost of the conflict and electricity rationing because of insufficient rain to fill hydroelectric reservoirs led to major economic problems. Confidence in both the economy and the political establishment was rocked by a huge corruption scandal which culminated with Vice-President Dahik fleeing the country in Oct 1996 in the face of charges of misuse of public funds. In all 23 ministers were impeached or resigned; at one stage the president himself was under threat of impeachment. The public's exasperation was amply demonstrated by the rejection in a referendum in Nov 1996 of all constitutional reforms, even those which, before the vote, were seen to have majority support.

By May 1996, the month general elections were due, it seemed likely that Durán Ballén's government would limp to the end of its term in Aug 1996. In the elections, the presidency was won by Abdalá Bucaram of the Roldosista party, who defeated Jaime Nebot, the Social Christian candidate. In the first three months of his presidency, Bucaram showed no intention of toning down his style, which contained all the flamboyance of his pre-election days and an erratic attitude to governing which left many bemused and caused his popularity ratings to fall dramatically.

In early February 1997, the people and Congress lost patience with the president. A 48-hour strike and mass demonstrations against the huge price rises in his economic austerity programme were followed by a congressional vote to remove Bucaram from office on the grounds of 'mental

An Ecuadorean political dynasty?

👣 Few newly elected Presidents have celebrated their victory by launching a career as a pop singer. Shortly after his election in Aug 1996, Abdalá Bucaram, who had campaigned as *El Loco* (the Madman) released an album called 'The Madman In Love' and was performing to packed audiences in Guayaquil. Unusual though Bucaram's political style may be, he is merely the latest member of Ecuador's most colourful political family to achieve fame.

Bucaram's father, Asaad, a man of humble origins who started his adult life as a travelling salesman for a textile company dominated Guayaquil politics for two decades. Elected to Congress in 1958 Asaad Bucaram soon made a name for himself with his unconventional debating methods, on one occasion brandishing a pistol in the chamber. After seizing control of the *Concentración de Fuerzas Populares* (CFP) in the early 1960s, he was twice elected mayor of Guayaquil. His fiery oratory and personal popularity among the poor of Guayaquil's shantytowns (where he was known affectionately as 'Don Buca') earned him the hatred and distrust of Ecuador's elite who saw him as a Communist. The Ecuadorean left regarded him as a fascist, pointing to his lack of real interest in redistributing power or wealth and to his practice of employing gangs of thugs to intimidate opponents.

He was arrested and exiled four times between 1963 and 1972 by the armed forces, who seized power in 1972 to prevent his election to the presidency after he had emerged as the leading candidate. On the return to civilian rule in 1978 the military and their civilian supporters insisted that the new constitution should stipulate that only those born of parents who were Ecuadorean citizens at the time of birth were eligeable as presidential candidates, thus excluding Bucaram, whose parents had been Lebanese citizens when he was born. Bucaram's nephew, Jaime Roldós, took his uncle's place as CFP candidate under the slogan 'Roldós to govern, Bucaram to power' but after Roldós's victory, the two men fell out: Roldós forming his own party (People, Change, Democracy) while Bucaram led the CFP in a bitter anti-government campaign which was cut short by his death in 1981.

incapacity'. Bucaram resisted his deposition for a few days, during which time Ecuador had three presidents: Bucaram, vice-president Rosalía Arteaga, who claimed the office, and Fabián Alarcón, chosen by Congress, of whom he was president. On 8 February the army withdrew its support for Bucaram and it was agreed that Arteaga should assume the presidency temporarily until Congress had resolved certain constitutional inconsistencies. Thereafter, a new president would be appointed by Congress prior to new elections brought forward to 1998.

BORDER DISPUTES

After the dissolution in the 1820s of Gran Colombia (largely present-day Venezuela, Colombia and Ecuador), repeated attempts to determine the extent of Ecuador's eastern jungle territory failed. While Ecuador claimed that its territory has been reduced from that of the old Audiencia of Quito by gradual Colombian and especially Peruvian infiltration, Peru has insisted that its Amazonian territory was established in law and in fact before the foundation of Ecuador as an independent state. The dispute reached an acute phase in 1941 when war broke out between Ecuador and Peru; the war ended with military defeat for Ecuador and the signing of the Rio de Janeiro Protocol of 1942 which allotted most of the disputed territory to Peru. Since 1960 Ecuador has denounced the Protocol as unjust (because it was imposed by force of arms) and as technically flawed (because it refers to certain non-existent geographic features). According to Peru, the Protocol demarcated the entire boundary and all the features are provable to US aerial photographic maps. Ecuador's official policy remains the recovery of a sovereign access to the Amazon. In Peru's view, the Protocol gives Ecuador navigation rights, but does not and cannot return land that Ecuador never had in the first place. Sporadic border skirmishes continued throughout recent decades and in January 1995 these escalated into an undeclared war over control of the headwaters of the Río Cenepa. Argentina, Brazil, Chile and the USA (guarantors of the Rio de Janeiro Protocol) intervened diplomatically and a ceasefire took effect after 6 weeks of combat, during which both sides made conflicting claims of military success. A multinational team of observers was dispatched to the region in Mar 1995 to oversee the disengagement of forces and subsequent demilitarization of the area of the conflict. In 1996 the bases for negotiations to end the dispute were being sought. Presidents Bucaram and Fujimori met informally in Sept 1996, although tangible results were not immediately apparent.

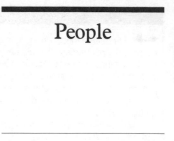

People

Roughly 48% of Ecuador's people live in the coastal region W of the Andes, and 47% in the Andean Sierra. Migration is occurring from the rural zones of both the coast and the highlands to the towns and cities, particularly Guayaquil and Quito, and agricultural colonization by highlanders is occurring in parts of the coastal lowlands and the Oriente. National average population density is the highest in South America. Average income per head has risen fast in recent years like that of other oil-exporting countries, but the distribution has not improved and a few citizens are spectacularly wealthy.

According to the 1980 census, about 50% of the population was classed as Quichua, 40% *mestizo*, 8.5% white and 1.5% other Amerindian. Different classifications state that there are 2-3 million Quichua-speaking Indians in the highlands and about 70,000 lowland Indians. The following indigenous groups maintain their distinct cultural identity: in the Oriente, Siona-Secoya, Cofán, Huaorani (also known as Aucas, which is a derogatory term), Záparo, Quichua, Achuar and Shuar; in the Sierra, Otavalo, Salasaca (province of Tungurahua), Puruha (Chimborazo), Cañar and Saraguro (Loja province); on the coast, Cayapas (also known as Chachi, Esmeraldas province), Tsáchilas (also known as Colorados, lowlands of Pichincha) and Cuaiquer (also known as Awas, Esmeraldas and Carchi provinces). Many Amazonian Indian communities are fighting for land rights in the face of oil

Day of the dead

One of the most important dates in the indigenous people's calendar is 2 Nov, the 'Day of the Dead'. This tradition has been practised since time immemorial. In the Incaic calendar, Nov was the eighth month and meant *Ayamarca*, or land of the dead. The celebration of Day of the Dead, or 'All Saints' as it is also known since the arrival of Christianity, is just one example of religious adaptation in which the ancient beliefs of ethnic cultures are mixed with the rites of the Catholic Church.

According to ancient belief, the spirit visits its relatives at this time of the year and is fed in order to continue its journey before its reincarnation. The relatives of the dead prepare for the arrival of the spirit days in advance. Among the many items necessary for these meticulous preparations are little bread dolls, each one of which has a particular significance. A ladder is needed for the spirit to descend from the other world to the terrestrial one. There are other figures which represent the grandparents, great grandparents and loved ones of the person who has 'passed into a better life'. Horse-shaped breads are prepared that will serve as a means of transport for the soul in order to avoid fatigue.

Inside the home, the relatives construct a tomb supported by boxes over which is laid a black cloth. Here they put the bread, along with sweets, flowers, onions and sugar cane. This latter item is an indispensable part of the table as it symbolizes the invigorating element which prevents the spirit from becoming tired on its journey towards the Earth. The union of the flowers with the onion ensures that the dead one does not become disoriented and arrives in the correct house.

The tomb is also adorned with the dead relative's favourite food and drink, not forgetting the all-important glass of beer as, according to popular tradition, this is the first nourishment taken by the souls when they arrive at their houses. Once the spirit has arrived and feasted with their living relatives, the entire ceremony is then transported to the graveside in the local cemetery, where it is carried out again, along with the many other mourning families.

This meeting of the living and their dead relatives is reenacted the following year, though less ostentatiously, and again for the final time in the third year, the year of the farewell. It does not continue after this, which is just as well as the costs can be crippling for the family concerned.

exploration and colonization. The main Indian organization is the National Confederation of Indigenous Nationalities of Ecuador, CONAIE, Casilla 17-17-1235, Quito, T 593-2-248-930, F 442-271. In July 1994 there was an uprising of indigenous groups in the Sierra and Oriente over proposed changes to land ownership laws, which were perceived as favouring landowners and agro-industrial interests to the detriment of native communities.

Indigenous Groups

The Quichua, Shuar and Siona-Secoya Indians in Pastaza welcome tourists in a controlled way, in order to sell their beautiful products; some work as guides. Contact the Organización de Indígenos de Pastaza (OPIP) in Puyo, T 885-461, they can also give you a list of indigenous museums and artesan workshops. Also contact Federación de Centros Shuar-Achuar, Domingo Comín 17-38, Sucúa, Morona-Santiago, T/F 593-7-740-108 (or in Quito 2-504-264). CONFENIAE, the confederation of Amazon Indians is another good contact at Km 5 outside Puyo, T 885-343, or at their office in

Quito, Av 6 de Diciembre y Pazmino, Edif Parlamento, p 4, of 408, T 593-2-543-973, F 220-325. Care is required when visiting the Oriente and taking tours to Huaorani villages without prior arrangement, the Huaorani are at great risk from the tourist invasion and do not appreciate being treated as a spectacle. ONHAE, the Huaorani Indigenous organization, has stated that it will only allow guides approved by them to enter their territories.

The term *cholo* refers to people in the Sierra who are an ethnic mixture of white and Indian. The same term is used in Peru. In Ecuador, however, it is also a name given to people of white/Indian/black descent who live in the Santa Elena peninsula, W of Guayaquil. Another, more common name is given to people of this three-way mixture in the area around Guayaquil and throughout the northern Pacific lowlands: *montuvio*. The *montuvios* (also spelt *montubios*) generally make their living from farming and fishing.

RELIGION

According to official statistics, 93% of the population belongs to the Roman Catholic faith. The remaining 7% covers those who are members of a variety of protestant churches and the Indian groups who still worship their traditional gods.

Culture

LITERATURE

Throughout its unsettled history, the Republic of Ecuador has suffered from many tensions. These started with the question of independence itself, leading to the rivalry between Liberals and Conservatives and between Costa and Sierra, and to the position of the Indian and the marginalized in society. Much Ecuadorean literature reflects these issues, with many writers in the 20th century adopting a strongly political line. In 1961, the writer Benjamín Carrión defined the major characteristics of the Republic as the tropics, the desire for liberty and a 'mestizaje incompleto' (not completely *mestizo*). All the main national cultural figures, he says, were fighters for liberty in their life and work, even to martyrdom. Such people were Francisco Eugenio de Santa Cruz y Espejo, who led a rebellion against Spain in 1795, José Joaquín de Olmedo, Federico González Suárez (archbishop of Quito) and Juan Montalvo. We shall return to Olmedo and Montalvo shortly. Carrión's theory of the Ecuadorean *mestizo* rests on two views of the Indian: the whites, in law and literature, love the Indian: Indians and *cholos* who have acquired a certain social standing detest the Indian. And the Indian who has remained in the fields does not know that they have made beautiful laws to protect him. He is systematically brutalized, destroyed by an ominous trilogy: the clergy wielding superstition, alcohol, purgatory, marriage and the dead, the *cacique* who wields extorsion, hunger, debt, prison and the whip, and political authority with its prisons, torture and forced labour. Carrión wrote this before the 1964 agrarian reform laws, but the vehemence of his sentiments has a great bearing on much of Ecuadorean literature's presentation of the Indian.

The 19th Century

José Joaquín de Olmedo (born Guayaquil 1780, died 1847) was a disciple of Espejo and was heavily involved first in the independence movement and then the formative years of the young republic. In 1825 he published *La Victoria de Junín, Canto a Bolívar*, a heroic poem glorifying the Liberator. Bolívar appointed him to represent Peru at the courts of London and Paris after the poem's appearance. Olmedo vowed to give up politics on his return to Guayaquil, but once relations between Peru and Gran Colombia broke down in the second half of the 1820s, he held many posts in the first Ecuadorean assemblies. His second famous poem was the *Canto al General Flores, Al Vencedor de Miñarica*. (Juan José Flores was the Venezuelan appointed by Bolívar to govern Ecuador, but for Benjamín Carrión at least, the state of Ecuador was not born until Flores' expulsion in 1845.) In addition to poetry, Olmedo wrote political works such as *Discurso sobre las mitas* and *Manifiesto político sobre la Revolución del Seis de Marzo*.

Juan Montalvo (born Ambato 1832, died 1889) was an essayist who was influenced by French Romantics such as Victor Hugo and Lamartine, also by Lord Byron and by Cervantes. As the accompanying box shows, one of his main objectives as a writer was to attack what he saw as the failings of Ecuador's rulers, but his position as a liberal, in opposition to conservatism such as García Moreno's, encompassed a passionate opposition to all injustice. 'Ojeada sobre América', for instance (in *El cosmopólita*, 1866-68), is a diatribe against the "natu-ral law" of man, namely war and killing. While it is indefensible, he does want war in Ecuador, war against the so-called peace which imprisons, suffocates and murders: "You can go to hell with that peace," he wrote. Other collections of essays included *Los siete tratados* (1881-82) and *El espectador* (1886), in which he wrote, "If my pen had the gift of tears, I would write a book called *The Indian*, which would make the whole world weep." He never wrote that book. His *Capítulos que se le olvidaron a Cervantes* (1895) was an attempt to imitate the creator of Don Quijote, translating him into an Ecuadorean setting.

Montalvo's contemporary and enemy, Juan León Mera (born Ambato 1832, died 1894), did write a book about the Indian, *Cumandá* (1979). But this dealt not so much with the humiliated Sierra Indians as the unsubjugated Amazonian Indians, "los errantes y salvajes hijos de las selvas" (the wandering and savage sons of the forests). He tells his readers (in Conservative, Catholic Quito) to forget society and venture into the world of these people who are cruel, ignorant of good and evil, but in their innocence potentially untainted Christians. The plot tells of a landowner, José Domingo Orozco, whose family is killed in an Indian uprising in 1790, provoked by his cruelty. Orozco becomes a missionary in the Amazon and takes his surviving son, Carlos, with him. Carlos falls in love with Cumandá, an Indian girl who saves him from death. Despite their love, her tribe enforce their separation in order to marry her to a chief. Eventually Carlos dies with her as she tries to escape the tribal custom of the chief's wife killing herself at her husband's death. It transpires that Cumandá was in fact José Orozco's lost daughter. A great deal of ink has been used in discussing the merits of *Cumandá*, its acceptance or rejection being almost a point of ideological principle. The novel conforms to the tastes of its

The pen is mightier than the sword

Gabriel García Moreno was assassinated in 1875, 6 years into his second term as president of Ecuador. He first held the post from 1861 to 1865. He promoted public works such as road improvement, railway construction and the introduction of the eucalyptus trees which add such a distinctive character to many Ecuadorean landscapes. He was also a devout Catholic, the influence of which is discussed in **History** above. At a time when politics was deeply split between Conservatives and Liberals, it was not surprising that García Moreno's forthright politics inspired intense support, or fervent antagonism. Among his supporters was Juan León Mera, who was a Catholic, Conservative politician and romantic novelist. In the opposite camp was another Juan from Ambato, Montalvo, the Liberal essayist.

Although no Ecuadorean leader was spared Montalvo's vilifications, especially Veintimilla (who followed García Moreno) in *Las Catilinarias*, the writer reserved some particularly choice insults for García Moreno. "Holy prostitute", "the saint of the scaffold" appear in *La dictadura perpétua*, an open letter to the US newspaper *Star and Herald*, which had called for García Moreno's reelection. In another essay ("A Don Gabriel García Moreno") he says: "García Moreno, you are called Gabriel: a sweet, pure name, an angel's name, which sounds harmoniously on the lips of God when He calls his chosen one: Gabriel, my friend, are you not my brother in Adam? Why do you want to kill me? Why do you want to kill your brothers?_After so many years of absolute domination, with so many ways to make yourself popular, so many resources to work your fellows' happiness_do we come to realize yet again that there is no place for men other than the scaffold? A lion is called a lion, a dove a dove; why are you called Gabriel? You do not hold the sword of the Lord in your right hand; you wield the lance and build the gibbet." For his opposition, Montalvo was exiled frequently. While in Ipiales, Colombia, he heard that García Moreno had been killed and announced: "My pen killed him."

time, but later critics have speculated about how much León Mera actually knew of the real jungle that he was describing. The debate revolves around the concepts of civilization and barbarism, how colonialism leads to exploitation, but also the value of using nature and the 'savage' solely for ideological ends so that characters are reduced to nothing more than symbols.

The 20th Century

In 1904, Luis A Martínez (1869-1909) published *A la costa*, the story of a middle-class man, Salvador Ramírez, and his family who move from the Andes to run a plantation on the coast. The action takes place during Eloy Alfaro's campaigns in the mid-1890s. The novel attempts to present two very different sides of the country and the different customs and problems in each. *Plata y bronce* (1927) and *La embrujada* (1923), both by Fernando Chávez, portray the gulf between the white and the Indian communities. In their distinct ways, the two writers moved beyond León Mera's use of an Ecuadorean setting for a Christian Romantic theme (shared, for example, by Chateaubriand in France – *René*) to books which are just Ecuadorean. These are, however, among the few examples of novel-writing in the century since the Republic's independence which begin to cast a serious eye on the reality of Ecuadorean society. Then, in 1930, everything changed.

For the next 15-20 years, novelists in Ecuador produced a realist literature heavily influenced by French writers like Zola and Maupassant, Russians like Gorki, the North Americans Sinclair Lewis, Dos Passos, Steinbeck and Hemingway, and, from Latin America, Mariano Azuela (Mexico), Alcides Arguedas (Bolivia) and Ricardo Güiraldes (Argentina). For the Ecuadoreans, the realism was taken to the point of 'beauty can wait'. They wrote politically committed stories about marginalized people in crude language and stripped-down prose. Some critics denominate three groups: Guayaquil (the best known), Quito and El Austro (Cuenca and Loja). The first indication of a radically different prose was *Los que van*, a collection of stories by Joaquín Gallegos Lara (1911-47), Enrique Gil Gilbert (1912-75 and Demetrio Aguilera Malta (1909-81). These 24 stories "del cholo y del montuvio" (stories of the *mestizos* of the coastal lowlands – see **People**) created a scandal. They describe incidents in the lives of poor people whose own violence and sexual passions bring about their tragedy. Their dialect is transcribed faithfully, adding to the realism. Interestingly, *Los que van* initiated a movement of protest literature without actually denouncing anyone or anything. The stories deal with social injustice, but in isolated, extreme cases.

Two other writers formed the Grupo de Guayaquil, José de la Cuadra (1903-41) and Alfredo Pareja Diezcanseco (1908). "There were five of us," said Gil Gilbert at de la Cuadra's funeral, "like a fist." A sixth member, Adalberto Ortiz (born 1914), joined later. Among the books of these writers are: Gallegos Lara, *Las cruces sobre el agua* (novel, 1946); Gil Gilbert, *Yunga* (stories, 1933), *Nuestro pan* (novel, 1941); Aguilera Malta, the novels *Don Goyo* (1933), *Canal zone* (1935), *La isla virgen* (1942), *La caballeresa del sol* (1964), *Siete lunas y siete serpientes* (1970) and *El secuestro del General*

(1973); de la Cuadra, many short stories, *Repisas* (1931), *Horno* (1934), and the novels *Los sangurinos* (1934), *Guasinto* (1938) and *Los monos enloquecidos* (1951). Pareja Diezcanseco's novels are concerned more with urban themes than the stories of his colleagues, eg *El muelle* (1933, set in Guayaquil and New York), *Baldomera* (1938), *Hombres sin tiempo* (1941), *Las tres ratas* (1944). He also wrote a group of books under the general title of *Los años nuevos* (including *La advertencia*, 1956, *El aire y los recuerdos*, 1959, *Los poderes omnímodos*, 1964) which show him breaking away from the Guayaquil Group, taking as his starting point the political events of 9 July 1925 and the founding of the Socialist Party. With *Las pequeñas estaturas* (1970) and *La manticora* (1974) he became more experimental with narrative forms, while introducing more imaginative material into the same historical lines. Adalberto Ortiz was born in Esmeraldas: his novel *Juyungo* (1943) relates the life of a black/Indian of that region. He also wrote *El espejo y la ventana* (1967), *La envoltura del sueño* (1981) and is a poet.

A slightly later Guayaquileño writer is Pedro Jorge Vera (born 1914), author of poetry in the 1930s and 1940s and novels such as *Los animales puros* (1946), *La semilla estéril* (1962), *Tiempo de muñecos* (1971) and *El pueblo soy yo* (1976), about Velasco Ibarra.

Of the writers of the 1930s and 1940s, outside Guayaquil, Pablo Palacio (1906-47) described himself as an observer. Besides the stories of *Un hombre muerto a puntapiés* and *Débora* (1927), in which Palacio approaches an individual, grotesque realism, Palacio's best known book is *Vida del ahorcado* (1932), which Jorge Enrique Adoum (more of whom later) describes as one of the rare cries of existential anguish in Ecuadorean literature. The Cuenca/Loja Group included Angel F Rojas (born 1909), a poet and novelist (*Banca*, 1940, *Un idilio bobo*,

1946, *El éxodo de Yangana*, 1949), G Humberto Mata (born 1904), writer of the indigenist novels *Sal* (1963), *Sumac-Allpa* and *Sanagüín*, and Alfonso Cuesta y Cuesta. Included in the Quito Group are Fernando Chávez (see above), Humberto Salvador (born 1909 – *Camarada*, 1933, *Trabajadores*, 1935, *Noviembre*, 1939) and Jorge Icaza (1906-78).

Leaving Icaza till last in this study of the 1930s-40s generation is not intended to diminish his importance. In fact, his novel of 1934, *Huasipungo*, has been described by Gerald Martin as a "literary bombshell...which may just be the most controversial novel in the history of Latin American narrative" (page 75, see bibliographical note below). Unlike some indigenist fiction (basically, writing about the Latin American Indian, especially in Peru and Bolivia), there is absolutely no attempt to portray the life of the Sierra Indians as anything other than brutal, inhuman, violent and hopeless. Even the landscape, cold, muddy, drenched in rain, has none of the beauty that is frequently the background to indigenist writing. Don Alfonso Pereira, the landowner of Tomachi, the town in which the story is set, is presented as a pathetic figure, governed by events outside his control. He and his retainers treat the Indians unspeakably, finally expropriating their *huasipungos* (shacks and plots of land) as part of his agreement with a foreign company to build a road for oil exploration. There are many degrading episodes before the Indians attempt a last-ditch resistance which inevitably fails. This is not Montalvo's book which will make the world weep, but it is a book that has aroused much anger, either at the Indians' plight, or at Icaza's motives as a novelist. He wrote many other novels, among them *En las calles* (1935), *Cholos* (1938), *Media vida deslumbrados* (1942) and *Huairapamuchcas* (1948), but none achieved the fame of *Huasipungo*.

The 1960s ushered in the so-called Boom, with writers such as Gabriel García Márquez, Mario Vargas Llosa, Carlos Fuentes and Julio Cortázar gaining international recognition for the Latin American novel. The Colombian García Márquez said that the revolutionary duty of any writer is 'to write well' and during those years of exploration, experimentation and celebration of all the possibilities of the novel, 'writing well' was a hallmark of these and other novelists. But, wondered Jorge Enrique Adoum (born 1923) the poet and novelist, what next? What can one write after James Joyce, after Cortázar's *Rayuela*? "It's not enough now to write well – obviously every honest writer must write well – ideas aren't enough...nor situations...nor the inventions of language that are becoming as boring as language itself. But that necessity for art in the man who sings in the shower or hangs a calendar of half-naked Italian 'Indians' on the wall...to invent something which until now did not exist and would not exist other than as you would do it yourself...for that which makes you feel fleetingly complete..." *Entre Marx y una mujer desnuda* (1976), which poses these questions, is an extraordinary novel, a dense investigation of itself, of novel-writing, of Marxism and politics, sex, love and Ecuador, loosely based around the story of the writer and his friends in a writing group, their loves and theorizing. "Here the only way to get read is by writing on the walls and door of the toilet, and why not, if it's a mass media as clean and worthy as the papers, the radio, the TV, why don't you go now and from the start, so as not to deceive the reader later, isolated like a voter – and there you have the two cabins – why don't you decide to be like everyone else, and have the courage even if in secret and write the first thing that comes into your head." Rather than attempt the impossible and summarize the book and all its targets, a few examples from it may give a flavour. In relation to some of the topics quoted from Carrión above, Adoum writes: "What happens to us as a country and as writers is that we don't have a destiny which overtook us, which was greater than us, and we never went to meet our own destiny when it was in play everywhere, in the decisive combats of other people, except those who are not 'us' because they opted for the side of shit...We are isolated, 6 million Robinson Crusoes and, yet, we believe ourselves to be the navel of the world...We don't know anything about the outside world and no one knows anything about us – except an earthquake, or, more frequently, a dictatorship...Or we describe the Indian who we only know from outside or in passing, as if we had looked at him from the window of a moving train, like a tree, stone, cow, or shack: an element of the geography but not history, nor literature. On the other hand, he doesn't know us either: neither the bosses nor the centuries of the whip have taught him to distinguish his enemy from the one who still kisses his hand."

Adoum has also written *Ciudad sin angel* (1995), and several collections of poetry, which is also intense and inventive (see for example *No son todos los que están, 1949-79*).

Other contemporary novelists include Abdón Ubidia (*Ciudad de invierno*; *Palacio de los espejos*; *Sueño de lobos*),Eliecer Cárdenas Espinosa (*Polvo y ceniza*; *Diario de un idolatra*), Raul Pérez Torres, writer of prose and poetry, Javier Vásconez (*El secreto*, *Ciudad lejana*), Miguel Donoso Pareja – who is also a poet (*Henry Black*, *El hombre que mataba a sus hijos*), Alicia Yáñez Cossío (*La casa del sano placer* – described as a satire of traditional sexual norms) and Nelson Estupiñán Bass (*Cuando los guayacanes florecían*). See also *Diez cuentistas ecuatorianos*, Libri Mundi, 1993.

20th Century Poetry

In *Lírica ecuatoriana contemporánea* (2 vols, Quito 1979), Hernán Rodríguez Castelo says that a generation of powerful lyric poets was born between 1890 and 1905. This included modernists like Ernesto Noboa y Caamaño and José María Egas, and many post-modernists. Among this second group were Miguel Angel Zambrano (born 1898, *Diálogo de los seres profundos*, 1956), Gonzalo Escudero (born 1903, *Estatua del aire*, *Materia de ángel*, *Autorretrato, Introducción a la muerte*, written in the 1950s and 1960s), Alfredo Gangotena (born 1904, *Poesía*, 1956) and Aurora Estrada y Ayala (born 1902,*Como el incienso*, 1925). The major figure, perhaps of all Ecuadorean poetry, was Jorge Carrera Andrade (1903-78). Son of a liberal lawyer, Carrera Andrade was involved in socialist politics in the 1920s before going to Europe. In the 1930s he started a diplomatic career, holding positions in Japan (whose culture and Zen philosophy strongly influenced his work), the USA and Venezuela. He was a firm opponent of many of Velasco Ibarra's policies and was often exiled in the 1940s and 1950s. In the 1930s and 1940s, Carrera Andrade moved beyond the socialist realist, revolutionary stance of his contemporaries and of his own earlier views, seeking instead to explore universal themes. He did not deny social concern in his poetry, but did rule out adherence to any one creed. Moreover, the poet's chief weapon in the struggle to save the world is beauty and Carrera Andrade's first goal was to write beautiful poetry. He published many volumes, including the haiku-like *Microgramas*; see *Registro del mundo: antología poética (1922-39)*, *El alba llama a la puerta* (1965-66), *Misterios naturales* and others. (See also *Selected Poems*, translated by H R Hayes, Albany, New York, 1972, and *Winds of Exile* by Peter R Beardsell, Oxford, 1977.) Of Carrera Andrade's view of the Indian and his environment, Hays writes, "The patient self-contained Indians of his native land, however, and the visual beauty of its snow-capped peaks and green valleys became for him a symbol of innocence and simplicity which he cherished during periods in which he felt overwhelmed by the cynicism and materialism of the world of highly developed technology." Compare this with Adoum, or *Huasipungo*.

From the 1940s onwards, many groups were writing in different parts of the country. A poet who was a major link between Carrera Andrade's generation and the new writers was César Dávila Andrade (1919-67: *Oda al arquitecto*, 1946; *Catedral salvaje*, 1951; *Arco de instantes*, 1959; *En un lugar no identificado*, 1963; *Materia real*, 1970). He was a member of the Madrugada group, as were Enrique Noboa Arízaga (*Orbita de la púpila iluminada*, 1947; *Biografía atlántida*, 1967) and Jorge Crespo Toral. There were two groups called Elan, in Cuenca and Quito. Other Quito groups were Presencia (eg Francisco Granizo Ribadeneira, *Muerte y caza de la madre*, 1978; Gonzalo Pesántez Reinoso, *Palabras*, 1951), Umbral (1952, including Alicia Yáñez Cossió) and Caminos, whose stated concern was for the Ecuadorean people, denouncing social disorder. In Guayaquil in the 1950s the Club 7 de Poesía included David Ledesma, Gastón Hidalgo Ortega, Sergio Román Armendáriz and Alvaro San Félix (both also playwrights) and Ileana Espinel, whose introspective, bitter poems confronted the meaninglessness of the 20th Century human condition. In the heat of the Cuban Revolution, Los Tzántzicos formed in Quito in 1961. They used shock tactics with direct, anti-bourgeois poetry, inciting people to revolution. A chief enemy was the conformist Caminos group. Some of the Quito Tzántzicos were Ulises Estrella, Iván Egüez, Rafael Larrea and Raúl Arias, while in Guayaquil Lenín Bohórquez, Sonia Manzano, Luis Delgadillo and others followed the same line. Many schools and workshops continue to promote poetry in Ecuador, notably the Centro Internacional de Estudios Poéticos del Ecuador (CIEPE), which has published collections like *Poemas de luz y ternura* (Quito 1993).

Bibliographical note Many sources have been used in the preparation of this brief survey. Apart from books quoted in the text above, mention should be made of: Jorge Enrique Adoum, *La gran literatura ecuatoriana del 30* (Quito: El Conejo, 1984); Benjamín Carrión, *El pensamiento vivo de Montalvo* (Buenos Aires: Losada, 1961); Jean Franco, *Spanish American Literature since Independence* (London, New York:Benn, 1973); Karl H Heise, *El Grupo de Guayaquil* (Madrid: Nova Scholar, 1975); Gerald Martin, *Journeys through the Labyrinth* (London, New York: Verso, 1989); Antonio Sacoto, *Catorce novelas claves de la literatura ecuatoriana* (Cuenca: 1990) and *The Indian in the Ecuadorian Novel* (New York: Las Americas, 1967); Darío Villanueva y José María Viña Liste, *Trayectoria de la novela hispanoamericana actual* (Madrid: Austral, 1991); Jason Wilson, *Traveller's Literary Companion: South and Central America* (Brighton: In Print, 1993). Thanks are also due to Anja Louis of Grant and Cutler, London, and Libri Mundi, Quito.

PAINTING AND SCULPTURE

The Quito School, 16th and 17th Centuries

Colonial Quito was a flourishing centre of artistic production, exporting works to many other regions of Spanish South America. Towards the end of the colonial era Humboldt reported that 264 crates of paintings and sculptures were shipped out of the port of Guayaquil during the eight-year period between 1779 and 1787. The origins of this trade date back to the year of the Spanish foundation of Quito, 1534, when the Franciscans established a college to train Indians in European arts and crafts. Two Flemish friars, Jodoco Ricke and Pedro Gosseal, are credited with teaching a generation of

Indians how to paint the pictures and carve the sculptures and altarpieces that were so urgently needed by the many newly-founded churches and monasteries in the region. The college's success, based on the Franciscans' liberal attitude towards the Indians, became a political issue and in 1581 control was transferred to the Augustinians. By that time however, Quito had an established population of indigenous craftsmen, and the legacy of the first Franciscan college is confirmed in the interior of San Francisco itself, lavishly furnished with 16th and early 17th century altarpieces, paintings and decorative carving. The influence of the ideology of the 16th century Franciscan missionary friars, their taste for images of ascetic penitent saints and badly wounded Christs, their fondness for theological allegory, and their devotion to the Virgin of the Immaculate Conception, can be discerned in religious art until the 19th century and beyond.

As well as the initial Flemish bias of the first Franciscans stylistic influences on the Quito school came from Spain, particularly from the strong Andalucian sculptural tradition. Quito churches preserve several works imported from Seville in the later 16th and early 17th century which served as models for local craftsmen, and there are records of Quiteñan craftsmen going to Spain to broaden their experience, but few Spanish craftsmen emigrated to Ecuador. The Toledan Diego de Robles (died 1594) who worked in Madrid and Seville before arriving in Quito in 1584 is an exception, important not so much for the quality of his few surviving works but because the workshop he ran together with the painter Luis de Ribera provided the expertise in the techniques of painted and gilded statuary for which Quito was to become so famous.

Colonial painting was as much influenced by Italy as by Spain. An important early figure in this was the Quito-born mestizo Pedro Bedón (1556-1621). Educated in Lima where he probably had contact with the Italian painter Bernardo Bitti, Bedón returned home to combine the duties of Dominican priest with work as a painter. He is best-known for his illuminated manuscripts, where his decorated initials include all manner of grotesque heads, but he also established a religious brotherhood attached to the church of Santo Domingo whose membership included many of the painters trained by the Franciscans, where the influence of his slightly archaic Italian manner was considerable.

Indigenous influence is not immediately apparent in painting or sculpture despite the fact that so much of it was produced by Indians. The features of Christ, the Virgin and saints are European, but in sculpture the proportions of the bodies are often distinctly Andean: broad-chested and short-legged. This is especially true of figures of Christ, such as the anonymous late 17th century *Ecce homo* in the San Francisco museum. In both painting and sculpture the taste – so characteristic of colonial art in the Andes – for patterns in gold applied over the surface of garments may perhaps be related to the high value accorded to textiles in pre-conquest times.

Important names in the field of 17th century colonial sculpture include the shadowy Padre Carlos active between 1620 and 1680 to whom is attributed the bleeding and emaciated San Pedro de Alcántara in the Franciscan chapel of the Cantuña. José Olmos known as Pampite, also very poorly documented but perhaps a pupil of Padre Carlos, produced gorey crucifixions, including one in the church of San Francisco and one now in the Museo del Banco Central where Christ's wounds are more like suppurating sores, contrasting starkly with the pale shiny flesh. In painting the mestizo Miguel de Santiago (died 1706) represents a break from the Italian mannerist style of Bedón. In 1656 he produced a monumental series of canvases on the Life of St Augustine for the Augustinian cloister based on engravings by the Flemish Schelte de Bolswert, but with local settings; and he later devised a set of eight ingeniously complex allegories on the theme of Christian Doctrine for the Franciscans (Museo de San Francisco). Santiago's daughter Isabel and nephew Nicolás de Goríbar (active 1685 – 1736) were also painters, influenced by the chiaroscuro of earlier Spanish artists particularly Zurbarán and Murillo. Painting in the later 18th century is dominated by the much lighter, brighter palette of Manuel Samaniego (died 1824), author of a treatise on painting which includes instructions on the correct human proportions and Christian iconography as well as details of technical procedures and recipes for paint.

Representations of the Virgin are very common, especially that of the Virgin Immaculate, patron of the Franciscans and of the city of Quito. This curious local version of the Immaculate Conception represents the Virgin, standing on a serpent and crescent moon as tradition dictates, but unconventionally supplied with a pair of wings. It was popularized by Miguel de Santiago in the mid 17th century (Museo del Banco Central) perhaps with earlier roots, and is best known from the cumbersome modern monument on the Panecillo hill while 18th century carved versions survive in churches throughout Ecuador. The prolific Bernardo de Legarda (died 1773) was responsible for many of these including that on the high altar of San Francisco (1734), a lively, dancing figure with swirling robes. The theatricality of 18th century Quiteñan sculpture is evident in Legarda's tableau in the old Carmelite convent (Carmen Alto) depicting the death of the Virgin, where sixteen life-size free-standing figures of saints and angels mourn at the bedside. In the later 18th century the sculptor

Manuel Chili known to his contemporaries as Caspicara 'the pock marked' continued the tradition of polychrome images with powerful emotional appeal ranging from the dead Christ (examples in the Museo del Banco Central) to sweet-faced Virgins and chubby infant Christs (Museo de San Francisco). Outside Quito the best-known sculptor was Gaspar Sangurima of Cuenca who was still producing vividly realistic polychrome crucifixions in the early 19th century (example in the Carmen de la Asunción, Cuenca). After the declaration of Independence in 1822 Bolívar appointed him Director of the first School of Fine Arts, so confirming Cuenca's importance as a centre of artistic activity, an importance the city retains to this day.

Independence and after

As elsewhere in Latin America the struggle for Independence created a demand for subjects of local and national significance portraits of local heroes. Antonio Salas (1795-1860) became the unofficial portrait painter of the Independence movement but his series of heroes and military leaders, each with minutely-observed details of uniform and regalia (Museo Jijón y Caamaño) is rather wooden. His portraits of notable churchmen are more sensitive and fluent. Antonio's son, Rafael Salas (1828-1906), was among those to make the Ecuadorean landscape a subject of nationalist pride, as in his famous birds-eye view of Quito sheltering below its distinctive family of mountain peaks (private collection). Rafael Salas and other promising young artists of the later 19th century including Luis Cadena (1830-1889) and Juan Manosalvas (1840-1906) studied in Europe, returning to develop a style of portraiture which brings together both the European rediscovery of 17th century Dutch and Spanish art and Ecuador's own conservative artistic tradition where the tenebrism of Zurbarán and his contemporaries had never been forgotten. They also brought back from their travels a new appreciation of the customs and costumes of their own country. The best-known exponent of this new range of subject matter was Joaquín Pinto (1842-1906) and although he did not travel to Europe and received little formal training his affectionate, often humorous paintings and sketches present an unrivalled panorama of Ecuadorean landscape and peoples.

The 20th Century

Pinto's documentation of the plight of the Indian, particularly the urban Indian, presaged the 20th century indigenist tendency in painting whose exponents include Camilo Egas (1899-1962), Eduardo Kingman (born 1913) and most famously Oswaldo Guayasamin (born 1919). Their brand of social realism, while influenced by the Mexican muralists, has a peculiarly bitter hopelessness of its own. Guayasamin's home also includes a museum which is well worth a visit. Their contemporary Manuel Rendón (1894-?) seems superficially more modern but his subject matter is traditional and often religious, the curvaceous patchwork designs reminiscent of stained glass windows. Several interesting artists of the subsequent generation have rejected social realism explored aspects of precolumbian and popular art. Aníbal Villacís (born 1927) and Enrique Tábara (born 1930) use textures and glyphic motifs to evoke ancient pottery and textiles while Osvaldo Viteri (born 1931) incorporates brightly-clad dolls into his compositions, contrasting the tiny popular figures with large areas of paint and canvas.

The civic authorities in Ecuador, particularly during the middle years of this century, have been energetic in peopling their public spaces with monuments to commemorate local and national heroes and events. Inevitably such sculpture is representational and often conservative in style, but within these constraints there are powerful examples in most major town plazas and public buildings are generously adorned with sculptural friezes, such as the work of Jaime Andrade (born 1913) on the Central University and Social Security buildings in Quito. Estuardo Maldonado (born 1930) works in an abstract mode using coloured stainless steel to create dramatic works for public and private spaces.

In recent years there have been lots of interesting artistic experiments which can be appreciated in museums and especially the galleries of the Casa de Cultura across the country: the lively expressionism of Ramiro Jácome, the hyperrealism of Julio Montesinos or the complex dramas of Nicolás Svistoonoff, for example, or the spare engravings of María Salazar and Clara Hidalgo. Jorge Chalco makes inventive use of popular motifs while Gonzalo Endara Crow's success has led to numerous imitators of his picturesque formula combining faux-naif landscapes with elements of surrealism. Cuenca hosts an important Bienial and Ecuador is unusual among the smaller Latin American countries for its lively international art scene.

MUSIC AND DANCE

Culturally, ethnically and geographically, Ecuador is very much two countries – the Andean highlands with their centre at Quito and the Pacific lowlands behind Guayaquil. In spite of this, the music is relatively homogeneous and it is the Andean music that would be regarded as 'typically Ecuadorean'. The principal highland rhythms are the Sanjuanito, Cachullapi, Albaza, Yumbo and Danzante, danced by Indian and mestizo alike. These may be played by brass bands, guitar trios or groups of wind instruments, but it is the *rondador*, a small panpipe, that provides the classic Ecuadorean sound, although of late the

Peruvian *quena* has been making heavy inroads via pan-Andean groups and has become a threat to the local instrument. The coastal region has its own song form, the Amorfino, but the most genuinely 'national' song and dance genres, both of European origin, are the Pasillo (shared with Colombia) in waltz time and the Pasacalle, similar to the Spanish Paso-doble. Of Ecuador's three best loved songs, 'El Chulla Quiteño', 'Romántico Quito' and 'Vasija de Barro', the first two are both Pasacalles. Even the Ecuadorean mestizo music has a melancholy quality not found in Peruvian 'Música Criolla', perhaps due to Quito being in the mountains, while Lima is on the coast. Music of the highland Indian communities is, as elsewhere in the region, related to religious feasts and ceremonies and geared to wind instruments such as the *rondador*, the *pinkullo* and *pifano* flutes and the great long *guarumo* horn with its mournful note. The guitar is also usually present and brass bands with well worn instruments can be found in even the smallest villages. Among the most outstanding traditional fiestas are the Pase del Niño in Cuenca and other cities, the Mama Negra of Latacunga, carnival in Guaranda, the Yamor in Otavalo, the Fiesta de las Frutas y las Flores in Ambato, plus Corpus Cristi and the Feast of Saint John all over the highlands. Among the best known musical groups who have recorded are Los Embajadores (whose 'Tormentos' is superb) and the Duo Benítez-Valencia for guitar-accompanied vocal harmony, Ñanda-Mañachi and the Conjunto Peguche (both from Otavalo) for highland Indian music and Jatari and Huayanay for pan-Andean music.

There is one totally different cultural area, that of the black inhabitants of the Province of Esmeraldas and the highland valley of the Río Chota. The former is a southern extension of the Colombian Pacific coast negro culture, centred round the marimba xylophone. The musical genres are also shared with black Colombians, including the Bunde, Bambuco, Caderona, Torbellino and Currulao dances and this music is some of the most African sounding in the whole of South America. The Chota Valley is an inverted oasis of desert in the Andes and here the black people dance the Bomba. It is also home to the unique Bandas Mochas, whose primitive instruments include leaves that are doubled over and blown through.

Economy

Structure of production In the 1970s, Ecuador underwent a transformation from an essentially agricultural economy to a predominantly petroleum economy. Substantial oil output began in 1972, from when economic growth has largely followed the fortunes of the international oil market.

The contribution of agriculture and fishing to gdp has dwindled from over 22% in 1972 to about 13% in the mid-1990s, but about one third of jobs are in farming and agro-exports generate around 40% of foreign earnings. Ecuador is the world's largest exporter of bananas. Efforts have been made to expand markets following the introduction of EU import restrictions, to introduce a variety of banana resistant to black sigatoka disease and to reduce costs and increase efficiency. Coffee is the most extensive of Ecuador's cash crops, accounting for over 20% of total agricultural land, but it is very low yielding. Cocoa yields have also fallen and a programme for better maintenance and replacement of old trees is under way. Several non-traditional crops are expanding rapidly, including roses and other flowers in the Sierra within reach of Quito airport, mangoes, strawberries, palm hearts, asparagus and other fruits and vegetables, many of which are processed before export.

The fishing industry is a major export earner, partly from the catch offshore of tuna, sardines and white fish, but mostly from shrimp farming along the coast. Shrimp farms offer employment in underdeveloped areas where other jobs are scarce, but their development is controversial and a large portion of Ecuador's mangroves has been destroyed. Most of the forest around Bahía and Muisne has gone but the Government has declared a large area of mangrove in Esmeraldas province a reserve, so several shrimp projects have been shelved. In the Gulf of Guayaquil, where most of the farms are, the shrimp have suffered from high mortality, allegedly because of the pollution from agrochemicals used intensively by banana growers.

Mining is not yet an important sector, but the discovery of about 700 tonnes of gold reserves around Nambija (Zamora) in the SE created intense interest and over 12,000 independent miners rushed to prospect there. Over 9 tonnes of gold are produced a year by prospectors along the Andean slopes, polluting the waters with cyanide and mercury. New legislation in 1991 was designed to encourage investors in large projects with better technology which would be less harmful and could be more strictly controlled. Foreign companies are interested in deposits of gold, silver, lead, zinc and copper in the S.

Although Ecuador's share of total world oil production is small (0.6%), foreign exchange earnings from oil exports are crucial, producing about 45% of exports and nearly half of government revenue. Ecuador left Opec in 1992 because of production quota disagreements and now produces 380,000 b/d, of which 209,000 b/d are exported. The main producing area is in the N Oriente, and a 495-km trans-Andean pipeline carries the oil to Esmeraldas on the coast, where it is refined and/or exported. A second pipeline takes oil directly to Colombia, but neither has the capacity required for planned development of new wells. The Durán Ballén administration opened millions of hectares of Amazon forest to exploration (disregarding Indian reserves and na-

Cocoa

In the late eighteenth century the Guayas basin, with its fertile soils, hot climate, abundant rainfall and easy river transport, became the most important area in the world for the production and export of *cacao*, a plant native to the Americas. At the time of independence *cacao* was the new Republic's only major export. The unhealthy coastal climate, especially notorious for yellow fever, and political instability hindered expansion of plantations until the 1870s. Meanwhile the demand for *cacao* was small until new processing techniques in Europe and the United States in the mid-19th century made chocolate cheaper and more widely available. As it ceased to be an expensive luxury in Europe and the USA and world consumption multiplied eightfold between 1894 and 1924, cocoa plantations expanded rapidly around the Río Guayas estuary. Grown on large plantations, cocoa made fortunes for a new coastal elite, who backed the Radical Liberal Party which seized power in 1895. By 1900 over 60% of government income came from taxes on cocoa exports. Great development schemes were begun, building roads, ports and railway lines, the most important of which, between Guayaquil and Quito, was completed in 1908.

Although Ecuador maintained its lead in cocoa production until the outbreak of the First World War, the planters were unprepared for a series of setbacks at the end of the war. Competition from African plantations in the British colonies hit the world cocoa price while witch broom disease swept through the plantations. Large areas of land were abandoned, most of the grand building projects were left incomplete and the Guayaquil elite was driven from power by a group of young army officers in the 1925 Revolution.

tional parks) in the mid-1990s, which could add 2 billion barrels of oil to existing reserves of 3.5 billion. The oil industry has had a considerable adverse affect on indigenous communities, who have seen their lands polluted and deforested. However, after a protracted campaign, Texaco, which ended two decades of operations in Ecuador in 1992, agreed in 1995 to pay for environmental and community development projects. Another oil company, Maxus, is also being asked for compensation.

Despite the abundance of oil, over two-thirds of electricity generation comes from hydropower. Hydroelectric projects on the Paute, Pastaza and Coca rivers could raise capacity from 2,300MW to 12,000MW. However, in the mid-1990s drought revealed the dangers of overdependence and power shortages were widespread. Several thermal plants came into operation in 1996 and the

Government eased restrictions on diesel imports. A new Energy Law was strongly opposed by unions in the power sector who took strike action in 1996 against the privatization of the state power utility, Instituto Ecuatoriano de Electrificación (INECEL). The Government proposed to sell 39% of the company to the private sector, with 10% allocated to INECEL workers and the state retaining 51%.

Recent trends After a sharp rise in debt in the 1970s, Ecuador joined other debtor nations in the 1980s in refinancing its external obligations. Adherence to free market economic policies in IMF programmes brought international approval and by 1985 Ecuador was widely acclaimed as a model debtor with sufficient creditworthiness to return to the voluntary market for loans. However, in 1986 oil prices crashed, cutting oil receipts by half, followed in 1987 by an earthquake which destroyed part of the trans-Andean pipeline and damaged other oil installations, halting oil exports. Huge amounts of finance were necessary for reconstruction, which put strain on public finances while inflation and poverty increased. Subsequent loss of confidence in the Government's economic management resulted in a massive demand for dollars and a heavy devaluation of the sucre. Arrears on debt payments to all creditors built up and it was only in 1989 that the Government felt able to begin negotiations with both official and private creditors. However, agreements were not made until 1994 when the IMF granted a standby facility, the Paris Club of creditor governments rescheduled maturities and commercial bank creditors restructured US$4.5bn of principal and US$3bn of overdue interest. The Government introduced reforms to streamline the public sector and liberalize trade and the financial markets. Debt remains a burden on the economy, representing 95% of gdp, but servicing costs have been halved to about 20% of exports of goods and services.

At the beginning of 1995 the border war with Peru caused direct costs to the budget of some US$300m, or 2% of gdp, but indirect costs were much higher. Despite approaching elections, the Government imposed austerity measures, allowed interest rates to rise and the sucre to devalue more rapidly. Confidence was restored and foreign reserves were soon back to the level before the war. However, economic reform stalled later in the year because of political upheaval. The impeachment of several ministers and the flight into exile of the Vice-President took priority in Congress over a backlog of legislation, while divisions within the Government led to delays in structural reform. The social security system, running at an estimated deficit of US$2bn, awaits reform and privatization of strategic areas of the

Ecuador : fact file	
Geographic	
Land area	272,045 sq km
forested	56.4%
pastures	17.9%
cultivated	10.9%
Demographic	
Population (1995)	11,460,000
annual growth rate (1990-95)	2.2%
urban	59.9%
rural	40.1%
density	42.1 per sq km
Religious affiliation	
Roman Catholic	93.0%
Birth rate per 1,000 (1993)	26.5
	(world av 26.5)
Education and Health	
Life expectancy at birth,	
male	67.5 years
female	72.6 years
Infant mortality rate	
per 1,000 live births (1994)	39.3
Physicians (1992)	1 per 836 persons
Hospital beds	1 per 623 persons
Calorie intake as %	
of FAO requirement	1113%
Population age 25 and over	
with no formal schooling	12.7%
Literate males (over 15)	90.5%
Literate females (over 15)	86.2%
Economic	
GNP (1993 market prices)	
	US$13,217mn
GNP per capita	US$1,170
Public external debt (1993)	
	US$9,935mn
Tourism receipts (1993)	US$230mn
Inflation (annual av 1989-94)	44.5%
Radio	1 per 3.5 persons
Television	1 per 12 persons
Telephone	1 per 19 persons
Employment	
Population economically active (1990)	
	3,359,767
Unemployment rate	1.3%
% of labour force in	
agriculture	30.8
mining	0.6
manufacturing	11.0
construction	5.9
Military forces	57,500
Source *Encyclopaedia Britannica*	

Constitutions and revolutions

Ecuador has often been seen as one of the most politically unstable countries in Latin America. Two features that stand out are its numerous constitutions and its frequent revolutions. Since independence in 1830 Ecuador has had 17 constitutions although few of the changes in these have made much difference to the lives of most of the population. One of the most notable was the so-called 'Black Charter' of 1869 decreed by Gabriel García Moreno, which enhanced the power of the Catholic church giving it complete control over education and denying citizenship to non-Catholics. The 1906 Constitution introduced by the Radical Liberal Eloy Alfaro separated church and state. Women gained the vote in the 1929 Charter but illiterates had to wait until the current Constitution, introduced in 1979.

Although there have been many violent and unconstitutional changes of government, it is hard to accept its image as a country of revolutions: few of these changes of power have led to anything more than a change of government and perhaps a new constitution. Only the Revolutions of 1895 and 1925 deserve the title: the first brought the coastal Radical Liberal Party to power and led to important social, political and economic changes; the second ended the rule of the Radical Liberals and brought the Conservatives of the *sierra* back into office.

economy slowed.

In 1996 President Bucaram announced a new economic programme modelled on the Argentine currency convertibility plan. Designed to be introduced in stages over a year, the plan would peg the sucre at 4 to the US dollar and keep foreign reserves equal to sucres in circulation. Inflation and interest rates would come down to international levels while economic growth would be 4-5% in 1997, rising thereafter. Privatization of the state oil and electricity companies would be speeded up, whole the energy and mining sectors would be developed. Fiscal discipline, on widening of the tax base and higher tariffs would improve the public accounts. There was considerable scepticism about the need for such a strongent programme and opponents feared that unemployment would rise to Argentine levels of 19%, Congressional support for reform could not be guaranteed.

GOVERNMENT

There are 21 provinces, including the Galápagos Islands. Provinces are divided into *cantones* and *parroquias* for administration.

Under the 1978 constitution, the vote was extended to include all citizens over the age of 18. The president and vice-president are elected for a 4-year term. The president may not stand for re-election. The legislative branch consists of a single Chamber of Representatives of 77 members, of which 65 are provincial representatives elected for a 2-year term and 12 are national representatives elected for a 4-year term. Constitutional amendments under consideration since August 1994 include permitting presidential re-election, the introduction of a bicameral congress, reorganization of the judiciary, and recognizing dual citizenship.

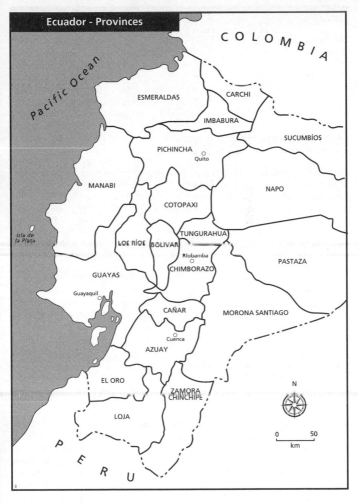

Ecuador - Provinces

COLOMBIA

Pacific Ocean

ESMERALDAS

CARCHI

IMBABURA

SUCUMBÍOS

PICHINCHA

Quito

NAPO

MANABI

COTOPAXI

Isla de
la Plata

LOS RÍOS

BOLIVAR

TUNGURAHUA

Riobamba

CHIMBORAZO

PASTAZA

GUAYAS

Guayaquil

CAÑAR

MORONA SANTIAGO

Cuenca

AZUAY

EL ORO

ZAMORA
CHINCHIPE

N

LOJA

0   50
km

P E R U

Responsible tourism

In April 1966, the National Tourism Convention, held in Loja, highlighted a number of important issues for the industry in Ecuador. Without doubt, the country offers a wonderful range of opportunities for the visitor. These include nature tourism, at altitude, at sea level, in the Amazonian lowlands and in the variety of habitats in between. 'Sea level' encompasses the unique Galápagos Islands. There are several colonial cities to be visited. Archaeological sites are not as widespread as in neighbouring Peru, for example, but the importance of the prehispanic coastal cultures is being recognized and facilities for the tourist are being opened up. There is ample scope for enjoying Ecuadorean culture at handicraft and other markets, at fiestas and in the controlled visits to indigenous peoples in the Oriente. Adventure tourism is described in detail below and the other options are given fully throughout this Handbook.

Growth in tourism has been rapid in recent decades for a variety of reasons. Chief among them have been the rise in numbers of tourists interested in nature, attracted by the Galápagos Islands and the contrasting mainland habitats; improved access to and within the country; the dramatic decline in tourism in Peru in the late 1980s, early 1990s. It should not be forgotten either that with so many Spanish language schools concentrated in Quito, visitors are keen to practice their new-found skills in the country-side nearby.

Reports from the Loja Convention indicated that concensus between private and state entities needs to be found in order to strengthen the tourist industry. A tourism law is before Congress and a special law for the Galápagos is being drafted with the aim of regulating fishing, conservation, immigration and tourism. The international airports require upgrading. Controls should be applied to potential harmful activities in zones whose ecology is protected. The private sector pressed the state representatives at the Convention for swift resolution of these matters.

Much has been written about the adverse impacts of tourism on the environment and local communities. It is usually assumed that this only applies to the more excessive end of the travel industry such as the Spanish Costas and Bali. However it now seems that travellers can have an impact at almost any density and this is especially true in areas 'off the beaten track' where local people may not be used to western conventions and lifestyles, and natural environments may be very sensitive.

Of course, tourism can have a beneficial impact and this is something to which every traveller can contribute. Many National Parks are part funded by receipts from people who travel to see exotic plants and animals, the Galápagos (Ecuador) and Manu (Peru)

National Parks are good examples of such sites. Similarly, travellers can promote patronage and protection of valuable archaeological sites and heritages through their interest and entrance fees.

However, where visitor pressure is high and/or poorly regulated, damage can occur. It is also unfortunately true that many of the most popular destinations are in ecologically sensitive areas easily disturbed by extra human pressures. This is particularly significant because the desire to visit sites and communities that are off the beaten track is a driving force for many travellers. Eventually the very features that tourists travel so far to see may become degraded and so we seek out new sites, discarding the old, and leaving someone else to deal with the plight of local communities and the damaged environment.

Fortunately, there are signs of a new awareness of the responsibilities that the travel industry and its clients need to endorse. For example, some tour operators fund local conservation projects and travellers are now more aware of the impact they may have on host cultures and environments. We can all contribute to the success of what is variously described as responsible, green or alternative tourism. All that is required is a little forethought and consideration.

It would be impossible to identify all the possible impacts that might need to be addressed by travellers, but it is worthwhile noting the major areas in which we can all take a more responsible attitude in the countries we visit. These include, changes to natural ecosystems (air, water, land, ecology and wildlife), cultural values (beliefs and behaviour) and the built environment (sites of antiquity and archaeological significance). At an individual level, travellers can reduce their impact if greater consideration is given to their activities. Canoe trips up the headwaters of obscure rivers make for great stories, but how do local communities cope with the sudden invasive interest in their lives? Will the availability of easy tourist money and gauche behaviour affect them for the worse, possibly diluting and trivialising the significance of culture and customs? Similarly, have the environmental implications of increased visitor pressure been considered? Where does the fresh fish that feeds the trip come from? Hand caught by line is fine, but is dynamite fishing really necessary, given the scale of damage and waste that results?

Some of these impacts are caused by factors beyond the direct control of travellers, such as the management and operation of a hotel chain. However, even here it is possible to voice concern about damaging activities and an increasing number of hotels and travel operators are taking 'green concerns' seriously, even if it is only to protect their share of the market.

Environmental Legislation Legislation is increasingly being enacted to control damage to the environment, and in some cases this can have a bearing on travellers. The establishment of National Parks may involve rules and guidelines for visitors and these should always be followed. In addition there may be local or national laws controlling behaviour and use of natural resources (especially wildlife) that are being increasingly enforced. If in doubt, ask. Finally, international legislation, principally the Convention on International Trade in Endangered Species of Wild Fauna and Flora (CITES), may affect travellers.

CITES aims to control the trade in live specimens of endangered plants and animals and also 'recognizable parts or derivatives' of protected species. Sale of Black Coral, Turtle shells, protected Orchids and other wildlife is strictly controlled by signatories of the convention. The full list of protected wildlife varies, so if you feel the need to purchase souvenirs and trinkets derived from wild-life, it would be prudent to check whether they are protected. Every country included in this Handbook is a signatory of CITES. In addition, most European countries, the USA and Canada are all signatories. Importation of CITES protected species into these countries can lead to heavy fines, confiscation of goods and even imprisonment. Information on the status of legislation and protective measures can be obtained from Traffic International, UK office T (01223) 277427, e-mail traffic@wcmc.org.uk.

Green Travel Companies and Information The increasing awareness of the environmental impact of travel and tourism has led to a range of advice and information services as well as spawning specialist travel companies who claim to provide 'responsible travel' for clients. This is an expanding field and the veracity of claims needs to be substantiated in some cases. The following organizations and publications can provide useful information for those with an interest in pursuing responsible travel opportunities.

Organizations Green Flag International: aims to work with travel industry and conservation bodies to improve environments at travel destinations and also to promote conservation programmes at resort destinations. Provides a travellers' guide for 'green' tourism as well as advice on destinations, T (UK 01223) 890250. **Tourism Concern**: aims to promote a greater understanding of the impact of tourism on host communities and environments; Southlands College, Wimbledon Parkside, London SW19 5NN, T (UK 0181) 944-0464, e-mail tourconcern@gn.apc.org). **Centre for Responsible Tourism**: CRT coordinates a North American network and advises on North American sources of information on responsible tourism. CRT, PO Box 827,

San Anselmo, California 94979, USA. **Centre for the Advancement of Responsive Travel**: CART has a range of publications available as well as information on alternative holiday destinations. T (UK – 01732) 352757.

Publications *The Good Tourist* by Katie Wood and Syd House (1991) published by Mandarin Paperbacks; addresses issues surrounding environmental impacts of tourism, suggests ways in which damage can be minimised, suggests a range of environmentally sensitive holidays and projects.

ECOTOURISM

Ecotourism has become a buzzword in recent years and it is certainly bandied about by several tour operators in Ecuador as well as elsewhere in Latin America. Guides with little or no experience of the environment and tour agencies out to make a fast buck all play a part in the destruction of the environment. It is worth 'checking out' guides and agencies and should you have doubts about any, or if you want to express your concern, you can contact the Asociación Ecuatoriana de Ecoturismo, Av 12 de Octubre y Cordero, Quito, T 508-575/222-389, F 222-390; the President is Andy Drumm.

VOLUNTEER PROGRAMMES

A number of bodies with nature reserves offer visitors to the country the chance to assist with their projects. Among them are:

Fundación Jatun Sacha, Av Río Coca 1734, Casilla 17-12-867, Quito, T 253-267/441-592, F 253-266. It has a well-organized volunteer programme which operates in their three reserves: at Jatun Sacha in the Ecuadorean Amazon, at the Bilsa reserve which is a lowland cloud forest in the Mache hills near Quininde, and at Guandera in high altitude inter-Andean cloud forest, near San Gabriel.

In all of these places they expect you to stay for a minimum of one month. In fact, there is so much interest in the Jatun Sacha reserve that they can often ask volunteers to commit for longer. You will have to pay for your food while there, which costs about US$10/day.

Los Cedros Reserve, CIBT, Casilla 17-7-8726, Quito, T/F 221-324: in the buffer zone for Cotocachi-Cayapas Reserve; takes volunteers on a similar basis to Jatun Sacha, and would like to know your areas of expertise or knowledge in advance.

Fundación Maquipicuna, Baquerizo 238 y Tamayo, Quito, Casilla 17-12-167, T 507-200, F 507-201, has a small volunteer programme, charging approximately US$15/day.

Bellavista Reserve, 1 Quito 509-255/223-381, c/o Richard Parsons, doesn't charge after the first few days if they are happy with your participation, but they can only cope with very small numbers. They also run a tourist lodge, so when there are visitors you are expected to help with them, mostly guiding.

The Chongon-Colonche Hills have several projects on environmental renewal, recycling, reforestation, and community work. They require you to pay your own expenses, and will help to find live-in situations with local families. They want a minimum of a month's commitment and there are two offices in Manglaralto, **Pro-pueblo**, T Manglaralto (4) 901-195, and **Fundación Eduardo Aspiazu**.

Fundación Natura, América 5653 y Voz Andes, Quito, T 447-341/4, has a programme at the Pasochoa forest just S of Quito.

Cerro Golondrinas, c/o *Casa de Eliza*, Isabel La Católica 1559, Quito, T 226-602, asks for volunteers; information can be obtained on arrival.

It is essential to check in advance exactly what you will be expected to do, how much time you will be required to work each day and so on, in order not to be disappointed. Opportunities may also be found on **teaching programmes**, several of which are run in the jungle, both English and general classes.

Genuine field biologists may be able to find employment at jungle lodges (eg **La Selva**, 6 de Diciembre 2816 y James Orton, Casilla 635/Suc 12 de Octubre, Quito, T 550-995, F 567-297), but it is necessary to enquire about terms in the first instance.

Quito

FEW CITIES have a setting to match that of Quito, the second highest capital in Latin America after La Paz, the administrative capital of Bolivia. It lies in a narrow valley running North-South, wedged between the slopes of the volcano Pichincha (4,794m) to the West and a steep canyon to the East, formed by the Machángara river. The city has spread northwards and southwards in a thin strip from its old colonial heart at the foot of Cerro Panecillo. More recently it has spilled eastwards into two much larger valleys, the Valles de los Chillos and Tumbaco.

The city's charm lies in its traditional centre, where pastel coloured colonial houses line a warren of steep and narrow cobbled streets. By day, the old town is a chaotic melee of Indian street vendors and slow-moving traffic belching toxic fumes into the faces of coughing, spluttering pedestrians (the trolley bus has helped reduce the pollution). By night, however, Old Quito is an altogether different place. Street vendors up and leave, the traffic all but disappears and everything closes. Their day's sightseeing done, the vast majority of Quito's visitors return to their hotel and the much livelier New City.

Modern Quito

Modern Quito extends N of the colonial city. It's broad avenues are lined with fine private residences, parks, embassies and villas. The district known as La Mariscal, or Mariscal Sucre, extends E from Av 10 de Agosto to 12 de Octubre, and N from Av Patria to Colón and comprises Quito's modern tourist and business area. Travel agencies, airlines, hotels and *residenciales*, exchange houses, smart restaurants, bars and cafés, arts and crafts stores and stalls, jewellery stores, bookshops, car rental agencies, and pastry shops are all clustered in this neighbourhood.

On Sunday, La Alameda, Carolina and El Ejido parks are filled with local families. There are exhibitions of paintings in El Ejido at the weekend, and aerobics, boating and horseriding in Carolina on Sunday. The Parque Metropolitano, behind Estadio Atahualpa, is reputed to be the largest urban park in South America and is good for walking, running or biking through the forest. Take a 'Batán-Colmena' bus from the city.

Air pollution has been an increasing problem in recent years and the municipal authorities finally began to take measures to control motor vehicle emisions in 1994. The situation was further helped by the introduction of a trolley bus service in early 1996 (see **Transport** below).

CLIMATE

Quito (*Pop* 1,100,847; *Alt* 2,850m; *Phone Code* 02) is within 25 km of the equator, but it stands high enough to make its climate much like that of spring in England – the days warm or hot and the nights cool. Because of the height, visitors may initially feel some discomfort and should slow their pace for the first day or so. The mean temperature is 13°C; rainfall, 1,473 mm. The rainy season is

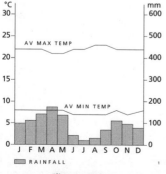

Climate: Quito

from Oct to May with the heaviest rainfall in April, though heavy storms in July are not unknown. Rain usually falls in the afternoon. The day length (sunrise to sunset) is almost constant throughout the year.

HISTORY

In pre-Inca times, this region was inhabited by several tribes, the most important of which were the **Caras**, who lived in the N, and the **Quitus**, who lived in the central area. By the beginning of the 16th century, the entire region was under the control of the Incas, and Quito became the capital of the northern half of their empire.

After the Spanish conquest, Quito became known as the **Real Audencia de Quito**. The colonial city of Quito was founded by Sebastián de Benalcázar, Pizarro's lieutenant, in 1534. It was built on the ruins of an ancient Inca city, seat of the government of Atahualpa. His general, **Rumiñahui**, razed the city prior to the conquistadors' arrival to ensure it wouldn't fall into their hands. The Spanish completed its destruction by using the rubble for their new buildings. Today, however, you can still find examples of Inca stonework in the facades and floors of some colonial buildings such as the Cathedral and the church of San Francisco.

The current layout of the Old City dates back to the late 18th century and there have been some changes over the centuries. For example, the current Government Palace was not part of the original city. Private homes which occupied the site were bought up by the King's treasury in order to build the present palace.

The Development of the Modern City

The 100th anniversary of Ecuador's independence in 1922 also marked the beginning of a new era in Quito's growth and a change in its style. A development

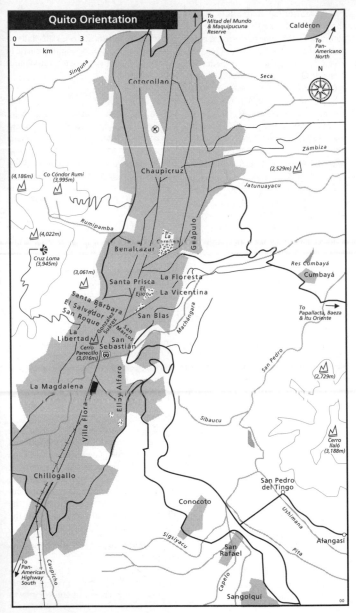

Quito Orientation

0   3
km

To
Mitad del Mundo
& Maquipucuna
Reserve

Calderón

To
Pan-
Americano
North

Singuna

Cotocollao

Seca

Zámbiza

N

Chaupicruz

Jatunuayacu

(2,529m)

(4,186m)

Co Cóndor Rumi
(3,995m)

Rumipamba

(4,022m)

Cruz Loma
(3,945m)

Benalcázar

El
Carolina

Guápulo

Res Cumbayá

(3,061m)

Santa Prisca

La Floresta

Cumbayá

Santa Bárbara

El
Ejido

La Vicentina

El Salvador

San Roque

San Blas

To
Papallacta, Baeza
& Itu Oriente

La
Libertad

San
Sebastián

San Marcos

Machángara

Gonzáles
Suárez

Cerro
Panecillo
(3,016m)

(2,729m)

La Magdalena

Elloy Alfaro

Villa Flora

Síbaucu

Cerro
Ilaló
(3,188m)

San Pedro

Chillogallo

San Pedro
del Tingo

Conocoto

Ushimana

Atangasí

Sigsiyacu

Pita

To
Pan-
American Highway
South

Caupicho

San
Rafael

Capelo

Sangolquí

plan for the northern part of the city was laid out in 1941. The 1950s saw the creation of a number of working-class districts such as **La Ferroviaria** and **La Villaflora** in the S and **La Vicenta** and **Belisario Quevedo** in the N. This growth to the N and S continued throughout the 1960s, peaking in the 1970s when the income from oil exports fuelled the development of many new upper, middle and working class districts. The city continues to grow, most notably in the **Valles de los Chillos** and **Tumaco** to the E.

PLACES OF INTEREST

The heart of the city is **Plaza de la Independencia**, dominated by the **Cathedral**, built 1550-1562, with grey stone porticos and green tile cupolas. The portal and tower were only completed in the 20th century. On its outer walls are plaques listing the names of the founding fathers of Quito. Inside is the tomb of the independence hero, General Antonio José de Sucre, in a small chapel tucked away in a corner, and a famous Descent from the Cross by the Indian painter Caspicara. There are many other 17th and 18th century paintings and some fine examples of the works of the Quito School of Art.

The interior decoration, especially the roof, shows Moorish influence. The Cathedral is open 0800-1000, 1400-1600.

Beside the Cathedral, round the corner, is **El Sagrario**, originally built in the 17th century as the Cathedral chapel, now reopened after restoration and very beautiful. Its inner doors are gold plated and built in the Churrigueresque style. Facing the Cathedral is the old **Palacio Arzobispal**, which has been renovated and now houses shops. On the NE side is the new concrete **Municipal Alcaldía** which fits in quite well, despite its material.

The low colonial **Palacio de Gobierno**, silhouetted against the flank of Pichincha, is on the NW side of the Plaza. It was built by Carondelet, president of the Crown Colony, in the late 18th century. On the first floor is a gigantic mosaic mural of Orellana navigating the Amazon. The balconies looking over the main square are from the Tuilleries in Paris and were sold by the French government shortly after the French Revolution. The palace is open 0900-1200, 1500-1800; admission is free but you can only see the patio.

Cerro Panecillo lies at the southern end of the Old City. From its top, 183m above

Plaza de la Independencia

Calle La Ronda

the city level, there is a fine view of the city below and the encircling cones of volcanoes and other mountains. There is a statue on the hill to the Virgen de Quito. Mass is held in the base on Sun. There is a good view from the observation platform up the statue; entry US$1.

NB On no account should you walk up Panecillo by the series of steps and paths to the Virgin which begin on García Moreno (where it meets Ambato) as assaults are very common. A taxi up and down with 30 mins' wait costs US$3, but even taxis have been robbed. Do not take valuables with you.

Calle Morales, the main street of La Ronda district, is one of the oldest streets in the city. This was traditionally called Calle La Ronda and is now a notorious area for pickpockets and bag slashers, which should be avoided after dark.

From Plaza de la Independencia two main streets, Calle Venezuela and García Moreno, lead straight towards the Panecillo to the wide Av 24 de Mayo, at the top of which is a new concrete building where street vendors are supposed to do their trading since the street markets were officially abolished in 1981. Street trading still takes place, however,

and there are daily street markets from Sucre down to 24 de Mayo and from San Francisco church W up past Cuenca.

Plaza de San Francisco (or Bolívar) is W of Plaza de la Independencia. On the NW side of this plaza is the great church and monastery of the patron saint of Quito, **San Francisco** (see below). **Plaza de Santo Domingo** (or Sucre), to the SE of Plaza San Francisco, has the church and monastery of **Santo Domingo**, with its rich wood-carvings and a remarkable Chapel of the Rosary to the right of the main altar. In the centre of the plaza is a statue to Sucre, pointing to the slopes of Pichincha where he won his battle against the Royalists. On the lower slopes of Pichincha, by Av América, is the modern University City.

Go past Plaza Santo Domingo to Calle Guayaquil, the main shopping street, and on to **Parque Alameda** at the northern end of the Old City, which has the oldest astronomical observatory in South America (open Sat 0900-1200). There is also a splendid monument to Simón Bolívar, various lakes, and in the NW corner a spiral lookout tower with a good view.

CHURCHES

There are altogether 86 churches in Quito. The fine Jesuit church of **La Compañía**, in Calle García Moreno, one block from Plaza de la Independencia has the most ornate and richly sculptured façade and interior. Of particular note are the coloured columns, the 10-sided altars and high altar plated with gold, and the gilded balconies. Several of its most precious treasures, including a painting of the Virgen Dolorosa framed in emeralds and gold, are kept in the vaults of the Banco Central del Ecuador and appear only at special festivals. Agree a price first if you use a guide; open 0930-1100, 1600-1800. In Jan 1996, during restoration work, the interior was badly damaged

Plaza San Francisco

by fire and will consequently need a lot more restoration work.

Not far away to the N is the church of **La Merced**, built at the beginning of the 17th century, in baroque and moorish style, to commemorate Pichincha's eruptions which threatened to destroy the city. General Sucre and his troops prayed here for the well-being of the nation, following the decisive battle which gave Ecuador her independence in 1822. In the monastery of La Merced is Quito's oldest clock, built in 1817 in London. Fine cloisters are entered through a door to the left of the altar. La Merced church contains many splendidly elaborate styles; note the statue of Neptune on the main patio fountain. The church is open at 1500.

The **Basílica**, on Plaza de la Basílica (Calle Venezuela), is very large, has many gargoyles, stained glass windows and fine, bas relief bronze doors (under construction since 1926).

The church of **San Francisco**, Quito's largest, is said to be the first religious building constructed in South America by the Spanish, in 1553. The two towers were felled by an earthquake in 1868 and rebuilt. A modest statue of the founder, Fray Jodoco Ricke, the Flemish Francis-can who sowed the first wheat in Ecuador, stands at the foot of the stairs to the church portal. See the fine wood-carvings in the choir, a magnificent high altar of gold and an exquisite carved ceiling. The church is rich in art treasures. Perhaps the best known is *La Virgen de Quito* by Legarda, which depicts the Virgin Mary with silver wings. The statue atop the Cerro Panecillo is based on this painting. There are also some paintings in the aisles by Miguel de Santiago, the colonial *mestizo* painter. His paintings of the life of Saint Francis decorate the monastery of San Francisco close by, where the collection of painting and sculpture by artists of the Quito School of Art was renovated in 1994. Adjoining San Francisco is the **Cantuña Chapel** with impressive sculptures. San Francisco is open 0600-1100, and 1500-1800.

Many of the heroes of Ecuador's struggle for independence are buried in the monastery of **San Agustín**, on Flores y Mejía. The church has beautiful cloisters on three sides where the first act of independence from Spain was signed on 10 August 1809, now a national shrine for Ecuadorians and a place of pilgrimage. The monastery was once the home of the

Universidad de San Fulgencio, Quito's first university, founded in the 16th century.

In the recently restored monastery of **San Diego** (by the cemetery of the same name, just W of the Panecillo) are some unique paintings with figures dressed in fabrics sewn to the canvas – a curious instance of present-day collage. Ring the bell to the right of the church door to get in; entrance US$0.75, 0900-1200, 1500-1700, all visitors are shown around by a guide.

Other churches of note are: **La Concepción**, at Mejía y García Moreno; and **San Blas**, Guayaquil y 10 de Agosto. The **Basílica of Guápulo**, perched on the edge of a ravine E of the city, is well worth seeing for its many paintings, gilded altars, stone carvings of indigenous animals and, above all, the marvellously carved pulpit, one of the loveliest in the whole continent. This 17th century church, built by Indian slaves and dedicated to Our Lady of Guápulo, was the founding spot for the famous Quito School of Art. Take bus 21 (Guápulo-Dos Puentes) from Mejía y Venezuela, or walk down the steep stairway near *Hotel Quito*. The district of Guápulo is popular with Quito's bohemian community and very interesting to visit.

NB A number of churches were temporarily closed after the 1987 earthquake and were still being restored in 1995-96. There are fears for the survival of La Compañía, El Sagrario and El Carmen Bajo, where the threat of subsidence from long term structural faults was compounded by earthquake damage. Money donated by Spain is helping to restore several churches.

MUSEUMS

Quito prides itself on its art and the city's galleries, churches and museums boast many fine examples. Check museum opening times in advance. In the Parque El Ejido, at the junction of 12 de Octubre

and Av Patria, there is a large cultural and museum complex housing the Casa de la Cultura and the museums of the Banco Central del Ecuador (entrance on Patria).

In addition to the many temporary exhibits, the following permanent collections are presented in museums belonging to the Casa de la Cultura (T 565-808): **Museo de Arte Moderno**, paintings and sculpture since 1830; **Museo de Traje Indígena**, a collection of traditional dress and adornments of indigenous groups; **Museo de Instrumentos Musicales**, an impressive collection of musical instruments, said to be the second in importance in the world. Open Tues-Fri 1000-1800, Sat 1000-1400; entry for the three museums, US$1.60, students with ISIC and national student card, US$0.70.

The museums belonging to the Banco Central del Ecuador (T 223-259), are also housed in the Casa de la Cultura. The **Museo Arqueológico** is particularly impressive. It consists of a series of halls with exhibits and illustrated panels with explanations in English as well as Spanish. It covers successive cultures from BC 4000 to AD 1534 with fine

Caspicara's Mater Dolorosa

diagrams and extensive collections of precolumbian ceramics and gold artifacts. There is a bookshop and cafeteria (good coffee), and guided tours every hour in English, French, German and Spanish; open Tues-Fri 0900-1700, Sat-Sun 1000-1500, US$3.35, US$1 for students with ISIC or national student card. **Museo Colonial y de Arte** consists of 3 sections; colonial, modern and contemporary art. Guided tours in English, French and Spanish; same hours and entrance fee.

Museo de Ciencias Naturales, Rumipamba 341 y Los Shyris, at E end of Parque La Carolina; open Mon-Fri

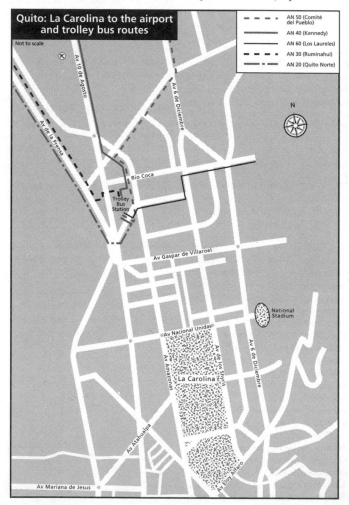

Quito: La Carolina to the airport and trolley bus routes

Not to scale

- – – – AN 50 (Comité del Pueblo)
- ——— AN 40 (Kennedy)
- ——— AN 60 (Los Laureles)
- – – – AN 30 (Ruminahui)
- – · – · AN 20 (Quito Norte)

Av 10 de Agosto
Av 6 de Diciembre
Av de la Prensa
Rio Coca
Trolley Bus Station
N
Av Gaspar de Villaroel
National Stadium
Av Nacional Unidas
Av Amazonas
Av de los Shyris
Av 6 de Diciembre
La Carolina
Av Atahualpa
Av Eloy Alfaro
Av Mariana de Jesus

Quito New City: North to La Carolina

Av Atahualpa
Rumipampa
LA CAROLINA
Av de los Shyris
Via Tombaco
Av de la República
Av Marianna de Jesús
Inglaterra
Río Amazonas
Diego de Almagro
6 de Diciembre
Fco de Orellana
Whymper
Baron de Humboldt
Av Cederico González Suárez
Av América
Antonio de Ulloa
Versalles
Av 10 de Agosto
9 de Octubre
La Rábida
La Mera
Reina Victoria
Av Cristóbal Colón
Alonso de Mercadillo
N
Carrión
Juan Morillo
Luis Tomayo
12 de Octubre
Isabela la Católica
Madrid
Toledo
Rafael León Larrea
GUÁPULO
0   200
metres

Hotels:
1. Oro Verde
2. Quito
3. Rincón de Castilla

0830-1630, Sat 0900-1300, US$2, students, US$1. **Museo Nacional de Arte Colonial**, Cuenca y Mejía, T 212-297, a small collection of Ecuadorean sculpture and painting, housed in the 17th-century mansion of Marqués de Villacís; open Tues-Fri 0830-1630, Sat and Sun 1000-1430, US$1. **Museo del Convento de San Francisco**, Plaza de San Francisco, T 211-124, has a fine collection of religious art which has been under restoration since 1991, those sections which have been completed are open to the public; open Mon-Sat 0900-1800, Sun 0900-1200, US$0.50.

There are similar collections in: **Museo de San Agustín**, Chile y Guayaquil, has an interesting exhibition of restoration work, open Mon-Sat 0830-1200, Mon-Fri 1500-1800, US$0.25; and **Museo Dominicano Fray Pedro Bedón**, on Plaza Santo Domingo. The **Museo Jijón y Caamaño**, now housed in the library building of the Universidad Católica, 12 de Octubre, has a private collection of archaeological objects, historical documents, portraits, uniforms, etc, which are very well displayed; open Mon-Fri 0900-1600, US$0.40. There is also a museum of jungle archaeology at the university; open 0830-1200.

There is a fine museum in Bellavista in the NE of Quito, **Museo Guayasamín**, Bosmediano 543, Bellavista, T 446-455, F 446-277. As well as the eponymous artist's works there is a precolumbian and colonial collection, highly rec; open Mon-Fri 0900-1230 and 1500-1830, Sun 0900-1430, US$1.50. Works of art may be purchased and also modern jewellery made by the artist. Ask to see the whole

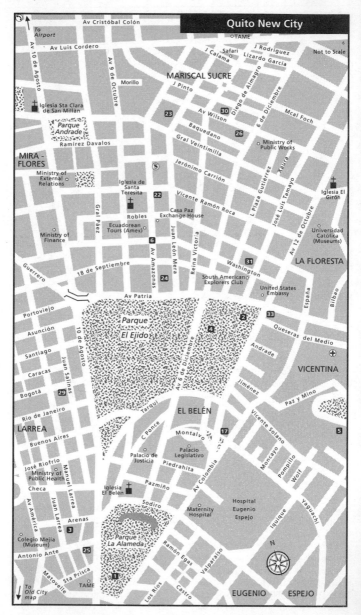

Quito New City

To Airport

Av Cristóbal Colón

Av Luis Cordero

OTAME

J Calama Safari J Rodríguez

Lizardo García

Not to Scale

Av 10 de Agosto

Av 9 de Octubre

Morillo

MARISCAL SUCRE

J Pinto

J Safari

Diego de Almagro

6 de Diciembre

Mcal Foch

Iglesia Sta Clara de San Millán

Parque Andrade

Ramírez Dávalos

23

Av Wilson

Baquedano

26

Gral Veintimilla

Ministry of Public Works

MIRA-FLORES

Ministry of External Relations

Iglesia de Santa Teresita

22

Jerónimo Carrión

Vicente Ramón Roca

Iglesia El Girón

Gral Páez

Robles

Ecuadorean Tours (Amex)

6

Casa Paz Exchange House

Reina Victoria

José Luis Tamayo

L Plaza Gutiérrez

Xaua

Universidad Católica (Museums)

Ministry of Finance

Juan León Mera

Av Amazonas

Guerrero

18 de Septiembre

24

Washington

31

South American Explorers Club

Av 12 de Octubre

LA FLORESTA

Av Patria

Portoviejo

Asunción

10 de Agosto

Parque El Ejido

4

2

33

United States Embassy

España

Bilbao

Santiago

Juan Salinas

Queseras del Medio

Andrade

VICENTINA

Caracas

Bogotá

29

Av 6 de Diciembre

Jiménez

Paz y Mino

Río de Janeiro

Tarqui

EL BELÉN

Vicente Solano

LARREA

Buenos Aires

C Ponce

Montalvo

17

5

José Riofrío

Ministry of Public Health

Palacio de Justicia

Palacio Legislativo

Piedrahita

Moncayo

Pompilio

Wolf

Av América

Juan Larrea

Manuel Larrea

Checa

Pazmiño

Av Colombia

Iglesia El Belén

Sodiro

Maternity Hospital

Hospital Eugenio Espejo

Iquique

Yaguachi

Arenas

3

Colegio Mejía (Museum)

25

Parque La Alameda

Ramón Egas

Valparaíso

N

Antonio Ante

Matovelle

Sta Prisca

TAME

1

Los Ríos

Castro

EUGENIO ESPEJO

To Old City map

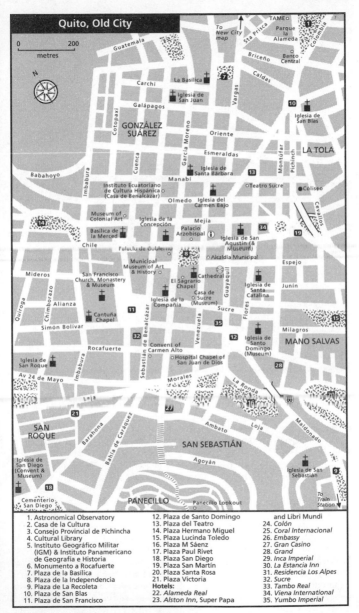

Quito, Old City

0 — 200
metres

N

Guatemala
Sta Prisca
TAME
Parque la Alameda
To New City map
Briceño
Colomba
Banco Central
Carchi
La Basílica
Vargas
Caldas
Iglesia de San Juan
Galápagos
Oriente
Iglesia de San Blas
GONZÁLEZ SUÁREZ
Cotopaxi
Imbabura
Cuenca
García Moreno
Esmeraldas
LA TOLA
Babahoyo
Manabí
Iglesia de Santa Bárbara
Montúfar
Pichincha
Instituto Ecuatoriano de Cultura Hispánica (Casa de Benalcázar)
Olmedo
Iglesia del Carmen Bajo
Teatro Sucre
Coliseo
Cevallos
Museum of Colonial Art
Iglesia de la Concepción
Mejía
Palacio Arzobispal
Iglesia de San Agustín (& Museum)
Basílica de la Merced
Chile
Palacio de Gobierno
Municipal Museum of Art & History
Alcaldía Municipal
Espejo
Mideros
San Francisco Church, Monastery & Museum
Cathedral
El Sagrario Chapel
Iglesia de Santa Catalina
Junín
Quiroga
Chimborazo
Alianza
Cantuña Chapel
Iglesia de la Compañía
Casa de Sucre (Museum)
Guayaquil
Sucre
Simón Bolívar
Rocafuerte
Convent of Carmen Alto
Venezuela
Flores
Iglesia de Santo Domingo (Museum)
Milagros
MANO SALVAS
Iglesia de San Roque
Hospital Chapel of San Juan de Dios
Imbabura
Av 24 de Mayo
Morales
La Ronda
SAN ROQUE
Barahona
Bahía de Caráquez
Ambato
Loja
Maldonado
SAN SEBASTIÁN
Iglesia de San Diego (Convent & Museum)
Agoyán
Iglesia de San Sebastián
Cementerio San Diego
PANECILLO
Panecillo Lookout
To Train Station

1. Astronomical Observatory
2. Casa de la Cultura
3. Consejo Provincial de Pichincha
4. Cultural Library
5. Instituto Geográfico Militar (IGM) & Instituto Panamericano de Geografía e Historia
6. Monumento a Rocafuerte
7. Plaza de la Basílica
8. Plaza de la Independencia
9. Plaza de La Recoleta
10. Plaza de San Blas
11. Plaza de San Francisco
12. Plaza de Santo Domingo
13. Plaza del Teatro
14. Plaza Hermano Miguel
15. Plaza Lucinda Toledo
16. Plaza M Sáenz
17. Plaza Paul Rivet
18. Plaza San Diego
19. Plaza San Martín
20. Plaza Santa Rosa
21. Plaza Victoria

Hotels:
22. Alameda Real
23. Alston Inn, Super Papa

and Libri Mundi
24. Colón
25. Coral Internacional
26. Embassy
27. Gran Casino
28. Grand
29. Inca Imperial
30. La Estancia Inn
31. Residencia Los Alpes
32. Sucre
33. Tambo Real
34. Viena International
35. Yumbo Imperial

Plaza Santo Domingo

collection as only a small portion is displayed in the shop. The museum is near the Channel 8 TV station; take Batán-Colmena bus No 3 marked Bellavista. The **Municipal Museum of Art and History**, at Espejo 1147, near the main plaza, was the old municipal offices; Tues-Fri 0800-1600, Sat-Sun 0900-1400, free entry. Underneath is the cell where the revolutionaries of 1809 were executed (waxwork); well worth a visit, but not for the claustrophobic. **Museum of Ethnology**, Dpto de Letras, Ciudad Universitaria, open Tues-Fri 0900-1230, Wed and Fri 1500-1700, Tues and Thur 1500-1830.

Museo Histórico Casa de Sucre, is the beautiful, restored house of Sucre, at Venezuela 573 y Sucre, with a museum; entry US$1, Tues-Fri 0830-1600, Sat-Sun 0830-1300. **The house of Benalcázar** is at Olmedo y Benalcázar, a colonial house with a courtyard and some religious statues on view to the public, 0900-1300, 1400-1600. **The house of Camilo Egas**, a recent

Ecuadorean artist, on Venezuela, has been restored by the Banco Central. It has different exhibitions during the year; entrance US$0.75, open Mon-Fri 1000-1300.

Museo de Artesanía, 12 de Octubre 1738 y Madrid, has a good collection of Indian costume, helpful guides and a shop, Mon-Fri 0800-1600. The **Museo-Biblioteca Aureliano Polit**, José Nogales y F Arcos, at the former Jesuit seminary beyond the airport, has a unique collection of antique maps of Ecuador; open Mon-Fri 0900-1200, 1500-1700, take a Condado minibus from Plaza San Martín in Av Pichincha. **Cima de la Libertad** is a museum at the site of the 1822 Battle of Pichincha, with a splendid view; open 0900-1200, 1500-1800, US$1.25. The Tourist Office recommends taking a taxi there (US$12) as the suburbs are dangerous, but you can take a bus to the S of the city and walk up. **Museo del Colegio Mejía** has natural science and ethnographic exhibits, it is at Ante y Venezuela, open Mon-Fri

0800-1200, 1400-1800, Sat 0830-1300.

Vivarium, run by Fundación Herpetológica Gustavo Orces, an organization whose aims are to protect endangered species through a programme of eduction, at Reina Victoria 1576 y Santa María, Casilla 17-03-448, E-mail: touzet@orstom.ecx.ec, T 230-988, F 448-425; they have an impressive number of South American and other snakes, reptiles and amphibians, displays are in Spanish but there is a leaflet in English, entry US$1.30 (children half price), open Tues-Sun, 0900-1300, 1430-1800.

In a similar vein is **Museo Amazónico**, Centro Cultural Abya Yala, 12 de Octubre 1430 y Wilson, T 506-247/562-633, which has interesting displays of Amazonian flora and fauna and tribal culture, shows effects of oil exploration and drilling; there is an extensive bookstore (mostly Spanish), open Mon-Fri 0830-1230, 1430-1830, Sat 0900-1200, entry US$0.40.

LOCAL FESTIVALS

The New Year is ushered in with life-size puppets, **Años Viejos**, on display throughout the country on 31 December. At midnight a will is read, the legacy of the outgoing year, and the puppets are burned. The celebrations, which involve much bitter satire about the county's politicians, are very entertaining and good humoured and best viewed from Amazonas, between Patria and Colón. New year's day is very quiet as everything is shut. 6 Jan is **Día de los Inocentes**, a time for pranks, which closes the Christmas – New Year holiday season.

27 Feb is **Día del Civismo** celebrating the victory over Peru at Tarqui in 1829. Students in graduating classes swear allegiance to the flag. **Carnival** at Shrovetide is celebrated, as elsewhere in the Andes, by throwing water at passersby, so be prepared to participate.

The solemn **Good Friday** proces-

sions are most impressive, with thousands of devout citizens taking part. 24 May is **Independence**, commemorating the Battle of Pichincha in 1822 with military and school parades, and everything closes. **Corpus Christi**, is held in late May or early June on a Thursday, in many small Indian communities, especially in Cotopaxi province.

Aug: Mes de los Artes, organized by the municipality, with dancing and music in different places throughout the city. **On the last Sat in Oct** fancy-dress parades for Hallowe'en are held along Av Amazonas.

The city's main festival, **Día de Quito**, is celebrated throughout the week ending 6 Dec. It commemorates the founding of the city with elaborate parades, bullfights, performances and music in the streets. Hotels are allowed to charge extra and everything except a few restaurants shuts. Foremost amongst the **Christmas** celebrations is the **Misa del Gallo**, midnight mass. Over Christmas Quito is crowded, hotels are full and the streets are packed with vendors and shoppers.

LOCAL INFORMATION

Price guide

L1	over US$200	**L2**	US$151-200
L3	US$101-150	**A1**	US$81-100
A2	US$61-80	**A3**	US$46-60
B	US$31-45	**C**	US$21-30
D	US$12-20	**E**	US$7-11
F	US$4-6	**G**	up to US$3

● **Warning**

Quito has become a tourist centre and unfortunately theft is on the increase, especially in the old city, some areas of which are very dangerous at night. The police are reported helpful. Harassment of single women also appears to be on the increase. Do not walk through city parks in the evening or in daylight at quiet times. This includes Parque La Carolina, where joggers are advised to stay on the periphery.

● **Accommodation**

Note that major hotels quote their prices in

dollars. In these establishments foreigners are expected to pay in dollars; there is a different price structure for Ecuadoreans and sometimes for citizens of other Latin American countries.

In the New City

L1 *Oro Verde*, 12 de Octubre 1820 y Cordero, T 566-479, F 569-189, Swiss-run, pool, casino, restaurants; **L1** *Holiday Inn Crowne Plaza*, Shyris 1757 y Naciones Unidas, T 445-305, F 251-985, luxury suites, non-smoking suites, restaurants, free transport to the airport; **L2** *Colón Internacional (Hilton)*, Amazonas y Patria, T 560-666, F 563-903, good discotheque, shopping arcade, casino and many useful services (post, exchange, etc), international newspapers in reading-room, food excellent (see **Places to eat** below), non-residents should dress neatly for best service; **L3** *Alameda Real*, Roca 653 y Amazonas, T 562-345, F 565-759, can be booked through KLM airline, most rooms are suites and many have kitchenettes, good breakfast buffet US$6, 24-hr cafeteria, business centre; **L3** *Quito*, T 544-600, high up on González Suárez, with nice pool, good view, often room on weekdays as business travellers prefer the more central *Colón*, good restaurant open to non-residents.

A1 *Akros Hotel*, 6 de Diciembre 3986, T 430-610, F 431-727, small, friendly, spacious rooms, excellent restaurant, bar; **A2** *Chalet Suisse*, Calama 312 y Reina Victoria, T 562-700, price negotiable in low season, only 12 safes, check availability, rooms on the street are very noisy Fri and Sat nights, restaurant; **A2** *Hostal Los Alpes*, Tamayo 233 y Washington, T 561-110, behind US Embassy, popular with Americans, 'alpine' interior, clean, friendly, comfortable, excellent restaurant with reasonable prices, breakfast inc, many handicrafts and artworks, free papers, English paperbacks, warmly rec; **A2** *Sebastián*, Almagro 822, T 222-400, F 222-500, comfortable, cable TV, rec; **A2** *Tambo Real*, 12 de Octubre y Patria opp US Embassy, T 563-822, F 554-964, rec, pleasant service, good rooms, TV, ideal for business visitors, casino, restaurant very good; **A3** *Hostal Barón de Carondelet*, Barón de Carondelet 313 parallel to Naciones Unidas, T 453-533/ 452-881, breakfast, cafeteria; **A3** *Santa Bárbara*, 12 de Octubre 2263, T 564-382, F 275-121, very nice; **A3** *Sierra Madre*, Veintimilla 464 y Luis Tamayo, T 505-687/505-688, F 505-715, colonial style, well furnished, comfortable rooms with private bath, romantic restaurant, inc breakfast, centrally located; **A3** *Hostal Villantigua*, Jorge Washington 237 y Tamayo, T 545-663, beautiful, renovated colonial house, open fire, friendly, quiet, all rooms with bath, suites available, furnished with antiques; **A3-B** *Sierra Nevada*, Pinto 637 y Amazonas, T 553-658/224-717, F 554-936, price inc breakfast in *Café Colibrí*, hot showers, coffee shop, laundry service, climbing wall, travel information.

B *Café Cultura*, Robles 513 y Reina Victoria, T/F 224-271, beautiful rooms, garden, luggage store, excellent breakfasts, shop with local crafts and foods, cultural events, rec; **B** *Embassy*, Wilson 441 y 6 de Diciembre, T 561-990, inc tax, clean, well furnished, parking, restaurant, noisy disco next door at weekends; **B** *Floresta*, Isabel La Católica 1005 y Salazar, T 236-874, bath, TV, phone, parking, restaurant, safe and very quiet, rec; **B** *Hostal de la Rábida*, La Rábida 227 y Santa María, T 222-169, F 221-720, Italian owner, bright and clean, big bathrooms, comfortable, excellent service, good restaurant, friendly, rec; **B** *Hostal La Pradera*, San Salvador 222 y Pasaje Republica Dominicana, T/F 226833, comfortable rooms with private bathroom, colour/cable TV, restaurant, located in a quiet and selective zone; **B-C** *Hostal La Quinta*, Cordero 1951, T 230-723, with bath and TV, large rooms, an old renovated mansion, Italian owner speaks English, excellent service, safe, parking, breakfast available, rec; **B** *Hostal Plaza Internacional*, Plaza 150 y 18 de Septiembre, T 522-735/549-397, F 505-075, clean, comfortable, multilingual staff, very helpful, good location; **B** *Residencial Cumbres*, Baquedano 148 y 6 de Diciembre, T 560-850, no credit cards, clean, helpful, inc large breakfast.

C *Alston Inn*, J L Mera 741 y Baquedano, T 229-955, with bath and hot water, TV, laundry service, many restaurants nearby; **C** *Ambassador*, 9 de Octubre 1046 y Colón, T 561-777, with bath, clean, rec; **C** *Camila's*, 6 de Diciembre y Roca, T 225412; **C** *Hostal Charles Darwin*, La Colina 304 y Orellana, T 234-323, F 529-384, cable TV, very quiet, safe, friendly, inc breakfast, rec; **C** *Hostal La Carolina*, Italia y Vancouver, T 542-472, suites **B**, friendly, helpful, very clean, safe deposit US$2.50, cable TV, hot water, credit cards, ask for quiet rooms at the back; **C** *Hostal Residencial Los Andes*, Muros 146 y González Suárez behind the British Embassy, T 550-839, good area for walking, spotlessly clean, hot water, cable TV in lounge, English spoken; rec; **C** *Palm Garten*, 9 de Octubre 923, T 526-263/523-960, German run, very clean, good breakfasts, beautiful house, luggage store; **C** *Rincón de Bavaria*, Páez 232 y 18 de Septiembre, T 509-401, clean, large rooms with colour TV, restaurant with good German food; **C** *Rincón Escandinavo*, Leonidas Plaza 1110 y Baquerizo, T 222-168, small, modern, well-furnished, convenient location, bathroom, friendly, English spoken; rec; **C** *San Jorge*, Reina y Cordero 1361, T 525-606, with bath, modern, clean, new 1996.

D *Casa Helbling*, Veintimilla 531 y 6 de Diciembre, T 226-013, good breakfast US$3.50, hot water even during power cuts, use of kitchen in afternoon, luggage store, use of washing machine US$3, very friendly and helpful, will help arrange medical help in the event of illness, German spoken, family atmosphere, good information on tours, highly rec; **D** *Dan*, Av 10 de Agosto 2482 y Colón, T 553737, F 225083, a/c, bath, hot water, clean, good food and laundry, rec; **D** *Hostal Amazonas*, Pinto 471 y Amazonas, T 225-

723, with bath, some sunny rooms, very clean; **D** *Hostal El Ciprés*, Lérida 381 y Pontevedra, T/F 549558/549561, inc breakfast, shared rooms, kitchen, very helpful owner; **D** *Hostal Estafany*, Reina Victoria 1343 y Rodríguez, T 524-612; **D** *Hostal Jardín Quiteño*, Versalles 1449, T 526-011, F 564-924, with bath and TV, carpeted rooms, restaurant, parking; **D** *Hostal Tatu*, 9 de Octubre 275 y J Washington, T 544-414, F 228-662, **F** in dormitory, sitting room with TV, kitchen facilities, safety box, fax service, hot water, big old mansion, very clean, luggage stored, rec; **D** *Hostal Vizcaya*, Rumipamba 1726 y Manuela Saenz, T 452-252, 450-288, owned by Sra Elsa de Racines, reservations essential, getting there involves a taxi ride but it's worth it, comfortable beds, bathroom, colour TV, good breakfast, evening meal on request, laundry service, English spoken, kind and friendly family, rec; **D** *La Estancia Inn*, Wilson 508 y D de Almagro, T 235-993, F 543-522, secure, clean, helpful; **D** *Loro Verde*, Rodríguez 241 y Diego de Almagro, T 226-163, with bath, clean, secure, friendly, good location; **D** *Majestic*, Mercadillo 366 y Versalles, T 543-182, F 504-207, well-furnished, bar, cafetería, restaurant, clean, hot water, quiet and friendly; **D** *Nueve de Octubre*, 9 de Octubre 1047 y Colón, T 552-424, modern, clean, very comfortable, bath, TV, phone, friendly, secure, night watchman, rec; **D** *Pensión Lotys*, Marchena 592 y América, T 522-531, F 226-438, with bath, garden, all rooms are on the ground floor and are a bit gloomy and cold, friendly, good value laundry, secure, peaceful, rec; **D** *Posada del Maple*, Rodríguez 148 y 6 de Diciembre, T 237-375, with bath, friendly, warm atmosphere, cable TV, inc breakfast, laundry, cooking facilities; the owners also run *Posada de Arupo*, **D**, at Berlin 147 y 9 de Octubre, bed and breakfast, family atmosphere, very helpful, English and French spoken; **D** *Quito Palace*, Av 18 de Septiembre 1117 y Av América, T 566-214, F 592-082, 5 mins' walk from Universidad Central, small but adequate rooms, with bath, clean, noisy, restaurant, laundry service; **D** *Residencial Carrión*, Carrión 1250 y 10 de Agosto, T 234-620, with bath, 2 or 3 rooms without private bath are **E** range, restaurant, bar, garden, luggage stored, friendly staff, good value, TV, accepts Visa, fills early, rec; **D** *The Magic Bean*, M Foch 681 y J L Mera, T 566-181, American owned, central, all except 2 rooms are dormitories, good beds, secure, hot water, restaurant, inc breakfast, highly rec; **D** *Versalles*, Versalles 1442 y Mercadillo, T 526-145, nice, clean, car park, restaurant.

E *El Cafecito*, Luis Cordero 1124 y Reina Victoria, T 234-862, Canadian-owned, relaxed atmosphere, café serves superb pancakes and pastries and an excellent vegetarian dish of the day, good information; **E** pp *El Centro del Mundo*, Lizardo García 569 y Reina Victoria, T 229-050, **F** pp in dormitory, clean, safe, modern, hot gas showers, laundry, restaurant with good home-cooked food, bar, cable TV in lounge, language school, notice board, good meeting place, "a real gringo hang-out", highly rec; **E** pp *El Taxo*, Foch 909 y Cordero, T 225-593, hostal-type, large family house, friendly, helpful, open fire, constant hot water, kitchen facilities, good meeting place; **E** *Hostal Los Frailes*, Guanguiltagua 234 y F Páez, nr La Carolina, T 455-052, beautiful guest house, inc breakfast, use of kitchen, luggage stored, free airport pick-up, family-run, friendly owners speak English, rec; **E** *La Casa de Eliza*, Isabel La Católica 1559, T 226-602, central, hot water, kitchen and laundry facilities, very popular and homely, Eliza organizes treks through the Cerro Golondrinas Cloudforest Reserve with research and volunteer opportunities, see page 156, rec; **E** *La Casona Albergue*, Andalucía 213 y Galicia, nr La Católica University, T 230-129/544-036, Argentine-run, shared room, comfortable, kitchen, laundry and storage facilities, big garden, cable TV, book exchange, very comfortable, highly rec; **E** *Pickett*, Wilson 712 y JL Mera, T 551-205, shared bathrooms not always too clean, **D** with bath and TV, hot water, all rooms have outside window, free coffee, laundry, friendly, popular, rec; **E** *Posada La Herradura*, Pinto 570 y Amazonas, T 226-340, kitchen and laundry facilities, clean, friendly, convenient location, rec; **E** *Rincón de Castilla*, Versalles 1127 y Carrión, T 224-312, F 548-097, shared bath, clean, friendly, safe, luggage stored, motorcycle parking, owner speaks German, French and English, laundry facilities, also travel agency and Spanish classes, highly rec.

F pp *Hostal Eva Luna*, Pasaje de Roca, C Roca entre Amazonas y JL Mera, T 234-799, women-only hostel, new, comfortable, kitchen facilities, secure, highly rec; **F** pp *Casa Paxee*, Romualdo Navarro 326 y La Gasca, T 500-441/525-331, price inc fruit for breakfast, use of kitchen area, laundry facilities, clean bathroom, 3 rooms only, discounts for longer stays, highly rec; **F** pp *Casapaxi*, Navarro 364 y La Gasca, PO Box 17-03-668, T 542-663, clean, hot water, friendly, will store luggage, TV, kitchen, owner Luigiana Fossati speaks perfect English and is very helpful, frequently rec as providing the best value in Quito for this price.

Youth Hostel: *Albergue Juvenil Mitad del Mundo*, Pinto 325 y Reina Victoria, T 543-995, F 226-271, HQ of Asociación Ecuatoriana de Albergues, take IYHA card, new building, modern, dormitory or private room with bath, **F** pp without bath for members, **E** with bath, inc breakfast, cafetería, laundry, hot water, safe deposit, luggage store, fax service, self-service laundrette next door, rec.

Near the airport

B *Aeropuerto*, opp the terminal, T 458-708, some rooms with kitchen, bath; **D** *Res Maromi*, Pedro del Solar 479 e Isla Seymour, T 433-822, shared bath, hot water, TV, laundry service, meals available, family run, quiet, in residential area; **E** *Hostal El Pinar*, Av La Prensa 2101 y N López, T 242-797, 1 room with bath, not too clean but friendly and helpful, safe, 3 mins from the airport; *Terraza Suites*, Isla San Cristóbal 880 y Río Coca, T 249-567, large rooms, hot water, TV, safe, good, breakfast on room service.

If you prefer not to stay in a hotel

Cecilia Rivera, a doctor, offers full board, **D**, at GF Salazar 327 y Coruña, T 548-006, 569-961, central, with a view across the valley, quiet, safe, hot water, laundry, luggage store; also Sra Anita Gomezjurado, Julio Zaldumbide 387 y Coruña, nr *Hotel Quito*, central, convenient (No 2 Colón-Camal bus), T 237-778, German and English spoken, friendly, clean, hot water, safe, full board available, massage by appointment; Sra Rosa Jácome has an apartment in the new city, T 503-180 (evenings), one double room with bath and 2 singles, **E** pp, use of kitchen and phone, she will arrange outings and is friendly and helpful, she meets most incoming flights at the airport in her taxi; Marcía de Sandoval, Galavis 130 y Toledo, T 543-254, rents small apartments, well equipped, US$180/month.

For longer stays with room, kitchen, TV, laundry service etc, the following have been rec:
A2 *Apart-Hotel Amaranta*, Leonidas Plaza 194 y Washington, PO Box 4967, T 560-585/586, comfortable, well-equipped suites, from US$900 a month, good restaurant. *Apartamentos Modernos*, Amazonas 2467 y Mariana de Jesús, T 553-136/543-509, 2 rooms and kitchen US$400/month, with extra room US$450, clean (nr La Carolina park)

English, French and German spoken, rec; **B** *Apart-Hotel Antinea*, Rodríguez 175 y Diego de Almagro, T 506-839, suites and apartments, lovely rooms; *Apartotel Mariscal*, Robles 958 y Páez, US$17 pp/night, 20% less a month, T 528-833.

Apartments for rent are advertised in *El Comercio*, especially in 'Suites (Sector Norte)' section, US$125-300/month, usually unfurnished.

In between the new and old cities

D *Coral Internacional*, Manuel Larrea 164, T 572-337, spacious, popular with families, clean, cafetería, open 0730-2200; **D-E** *Residencial Margarita*, Elizalde 410 y Colombia (nr Los Ríos), T 512-599/510-441, clean, with bath, helpful, baggage stored, rec.

E *Baraka*, Asunción y América, T 509-260, clean, friendly, noisy, good value; **E** *Hostal El Ejido*, Juan Larrea 535 y Riofrío, T 526-066, **D** with bath, clean, friendly, hot water, good value; **F** *Residencial Marsella*, Los Ríos 2035 y Espinoza, T 515-884, clean, hot water 0600-1200, 1800-2000, some rooms with bath, good rooftop terrace with views over Parque La Alameda, top floor rooms best, luggage stored for US$1/bag/15 days, convenient location, often full by 1700, expensive laundry, safe deposit, notice board, good value, doors may be locked as early as 2100, otherwise rec; **E** *Residencial Portoviejo*, Portoviejo y América, T 235-399, Chilean owner, friendly, safe, clean, use of kitchen for breakfast, cheap laundry service, luggage stored, rec; the owner has another rec hotel on América y Colombia 558, no sign, knock on the door, popular with Iraelis.

F *Casa Patty*, Tola Alta, Iquique 2-33 y Manosalvas, T 510-407, son of *Pensión Patty* in Baños, large rooms, hot shower in the morning, kitchen, terrace, laundry facilities, friendly, helpful, safe for left luggage, it is at the top of a steep hill, take bus no 8, 'Tola-Pintado' from the old town, take a taxi at night; **F** *Hostal Farget*, Pasaje Farget, T 570-066, clean, friendly, helpful; **F** *L'Aubergine*, Av Colombia 1138 y Yaguachi, T 569-886, shared rooms, laundry and cooking facilities; **F** *Oriente*, Yaguachi 824 y Llona (nr Instituto Geográfico Militar), T 546-157, with bath and kitchen, safe, family-run, weekly or monthly rentals only, rec.

G *Atahualpa*, Manuel Larrea y Riofrío, convenient location, basic, no hot water, clean, safe, friendly.

Accommodation in the Old City
Note that there can be water shortages in Aug.
C *Real Audiencia*, Bolívar 220, T 512-711, F 580-213, recently refurbished, spacious, well furnished rooms, TV, laundry service, baggage stored, restaurant/bar on top floor, great views, highly rec, convenient for the Trolley bus; **C** *Viena Internacional*, Flores y Chile, T 519-611, English spoken, clean, large rooms, hot water, good value, phone, laundry, good meals, safe.

D *Catedral Internacional*, Mejía 638 y Cuenca, T 683-119, hot shower, very clean, good rooms; **D** *Hostal La Casona*, Manabí 255 entre Flores y Montufar, T 514-764, F 563-271, renovated, good beds, TV, phone, safe, use of kitchen, discount for longer stays, rec; **D** *Huasi Continental*, Flores 3-22 y Bolívar, T 517-327, with bath, cheaper without, TV, phone, hot water, clean, safe, luggage stored, helpful, good restaurant; **D-E** *Plaza del Teatro Internacional*, Guayaquil, 1373 y Esmeraldas, T 514-293/512-980, F 519-462, Casilla 3443, with bath, clean, good service, restaurant, bar, café, conference room, parking, rec; **D-E** *Residencial San Marcos*, Junín 452 y Almedia, T 212-913, hot shower, cooking and washing facilities, safe, clean, friendly, rec.

E-F *Flores*, Flores 355 y Sucre, T 580-148, with bath, hot water, ask for a room on the 1st floor, safe, laundry facilities, friendly, convenient for bus station; **E** *Gran Casino Internacional*, 24 de Mayo y Loja, T 514-905, clean, rooms with private bath, cold water, luggage store, good restaurant, they have their own travel agency which sells trips to the Galápagos and Oriente (see under Travel Agencies), good value for the price; **E** *Hostal Belmonte*, Antepara 413 y V León, T 519-006, 1 block from La Marín underpass, good meeting place for backpackers, clean, safe, friendly, family-run, hot showers, phone for incoming and outgoing calls, nice terrace, use of kitchen and laundry facilities, laundry service, book exchange, free luggage storage, son has opened Spanish school (see below), repeatedly rec; **E** *La Posada Colonial*, Paredes 188 y Rocafuerte, T 212-859, bar, restaurant, garage, rec; **E** *Rumiñahui*, Montúfar 449 y Junín, T 211-407/219-325, with bath, hot water, safe deposit box, laundry facilities; **E** *San Agustín*, Flores 626 y Chile, T 212-847, with bath, clean, hot water, restaurant variable; **E** *Santo Domingo*, Plaza Santo Domingo, T 512-810, with bath, cheaper without, hot water, noisy, best rooms 8a or 9a, luggage store, not a safe area at night or early morning.

F *Gran Casino Colonial*, García Moreno 337 y Loja, T 211-914, converted colonial house, TV, restaurant, luggage stored, second-hand books, shared showers have hot water; **F** *Montúfar*, Sucre 160 y Flores, T 211-419, without bath, hot water, clean, safe, good value; **F** pp *Yumbo Imperial*, Guayaquil 647 y Bolívar, nr Plaza Santo Domingo, T 518-651, with bath, cheaper without, clean, safe luggage store, friendly, laundry facilities, top rooms overlook the old city; **F** *Venezia*, Rocafuerte y Venezuela, with bath, cheaper without, clean, water tepid, basic, often full.

G pp *Hostal Junín*, Junín y Flores, T 500184, clean, friendly, hot water; **G** pp *Hostal Félix*, Guayaquil 451, nr Plaza Santa Domingo, hot shower in basement, friendly, reliable; **G** *Residencial Sucre*, on Plaza San Francisco, corner of Bolívar and Cuenca, cold showers, a bit noisy, has terrace with great views over the old city, laundry facilities, not for the hygenically-minded but very cheap.

In the vicinity of the Terminal Terrestre
E *Gran*, Rocafuerte 1001, T 519-411, with or without bath, run down, some rooms dingy, clean, secure, friendly, free bag storage, same-day laundry attached, good breakfast in restaurant, Spanish school attached; **E** *Juana de Arco*, Rocafuerte 1311 y Maldonado, T 214-175, only back rooms with shower, front rooms cheaper but noisier, good restaurant next door.

On Calle Morales
D *Cumandá*, No 449, T 516-984/513-592, comfortable, hot showers, TV, phone, travel agency, laundry, restaurant, garage, excellent service, clean, safe, noisy from proximity to bus station but quieter at the back, rec; **F** *Los Shyris*, No 691, T 515336, shared bath, hot water, clean, spacious rooms, secure, laundry, restaurant downstairs.

On Maldonado
E *Colonial*, No 3035 (at the end of an alley), T 580-762, with bath, hot water most of the time, safe although not a safe area at night, quiet, laundry; **E** *Piedra Dorada*, No 3210, T 517-460, modern, with bath, hot shower, phone, TV, laundry service unreliable, clean, restaurant; **F** *Guayaquil No 1*, No 3248, hot water, will store luggage for small fee, safe, basic. There are also many hotels on Loja in the red light district.

NB Those travelling by car may have difficulty parking in the centre of Quito and are therefore advised to choose the less central hotels.

● **Places to eat**

There are few restaurants in the Old City, although these tend to be cheaper, with more local and fast food types than in the New City, where more foreign styles can be found. It is difficult to find places to eat in the Old City in the evenings, especially after 2200. Fast food in Quito is usually hamburgers or chicken, spit roasted. Note that hygiene in hamburger and *salchipapa bars* is sometimes poor. Many restaurants throughout the city close on Sun. **NB** Prices listed are often inaccurate. Restaurants with stickers indicating acceptance of credit cards do not necessarily do so; check first. In many of the more expensive restaurants 20% tax and service is added to the bill. The following list is by type and all restaurants are in the New City unless otherwise stated. In all cases, assume good food, service and value. All have been rec.

International: the *Oro Verde* has a superb international restaurant, a very expensive but good Japanese restaurant, and *Café Quito*, with lunch and breakfast buffets. Excellent food at *Hotel Colón Internacional*, spectacular Sun buffet, all you can eat for US$12, drinks very expensive, also buffet breakfast in the restaurant, cheaper in snack bar, good pastry shop and ice cream. In the *Hotel Quito*, buffet breakfast is excellent value. *La Casa de al Lado*, Valladolid 1018 y Cordero, with bar and cinema Mon-Sat 1100-0100, classy; *Excalibur*, Calama 380, expensive; *Palladino*, 10 de Agosto 850 y Patria, p 19, continental cuisine, expensive but good view over old and new town; *Barlovento*, 12 de Octubre y Orellana, seafood and inexpensive steak, outside seating; *El Arabe*, Reina Victoria y Carrión, good Arabic food.

Ecuadorean: *Mamá Clorinda*, Reina Victoria y Calama, large portions, moderately priced; *Inti*, Mariana de Jesús y Hungria; *La Choza*, 12 de Octubre 1821 y Cordero, T 230-839; *La Querencia*, Eloy Alfaro 2530 y Catalina Aldaz, good views and atmosphere. In the Old City: *El Criollo*, Flores 825, clean, cheap, tasty, chicken specialities; *La Vieja Colonia*, García Moreno 8-34, clean, nice atmosphere; *La Cueva del Oso*, elegant covered court of Edif Pérez Pallares on Chile y Venezuela across from the Plaza de la Independencia, reasonable prices, art deco interior, great atmosphere.

General: *Terraza del Tártaro*, Veintimilla 1106 y Amazonas (no sign), at the top of the building, good views, steaks, pleasant atmosphere, rec;

Taller del Sol, Salazar 1063 y Camilo Destruge, always busy, great atmosphere, US$40 for two inc wine; *Rincón del Amazonas*, Ramírez Dávalos 152, great *parrilladas*, moderately priced; *Café Stop*, Amazonas y Moreno Bellido, very good atmosphere, moderate prices; *Matrioshka*, Pinto 376 y León Mera, cheap set lunch; *El Frutal*, Reina Victoria 328, excellent fresh fruit juices and set lunches; *Super Papa*, J L Mera 761 y Baquedano, stuffed baked potatoes, some vegetarian, sandwiches and salads, excellent cakes, takeaway service, great breakfasts, popular for notices and advertisements, open every day, 0730-2100; *Café 3.30*, Whimper 330 y Coruña, first class; *Super Ola*, JL Mera 1333 y Cordero, small, serves good, cheap lunches Mon-Sat, also seafood. In the Old City: *Viena*, Chile y Flores, for breakfasts; *Monaco*, García Moreno y 24 de Mayo, cheap; *El Amigo*, Guayaquil, between Esmeraldas y Oriente, good food and coffee; *Café Madrillón*, Chile 1270 y Mejía; *Shangay*, Mejía, nr Flores, cheap; *Cafetería Dimpy*, Venezuela y Mejía, cheap lunches, snacks, juices, breakfast and coffee. You can find cheap meals in the market behind the shoe shops on Flores y Olmedo between 1130 and 1400.

French: these are usually very smart and used by businessmen on expense accounts. *Rincón de Francia*, Roca 779 y 9 de Octubre, excellent but very expensive, reservation essential, slow service; *Le Bistrot*, González Suárez 139, T 523-649, best gourmet food in town, expensive, live music at 2100, closed Sun; a sister restaurant is *Amadeus Restaurant and Pub*, Coruña 1398 y Orellana, T 230-831 and 566-404, very good French cuisine and concerts, usually at 2300 on Fri, rather formal; *La Marmite*, Mariano Aguilera 287; *La Pêche Mignon*, Belo Horizonte 338 y 6 de Diciembre, expensive; *Rincón de Borgoña*, Eloy Alfaro 2407, excellent; *Chantilly*, Roca 736 y Amazonas, restaurant and bakery, reasonably priced, they have a second branch at Whimper 394; *La Fite*, La Niña 559 y J L Mera; *La Crêperie*, Calama 362, not cheap; *La Belle Epoque*, Whimper 925 y 6 de Diciembre, expensive; *Chalet Suisse*, Calama 312 y Reina Victoria, steaks and some Swiss dishes, expensive; *Grain de Café*, Baquedano 332 y Reina Victoria, T 234-340, excellent cheesecakes, pies, lunch, vegetarians catered for, good coffee, book exchange, films in English on Tues pm, informative owner (Daniel – French Canadian), good meeting place for francophones.

German: *El Ciervo*, Dávalos 270 y Páez, slow service, southern German food, German newspapers available.

Spanish: *Costa Vasca*, 18 de Septiembre 553 y 9 de Octubre; *El Mesón de la Pradera*, Orellana y 6 de Diciembre, converted hacienda, also has tapas bar; *La Vieja Castilla*, Pinto 435 y Amazonas, expensive; *La Paella Valenciana*, República y Almagro, huge portions, superb fish and paella, US$10-12/dish; *La Puerta de Alcalá*, Lizardo García 664 y J L Mera, delicious *tapas*. **In the Old City**: *Las Cuevas de Luis Candela*, Benálcazar y Chile and Orellana y Coruña, reasonable prices, closed Sun.

Italian: *Vía Margutta*, San Ignacio 1076 y González Suárez, expensive; *La Gritta*, Santa María 246 y Reina Victoria, smart, home made pasta, expensive for Ecuador; *Il Grillo*, Baquerizo 533 y Diego de Almagro, closed Mon, US$5-7/dish; *La Scala*, Salazar y 12 de Octubre, good atmosphere, not cheap; *Taberna Piemonte*, Eloy Alfaro, above the stadium, expensive; *La Trattoria de Renato*, San Javier y Orellana, nice atmosphere, expensive; *Vecchia Roma*, Roca 618 y J L Mera, good atmosphere, excellent antipasti, US$10-12 pp inc drinks; *Michele*, Páez 259 y J Washington; *Portofino*, Calama 328 y Reina Victoria, good pasta selection; *Marina Yate*, Calama 369 y J L Mera, moderate prices; *Il Risotto*, Pinto 209 y Diego de Almagro, T 220-400, very good Italian specialities, no pizzas; *Spaghetti Café*, Portugal y Eloy Alfaro, nice atmosphere.

Pizza: *El Hornero*, at Veintimilla on Amazonas, expensive for budget travellers, closed Sun; *Che Farina Pizzería*, Carrión, entre J L Mera y Amazonas and Naciones Unidas y Amazonas, fast service, popular with locals, expensive, open Sun; *Eccos Pizzas*, Los Shyris nr Parque La Carolina, large-screen video; *Pizza Pizza*, Santa María y Diego de Almagro, relatively cheap; *Pizza Hut*, Av Naciones Unidas y Amazonas, 24 hrs, excellent, also JL Mera y Carrión, not 24 hrs.

Latin American and US: *La Guarida del Coyote*, Carrión 619 y Amazonas, and at Jápon 542 y Naciones Unidas, Mexican, small portions, pleasant atmosphere; *El Coyote de Eduardo*, El Universo 645 y Los Shyris, T 432-580, Mexican, very popular; *La Posada*, González Suárez 135, T 523-649, 1100-2300, Mexican, in front of *Hotel Quito*; *Rincón de México*, Amazonas y Cordero, upstairs terrace; *Churrascaría Tropeiro*, Veintimilla 564

y 6 de Diciembre, Brazilian-style, salad bar; *Rincón del Gaucho*, Almagro 422 y García, T 547-846; *Tex Mex*, Reina Victoria y Pinto, US$3-4/dish, the Tex Mex Mixta is especially rec at US$5, lively, draught beer, open daily; *Rincón Ecuatoriano Chileno*, 6 de Diciembre y Orellana, delicious, very good value, rec; *Rincón Cubano*, Amazonas 993 y Veintimilla, rec; *La Bodeguita de Cuba*, Reina Victoria y Pinta, good food and music, reasonably priced; *The Magic Bean Restaurant and Coffee House*, Foch 681 y J L Mera, excellent atmosphere, outdoor eating, specializes in fine coffees and natural foods, more than 20 varieties of pancakes, salads are relatively expensive at US$3.50, but are "safe", slow service but rec; *Hyatt*, J L Mera y Bruna, southern US menu, very select; *Adam's Rib*, Calama y Reina Victoria, American ribs, Reuben sandwiches, good atmosphere, poor service, closed Sat; *The Taco Factory*, Foch 713 y J L Mera, relatively cheap, generous portions, US TV; *Fried Green Bananas*, L Plaza y Washington, US, Tex-Mex; *Coconut Willy's*, Calama y J L Mera, salads, sandwiches and burgers, lively atmosphere; *Clancy's*, Toledo y Salazar, classy.

Steak: *Casa de mi Abuela*, J L Mera 1649, T 565-667, steak and salad US$7; *Columbia*, Colón 1262 y Amazonas, popular, open Sun; *Shorton Grill*, Calama 216 y Almagro, huge platter US$5-6; *Martín Fierro*, Inglaterra 1309 y República, friendly service; *Texas Ranch*, JL Mera y Calama, for steak, also good burgers and seafood, moderately priced, rec. **In the Old City**: *La Vieja Colonia*, García Moreno y Sucre, cheap.

Seafood: *Pedro El Marino*, Lizardo García 559 y Reina Victoria, rec for lunch; *Los Redes de Mariscos*, Amazonas 845 y Veintimilla, lovely atmosphere, closed Sun. Under the same management but more upmarket, *Mare Nostrum*, Foch 172 y Tamayo, cold rooms; *El Cebiche*, J L Mera 1232 y Calama, and on Amazonas, delicious seafood, best ceviche in town; *Maremoto*, Diego de Almagro y Ponce Carrasco 282, T 528-351, seafood and ceviche; *El Viejo José*, Reina Victoria y Pinto, cheap, highly rec, same menu at *El Viejo Jorge*, Calama y Reina Victoria; *Cevichería Puerto Manabí*, Amazonas y Calama 461, seafood, paella and *parrillada de mariscos*; *Ceviches y Banderas*, Av 12 de Octubre 1533 y Foch, reasonably priced; *Bar y Grill Buon Gustaio*, Isla San Cristóbal 881, seafood and local, rec; *Puerto Camarón*, Centro Comercial

Olímpico, 6 de Diciembre N of the stadium, try *viche* (fish soup), Mon-Fri lunch and dinner, Sat-Sun lunch only; *Ceviches de la Rumiña-hui*, 3 branches: Nazareth 1777 y Dalias; Real Audiencia, Manzana 12, casa 38 entre Av del Maestro y Tufiño (the original branch and less clean), these two are N of the airport runway; Quicentro Shopping Centre, Naciones Unidas y Shyris (a bit more expensive than the others): all three are popular for *ceviche* (US$2-3), seafood and fish.

Oriental: *Casa Asia*, Amazonas by bullring, excellent, Korean, private rooms and main restaurant; *La Casa China*, Cordero y Tamayo, expensive, service not consistently good; *Chifa Mayflower*, Carrión 442 y 6 de Diciembre, T 550-630, good food, excellent service, 30-mins' home delivery service till 2200; *China Town*, Mariana de Jesús 930 y Amazonas, not cheap; *Gran Ciudad de China*, Carrión 1238, cheap, good service, great value; *Chifa China*, Carrión y 10 de Agosto, authentic; *Hong Kong*, Wilson 246 y G Córdova, T 225-515, good; *Tanoshii*, Japanese in *Hotel Oro Verde*, see above; *Palacio Real de China*, Calama 434 y Amazonas, cheap, large portions, good; *Hong Tai*, Niña 234 y Yanez Pinzon, reasonable prices; *Casa Guang Zhou*, 18 de Septiembre y Amazonas, good food for US$3-4. **In the Old City**: *Chifa El Chino*, Bolívar y Venezuela, cheap, good lunch.

Vegetarian: *El Márquez*, Calama 433, between J L Mera and Amazonas, good, cheap set lunch, Mon-Fri; *Girasol*, Oriente 581 y Vargas, cheap, closes 1700; *Windmill*, Versalles y Colón 2245, reasonable prices; *Maranatha*, Riofrío y Larrea, lunch Mon-Fri, clean and cheap; *El Maple*, Paez 485 y Roca, lunch US$1.25, open daily except Sun for dinner,

good natural yoghurt at the shop next door, rec; *Casa Naturalista*, Lizardo García 630, is also a health food store; *Chapati*, Calama y Diego de Almagro, vegetarian *almuerzos*; *El Holandés*, Reina Victoria 600 y Carrión, cheap, delicious, also Indian, Indonesian, Greek and Italian, dishes US$3.50, wine expensive, open Mon-Fri, highly rec; *Manantial*, at 9 de Octubre 591 y Carrión and Luis Cordero 1838 y 9 de Octubre, good, cheap set lunch.

Cafés/Pastry Shops/Bakeries: *Café Cultura*, Robles y Reina Victoria, nice atmosphere, converted colonial building, expensive but excellent cakes, homemade bread, open daily for breakfast (0800-1130) and afternoon tea (1500-1700). *Crepes y Waffles*, Orellana y Rábida, a Colombian chain, good desserts and ices; *Galería de Arte Libri Mundi*, JL Mera 804 y Baquedano, good art exhibits in lovingly restored building, nice garden café; *La Cosecha*, main bakery on Los Shyris nr Villaroel across from Parque Carolina, several other outlets for homemade breads, doughnuts, oatmeal cookies; *El Cyrano*, Portugal y Los Shyris, wholemeal bread, pastries, French owner also runs excellent ice cream shop; *Corfu* next door, try *Corfu con crema*; *Bangalô*, Carrión 185 y Tamayo, excellent cakes, quiches, coffees, Mon-Sat, open at lunchtime and 1600-2000, great atmosphere, good jazz at weekends; *Gustapan*, Colón y 10 de Agosto and several other locations, good bread and pastries; *Tip Top*, Cordero y Almagro, teashop, open weekdays; *Los Bocadillos*, Cordero, just off Amazonas, delicious hot sandwiches on crusty French bread and other light meals; *Café Colibrí*, Pinto 619 y Cordero, T/F 564-011, German-owned, breakfast, coffee and snacks, good atmosphere, German and English newspapers, open 0700-2100;

Watch the hummingbird during breakfast, lunch or teatime.
Open every day from 7h00 to 21h00
Pinto 619 y Cordero Quito Telefax (02)564011
Next to Hostal "Sierra Nevada" Bed&Breakfast ★★★

Haripan, Wilson y 6 de Diciembre, good breads and pastries; *San Fernando*, Asunción 136, excellent; *Baguette*, Amazonas 2525 y Mariana de Jesús, sells excellent bread, pasteurized cheeses, another branch in Colón 900 block, rec; *Delicatessen Español* next to Libri Mundi, J L Mera y Wilson, sandwiches, sausages, salmon, cheese, etc; *Pastelería Frederica*, 10 de Agosto 679, rec for very fresh *cachos*; *Top Cream*, Naciones Unidas, nr Amazonas, and on 6 de Diciembre, for high-quality ice cream, milkshakes; *Gelatería Uno*, Centro Comercial Olímpico, 6 de Diciembre, excellent sherbet and ice cream. **In the Old City**: *Café del Teatro*, Flores y Manabí in Old City, nr Teatro Sucre, great atmosphere, coffee, desserts; *Pastelería Dulce*, Rocafuerte y García Moreno, good bakery; *Café Modelo*, Sucre y García Moreno, cheap breakfast; *Su Café*, Flores 5-46, small coffee shop, rec for breakfast; *Las Cerezas* fruit bar, García Moreno 1355 y Olmedo, nice patio, friendly, good juices and fruit salads; *Heladería Zanzibar*, on Guayaquil, nr Plaza Santo Domingo and on Benalcázar 860, excellent ice cream; *Jugos Naturales*, Oriente 449 y Guayaquil, safe juices and extracts, rec.

● **Bars**
In the New City: *Rumors*, J L Mera at Veintimilla, relatively cheap, good atmosphere, open daily 1700-0200; *El Pub*, San Ignacio y Gonzalez Suárez, English menu, including fish and chips; *Reina Victoria*, on Reina Victoria 530 y Roca, open Mon-Sat from 1700, darts, relaxed atmosphere, English beer in cans for US$2.50, happy hour 1700-1800, moderately priced bar meals, both places are meeting points for British and US expats; *Night Rider's*, J Martínez 489 y Portugal, nice atmosphere, US, popular; the *Hotel Colón* is good for cocktails with canapés and a resident jazz band; *Ghoz Bar*, La Niña 425 y Reina Victoria, T 239-826, Swiss owned, excellent Swiss food, pool, darts, videos, games, music, German book exchange; *Pym's*, 12 de Octubre y Baquerizo Moreno, varied menu, good sandwiches; *El Pobre Diablo*, Santa María, nr *La Gritta* restaurant, popular, trendy, also serves good local food and plays great music, good atmosphere; *Papillon*, Almagro y Santa María, open every day, very popular for 'casual assignments', selective admission policy, passport needed at door; a few yards away is *Tequila Bar*, packed every night with young professionals, good atmosphere; *Bar People's*, Amazonas 585 y Carrión, rock and reggae, open 0800 for breakfast and 1600-0300; *Arribar*, JL Mera 1238 y Lizardo García, pool table, trendy, rap and other music, happy hour 1600-1800, Swiss-owned, more gringos than locals; *Cats*, Lizardo García y Almagro, quaint hideaway, good selection of music; *Ogui's World*, Baquedano 358 y JL Mera, bar and disco, dancing on the tables, loud and raucous, popular with local teenagers, happy hour 1800-2000; *Kizomba*, Almagro y L García, rec for atmosphere and creative drinks, good music; *L'petit Tango*, Almagro y Colón, live tango music, no beer served; *Patatus*, Pres Wilson y Amazonas, outdoor seating, fireplaces, nice; *The Lion of Judah Reggae Bar*, Amazonas y Orellana, p 2, good for a dance and drinks, funky reggae; *Blues*, La Granja 112 y Amazonas, good, passport needed at door; *No Bar*, Calama between Amazonas and JL Mera, always packed, latin and rock, rec; *El Taller del Sol*, on Luis Tamayo, is an excellent bar. Try the *Cervecerías* around the Universidad Central for salsa and merengue. **In the Old City**: Teatro Bolívar has a good wine bar.

● **Airline offices**
Local: *Aerogal*, Italia 241 y Eloy Alfaro, T 563-646; *Ecuatoriana*, Torres de Almajro, Reina Victoria y Colón, T 563-923, F 563-931; *Saeta*, Santa María y Amazonas, T 542-148 (British Airways agents, T 540-000); *SAN*, Santa María y Amazonas, T 564-969; *TAME*, Colón y Rábida, T 509-382, also 10 de Agosto 239.

Foreign airlines: *AeroPerú*, Jorge Washington 718, T 561-699/700; *Air France*, Amazonas y 18 de Septiembre, T 523-596; *Alltalia*, Ernesto Novoa 474 y Av 6 de Diciembre, T 509-061; *American Airlines*, América y Robles, T 561-144, 561-526; *Americana*, Eloy Alfaro 266, Edif Doral, p 10, internal Peru airlines, T 549-478, rec; *AOM*, 12 de Octubre 394, T 541-627; *Avensa Servivensa*, Naciones Unidas y Amazonas, Edif Previsora, Torre B, of 410, T 466-461; *Avianca*, 6 de Diciembre 511 y 18 de Septiembre, T 508-842; *KLM*, Edif Xerox, Amazonas 3617 y Juan Pablo Sanz, T 455-233; *Lacsa*, Av 12 de Octubre 394, T 504-691; *Lufthansa*, Av 6 de Diciembre 955 y 18 de Septiembre, T 508-682; *TAP Air Portugal*, Edif de los Andes, Amazonas 477 y Roca, on p 7, opp Lloyds Bank, T 550-308; *Varig*, Amazonas 1188 y Calama, T 543-257.

● **Banks & money changers**
Banking hours are 0900-1400. (Some banks open till 1530 for dollar services.) You can withdraw inward transfers in US dollars.

Lloyds Bank, Av Amazonas 580 y Carrión, with Torres de Colón and Jipijapa agencies, quick service, no commission, rec, closes 1530; Citibank, Reina Victoria y Patria, can only use their own cheques, money transfers from most European countries; Bank of America, Patria y Amazonas, gives cash only on its own Visa cards; Filanbanco, 10 de Agosto, opp Central Bank, and other branches, provides cash against all Visa cards, helpful if cards are lost; Banco Internacional, opp Bank of America, cash only; Banco de Pichincha, Amazonas y Colón branch gives good exchange rates for cash, also on Venezuela in the old town, half a block from Plaza de la Independencia; Banco Guayaquil, Colón y Reina Victoria, p 3, arranges cash advances on Visa without limit (but depends on limit set by your own country), fast and efficient, cash advances from Ban NET ATM at rear of bank in sucres only, with Visa, maximum withdrawal US$100; Banco Popular, Amazonas 648, Mastercard, good service.

Banco del Pacífico, at their Japón branch, W of Shyris, good rates for TCs, no commission changing into dollars, cash advance on Mastercard in dollars or sucres; at the branch at Centro Comercial El Jardín, Amazonas y Av República it is possible to buy TCs with Mastercard, excellent service; there is also a branch nr the airport, and in Hotel Oro Verde, which charges no commission for cashing dollars and is open until 1800 weekdays.

Banco Consolidado, Guayaquil y Olmedo, good rate for cash only. Good rates at Banco de la Producción, Amazonas, opp Ecuadorean Tours, open 0900-1330, closed Sat. The American Express representative is Ecuadorean Tours, Amazonas 339, T 560-488, no cash advances. Amex cheques available at Casa Paz, Amazonas 370. Master Card is at Amazonas y Veintimilla, in Banco Pacífico building. The bank in the departure lounge at the airport is open Sat and Sun. It is possible to change German mark TCs without problems. US$ money orders of any kind are not accepted anywhere in Ecuador.

Money changers: Casa Paz, Sucre y García Moreno, T 518-500, Amazonas 370 y Robles (open also Sat morning), T 563-900, Centro Comercial El Bosque, T 455-075, Centro Comercial Plaza Aeropuerto, T 241-865, airport lobby and Hotel Colón, will change TCs into US$ cash up to US$300, 1% commission, plus all major currencies, slightly better rates for holders of international student cards,

open 0900-1300, 1500-1800, Mon-Fri, branches also in Multicentro, 6 de Diciembre y Orellana (T 525-153, Mon-Fri 0915-1800, Sat 0930-1330) and in Centro Comercial Iñaquito, open Sat to 2000 and Sun to 1200.

Multicambio, Venezuela 689, T 511 364, Roca 720, T 567-344, and Colón 919 y Reina Victoria, T 561-747, open Mon-Fri, 0830-1330, 1430-1730 and Sat morning, also at the airport, no commission charged, good rates, no queues, better rate with ISIC card, change Citibank and Thomas Cook TCs. Delgado Travel, Av Amazonas 1225 y Foch.

Casa Paz, Centro Comercial Iñaquito and the Hotel Colón are the only places you can change money on Sat afternoon and Sun (Hotel Colón, Sat 0800-1300 and 1500-1800, Sun 0900-1300, quick service, no commission). The airport cambio is also open at these times and late at night.

Vazcambios, Amazonas y Roca, Hotel Alameda Real, T 548-010, good rate for TCs; Ecuacambio, República 192 y Almagro, T 540-129, change TCs to dollars cash for 1% commission, best rate for a casa de cambio. If you have trouble cashing American Express or Thomas Cook's TCs, try the Banco Popular. You are advised not to buy Peruvian soles until you get to the border; you will get a much better rate in Peru.

● Cultural centres
British Council: Amazonas 1646 y La Niña, T 232-421, F 565-720, Casilla 1197. There is a library, open Mon-Fri, 0800-1915, and back copies of British newspapers are stocked in the La Galería café which serves a full English breakfast for US$3, also book exchange, vegetarian restaurant, tea and cakes, free films every Wed, E-mail service. Books are loaned if you join the library and pay a returnable deposit.

Alliance Française: at Eloy Alfaro 1900, French courses, films and cultural events. Casa Humboldt, Vancouver y Polonia, T 548-480, German centre, films, talks, exhibitions.

● Embassies & consulates
Argentina, Amazonas 477, Edif Banco Pacífico, T 562-292; Bolivia, Borja Lavayen y J P Sanz, T 458-863; Chile, Juan Pablo Sanz 3617 y Amazonas, T 249-403, 453-327, open 0900-1300; Colombia, Colón 133 y Amazonas, T 553-263, insists on a ticket to leave Colombia before issuing a visa; Costa Rica, Francisco de Nates 165, T 568-615; Cuba, 6

de Diciembre 5113, T 458-282; **El Salvador**, Los Shyris 1240, T 433-823; **Dominican Republic**, Patria 850 y 10 de Agosto, T 552-300; **Guatemala**, República 192 y Almagro, T 545-714, visa for 30 days issued at once, fee depends on nationality; **Haiti**, Whimper 493, T 561-861; **Honduras**, Italia 420 y Mariana de Jesús, p 3, T 503-220; **Mexico**, 6 de Diciembre 4843 y Naciones Unidas, T 457-820; **Nicaragua**, Iñaquito 275 y Atahualpa, T 240-559; **Panama**, Diego de Almagro 1550 y La Pradera, T 566-449; **Peru** (T 520-134, 554-161) and **Brazil** (T 563-086, 563-141) both in Edif España, Av Colón y Av Amazonas; **Uruguay**, Lizardo García 1025, T 541-968; **Venezuela**, Coruña 1609 y Belo Horizonte, T 564-626, 562-038, visa US$30 plus 1 photo, it can take from a full morning up to 3 working days.

USA, Av 12 de Octubre y Patria, T 562-890. An official copy of a US passport, US$2. (The US embassy does not hold mail for US citizens.) **Canadian Consulate**, Edif Josueth González, 6 de Diciembre 2816 y James Orton, p 4, T 543-214, F 503-108.

Austria, Veintimilla 878 y Amazonas, T 524-811, PO Box 17-01-167, T 503-456; **Belgium**, JL Mera 863 y Wilson, T 545-340, F 507-367, Apdo Postal 17-21-532; **Bulgaria**, De Los Cabildos 115, T 444-873; **Czech Republic/Slovakia**, Grecia 210, T 460-220; **Denmark**, Av República del Salvador 733 y Portugal, Edif Gabriela 3, T 458-585/786, 437-163, open 0900-1700; **Finland**, Av 18 de Septiembre 368, p 3, T 523-493; **France** Diego de Almagro y Pradera, Edif Kingmann, p 2, T 569-883 for the consulate, the embassy is at Gen Plaza 107 y Patria, T 560-789, 562-270, they will hold letters for French citizens; **Germany**, Av Patria y 9 de Octubre, Edif Eteco, p 6, T 232-660, 567-231; **Honorary Irish Consul**, Montes 577 y Las Casas, T 503-674; **Hungary**, República de El Salvador 733, T 459-700; **Italy**, La Isla 111 y H Albornoz, T 561-077/074; **Netherlands**, 12 de Octubre 1942 y Cordero, World Trade Center, T 229-229; **Norway**, Pasaje Alonso Jerves 134 y Orellana, T 566-354; **Poland**, Eloy Alfaro 2897, T 453-466; **Russia**, Reina Victoria 462 y Roca, T 505-089; **Spain**, La Pinta 455 y Amazonas, T 564-373/377/390; **Sweden**, Amazonas s/n y República, Edif Las Cámaras, p 20, T 452-010, open mornings only; **Switzerland**, Amazonas 3617 y Sanz, T 434-948; **UK**, Av González Suárez 111 y 12 de Octubre (opp *Hotel Quito*), letters to Casilla 314, T 560-309/669/670/671. The Consulate is in a separate building a few doors away, it has travel information on Peru, helpful, open 0930-1200, 1430-1600.

China, Av Atahualpa 349 y Amazonas, T 458-337; **Egypt**, Baquedano 922 y Reina Victoria, T 225-240; **Israel**, Eloy Alfaro 969 y Amazonas, T 565-509/512; **Japan**, JL Mera 130 y Av Patria, Edif Corp. Financiero Nacional, p 7, T 561-899; **Korea**, Reina Victoria 1539 y Colón, T 528-553.

● **Entertainment**

Cinema: *Colón*, 10 de Agosto y Colón; *República*, on República; *Universitario*, América y A Pérez Guerrero, Plaza Indoamérica, Universidad Central; *Benalcázar*, 6 de Diciembre y Portugal; *24 de Mayo*, Granaderos y 6 de Diciembre. *Colón* often has documentaries with Latin American themes. The Casa de la Cultura often has film festivals, as well as showing foreign films. *Cine Metro*, Venezuela, good sound, interesting films. Expect to pay around US$2.60 in these cinemas. There are many others, especially in the Old City, mostly showing violent films; usually there is a standard entry charge (US$0.75 or less) and you can stay as long as you like. Section D of *El Comercio* lists the films every day.

Music: local folk music is popular and the entertainment is known as a *peña*. Places inc *Dayumac*, J L Mera y Carrión, a meeting place for local music groups, dark, bohemian, warms up after 2400; *Cuerdas Andinas Disco Bar*, Carrión y J L Mera, entrance only for couples; *Ñucanchi*, Av Universitaria 496 y Armero, Thur-Sat 2230-0300. Most places do not come alive until 2230.

Nightclubs: Most of the places below are open until 0300. *Licorne*, at Hotel Colón Internacional; discos at *JK*, Amazonas 541, *Tobujas*, Amazonas y Santa María; *Dreams*, Naciones Unidas y Los Shyris; *Río Club*, Av 12 de Octubre y Colón; *Le Pierrot*, Carrión 617 y Amazonas; *Carpenix*, Almagro y La Niña, cover charge, popular with young crowd; *Cali Salsoteca*, Almagro y Orellana, great atmosphere; *Seseribó*, Veintimilla y 12 de Octubre, salsa and rock, rec, Thur-Sun, US$2; *El Solar*, Amazonas 2563 y Mariana de Jesús, salsa, Wed-Sat, good music, popular; *Tropicana*, Whimper y Coruña; *Footloose*, Baquerano 188 y J L Mera, gay disco, cover charge US$4; *Ku*, Orellana y 6 de Diciembre, popular disco.

Theatre: *Teatro Sucre*, Flores with Guayaquil, the most elegant. Symphony concerts are free. Advance tickets from Metropolitan Touring, no need to book in April or May, the cheapest unreserved seats are OK (row 1-8 US$4.20; circle US$8), but arrive early; the theatre was closed for major renovation in mid 1996. *Teatro San Gabriel*, América y Mariana de Jesús, Ecuadorean folk ballet 'Jacchigua' presented Wed and Fri 1930, entertaining, colourful and loud. *Teatro Prometeo* adjoining the Casa de la Cultura Ecuatoriana, 6 de Diciembre y Tarqui, also closed for renovation in mid 1996. *Agora*, open-air theatre of Casa de la Cultura, 12 de Octubre y Patria, stages many concerts. There are also plays at the *Patio de Comedia*, 18 de Septiembre, between Amazonas and 9 de Octubre. Good music at *Teatro Equitorial Experimental*; check posters in Plaza Teatro for details. *Centro Cultural Afro-Ecuatoriano* (CCA), Tamayo 985 y Lizardo García, Casilla 352, Sucursal 12 de Octubre, T 522318, sometimes has cultural events and published material, a useful contact for those interested in the black community. There are always many cultural events taking place in Quito, usually free of charge; see the listings section of *El Comercio* for details.

● **Hospitals & medical services**
Most embassies have the telephone numbers of doctors who speak non-Spanish languages. **Hospital Voz Andes**, next to Voz Andes radio station, Villalengua 267, T 241-540, emergency room, quick, efficient, staffed by US, British and Ecuadorean doctors and nurses, fee based on ability to pay, run by Christian HCJB organization, has out-patient dept, reached by No 1 bus to Iñaquito. **Metropolitano**, Av Mariana de Jesús y Av Occidental, T 431-520, just E of the western city hypers, has also been rec, but prices are almost the same as in the USA; catch a Quito Sur-San Gabriel bus from El Tejar downtown, via Av Universitaria and Av América, or a bus on 10 de Agosto or Av América and walk up, or take a taxi, about US$0.60; very professional, not cheap, gamma globulin costs about US$12. A rec paediatrician is Dr Ernesto Quiñones, at ProSalud, Coruña 1761 y Novoa Camaño, T 223-591/223-593, F 223-590, E-mail: 04150,1472@compuserve.com.

Among the rec health centres are: **Centro Médico Alemania**, Eloy Alfaro y Alemania; **Clínica Pichincha**, Veintimilla 1259, T 561-643, amoebic dysentry tests, results within hours, US$15; **Clínica Americana Adventista** (some English spoken), 10 de Agosto 3366, 24 hrs, US$5; **Clínica San Francisco**, 6 de Diciembre y Colón, 24 hrs, x-rays.

For amoebic dysentery tests, **Análisis Médicos**

Automatizados, Alpallana 477 y Whymper, Ramírez Dávalos 202, T 545-945. **Dra Johanna Grimm**, Salvador 112 y Los Shyris, T 240-332, Lab 462-182; **Lab León**, Edif Torrealba, Amazonas, facing British Council, Dr León speaks English, does test and can prescribe, popular with foreign residents; **Centro Médico Martha Roldós**, Plaza Teatro, Hepatitis B injections for US$0.30, but to buy your own syringe, needle and phial from *Fybeca* chemist (see below). **Dr Vargas Uvidia**, Colombia 248, T 513-152, speaks English and French; **Dr Rodrigo Sosa**, Cordero 410 y 6 de Diciembre, T 525-102, English-speaking; **Dr Wilson Pancho**, Av República de El Salvador 112, T 463-139/469-546, speaks German.

Dr John Rosenberg, internal and travel medicine, he has a wide range of vaccines, consultation US$20, Hepatitis A vaccine costs US$25, speaks English and German, very helpful general practitioner, office at Med Center Travel Clinic, Foch 476 y Almagro, T 521-104, paging service 506-856 beeper 135, home 441-757.

For treatment of leishmaniasis and other tropical cutaneous horrors, Dr Rodrigo Armijos at the pathology laboratory in the Medical Faculty below Iquique.

Chemist: all-night **chemist**, Farmacia Alaska, Venezuela 407 y Rocafuerte, T 210-973; *Droguería Doral*, on Amazonas, is a well-stocked, inexpensive pharmacy/chemist; also *Fybeca* on Guayaquil in the Old City (sells typhoid/paratyphoid pills – Vivatif, Swiss); *Fybeca* at Venezuela y Mejía sells tampons. Check the listing of *farmacias en turno* in *El Comercio* on Sat for 24-hr chemists in the following week. Chloroquine is available for malaria prevention but not Paludrine. For injections and prescriptions, Rumipampa 1744 y Vasco de Contreras, opp Coliseo de Colegio San Gabriel (old city), T 457-772.

Dentists: *Dr Aldo Grundland*, Rep de El Salvador 210 y Av de Los Shyris, Edif Onix p 7, speaks English, Hebrew, Italian, good value and efficient, great view of Pichincha from his chair; *Drs Sixto y Silvia Altamirano*, Av Amazonas 2689 y Av República, T 244-119, excellent; *Dra Rosa Oleas*, Amazonas 258 y Washington (T 524-859); *Dr Fausto Vallejo*, Madrid 744 (1 block from the end of the No 2 Carnal/Colón bus line), T 554-781, rec, very reasonable; *Dr Roberto Mena*, Tamayo 1237 y Colón, T 525-329, speaks English and German; *Dr Víctor Peñaherrera*, Edif Banco Amazonas 4430 y Villalengua, T 255-934/5, speaks English, rec.

Gynaecologist: *Dr Steven Contag*, Cordero 410 y 6 de Diciembre, T 560-408, speaks English.

Opticians: *Optica Luz*, Amazonas y Colón, T 521-818, also 10 de Agosto y Riofrío, professional, helpful, good value for repairs, eye tests and new glasses; *Optica Gill*, Amazonas, opp the British Council, English spoken, glasses, contact lenses, helpful.

● **Language courses**
At the *Universidad Católica*, Octubre 1076 y Carrión, *Instituto de Lenguas y Lingüística*, T 529-240: 5-week Spanish courses, US$425, large classes; courses in Quechua. They will provide student cards, which are valid for reductions in Peru.

Language schools: *The South American Explorers Club* provides a free list of rec schools and these may give club members discounts. It is impossible to list all the schools offering Spanish courses in Quito. We list schools for which we have received positive recommendations each year. This does not necessarily imply that schools not mentioned are not rec. Although few schools are registered with the Ministry of Education, many of the others offer a high standard of teaching. Schools usually offer courses of 7 hrs or 4 hrs tuition/day, either

in groups or on a one-to-one basis. Many correspondents have suggested that 4 hrs a day is normally sufficient. Charges range between US$1.50 and US$8/hr for one-to-one classes, but beware of extras which may not be mentioned in the initial quote.

Some of the most expensive schools spend a great deal on multi-media equipment and advertising abroad, check how much individual tuition is provided. It is possible to arrange some trial lessons. If staying with a family book 1 week initially; if you are pressed too hard to sign a long-term contract go elsewhere. Do not arrange accommodation through intermediaries or 'fixers' and make sure you get a receipt for money paid. It is normally more expensive and not necessary to book from abroad. Most schools can arrange accommodation with families from US$10 to US$25 a day, full board. Many also offer excursions.

Favourable reports in 1996 were received on the following schools In the New City: *Mitad del Mundo*, Terán 1676 entre Versalles y 10 de Agosto, T/F 567-875, PO Box 17-15-389C, repeatedly rec; *Academia Latinoamericano*, José Queri 2 y Eloy Alfaro, PO Box 17-17-593, T 452-824, F 4633-820; *Amazonas One to One Spanish School*, Washington

ÆCE ASOCIACION ECUATORIANA

Q U I T O

The **AECE** is an institution legally constituted and recognized by the Ecuadorian government. The member schools are recognized by
Ecuador's Ministry of Education and Culture.
They are a guarantee for foreigners who wish to
learn Spanish because all have been previously
qualified by the Association and the authorities
of the Ecuadorian government.

The courses taught by the Spanish learning centers follow the system of individual
classes, in accordance with the established
methods and politics af each center.

● THE ORDER IN WICH THEY ARE LISTED IS STRICTLY ALPHABETICAL ●

ACADEMIA DE ESPAÑOL "AMISTAD"
9 de Octubre 712 y Ramirez Dávalos ● Telf.: (593-2) 524-575 Fax: (593-2) 568-664
P.O.Box 248-C

ACADEMIA DE ESPAÑOL "EQUINOCCIAL"
Roca 533 y Juan León Mera ● Inter: E.Mail eee@eee.org.ec
http: //www.qni.com.~~mj equinox ● Fax: (593-2) 529-460/564-488 ● Telf: 525-690

ACADEMIA DE ESPAÑOL "MITAD DEL MUNDO"
Gustavo Darquea Terán 1676 y Versalles (2nd floor) ● Telf & Fax: (593-2) 567-875
Telf.:546-827 Telex:21215 Woc. Ed. ● P.O.Box 17-15-389 C

ACADEMIA DE ESPAÑOL QUITO
130 Marchena St. and 10 de Agosto Ave. ● Telf: (593-2) 553-647 ● Fax: (593-2) 506-474
E-Mail edalvare@pi.pro.ec P.O.Box 17-15-0039-C ● http: //mia.lac.net/acaquito/htm/spanish/htm

"AMAZONAS" SPANISH SCHOOL
718 Jorge Washington St. and Amazonas Avenue ● Building: Rocafuerte, Washington
block, 3rd floor ● Phone & Fax (593-2) 504-654 ● P.O.Box 17-21-1245

AMERICAN SPANISH SCHOOL
Carrión 768 y 9 de Octubre 2nd floor ● Telf /Fax: (593-2) 229-165/229-166
P.O.Box 17-03-1588 ● E-Mail jproano@srv1.telconet.net

ASOCIACION ECUATORIANA DE CENTROS DE ENSEÑANZA DE ESPAÑOL

DE CENTROS DE ENSEÑANZA DE ESPAÑOL

E C U A D O R

ATAHUALPA SPANISH INSTITUTE
Juan León Mera 935 y Pinto
Phone & Fax: (593-2) 523-306/505-151 • P.O.Box 17-07-9581

BELMONTE SPANISH SCHOOL
331 Jose Riofrío and Manuel Larrea
Phone: (593-2) 520-177 • P.O.Box: 17-15-133B

COLONIAL SPANISH SCHOOL
518 Sucre and Benalcazor
Phone & Fax: (593-2) 582-237 • P.O.Box: 17-01-3739

ESTUDIO DE ESPAÑOL "PICHINCHA"
Andrés Xaura 182, between Lizardo García y Foch • Inter: http//www.qni.com/~mj/pichinch.
htm#PICHINCHA • P.O.Box: 17-03-0936 • Phone: (593-2) 452-891 • Fax: (593-2) 601-689

GALAPAGOS SPANISH SCHOOL
258 Amazonas Av. and J. Washington St. 2nd floor • Phone & Fax: (593-2) 540-164/220-939
P.O.Box: 1703744 E-Mail: mbr@galapago.ecx.ec • Internet: http://www.qni.com/~mj/galapagos

INSTITUTO SUPERIOR DE ESPAÑOL
Ulloa 152 y Jerónimo Carrión • Phone: (593-2) 223-242 Fax: (593-2) 221-628
P.O.Box:17-03-00490 • E-Mail: institut@superior.ecx.ec • Internet: http.//www.qni.oom. mj ise

LA LENGUA
Colón 1001 & Juan León Mera
Building "Avé María" 8th Floor • Phone & Fax: (593-2) 501-271 • P.O.Box: 17-07-9519

"RENOVACION" SPANISH SCHOOL
18 de Septiembre 413 y Amazonas (In front of the Hotel Colón)
Phone & Fax: (593-2) 220-385 • E-Mail: 103726.452@COMPUSERVE.COM

SPANISH INSTITUTE "SAN FRANCISCO"
Veintimilla 11-06 y Amazonas, Ed. Amazonas 7 Piso, Of. 703 • Phone & Fax: (593-2) 553-476
Internet: http: 200.6.8.62/otros/essanf.htm • E-Mail: lKennedy@L2.Lonet.Ca (Canada)

SOUTH AMERICAN SPANISH INSTITUTE
Av. Amazonas 1549 and Santa María P.O.Box:17-21-373 • Phone: (593-2) 544-715
Fax: (593-2) 226-348 • E-Mail: mlramire@srv1.telconet.net • Internet: http: //www.qni.com/~mj/samerica

718 and Amazonas, Edif Rocafuerte, p 3, PO Box 17-21-1245, T/F 504-654; *Instituto Superior de Español*, Ulloa 152 y Jerónimo Carrión, PO Box 17-03-00490, T 223-242, F 221-628, E-mail: Institut@superior.ecx.ec (they have also opened a school in Otavalo and can arrange voluntary work with La Cruz Roja Ecuatoriana, at Mindo, Fundación Jatun Sacha and others); *Galápagos Spanish School*, Amazonas 258 y Washington, PO Box A744, T/F 540-164/220-939; *Estudio de Español Pichincha*, Andrés Xaura 182, entre Lizardo García y Foch, PO Box 17-03-0936, T 452-891/528-081, F 601-689; *Academia de Español Quito*, Marchena 130 y Av 10 de Agosto, T 553-647/554-811, F 506-474/504330; *Asociación Ecuatoriana de Enseñanza de Español*, Av Amazonas 629 y Carrión, T/F 547-275; *South American Spanish Institute*, Av Amazonas 1549 y Santa María, T 544715/226348, F 436-200; *Rainbow Spanish Centre*, Armero 749 y Sta Rosa, PO Box 1721-01310, T 548-519, F 440-867; *New World Spanish School*, Orellana 290, PO Box

17-04-1052, F 502066; *World Wide Language School*, Versalles 1449, T 656-573/526-001, F 564-924; *Belmonte*, Ríofrio y J Larrea, T 520-177, PO Box 17-15-133B; *San Francisco*, Veintimilla 1106 y Amazonas, Edif Amazonas, p 7, T 553-476; *Atahualpa*, Veintimilla 910 y J L Mera, T 545-440, F 505-151, PO Box 17-07-9581; *La Lengua*, Colón 1001 and J L Mera, p 8, PO Box 17-07-9519, T/F 501-271; *Cumbre Andina*, Av América 1530 y Ramírez Dávalos, T/F 552-072; *Academia de Español Equinoccial*, Roca 533 y J L Mera, T 564-488, F 529-460; *Bipo & Toni's Academia de Español*, Carrión 300 y Plaza, T/F 547-090; *America Spanish School*, 768 Carrión and 9 de Octubre, T 229-166, F 568-664; *Simón Bolívar*, Andalucía 565 y Salazar, Sucursal 12 de Octubre, T/F 502-640, also salsa lessons on Fri; *Escuela de Español Ecuador*, Queseras del Medio 741 y Av 12 de Octubre, p 2, T 502-460, F 520-667.

In the Old City: *Beraca School*, Vargas 275 y Oriente, T 518-873, they also have a new school in Mindo; *Pacha Mama*, Guayaquil 1258 y Manabí, Plaza del Teatro, p 3, Of 305, PO Box 17-01-2535, T 218-416; *Los Andes*, 1245 García Moreno entre Mejía y Olmedo, p 2, F 583-086; *Nueva Vida*, Venezuela 1389 y Oriente, PO Box 17-01-2518, T 216-986; *Interandina*, García Moreno 858 y José Antonio Sucre, F 583-086; *Quito's Information Center*, Guayaquil 1242 y Olmedo, p 2, F 229-165, PO Box 17-03-0062, for information and world-wide phone and fax service.

Recommended course books: *Español, Curso de Perfeccionamento*, by Juan Felipe García Santos (Universidad de Salamanca, Sept 1990). *Learn Spanish One to One*, by José Aguirre and *1001 Ejercicios* by Marcia García, PO Box 17-03-543, T 449-014. In 1996 José Aguirre opened the *Cristóbal Colón* school, Av Colón 2088 y Versalles, T 506-508, F 222-964, PO Box 17-17-1051, flexible courses, hostel accommodation (**E** pp) next door.

National Registration Centre for Study Abroad, 823N 2nd St, PO Box 1393, Milwaukee, WI 53203, USA, T 414-278-0631, F 271-8884, and *AmeriSpan Unlimited*, PO Box 40513, Philadelphia, PA 19016-0513, T 800-879-6640 (USA and Canada), 215-985-4522 (worldwide), F 215-985-4524, E-mail: info@amerispan.com (http:/www.amerispan.com) have information on courses and will make bookings, free newsletters.

● **Laundry**
Lavanderías Modernas, 6 de Diciembre 24-

00 y Colón, T 527-601, expensive; *Lavyseca*, Cordero y Tamayo, laundry and dry cleaning, US$7 for 12 kg, same day; *Lavandería*, 552 Olmedo, T 213-992, will collect clothes; *Lavahotel*, Almagro 818 y Colón, good value, US$1.65/load, including soap powder, US$1.65/dryer; *Lavandería Opera de Jabón*, Pinto 325, next to IYH, US$1.50/kg, open 7 days, 0700-2000. The laundry next to *Hotel Pickett Inn* does a good deal, US$0.60/kg; *La Química*, Mallorca 335 y Madrid; *Norte*, Amazonas 7339, and Pinzón y La Niña; *Almagro*, Wilson 470 y Almagro, T 225-208, laundry by weight.

Dry-cleaning: *Martinizing*, 1 hr service, 12 de Octubre 1486, Diego de Almagro y La Pradera, and in 6 shopping centres, plus other locations, expensive.

● **Places of worship**
Joint Anglican/Lutheran service is held (in English) at the Advent Lutheran Church, Isabel la Católica 1419, Sun, 0900. Synagogue at 18 de Septiembre y Versalles, services Fri 1900 and Sat 0900.

● **Post & telecommunications**
Post Office: the old sucursal mayor (main branch) is in the old city, on Espejo, entre Guayaquil y Venezuela. The new head office (philatelic service 7th floor) is located at Eloy Alfaro 354 y 9 de Octubre. For parcels and surface-air-lifted reduced priority (SAL/APR, replacing sea mail which is no longer available), Correo Marítimo Aduana, Ulloa 273 y Ramírez Dávalos, next to Santa Clara market.

Other offices at: Japón y Naciones Unidas (fax service); Colón y Almagro (fax service); Ulloa y Ramírez Dávalos (fax service); and at the airport (national departures). All sell stamps Mon-Fri 0730-1930, Sat 0800-1400; special services, eg parcels, collection of registered mail until 1530 only. *Poste Restante*, at the post offices at Espejo and at Eloy Alfaro; all *poste restante* letters are sent to Espejo unless marked 'Correo Central, Eloy Alfaro', but you are advised to check both *postes restantes*, whichever address you use (the one at Eloy Alfaro is reported unhelpful and chaotic). Letters can be sent care of American Express, Apdo 2605, Quito. The *South American Explorers Club* holds mail for members. For more details and for parcels service and letters to Europe via Lufthansa, see page 375.

Telecommunications: international and interprovincial calls are possible from the Emetel offices at Av 10 de Agosto y Colón, and in the Old City from Benalcázar y Mejía, and the Terminal Terrestre, open 0800-2200; also at the airport, open 0800-1900. People at the airport try to sell you phone cards, but as international calls can only be made at Emetel offices it is better to buy them only when you need them. *Hotel Oro Verde* will send faxes, *Hotel Colón* is cheaper but only for residents. You can also send faxes from the postcard shop at the end of the passage next to Ecuadorean Tours.

Fax service and 1-min international phone calls (Europe US$7/minute; Canada US$5.10) so that you can be called back if necessary, are available through Intimexpo, Amazonas 877 y Wilson, Edif Visecom, Oficina 306, T 568-617/632, F 568-664; Mon-Fri 0900-1800. It is also possible to make a collect call to some, but not all, countries. Note that Emetel offices charge only US$0.70 for an unsuccessful transmission, unlike some offices which advertise fax service and charge per minute whether successful or not.

● **Shopping**
Most shops in the Old City are shut on Sat afternoon. Articles typical of Ecuador can be bought in the main shopping districts of Avenidas Amazonas and Guayaquil. There are carved figures, plates and other items of local woods, balsa wood boxes, silver of all types, Indian textiles, buttons, toys and other things fashioned from tagua nuts, hand-painted tiles, hand-woven rugs and a variety of antiques dating back to colonial days. Panama hats are a good buy. Indian garments (for Indians rather than tourists) can be seen and bought on the N end of the Plaza de Santo Domingo and along the nearest stretch of C Flores.

Handicrafts: *Hilana*, 6 de Diciembre 1921 y Baquerizo, beautiful unique 100% wool blankets in Ecuadorean motifs, excellent quality, purchase by metre possible, inexpensive. Near *Hotel Quito* at Colón 260 is *Folklore*, the store of the late Olga Fisch, a most attractive array of handicrafts and rugs, but distinctly expensive, as accords with the designer's international reputation; also at *Hotel Colón*, where *El Bazaar* also has a good selection of crafts, and *Hotel Oro Verde*.

Productos Andinos, an artisans' co-operative, Urbina 111 y Cordero, good quality, reasonably priced, rec; *La Bodega Exportadora*, J L Mera 614 y Carrión, is rec for antiques and handicrafts, as is *Renacimiento*, Carrión y J L Mera; *Fundación Sinchi Sacha*, Reina Victoria 1780 y La Niña, T 230-609,

F 567-311, PO Box 17-07-9466, cooperative selling select ceramics and other arts and crafts from the Oriente, rec; *MCCH Women's Co-op*, JL Mera y Robles; *Marcel Creations*, Roca 766, entre Amazonas y 9 de Octubre, good panama hat selection; *Artesanías Cuencanas*, Av Roca 626 entre Amazonas y J L Mera, friendly, knowledgeable, wide selection; *Galería Latina*, next to Libri Mundi at J L Mera 823 y Veintimilla, has a fine selection of handicrafts from Ecuador, Peru and Bolivia; *Centro Artesanal*, J L Mera 804, *El Aborigen*, Washington 536 y J L Mera, and *Ecuafolklore*, Robles 609 entre Amazonas y J L Mera (also stocks guide books) have all been rec. *Coosas*, J L Mera 838, the factory outlet for Peter Mussfeldt's attractive animal designs (bags, clothes etc); *The Ethnic Collection*, esq Amazonas 1029 y Pinto, PO Box 17-03-518, T 522-887, F 567-761, wide variety, clothing, leather, bags, jewellery, etc (in UK contact Richard Hartley, The Alpaca Collection, 16 Warstone Parade East, Hockley, Birmingham B18 6NR, T 0121 212 2550, F 0121 212 1948).

Goldwork from *Antigüedades el Chordeleg*, 6 de Diciembre y Cordero. *Handicrafts Otavalo*, Sucre 255 and García Moreno, good selection, but expensive; *Nomada*, Reina Victoria 909 y Roca, excellent quality T-shirts at factory prices, also factory shop at Pinzón 199 y Colón; *Amor y Café*, Foch 721 y JL Mera, quality ethnic clothing; *Los Colores de la Tierra*, JL Mera 838 y Wilson, hand-painted wood items and unique handicrafts; *Gran Cacao*, Foch 721, a gallery collection of quality art.

Mercado Ipiales, on Chile from Imbabura uphill, or *Mercado Plaza Arenas* on Vargas are where you are most likely to find your stolen camera for sale – or have it stolen, also try *Grau* camera shop, Plaza Santo Domingo, on your left as you face the church. The other market is on 24 de Mayo and Loja from Benalcázar onwards.

There is an exhibition and sale of paintings in El Ejido park, opp *Hotel Colón*, on Sat mornings. On Amazonas, NE of *Hotel Colón*, are a number of street stalls run by Otavalo Indians, who are tough but friendly bargainers. Bargaining is customary in small shops and at street stalls.

Leather goods at *Chimborazo*, Amazonas (next to Espinal shopping centre) and *Aramis*, Amazonas 1234; *Su Kartera*, Sucre 351 y García Moreno, T 512-160, with a branch on Veintimilla 1185 between 9 de Octubre y Amazonas, manufacturers of bags, briefcases, shoes, belts etc; *Casa Indo Andina*, Roca y J L Mera, alpaca, wool fashions, good quality. *Camari*, Marchena 260, is a direct sale shop run by an artisan organization. See *H Stern's* jewellery stores at the airport, *Hotel Colón* and *Hotel Quito*.

Other jewellery shops: *Alquimia*, Juan Rodríguez 139, high quality silversmith; *Edda*, Tamayo 1256 y Cordero, custom-made jewellery, rec; *Argentum*, J L Mera 614, reasonably priced. *La Guaragua*, Washington 614, sells *artesanías* and antiques, excellent selection, reasonable prices.

Foodstuffs: *Supermaxi* supermarkets offer 10% discount on purchases if you buy a Supermaxi card; this is available at the main counter. There are Supermaxi stores at the Centro Comercial Iñaquito, Centro Comercial El Bosque (Av Occidental), Centro Comercial Plaza Aeropuerto (Av de la Prensa y Homero Salas), at the Multicentro shopping complex on 6 de Diciembre y La Niña, about 2 blocks N of Colón, and at Centro Comercial El Jardín at Amazonas y Mariana de Jesús; all open Mon-Sat 0930-2000, Sun 0930-1300; *Mi Comisariato*, Centro Comercial Quicentro, Naciones Unidas y 6 de Diciembre, supermarket and department store, also sells 10% discount cards; *La Feria* supermarket, Bolívar 334, between Venezuela y García Moreno sells good wines and spirits, and Swiss, German and Dutch cheeses. Macrobiotic food is available at *Vitalcentro Microbiótico*, Carrión 376 y 6 de Diciembre. *Sangre de Drago*, the Indian cure all, is sold at the juice bar at Oriente y Guayaquil.

Miscellaneous: *Audio-Video*, several branches, national and international. Excellent art supply shops *S Bandra*, Calama 221, between Almagro y Reina Victoria, T 525-353; *Papelería Chávez*, Veintimilla y 12 de Octubre, is cheaper, they also have large envelopes and boxes; good quality drawing paper is hard to find, better to take supplies with you. There is a chain of hardware stores called *Kywi* which have a good selection of items such as padlocks; one is on Av 10 de Agosto, just S of Colón.

Bookshops: the *South American Explorers Club* in Quito and USA (see page 122) has the best selection of guidebooks in English (new and second-hand at good prices) and maps covering Ecuador and the rest of South America. *Libri Mundi*, J L Mera 851 y Veintimilla, open Mon-Sat, 0800-1800, and at the *Hotel Colón Internacional*, open Mon-Fri, 0800-

1800, Sat-Sun, 1700-2000, Spanish, English (some second-hand available), French, some Italian books, records, Ecuadorean maps when in stock, though these are cheaper at other bookshops, has a notice-board of what's on in Quito; very highly rec. *The Travel Company*, JL Mera 517 y Roca and JL Mera 1233 y Lizardo García, for books (secondhand at No 1233), postcards, T-shirts, videos, rec; *Imágenes*, 9 de Octubre y Roca, for books on Ecuador and art, postcards; *Libro Express*, Amazonas 816 y Veintimilla, has a good stock of maps, guides and international magazines; *Confederate Books*, Calama 410 y JL Mera, open 1000-1900, excellent selection of second-hand books, inc travel guides, mainly English but German and French are also available, the owner Tommy will exchange damaged dollar bills; *Librería Científica*, Colón y J L Mera; *Librería Cima*, 10 de Agosto 285 y Sta Prisca, good selection in Spanish; *Ediciones Abya-Yala*, 12 de Octubre 14-36 (T 562-633), also has excellent library and museum (see **Museums** above). *Biblioteca Luz*, Oriente 618 y Vargas, runs a book exchange (mainly Spanish) charge US$1. Bookshop at Centro Comercial Popular, Flores 739 y Olmedo, T 212-550, sells half price books and magazines, some French and English books, also book exchange. Foreign newspapers are for sale at the news stand in *Hotel Colón* (approx US$3). Lufthansa will supply German newspapers if they have spare copies.

Camera repairs and equipment: *Difoto*, Amazonas 893 y Wilson, professional processing, English and German spoken; *El Globo*, 10 de Agosto in departmental store, sells Fuji slides and print film, stored properly, refrigerated; *Japon Color Express*, Amazonas 507, slide film, Fuji RD 100-36, US$7, check the dates; *Kis Color*, Amazonas 1238 y Calama, will develop and print 36 exposure film for US$8, better quality for 24-hr printing than 1 hr service, passport photos in 3 mins. There are several places for cheap processing on Plaza Santo Domingo.

Suba Foto, Maldonado 1371 y Rocafuerte, sells second-hand cameras, and *Foto Estudio Grau*, Bolívar 140 y Plaza Santo Domingo for repairs and parts; *Cemaf*, Asunción 130 y 10 de Agosto, Edif Molina, p 1, T 230 855, helpful, also repairs video cameras. Film is cheap but only ASA100, 200, 400 and Kodak Gold 35 mm are available, no Kodachrome. Lots of shops on Amazonas sell film at good prices. *Ecuacolor/Kodak*, Amazonas 888 y Wilson,

Orellana 476 y 6 de Diciembre, and 10 de Agosto 4150 y Atahualpa. The Kodak processing laboratory has been criticized as dirty and careless.

A rec processing lab is that of Ron Jones, Brieva 641 y Diguja (Granda Centeno), take a bus to Av América, get off at TV channel 4, then walk up the hill, he develops Fuji and Kodak, slides/prints, B/W or colour, helpful and informative. *Naun Briones*, Cordero 1167 y J L Mera. Also for black and white, *Fotomania*, 6 de Diciembre y Patria, for new and second-hand cameras. The average price for processing US$6.50 for 24, US$8.50 for 36.

● **Sports**

Dance classes: *Ritmo Tropical*, Av 10 de Agosto 1792 y San Gregorio, Edif Santa Rosa, of 108, T 227-051, teach Salsa, Merengue, Cumbia, Vallenato and Folkloric dance in groups or one-to-one, US$5/hr.

A local game, *pelota de guante* (glove ball), is played, Sat afternoon and Sun at Estadio Mejía. **Football** is played Sat afternoons (1200 or 1400) and Sun mornings (maybe as early as 0800) at Estadio Atahualpa, 6 de Diciembre y Naciones Unidas, any northbound bus on 6 de Diciembre marked 'Estadio' goes there. **Basketball** is palyed in the Coliseo.

The first week of Dec is the main **Bullfighting** season. Tickets are on sale at 1500 the day before the bullfight; an above-average ticket costs US$8 but you may have to buy from touts. The Unión de Toreros, Edif Casa Paz, Av Amazonas, has information on all bullfights around the country; these take place all year, except Christmas to March. They do not have details of the parochial *corridas del pueblo*. **Cockfighting** takes place in the Pollodrome, C Pedro Calixto y Chile, Sat, 1400-1900, US$0.25 plus bet.

There is a cold spring-water **Swimming pool** on Maldonado beyond the Ministry of Defence building (US$0.10), hot shower (US$0.10). A public heated, chlorinated pool is in Miraflores, at the upper end of C Universitaria, corner of Nicaragua, a 10-min walk from Amazonas, you must take swimming cap, towel and soap to be admitted, open Tues-Sun, 0900-1600, US$1.50. There is another public pool at Batán Alto, on Cochapata, nr 6 de Diciembre and Villaroel, very good but expensive at US$3.

Rugby is played at Colegio Militar on Sun 1000; enquire at *El Pub*. The Hash House Harriers is a club for **Jogging**, runners and walkers, enquire at *Reina Victoria Pub*, T 233-369. **Bowling** centre, pool, at Amazonas y Alfaro. **Paragliding**, *Escuela Pichincha*, Alemania 339 y Eloy Alfaro, T Jaime 540-347, Cicque 455-076, US$250 complete course, good (see also page 22). **Bungee jumping**, every Sun at 1000 with Andes Bungee, T 226-071/524-796, US$40 for 2 jumps.

Climbing: for climbing the volcanoes, proper equipment and good guidance are essential. The dangers of inadequate acclimatization, snow blindness, climbing without equipment or a guide must be taken very seriously, especially on Chimborazo and Cotopaxi, which are not technically difficult and tempting targets for the less experienced, as many letters show. The Quito climbing clubs welcome new members, but they do not provide free guiding service. It is not really worth joining if you are in Ecuador for only a few weeks. The clubs are a good source for locating professional guides. Newly established is **Aseguim**, The Mountain Guide Association, which provides courses for their members and checks standards and equipment. You can check the validity of any guide through any of the rec climbing stores. Aseguim also organizes mountain rescues. The Association is not-for-profit and its members appreciate donations (see also page 18). Mountain rescue facilities are inadequate, it can take many hours to start a rescue operation and lack of equipment severely hinders success.

Safari Tours, Calama 380 y J L Mera, T 552-505, F 223-381, chief guide Javier Herrera speaks English, uses only ASEGUIM guides, maximum 2 climbers/guide, several languages spoken, very knowledgable, well organized and planned, small groups. *Surtek*, Amazonas y Ventimilla, T 561-129, branch of original Ambato office, chief guide Camilo Andrade, 8 languages spoken, all guides ASEGUIM, large and small groups, experienced; *La Compañía de Guías*, Jorge Washington y 6 de Dicembre, T 533-779, seven ASEGUIM guides, several languages spoken, Julio Mesías, José Luis Peralvo, Reno Román, Edison Salgado, Iván Vallejo, Mario Vascónez, Diego Zurita, new, expensive; *Sierra Nevada*, Pinto 637 y Amazonas, T 553-658/224-717, F 554-936, chief guide Freddy Ramírez uses mostly ASEGUIM guides, has own equipment, professional, mostly large groups; *Pamir*, JL Mera, 741 y Ventimilla, T 322-331, F 569-741, chief guide Hugo Torres, very experienced, speaks English; *Agama*, Venezuela 1163 y Manabí, T 518-191, chief guide Eduardo Agama, large groups, few guides, inexpensive.

Independent guides do not normally provide transport or full service, ie food, equipment, insurance, all ASEGUIM: Cosme León, T 603-140; Oswaldo Friere, T 265-597; Benno Schlauri, T 340-709; Gabriel Llano, T 450-628. The only woman guiding at this time is Damaris Carlisle, T 220-674.

Climbing clubs: Padre José Ribas at *Colegio San Gabriel Climbing Club* is helpful, their club meets Wed 1930. *Club de Andinismo* of the University Católica meets every Tues and Thur at 1930 and welcomes visitors, it is probably the most active club at this time. *Nuevos Horizontes Club* at Colón 2038 y 10 de Agosto, T 552-154, welcomes non-members onto their increasingly infrequent trips and will provide climbing information. *Sadday* is at Alonso de Angulo y Galo Molina. Climbing clubs do not provide guiding services.

Climbing, camping & trekking equipment: useful climbing equipment stores (and sources of information) are: *Equipo Cotopaxi*, 6 de Diciembre y Patria, equipment rentals, rec but expensive; *Campo Abierto*, Baquedano y Reina Victoria, Casilla 17-03-671, T 524-422, publishes a guide to climbing Ecuador's mountains, *Montañas del Sol* (US$6.75, 1994); *Altamontaña*, Jorge Washington 425 y 6 de Diciembre, F 524-422, climbing equipment, reasonable prices, good advice; *Altamontaña* and *Campo Abierto* both sell imported gear. Usual charge for hiring equipment is US$1-2/item/day, plus US$60 deposit in cash or cheques; stores may buy your used equipment.

Camping: *Cotopaxi*, Av Colón 942 y Reina Victoria, Mon-Fri 0900-1300, 1500-1900, T 563-560, good value equipment and camping gas. *The Explorer*, Reina Victoria y Pinto, reasonable prices for renting or buying, very helpful, will buy US or European equipment.

'*Bluet Camping Gas*' is reported to be easily obtainable: try *Importadora Vega* opp Banco Central, *Deportes Cotopaxi*, 6 de Diciembre y 18 de Septiembre, or *Globo*, 10 de Agosto, sometimes have it in stock but it's expensive. *Globo* shops also stock cheap snorkelling gear, also *Importaciones Kao*, Colón y Almagro, and *Casa Maspons*, Orellana entre 6 de Diciembre y Pinzón. *Captain Peña*, on the corner of Plaza Santo Domingo and Flores, also sells snorkelling equipment and for your personal security they stock C S Gas spray.

There are several new camping stores on Colón, E and W of Amazonas, which stock camping gas. For primus stoves and parts try

Almacenes Jácome, Chile 955 (nr Guayaquil). White gas is impossible to find in Ecuador; better to have a multifuel stove. Kerex or kerosene can be found on the corner of Bogotá y Uruguay, knock on the back gate. Those stoves which burn kerex work with unleaded gasoline (from Eco 82 or Super SP pumps in larger cities).

For hiking boots, *Calzado Beltrán*, Cuenca 562, and other shops on the same street. For a lockable rucksack cover *Equipos Cotopaxi*, Alianza 351 y Chimborazo, T 517626, made to measure, around US$25.

Mountain biking: *Pedal Andes*, T 220-674, E-mail: explorer@saec.org.ec, run back-road mountain bike tours, cultural as well as physical, highly rec, can combine with whitewater rafting; *Bike Tech*, Andagoya 498 y Ruiz de Castilla, owners Santiago and Regis have informal 'meets' every Sun, anyone is welcome, no charge, they ride 20 or more routes around Quito, they also have a good repair shop and cheap parts, they are friendly and glad to advise on routes; *Biking Dutchman Mountain Bike Tours*, Foch 714 y JL Mera, T 542-806, T/F 449-568, 1-day and 2-day tours, great fun, good food, very well organized, English, German and Dutch (of course) spoken; *Páramo Mountain Bike Shop*, 6 de Diciembre 3925 y Checoslovaquia, T 255-403/404, F 465-507, stocks high quality bikes. A rec mechanic is Alex Morillo, T 434-570; *Bicisport*, Los Shyris 1300 y Portugal, T 442-984, rec. Also *Biciteca y Renta Bike*, Av Brasil 1612 y Edmundo Carvajal, T/F 241-687, subida al Bosque, for sales, spares, repairs, tours, rentals and information, rents high quality bikes for US$20/day; *Safari* (see **Tour companies**, below) rents bikes and has free route planning.

Whitewater rafting: *Sierra Nevada*, Pinto 637 y Amazonas, T 553-658/554-936, F 659-250, excellent trips from 1 to 3 days; *Ríos Ecuador*, based in Tena, T 06-887-438 (see **Oriente** section), Gynner Coronel has equipment, lessons and information on kayaking, rafting trips in the jungle, highly rec, very experienced, T 553-727, or book through Quito agencies; *Row Expediciones*, Noriega 374 y Villaroel, T 458-339, contact Juan Rodríguez for 1-day trips on the Río Blanco and Toachi, depending on the water levels, very professional operation; also connected to *ROW* (River Odysseys West) of the USA, offering 6-day professionally-guided trips down the Río Upano in the southern Oriente (T 1-800-451-6034, or PO Box 579, Coeur d'Alene, ID 83816); *Eco-Aventur*, Alfredo Meneses runs day trips on the Ríos Blanco and Toachi, T 524-715, F 223-720, also affiliated with *Small World Adventures* in the USA; *Andean River Tours*, T 543-954, or contact through the SAEC. All these outfits charge US$50-70/day.

NB Only one resident guide is trained to Class V, Gymer Coronel, and one to Class IV, Alfredo Meneses; all others are to Class III.

● **Tour companies & travel agents**
Note that many agencies offer 'nature tourism', which is not the same as 'ecotourism'. The difference is that, while nature tourism may offer trips to natural areas, there is no commitment to the environment, or economic benefits to indigenous groups. This is particularly true of the Oriente region. Very few of the tour operators along Av Amazonas actually offer ecotourism.

Fruadorean Tours (American Express agent), Av Amazonas 339, T 560-488, also sell local student cards, US$17, to those with proof of home student status, useful for discounts (Poste Restante can be sent to Aptdo 2605, Quito), office at *Hotel Colón* helpful; *Metropolitan Touring*, Av República de El Salvador 970, PO Box 17-12-310, T 464-780, F 464-702; also Amazonas 239 y 18 de Septiembre and at *Hotel Quito*; Thomas Cook representative; general agents for Galápagos Cruises and Transturi; runs tours to the Galápagos, also arranges climbing, trekking expeditions led by world-known climbers, as well as tours of Quito, Machalilla National Park, rail journeys to Cuenca and Guayaquil, jungle camps, generally rec, *Transturi*, part of Metropolitan Touring, operate a cruise ship, the *Flotel Francisco de Orellana*, in 4-5 day trips along the jungle rivers; *Ecoventura*, Av Colón 535 y 6 de Diciembre, T 507-408, F 507-409, has tours throughout Ecuador and to the Galápagos, including the Northern Andes, Indian markets, Cuenca, Ingapirca, bird-watching, the Amazon and the Pacific coast; *Ecuaviajes*, Av Eloy Alfaro 1500 y Juan Severino, T 233-386, F 504-830, highly rec for everything, Cristina Latorre de Suárez speaks excellent English, very helpful if trying to find a cheap way home.

Angermeyers Enchanted Expeditions, Foch 726 y Amazonas, T 569-960, F 569-956, for Galápagos cruises on a variety of boats, and tours of jungle, sierra and costa (including economy); *Rolf Wittmer*, Amazonas 621 y Carrión, PO Box 17-07-8989, T 553-460, F 448-173, 2 yachts for tours of the Galápagos; *Sierra Nevada Expeditions*, Pinto 637 y Amazonas, T 553-658, F 554-936, specialized tours, river rafting, treking, mountaineering, jungle expeditions; *Golondrina Tours*, J L Mera 639 y Carrión, T 528-616, F 528-570, also in Puerto Ayora, rec for 8 day trip to Galápagos from Quito; *Napo Tour*, J L Mera 1312 y Cordero, T 545-426/547-283, has been rec as efficient and cheap, it is better value to book Napo's *Anaconda Hotel* (nr Misahuallí) in Quito than to book in Misahuallí (it is also cheaper to make your own way there than to go with Napo Tour); *Neptunotour*, 290 Gangotena Enrique St, PO Box 17-04-10502, F 502-066, Galápagos cargoboat tour; *Alpa Tours*, Amazonas y Foch, rec, very helpful, T 562-436/7; *Etnotur*, Luis Cordero 1313 y J L Mera, T 564-565, F 502-682, helpful, English and German spoken, jungle, mountain, rafting and Galápagos tour, rec.

La Moneda Tours, Av Naciones Unidas 825 y Av de Los Shyris, Mastercard building, 4 p, T 256-214/5, F 256-113, also has offices in Guayaquil and Machala, specializes in coastal and archaeological tours; *Eco Adventours*, Calama 339 entre R Victoria y JL Mera, T 524-715, F 223-720, organizes trips to more unusual areas with rafting on various rivers a speciality; *Latin Tour*, office at airport and in Av Amazonas, T 508-811/528-522, various trips around the country in a jeep and by motorbike, eg to Cotopaxi, English speaking, ask for Juan López, very friendly staff, frequently rec; *Free Biker Tours*, Guipuzcoa 339 y La Floresta, T 560-469, or in Switzerland, Grenzweg 48, 3645 Gwatt, T 033-365-128, run by Patrick Lombriser, Enduro-Motorcycles 600cc, good tours, spectacular roads, rec; *Andean Sports*, Roca 549 y J L Mera, T 520-442, English, French, German spoken, climbing, tours, equipment provided, rec; *Elinatour*, Bejarano 150 y Suárez, T 525-352, 7 blocks from *Hotel Quito*, gives time and effort to finding what people want; *Naturgal*, Foch 635 y Reina Victoria, T 522-681, T/F 224-913, English spoken, specializes in trips to the Llanganates, rec as good value for Galápagos; *Pablo Prado*, Rumipamba 730 y República, T 446-954, for tours in 4WD vehicle, nature adventures, ecological excursions, Galápagos, rainforests; *Volker*, organizes walking, cycling and river rafting tours to Mindo, Muisne and other places, rec, contact him in *Ghoz* bar or *Arribar*; *Agama Expediciones*, Venezuela 1163 y Manabí, climbing, trekking, some equipment for sale and rent, rec.

Ecuagal, Amazonas 1113 y Pinto, T 229-579, F 550-988, own 2 boats in Galápagos; *Klein Tours*, Av Los Shyris 1000 y Holanda, T 430-345, F 442-389, Galápagos and mainland tours, tailor-made, specialist and adventure, English, French and German spoken; *Nixe Cruises*, El Comercio 125 y Av de los Shyris, T 467-980, F 437-645, PO Box 6646 CCI, catamaran cruises of Galápagos, maximum 10 passengers, 4 crew, 1 guide, diving available, also tours of the coast, Machalilla National Park and the Oriente; *Palmer Voyages*, Alemania 575 y Mariana de Jesús, T 506-915, small specialist company, good rates, speak to Dominique Olivares; *Nature Life*, Joaquín Pinto 446 y Amazonas, PO Box 17-03-504, T 505-158, F 550-836, specializes in jungle tours based around Nativo Lodge on Napo River; *Fantasía Tours*, Roca 736 y Amazonas, Pasaje Chantilly, T 567-186, F 554-454, PO Box 9249, rec for booking Galápagos trips efficiently; *Sudamericana de Turismo*, Av Amazonas 11-13 y Pinto, good, Ricardo speaks German. *Tropic Ecological Adventures*, Av

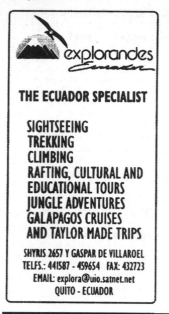
12 de Octubre 1805 y Cordero, Edif Pallares, T 508-575/222-389, F 222-390, E-mail Larry@lziegler.ecx.ec. Run by Welshman Andy Drumm, a naturalist guide and divemaster on the Galápagos. He is also director of the Amazon Project run by the *Asociación Ecuatoriana de Ecoturismo* and works closely with conservation groups. This small company runs ecologically responsible and educational jungle tours and is rec for anyone seriously interested in the environment; a sizeable percentage of each fee is given to indigenous communities and ecological projects. *Andes Discovery Tours*, Av Amazonas 645 y Ramírez Dávalos, T 550-952, F 437-470, Galápagos tours, helpful, rec.

Safari, Calama 380 y J L Mera (also in the cul-de-sac opp *Hotel Alameda Real* on Roca), T 552-505, F 220-426, E-mail admin@safariec.ecx.ec, David Gayton and Jean Brown, excellent adventure travel, customized trips, mountain climbing, rafting, trekking, 4WD jeeps available (Fabian Espinosa is an excellent guide), open 7 days; *Explorer Tours*, Reina Victoria 1235 y Lizardo García, T 522-220/508-871, F 508-871, owns *Sacha Lodge* and *La Casa del Suizo* on the Río Napo, first

rate educational jungle tours; *The Galápagos Boat Company*, Pasaje Roca 630, T 220-426, is a broker for up to 80 boats in the islands, purchase in Quito for non-commissioned prices, good deals; *Explorandes*, Shyris 2657 y Gaspar de Villaroel, T 441-587, F 432-723, Email explore@uio.satnet.net, trekking, rafting, climbing, jungle tours; *Taurus Viajes*, Amazonas 678 y Ramirez Davalos, p 2, T 223-639, rec for Galápagos tours, Luis Tipan speaks English; *Galatravel*, Amazonas 519 y Roca, Galápagos tours, and *Eurogalápagos*, Amazonas 330 y Washington; *River Tour*, Washington y Amazonas, Edif Rocafuerte, local 10, T 505-706, highly rec for good value Galápagos tours, small boats and groups, staying overnight in hotels; *Terracenter*, Reina Victoria 1343 y J Rodríguez, T/F 507-858, all variety of tours, inc to the Galápagos (special arrangement with Simón Bolívar language school). *Icelandair*, Av Diego de Almagro 1822 y Alpallana, T 561-820 for tickets to Europe via Iceland, student discounts. There are many agencies in the Av Amazonas area. Shop around for best deals for the Galápagos and jungle lodges.

Galasam Cía Ltda, Pinto 523 y Av Amazonas, and Amazonas 1316 y Cordero, T 507-080/1/2, F 567-662, operates Economic Galápagos Tours as well as Condor Tours, Uniclán, Yanasacha, Sol Mar Tours. 4-star hotel due open at Amazonas y Cordero in 1996. Their tours can be purchased in Switzerland: Mondorama, T (01) 261-5121, F (01) 262-2306; Holland, Cross Country Travel, T (025) 20-77-677, F (025) 20-23-670; Australia, Latin American Travel, T (61) 33-29-5211, F (61) 33-29-6314; USA, Galapagos Worldwide, T (305) 1-800-327 9854, F (305) 661 1457; Latin American Specialized Tours, T (410) 922-3116, F (410) 922-5538; Galapagos Yacht Cruises, T 1-800-GALA-PRO (1-800-425-2778); Forum Travel, T (510) 671-2993, F (510) 946-1500, exclusive representatives, prices are the same as in Ecuador. Galasam offer 3, 4 and 7 night Galápagos cruises, 6-day/5-night cruises with 2 extra nights in Santa Cruz or San Cristóbal.

Galapagos Network, 7200 Corporate Center Drive, Suite 404, Miami, Florida, T (305) 592-2294, F (305) 592 6394, in Quito T 564-969, F 564-592, Guayaquil, T 201-516, F 201-153, modern yachts. For other agencies organizing tours to the Galápagos, see page 331.

NB When booking tours, note that National Park fees are rarely inc.

● **Tourist offices**

Corporación Ecuatoriana de Turismo (Cetur), Eloy Alfaro 1214 y Carlos Tobar (between República and Shyris), T 507-559/560, F 507-564, and at Venezuela 976 nr Mejía, p 1, open Mon to Fri, 0830-1700, T 514-044; and at airport, 0700-1900 (last two can make hotel bookings; provide maps and other information, very helpful. Some staff speak English.

Maps: Instituto Geográfico Militar on top of the hill to the E of El Ejido park. From Av 12 de Octubre, opp the Casa de la Cultura, take Jiménez (a small street) up the hill. After crossing Av Colombia continue uphill on Paz y Miño behind the Military Hospital and then turn right to the guarded main entrance; you have to deposit your passport or identification card. There is a beautiful view from the grounds. Map and air photo indexes are all laid out for inspection. The map sales room (helpful staff) is open 0800-1600, Mon-Fri. They sell the best topographic maps, covering most areas of Ecuador, scales 1:250,000, 1:100,000, 1:50,000, 1:25,000, US$2 each. Maps of border areas are 'reservado' (classified) and not available for sale without a military permit (requires approx 6 weeks). Many large-scale topographical maps are reported out of print, but there are four new sheets covering the Oriente, 1:250,000 Mapas Amazónicas, very accurate, US$2.75 each. Buy your maps here, they are rarely available outside Quito. If one is sold out you may order a photocopy. Map and geographic reference libraries are located next to the sales room. Many maps are now available at the **Centro de Difusión Geográfica** in the Casa de Sucre, Venezuela 573, helpful. All IGM maps are available by mail order from **Latin American Travel Consultants**, PO Box 17-17-908, Quito, Ecuador, F 593-2-562-566, Internet: LATA@pi.pro.ec. See also next paragraph and **Maps and Guide Books**, page 380.

South American Explorers Club: Jorge Washington 311 y Leonidas Plaza, T/F 225-228, Mon-Fri 0930-1700, is a non-profit organization staffed

by volunteers which provides a wide range of information on South America through its resource centre, library and quarterly journal as well as selling guidebooks, maps and equipment, both new and used. Clubhouse services are only available for members. Highly rec. Annual membership US$40 single, US$60 for a couple. See below for Quito and Ithaca addresses or you can join on arrival in Quito.

The Club has new, enlarged premises in a beautiful colonial house. Also has information on mountain biking in Ecuador. You can arrange incoming faxes through SAEC. Write to Apdo 17-21-431, Eloy Alfaro, Quito; E-mail: explorer@saec.org.ec (to send E-mail to a member, send to member @saec.org.ec and put member's full name in Subject field). In USA, 126 Indian Creek Rd, Ithaca, NY 14850, T (607) 277-0488, F 607-277-6122; E-mail: explorer@samexplo.org. US office offers books, maps, trip-planning service and can ship books and maps worldwide. For information and travel tips on-line: http://www.samexplo.org. Official representatives in UK: Bradt Publications, 41 Nortoft Rd, Chalfont St Peter, Bucks, SL9 0LA, T/F 01494-873478.

● **Useful addresses**
Immigration Office: tourist visas will only be extended on the last valid day. **Policía Nacional de Migración**, Amazonas 2639, Mon-Fri 0800-1200 and 1500-1800; take bus 15 or a double-decker bus along Amazonas; go early and be prepared to wait. Those with visas other than tourist may obtain information from the **Cancillería** (Asuntos Migratorios, Sección Visas, Edif Zurita, Páez y Carrión, p 1, T 561-010, Mon-Fri 0930-1230), the **Extranjería** (Carrión y Páez, diagonally across from Asuntos Migratorios, T 563-353, Mon-Fri 0800-1300), and **Policía Nacional de Migración** (as above). Paperwork at any or all of these offices may be required to change, extend, or renew non-tourist visas.

Police: Criminal Investigations, Cuenca y Mideros, in the Old City. To report a robbery, make a *denuncia* within 48 hrs on official paper; if one officer is unhelpful, try another. If you wait more than 48 hrs, you will need a lawyer. Centralized number for all emergency services, T 101.

● **Transport**
Buses Standard fare on local buses and

busetas is US$0.10. Red and blue municipal buses on El Ejido-Quito Norte route (along Amazonas and by airport) US$0.25; *selectivos* and *ejecutivos* (sitting only), US$0.16-25. All tickets are bought on the bus; exact fare is sometimes expected. Buses are very slow in the Old City owing to traffic jams.

Trolley bus: a new trolley bus system ('El Trole') has been running since May 1996. The various routes serve the southern and northern parts of the city, and two routes cross the city along 10 de Agosto (see map); one running N to S and the other S to N. The northern station is at 'La Y', the junction of 10 de Agosto, Av América and Av de la Prensa, and the southern station is at El Recreo, on Av Maldonado. Running N from the southern station, there is a stop outside the train station, called Chimbacalle. Heading S you need to get off at the stop before, Machángara, and walk uphill along Maldonado. The main bus terminal is served on both the northern and southern routes by the Cumandá stop, at Maldonado y 24 de Mayo. In the N, some services run past the airport. The fare is US$0.25; US$0.15 for students. There is a special entrance for wheelchairs. Though the trolley bus is not designed for heavy luggage, it's just about possible to squeeze on with a backpack.

Car rentals: all the main car rental companies are at the airport (Hertz, Avis, International, Ecuacar, Budget, Carros Diligentes and Arrancar). City offices: **Budget**, Colón y Amazonas, T 548-237 and *Hotel Colón* (closed Sat-Sun), T 525-328. **Avis**, Colón 1741 y 10 de Agosto, T 550-238. **Dollar**, Juan de Ascaray 281 y 10 de Agosto, T 430-777. **Ecuacar**, Colón 1280 y Amazonas, T 529-781. **Premium**, Orellana 1623 y 9 de Octubre, T 552-897. **Localiza**, 6 de Diciembre 1570 y Wilson, T 505-986. **Santitours**, Maldonado 2441, T 212-267/251-063 also rent minibuses, buses and 4WD, chauffeur driven rental only. Budget and Ecuacar have been particularly rec, helpful staff.

In 1996, a small car at Budget cost, including 10% tax, US$10/day, plus US$0.10/km or US$168 for a week with unlimited kms. A 4WD Trooper (rec for trips to the Oriente and the higher peaks) cost US$19/day inc tax, plus US$0.19/km or US$328 for a week with unlimited kms. A 10% tax is always added to the posted prices, insurance is in the range of US$5.50-7/day, drop off charge (for returning the vehicle in a city other than where it was rented) US$70.

In order to rent a car you must be 25 and have an international credit card. You may pay cash, which is cheaper and may allow you to bargain, but they want a credit card for security. You may be asked to sign two blank credit card vouchers, one for the rental fee itself and the other as a security deposit, and authorization for a charge of as much as US$1,000 may be requested against your credit card account. These arrangements are all above board and the uncashed vouchers will be returned to you when you return the vehicle, but the credit authorization may persist on your account (reducing your credit limit) for up to 30 days. Always make certain that you fully understand the rental arrangements before signing the contract, and be especially careful when dealing with some of the smaller agencies.

AMIPA, *Auxilio Mecánico Inmediato para Automóviles*, T 238-032 or through paging service at 228-444 *receptor* No 958, is a reliable roadside mechanical assistance in the Quito metropolitan area (including Los Chillos and Tumbaco valleys), service for members and non-members, also run a good repair shop. Unleaded fuel is now widely available in the city. **Land rover**: specialists at Inglaterra 533, Talleres Atlas. Also Luis Alfredo Palacios, Iturralde y Av de la Prensa, T 234-341. **Motorcycle repairs**: Sr Lother Ranft, Euro Servicio, Av Los Shyris y Río Coca, T 454-261; main business is BMW, Mercedes and Porsche cars (very busy) but is a bike enthusiast and can get BMW motorcycle parts from Germany in 2 weeks. Paco Olmedo, Domingo Espinar 540 y La Gasca, T 550-589, has a well-equipped mechanical shop. Talleres Kosche, Eiffel 138 y Los Shyris, T 442-204, rec. Juan Molestina, Av 6 de Diciembre y Bélgica, T 564-335, fuel and travel equipment shop, helpful for motorbike spare parts.

Taxi: standard taxi tariff in the city is US$0.50 to US$4 and not more than double by night; no increase for extra passengers; by the hour, from US$5. Although the taxis now have meters and are required by law to use them, drivers sometimes say they are out of order. Insist on the meter being used, it is always cheaper. If they have no meter, it is imperative to fix the fare beforehand. Taxis for local journeys in front of the big hotels nearly always ask more. After dark expect surcharges. Negotiate the fare first; if quoted in dollars check the rate, it may be cheaper in sucres. Insist that the taxi drops you precisely where you want to go. A negotiated fare from the airport of

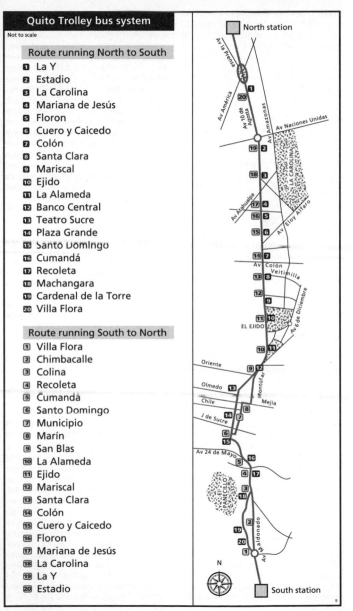

Quito Trolley bus system

Not to scale

Route running North to South

1. La Y
2. Estadio
3. La Carolina
4. Mariana de Jesús
5. Floron
6. Cuero y Caicedo
7. Colón
8. Santa Clara
9. Mariscal
10. Ejido
11. La Alameda
12. Banco Central
13. Teatro Sucre
14. Plaza Grande
15. Santo Domingo
16. Cumandá
17. Recoleta
18. Machangara
19. Cardenal de la Torre
20. Villa Flora

Route running South to North

1. Villa Flora
2. Chimbacalle
3. Colina
4. Recoleta
5. Cumandá
6. Santo Domingo
7. Municipio
8. Marín
9. San Blas
10. La Alameda
11. Ejido
12. Mariscal
13. Santa Clara
14. Colón
15. Cuero y Caicedo
16. Floron
17. Mariana de Jesús
18. La Carolina
19. La Y
20. Estadio

US$4-5 to the new city and US$5-6 to the old city is reasonable but they will often try to charge up to US$10. If arriving on an international flight before 1830 walk back to domestic arrivals where they charge less, or walk out of the airport to Av de la Prensa and hail a taxi which will use a meter, or catch a bus. At night there are only taxis parked outside the airport (no cruising taxis), and they charge more.

All legally registered taxis have the number of their co-operative and the individual operator's number prominently painted on the side of the vehicle. Note these and the license plate number if you feel you have been seriously overcharged or mistreated. You may then complain to the transit police or tourist office, but be reasonable as the amounts involved are usually small and the majority of taxi drivers are honest and helpful. For trips outside Quito taxi tariffs should be agreed beforehand: usually US$50-70 a day. Outside main hotels co-operative taxi drivers have a list of agreed excursion prices which can be as little as 20% off tourist excursion prices; most drivers are knowledgeable. For taxi tours with guide, Hugo R Herrera, T 267-891/236-492, speaks good English, rec. To order taxis by phone, Teletaxi T 220-800.

Air Mariscal Sucre Airport. From the airport catch bus 16 to go to Plaza Santa Domingo. The No 1 Iñaquito and Aeropuerto buses go to the airport, look for a sign 'Aeropuerto' on the windscreen; also No 43, Marín-Carcelén. The trolley bus service runs from outside the airport to the northern terminal at La Y. See also **Local buses** above for buses on Amazonas and taxis.

Beware of self-styled porters: men or boys who will grab your luggage in the hope of receiving a tip. There are no facilities for long-term left luggage at the airport, but there are at *Hotel Aeropuerto*, just outside the terminal, US$2/day. Watch bags at all times and watch out for theft by security officials when searching your bags; it has been reported that while you walk through the metal detector they remove money from your hand baggage. After checking in and before going through immigration, pay airport tax. The *Casa de cambio* opens at 0700. There are duty-free shops in the international departure lounge, also travel videos of Ecuador and frozen shrimp packed to travel are on sale here.

There is a monthly transport guide which gives details of international and national flights, and phone numbers of airlines in Quito and Guayaquil.

Internal flights: there are about 14 flights a day to and from **Guayaquil**, book in advance for daytime flights and check in promptly (with TAME, Saeta and SAN) and 3 to **Cuenca**. There are flights to **Esmeraldas, Manta, Bahía de Caráquez, Tulcán, Loja, Lago Agrio, Coca,** the **Galápagos, Portoviejo, Macas** and **Machala**. Prices are payable in US$ or sucres and are increased every 6 months, all airlines charge the same. Cancellations are frequent. Student discounts may be given on Galápagos flights to those under 26 with a student card from their home country, not an international card.

Trains The railway station is 2 km S of the centre, along the continuation of C Maldonado, reached by buses along that street (eg Iñaquito-Villa Flora No 1 or Colón-Camal, No 2), and the trolley bus (see above). The ticket office at this beautiful but decrepit old station is frequently closed and employees are not well-informed.

There are no trains going straight through from Quito to Durán (Guayaquil), an overnight stay in Riobamba is necessary. The passenger service between Quito and Riobamba is limited to one train a week: Quito-Riobamba, Sat 0800, US$10. This route provides spectacular views along the 'Avenue of the Volcanoes'. There is a service Riobamba-Durán (details under Riobamba **Transport**). There is no longer any service Quito-Cuenca or Riobamba-Cuenca as the Sibambe-Cuenca rail line was permanently closed in Mar 1995.

A tourist train, pulled by a steam locomotive runs from Quito to Parque Nacional Cotopaxi, Sun 0800, return 1430, US$20 return, for information T 513-422. Special arrangements can be made for group excursions from Quito to Riobamba and further S as far as Chunchi (118 km from Riobamba). A written request (*oficio*) must be presented at least 10 days prior to the date of the trip.

Metropolitan Touring (T 464-780) offers the following tours involving train travel: 1) a 2-day tour to Riobamba by train on Tues, Thur or Sat, overnight in Riobamba, back by bus US$285 pp based on double occupancy. The tour includes several stops along the way, visits to towns, Laguna de Yambo, a market and side trips to Guano and Baños, first class accommodations and meals. 2) An extension by train from Riobamba to Guayaquil over the famous *Nariz del Diablo* (Devil's Nose) the following day, Quito-Guayaquil US$374 pp (hotel in

Guayaquil and return to Quito not included, minimum 10 passengers required to run this portion). 3) A 4-day trip to Cuenca, starting in Quito Tues, Thur or Sat, involving bus, train and plane, including a visit to Ingapirca, US$627pp plus return flight to Quito US$29.

Road Bus: most main roads are paved, so interurban buses are fast and tend to be reliable. The Terminal Terrestre, at Maldonado and Cumandá (S of Plaza Santo Domingo), handles most long-distance bus services and is really the only place to get information on schedules. 24-hr luggage store, US$0.15 to use terminal. It is unsafe at night and in queues. Buses within the province of Pichincha leave from 'La Marín', which extends the length of Av Pichincha; a few others leave from Cotocollao (Trans Minas), Villaflora, or nr the Patria/10 de Agosto intersection.

From Terminal Terrestre to anywhere in the city, take a taxi, or the trolley bus along 10 de Agosto almost to the airport (if it does not go where you want, change at Marín or San Blas). No buses are allowed on Maldonado. There are company booking offices but staff about destinations of buses leaving; you can pay them and get on board. For buses out of Quito it is often advisable to reserve the day before as they may leave early if they are full. See under destinations for fares and schedules.

Several companies now run luxury coaches on the longer routes; those which have stations in the new city are: Flota Imbabura, Manuel Larrea 1211 y Portoviejo, T 236940, for Cuenca and Guayaquil; Transportes Ecuador, JL Mera 330 y Jorge Washington, to Guayaquil; Panamericana Internacional, Colón 852 y Reina Victoria, T 501584-5, for Huaquillas, Machala, Cuenca, Loja, Guayaquil, Manta and Esmeraldas, they also run an 'international' bus to **Bogotá**, but this involves many changes and greater expense; it is better to take a bus to the border and change. The route for crossing the Peruvian border via Loja and Macará takes much longer than the Machala route. Tepsa has an office at Pinto 539 y Amazonas; do not buy Peruvian bus tickets here, they are much cheaper in Peru, the same is true for tickets sold for other South American destinations.

Drivers should note that there is a ring road around Quito, and a by-pass to the S via the Autopista del Valle de Los Chillos and the Carretera de Amaguaña.

SHORT EXCURSIONS FROM QUITO

Mitad del Mundo

23 km N of Quito is the **Mitad del Mundo** Equatorial Line Monument at an altitude of 2,483m near San Antonio de Pichincha. The exact equatorial line here was determined by Charles-Marie de la Condamine and his French expedition in 1736.

The monument forms the focal point of a park and leisure area built as a typical colonial town, with restaurants, gift shops, Post Office with philatelic sales, tourist office (open 0900-1600), international pavilions (mostly not open) etc. It also has a museum inside; open Tues-Sun, 1000-1600, very crowded on Sun. Admission to the monument and the museum is US$1.60. The museum is run by the Consejo Provincial. A lift takes you to the top, then you walk down with the museum laid out all around with different Indian cultures every few steps.

There is a Planetarium with hourly 30-min shows and an interesting model of old Quito, about 10m square, with artificial day and night, which took 7 years to build, and is very pretty; entry US$0.65. 2 mins' walk before the Monument is the restaurant *Equinoccio*, which charges about US$10 a meal, live music, open from 1200 daily, T 394-091, F 545-663. Available at the restaurant, or at the stalls outside, are 'certificates' recording the traveller's visit to the Equator. These are free if you have a meal.

● **Accommodation D** *Hostería Alemana*, on the approach road from Quito, 4 blocks S; **E** *Res Mitad del Mundo*, in village of San Antonio de Pichincha.

● **Transport** From Quito: a paved road runs from Quito to the Monument, which you can reach by a 'Mitad del Mundo' bus (US$0.35, 1 hr) from Av América or the Parque Hermano Miguel (see Old City map, No 14). The bus fills instantly, but outside rush hour you can board anywhere along 10 de Agosto; beware of pickpockets on the bus. An excursion to Mitad del Mundo by taxi with a 1-hr wait is about US$25/taxi.

Pululahua

A few kilometres beyond the Monument, off the paved road to Calacalí, is the Pululahua crater, which is well worth visiting. It is a geobotanical reserve, entry US$6.60 (if you go in by the road). Try to go in the morning, as there is often cloud later. Trucks will take you from the Mitad del Mundo bus stop, round trip US$5. *Calimatours*, Manzana de los Correos, Oficina 11, Mitad del Mundo, T 394-796 in Quito, PO Box 17-03-638, organizes tours to all the sites in the vicinity, US$5 pp, rec.

Continue on the road past the Monument towards Calacalí. After a 4.7 km (1 hr walk) the road bears left and begins to climb steeply. The paved road to the right leads to the rim of the volcano and a view of the farms on the crater floor. There are infrequent buses to Calacalí which will drop you at the fork, from where it is a 30-min walk. There is plenty of traffic at weekends for hitching a lift. There is a rough track down from the rim to the crater, to experience the rich vegetation and warm micro-climate inside. Continuing past the village in the crater, turn left and follow an unimproved road up to the rim and back to the main road, a 15-20 km round trip. **D** *Hostería La Rinconada de Pululahua*, at the N end of the crater (turn right at the bottom of the valley if you walked down the path), with bath, restaurant open weekends only, camping US$2.

It is also possible to drive to the reserve: 8 km from the Mitad del Mundo monument on the way to Calacalí, take the turn off to the right past the gas station; it is 2.4 km to the Moraspungo Park gate where a very scenic drive into the crater begins. In 8 km you reach the valley floor. From there you can turn right towards the village of Pululahua, or left and continue downhill to the

sugar-cane growing area of Nieblí. There are two cabins near the Moraspungo entrance, US$0.65 pp, take sleeping bag, warm clothing and food.

Other Excursions from Quito

Also in the vicinity of the Mitad del Mundo Monument, 3 km from San Antonio beyond the Solar Museum, are the Inca ruins of **Rumicucho**. Restoration of the ruins is poor, but the location is magnificent. Investigations are under the auspices of the Museum of the Central Bank; entry US$1.25. Start early if you want to visit all these in a day.

8 km from Quito on the road to San Antonio de Pichincha, is the village of **Pomasqui**, near where was a tree in which Jesus Christ appeared to perform various miracles, El Señor del Arbol, now enshrined in its own building. In the church nearby is a series of paintings depicting the miracles (mostly involving horrendous road accidents), which is well worth a visit. You may have to find the caretaker to unlock the church (we are grateful to Hilary Bradt for this information).

From San Antonio a dirt road heads N towards Perucho. South of Perucho another road turns sharply SE to Guayllabamba via **Puéllaro** (eat at the house on the plaza which is also a radio/TV workshop). A left turn (NE) off this road, just before Guayllabamba, goes to Malchinguí, Tocachi and Cayambe (see page 138).

The Equator line also crosses the Pan-American Highway 8 km S of Cayambe, where there is a concrete globe beside the road. Take a Cayambe bus (2 hrs, US$0.80) and ask for Mitad del Mundo by Guachala.

● **Accommodation** For nearby accommodation, see *Hostería Guachala* and *Hostal Mitad del Mundo*, under Cayambe.

Sangolquí

Another day-trip is to Sangolquí (*Pop* 18,000), about 20 mins from Quito by

The middle of the world

👣 At the *Mitad del Mundo*, or Middle of the World, the imaginary 38,600 km equatorial line around the world has been turned into a 10 cm wide strip of white pebbles set into the ground. Here you can have your photograph taken with a foot in either hemisphere, or shake hands across the Equator, kiss across the Equator, or even read your Handbook across the Equator (if you've no one to kiss or shake hands with).

The French aristocrat and friend of Voltaire, Charles-Marie de la Condamine, was commissioned by the French Academy of Sciences to test Isaac Newton's theory that the Earth bulged at the Equator. In the process of testing this, La Condamine and his team determined the precise location of the line and the unit of measurement which resulted in the metric system.

The original monument, erected in 1936 to celebrate the 200th anniversary of the famous discovery, was replaced in 1986 by the much larger present one (the largest Equator marker in the world). Leading up to it is an impressive avenue lined with the busts of the members of the expedition. One of its number, the Ecuadorean scientist, Pedro Vicente Maldonado, also accompanied La Condamine on a raft journey down the Amazon in 1743. They were the first scientists to make this epic journey, and their map of the mighty river remained almost unchanged until the 20th century.

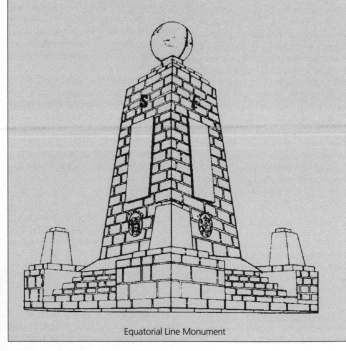

Equatorial Line Monument

bus. There is a busy Sun market (and a smaller one on Thur) and few tourists. There are thermal baths nearby, though they are reported dirty.

● **Accommodation C** pp *Hostería Sommergarten*, Urb Santa Rosa, Chimborazo 248 y Río Frío, 30 mins by bus from Quito in the valley of Los Chillos, T 332-761, F 330-315, or T/F 221-480, a colonial-style bungalow resort surrounded by a subtropical park, price inc breakfast, lots of activities are available, sauna, pool.

CLIMBING NEAR QUITO

Cruz Loma is the low, southern one of the two antenna-topped peaks overlooking Quito from the W (to the N is a peak with loads of antennae, known as Las Antenas). On a clear day you can see about 50 km down the central valley and to the E.

Rucu Pichincha

Rucu Pichincha (4,627m) can be seen from some parts of Quito, and can be climbed either via Cruz Loma or via its neighbour. The path to its foot runs due W over and around hummocks on the rolling, grass-covered *páramo*. The climb up to the peak is not technical, but it is rocky and requires a bit of endurance. From Cruz Loma to Rucu Pichincha peak takes about 4 hrs up and 2 down. Take rainproof and cold-weather gear just in case. You can continue from Rucu to Guagua Pichincha, the higher of the two peaks, be careful at Paso de la Muerte, a narrow ledge, about half an hour beyond Rucu Pichincha.

● **Safety** Do not to walk in this area without checking safety first, ask at the South American Explorers Club. Do not walk up from Av 24 de Mayo in central Quito as this is extremely dangerous (frequent attacks reported – on no account go alone). Also be vigilant if taking the route up from C Mañosa.

● **NB** No water is available so be sure to carry adequate supplies, especially if going to Rucu Pichincha. Please pick up your flotsam; the area is rubbish-strewn enough as it is.

● **Transport** To save time and energy take a taxi or bus, eg No 14, to Toctiuco, to the upper reaches of the city and start climbing to Cruz Loma from there (allow at least 5 hrs to reach the summit). There are poor roads up to both peaks, but traffic is sparse. Try hitching early in the morning, but remember that it is difficult to hitch back after about 1730 and you will have to walk in the dark. The road to the radio station on the northern hill is better for hitching.

Guagua Pichincha

A recommended route for climbing Guagua Pichincha volcano (4,794m) is to take a bus to Mena 2 at Calle Angamarca (dump trucks go to a mine near Lloa on weekdays), or to Chillogallo (US$1), from where the road goes to the town of **Lloa**, then a 4 x 4 track goes to the rim of the crater. There are no regular buses to Lloa. It is possible to catch a lift on a truck or *camioneta*, but, if you're in a small group, it is better to take a taxi to Lloa, which costs around US$12. Set off early as you will need all day to walk up to the *refugio*, just below the summit at 4,800m.

Lloa is a small, friendly village set in beautiful surroundings. The road to the summit is signposted from the right-hand corner of the main plaza as you face the volcano, and is easy to follow. There are a couple of forks, but head straight for the peak each time. It can take up to 8 hrs to reach the *refugio*, allowing for a long lunch break and plenty of rests. The *refugio*, which is maintained by the Defensa Civil, is manned and will provide a bed and water for US$2 pp. The warden has his own cooking facilities which he may share with you. It gets very cold at night and there is no heating or blankets. Be sure to keep an eye on your things.

The walk from the *refugio* to the summit is very short. You can scramble a bit further to the 'real' summit (above the *refugio*) which is tricky but worth it for the views; many other volcanoes can be seen on a clear morning. The descent into the crater is prohibited (since 1994) owing to increased volcanic activity (see **Hot Springs**, page 41). The University Hiking Clubs have details on 3-day hikes around the Pichincha peaks, with overnight stops in caves.

The descent back to Lloa takes only 3 hrs, but is hard on the legs. There is a restaurant in Lloa, on the main road to Quito, which sells good but expensive soup. To get back to Quito, walk a few hundred metres down the main road until you reach a fork. Wait here for a truck, which will take you to the outskirts of the city for around US$1. A taxi from the southern outskirts to the New City costs around US$4.

HOT SPRINGS NEAR QUITO

In the valley of Los Chillos (to the SE, 1 hr by car) are the thermal pools of **La Merced** and **El Tingo**. Take a 'La Merced' bus from La Marín (lower end of Av Pichincha). If driving, take Autopista de Los Chillos to San Rafael, where the divided highway ends, turn left at the traffic lights, it is 4 km to El Tingo where there are thermal baths, which are crowded and dirty at weekends. There is excellent food and a good atmosphere at the German-owned *Mucki's Garden* restaurant, T 320-789. 7 km past El Tingo is La Merced, which also has thermal baths, but avoid going at weekends (see **Hot Springs**, page 41). 4 km from La Merced is Ilaló, privately owned pools, admission US$2, these are cleaner, with fewer mosquitoes and people, but also best on weekdays. **Accommodation** E *Hostal San Pedro*, beside springs, also serves food.

From Alangasí, along the road to La Merced, a good paved road branches 10 km SE to **Píntag**. The road then turns to rough gravel and divides, the right fork goes to the base of Sincholagua (4,899m), the left fork goes to Laguna La Mica at the base of the snow covered volcano Antisana (5,704m). This is a magnificent area for hiking and camping where condors may be seen. There are no services, so visitors must be self

sufficient. An access permit from the landowner is required; enquire beforehand in Píntag, or from Fundación Antisana, Mariana de Jesús y Carvajal, T 433-851.

PAPALLACTA

At the Baños de Papallacta, 80 km E from Quito, 1 km from the road to Baeza, there are eight thermal swimming pools and two cold pools fed by a river, open 0700-2300, entrance US$3. There are showers, toilets, steam room, changing rooms and restaurant serving trout and other dishes (US$4-5). The baths are crowded at weekends but usually quiet through the week. The view, on a clear day, of Antisana from the Papallacta road or while enjoying the thermal waters is superb. In the village are municipal pools, simple, clean, US$1. (See also **Hot Springs**, page 41.)

The Fundación Ecológica Rumicocha has a small office on the main street, run by Sra Mariana Liguia, who is friendly (open 0800-1200, 1400-1600). There are leaflets on the Cayambe-Coca reserve. Permission cannot be given (1996) to walk to the lakes in the reserve while the state water company is working in the area. The circuit of the lakes (Papallacta, 3,450m, Sucus, 3,800m, and Tarugacocha, 3,850m) would be a wonderful hike for those wishing to acclimatize for climbing volcanoes. With luck condors can be seen.

● **Accommodation** There are two newly-built cabins for 6 people, 1 with private thermal bath, the other with kitchen facilities, US$50/cabin, 10 more rooms are available, for reservations T (Quito) 435-292 (Núñez de Vela 903, edit El Doral 2, p 1, of 15). C *Hostal La Posada Papallacta*, inc entry to the pools, fireplace, shared bunk rooms, restaurant at pools, food expensive. **In town:** F *Residencial El Viajero*, basic, shared bath, restaurant with reasonable meals, avoid the rooms in the old building. You can also stay in the village at G *Hotel Quito*, clean and friendly, restaurant also with reasonable meals, or ask the *alcalde*. There are also a couple of shops. **Camping:**

limited facilities, due for expansion 1996, US$5 per tent, clean, emphasis on recycling of rubbish, management prefers campers not to cook until washing-up facilities have been built.

● **Transport** Buses from Quito, Terminal Terrestre, 2 hrs, US$1.75: to Lago Agrio or Baeza (drivers sometimes charge full fare). Ask to be let off at the road to the springs; it's a steep 1 km walk up to the baths. On Sat and Sun there is a bus from Plaza San Blas at 0800, returning 1430.

PROTECTED AREAS NEAR QUITO

Maquipucuna Biological Reserve

2 hrs NW of Quito lies an 14,000 acre reserve established by the Maquipucuna Foundation, a non-profit organization dedicated to conservation activities. The cloud forest at 1,200-2,800m contains a tremendous diversity of flora and fauna, including over 325 species of birds. The reserve has five trails of varying length (15 mins to 5 hrs), including Sendero del Río and Sendero de la Unión de los Ríos (4-5 hrs with a wade through a river and swimming in a rock pool). There is also a research station and an experimental organic garden. Entry fee for foreigners, US$5 pp; one night's accommodation, 3 meals and entry, US$45; guide, US$8.50.

● **Access** Take the road from Quito to Mitad del Mundo, past Pululagua and Calacalí, the new road to Mindo, down the Western Cordillera to the coast. At Nanegalito turn right to a dirt road to Nanegal; keep going until a sign on the right to the reserve (before Nanegal). Pass through the village of Marianitas and it's another 20 mins to the reserve. The road is poor, especially in the Jan-May wet season, 4WD rec.

● **Reservations** Fundación Maquipucuna, Baquerizo 238 y Tamayo, Quito, Casilla 17-12-167, T 507-200, F 507-201, e-mail: root@maqui.ecx.ec. The British charity, **Rainforest Concern**, can also be contacted for information (and fund-raising), c/o Peter Bennett, 27 Lansdowne Crescent, London W11 2NS, T 0171-229-2093, F 0171-221-4094.

At Km 68 on the old road to Mindo via Tandayapa is Bellavista, with **C** pp *Finca Bellavista* (Cabins in the Clouds), with or without full board, hot showers, cheaper with shared facilities, vegetarian food, good views, excellent birdwatching and botany, T Quito c/o Richard Parsons (593-2) 509-255, or T/F 223-381. Advance booking essential. For Maquipucuna and Bellavista take a bus to Nanegalito then hire a truck, or arrange everything with the lodges or in Quito.

Aldea Salamandra

140 km NW of Quito, this beautiful nature reserve is set in tropical rainforest. Accommodation is in bamboo and thatch cabins, some of which are built in the trees on the riverbank. This is a great place to take a birdwatching excursion (over 300 species including toucans and hummingbirds), swim in the river, trek through the forest to isolated waterfalls, take a kayak trip or simply relax and enjoy nature. Note that weekends tend to be busy when it is used as the local beach. Aldea Salamandra work with Fundación Natura to preserve the environment and raise awareness of environmental issues.

The price of US$15 pp/day includes all meals and excursions; accommodation only is US$7 pp. Vegetarian food is available, as well as typical dishes. Discounts are available for groups of 15 or more and IYHA members; payment in dollars, sucres or TCs. For reservations T 551-188 (Quito).

● **Access** 3 hrs by bus from Quito. Take any Esmeraldas bus and ask the driver to stop 2 km before Puerto Quito. It is a 10-min walk from the main road; well signposted. You can also go from Esmeraldas with Trans Esmeraldas, 2 hrs; tell the driver to stop 2 km after Puerto Quito.

MINDO

Mindo is a small town (*Pop* approx 1,700) surrounded by dairy farms and lush cloud forest climbing the western slopes of Pichincha. 19,200 ha, ranging in altitude from 1,400 to 4,780m (the rim of the crater of Guagua Pichincha) have been set aside as a nature reserve: **Bosque Protector Mindo-Nambillo**. The reserve features spectacular flora (many orchids and bromeliads), fauna (butterflies, birds including the cock of the rock) and spectacular cloud forest and waterfalls. There has been some conflict in the area over the future of the reserve which includes both state and private land. Two ecological organizations are involved in the reserve: *Amigos de la Naturaleza de Mindo* and *Fundación Pacaso*, both with offices in Mindo. The former runs 2 refuges: one, Centro de Educación Ambiental (CEA), 4 km from town, within the 5 ha buffer zone at the edge of the reserve, has capacity for 25-30 people. The second, Refugio Enrique Grosse-Leumern, 12 km from Mindo, with capacity for 15. Guide service, lodging and food are available at these shelters.

Admission to the reserve is US$2, lodging US$6 pp, full board US$18 pp. Take sleeping gear (none provided) and food if you wish to prepare your own (nice kitchen facilities available). There are well maintained trails near the shelters. Arrangements have to be made in advance, contact in Mindo: Amigos de la Naturaleza de Mindo, on the main road into town, before reaching the plaza, on the left (signposted). If closed, enquire about Pedro Peñafiel or his family. In Quito: Sra María Guerrero, Casilla 17-03-1673, T 455-907. Visitors are recommended to stop at the office in Mindo before heading towards the reserve to get directions and information about the road. During the rainy season, access to the reserve can be very difficult or impossible. Be prepared to wade thigh-deep through rivers. However, even a visit to the buffer zone is well worthwhile. Vinicio Pérez is an excellent resident birding guide, Spanish only, rec.

● **Accommodation B** pp *Hostería El Carmelo de Mindo*, in 32 ha, 700m from the town centre, T/F 408-355, cabins or room with or without bath, **E** pp dormitory, bring sleeping

bag, **F** pp camping, US$ prices for foreigners, meals available, horse rental, excursions, 50% discount for IYHA card holders; **E** pp *Hacienda San Vicente*, 'Yellow House', 500m S of the plaza, inc all meals, family-run, very friendly, clean, nice rooms, TV, excellent food, good walking trails nearby, great value, rec; **E** *El Bijao*, on the left approaching the village, good, rec; **E-F** *Familia Patiño*, 2 attractive cabins, new, cheap, clean, friendly, ask at *Restaurant Omarcito*; **F** *Noroccidental*, basic, clean, some rooms with private bath; **F** *El Guadual*, clean, hot shower, good food to order.

● **Places to eat** *Salón Noroccidental, El Guadual, La Choza*; *Omarcito*, also has rooms for 10.

● **Transport** Bus Cooperativa San Pedro de Cayambe, Av Pérez Guerrero 150, T 508-947, daily at 1500 and at 0800 Thur-Sun, US$1.90, 2½ hrs (up to 7 hrs in the wet; road under repair 1996). From Santo Domingo de los Colorados, daily 1200 and Sat 0800, US$3, 4 hrs. The most direct access from Quito is along the road to San Miguel de los Bancos, Puerto Quito (accommodation available in both towns) and La Independencia where it joins the Santo Domingo- Esmeraldas road. It is now paved. If driving go to Mitad del Mundo, follow the signs for Calacalí and continue on to Nanegalito. It is a beautiful ride through native cloud forest. 24 km beyond Nanegalito, to the left is the turnoff for Mindo. It is about 7 km along a new road to the town. It can also be reached on a 2-day walk from the town of Lloa (10 km W of the the southern end of Quito).

BOSQUE PROTECTOR PASOCHOA

45 mins SE by car from Quito, is a subtropical natural park set in mountain forest, run by the Fundación Natura, América 5653 y Voz Andes, T 447-341/4, who provide further information (entrance for foreigners US$7, Ecuadoreans US$1.70; very touristy at weekends). The reserve is classified as humid Andean forest, with more than 120 species of birds (three condors often seen) and 50 species of trees, situated between 2,700 and 4,200m. Its average temperature is 10°C and its dry season occurs between June and September. Half of the plants have medicinal and/or traditional value.

There are walks of 30 mins, 1 hr, 2, 4 and 8 hrs. Camping is permitted in the park (US$3 per tent); take food and water as there are no shops and take your rubbish away with you. There is also a refuge (US$5 pp/night, with shower, has cooking facilities), but you will need a sleeping bag. Much of the fauna has been frightened away by the noise of visitors.

● **Transport** From Quito buses run from Marín to Amaguaña (ask the driver to let you off at the 'Ejido de Amaguaña'); from there follow the signs for the Bosque Natural Pasochoa. It's about a 8 km walk, with not much traffic for hitching, except at weekends. There is a short-cut 45 min walk nr Tambillo; maps at South American Explorers Club or *Safari*, Calama 380 y Jl Mera, Quito. By car, take the highway to Los Chillos, at San Rafael (traffic light) continue straight towards Sangolquí and on to Amaguaña. 1.4 km past the sign 'Amaguaña Os Da La Bienvenida' turn left onto cobblestone road and follow the signs to Pasochoa, 5.4 km to the park. Tours with Safari Tours in Quito cost US$40 pp; a price negotiated with a taxi driver from a good hotel is about US$15 pp; a pick-up truck from Amaguaña is about US$6.

Northern Ecuador

FOR MANY, the North of Ecuador, from Quito to the border with Colombia, contains a good tourist market at Otavalo, a route to the coast and little else. But that's their loss. This is an area of outstanding ecological importance and natural beauty, where several organizations are working to protect its precious assets. The landscape is mountainous, with views of the Cotacachi, Imbabura, Chiles and glacier-covered Cayambe, interspersed with lakes. This is also a region renowned for its artesanía. Countless villages specialize in their own particular product, be it hats, woodcarvings, bread figures or leather goods. And, of course, there's Otavalo, with that famous Saturday market, a must on everyone's itinerary.

ROUTES The Pan-American Highway and a railway line run NE from Quito to Otavalo (94 km) and Ibarra (114 km). Train services to Otavalo are indefinitely suspended. North of Ibarra, the railway and Highway separate. The railway goes NW to the Pacific port of San Lorenzo, a very spectacular trip, though passenger services were all but terminated in 1996. The highway runs N for another 108 km to Tulcán and on to Ipiales in Colombia. The Pan-American Highway is paved for the whole stretch Quito-Tulcán.

QUITO TO CAYAMBE

Calderón

32 km N of Quito, Calderón is the place where miniature figurines are made of bread. You can see them being made, though not on Sun, and prices are much lower than in Quito. Especially attractive is the Nativity collection. Prices range from about US$0.10 to US$4, which is excellent value. The figures can be seen in the Indian cemetery on 1-2 Nov, when

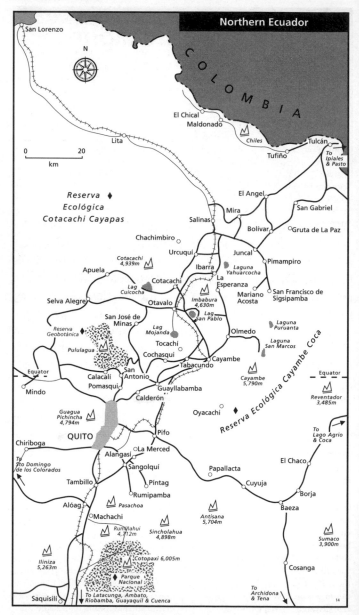

Northern Ecuador

San Lorenzo

COLOMBIA

N

El Chical
Maldonado
Chiles
Tulcán
Lita
Tufiño
To Ipiales
& Pasto

0   20
km

El Angel
San Gabriel

Reserva
Ecológica
Cotacachi Cayapas

Salinas
Mira
Bolívar
Gruta de La Paz

Chachimbiro
Urcuquí
Juncal
Pimampiro

Cotacachi
4,939m
Ibarra
Laguna
Yahuarcocha

Apuela
La
Esperanza
San Francisco de
Sigsipamba

Lag
Cuicocha
Cotacachi
Imbabura
4,630m
Mariano
Acosta

Selva Alegre
Otavalo

San José de
Minas
Lag
San Pablo
Laguna
Puruanta

Reserva
Geobotánica
Lag
Mojanda
Olmedo
Laguna
San Marcos

Pululahua
Tocachí

Cochasqui
Cayambe

San
Antonio
Tabacundo

Equator
Calacalí
Pomasqui
Guayllabamba
Cayambe
5,790m
Equator

Mindo
Calderón
Reventador
3,485m

Guagua
Pichincha
4,794m
Oyacachi
Reserva Ecológica Cayambe Coca

QUITO
Pifo
To Lago Agrio
& Coca

Chiriboga
La Merced
El Chaco

To
Sto Domingo
de los Colorados
Alangasí
Sangolquí
Papallacta

Tambillo
Píntag
Cuyuja
Borja

Alóag
Rumipamba
Pasachoa
Antisana
5,704m
Baeza

Machachi
Sumaco
3,900m

Rumiñahui
4,712m
Sincholahua
4,898m

Iliniza
5,263m
Cotopaxi 6,005m
Cosanga

Parque
Nacional
To
Archidona
& Tena

Saquisilí
To Latacunga, Ambato,
Riobamba, Guayaquil & Cuenca

14

Making money out of dough

🐾 The inhabitants of the town of Calderón, NE of Quito, know how to make dough. The main street is lined with shops selling the vibrantly-coloured figures made of flour and water which have become hugely popular in recent years.

The origins of this practice are traced back to the small dolls made of bread for the annual celebrations of All Soul's Day. The original edible figures, made in wooden moulds in the village bakery, decorated with a simple cross over the chest in red, green and black and were placed in cemeteries as offerings to the hungry souls of the dead.

Gradually, different types of figures appeared and people started giving them as gifts for children and friends. Special pieces are still made for All Soul's Day, such as donkeys and men and women in traditional costume.

(From *Arts and Crafts of South America*, by Lucy Davies and Mo Fini, Tumi).

the graves are decorated with flowers, drinks and food for the dead. The Corpus Christi processions are very colourful. Many buses leave from Plaza San Martín in Quito, but drivers are often unwilling to take backpackers.

After Calderón the road for the N descends into the spectacular arid Guayllabamba gorge and climbs out again to the fertile oasis of **Guayllabamba** village, noted for its avocados and delicious chirimoyas (**D** *Hostería Guayllabamba*, cabins on eastern outskirts of town). At Guayllabamba, the highway splits into two branches. To the right, the Pan-American Highway runs NE to Cayambe. The left branch goes towards the town of Tabacundo, from where you can rejoin the Pan-American travelling E to Cayambe or NE to Cajas.

Tolas de Cochasquí

10 km past Guayllabamba on the road to Tabacundo (8 km before Tabacundo), a gravel road to the left (signed Pirámides de Cochasqui) leads to Tocachi and further on to the national Tolas de Cochasqui archaeological site, administered by the Consejo Provincial de Pichincha. The protected area contains 15 truncated clay pyramids, nine with long ramps, built between 900 and 1500 AD by Indians of the Cara or Cayambi-Caranqui tribe. The pyramids are covered by earth and grass but one or two have been excavated, giving a good idea of their construction. Festivals take place with dancing at the equinoxes and solstices. There is a site museum with interesting historical explanations in Spanish. The views from the site, S to Quito, are marvellous.

● **Access** Only with a free 1½-hr guided tour; open 0900-1530. Be sure to take a bus that goes on the Tabacundo road and ask to be left off at the turnoff. From there it's a pleasant 8 km walk through an agricultural landscape. If you arrive at the sign between 0900-0930, you should get a lift from the site workers. A taxi from Cayambe costs US$8 for the round trip. Sometimes there is a colectivo taxi to Tabacundo or La Esperanza; it's then 15 km to the site.

El Quinche

6 km SE of Guayllabamba is the small village of El Quinche, where there is a huge sanctuary to Nuestra Señora de El Quinche in the plaza. The image was the work of the sculptor Diego Robles around 1600 in Oyacachi. It was brought to El Quinche because the local Indians did not wish to worship the image. There are processions on 21 Nov in El Quinche. There are many paintings illustrating miracles, ask the caretaker for the details. There is a bus service from Guaylla-bamba and direct buses from Quito via Cumbayá and Pifo (*Pensión Central*, basic, clean).

CAYAMBE

Cayambe (*Pop* 16,849), on the righthand branch of the highway, NE of Guayllabamba, is dominated by the snow-capped volcano of the same name. The town itself is fairly unremarkable, but quiet and pleasant. Worth a visit are the pyramids of the Sun and Moon at Puntiachil; a descriptive route for the Pyramid of the Sun is displayed.

The surrounding countryside consists of rich dairy farms which produce a fine range of European-style cheeses. Cayambe is the Agrarian Reform Institute's showplace and its only major project. The local Nestlé factory is such a dominant factor that locals will automatically assume foreigners are of Swiss origin. The area is noted for its *bizcochos*, which are little, shortbread-type biscuits. Particularly tasty are the *bizcochos con queso*. There is a *Fiesta* in Mar for the equinox with plenty of local music. Another important festival is IntiRaymi, during the last weekend in July.

Local information
● **Accommodation**
Hotels may be full on Fri during June-September.

B *Hacienda Guachala*, S of Cayambe on the road to Cangahua, a beautifully restored hacienda built in 1580, owned by Diego Bonifaz, ex-Agriculture Minister, spring-fed swimming pool, basic but comfortable rooms with fireplaces, delicious food, good walking, Anglo-Arabian horses for rent, excursions to nearby pre-Inca ruins, highly rec, reservations in Quito: Reina Victoria 1138 y Foch, T 563-748.

D *Cabañas Nápoli*, Panamericana Norte Km 2, good restaurant.

E *Hostal Cayambe*, Bolívar 23 y Ascázubi, T 361-007, Youth Hostel, clean, friendly, stores luggage; **E** *Hostal Mitad del Mundo*, on the Panamericana, clean, pool, sauna, restaurant.

● **Places to eat**
Restaurant El Unicorno, nr the market, serves a good meal for US$0.65. There are several cheap restaurants on Bolívar. *Casa de Fernando*, Panamericana Norte, good.

● **Transport**
Cayambe-Olmedo every 30 mins, till 1600 Mon-Fri, and 1800 Fri-Sun, 1 hr, US$0.35; bus to Ibarra 0700 only, 1½ hrs, US$0.50, returns 1230. Otavalo-Quito buses stop in Cayambe; they depart every few minutes, 40 mins to Otavalo.

CAYAMBE VOLCANO

At 5,790m, Cayambe is Ecuador's third highest peak and the highest point in the world which lies directly on the Equator. About 1 km S of Cayambe is an unmarked cobbled road heading E via Juan Montalvo, leading in 26 km to the Ruales-Oleas-Berge refuge at about 4,800m. The *refugio* costs US$10 pp/night, it can sleep 37 people in bunks, but bring a sleeping bag, it is very cold. There is a kitchen, fireplace, and eating area with tables and benches, running water, electric light and a radio for rescue. It is named after three Ecuadorean climbers killed by an avalanche in 1974 while pioneering a new

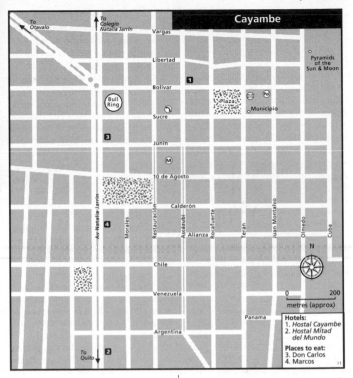

Cayambe

Hotels:
1. *Hostal Cayambe*
2. *Hostal Mitad del Mundo*

Places to eat:
3. *Don Carlos*
4. *Marcos*

route up from the W.

This is now the standard route, using the refuge as a base. The route heads off to the left of a rocky outcrop immediately above the *refugio*. To the right of the outcrop is an excellent area of crevasses, seracs and low rock and ice walls for practising technical skills. The climb is heavily crevassed, especially near the summit, there is an avalanche risk near the summit and south-easterly winds are a problem. It is more difficult and dangerous than either Chimborazo or Cotopaxi. An alternative route is to the NE summit (5,570m), which is the most difficult, with the possible need to bivouac.

● **Access** You can take a camioneta from Cayambe to *Hacienda Piemonte El Hato* (at about 3,500m) or a taxi for US$15. From the *hacienda* to the *refugio* it is a 3-4-hr walk, sometimes longer if heavily laden, the wind can be very strong but it is a beautiful walk. It is difficult to get transport back to Cayambe. A milk truck runs from Cayambe hospital to the *hacienda* at 0600, returning between 1700-1900. 4WD jeeps go to the refugio (eg *Safari Tours*), 1½ to 2 hrs. An alternative route is via Olmedo, through *Hacienda La Chimba* to Laguna de San Marcos, which is the end of the vehicle track. This gives access to the NE summit.

CAYAMBE TO OTAVALO

The road forks N of Cayambe. **To the right**: a cobbled road, the very scenic *carretera vieja*, runs in good condition to **Olmedo**. There are no hotels or restaurants in Olmedo, but there are a couple of shops and lodging with the local nuns

– but ask first. There is also an Emetel office, in the old Tenencia Política, on the plaza. The surrounding countryside is pleasant for strolling. A road runs E from Olmedo to the **Laguna de San Marcos**, 40 mins by car, 3 hrs on foot.

After Olmedo the road is not so good (4WD rec). It is 9 km from Olmedo to **Zuleta**, where beautiful embroidery is done on napkins and tablecloths. There is a *feria* on Sun. You can see the beautiful *hacienda* of the former president. Officially, this can only be visited as part of a tour from Quito, but the caretaker may let you wander round. 15 km beyond Zuleta is La Esperanza (see **Excursions** from Ibarra), and 8½ km further on is Ibarra.

To the left: the main paved road crosses a *páramo* and suddenly descends into the land of the Otavalo Indians, a thriving, prosperous group, famous for their prodigious production of woollens. **An alternative route from Quito to Otavalo** is via San Antonio de Pichincha, past the Inca ruins of Rumicucho and San José de Minas. The road curves through the dry but impressive landscape down to the Río Guayllabamba, then climbs again, passing some picturesque oasis villages. After Minas the road is in very bad condition and a jeep is necessary for the next climb and then descent to join the Otavalo-Selva Alegre road about 15 km W from Otavalo. The journey takes about 3 hrs altogether and is rough, but the magnificent scenery more than compensates for any discomfort.

OTAVALO

Otavalo (*Pop* 21,548; *Alt* 2,530m; *Phone code* 06) is set in beautiful countryside which is worth exploring for 3 or 4 days. The town itself is nothing to write home about, consisting as it does of rather functional concrete buildings. But then visitors don't come here for the architecture. The town is notable for its textiles and its enormous Sat market. It's best to travel on Fri, in order to avoid overcrowded buses on Sat and to enjoy the nightlife. In the Plaza Bolívar is a statue of Rumiñahui, Atahualpa's general, who was instrumental in the war between Atahualpa and Huáscar, and in the resistance to the Spaniards.

Otavalo men wear their hair long and plaited under a black trophy hat; they wear white, calf-length trousers and blue ponchos. The women's colourful costumes consist of embroidered blouses, shoulder wraps and a plethora of coloured beads. All families speak Quichua (the Ecuadorean equivalent of Quechua) as their first tongue and Spanish as their second. There is some debate over the origin of the Otavaleños. In present-day Imbabura, pre-Inca people were Caranquis, or Imbaya, and, in Otavalo, the Cayambi. They were subjugated by the Caras who expanded into the highlands from the Manabí coast. The Caras resisted the Incas for 17 years, but the conquering Incas eventually moved the local population away to replace them with Mitimaes from Peru and Bolivia. One recent theory is that the Otavaleños are descended from the Mitimaes and Chibcha salt traders from Colombia. Others say they are only Mitimaes.

Places of interest
The Sat market actually comprises three different markets in various parts of the town and the central streets are filled with vendors. The *artesanías* market is held 0700-1800, and based around the Plaza de Ponchos. The livestock section begins at 0600 until 1000, and takes place outside town in the Viejo Colegio Agricultural; go W on C Colón from the town centre. The produce market lasts from 0700 till 1400, in Plaza 24 de Mayo and E across town to the Plaza Copacabana.

The *artesanías* industry is so big that the Plaza de Ponchos is now filled with vendors every day of the week.Bargaining is appropriate in the market and in the shops. The Otavaleños not only sell goods they weave and sew themselves, but they bring *artesanías* from throughout Ecuador and from Peru and Bolivia. Mestizo and indigenous vendors from Otavalo, and from elsewhere in Ecuador and South America sell paintings, jewellery, shigras, baskets, leather goods, woodcarvings from San Antonio de Ibarra and the Oriente, ceramics, antiques and almost anything else you care to mention.

The *artesanía* market has more selection on Sat but prices are a little higher than Wed or Sun when the atmosphere is more relaxed. Look out for the Mickey Mouse tapestries – yes, Mickey Mouse! Some tourist order these specially, in preference to traditional local designs: all tastes, it seems, are catered for. There is a good book market also at Plaza de Ponchos. Indigenous people in the market respond better to photography if you buy something first, then ask politely. Reciprocity and courtesy are important Andean norms.

Museums

Instituto Otavaleño de Antropología, exhibition, W of the Panamericana

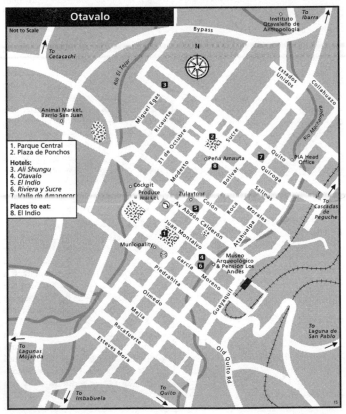

Otavalo

Not to Scale

1. Parque Central
2. Plaza de Ponchos

Hotels:
3. Ali Shungu
4. Otavalo
5. El Indio
6. Riviera y Sucre
7. Valle de Amanecer

Places to eat:
8. El Indio

To Cotacachi

To Ibarra

Instituto Otavaleño de Antropología

Bypass

Río El Tejar

Miguel Egas

Ricaurte

Estados Unidos

Coljahuazo

Río Machangara

Animal Market, Barrio San Juan

31 de Octubre

Sucre

Quito

PIA Head Office

Peña Amauta

Modesto

Bolívar

Quiroga

Salinas

Cockpit Produce Market

Zulaytour

Colón

Roca

Morales

To Cascadas de Peguche

Av. Abdón Calderón

Atahualpa

Juan Montalvo

Municipality

García

Moreno

Museo Arqueológico & Pensión Los Andes

Piedrahita

Olmedo

Guayaquil

Mejía

Rocafuerte

To Laguna de San Pablo

Esteves Mora

Old Quito Rd

To Lagunas Mojanda

To Imbabuela

To Quito

15

Norte. The **Museo Arqueológico César Vásquez Fuller** is at *Pensión Los Andes*, Roca y Montalvo, Mon-Sat 1400-1800, US$1, rec. **Museo Jaramillo**, is at Bolívar, off Parque Central. **Centro Histórico**, is just outside town, in the direction of Cotacachi.

Excursions

Otavalo weavers come from dozens of communities, but it is easiest to visit the nearby towns of Peguche, Ilumán, Carabuela and Agato which are only 15-30 mins away and all have a good bus service; buses leave from the Plaza Copa-

The weavers of Otavalo

Otavalo is a nucleus of trade for more than 75 scattered Otavaleño communities. The history of weaving in Otavalo goes back to the time of conquest. Owing to Ecuador's lack of mineral wealth, the Spanish instead exploited the country's human resources. Soon after conquest, grants, or *encomiendas*, were given to the *conquistadores*, entitling them to the use of the native labour in return for converting them to Christianity. A textile workshop (*obraje*) was soon established in Otavalo using forced indigenous labour. *Obrajes* were also set up elsewhere in the region, for example in Peguche and Cotacachi, using technology exported from Europe: the spinning wheel and treadle loom. These are still in use today.

At the end of the 17th century, the *encomiendas* were abolished by the Spanish Crown, but the land merely passed to those of European descent. Many of the indigenous people entered the infamous *huasipungo* system, rendering them virtual serfs on the large *haciendas*. Many of these estates continued to operate weaving workshops, producing cloth in huge quantities for commercial purposes.

The textile industry as it is known today was started in 1917 when weaving techniques and styles from Scotland were introduced to the native workers on the Hacienda Cusín. These proved successful in the national market and soon spread to other families and villages in the surrounding area. The development of the industry received a further boost with the ending of the *huasipungo* system in 1964; the *indigenas* were granted title to their plots of land, allowing them to weave at home.

The Otavaleños are not only renowned for their skilled weaving, but also for their considerable success as traders. They travel extensively, to Colombia, Venezuela, North America and as far afield as Europe, in search of new markets for their products.

(Adapted from *Arts and Crafts of South America*, by Lucy Davies and Mo Fini, Tumi.)

cabana. You can also negotiate a price with a taxi driver.

In Ilumán, the Conterón-de la Torre family of *Artesanías Inti Chumbi*, on the NE corner of the plaza, gives backstrap loom weaving demonstrations and sells crafts. There are also many felt hatmakers in town who will make hats to order. In Agato, the Andrango-Chiza family of *Tahuantinsuyo Weaving Workshop*, gives weaving demonstrations and sells textiles. In Carabuela many homes sell crafts including wool sweaters. In Peguche, the Cotacachi-Pichamba family, off the main plaza behind the church, sells beautiful tapestries, finished with tassels and loops, ready to hang. (With thanks to Lynn A Meisch.)

To reach the **Cascadas de Peguche** follow the old railway track through the woods in the direction of Ibarra until the track drops away to the left and a dirt path continues up the hill towards the waterfall. Allow 1-1½ hrs each way. A wooden bridge at the foot of the falls leads to a steep path on the other side of the river which leads to Ibarra. From the top of the falls you can continue the walk to Lago de San Pablo (see below).

4 km N of Otavalo are cold ferrous baths at the **Fuente de Salud**, said to be very curative, but opening hours are very irregular.

Local festivals

From 24 to 29 June, at the *Fiesta de San Juan*, there are bullfights in the plaza and regattas on the beautiful Lago de San Pablo, 4 km away, see below (bus to Espejo, US$0.20). There is the *Fiesta del Yamor* **from 3 to 14 Sept**, when local dishes are cooked, roulette played and bands in the plaza, as well as bullfights. If you wish to visit fiestas in the local villages, ask the musicians in the tourist restaurants, they may invite you. The music is good and there is a lot of drinking, but transport back to Otavalo is hard to find.

There is an annual 2-day hike from Quito over Mojanda to reach Otavalo for the 31 Oct foundation celebrations. Called **Mojandas Arriba**, it is walked by hundreds each year and follows the old trails with an overnight stop at Malchingue.

Local information
● Accommodation
Hotels may be full on Fri nights, before market, when prices go up. Water is not always available in Otavalo.

A3 *Casa de Mojanda*, Vía Mojanda Km 3, Apdo Postal 160, Otavalo, E-mail: mojanda@uio.telconet.net, T (cellular) 09-731-737, F (06) 922-969, beautiful setting on a mountainside nr the main road on 25 acres of farmland and forested gorge, organic garden, 7 cottages and 1 dormitory for 12, price includes all meals, healthy cooking, cosy, comfortable, quiet, library, horse riding, mountain bikes, highly rec.

B *Ali Shungu*, Quito y Miguel Egas, Casilla 34, T 920-750, run by friendly US couple, lovely garden, firm mattresses, hot water, safe deposit boxes, good restaurant with vegetarian dishes on request, folk music at weekends, popular, new apartment suites, **A2**, highly rec. **C** *El Indio*, Bolívar 904, T 920-325, private bath, also has suites with sitting room, hot water, clean, very attractive; also at C Sucre next to Plaza de Ponchos, T 929-960, and Colón 507 y Sucre, T 920-161; **C** *Yamor Continental*, at the N end of Bolívar nr the bus terminal, T 920-451, pool, parking, pleasant gardens, comfortable, restaurant.

D pp *El Coraza*, Calderón y Sucre, T 921-225, F 920-459, with bath, hot water, very clean, friendly, nice rooms, quiet; **D** *Los Pendoneros*, Av Abdón Calderón 510 y Bolívar, T 921-258 clean, safe, hot showers, some rooms can be noisy, **E** without bath, rec; **D** *Otavalo*, Roca 504 y J Montalvo, T 920-416, **E** without bath or outside window, attractive patio, car and motorbike park, indigenous music on Fri nights, set menu with infrequent changes, homemade ice cream in the *Golden Eagle* coffee shop; **D** *Residencial Centenario*, Pasaje Saona 7-03 y Jaramillo, nr Plaza de Ponchos, clean, good parking.

E *El Cacique* and *El Gran Cacique*, both on 31 de Octubre, entre Quito y Panamericana Norte, T 921-740, F 920-930, heading out of town, same owner, the latter is newer and better, private bath, TV, parking clean, spacious, friendly, laundry, hot water, nice rooftop area; **E** *La Cascada*, Colón y Sucre, T 920-165, small rooms, hot water, clean, safe; **E** *Residencial San Luis*, Abdón Calderón 6-02 y 31 de Octubre, T 920-614, shared bath, family run, safe, café, friendly; **E** *Riviera Sucre*, García Moreno 380 y Roca, T 920-241, cheaper with shared bath, hot water, laundry facilities, cafetería, good breakfasts, book exchange, safe, nice garden, staff not always helpful, nice place, mostly rec; **E** *Rincón de Belén*, Roca 8-20 y J Montalvo, T 920-171/921-860, nice, modern, private bath, TV, parking, restaurant.

F *Hostal Ingrid*, 31 de Octubre y Colón, T 920-191, quiet, clean, friendly; **F** *Inti Ñan*, J Montalvo 602 y Sucre, shared bath, nice clean rooms, small, friendly, noisy; **F** *Isabelita*, Roca 1107 y Quiroga, 2 shared gas showers, laundry facilities, clean, helpful, basic, parking space, noisy Sat night, good value; **F** *La Herradura*, Bolívar 10-05, T 920-304, shared bath, clean, hot water, rec; **F** *Pensión Los Angeles*, Colón 4-10, friendly, cold showers, nice patio; **F** *Residencial Colón*, Colón 7-13, hot water, good; **F** *Residencial Irina*, Jaramillo 5-09 y Morales, T 920-684, clean, friendly, shared bath, tepid showers, laundry facilities, excellent breakfast, discount for longer stay, top rooms best, mountain bike hire, rec; **F** *Residencial Otavalo*, J Montalvo 4-44, shared bath, basic, friendly, small rooms; **F** *Residencial Santa Martha*, C Colón, pretty courtyard, some large rooms, ask for hot water, not enough toilets or bathrooms, safe, unfriendly, new double rooms small and less comfortable; **F** *Samaj Huasy*, Jaramillo 6-11 y Salinas, half a block from Plaza de Ponchos, T 920-126, shared bath, hot water, clean, safe, friendly, rec; **F** pp *Valle del Amanecer*, Roca y Quiroga, T 920-990, F 920-286, with bath, hot water, relaxed atmosphere, nice colonial building, very clean, popular, good restaurant, *peña* on Fri evening, mountain bike hire, friendly, cheap laundry, rec.

Out of town: in Peguche (see **Excursions** above) is **E** *Aya Huma Hotel* with a good restaurant, on the railway, 5 mins from the falls, T 922-663, F 922-664, excellent restaurant with vegetarian food and delicious pancakes, lovely place, hot water, clean, quiet, run by a Dutch lady, great place to make contact with local indigenous culture, live folk music on Sat, highly rec. Closer to the centre of the village is *Tío Peguche*, T 922-619, same prices, new. Ask to leave the Otavalo-Ibarra bus at Peguche village.

Also out of town, 5 mins on the road to Lagunas Mojanda, is *Hospedaje Camino Real*, T 920-421, in a eucalyptus wood, cabins, hot water, kitchen, laundry, good meals, library, rec. 3.5 km N of Otavalo is **A3** *Hacienda Pinsaqui*, T/F (06) 920-387, 7 immaculate rooms, one with private sunken jacuzzi, beautiful original antiques, lovely dining room, lounge with fireplace, stylish colonial ambience, beautiful gardens, horse riding. By Carabuela is **C** *Troje Cotama*, T/F (06) 922-980, inc breakfast, converted grain house, very attractive, fireplace in rooms, good food, horses available.

● **Places to eat**

The restaurant of *Hotel Ali Shungu* (see above) serves all meals, open 0700-2100, wide variety, rec; *El Indio*, Sucre y Salinas, good fried chicken (weekends especially) and steaks; *El Tabasco*, Salinas 4-8, entre Sucre y Bolívar, overpriced Mexican food; *Quino Pequeño*, Roca 740 y Juan Montalvo, good typical food, good value; *Fontana di Trevi*, Sucre entre Salinas y Morales, open 0600 to midnight, good pizzas and pasta, good juices, good views from top balcony, friendly service, helpful;

Pizza Siciliana, Sucre 10-03 y Calderón, good large pizzas, vegetarian dishes, good juices, friendly; *Fuente del Mar*, Bolívar 815, half a block from main plaza, seafood, also has some rooms with hot showers, rec; *La Familia Sucre*, Mercado Centenario 13-06, at the Plaza de Ponchos, good; *Jack Daniels Rock Café*, next to Plaza de Ponchos, good music, good, cheap set meals, crêpes not so good; *Mi Otavalito*, Sucre y Morales, good for lunch; *Cafetería Shanandoa Pie Shop*, Salinas y Jaramillo, good pies, milk shakes and ice cream, expensive, good meeting place, popular and friendly, rec for breakfast, book exchange, daily movies at 1700 and 1900; *Tapiz Café*, Morales 5-05 y Sucre, good, friendly, breakfast and Sat lunch rec; *Royal*, on main plaza, clean (even the toilets), meal with soft drink about US$1.40; *L'Olivier*, on Roca, good cheap breakfasts, crepes, evening meals, run by French lady, rec; *SISA*, Abdón Calderón 409 entre Bolívar y Sucre, coffee shop, cappuccino, excellent food in clean restaurant upstairs, cultural centre and bookstore; *Quindi Bar*, Morales opp *Peña Tucano*, cheap drinks, food, nice atmosphere; *Plaza Café*, Plaza de Ponchos, good food and atmosphere, free coffee refill, safe storage for shopping goods, rec for hanging out; *Café Galería*, Plaza de Ponchos, vegetarian, mainly snacks, open Mon, Wed, Fri, Sat only, good music and atmosphere. *Oraibi Bar*, Colón y Sucre, open Thur, Fri, Sat July and Aug, Swiss owner, pleasant courtyard, snacks, live music Fri and Sat evenings, good service, book exchange. Cheap food can be found in the fruit and vegetable market (suitable for vegetarians).

● **Banks & money changers**
Imbacambios, Sucre 1205. There are several other Cambios on Sucre and Morales, good rates. **Banco Previsora**, on Sucre, Visa ATM, cash advance.

● **Entertainment**
Peña Amauta, Jaramillo y Salinas, and Jaramillo y Morales, the best, good local bands, friendly and welcoming, mainly foreigners, Italian food upstairs; *Peña Tucano*, Morales 5-10 y Sucre, nice place, good music, friendly, restaurant; *Peña Tuparina*, Morales y 31 de Octubre, rec. Peñas normally only on Fri and Sat from 2200, entrance US$1. *Habana Club*, Quito y 31 de Octubre, lively disco.

● **Language schools**
Instituto Superior de Español, have a school at Sucre 11-10 y Morales, p 2, T (06) 992-414, F 922-415 (see also **Quito language schools**). Classes also with Helena Paredes Dávila, at C Colón 6-12, T 920-178, rec.

● **Laundry**
Lavado en Seco, C Olmedo 32. Also laundry at Roca 942 y Calderón, US$1.20/kg.

● **Post & telecommunications**
Post Office: behind the Municipal building, approach from Piedrahita.

● **Security**
We have received many reports of stealing from Otavalo hotel rooms and cars. Ensure that your door is always locked, even if your absence is very brief and never leave anything in your car or taxi, even if it is being watched for you. The streets of Otavalo are safe at night, but the surrounding areas are not. Lone walkers have been attacked on some of the trails around the town which are described below, so it's best to go in company. Also take a stick to fend off dogs.

● **Shopping**
Jatun Pacha, Av 31 de Octubre 19 y Panamericana, cooperative, select handicrafts, mountain bike tours and Spanish classes.

● **Sports**
There is a cockpit (*gallera*) at 31 de Octubre y Montalvo, fights are on Sat and Sun 1500-1900, US$0.50. On the Panamericana, *Yanuyacu* has 3 swimming pools, volleyball courts and is full of Otavaleños on Sun.

Near the market, a ball game is played in the afternoons. It is similar to the game in Ibarra described below except that the ball is about the size of a table-tennis ball, made of leather, and hit with the hands, not a bat.

Mountain bikes: for hire at *Ecoturismo*, Jatun Pacha, 31 de Octubre y Panamericana, T 548-068, US$5 for 5 hrs or US$8/day. *Taller Ciclo Primaxi*, García Moreno y Atahualpa 2-49, has good, new bikes for rent, US$5/day, rec.

● **Tour companies & travel agencies**
Zulaytur, Sucre y Colón, T 921-176, run by Rodrigo Mora, English spoken, information, map of town, slide show, horse-riding, tours, interesting 1-day tour of local artesan communities, US$10 pp, repeatedly rec; *Intiexpress*, Sucre 11-06, rec for 3/4-hr trek on horseback, less if you gallop, US$15 pp, ask them to prepare the horses before you arrive or time is wasted, good for those with or without

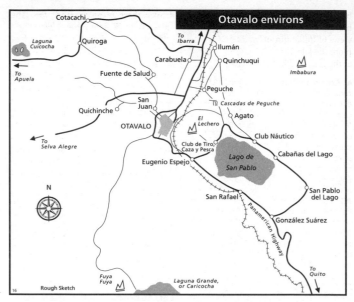

experience, beautiful ride; *Zulay Diceny Viajes*, Sucre 1014 y Colón, T 921-217, run by an indigenous Otavaleña; *Lassotur*, Calderón 402 y Bolívar, T 902-446, also organizes local tours and horseriding; *Ecuapanorama*, Calderón y Roca, T 920-889/563, ecological tours of Intag, horseriding, hikes. All these agencies run tours with English-speaking guides to artisans' homes and villages, which usually provide opportunities to buy handicrafts cheaper than in the market. We have received favourable reports on all, especially Zulaytur.

● **Transport**

Trains There is a regular ferrobus service to Ibarra, several daily, 1 hr.

Road There is a new bus station at the intersection of Atahualpa and Ordóñez, by the Police HQ. Bus to **Ibarra**, every 15 mins, US$0.35, 30 mins. From **Quito** by taxi takes 1½ hrs, US$30-40; *Hotel Ali Shungu* (see above) runs a shuttle bus from any hotel in the new city, Quito, to Otavalo, US$12 pp, not restricted to *Ali Shungu* guests, dependable service; by minibus, 1½ hrs, US$2.35, with Transportes Andinos, they depart from 18 de Septiembre and Av Pérez Guerrero, and bypass the centre of Otavalo, you have to tell the driver when you want to get off; by bus from the

Terminal Terrestre (Cooperativa Otavalo, Coop Las Lagos), or any Ibarra bus from Av América, 1¾-2½ hrs, US$2, leave every 15 mins on Sat, the last bus is about 1800. To **Tulcán**, via Ibarra, frequent departures. Buses and trucks to Apuela, Peñaherrera, García Moreno and points W leave from Colón y 31 de Octubre. The Tourist Office in Quito will help with transport reservations. The organized tour sold by the hotels is expensive. Travelling on Fri is rec.

AROUND OTAVALO

LAGO DE SAN PABLO

There is a network of old roads and trails between Otavalo and the Lago de San Pablo area, none of which takes more than an hour or 2 to explore. It is worth walking either to or back from Lago de San Pablo for the views. The walk there via El Lechero is recommended, though you will be pestered by children begging. The walk back via the outlet stream from the lake, staying on the right hand side of the gorge, takes 2-3 hrs, is also recommended, or you can flag down a passing bus. Alternatively, take a bus to San Pablo, then walk back towards the lake. The views of Imbabura are wonderful. To explore the lake itself, canoes can be hired at the *Club de Tiro, Caza y Pesca*.

● **Accommodation At the lake: A1** *Hostería Cusín* in a converted 17th century *hacienda* on the E side of the lake, San Pablo del Lago, T 918-013, F 918-003, 25 rooms with fireplaces, US$70 pp extra full board plus use of sports facilities (horses, mountain bikes, squash court, pool, games room), library, large screen TV, lovely courtyard and garden, book in advance, 2 nights minimum, run by an Englishman, Nick Millhouse, French and German also spoken, credit cards not accepted; **A3** *Hostería Puerto Lago Country Inn*, Panamericana Sur, Km 5½ y Lago San Pablo on the W side of the lake, T 920-920, F 920-900, beautiful setting, a good place to watch the sunset, very hospitable, restaurant, **A2** inc dinner; **B** *Cabañas del Lago*, on NE side of the lake, T 918-001 (in Quito, Unicentro Amazonas, Amazonas y Japón, PO Box 17-11-6509, T 435-936/461-316), price includes breakfast, on the lakeside, has cabins with bunk beds, clean, mediocre restaurant, boats and pedalos for hire; **D** *Hotel Chicapán*, T 920-331, on the lakeshore, a bit run-down, the restaurant is very good, though expensive, there is a fine view of the lake and Imbabura mountain. There are also restaurants and other places to stay, ask around.

From **San Pablo del Lago** it is possible to climb the **Imbabura** volcano, at 4,630m and almost always under cloud – allow at least 6 hrs to reach the summit and 4 hrs for the descent. Easier, and no less impressive, is the nearby Cerro Huarmi Imbabura, 3,845m.

● **Transport** Buses from Otavalo-San Pablo del Lago every 30 mins, US$0.15, from esq Montalvo y Atahualpa; taxi US$1.70.

LAGUNAS DE MOJANDA

It is possible to hike S to an impressive crater lake 18 km from Otavalo. **Caricocha** (or Laguna Grande de Mojanda) is 1,200m higher than Otavalo. 25 mins walk above Caricocha is **Laguna Huarmicocha** and a further 25 mins is **Laguna Yanacocha**. Take a warm jacket, food and

drinks; there is no entrance fee. The views on the descent are excellent.

From Caricocha the route continues S about 5 km before dividing: the left-hand path leads to Tocachi, the right-hand to Cochasqui (see page 137). Both are about 20 km from Laguna Grande and offer beautiful views of Quito and Cotopaxi (cloud permitting). You can climb Fuya Fuya (4,263m) and Yanaurco (4,259m) but the mountain huts on the shore of Laguna Grande and on the path to Fuya Fuya are derelict. (See Otavalo **Accommodation** for *Casa de Mojanda*.)

● **Access** By car on a cobbled road. Take a tent, warm sleeping bag, and food; there is no accommodation. Or take a Quito bus as far as Tabacundo, hitch to Lagunas (difficult at weekends), then walk back to Otavalo by the old Inca trail, on the right after 2 or 3 km. A taxi or camioneta from Otavalo is US$18 return, arrange in advance but don't pay full fare; one way is US$7.

COTACACHI

West of the road between Otavalo and Ibarra is **Cotacachi**, where leather goods are made and sold, although quality varies a lot. The collapsible leather duffle bags are recommended. Credit cards are widely accepted but you have to pay a 10% surcharge.

● **Accommodation L2-3** *La Mirage*, ex-hacienda 500m W of town, T 915-237, F 915-065, beautiful garden, pool and gymnasium, very good suites with fireplace and antiques, lovely restaurant, excellent chocolate cake, arrive early for lunch as tour parties stop here, expensive, good excursions, price inc breakfast and dinner, rec; **L2** *Hostería La Banda*, W of town along 10 de Agosto, T 915-176, F 915-873, lavish bungalows and suites, country estate style, restaurant, cafeteria, tours, horse riding; **A2** *El Mesón de las Flores*, T 915-009, F 915-828, bath, parking, converted ex-hacienda off main plaza, meals in a beautiful patio, often live music at lunch, highly rec; **B** *Gran Hotel Primitivo*, on the road between the Panamericana and Cotacachi, approx 4 km before town, Inca style fortress, private bath, terrace cafeteria; **E** *Hostal Cuicocha*, 10 de Agosto y Bolívar, Edif de la Sociedad de Artesanos, p 3, T 915-327, unfriendly, bar, restaurant, expensive breakfast, cafetería, parking, theft reported from rooms in 1996; **F** *Bachita*, Sucre y Peñaherrera, modern, bath, clean, rec; **G** *Residencial Santa Marta*, luggage stored, rec.

● **Places to eat** *Don Ramiro*, Sucre y 9 de Octubre, nice, clean, trout is a speciality; *Asadero La Tola*, Rocafuerte, in an old courtyard; *Chifa Nueva*, González Suárez y 10 de Agosto, authentic Chinese; *La Choza* restaurant, typical local dishes, *carne colorada*, for US$1.50.

● **Transport** Frequent buses run from Otavalo, Calderón y 31 de Octubre, US$0.20.

LAGUNA CUICOCHA

The lake lies about 15 km beyond Cotacachi, past the town of Quiroga, at an altitude of 3,070m. The area has been developed for tourism and is part of the **Parque Nacional Cotacachi-Cayapas**, which extends from Cotacachi volcano to the tropical lowlands on the Río Cayapas in Esmeraldas. The US$7 park fee need not be paid. This is a crater lake with two islands, although these are closed to the public for biological studies.

There is a well-marked, 8 km path around the lake, which takes 4-5 hrs and provides spectacular views of the Cotacachi, Imbabura and, occasionally, glacier-covered Cayambe peaks. The best views are to be had in the early morning, when condors can sometimes be seen. There is lookout at 3 km, 2 hrs from the start. It's best to do the route in an anticlockwise direction and take water and a waterproof jacket. Motor boats can be hired for groups, US$17.50 for minimum 6 persons. The slopes of Cerro Cotacachi, N from the lake, are a nature reserve. If you wish to climb Cotacachi (4,944m), it's best to approach from the ridge, not from the side with the antennae which is usually shrouded in cloud. New detailed maps of the Otavalo-Ibarra region are available from the IGM in Quito.

● **Warning** Many people have been badly poisoned by eating the blue berries which grow near the lake. They are *not* blueberries; they render the eater helpless within 2 hrs, requiring at least a stomach pump. **NB also** On the road between Cotacachi and Cuicocha, children stretch string across the road to beg, especially at weekends.

● **Accommodation & places to eat** **F** pp *El Mirador*, with food, rooms with hot water and fireplace, friendly service, camping possible, hikes arranged with knowledgeable guide up Cotacachi, but you must be fit, excellent view, return transport to Otavalo provided for US$7, the restaurant, *Muelle*, has a dining room overlooking the lake, clean, moderate prices.

● **Transport** Bus Otavalo-Quiroga US$0.20 (from Calderón y 31 de Octubre), Cotacachi-Quiroga US$0.10; camioneta Quiroga-Cuicocha US$2.50, Cotacachi-Cuicocha US$3.50. Alternatively, hire a taxi (US$12.50) or camioneta in Otavalo for Laguna Cuicocha, US$7. A taxi costs US$4 one way from Cotacachi. The 3-hr walk back to Cotacachi is beautiful; after 1 km on the road from the park entrance, turn left (at the first bend) on to the old road. You can also walk from Otavalo.

On the SW boundary of the Cotacachi-Cayapas park is **Los Cedros Research Station**, 6,400 ha of pristine cloudforest. Contact CIBT, Casilla 17-7-8726, Quito, T/F 221-324 for details on research and accommodation; US$25/day, including food, negotiable for researchers. To get there, take a bus from Quito (the plaza at Cotocollao) to Saguangal, 6 hrs, then it's a 6-hr walk; or through Safari Tours in Quito. A 4WD can reach the road-end.

● **Accommodation** **C-D** *Reserva Río Guaycayacu*, exotic fruit farm, birdwatching, several hours' hike, maximum 8, booking essential, write to: Galápagos 565, Quito (includes 3 hearty vegetarian meals a day).

Near **Apuela**, in the lush tropical valley of the Zona del Intag (see **Birdwatching**, page 35, are the thermal baths of Nangulví; there is accommodation in **G** *Cabañas*, basic (see **Hot Springs**, page 40). Buses for Apuela leave from Otavalo on a bumpy, dusty dirt road; 3 hrs, 5 a day, book in advance as they are usually crowded, three of the buses pass Nangulví. It's a beautiful trip.

• **Accommodation & places to eat** Before Apuela is **B-C** pp *Intag Cloud Forest/Hacienda La Florida*, price includes all meals, they offer a wide range of nature walks in primary subtropical rainforest and excursions, it's essential to book in advance, at: Casilla 18, Otavalo, Imbabura, Ecuador; **D** *Gualiman*, T 953-048, new cabins up the road to Peñaherrera overlooking the Nanguluí area, pre-Inca *tolas* and archaeological finds. In town are **G** *Pensión Apuela*, grim; and *Residencial Don Luis*, basic, cold showers, fairly clean, friendly.

IBARRA

(*Pop* 80,990; *Alt* 2,225m). This pleasant colonial town, founded in 1606, has many good hotels and restaurants. Prices are lower than Otavalo and there are fewer tourists. The city has an interesting ethnic mix, with blacks from the Chota valley and Esmeraldas alongside Otavaleños and other highland Indians.

Places of interest
The city has two plazas with flowering trees. On **Parque Pedro Moncayo**, stand the Cathedral and Casa Cultural, the Municipio and Gobernación. One block away is the smaller **Parque Dr Victor Manuel Peñaherrera**, at Flores y Olmedo, more commonly called Parque de la Merced after its church. It is also flanked by the Ministerio de Agricultura y Ganadería.

Some interesting paintings are to be seen in the church of **Santo Domingo** and its museum of religious art, at the end of Cra Simón Bolívar, Mon-Sat 0900-1200, 1500-1800, US$0.15. At García Moreno y Rocafuerte is the back of **San Agustín** church, whose façade is on the small Parque Abdón Calderón. On Sucre, at the end of Av A Pérez Guerrero is the **Basílica de La Dolorosa**, damaged by an earthquake in May 1987, but reopened in Dec 1992. A walk down Pérez Guerrero leads to the large covered **market** on Cifuentes, by the railway station, open daily. Take care in the downtown area, especially at night.

Excursions
La Esperanza A pretty village to visit close to Ibarra, 10 km directly S on the road to Olmedo, is La Esperanza, set in beautiful surroundings on the pre-Inca road which goes to Cayambe. Eugenio makes good quality leather bags and clothes cheaply to measure, eg US$60 for trousers. One particular lady does extremely fine embroidery; ask in the village for her house.

You can climb **Cubilche** volcano in 3 hrs from La Esperanza for beautiful views. From the top you can walk down to Lago de San Pablo, another 3 hrs.

You can also climb Imbabura volcano more easily than from San Pablo del Lago. Allow 10-12 hrs for the round trip, take a good map, food and warm clothing. The easiest route is to head right from *Hotel Casa Aída*, take the first road to the right and walk all the way up, following the tracks up past a water tank. It's a difficult but enjoyable walk with superb views; watch out for some loose scree at the top. You can go back to La Esperanza from the summit or go on to Otavalo, which is about another 3-4 hrs.

• **Accommodation & transport G** pp *Casa Aída*, with bath, clean, hot water, friendly, Aída speaks some English and cooks good vegetarian food, Sr Orlando Guzmán is rec for Spanish classes, $2.40/hr; next door is **G** pp *Café María*, basic rooms, will heat water, friendly, helpful, use of kitchen, laundry facilities. The bus from Parque Germán Grijalva in Ibarra passes the hotels, US$0.17, 1 hr; taxi from Ibarra, US$5.

Urcuqui is a pretty little town with a basic hotel and a park. On Sun the locals play unusual ball games. To get there, a bus from Ibarra leaves from the open space opposite the old bus station (now a car showroom). Urcuqui is the starting point for walking to the Piñán lakes.

Cuajara, NW of Ibarra, is reached by bus from Ibarra railway station (US$0.10). The people are friendly, the mountains beautiful and hitchhiking very possible. About 2-hrs' drive (bumpy track) from

Ibarra are the clean, hot mineral swimming pools of **Chachimbiro** in the parish of Tumbabiro (see **Hot Springs**, page 40).

San Antonio de Ibarra Off the main road between Otavalo and Ibarra is, San Antonio de Ibarra, well known for its wood carvings. The trade is so successful that the main street is lined with galleries and boutiques. Bargaining is difficult, but it is worth seeing the range of styles and techniques and shopping around. Visit the workshop of Moreo

Santacruz, and the exhibition of Osvaldo Garrido in the Palacio de Arte. Luís Potosí's gallery on the main plaza has some beautiful carvings.

● **Accommodation & transport F** *Hostal Los Nogales*, T 955-000, cheaper without bath, restaurant, good value. Buses leave from Ibarra, 13 km, 10 mins.

Lago Yahuarcocha It is possible to walk the 4 km to Lago Yahuarcocha in about 1½ hrs. Follow Calle 27 to the end of town, cross the river and walk to the right at the first junction. At the end of

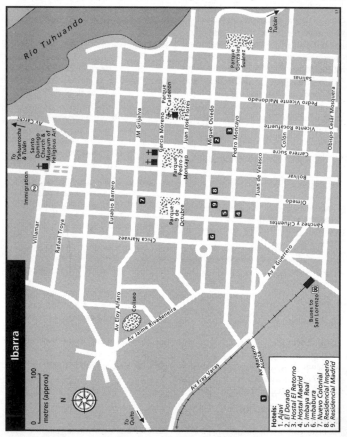

A one trade town

During the colonial era, uses of woodcarving were extended to provide the church with carved pieces to adorn the interiors of its many fine edifices. Wealthy families also commissioned work such as benches and chairs, mirrors and huge *barqueños* (chests) to decorate their salons.

In the 16th and 17th centuries woodcarvers from Spain settled N of Quito and San Antonio de Ibarra has become the largest and most important woodcarving centre in South America.

Initially the *mudéjar*, or Spanish-Moorish styles were imported to the New World, but as the workshops of San Antonio spread N to Colombia and S to Chile and Argentina, they evolved their own styles. Today, everyone in San Antonio is involved with woodcarving and almost every shop sells carved wooden figures, or will make items to order.

(From *Arts and Crafts of South America*, by Lucy Davies and Mo Fini, Tumi.)

this road, behind two low buildings on the left, there is a small path going steeply uphill. There are beautiful views of Ibarra and then, from the top of the hill, over the lake surrounded by mountains and the village of the same name. The beauty of the lake has been disfigured by the building of a motor-racing circuit round its shores. The lake is gradually drying up with *totora* reeds encroaching on its margins. They are woven into *esteras* (mats) and sold in huge rolls at the roadside. Reed boats can sometimes be seen.

● **Accommodation & places to eat** D *Parador El Conquistador*, 8 rooms, large restaurant, rec, run by Cetur; *Hotel del Lago*, no accommodation, only refreshments; *Rancho Totoral*, T/F 955-544, excellent cooking, many local dishes, US$3-4 for a meal, beautiful, tranquil setting, accommodation planned. Camping on the lakeside is possible.

● **Transport** There are frequent buses between Ibarra (market area) and the village, 30 mins, US$0.08.

Local festivals
Fiesta de los Lagos is held over the last weekend of Sept, Thur-Sun, it begins with *El Pregón*, a parade of floats through the city. On 16 July is **Virgen del Carmen**.

Local information: Ibarra
● **Accommodation**
The better class hotels tend to be fully booked during Holy Week, Fiesta de los Lagos and at weekends. Along the Pan-American Highway S towards Otavalo are several country inns, some in converted haciendas

From South to North are: C *Hostería Natabuela*, Km 8, PO Box 683 (Ibarra), T 957-734, F 640-230, comfortable rooms, covered pool, sauna, restaurant; C *Hostería San Alfonso de Moras*, Km 4½, T 935-499, nice cabins, friendly; B *Hostería Chorlaví*, set in a converted hacienda, Km 4, PO Box 828, T 955-777, F 956-311, US$2.50 for extra bed, also cabins, excellent *parrillada* and folk music and crafts on Sun, disco at weekends, sauna, good restaurant, pool open to non-residents US$0.30; next door, up the same drive is B *Rancho Carolina*, PO Box 78, T 953-215, F 955-215, nice cabins, restaurant; D pp *Hostería San Agustín*, Km 2½, T 955-888, clean, friendly, good service, hot water, good food; C *Hostería El Prado*, off the Pan-American at Km 1, barrio El Olivo, T/F 959-570, inc tax, luxurious, set amongst fruit orchards, restaurant, pool; C *Ajaví*, Av Mariano Acosta 16-38, T 955-555, F 952-485, along main road into town from S, pool and restaurant.

In town: C *Montecarlo*, Av Jaime Rivadeneira 5-63 y Oviedo, T 958-266, F 958-182, inc tax, restaurant, heated pool, Turkish bath, jacuzzi, same management as *Hostería El Prado* (see above).

D *El Dorado*, Oviedo 5-47 y Sucre, T 950-699, F 958-700, clean, good restaurant, parking; D *Imbaya Real*, Pedro Moncayo 7-44, T 959-729, with bath, nice, modern, good value, smaller rooms cheaper.

E *Hostal Madrid*, Moncayo y Sánchez, T 952-

177, clean, comfortable, with bath, TV, parking, doors locked at 2300, rec; **E** *Los Alpes*, Velasco 732 y Bolívar, clean, with bath; **E** *Nueva Colonial*, Carrera Olmedo 5-19, T 952-918/543, clean, restaurant, parking.

F *Hostal El Retorno*, Pasaje Pedro Moncayo 4-32, between Sucre and Rocafuerte, T 957-722, without bath, hot water, clean, nice view from terrace, restaurant, friendly, rec; **F** *Imbabura*, Oviedo 9-33 y Narváez, T 950-155, shared bath, cheap, clean, will store luggage, splendid showers, big rooms, breakfast and snacks in the patio, basic, take your own padlock, the owner has considerable local knowledge, very friendly, recently refurbished, highly rec; **F** *Residencial Astoria*, Velasco 809, safe, can store luggage, friendly, basic, not very clean, large terrace, laundry facilities; **F pp** *Residencial Colón*, Narváez 5257 y Velasco, with bath, hot water, pleasant, clean, friendly, laundry facilities, stores luggage, will change money, rec; **F** *Residencial Imperio*, Olmedo 8-62 y Oviedo, T 952-929, with bath, hot water, TV in lobby, reasonable value, disco at weekends till 0400; **F pp** *Residencial Madrid*, Olmedo 857 y Oviedo, T 951-760, with bath, hot water, TV, friendly, parking, good views from upper rooms; **F** *Residencial Majestic*, Olmedo 763 y Flores, T 950-052, with or without bath, hot water, not too secure, friendly.

There are several others in the **F** and **G** categories along Bolívar, Moncayo and Olmedo.

● **Places to eat**
Hostería Chorlaví restaurant rec (but it is crowded with tour buses on Sat lunchtime), likewise *Hotel Ajaví. El Chagra*, Olmedo 7-48, *platos típicos*, good river trout, reasonable prices, rec; *Marisquería Los Redes*, Moreno 3-80, seafood, accepts US$ at top rate; *Marisquería Rosita*, Olmedo 7-42, cheap fish and seafood. Breakfast with good bread at *Café Pushkin*, Olmedo 7-75, opens 0730; *Rith's*, Olmedo 7-61, good set meals and à la carte.

There are many other restaurants on Olmedo: eg *Miravalle*, No 7-52, good value *almuerzo* and *merienda*; *El Cedrón*, No 7-37, vegetarian food, poor coffee and breakfast. There are also many Chinese restaurants on Olmedo, but choose carefully: *Chifa Muy Bueno*, No 7-23, does a good *Chaulafan*; and also worth mentioning is *Chifa Gran Kam*, at No 7-62, exceptionally good food, not expensive. *Mr Peter's*, Oviedo 7-30 y Bolívar, good pizza, wide ranging à la carte, modern surroundings,

good service, nice atmosphere, reasonable prices, open 1100-2200; *Casa Blanca*, Bolívar 7-83, excellent, family-run, located in colonial house with seating around a central patio with fountain, open for breakfast and on Sun, delicious food, "amazingly cheap", US$2/dish, warmly rec; *Mesón Colonial*, Rocafuerte 5-53, at Parque Abdón Calderón, also in a colonial house, extensive à la carte menu, good food and service, most main dishes around US$3-4, rec; *MacPollo*, Cifuentes 11-66, clean, popular with local kids; *El Torreón*, Oviedo 7-62 y Olmedo, smart, expensive, extensive à la carte, good service, good wine list.

Café Floralp, Bolívar y Gómez de la Torre, open 0700-2100, Swiss-owned, good breakfast, bread, has its own cheese factory behind the restaurant, yoghurt, excellent coffee, good selection of Chilean wines, warmly rec; *Café Moliendo*, Velasco 7-12 y Bolívar, excellent coffee and cappuccino, good breakfasts and pastries, friendly; *La Estancia*, García Moreno 7-66, very good grill but not cheap; *Pizzería*, at Av Gómez de la Torre s/n, nr the Bolívar intersection, smart, open late, also serves lasagne, spaghetti and beer; *George's Snack Bar*, Bolívar 10-84, cable TV with giant screen, open late.

There are several excellent *heladerías*, including: *La Bermejita*, at Olmedo 7-15; directly opp is *Hielo y Dulce*, at Olmedo 7-08; also *Heladería Rosalía Suárez*, Oviedo y Olmedo (100 years old in 1996), good home made *helados de paila*, also try *mora* or *guanábana*.

Local sweet specialities inc walnut nougat and bottled blackberry syrup concentrate (*arrope de mora*). These are both made locally and sold in the small shops along Olmedo 700 block. The best selection of these, plus others such as guava jam, are to be found in the line of kiosks opp the Basílica de la Merced, in Parque Peñaherrera. *Helados de paila*, which are fruit sherbets made in large copper basins (*pailas*), are available in many *heladerías* throughout the town.

● **Banks & money changers**
Banco Continental, Olmedo 11-67; **Filanbanco**, Olmedo 11-49; **Banco del Pacífico**, Moncayo y Olmedo; **Banco la Previsora**, Olmedo y Oviedo; **Banco del Austro**, Colón 7-51; all have ATMs and are open Mon-Fri 0845-2000. Only *Casas de Cambio* change TCs: **Ecuafactor**, Pedro Moncayo 6-35, T 641061, F 955-258; **Imbacambios**, Oviedo 7-13 y Bolívar, p 2, T 955-129. Many shops

change US$ notes: eg, *Las Redes* restaurant, *Residencial Colón*, *Farmacia Sudamericana*, Olmedo 8-64 y Moncayo, and *Delgado Travel* (see below); some also change Colombian pesos.

● **Entertainment**
Nightlife: piano bar, *El Encuentro*, Olmedo 9-59, interesting drinks, pleasant atmosphere, unusual décor; *Nexus*, Velasco y Bolívar; *Studio 54*, Autopista y Yahuarcocha. Ibarra is very quiet, even on Sat nights, as the locals go to Otavalo for the *peñas* and bars.

● **Hospitals & medical services**
Clínica Médica del Norte, at Oviedo 8-24, is open 24 hrs.

● **Language courses**
Centro de Español Imbabura, PO Box 10-01505, T 959-429.

● **Post & telecommunications**
Post Office: Salinas 6-64, between Oviedo y Moncayo. **Emetel**: at Sucre 4-56, just past Parque Pedro Moncayo, opens 0800.

● **Shopping**
There are a number of good supermarkets in the centre of town: *Supermercado El Rosado*, at Olmedo 9-46; *Supermercado Universal*, Cifuentes y Velasco; *Mi Supermercado*, Bolívar 7-83.

● **Sports**
A unique form of paddle ball is played on Sat and Sun nr the railway station and other parts of town; ask around for details. The players have huge spiked paddles for striking the 1 kg ball. On weekdays they play a similar game with a lighter ball.
Balneario Primavera, Sánchez y Cifuentes 3-33, heated pool, turkish bath, also offers aerobics classes and remedial massage, for membership T 957-425; also *Baños Calientes*, at Sucre 10-68; *Ibarra Tennis Club*, at Ciudad Jardín, T 950-914.

● **Tour companies & travel agents**
Nevitur Cia Ltda, Bolívar 7-35 y Oviedo, T 958-701, F 640-040, excellent travel guides, new vans for trips throughout the country, as well as the Pasto region of Colombia; *Turismo Intipungo*, Rocafuerte 4-47 y García Moreno, T 955-270; *Delgado Travel*, Moncayo y Bolívar, T/F 640-900, excellent service; *Imbaviajes*, Oviedo 8-36. A rec **taxi driver** for excursions is Luis Cabrera Medrano, Cooperativa de Taxis, Pascual Monge, 'El Obelisco'.

● **Tourist offices**
Cetur, J Rivadeneiro 6-48 y Mariano, p 2, T 958-547, F 955-711, very helpful, free city map and various tourist leaflets, English spoken, open Mon-Fri usual business hours.

● **Useful addresses**
Immigration: Olmedo y LF Villamar (T 951-712), very quick for extensions.

● **Transport**
Trains Ferrobus service to **Otavalo** several times daily, 1 hr.

Buses There are four separate terminals, each for a different company: Flota Imbabura is at Flores y Cabezas Borja; Trans Andina, Av M Acosta y L C Borja; Expreso Turismo, Flores y Moncayo; Trans Otavalo, Av F E Vacas cuadra 3 (beside the railway track). Other bus companies leave from alongside the railway tracks nr the obelisk, on the corner of Velasco, at the entrance to the city; beware of bagslashers here.
To/from **Quito** 2-3 hrs, US$1.95, about 50 departures a day; colectivo taxis (Taxis Lagos de Ibarra) for about US$2.65, taxis US$20. To **Tulcán**, US$2, 2 hrs. To **Otavalo**, 30 mins, US$0.35; most of the companies above go to Otavalo, and to **Cotacachi** (US$0.25, 1 hr) and **Quiroga**.

IBARRA TO THE COAST

5 hrs by train, 3 hrs by road from Ibarra is **Lita** *(Alt* 512m), 93 km before San Lorenzo on the Pacific coast. The tropical forests on the surrounding hill tops contain an immense variety of plants. Be careful taking photos in Lita, due to its proximity to the Colombian border.

● **Accommodation & places to eat In Lita**: 1 km uphill from the station is a *residencia*, **G** pp, adequate, clean, frequent water cuts. There are now several restaurants owing to the increase in road traffic. Lights go out at 2200.

● **Transport Trains** The Ibarra-San Lorenzo train service has been replaced by buses on the new road from Ibarra to the Pacific. It is doubtful if rail services will resume, although the travel agency *Ecuagal* has bought a carriage with a view to running tourist trips. **Road** The road to San Lorenzo is paved as far as Guallupe, 20 km before Lita. From there it is in poor condition during and after the rainy season and often blocked by landslides. To **San Lorenzo**, buses depart at 0700 and 1000, 6 hrs, US$5.75; and return at 0700 and 1430; Coop Valle de Chota. Also Coop Espejo from Quito. To Lita, buses depart at 0600, 0900 and 1300, 3 hrs, US$2.30; return to Ibarra 0600, 1000, 1300; the last San Lorenzo-Ibarra bus passes Lita at 1800. Buses depart from behind the train station.

PIMAMPIRO

The quiet town of **Pimampiro** lies NE of Ibarra, 8 km off the Panamericana along a paved road; take the turnoff at Juncal. The surrounding countryside offers excellent walking. There is a Sun market.

● **Accommodation & places to eat** G *Residencial* run by the Hurtado family on C Flores, no sign, ask around, basic, friendly, poor water supply. *El Forastero*, on the corner of Flores and Olmedo, good food; also *El Vecino*, Espejo 3-028; and *Picantería Riobambeñita*, Espejo 3-054.

● **Transport** Buses from Ibarra, Cooperativa Oriental, leaves every 20 mins, US$0.60, 45 mins; also Expreso Turismo from P Moncayo y Flores.

From Pimampiro follow a steep dirt road along the beautiful canyon of the Río Pisquer 20 km to the village of **Sigsigpamba**. There are many forks in the road, so you'll need to ask directions frequently if you're walking. The views are magnificent. 4WD is recommended if driving. There are no hotels or restaurants in Sigsigpamba, only a few basic shops. Bus from Pimampiro at 1100, Thur to Sun, crowded.

Sigsigpamba is the best access to the **Laguna de Puruanta**, a 4-5-hr strenuous hike. The lake is set amid the high *páramo* and you can camp and fish for trout. The area is very muddy during the rainy season (Nov to May). From the lake you can walk to the village of Mariano Acosta, from which buses run back to Ibarra through Pimampiro. The direct road from Mariano Acosta to Ibarra is in very poor shape and no longer has a bus service. Allow 3 or more days for the excursion and take a tent, sleeping bag, warm waterproof clothing, food, stove and fuel.

NORTH TO COLOMBIA

ROUTES The Pan-American Highway goes past Laguna Yahuarcocha and then descends to the hot dry Chota valley. 24 km N of Ibarra is the turnoff W for Salinas and Lita along the new road to San Lorenzo. 6 km further N, at Mascarilla, is a police checkpoint (have your documents at hand), after which the highway divides. One branch follows an older route NE through Mira and El Angel to Tulcán on the Colombian border. This road is paved and in excellent condition as far as El Angel, but deteriorates rapidly thereafter. The El Angel-Tulcán section is unpaved and in very poor condition but the scenery is beautiful. It is now seldom used and there are no facilities along its 49 km. The second branch (the modern Pan-American Highway), in good repair but with many heavy lorries, runs E through the Chota valley to Juncal, before turning N to reach Tulcán via Bolívar and San Gabriel. An excellent paved road runs between Bolívar and El Angel, connecting the two branches. A second lateral road, between San Gabriel and El Angel, is in poor shape and is often impassable during the rainy season.

THE OLD ROUTE TO THE BORDER

MIRA

Along the old route, which climbs steeply from Mascarilla, is the town of **Mira** (*Pop* 5,500), 15 km past the fork. Some of the finest quality woollens come from this part of the country. There are two women in Mira who produce them for export and a cooperative up the hill opposite the bus station which sells them in the town at export prices. There are two carnivals held each year, on 2 Feb, and 18 Aug, with fireworks and free flowing Tardón, the local *aguardiente*.

● **Accommodation & places to eat** G *Residencial Mira*, basic but clean, good beds. There are very few restaurants; the best is the *Bar Latino*.

● **Transport** Bus from Ibarra, US$0.55, 1 hr; from Tulcán, 1600, 1½ hrs, US$1.

EL ANGEL

20 km NE along the old Panamericana is **El Angel** (*Pop* 5,700; *Alt* 3,000m), a sleepy highland town that comes to life during its Mon market. It is the birthplace of José Franco, designer of the famous topiary in the Tulcán cemetery, and the main plaza retains a few trees that were originally sculpted by him.

● **Accommodation & places to eat E** pp *Hostería El Angel*, at the village entrance, T (06) 977-584, new, inc breakfast, 7 rooms with hot showers and living room, they run 1-day ecological trips by jeep into the reserve (see below), US$20 pp (minimum 4 people), reservations in Quito T 221-489, F 221-480; **G** *Residencial Viña del Mar*, José Grijalva 05-48 on main plaza, shared bath, basic, restaurant next door; **G** *Residencial Alvarez*, run by Sra Ofelia López Peñaherrera, José Grijalva 02-59, basic, shared bath, cold water, no shower, but very friendly, rec. *Asadero Los Faroles*, José Grijalva 5-96, roast chicken and trout, expensive. Several other chicken places in town. *Pastelería Mi Pan*, José Grijalva corner Bolívar, very good bread and pastries. The shops are well stocked with provisions. *Photo Estudio Narváez*, José Grijalva by plaza, sells nice photos of the surrounding area.

● **Transport** Trans Espejo, hourly to **Quito** via Ibarra, US$2.50, 4 hrs; to **Tulcán** at 0530 and 0700 daily, US$0.95. Trans Mira, hourly to **Mira** and **Tulcán**.

3 km S of town, along the road to Mira, is the turnoff for the thermal baths of **La Calera**. From here a steep but good cobbled road descends for 6½ km into a lovely valley to the baths themselves, with good views along the way. There are two pools with warm water in pleasant surroundings, admission US$0.50. The baths are deserted during the week, when only the smaller pool is filled. There is no public transport, US$15 round trip to hire a jeep from El Angel; camioneta Fernando Calderón, T 977-274. The baths are crowded with locals on weekends and holidays, when the same jeeps charge US$0.50 pp. With a sleeping bag it is possible to stay the night in the main building; take food.

RESERVA ECOLOGICA EL ANGEL

El Angel is the main access point for the Reserva Ecológica El Angel, created in 1992 to protect 15,715 ha of *páramo* ranging in altitude from 3,400 to 4,150m. The reserve contains the southernmost large stands of the velvet-leaved *frailejón* plant, also found in the Andes of Colombia and Venezuela. Also of interest are the spiny *achupallas* with giant compound flowers, related to the *Puya Raymondii* of Peru and Bolivia. The fauna includes *curiquingue* hawks, deer, foxes, and a few condors. There are several small lakes scattered throughout the reserve. It can be very muddy during the rainy season and the best time to visit is May to August.

The reserve is administered by *Inefan* (the Forestry Institute of the Ministry of Agriculture), El Angel office José Grijalva 04-26, in an old school, upstairs to the left. The staff is friendly and helpful. The Reserve entry fee is US$7 for foreigners. The *Fundación El Angel*, offices in the municipal building, can also provide information about visiting the reserve. Gerardo Miguel Quelal knows the area well and can be hired as a guide. Contact him through either of the above offices.

Excursions into the reserve: from El Angel follow the poor road N towards Tulcán for 16 km to **El Voladero** (parking area but no sign) where a trail climbs over a low ridge (30 mins' walk) to two crystal clear lakes. Camping is possible here, but you must be self-sufficient and take great care not to damage the fragile surroundings. Jeeps can be hired in the main plaza of El Angel for a day trip to El Voladero, US$40 return, but bargain.

Another, longer, excursion follows an equally poor road to Cerro Socabones, beginning in the town of **La Libertad**, 3½ km N of El Angel. This route climbs gradually through haciendas, where fighting bulls are bred, to reach the high *páramo* at the centre of the reserve. After

Socabones, in the village of **Morán**, the local guide Hugo Quintanchala can take you further through the valley. There are many paths criss-crossing the *páramo* and it is easy to get lost. Jeeps from El Angel to Cerro Socabones, US$50 return. A helpful driver is Sr Calderón, T 977-274.

A third access to the reserve is from the N along the Tufiño-Maldonado road (see below) from which the Lagunas Verdes (green lakes) can be seen. Like many of the lakes in the *páramo* these are gradually drying. According to local legend, they are enchanted. There are sulphur gas vents here, so take care.

CERRO GOLONDRINAS

Beyond the Morán valley, in the forested hills towards the Mira valley, **Fundación Golondrinas** is working to protect the fragile environment in the **Bosque Protector Cerro Golondrinas**. The foundation's main sources of income to finance their different activities come from their *Hostal La Casa de Eliza* in Quito and the recently-opened *Hostal El Tolondro*, in Guallupe (see page 153). The foundation also organizes a 4-day trek from El Angel, at 4,000m, through the **Golondrinas Reserve**, down to the village of Guallupe on the Ibarra-San Lorenzo road that parallels the rail line, in the subtropical lowlands. The trek costs US$50/day and is

The Golondrinas foundation

The precious Cerro Golondrinas cloudforest region is Ecuador's last intact rainforest that stretches from the *páramo* down to nearly sea level. This is a fascinating area, one of the most biologically diverse with endless opportunities for scientific research – more than 20% of the species are endemic. The region encompasses three different ecosystems: the *páramo* (3,800-4,200m), montane forest (1,500-3,800m) and premontane forest (less than 1,500m). In this part of the Chocó Bioregion, the extraordinary biological diversity is the result of high levels of precipitation.

As well as being one of the most biologically diverse regions, however, it is one of the most endangered. The remaining patches of forest are constantly under the threat of deforestation, through a combination of poverty, population pressure and lack of awareness of less destructive farming methods. Which is where the *Fundación Golondrinas* plays its part. The foundation works both in the conservation of highland cloudforest (the Cerro Golondrinas Cloudforest Conservation Project) and in the implementation of permaculture/agroforestry in deforested areas under agriculture.

The project was initiated in the village of Guallupe, or La Carolina, in the Mira valley, 4 years ago by Ecuadorean environmentalist, Eliza Manteca Oñate and her Belgian husband, Piet Sabbe. Since then, things have expanded considerably to the present level, with seven founding members and eight staff. The foundation manages an 1,800 ha reserve and aims to enlarge the protected area to 25,000 ha. They have been implementing small scale activities in several parts of the area, such as tree nurseries and three demonstration sites where permaculture and agroforestry techniques are applied in order to teach local farmers sustainable productive methods.

Moreover, the *Fundación Golondrinas* is not only working to preserve primary forests from further destruction but also to create and implement a long-term regional development plan to improve the living standards of local residents through education in alternative forestry management.

well worth it; the project has 2 simple cabins to stay in during the trek.

There are opportunities for volunteers on the conservation project on a short-term (minimum 1 month) or full-time basis (minimum 1 year). Those interested in working, or merely visiting the reserve, contact: *La Casa de Eliza*, Quito, T (02) 226-602, F 502-640, E-mail: member@saec.org.ec; or Hugo in Morán.

THE NEW ROUTE TO THE BORDER

EL CHOTA

Following the new route of the Pan-American Highway E past Mascarilla for 2 km, is the turnoff for the town of **El Chota** with the **Honka Monka** museum of Afro-Ecuadorean culture. A further 8 km leads to a series of tourist complexes for Colombians and Ecuadoreans who come down from the highlands for the *sabor tropical*.

● **Accommodation** B *Aruba Hostería*, T (06) 937-005, modern, small pool, very smart restaurant, expensive; D *Hostería Oasis*, Casilla 208, Ibarra, T (06) 937-001, F (06) 996-304, cabins for up to 6 and mini-cabins for 2, best facilities incl 3 large pools (one is a wave pool), waterslide, playground, several snack bars, disco, good restaurant with live music on weekends, good value, day use US$3 pp; E *Hostería El Jordán*, T (06) 937-002, similar but not as elaborate. There are several others. Next to the *hosterías* is a roadside kiosk run by Cetur (tourist office) with limited information.

Just beyond is **El Juncal**, the turnoff E to Pimampiro (see above), after which the highway turns N to cross the Río Chota into the province of Carchi and begins its steep climb out of the valley.

BOLIVAR

A further 17 km N is Bolívar (*Pop* 15,175), a neat little town with houses and the interior of its church painted in lively pastel colours, a well kept plaza and a Fri market.

● **Accommodation & places to eat** G *Hospedaje* run by Sra Lucila Torres, Carrera Julio Andrade s/n, 1 block N of the plaza, no sign, shared bath with electric shower, basic. *Restaurant Los Sauces*, by highway, good food, good value, rec. *Salón Andaluz*, C García Moreno 5-47, 2 blocks W of the plaza. There's a good bakery on the main plaza at García Moreno esq Julio Andrade.

LA PAZ

5 km N of Bolívar is the turnoff E for the town of **La Paz**, from which a steep but good cobbled road descends for 5 km to the **Gruta de La Paz**. Views along the road are breathtaking, including two spectacular waterfalls. The place is also called *Rumichaca* (Quichua for stone bridge) after the massive natural bridge which forms the *gruta* (grotto); not to be confused with the Rumichaca on the Colombian border.

The entire area is a religious shrine, receiving large numbers of pilgrims during Holy Week, Christmas, and especially around 8 July, feast day of the Virgin of La Paz. In addition to the chapel in the grotto itself, there is a large basilica, a Franciscan convent, a guest house for pilgrims **F**, a restaurant, and shops selling religious articles. These are open on weekends and pilgrimage days only, and there are very few visitors at other times. It is possible to camp for free opposite the convent. The river which emerges from the grotto is rather polluted, and the sewer smell detracts from its otherwise great natural beauty.

There are clean thermal baths (showers and one pool) just below the grotto, open Wed to Sun (crowded at weekends), admission US$0.50, showers US$0.25; look for the caretaker if the gate to the pool is locked. Several scenic trails through the valley start from behind the hotel.

● **Access** Excursions to La Paz from Tulcán on Sat and Sun. Also jeeps from San Gabriel, US$0.60 pp (20 mins) on weekends; US$10 to hire a vehicle during the week. A second, signposted access road has been built from the Panamericana, 3 km S of San Gabriel.

SAN GABRIEL

10 km N of La Paz is San Gabriel (*Pop* 19,500), an important commercial centre. The spectacular 60m high **Paluz** waterfall is 4 km N of town; follow C Bolívar out of the main plaza and turn right after the bridge. It's well worth the walk. There is a rather chilly 'thermal' bath along the way.

- **Accommodation G** *Residencial Ideal*, Montúfar 08-26, basic, hot water US$0.25 extra, a bit smelly, lousy beds; **G** *Residencial Montúfar*, Colón 03-44, some rooms with private bath, hot water, clean, safe, motorcycle parking, basic, "has seen better days".

- **Places to eat** *Su Casita*, Bolívar 12-07, good set meal; *Asadero Pío Riko*, Bolívar 10-15, chicken and others. *Heladería Zanzibar*, Colón 3-16, for ice-cream.

- **Transport** Jeeps for Iulcán leave from main plaza when full. Also **buses** to Quito, every 45 mins, US$2.50, 4 hrs.

20 km E of San Gabriel is the tiny community of **Mariscal Sucre**, also known as Colonia Huaquenia, which has no tourist facilities but is very hospitable. This is the gateway to the **Guandera Cloudforest Reserve**, where you can see bromeliads, orchids, toucans and other wildlife. The reserve is part of the **Fundación Jatun Sacha**, which also owns a station at Misahuallí, in the Oriente, and at Bilsa, near Quinindé, in Esmeraldas province. There is a small cabin at the entrance to the reserve, where visitors can sleep. Reservations should be made at the Jatun Sacha office in Quito; Av Río Coca 1734, T 441-592.

José Cando, in Mariscal Sucre, will act as a guide for hikes in the reserve. From San Gabriel, take a taxi to Mariscal Sucre, US$8, or one of the 'blue patrols' which leave from the plaza, US$0.50.

Julio Andrade (**G** *Residencial Bolivia*, very basic), a small town before Tulcán, is the access for El Carmelo and La Bonita. The former is a back way for contraband into Colombia, the latter the road head for a new road into Sucumbíos province. It will connect to Lumbaqui and Lago Agrio.

TULCAN

The old and new branches of the Panamericana join at Las Juntas, 2 km S of **Tulcán** (*Pop* 37,069; *Alt* 2,960m), a commercial centre and capital of the province of Carchi. It is always chilly. For decades the economic life of the town revolved around smuggling between Ecuador and Colombia. It was therefore expected to go bust following the implementation of a free trade agreement between the two countries in 1992, as part of the *Pacto Andino*. Tulcán continues to thrive however, now as a shopping destination for Colombians who arrive by the busload from as far away as Bogotá and Medellín. There is a frantic textile and dry goods fair on Thur and Sun. Prices are generally lower than Colombia, but higher than other parts of Ecuador.

Places of interest

In the cemetery, 2 blocks from Parque Ayora, the art of topiary is taken to incredible, beautiful extremes. Cypress bushes are trimmed into archways and fantastic figures of animals, angels, geometric shapes, etc, in *haut* and *bas* relief. Note the figures based on the stone carvings at San Agustín in Colombia, to the left just past the main entrance. To see the various stages of this art form, go to the back of the cemetery where young bushes are being pruned. The artistry, started in 1936, is that of the late Sr José Franco, now buried among the splendour he created. His epitaph reads: "In Tulcán, a cemetery so beautiful that it invites one to die!" The tradition is carried on by his sons. There is also an amazing cantilevered statue Abdón Calderón and his horse leaping into mid-air in the Parque.

Local information
● **Accommodation**

On Fri nights and at weekends it can be difficult to find a room as the town is usually busy with Colombian shoppers.

C *Parador Rumichaca*, on old road to the frontier, a short walk from the old bridge, T 980-276, swimming and thermal pools,

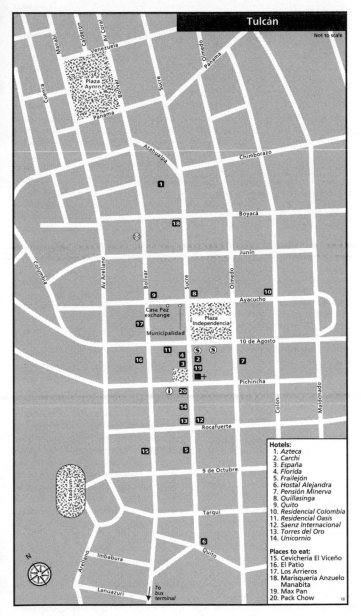

Tulcán

Not to scale

Hotels:
1. *Azteca*
2. *Carchi*
3. *España*
4. *Florida*
5. *Frailejón*
6. *Hostal Alejandra*
7. *Pensión Minerva*
8. *Quillasinga*
9. *Quito*
10. *Residencial Colombia*
11. *Residencial Oasis*
12. *Saenz Internacional*
13. *Torres del Oro*
14. *Unicornio*

Places to eat:
15. Cevichería El Viceño
16. El Patio
17. Los Arrieros
18. Marisquería Anzuelo Manabita
19. Max Pan
20. Pack Chow

popular, reservations required, rec; **C-D** *Frailejón*, Sucre y Rocafuerte, T 981-129/980-149, with bath, hot water, TV, good but expensive restaurant.

D *Sáenz Internacional*, Sucre y Rocafuerte, T 981-916, F 983-925, very nice, modern, friendly, good value.

E *Azteca*, Bolívar y Atahualpa, T 981-447, F 980-481, TV, restaurant, good, clean rooms, but noisy from the disco downstairs; **E** *España*, Sucre entre 10 de Agosto y Pichincha, T 983-860, modern, some rooms with bath; **E** *Florida*, Sucre y 10 de Agosto, T 983-849, with bath, **F** without, modern section at back, good value; **E** *Hostal Alejandra*, Sucre y Quito, T 981-784, bath, clean, hot water, TV, safe indoor parking, restaurant, good value, rec; **E** *Los Alpes*, opp the bus station, with hot shower, TV, clean, rec; **E** *Quillasinga*, Sucre y Ayacucho by main plaza, T 981-892, with bath, basic; **E** pp *Torres de Oro*, Esq Sucre y Rocafuerte, T 980-226, with bath and TV.

F *Carchi*, Sucre 50-044, shared bath, cold water, basic; **F** *Pensión Minerva*, Olmedo 40-50, hot water, a bit smelly but otherwise clean, beds not too comfortable, friendly, quiet; **F** *Residencial Colombia*, Colón 52-017 y Ayacucho, T 982-761, shared bath, simple; **F** pp *Residencial Oasis*, 10 de Agosto 6-39, T 980-342, large rooms.

G *Quito*, Ayacucho 450, T 980-541, OK.

● **Places to eat**
Terminal, in bus station, reasonable. You can find Colombian specialities at *Los Arrieros*, Bolívar 51-053; and *El Patio*, on Bolívar, more expensive. Seafood at: *Cevichería el Viceño*, Bolívar 48-049; *Marisquería Los Alpes*, by the bus station; *Marisquería Anzuelo Manabita*, Sucre y Boyacá. There are various Chinese restaurants on Sucre; *Café México*, Bolívar 49-045, excellent vegetarian dishes, good value, friendly staff, rec; *Parrilladas*, Sierra y Bolívar, good typical food, nr the cemetery. There are many other places to eat in town.

● **Banks & money changers**
There is an association of informal money changers in Tulcán, look for photo ID and note down the name in case of any disagreement. A good place to change cash is in the main plaza, where the rates are better than at the border. It is reportedly difficult to change TCs, but try **Casa Paz cambio**, on Ayacucho in front of *Hotel Quito*, or **Carlos Burbano**, Bolívar y Junín. *Casas de cambio* in Tulcán give better rates than Ipiales. For those arriving in Ecuador, change only what you need to get to Quito or Ibarra, where the rate is better. **Filanbanco**, Sucre y Junín and **Banco de Préstamos**, in front of the park, will undertake foreign currency transactions. Few places accept credit cards.

● **Security**
Tulcán and the traditionally tranquil border province of Carchi have seen an increase in drug trafficking and a corresponding decline in public safety. The area is still safer than Quito or Guayaquil, but it is prudent not to wander about late at night (ie after 2200).

● **Transport**
Air The airport is on the new road to Rumichaca. TAME flies to Cali and to Quito.

Buses Bus to **Quito**, 5 hrs, US$4.10, every 15 mins; to **Ibarra**, 2 hrs, US$1.95. **Otavalo**, US$1.95, 3 hrs (make sure the bus is going to Otavalo; if not get out on the Highway at the turnoff), or take a bus to Ibarra and then a colectivo. To **Guayaquil**, 20 a day, 11 hrs, US$7. To **Huaquillas**, with Panamericana Internacional, 1 luxury coach a day. There are also plenty of colectivos. The bus terminal is a long uphill walk 1½ km from centre; best to take a taxi, US$1.50, or a little blue bus from Parque Ayora; keep a sharp look out on the right for the terminal, or the bus will not stop.

HOT SPRINGS NEAR TULCAN

TUFIÑO

The area surrounding Tufiño has various hot mineral springs arising from the nearby Chiles volcano and geothermal energy projects are planned here. Up the hill from Tufiño, 1.2 km W then take turnoff left, are two pools by the river in a pretty setting. The water is barely tepid and the site has fallen into great disrepair; free admission, camping possible.

Crossing the border from Tufiño towards Chiles, in Colombia, turn left at the large green sign for the *Balneario* and continue uphill for 1½ km. There are no formalities at the border, but you must return the same day. The water here is warm, the public baths are free and dirty, the private *Baños Termales 'Juan Chiles'* cost US$0.65 and are somewhat cleaner. There are many other springs all along this hillside; just follow the trail from behind the public pool.

● **Transport** Buses every 2 hrs from opp Colegio Nacional Tulcán, C R Sierra, US$0.50, 45 mins; it's a rough road, with a military checkpoint just before the village. Last bus back at 1700. No hotels in Tufiño, just one basic restaurant and several shops.

AGUAS HEDIONDAS

By far the best hot springs of the region are Aguas Hediondas (stinking waters), a stream of boiling sulphurous mineral waters in a wild, impressive, lonely valley. An ice-cold irrigation channel of melted snow water passes nearby; you need to direct it to make the hot water cold enough to enter. These waters are said to cure everything from spots to rheumatism but are reported as rubbish-strewn. The baths are deserted on weekdays. Condors can sometimes be seen hovering above the high cliffs surrounding the valley (see also **Hot Springs**, page 40).

● **Warning** Several visitors have died after being overcome by fumes from the source of the sulphurous water. Bathe in the lower pools and do not follow the stream uphill. Do not go alone.

● **Access** Follow the winding road 3 km W of Tufiño, to where a rusting white sign marks the turnoff to the right. From here it is 8 km through strange scenery to the magnificent natural hot river. Only the midday Tulcán-Tufiño bus goes up the hill to the turning to Aguas Hediondas.

Past the turnoff for Aguas Hediondas the road climbs to the *páramo* on the southern slopes of **Volcán Chiles**, whose summit is the border with Colombia. The volcano can be climbed in about 6 hrs, but you must be self-sufficient. Enquire about the route in Tufiño, where guides can sometimes be hired.

To the S lies the Reserva Ecológica El Angel and the Lagunas Verdes (see above). The road then begins its long descent to **Maldonado** and Chical in the subtropical lowlands. **NB** In Feb 1994

there was an incursion of Colombian guerrillas into the previously tranquil Maldonado area and the region was subsequently militarized. Enquire before heading out.

● **Transport** One bus leaves from opp Colegio Nacional Tulcán, C Sierra, daily at noon, US$2.20, 5 hrs, returning early next morning.

FRONTIER WITH COLOMBIA
● **Ecuadorean immigration**
Border hours are 0600 to 2100. The Ecuadorean side is older and more chaotic than the modern Colombian complex, but nonetheless adequate. There is a modern Emetel office for phone calls. 90 days are given on entering Ecuador.

NB You are not allowed to cross to Ipiales for the day without having your passport stamped. Both Ecuadorean exit stamp and Colombian entry stamp are required. Although no one will stop you at the frontier, you risk serious consequences in Ipiales if you are caught with your documents 'out of order'.

● **Exchange**
The many money changers on both sides of the border will exchange cash; good rates have been reported at the Rumichaca bridge, but double-check all calculations.

● **Transport**
Colectivos Tulcán-border (blue and white minivans) leave when full from Parque Ayora (near the cemetery) US$0.50; from terminal to border, US$1. A city bus from the terminal to Parque Ayora, US$0.07, though this is often too crowded for luggage. Taxis to border US$0.85 pp from Parque Ayora; US$3.50 to hire a cab from anywhere in town (including the bus terminal, though it's cheaper from the upper level).

INTO COLOMBIA

2 km from the border bridge is the Colombian town of **Ipiales**, "the city of the three volcanoes". It has an Indian market every Fri morning. There is a good selection of hotels and transport links by air and road into Colombia are frequent. 7 km E of Ipiales is the famous Sanctuary and pilgrimage centre of **Las Lajas**, on a bridge over the Río Guáitara, which is definitely worth a visit for its architecture and setting.

The Central Sierra

SOUTH FROM QUITO is some of the loveliest mountain scenery in Ecuador, running in a series of intermontane basins between the Western and Eastern Cordilleras. This part of the country was named the 'Avenue of the Volcanoes', by the German explorer, Alexander Von Humboldt. Unsurprising, given the preponderence of peaks lining the route South: Cotopaxi, the Illinizas, Carihuarazo and Chimborazo to name but a few. The Central Sierra obviously attracts its fair share of trekkers and climbers while the less active tourist can browse through the many colourful Indian markets and colonial towns that nestle among the high volcanic cones. Snaking its way through all this majestic scenery is one of the few remaining lengths of railway still in use, from Quito South to Riobamba and then on to the Pacific lowlands by Guayaquil: one of the great Andean journeys.

ROUTES The Pan-American Highway and the railway to the S climb gradually out of the Quito basin towards Cotopaxi. At Alóag, a road heads W to Santo Domingo de los Colorados and the Pacific lowlands.

MACHACHI

In a valley below the bleak *páramo* lies the town of **Machachi**, famous for its mineral water springs and icy cold, crys-

tal clear swimming pool. It is open 0700-1600 daily, US$0.25, and lies in a nice setting. The water, 'Agua Güitig', is bottled in a plant 4 km from the town and sold throughout the country. Free, self-guided tours of the plant are 0800-1200 (take identification). Machachi produces a very good cheese. Cockfights are held on Sun and an annual highland 'rodeo', La Chagra, can be seen in July.

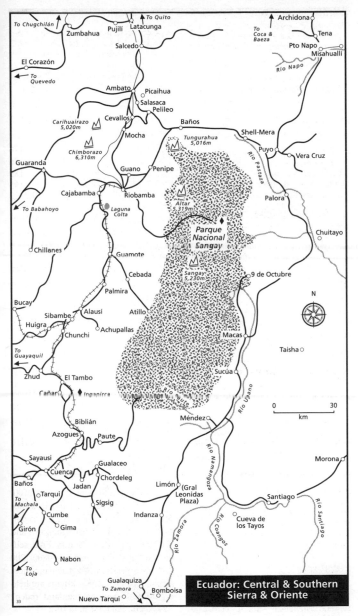

Ecuador: Central & Southern
Sierra & Oriente

33

● **Accommodation** D *La Estación de Machachi*, T 315-246, across the highway in the village of Aloasi, beautiful, family-run, fireplaces, access to Volcán Corazón; E *Hacienda San José del Chaupi*, between Machachi and Lasso, T (09) 737-985, or T 891-547 (Rodrigo), good base for climbing Illiniza, horse riding US$5/hr, US$20/day; E *Tambo Chisinche*, 150m from the Panamericana, T 315-041, small sign, horse riding on Rumiñahui, clean, spartan, hot water; F pp *Mejía*, dirty, noisy, no door lock, no water; G pp *Miravalle*, shared bath, quite dirty.

● **Places to eat** *Restaurante Pedregal*, good, cheap, basic food, log-cabin style, located off the park on the bus road into town; *El Chagra*, good typical food, reasonably priced, take the road that passes in front of the church, on the right-hand side, about 5 km from church; *Cafe de la Vaca*, on the Highway, open Wed-Sun, fresh produce from a farm.

● **Transport** Bus to **Quito** (Villaflora), 1 hr, US$0.45. Taxi to **Cotopaxi**, about US$30/car.

Climbing the Illinizas

Machachi is a good starting point for climbing **Illiniza**. Illiniza Norte can be climbed without technical equipment in the dry season but a few exposed, rocky sections require utmost caution, allow 2-4 hrs for the ascent, take a compass, it's easy to mistake the descent.

Illiniza Sur (5,305m) is a 4-hr ice climb. There are some steep, technical sections on this route, especially a 50-65° 400m ice slope, and full climbing gear and experience are absolutely necessary. There is a *refugio* below the saddle between the two, at 4,750m, fully equipped with beds for 12 and cooking facilities, take a mat and sleeping bag because it fills quickly, US$10/night (the caretaker closes the shelter when he is out).

● **Access** A pick-up truck along the deteriorating road to the 'Virgen' is about US$20, from there it is 4 hrs' walk to the refuge. It's cheaper to get a bus from Machachi to El Chaupi, 10 km S and about 7 km from the Panamericana. From El Chaupi it is an 8-hr walk to the refuge, with a beautiful view of the peaks. The refuge can be reached in a day from Quito, but start very early. (With thanks to Dan Walker). Horses can be hired at *Haciendas San José*, or *Las Nieves* (see below).

● **Accommodation** E *Hacienda Las Nieves*, T 330-872 (Mario), in village of El Chaupi, horse riding on Illiniza and Corazón.

COTOPAXI NATIONAL PARK

Cotopaxi volcano (5,897m) is at the heart of a much-visited national park. The park authorities are breeding a fine llama herd on the pine clad lower slopes. There was a major forest fire here in Sept 1994. Visitors to the Parque Nacional Cotopaxi must register at the main entrance; fee US$7. The park gates are open 0700-1500, although you can stay until 1800. The park administration and a small museum are located 10 km from the park gates, just before the plateau of Laguna Limpio Pungo, where wild horses may be seen. The museum has a 3D model of the park and stuffed animals; open 0800-1200 and 1400-1600.

Park information
● **Access**
There are three entrances to the Cotopaxi National Park. The first, 16 km S of Machachi, is near a sign for the Clirsen satellite tracking station, which cannot be visited. This route goes past Clirsen, then via El Boliche National Recreation Area (shared entry fee, US$7 for foreigners), for over 30 km along a signposted dirt road, through the National Park gates, past Laguna Limpio Pungo to a fork, where the right branch climbs steeply to a parking lot (4,600m). From here it is 30 mins to 1 hr on foot to the José Ribas refuge, at 4,800m; beware of altitude sickness.

The second entrance, about 9 km further S, near the village of Mulaló, is marked by a small Parque Nacional Cotopaxi sign. It is about 36 km from here, through the main park gates, to the refuge. Nearly 1 km from the highway, turn left at a T junction and a few hundred metres later turn sharp right. Beyond this the road is either signed or you take the main fork. It is shorter and easier to follow than the first route which you join just before the Park gates. Walking from the highway to the refuge may exhaust you for the climb to the summit.

Cyclists should approach Cotopaxi from the northern end (the third entrance), rather than from the S because the latter route, 36 km, is too soft to climb on a bike. From Machachi it is 13 km on a cobbled road, then 2 km of sand to Santa Ana de Pedregal. Five more kilometres of sand lead to the park entrance, then it's 15 km to the parking lot. The last 7 km is steep and soft. The descent takes 1½ hrs, as opposed to 7 going up. Trips to this point on a motorcycle are possible, ask Jan But, 'The Biking Dutchman', T 542-806, F 449-568, Quito (see **Mountain Biking**). He has all the equipment. Also book through Pedal Andes, T 220-674, F 566-076, Quito, they have equipment.

If you don't have a car it is best to take a **Quito-Latacunga** bus (or vice-versa) and get off at **Lasso** (see below). Do not take an express bus as you cannot get off before Latacunga. A truck from Lasso to the parking lot costs US$30 for 4 people, one-way, no bargaining. If you do not arrange a truck for the return you can sometimes get a cheaper ride down in a truck which has just dropped off another party. Alternatively, get off the bus at the southern entrance and hitchhike into the park from there. This is usually possible at weekends. Trucks and a jeep are available from Latacunga for about US$30 round trip – ask at the *Hotel Estambul*, leaves 0700 (see page 116 for guides).

● **Accommodation**

There are two rustic *cabañas* (register at administration, US$0.65 pp) and many campsites (US$0.65 pp) in the Park. A good spot is below Laguna Limpio Pungo, but it is very cold, water needs to be purified, and food should be protected from foxes. Camping is not permitted around the Laguna. The José Ribas refuge has a kitchen, water, and 30 beds with mattresses; US$10 pp/night, bring sleeping bag and mat, also padlock for your excess luggage when you climb, or use the lockable luggage deposit, US$2.50.

CLIMBING COTOPAXI

Check about snow conditions with the guardian of the refuge before climbing. In April 1996, an avalanche buried about 30 people just behind the refuge. The ascent from the refuge takes 5-8 hrs, start climbing at 0100 as the snow deteriorates in the sun. A full moon is both practical and a magical experience. Equipment and experience are required. Take a guide if you're inexperienced on ice and snow. Climb the sandy slope above the hut and head up leftwards on to the glacier. The route then goes roughly to the right of Yanasacha and on to the summit. Allow 2-4 hrs for the descent.

Dr Sverre Aarseth writes that the best season is Dec-April. There are strong winds and clouds in Aug-Dec but the ascent is still possible for experienced mountaineers. The route is more difficult to find on Cotopaxi than on Chimborazo (see page 195) and the snow and ice section is more heavily crevassed and is also steeper, however the climbing time is less. It is advisable to seek information from Quito climbing clubs.

From the left branch at the fork for the José Ribas refuge, a narrow dirt road continues along the *páramo*, making an incomplete circuit around the Cotopaxi volcano. Beautiful views and undeveloped archaeological sites may be found in this area, but 4WD is advised as parts are washed out. Just N of Cotopaxi are the peaks of Sincholahua (4,893m), Rumiñahui (4,712m) and Pasochoa (4,225m).

CLIMBING RUMIÑAHUI

Rumiñahui can be climbed from the park road, starting at Laguna Limpio Pungo. The area around the base of the mountain is excellent for birdwatching and it's possible to see several species peculiar to the *páramo*. However, you should also watch out for wild horses, mountain lions and, most of all, wild bulls. From Laguna Limpio Pungo to the mountain base takes about 1-1½ hrs.

The climb itself is straightforward and not technical. There is no difficulty, though it is quite a scramble on the rockier parts and it can be very slippy and muddy in places after rain. There are three summits: *Cima Máxima* is the highest, at 4,722m; *Cima Sur* and *Cima Central* are the others. The quickest route to *Cima Máxima* is via the central summit, as the climb is easier and not as steep. There are excellent views of Cotopaxi and the Illinizas. From the base to the summits takes about 3-4 hrs. Allow around 3-3½ hrs for the descent to Limpio Pungo.

This is a good acclimatization trek. Take cold/wet weather gear. Even outside the winter months there can be showers of sleet and hailstones.

LASSO

The railway and the Pan-American Highway cross one another at **Lasso** a small village, 33 km S of Alóag, with a milk bottling plant and two recommended cafés serving dairy products. Just N of Lasso, E of the highway, is the San Agustín hill, thought to be a prehistoric monument.

The area around San Agustín is owned by the Plaza family, which has two large *haciendas* and breeds bulls for the bullfights in Quito in December. One of the two *haciendas* is actually at the base of the San Agustín hill and includes some converted Inca buildings (limited accommodation in Inca rooms, **A1**, T 03-719-160).

- **Accommodation & transport B** *Hostería La Ciénega*, 2 km S of Lasso, an old *hacienda* with nice gardens, an avenue of massive, old eucalyptus trees leads to the hacienda and a small private chapel, nice rooms with heater, expensive restaurant, reserve accommodation in advance on Thur and at weekends; horse-riding US$1.50/hr; it belongs to the Lasso family (whose land once spread from Quito to Ambato), but is administered by others. The place now has an air of faded glory, T (03) 719-052. Camioneta to Cotopaxi park-

ing area, US$22. **C** *Hostería San Mateo*, new, S of Lasso on the Panamericana. **D** *Parador Cotopaxi*, Km 13 S of Lasso, T 719-046, simple cabins by the roadside.

LATACUNGA

Capital of Cotopaxi Province (*Pop* 39,882), a place where the abundance of light grey pumice has been artfully employed. Cotopaxi is much in evidence, though it is 29 km away. Provided they are not hidden in the clouds, which unfortunately is all too often, as many as nine volcanic cones can be seen from Latacunga. The best opportunity is early in the morning. The colonial character of the town has been well preserved. Latacunga, and more especially the surrounding countryside to the W, were seriously affected by an earthquake in April, 1996, which left nearly 4,000 families homeless.

Places of interest

The central plaza, **Parque Vicente León**, is a colourful and beautifully maintained garden. It is locked at night. There are several other gardens in the town including **Parque San Francisco** and **Lago Flores**. On Av Amazonas, by the Palacio de Justicia, is an interesting statue of a market vendor.

Casa de los Marquéses de Miraflores, at Sánchez de Orellana y Abel Echeverría, is housed in a restored colonial mansion with a lovely inner courtyard and gardens, some of the rooms have been converted into a modest museum, it includes exhibits about the Mama Negra celebrations (see below), colonial art, archaeology, numismatics and a library. The house itself is worth a visit; admission free.

Casa de la Cultura, on Antonio Vela 71-53 y Padre Manuel Salcedo, was built in 1993 around the remains of a Jesuit Monastery and incorporates the old Monserrat watermill. The finely designed modern building contains an excellent museum with precolumbian ceramics, weavings, costumes and

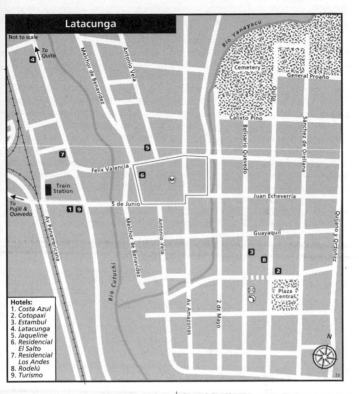

Latacunga

Not to scale

To Quito

Cemetery

General Proaño

Calixto Pino

Felix Valencia

Train Station

To Pujilí & Quevedo

5 de Junio

Juan Echeverria

Guayaquil

Plaza Central

N

Hotels:
1. *Costa Azul*
2. *Cotopaxi*
3. *Estambul*
4. *Latacunga*
5. *Jaqueline*
6. *Residencial El Salto*
7. *Residencial Los Andes*
8. *Rodelú*
9. *Turismo*

models of festival masks; also an art gallery, library and theatre. The complex is open Tues-Sat 0900-1200 and 1400-1730, admission US$0.35. The Casa de la Cultura presents a *fiesta de música indígena* on 5 May.

Escuela Isidro Ayora, Sánchez de Orellana y Tarqui, and the **Cathedral** both have museums.

There is a Sat **market** on the Plaza de San Sebastián. Goods for sale include *shigras* (fine stitched, colourful straw bags) and homespun wool and cotton yarn. There is also an important market along C Guayaquil, between Quevedo y 2 de Mayo, held on Tues. The quality of *artesanía* is rated by some as better than Saquisilí.

Local festivals

The **Fiesta de la Mama Negra** is held on 24 Sept, in homage to **Nuestra Señora de la Merced**. It celebrates the black slaves brought by the Spanish to work on the plantations (similar to the *morenada* at Oruro in Bolivia). There is dancing in the streets with colourful costumes, headdresses and masks. The civic festival of Mama Negra is on the first Sun in Nov; all the elected officials of the Municipio participate.

Local information
● Accommodation

C *Rodelú*, Quito 7331, T 800-956, F 812-341, with bath, TV, clean, excellent restaurant, private parking, rec.

D *Central*, Sánchez de Orellana y Padre

Bus travel in the Andes

Stepping onto a bus at the beginning of a journey in the Ecuadorean Andes can be an unnerving experience. Maybe it's the sight of those shiny, bald tyres which look as if they haven't seen tread since the driver was last in short trousers. Or maybe it's the comprehensive collection of religious imagery decorating the driver's cab, leaving one to contemplate prayer as the best means of ensuring a safe trip. On the other hand, it could simply be the fact that the bus is packed to suffocation point. For you can bet your last banana pancake that, on board there will be enough passengers, luggage and livestock to fill your average super-tanker. Overcrowded, it seems, is a word not included in the Andean vocabulary.

As the bus heads off and you settle down into your 10 sq cm of available space, thoughts may turn to the road. In the Andean backwoods roads tend to range from badly pot-holed dirt tracks, barely wide enough for two buses to pass, to badly pot-holed dirt tracks, barely wide enough for two anorexic llamas to stand shoulder-to-shoulder without one of them falling off the side.

The term pot hole comes from a time before roads began to be paved and refers to the common practice of digging holes in the roads in order to provide sufficient material for pot-making. Such a prevalence of pot holes does have its compensations, though. It makes for some amusing near head-on collisions as your driver veers back and forth across the carriageway in an attempt to avoid them. In places, the pot holes join up, so that the road becomes one giant pot hole with the driver veering wildly from one side to the other in a desperate attempt to avoid hitting the few remaining bits of original road that stick up like stalagmites, turning the road into a kind of obstacle course.

But pot holes are only a minor distraction. Rather more worrying are the crosses that all-too frequently appear by the side of the road. These are placed by the relatives of those who have perished in road accidents at the precise spot where the vehicle plunged over the side. This means that they can serve as some macabre point-scoring system to indicate the degree of difficulty of any particular

Salcedo, T 802-912, with bath; **D** *Cotopaxi*, Salcedo 42-32, on Parque Vicente León, T 801-310, with bath, parking nearby, hot water after 0700, rooms with view over plaza are noisy at weekends. *El Aventurero*, Echeverría y 2 de Mayo, T 801-866, new. Along the Pan-American Highway, known as Av Eloy Alfaro are: **D** *Hostal Quilotoa*, No 78A-17, T 800-099, F 802-090, with bath, *Pollo a la Brasa* restaurant downstairs; **D** *Llacta Cunga*, No 79-213, T/F 811-461, with bath, TV, hot water, restaurant, parking, request rooms away from the road, group discounts; in the same building is **D** *Los Ilinizas*, No 79-213, T/F 801-895, with bath, TV, hot water, parking; **D** *Residencial Los Andes*, Eloy Alfaro 78A-51 y Flavio Alfaro, T 800-983, with bath, hot water, restaurant; **D** *Residencial Santiago*, 2 de Mayo y Guayaquil, T 802-164, with bath, comfortable, good value; **D** *Tilipulo*, Guayaquil y 2 de Mayo, T 802-130, with bath,

TV, parking, spacious well-furnished rooms, comfortable, good restaurant, friendly, helpful, Nestor Cueva is a rec mountain guide and can be contacted here.

E *Estambul*, Belisario Quevedo 7340 y Salcedo, T 800-354, shared bath, clean, quiet, luggage store, public parking at rear, trips to Cotopaxi National Park, highly rec; **E** *Los Nevados*, Av 5 de Junio 53-19 y Eloy Alfaro, T 800-407, with bath, hot water, **F** with shared bath, restaurant; **E** *Los Rieles*, Av Los Nevados, by the railway tracks, T 801-254, with bath, **F** with shared bath.

F *Costa Azul*, Av 5 de Junio, very basic, good meals; **F** *Jackeline*, Antonio Vela 78-33, T 801-033, friendly, basic, hot water, clean; **F** *El Turismo*, 5 de Junio 53-09 esq Alfaro, T 800-362, friendly, basic, very cold shower.

G *Residencial El Salto*, Valencia 47 s/n, warm showers, clean, noisy, safe, restaurant, small

bend. On the most dangerous bends, there may be so many that they form a makeshift crash barrier, preventing others from suffering the same fate.

Guiding you along these thin strips of mountain roads which coil their way through the Andes are people you will come to fear and respect – the drivers. At times you may be convinced that many of these drivers are members of a strange religious cult whose sole aim is to wipe out the entire travelling public. What other explanation could there be for hurtling at breakneck speed along roads that would make a tortoise slow down?

Some drivers manage to combine their formula one racing skills with a nice line in sadistic humour. There you'll be, crawling along behind an excruciatingly slow-moving farm vehicle on a road as straight as a pool cue. Then, as you approach the first bend for miles, the driver will suddenly pull out to overtake. Just as suddenly, he pulls back in, comfortably missing the onrushing 10-ton truck by, oh, at least 2 mm. You have to laugh.

Though you will often curse the driver's apparent disregard for your well-being, you'll also have occasion to sing his praises. For when the bus breaks down (as it invariably does), he can display his breathtaking mechanical genius. More often than not, this will happen in the middle of the night, far from the nearest dwelling, with the temperature outside well below zero. The engine has blown up, the wheels fallen off and the driver disappears into a cloud of black smoke wielding nothing more than a metal pipe, an old cigarette packet and a length of string. Miraculously, an hour later, you're on your way once more. Uncanny.

But it's not all discomfort and near-death experiences. The intimacy of bus travel makes for some interesting encounters and, if your Spanish is up to it, can prove the beginning of many a beautiful friendship. Buses can also be a unique insight into Andean life. And at dinner parties in years to come, it'll be these experiences that have your guests glancing anxiously at their wristwatches and reaching for their jackets.

rooms; next door is *Amazonas*, Valencia 47-36, T 801-156, which is a better place to stay, good restaurant, best place to eat around the mercado central.

● **Places to eat**
Los Copihues, Quito 70-83, slow service, lunch US$4, popular with businessmen; *Rodelú* (see hotel above), good breakfasts, steaks and pizzas, popular with travellers; *El Fogón*, S of the centre, large, varied menu; *El Mashca*, C Valencia 41-54, good value, open until 2200, reasonable prices, rec; *Chifa Tokio*, Guayaquil 45-58, moderate prices, good value; *Chifa Casa China*, Av Amazonas 70 s/n, between Maldonado y Tarqui, smart, open-air seating on terrace, good food and service, open late; *El Portón*, Quito 73-107, cheap, open for breakfast, popular with travellers, no sign, rec; *Pizzería Santa Bárbara*, Orellana 74-49, good; *La Borgoña*, Valencia 41-40,

good value, friendly *Pingüino*, Quito 73-106, 1 block from Parque Vicente León, good milk shakes and coffee; *Beer Center*, Orellana 74-20, good atmosphere, cheap beer. Two well-stocked supermarkets on C Quito. For breakfast before 0800-0900 try the *comedor* in the mercado central. A local dish is *chugchucaras*, fried pork with corn, bananas, potatoes, popcorn and porkskin (best at *Mama Rosa* on the main road).

● **Banks & money changers**
Banco de Pichincha on Parque Vicente León, cash only 0900-1300, poor rate; **Banco Popular** opp changes cash and TCs, only 0900-1300, good rate. Many shops on the Quito/Salcedo intersection buy dollars.

● **Post & telecommunications**
Post Office and Emetel: both at Belisario Quevedo y Maldonado.

● **Travel agencies**

Metropolitan Touring, Guayaquil y Quito, T 802-985/810-334, Thomas Cook representative.

● **Transport**

Buses to **Quito** from *mercado central*, every 15 mins, 2 hrs, US$1; to **Ambato**, ¾ hr, US$0.70; to **Guayaquil**, US$3.35, 6 hrs. To **Saquisilí** from C Melchor de Benavides 78-35 next to *mercado central*, every 20 mins (see below). To Quevedo (US$2.75), from Av 5 de Junio y Eloy Alfaro. Buses to **Chugchilán**, go via **Sigchos**, daily (except Thur) at around 1030, from C Melchor de Benavides, 4 hrs (may leave early if full). On Sat at 1030 and 1300 buses leave from opp the *Residencial Costa Azul* for Chugchilán, via Zumbahua and Quilotoa, US$1.75. Day trips to **Cotopaxi** (see page 164) can be arranged with a taxi for about US$30. Day-trip by taxi to **Zumbahua, Quilotoa**, return to Latacunga is US$40.

THE QUILOTOA CIRCUIT

If driving, it is possible to do a round trip: Latacunga-Pujilí-Zumbahua-Quilotoa crater-Chugchilán-Sigchos-Toacazo-Saquisilí-Latacunga. The whole loop is 200 km in total and would take a minimum

of 7 hrs of non-stop driving. It's a better idea to break it up into 2-3 days or more. There is accommodation in Saquisilí, Sigchos, Chugchilán, Laguna Quilotoa and Zumbahua. The area is criss-crossed by many small, primitive roads that make for great back-country hiking, biking, trekking and 4WD driving. **NB** All bus times quoted are approximate; buses are often late owing to the rough roads.

Festivals in all the villages are quite lively; *Año Viejo* (New Year), *Día de los Ramos* (Palm Sunday), Carnival (Mardi Gras), *Semana Santa* (Easter Week), *Corpus Cristi* (bullfighting), *Mama Negra*, *Finados* (Day of the Dead). For the poor people of these small villages life can be quiet, so they really come alive during their festivals, which are genuine and in no way designed to entertain tourists.

LATACUNGA TO ZUMBAHUA

A fine paved road leads W to **Pujilí** (15 km, bus US$0.30), which has a beautiful church but it is closed most of the time (the town was damaged in the April 1996 earthquake). There is some local ceramic

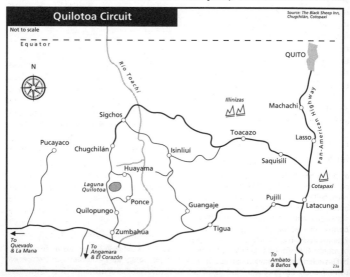

work, a good market on Sun, and a smaller one on Wed. Beware of local illicit liquor and pickpockets. The town boasts excellent Corpus Christi celebrations with masked dancers (*danzantes*) and *castillos*, 5 to 20m high poles which people climb to get prizes suspended from the top (including sacks of potatoes and live sheep!).

The road goes on over the Western Cordillera to Zumbahua, Macuchi and Quevedo. Quevedo can also be reached by turning off this road through El Corazón. Transporte Cotopaxi (C 5 de Junio 53-44) runs several buses daily to El Corazón via Angamarca; a spectacular ride.

ZUMBAHUA

This small indigenous village lies 1 km from the main road, 65 km from Pujilí. It has an excellent hospital, a school, *colegio* and a large church with new woodcarvings by local artesans. It is quite sleepy for most of the week, but comes alive on weekends, festivals and market day, which is Sat. The market starts at 0600, and is only for local produce and animals, not tourist items. It is interesting nevertheless. Fri nights involve dancing and drinking. Take a windcheater, as it can be windy and dusty. Many interesting crafts are practised by the Indians in the neighbouring valley of Tigua, such as skin paintings, hand-carved wooden masks and baskets.

The Sat trip to Zumbahua market and the Quilotoa crater is one of the best excursions in Ecuador, despite the poor accommodation in Zumbahua (see below). The walk from Zumbahua to Pujilí, 6 hrs, is also recommended.

● **Accommodation** In general, accommodation is poor. **F** *Pensión Quilotoa*, owned by Pachito Chaluisa, grey, 2-storey building at the bottom of the plaza, look out for the small sign, clean, with hot shower; **G** *Pensión Zumbahua*, owned by César Guantuña, green 2-storey building at the top of the plaza, lots of rooms; **G** *Residencial Oro Verde*, owned by Luis Rubio, first place on the left as you enter town, friendly, has small store and restaurant,

sells purified water. There is also an unnamed *pensión*, a white 2-storey house behind the church and up the hill a bit; look for someone to open it up for you. The only restaurant is on the main road outside the village, or you can find a cheap meal in the market. Just below the plaza is a shop selling dairy products and cold drinks.

● **Transport** There are many buses daily, and into the evening, on the Latacunga-Quevedo road and transport to and from Latacunga is easy at almost any time. Buses leave every 2 hrs from 0600 (check evening before) from Av 5 de Junio, opposite the *Residencial Costa Azul*, across the river; US$1.25. Four buses daily with Trans Vivero also leave from here, starting at 1100 and then every 30 mins, 2½ hrs. These buses continue up to Laguna Quilotoa, if there are passengers who wish to go, which takes another hour, US$0.75. Vivero buses also go to Guangaje once a day and to Ponce a few times a week. On Thur and Sat buses leave from La Maná and Pucayacó for Sigchos, via Zumbahua, Quilotoa and Chugchilán; they pass Zumbahua at around 1000-1200. A pick-up truck can be hired from Zumbahua to go to Quilotoa for US$10-15; also to Chugchilán for around US$25-30. On Sat mornings there are many trucks leaving the Zumbahua market for Chugchilán which pass Quilotoa. Return buses from Quevedo are every 2 hrs until 1900. The first 30-40 km of road from Pujilí is paved and compacted gravel thereafter; a bit bumpy but not too dusty.

QUILOTOA

Zumbahua is the point to turn off for a visit to **Quilotoa**, a volcanic crater filled by a beautiful emerald lake, to which there is a steep path from the rim. From the rim of the crater several snowcapped volcanoes can be seen in the distance.

The crater is reached by a road which runs N from Zumbahua. Go down from the village and cross the river. After a few kilometres along the dusty (during the dry season, June-Sept) road turn right and over the bridge at the fork in the road; there are no road signs. Keep climbing past Quilopungo, a small school and playground, and continue past the Ponce turn-off on the right. Then head up to a colourfully-painted tombstone-shaped sign for Quilotoa, where there is a road to the right towards a small group of houses (see **Accommodation** below). The crater is just beyond; it can only be recognized when you are on top of it.

Zumbahua to Quilotoa is about 14 km, 3-4 hrs walk. To walk round the crater rim will take you 6-7 hrs, but this is not advisable following the April 1996 earthquake. Parts of the path have been destroyed, others are very slippery and dangerous. If visiting the lake, do not drink its water as it is sulphurous. Do not walk alone or after dark; also take a stick to fend off dogs on the road. Also be prepared for sudden changes in the weather. During the wet season, the best views are in the early morning so those with a tent may wish to camp.

You can walk from Quilotoa to Chugchilán along the road, 22 km, about 6 hrs. Or walk around part of the crater rim, then down to Huayama, and across the canyon (Río Sihui) to Chugchilán, 11 km, about 5 hrs.

Everyone at the crater tries to sell the famous naïve Tigua pictures and carved wooden masks, so expect to be besieged. The best artists in the area are the Toaquiza family, at Chimbacucho, by the road at Km 53 on the way to Zumbahua. The father of the family, Julio, began the paintings at the request of Olga Fisch, who has a handicrafts store in Quito (see page 113). Julio's sons and daughters are now regarded as the most accomplished of the Tigua painters, with exhibitions in the USA and Europe.

● **Accommodation** *Cabañas Quilotoa*, owned by Humberto Latacunga (no relation to Jorge below), very friendly, warm fireplace, beds and wool blankets, cooks traditional food, vegetarian or *cuy* on request, Humberto will lead treks and provide mules, he is a good painter and has a small store, rec; *Refugio Quilotoa*, owned by Jorge Latacunga, take a sleeping bag as you sleep on the floor, he will cook food and take you on a day trek round the lake if you wish, he also paints masks;

Hostal Quilotoa, owned by José Guamangate, friendly, with giant fireplace, offers bicycle rental, food, paintings and excursions. There is stiff competition for your custom in all three of these basic places. Rumour has it that a fourth is opening.

● **Transport** A daily bus, Trans Vivero, takes teachers to schools in Zumbahua and Quilapungo, leaving at 0600 arriving 0815 in Quilapungo (0750 in Zumbahua), from where it is about 1 hr walk to the crater. Alternatively, hitch a truck on Sat morning from Zumbahua market bound for Chugchilán; you will be dropped close to the volcano. Hitching a return trip should not be left till late in the afternoon. Buses bound for Chugchilán/Sigchos drop the traveller 5 mins from the lake. Trans Vivero services Ponce a few times a week; from the Ponce turnoff it is about a 40-min walk N. There is a daily milk truck which returns from Latacunga, via Zumbahua/Quilotoa, to Moreta, which is a *hacienda* with a bullring, 4 km before Chugchilán. It passes through Zumbahua around midday.

CHUGCHILAN

It is 20 km by road from the Quilotoa crater to **Chugchilán**, a very poor village in one of the most scenic areas of Ecuador. It is a beautiful but tiring walk along the edge of a canyon (5 hrs, shorter than the road). Water is available from small streams, but take a purifier.

● **Accommodation** F pp *The Black Sheep Inn*, a few minutes below the village, run by Andy Hammerman and Michelle Kirby, hot showers, accommodation comprises 2 bunk rooms and 2 private rooms at a slightly higher rate, excellent gourmet vegetarian restaurant, book exchange, they have an organic garden, and various animals, very friendly environment, there are plans to build a sauna (end 1996), highly rec, a good base for hiking to Quilotoa, Toachi canyon and Inca ruins (Apdo 05-01-240, Correos Central Latacunga, Provincia Cotopaxi).

● **Transport** Buses depart daily (except Thur) from Latacunga at 1030 from C Melchor de Benavides, US$1.75, 4 hrs. On Thur the bus leaves from Saquisilí market. On Sat two Illinizas buses leave Latacunga at 1030 and 1300. On Fri and Sat a 14 de Octubre bus leaves from opposite *Residencial Costa Azul* in Latacunga at 1030, via Zumbahua and Quilotoa, 3-4 hrs, US$1.75. Buses return to Latacunga at 0300, via Sigchos. On Sat another bus leaves at 0300 for Latacunga, via Zumbahua. A bus leaves for Quito, via Zumbahua, on Sun at 1030; also on Sun to Sigchos at 1200 and to Latacunga, via Zumbahua, at 0600.

SIGCHOS

Continuing from Chugchilán the road runs through **Sigchos**, with its Sun market. The road E to Toacazo has been improved and from there to Saquisilí it is paved. Sigchos is the starting point for walks in the Río Toachi Valley. There are a few campsites, and you may be able to sleep on the school floor in Asache. There is a basic hotel and restaurant in San Francisco de las Pampas, from where a 0900 bus leaves daily to Latacunga.

● **Accommodation & places to eat** E *Residencia Sigchos*, basic but clean, large rooms, shared bath, hot water; **G** *Hostal Tungurahua*, shared bath, cold water. There are a few restaurants in Sigchos, but ask in advance for food to be prepared.

● **Transport** There are 3-5 buses daily to and from Latacunga, US$1.25, 3 hrs, they leave from C Melchor de Benavides in Latacunga. On Wed to Pucayaco, via Zumbahua, Quilotoa and Chugchilán, at 0400, 9 hrs (returns Thur at 0400); and to La Mana, via Zumbahua, Quilotoa and Chugchilán, at 0500, 9 hrs (returns Thur at 0500 and Sat at 0400).

SAQUISILI

Some 16 km S of Lasso, and a couple of km W of the highway, is the small but very important market town of **Saquisilí**. Its Thur market (0700-1400) is famous throughout Ecuador for the way in which its plazas and most of its streets become jam-packed with people, the great majority of them local Indians with red ponchos and narrow-brimmed felt hats.

Dan Buck and Anne Meadows describe the market thus: "Trucks brimming with oranges and yellow and red bananas; reed tubes, fans and baskets. Beef, pork and mutton parts are piled on tables. Indian women squat down beside bun-dles of onions, radishes and herbs and little pyramids of tomatoes, mandarin oranges, potatoes, okra and avocados. *Cabuya* and *maguey* ropes are laid out like dead snakes, and a food kiosk every few metres offers everything from full *almuerzos* to *tortillas de papa*."

The best time to visit the market is between 0900 and 1200. Be sure to bargain, as there is a lot of competition for your custom. The animal market is a little way out of the village and it's best to be there before 0900. Saquisilí has colourful Corpus Christi processions. The bank near the main square exchanges dollars at poor rates.

● **Accommodation** D *Hostería Rancho Muller*, 5 de Junio y González Suárez, at the S end of town, T 721-380, F 721-103, cabins with bath and TV in a country setting, restaurant overpriced, German owner organizes tours and rents vehicles, rec; **F** *Pensión Chavela*, main plaza, very basic, friendly, beds are like rock, good views, billiards and gambling hall downstairs, noisy; **F** *Salón Pichincha*, Bolívar y Pichincha, restaurant-bar below, good beds, cheap meals, basic but friendly, secure motor cycle parking.

● **Places to eat** Some basic restaurants can be found at the entrance to the village, beware of overcharging. Try *colada morada*, a sweet, warm blueberry drink, with bread.

Narrow-brimmed felt hats

Built to last

🐾 Plant fibre is used not only for weaving but is also sewn into fabric for bags and other articles. *Mochilas* (bags) are used throughout the continent as everyday holdalls.

In Cotopaxi province, *shigras*, which are bags made from sisal, were originally used to store dry foodstuffs around the home. It is said that very finely woven ones were even used to carry water from the wells, the fibres swelling when wet to make the bags impermeable. These bags almost died out with the arrival of plastic containers, until Western demands ensured that the art survived. *Shigras* can be found at the market in Salcedo.

Like the small backstrap looms and drop spindles of the Andes, the bags are portable and can be sewn while women are herding animals in the fields. Today, women's production is often organized by suppliers who provide dyed fibres for sewing and later buy the bags to sell. A large, blunt needle is used to sew the strong fibres and the finished article is likely to last a lot longer than the user.

(From *Arts and Crafts of South America*, by Lucy Davies and Mo Fini, Turni.)

• **Transport** The Saquisilí and Cotopaxi bus companies have frequent services between **Latacunga** and Saquisilí, US$0.15, 30 mins; many buses daily from **Quito**, depart from the bus terminal, 0530 onwards, US$1.50, 2½ hrs. Alternatively you can catch an Ambato bus from Quito, ask the driver to let you off at the junction for Saquisilí and get a passing pick-up truck (US$0.35) from there. On Thur a bus goes to **Chugchilán**, via **Sigchos** at 1100, 4 hrs, though it is always crowded. The *Hotel Quito* and the *Hotel Colón* in Quito both organize efficient but expensive taxis for a 2-hr visit to Saquisilí market on Thur. Bus tours cost about US$26 pp, taxis can be found for US$45, with 2 hrs wait at market. Buses and trucks to many outlying villages leave from 1000 onwards.

SALCEDO

11 km S of Latacunga is **Salcedo**, with good Thur and Sun markets. The town's Mama Negra festival is on 1 November.

• **Accommodation & places to eat** At Rumipamba, 1 km N, is **A3 Hostería Rumipamba de las Rosas**, T (03) 726-128, F 727-103, hot showers, clean, guarded, nice garden with small zoo, swimming pool, tennis, table tennis, lake, good restaurant, highly rec; **C Los Molles**, T 727-133, converted family house behind *Rumipamba*; **F Residencial Las Vegas**, Bolívar y Paredes, hot water, private showers. *Restaurant Ritz*, Bolívar y Sucre, chicken; *Iguazú* for breakfast, on Parque behind *Municipio*.

AMBATO

The city (*Pop* 124,166), was almost completely destroyed in the great 1949 earthquake. It has, therefore, lost the colonial charm found in other Andean cities. It is the capital of the Province of Tungurahua, an important commercial centre for the leather industry and a market for nearby fruit growing valleys. The city comes alive during festivals and market days.

Because of its many orchards, flower and tree lined avenues, parks and gardens, its nickname is "the city of fruits and flowers". Since it is the birthplace of the writers Juan Montalvo, Juan León Mera and the artist Juan Benigno Vela, it is also known as the "city of the three Juanes". On a clear day Tungurahua and Chimborazo can be seen from the city.

Places of interest

The modern cathedral faces the pleasant **Parque Montalvo**, where there is a statue of the writer Juan Montalvo (1832-1889) who is buried in a memorial in a neighbouring street. His house (Bolívar y Montalvo) is open to the public; entrance free (T 821-024).

In the **Colegio Nacional Bolívar**, at Sucre entre Lalama y Martínez, there is a Museo de Ciencias Naturales with stuffed birds and other animals and items of local historical interest; US$1.65, open Mon-Fri 0800-1200 and 1400-1800, closed for school holidays, rec. The **Quinta de Mera**, an old mansion in beautiful gardens in Atocha suburb. It is open 0900-1200, 1400-1800, and can be reached by bus from Espejo y 12 de Novembre.

Out along the Río Ambato, a pleasant walk from the centre, is the prosperous suburb of Miraflores, which has several hotels and restaurants. Buses leave from the centre to Av Miraflores. It is an important centre for the manufacture of leather goods and has some excellent tourist shops, look for colourful and good-quality cloth shoulder bags. Leather clothes can be specially made quite cheaply.

The main market, one of the largest in Ecuador, is held on Mon, and smaller markets on Wed and Fri. They are interesting, but have few items for the tourist. Most of the action takes place in the streets although there are also two market buildings.

Excursions

To **Picaihua** by frequent bus to see the local work from *cabuya* fibre, and to Pinllo to see the leather work. At Pillaro outside the city there is a bull run and fight in early August.

Local festivals

Ambato has a famous festival in Feb, the **Fiesta de frutas y flores**, during carnival when there are 4 days of bullfights, parades and festivities. It is impossible to get a hotel room unless you book ahead. The town has taken the bold and novel step of prohibiting water-throwing at carnival (see **Holidays and festivals**, page 377).

Local information
● Accommodation

NB A new street numbering system was being implemented in mid-1996, causing consider-able confusion. Some numbers shown here correspond to the new system, while others to the old one.

A2 *Ambato*, Guayaquil y Rocafuerte, T 827-598, F 827-197, clean, good restaurant, casino, squash court, rec; **A2** *Miraflores*, Av Miraflores 2-27, T 843-224, F 844-395, clean, heating, fridge, cable TV, refurbished in 1996, good restaurant, parking; **A3** *Villa Hilda*, Av Miraflores 09-116 y Las Lilas, T 840-700, F 845-571, a bit faded but nice, undergoing renovations in 1996-97, cheaper rooms in older building, 2 and 3 bedroom furnished apartments also available, German, Italian and Czech spoken, laundry, ask if you want hot water before 0700, restaurant good, limited menu but generous portions (it is acceptable to order 1 set meal for 2 people to share), nice big garden.

B *De las Flores*, Av El Rey y Mulmul, nr bus terminal, T 851-424, F 850-593, modern, nice, cafeteria, restaurant; **D** *Florida*, Av Miraflores 1131, T 843-040, F 843-074, with bath, TV, pleasant, clean, set meal good at US$3, sauna US$2.60, buses from the centre stop outside.

C *Colonial*, Sucre y Martínez, opp Parque Cevallos, T 827-134, with bath, TV, in restored colonial building, elegant, ask for a room away from the street; **C** *Gran*, Lalama y Rocafuerte, T 824-235, with bath, hot water, TV, friendly; **C** *Hostal Señorial*, Cevallos y Quito, T 826-249, F 829-536, with bath, hot water, TV.

D *Bellavista*, Oriente y Napo Pastaza, T 847-535, by Bellavista stadium, with bath, TV, rec; **D** *Cevallos*, Montalvo y Cevallos, T 847-457, F 824-877, with bath, TV, good; **D** *Ejecutivo*, 12 de Noviembre 12-30 y Espejo, T 825-506, bath, hot water, parking; **D** *Imperial Inn*, 12 de Noviembre 24-92 y Av El Rey, nr the bus terminal, T 844-837, with bath, fridge, TV, restaurant; **D** *Pirámide Inn*, Cevallos y Mariano Egüez, T 825-252, F 854-358, with bath, TV, clean, comfortable, owner speaks fluent English and is very helpful, rec; **D** *San Ignacio*, Maldonado y 12 de Noviembre, with bath, TV, cafeteria, rec; **D** *Tungurahua*, Cevallos 06-55 y Ayllón, T 823-784, with bath, hot water TV, overpriced; **D-E** *Vivero*, Mera 504 y Cevallos, T 841-000, F 826-457, with bath, TV, cheaper with shared bath, old building, cafeteria, good, but expensive.

E *Garibaldi*, Av Paraguay y Estados Unidos, T 849-567, opp bus terminal, with bath, hot water, disco downstairs; **E** *Guayaquil*, Mera

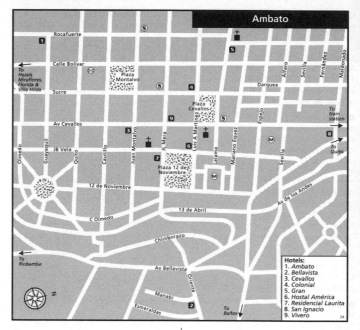

Ambato

To
Hotels
Miraflores,
Florida &
Villa Hilda

Rocafuerte

Calle Bolívar

Sucre

Plaza
Montalvo

Av Cevallos

JB Vela

Olmedo

Guayaquil

Quito

Cautillo

Juan Montalvo

JL Mera

Luis A Martínez

Lalama

Mariano Eguez

Sevilla

Espejo

Darquea

Alfaro

Sevilla

Fernández

Maldonado

Plaza
Cevallos

12 de Noviembre

Plaza 12 de
Noviembre

C Olmedo

13 de Abril

Chimborazo

Av Bellavista

Manabi

Oriente

Esmeraldas

To
Riobamba

To
Baños

To
train
station

To
Quito

Hotels:
1. *Ambato*
2. *Bellavista*
3. *Cevallos*
4. *Colonial*
5. *Gran*
6. *Hostal América*
7. *Residencial Laurita*
8. *San Ignacio*
9. *Vivero*

24

07-82 y 12 de Noviembre, good basic, **F** with shared bath; **E** *Madrid*, Juan Cajas 06, nr bus station, T 828-298,with bath, hot water, TV, cheaper with shared bath, restaurant, disco; **E** *Portugal*, Juan Cajas 05, nr bus station, T 823-218, F 840163, with bath, hot water, TV, good value; **E** *San Francisco*, Egüez 8-37 y Bolívar, T 821-739, with bath, electric shower, cheaper with shared bath, central; **E-F** *Hostal La Liria*, Atahualpa y Caspicara, rec.

F *América*, Vela 06-46 y Mera, basic, shared bath, hot shower; **F** *Carrillo*, Av Colombia, above bus terminal, T 827-200, shared bath, basic; **F** *Europa*, Vela y Mera, shared bath, hot shower, basic; **F** *Laurita*, Mera 333 y Vela, shared bath, basic; **F** *Nueve de Octubre*, Mera 07-56 y 12 de Noviembre, shared bath, hot water, good basic. There are a lot of cheap *residenciales*, hotels and restaurants around Parque 12 de Noviembre.

● **Places to eat**
El Alamo Chalet, Cevallos 560 y Montalvo, Swiss-owned, good meals; also *El Alamo*, at Sucre 660 y Mera, more economical, and *Gran Alamo*, Montalvo 535 y Sucre; *La Borgoña*, 13 de Abril y Luisa Martínez, French; *La Buena Mesa*, Quito 924 y Bolívar, French, rec; *La Piel de Toro*, Ficoa El Sueño, Av Los Capulíes, Spanish; *Café Alemán*, Quito 778 y Bolívar, good food, ice cream, rather old German magazines; *Happy Chicken*, Mera 502 y Cevallos, clean, cheap, fast food; *Marisquería del Pacífico*, Cevallos y Eloy Alfaro, seafood; *La Casa Brasilera*, Rocafuerte 1513 y Castillo, Brazilian, good; *Vegetariano*, Lalama y Bolívar esquina, vegetarian meals and health food products. Typical food at *Los Cuyes*, Los Guaytambos y Los Manzanos, Barrio Los Huertos in the suburbs, *cuy* and rabbit specialities; *Miramar*, 12 de Noviembre y Juan Cajas, Redondel de Cumandá, nr the bus terminal, good; *Casa del Cangrejo*, Los Guaytambos y Los Manzanos, Barrio Los Huertos, crabhouse.

Mexican at *Tacolandia*, Martínez y Bolívar, good food; *El Coyote Disco Club*, Bolívar y Guayaquil, Mexican-American food, disco at weekends. Pizzas at *Cominos*, Guayaquil 9-34 y Bolívar, good pizza and home-made desserts; *Carlinho's*, Mariano Egüez y Bolívar, pizza and good set meals; *Los Charnas*, Av Atahualpa y Los Shyris, rec; *El Gaucho*, Bolívar y Quito, rec;

Caracol, Matiano Egüez y Bolívar, good set meals. Oriental at *Chifa Nueva Hongkong*, Bolívar 768 y Martínez, good; *Chifa Jao Fua*, Cevallos 756, popular. There are many good cafeterías and snackbars: eg *Las Cañas*, 13 de Abril y Mera, open 24 hrs; and *Mama Miche*, 13 de Abril y Mera, Centro Comercial, open 24 hrs. For those who prefer low prices to hygiene, try the markets.

● **Banks & money changers**
Banco de Guayaquil, Sucre y Mera, cash and TCs, gives cash advance on Visa but charge commission; **Banco del Pacífico**, Cevallos y Lalama, and Cevallos y Unidad Nacional, cash and TCs, cash advance on Mastercard, 3% commission; **Banco del Tungurahua**, Montalvo 603 y Rocafuerte; **Banco Internacional**, Bolívar y Martínez; **Banco del Pichincha**, Lalama y Cevallos, on Parque Cevallos and Av El Rey y Av de las Américas, nr the bus terminal, cash and TCs. **Cambiato**, Bolívar 17-15, changes Visa and Amex cheques, cash, European and Latin American currencies, no commission, Mon-Fri 0900-1300 and 1430-1800, Sat 0900-1230. Money exchange at *Café Español*, Montalvo 607, Mon-Sat, 0900-1800.

● **Entertainment**
There is a *peña* on Fri and Sat, *Peña del Tungurahua*, in block 2 of the Centro Comercial.

Discos: *El Coyote*, Bolívar y Guayaquil; *CowBoys*, Paccha y Los Incas; *El Galeón*, Castillo y Av Cevallos; *Imperio Club*, Paccha y Saraguro, international music; *Villa Blanca*, Vía a Baños Km 5, international music restaurant snackbar.

● **Post & telecommunications**
Post Office: Castillo y Bolívar, at Parque Montalvo, 0730-1930; fax service at EMS express mail office, national US$1.10/pg, Americas US$8/pg, Europe US$10/pg, other US$12/pg. **Emetel**: Castillo 03-31 y Rocafuerte, national and international calls, 0800-2130.

● **Shopping**
Supermercado, Centro Comercial Ambato, Parque 12 de Noviembre, or *Supermaxi*, Centro Comercial Caracol, Av de los Capulíes y Mirabales, in Ficoa, for buying provisions. Good leather hiking boots from *Calzado Piedrahita*, Bolívar 15-08 y Lalama. Leather jackets, bags, belts on Sucre between Lalama and Eloy Alfaro and Vela between Lalama and Montalvo. Many stores for leather shoes along Bolívar.

● **Tour companies & travel agents**
Metropolitan Touring, Bolívar 19-22 y Castillo, T 824-084, F 829-213 and in Centro Comercial Caracol; *Coltur*, Cevallos 15-57; 471 y Castillo and Páez 370 y Robles, T 548-219, F 502-449; *Ecuadorean Tours*, Cevallos 428, Amex agent, but no help with TCs, go instead to Banco del Tungurahua. *Surtrek*, Av Amazonas 897 y Wilson, Quito, T 561-129, F 561-132, is a climbing agency, arranges guided climbs of most major peaks, rents and sells equipment, manufactures good quality backpacks to order, German, Spanish, English spoken, rec. For airline reservations *TAME*, Sucre 09-62 y Guayaquil, T 826-601; *SAN/Saeta*, Bolívar 17-52, across from the Cathedral, T 825-028.

● **Tourist offices**
Cetur is next to the *Hotel Ambato*, Guayaquil y Rocafuerte, T 821-800, open 0800-1200, 1400-1800, Mon-Fri, helpful, will assist with any complaints about services.

● **Useful addresses**
Immigration: Av Fermín Cevallos y Juan León Mera, T 820-000, Edif Asociación de Empleados, p 2, open Mon-Fri 0830-1230, 1430-1800.

● **Transport**
Buses To Quito, 2¾ hrs, US$1.90. To Guayaquil, 6½ hrs, US$3.95. To Cuenca, US$4.60, 7 hrs. To Guayaquil, 6½ hrs, US$6; to Baños, paved road, lovely scenery, 45 mins, US$0.60. To Riobamba, US$0.80, 1 hr. To Guaranda, US$1.50, 1 hr. To Latacunga, ¾ hr, US$0.70. To Santo Domingo de los Colorados, 4 hrs, US$2.65. To Tena, US$4, 6 hrs. To Puyo, US$2.60, 3 hrs (see **Routes** below). To Macas, US$3.30, 6½ hrs. To Esmeraldas, US$4.80, 8 hrs. To Loja, US$6.90, 12 hrs. To Machala, US$5.30, 7 hrs. The main bus station is on Av Colombia y Paraguay, 2 km N from the centre, nr the railway station. Town buses go there from Plaza Cevallos in the city centre.

ROUTES To the E of Ambato, an important road leads to Salasaca, Pelileo, and Baños and then on along the Pastaza valley to Mera, Shell Mera, Puyo and Tena in the Oriente (see page 314). In 1996 work was in progress to rebuild the road from Baños to Puyo and construction is expected to continue into 1997. It was open to vehicular traffic only Sun 1900 to Tues 0600. Buses to the Oriente take an alternate, longer routes the rest of the week. **NB** Motorists driving through Ambato to other cities should avoid going into the centre as traffic is very slow.

SALASACA

This small, modernized village is 14 km (30 mins) from Ambato. The Salasaca Indians wear distinctive black ponchos with white trousers and broad white hats. This is said to reflect perpetual mourning for the death of their Inca, Atahualpa. Most of them are farmers, but they are best known for weaving *tapices*, strips of cloth with remarkable bird and animal shapes in the centre. A co-operative has

Examples of bird and animal shapes used on *tapices*

fixed the prices on the *tapices* it sells in its store near the church. Throughout the village the prices are the same, somewhat cheaper than in Quito, and the selection is much better. If you have the time you can order one to be specially made. This takes 4 to 6 weeks, but is well worth the wait. You can watch the Indians weaving in the main workshop opposite the church. Fine backstrap weaving can also be seen at Alonso Pilla's, ask around.

PELILEO

Pelileo, 5 km beyond Salasaca, is a lively little market town which has been almost completely rebuilt on a new site since the 1949 earthquake. In all, Pelileo has been destroyed by four earthquakes during its 400-year history. The new town springs to life on Sat, the main market day. This is the blue jean manufacturing capital of Ecuador. The ruins of Pelileo Viejo can be seen about 2 km E of the present site, on the N side of the road to Baños. The town's *Fiesta* is held on 22 July. There are regular buses from Baños making the 25-mins' journey.

ROUTES From Pelileo, the road gradually descends to Las Juntas, the meeting point of the Patate and Chambo rivers to form the Río Pastaza, and where the road from Riobamba comes in. The road then continues along the lower slopes of the volcano Tungurahua to Baños (25 km from Pelileo). The road gives good views of the Pastaza gorge and the volcano.

BAÑOS

(*Pop* 12,984; *Alt* 1,800m; *Phone code* 03) The town of Baños, with its beautiful setting and pleasant sub-tropical climate, has grown into a major holiday resort. It is bursting at the seams with hotels, *residenciales* and restaurants. Tourists come here for the hot springs, from which the town derives its name, or to climb Tungurahua (see below), or simply to escape the Andean chill.

It is also the gateway to the central Oriente. However, in 1996 work was in progress to rebuild the road from Baños to Puyo and construction is expected to continue into 1997. It is open to vehicular traffic only from Sun 1900 to Tues 0600. Buses to the Oriente take an alternate, longer routes the rest of the week.

The Río Pastaza rushes past Baños to the Agoyán falls 10 km further down the valley, nearly dry now because of the construction of a hydroelectric dam. The whole area between Pelileo and Baños has a relaxing sub-tropical climate. The rainy season is usually from May to Oct, especially July and August.

Places of interest

The **Basilica** attracts many pilgrims. The paintings of miracles performed by Nuestra Señora del Agua Santa are worth seeing and there is a museum with stuffed birds and Nuestra Señora's clothing; open 0800-1600.

Three sets of thermal baths are in the town. The **Baños de la Virgen** are by the waterfall opposite the *Hotel Sangay*. The water in the hot pools is changed three times a week, and the cold pool is chlorinated. The best time to visit is early in the morning. The **Piscinas Modernas** are next door and are open weekends and holidays only. The **El Salado** baths are 1½ km out of town off the Ambato road; entrance to each, US\$0.75; open 0400-1700. There are regular buses every 30 mins between the Salado baths and the Agoyán Falls, passing by the centre of town. All the baths can be crowded at weekends, but the water is usually clean (its brown colour is the result of mineral content) and is almost always hot. There are also the **Santa Clara baths**, which are thermal, but only tepid. They are popular with children and have a gym and sauna. (See also **Hot Springs**, page 41.)

Excursions

There are many interesting **walks** in the Baños area. You can cross the Pastaza by the San Francisco suspension bridge across the main road from the bus station. It is possible to recross the river by another suspension bridge, a round trip of 2-3 hrs. Note that robberies have been reported near the bridge. It is a 45-min hike to the new statue of the Virgin. Take the first path on the left after the hospital. There are good views of the valley from the statue.

Other short hikes include the **Bella Vista cross** overlooking Baños. It is a steep climb from C Maldonado, 45 mins-1 hr. Watch out for unfriendly dogs and be aware that robberies have also been reported on this route. **Illuchi** village is a steep 1¾ hr climb with marvellous views over the valley and Tungurahua. The **San Martín shrine** is a ¾ hr walk away and overlooks a deep rocky canyon with the Río Pastaza thundering below. Beyond the shrine is a path to the **Inés María waterfall**, a thundering cascade which smells of raw sewage. The round trip takes 2 hrs. 50m from Inés María is the **zoo**, with a large variety of animals but small cages; entry US\$1.25.

There are also walks along the old road from Ambato to **Lligua**, a flowery little village straddling the Río Lligua at its junction with the Pastaza, and to **Runtún**. The latter is a village of a dozen mud dwellings, from which there is a splendid view of Tungurahua. It is a 5-6 hrs round trip. Cold drinks are sold at the billiard hall. There are two paths from Baños to Runtún, one from S end of Calle 9, the other from Calle 6. See Baños **Hotels** for *Hostería Luna Runtún*.

20 km from Baños on the Puyo road are the spectacular **Río Verde** falls, better known as El Pailón del Diablo. A bus goes from the Baños terminal, 30 mins, US\$0.25. For a thrill, ride on the roof. A worthwhile trip is to cycle to Río Verde and take a bus back to Baños (see above for road conditions). It is possible to cycle to Puyo (4-5 hrs) but very difficult with paniers trying to get around the

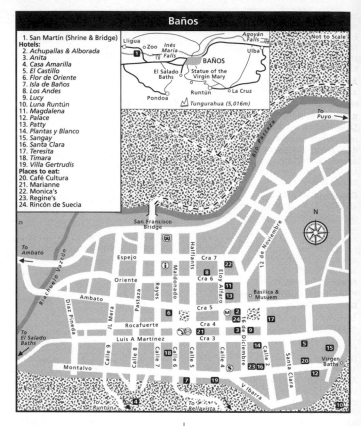

Baños

1. San Martín (Shrine & Bridge)
Hotels:
2. Achupallas & Alborada
3. Anita
4. Casa Amarilla
5. El Castillo
6. Flor de Oriente
7. Isla de Baños
8. Los Andes
9. Lucy
10. Luna Runtún
11. Magdalena
12. Palace
13. Patty
14. Plantas y Blanco
15. Sangay
16. Santa Clara
17. Teresita
18. Timara
19. Villa Gertrudis
Places to eat:
20. Café Cultura
21. Marianne
22. Monica's
23. Regine's
24. Rincón de Suecia

roadworks. In Río Verde, cross the river and take the path to the right after the church, then follow the trail down to the suspension bridge with a view of the falls. Alternatively, hike from the bridge below the dam on old contraband trails.

● **Accommodation** *El Otro Lado*, on the other side of the bridge, beautiful *cabañas* run by an Israeli couple, surrounded by waterfalls and mountains, will be closed until the reopening of the road to Puya. Enquire at *Café Cultura* in Quito.

Local festivals

There is a *fiesta* in honour of **Nuestra Señora del Agua Santa** in Oct with pro-

cessions, bands, fireworks, sporting events and a lot of general partying. There is another civic *fiesta* on 15 Dec to celebrate the town's anniversary when each *barrio* hires a *salsa* band and there are many processions. The following day there is a parade in which spectators are outnumbered by participants.

Local information
● **Accommodation**

A2 *Hostería Luna Runtún*, Caserío Runtún Km 6, T 740-882/3, F 740-376, also suites **L3**, rustic design, beautiful setting, gardens but no outside seats or benches, very comfortable rooms with balconies, wonderful views of the town and surrounding mountains, delicious meals on request US$15-25, excellent service, English, French and German spoken, hiking, horse riding and biking tours, laundry, sports and nanny facilities, videos, internet service, luxurious, very highly rec.

A3 *Villa Gertrudis*, Montalvo 2975, T 740-441, with lovely garden, pool, demi-pension, reserve in advance, rec.

B *Cabañas Bascún*, on the edge of town, nr El Salado baths, T 740-334, **A3** for a cabin for 5, quite comfortable, pools (cold), sauna, health spa (US$5 to non-residents) and service; **B** *Monte Selva*, Halflants y Montalvo, T 740-566, private cabins, sauna, bar, restaurant, pool, excellent service.

C *Sangay*, Plazoleta Isidro Ayora 101, T 740-490, F 740-056, with bath, beautifully situated close to the waterfall, good restaurant, sauna, whirlpool, steam bath and pool all open to non-residents (US$5), tennis and squash courts, also more luxurious chalets, **A3**, a few rooms in the basement are cheaper, but sometimes no warm water, information and some equipment for expeditions to the jungle and volcanoes may be provided.

D *Flor de Oriente*, Ambato y Maldonado, T 740-418, F 740-717, inc breakfast, bath, accepts credit cards, very good, 3 rooms have balconies, can be noisy at weekends, clean, electric showers, *Su Café* downstairs, rec; **D** *Isla de Baños*, Halflants 1-31 y Montalvo, T/F 740-609, owned by Christian and Gabby Albers Weltz (see **Horse riding** below), 10 clean rooms with bath, nice atmosphere, garden with parrots and monkeys, rec; **D** *La Casa Amarilla*, yellow house on mountainside on path to Runtún, T 740-017, 15-mins' walk uphill from Baños, lovely and quiet, being converted into yoga and meditation centre (1996), bed and breakfast, 3 rooms, longer stays encouraged, organic garden; **D** pp *Palace*, opp *Sangay* (even closer to waterfall), T 740-470, lots of beds, good for groups, old-fashioned, a little dark, choose an airy room at the front with balcony, nice garden and pool, Turkish bath, sauna and jacuzzi, open to non-residents for US$5, friendly, restaurant, breakfast US$2, dinner US$4; **D** *Petit Auberge*, 16 de Diciembre y Montalvo, T 740-936, inc breakfast, hot showers, homely, rooms with fireplace, quiet.

E *Achupallas*, 16 de Diciembre y Ambato, T 740-389, clean, hot showers, laundry; **E** *Alborada*, on the plaza nr the Basilica, T 740-614, with shower, modern, clean, friendly, safe, luggage store, rooms have balconies; **E** pp *Café Cultura*, Montalvo y Santa Clara, T 740-419, beautiful, colonial-style house, large balcony, garden, 4 rooms with shared bath, clean, excellent breakfasts, closed Thur, highly rec; **E** *El Castillo*, Martínez y Santa Clara, with bath, nr the waterfall, quiet, clean, hot water, good beds, parking, restaurant, rec; **E** *Hospedaje Santa Cruz*, 16 de Diciembre y Martínez, T 740-648, with bath, hot water, clean, modern, nice, noisy, friendly, rec; **E** *Hostal Magdalena*, Oriente y Alfaro, T 740-233, with bath, clean, warm water, rec, but closes at 2200; **E** *Hostal Plantas y Blanco*, 12 de Noviembre y Luis Martínez, Casilla 1980, T/F 740-044, European owners, laundry, change cash and TCs at good rates, excellent breakfast on roof terrace, good restaurant (*El Artesano*), try the fresh fruit pancakes, steam bath 0730-1100, US$2, jeep, motorbike and mountain bike hire, fax service, luggage store, front door keys provided, very clean, friendly, warmly rec; **E** *Las Esteras*, Montalvo 20-13 y 12 de Noviembre, hot showers, good beds, good value, breakfast, nice view from balcony; **E** *Las Orquídeas*, Rocafuerte y Halflants, T 740-911, with bath, clean, good beds, friendly; **E** *Mario's Place*, JL Mera y Rocafuerte, **G** pp in dormitory, inc breakfast, clean, comfortable, Mario speaks good English, offers jungle tours which are rec; **E** *Posada El Marqués*, Montalvo, T 740-053, spacious, bright rooms, hot water, bath, clean, view of waterfall, laundry, use of kitchen, garden, good restaurant; **E** *Venus & Bacchus*, Montalvo entre Reyes y Pastaza, quiet, clean, friendly, excellent breakfast, terrace and tearoom serving imported teas and delicious homemade cakes and pies, Canadian owners, massages by appointment, rec; **E** *Victor's House*, Martínez y 16 de Diciembre, T 740-913, with bath, hot water, inc breakfast, comfortable, restaurant with vegetarian food, rec.

F *Anita*, Rocafuerte y 16 de Diciembre, behind the market, moderately clean, friendly, use of kitchen, parking for motorcycles; **F** *Cordillera*, 16 de Diciembre y Luis A Martínez, great view from front rooms, clean, cold water; **F** *El Oro*, Ambato y Mera, with bath, towels and soap provided, very clean, use of kitchen, laundry facilities, good value, rec; **F** *Lucy*, opp *Anita*, T 740-838, with bath, **G** without, friendly, comfortable beds, parking for motorcycles; **F** *Los Andes*, Oriente 1118 y Alfaro, without bath, 24-hr hot water, clean, friendly, restaurant (*Le

Gourmet); **F Pensión Patty**, Alfaro 556, nr the market, T 740-202, clean, basement rooms poor, otherwise good facilities, use of kitchen, laundry, comfortable and quiet, family-run, popular, safe, motorcycle parking, rec; **F Residencial Angely**, Alfaro 553 y Ambato, opp *Patty*, hot showers, top rooms quieter, friendly; **F Residencial Baños**, Ambato y Alfaro, T 740-284, good, washing facilities, luggage store, clean, ask for a top room; **F Residencial El Rey**, Oriente y Reyes, nr the bus station, motorbike parking, rec; **F Residencial Kattyfer**, 16 de Diciembre entre Luis A Martínez y Montalvo, T 740-856, with bath, hot water, nice rooms, clean, TV, safe, very friendly and helpful with local information, laundry facilities, rec; **F Residencial Timara**, Maldonado 381, T 740-709, friendly, hot water, use of kitchen, laundry facilities, nice garden, rec; **F Residencial Rosita**, opp *Bamboos Bar* on 16 de Diciembre, T 740-396, hot water, big rooms with sitting room, kitchen for every 2 rooms, motorcycle parking, highly rec; **F Santa Clara**, Santa Clara, T 740-349, without bath, rooms in new part with bath, **E**, or *cabañas*, clean, hot water, use of kitchen, washing facilities, nice garden, motorcycle parking, friendly, good value, rec.

G Familia Reyes y Alvarez, J L Mera y Ambato, T 740-017, rent apartments in the green house, hot water, helpful; **G pp Residencial Dumary**, Halflants 656, T 740-314, very clean, hot water, only one shower, small rooms, friendly, private Spanish lessons from English/German speaking daughter, rec; **G Residencial Teresita**, Parque de la Basílica, hot water, prices vary, shuts early.

● **Places to eat**

Many close by 2130. *Monica's*, Alfaro y Espejo, good, very slow service; *Closerie des Lilas*, Oriente 620 y Eloy Alfaro, excellent Fench cuisine at reasonable prices; *Donde Marcelo*, Ambato nr 16 de Diciembre, good breakfasts, friendly gringo bar; *Le Petit Restaurant*, 16 de Diciembre y Montalvo, Parisian owner, excellent food, US$7 for 2 courses, great atmosphere, also rents rooms; *Marianne*, on Martínez, opp Emetel, French and North African, excellent food, reasonable prices, closed Mon; *El Jardín*, 16 de Diciembre y Rocafuerte, good garden, vegetarian food, excellent chicken and oregano, juices and bar, hammock for siesta; *Central Chifa*, on main street, *jugos*, pastas and meat, huge portions for US$2; *Bella Italia*, at the back of the market, excellent Italian sauces on pasta; *Rincón de Suecia*, Carrera 5 y Parque Basílica and Rocafuerte y 16 de Diciembre, pizzas, good, Swedish and English spoken; *Regines Café Alemán*, 12 de Noviembre y Montalvo, good breakfasts, cakes, meeting place, very popular, expensive; *Mi Pan*, 16 Diciembre y Ambato, good meeting place, excellent fresh bread, pastries and coffee, 3 tables, not cheap; *Cafetería Chushi*, on Maldonado opp bus station, good and cheap breakfast and snacks, fast service, notice board; *Rico Pan*, Ambato y Maldonado, cheap breakfasts, hot bread, good fruit salads and pizzas.

La Abuela, nr Ambato 636, small, good pizzas, good breakfasts; next door is *Café Blah Blah*, good coffee, snacks, small, cosy, popular; *Karson Bar*, on Alfaro opp *Pensión Patty*, friendly; *Higuerón*, 12 de Noviembre 270 y Luis Martínez, open daily 0900-2230 except Wed, good European, local and vegetarian food, nice garden, friendly; *Café Cultura*, Montalvo y Santa Clara, book exchange; *Café Hood*, 16 de Diciembre y Martínez, excellent vegetarian food, dishes around US$1.50, all water and milk boiled, English spoken, always busy, American/Ecuadorean run, owner Ray Hood also has bookstore, shows movies at cultural centre, closed Tues; next door is *Paolo's Pizzería*, good pizzas, very friendly, nice ambience.

● **Banks & money changers**

Banco del Pacífico, Montalvo y Alfaro, changes US$ TCs and currency, best rates for TCs, Mon-Sat from 0900-1800, very slow on Mon morning. **Banco del Pichincha**, Ambato y Halflants; and **Banco Tungurahua**, Ambato y Maldonado, ground floor, both good rates for TCs. **Cambiaria Torres**, Parque Palomino Torres.

● **Entertainment**

Peñas La Burbuja, Pasaje interior de la Ciudadela and *Agoyán* (nr the main baths), Fri and Sat; *Ilusion Bar*, Montalvo y 16 de Diciembre, *peña*; *Hard Rock Café*, Eloy Alfaro nr the market, a favourite travellers' hangout, fantastic *piña colada* and juices; *Bamboos Bar*, Rocafuerte y 16 de Diciembre, good music, friendly, pool table, strong drinks. Films are shown at Centro Cultural, programme available at *Café Hood*. The police make late night passport checks in bars; without a passport you may spend a night in prison.

● **Language classes**

Spanish is taught by José M Eras, Montalvo 5-26 y Santa Clara, T 740-453/740-232, English speaking retired teacher, US$4/hr; *Baños Spanish School*, run by Elizabeth Barrionuevo, at Calle 2 y Av Oriente, T 740-632, English and German speaking, US$4/hr, flexible and rec; Sandra Alvarez Solís, next to Familia Reyes Alvarez (see hotels) T 740-531, private lessons in afternoons, under US$3.50/hr; Esther Romo, Maldonado opp bus terminal, T 740-703; Martha Vacas Flores, 16 de Diciembre y Espejo, T 740-612, university trained, US$3/hr; *Instituto de Español Alternativo*, Montalvo y Alfaro, T/F 740-799.

● **Laundry**

You can have clothes washed at the municipal washhouse next to the main baths for US$1.20 a bundle, or do it yourself there for free. *El Marqués*, next to *Hotel Palace* has laundry service; also *Plantas y Blanco*, which charges US$3.60 for a full load.

● **Shopping**

Street vendors sell *canelazo*, a sweet drink of *aguardiente*, naranjilla, water and cinnamon, and *canario*, aguardiente with egg, milk and sugar. Look out for jawsticking toffee (*taffy*, also known as *melcocha de caña* or *alfeñique*) made in ropes in shop doorways.

For painted balsa-wood birds see *El Chaguamango* shop by the Basílica, open 0800-1600. *Tucán*, Maldonado y Ambato, T 740-417/114, good for handicrafts. *Monilu T-shirts*, Rocafuerte 275 y Alfaro, large selection of good quality handicrafts and t-shirts, reasonable prices, friendly service. The small factory on C 6, just before road to Bella Vista, demonstrates carving. Ask for the weaver José Masaquiza Caizabanda, Rocafuerte 2-56, who sells Salasacan weaving, gives demonstrations and explains the designs, materials, etc to visitors. *Galería de Arte Contemparáneo Huiliac Cuna*, next to *Café Cultura* on Montalvo, has modern art exhibits and a pizza restaurant, owner Marcelo Mazo organizes jungle trips. Maracas are made to order by a family business (everyone is involved) on the road E from behind the church; most are exported to the Caribbean.

There is a fruit and vegetable market on Sun morning, and to a lesser extent on Wed, in Plaza 5 de Junio on C Ambato.

Book exchange: *Café Cultura, Artesania El Tucán, Cafetería Chushi*.

Camping equipment: *Varoxi*, Maldonado 651 y Oriente, T 740-051, also makes daypacks, windproof jackets, larger backpacks, backpack covers and repairs luggage, rec.

Cycle hire: *Sierra Salva Adventures*, Maldonado y Oriente, T 740-298, for mountain bikes and motorcycles, friendly owner Adrián Carrillo, reliable machines. Many other places rent bikes but quality is variable, so shop around. Expect to pay US$4/day; check the brakes and tyres, find out who has to pay for repairs, and insist on a puncture repair kit and pump.

● **Sports**

Horse riding: Christian and Gabby Albers Wetzl have excellent horses for rent, 5 hrs with a guide costs US$20 pp English, Spanish, German spoken, not rec for novices, contact Christian at *Hostería & Cafetería Isla de Baños* (with pool table and bar), Calle T Halflants 1-31 y Juan Montalvo, T/F 740-609. Also Caballos José, Maldonado y Martínez, T 740-746, friendly, good rates, flexible hours; and Angel Aldaz, Montalvo y JL Mera, US$3/hr (on road to the Virgin).

River rafting: is organized in Baños by Esther and Héctor Romo-Oester; trips down the Patate and Pastaza rivers, half day, US$30, full day, US$60. Check with Geotours, C Maldonado, Terminal Terrestre, or write to Casilla 18-02-1933, Baños, T 740-703.

● **Tour companies & travel agents**

Baños is a good meeting place to form a group to visit the Oriente. It is more interesting than Misahuallí, if you have to wait a few days, but can be more expensive. It's a good idea to leave messages in the popular travellers' restaurants. While the road to Puyo is closed, fewer tours are using this route.

There are many unqualified and unscrupulous guides operating. Only use qualified guides and seek advice, eg from the *South American Explorers Club*, or recommendations. In Baños, the Club says, mountain guides are not of the same standard regarding equipment or technique as in other climbing centres, even though they may be cheaper. For exceptions see below.

Guides in Baños: Carlos Saant Mashu, *Agencia de Viajes Kaniats Cia Ltda*, Residencial Santa Clara, T 740-349, knowledgeable, honest, friendly, rec, US$40/day inc transport. Sebastián Moya can be found at *Tsantsa Expeditions*, Oriente y Eloy Alfaro, T 740-957, he is a Shuar Indian who will lead tours anywhere, careful planning is needed to minimize travelling time, US$45/day, not inc optional air travel. You may have to wait some weeks for him to be free, but *Tsantsa* have other good jungle guides, Spanish-speaking only, and they can arrange fly-in trips. *Julio Verne*, Oriente 11-69 y Alfaro, T 740-249, climbing, trekking, equipment rental and sale, good laundry service US$3.25/load, Ecuadorean-Dutch run, rec.

Contactable through *Pensión Patty* (where equipment can be hired, helpful) is mountain guide Carlos Alvarez, who takes climbs in both the Sangay and Cotopaxi National Parks. Also contacted through *Patty* is Fausto Mayorga, who is safe and good. *Geovanny Romo*, is a small, experienced agency on Maldonado who arrange jungle tours, as well as horseback tours from Baños. Juan Medinas and Daniel Vasco (based in Misahuallí), are at *Vasco Tours*, Eloy Alfaro y Martínez, T 740-017, PO Box 18-02-1970, 6-28 trips days available, also mountains and national parks, 6-8 people needed, excellent and plentiful food, up to 4 guides/tour. *Auca Tours*, 12 de Noviembre y Rocafuerte, owned by Marco Bermeo, rec for jungle trips.

NB There are four tour agencies in Baños who are recognized by Cetur and who use qualified guides; they are the above-mentioned Tsanta Expeditions, Sangay Touring (excellent trips down the Curaray Amazonas y Cordero esquina, Quito, T 542-476, F 230-738), Aventurandes and Marcelio Turismo. The above mentioned Juan Medinas of Vasco Tours is also recognized. We have received some critical reports of tours out of Baños; in all cases, insist on a written contract and pay half after the tour. In late 1996 only 5 guides were authorized to enter Huaorani territory in the Oriente; Juan Medinas, Carlos Sevilla, Canadian Randy Smith, Juan Enomenga and Caento Padilla (both Huaoranis).

Guides and equipment for climbing: check all equipment carefully before hiring (see also page 116). *Willie Navarrete*, at *Café Higuerón*, is highly recommended for climbing and is the only ASEGUIM member in Baños. Other guides who are safe to take climbers to Tungurahua are: Fabian Pineda of *Selvanieve*, in Francisco Alomoto, W of Halflants. Dosto Varela of *Expediciones Amazónicas*, in C Oriente, T 740-506. For a guide and pack animals enquire at Baños tourist office or Pondoa shop; guide and mule for 1 pack US$5, for 2 packs, US$7. Horses can be hired for

US$0.90 an hour; contact Julio Albán, Segundo Sánchez or Víctor Barriga through the tourist office.

● **Tourist offices**
Tourist information office is nr the bus terminal, friendly, helpful, but not state-run. Good maps, town map US$1, hiking maps US$0.30, but distances and times reported incorrect; also high-pressure selling of jungle tours. Local artist, J Urquizo, sells an accurate Baños map, 12 de Noviembre y Ambato, T 740-589.

● **Buses**
The bus station is on the Ambato-Puyo road a short way from the centre, and is the scene of vigorous volleyball games most afternoons. To/from **Quito**, via Ambato, US$3, 3½ hrs, Trans Baños half hourly; going to Quito sit on the right for views of Cotopaxi, buy tickets early for weekends and holidays. To **Ambato**, from the market place, 45 mins, US$0.60; to **Riobamba**, 1 hr, US$1; to **Latacunga**, 2-2½ hrs, US$0.80; to **Puyo**, 2 hrs, US$1.50; pack your luggage in plastic as all goes on top of the bus. The road to Puyo is currently closed till 1998, except Sun 1900 to Tues 0600. To **Macas**, some direct buses or change at Puyo, 0830, US$1.75, 6 hrs, magnificent scenery, sit on the right; to **Tena**, 5½ hrs, US$2.50, with Coop Riobamba, rec, or US$2.65 by *buseta*. There are only 3 direct buses Baños-Tena, otherwise passing buses from Riobamba and Ambato, or change at Puyo. Seat reservations are rec but buses don't always leave. To **Misahuallí**, change at Tena, or at the Río Napo crossing, see page 310.

CLIMBING TUNGURAHUA

From Baños it is possible to climb **Tungurahua**, 5,016m – part of Sangay National Park, entry US$7. A guide is highly recommended for this climb; see **Tour companies & travel agents** above. Depending on the season, you may need rubber boots to get to the refuge and crampons for the summit, check in Baños beforehand. The best season is Dec to Mar, though in Dec it can be cloudy in the mornings; check conditions locally.

Access
Follow the road opposite the police control on the Ambato side of town, then take the first mule track to the right of the

store and follow the path to **Pondoa**; do not follow the road up to the baths. If you are driving to Pondoa, take the main Ambato road and turn off to the left about 1 km from the town centre. The road runs parallel to the main road for several kilometres before turning E into the mountains. Park the car at the shop in Pondoa. The walk from the shop to the beginning of the trail takes 30 mins. There is an occasional bus from Baños around 0900 to Pondoa; and a milk truck leaves at 0800 daily from *Pensión Patty* to the Park office, 1 hr, US$1.75. Trucks return from Pondoa around 1300-1400. A pickup truck and driver from Coop Agoyán on central park, C Maldonado, costs US$15 to the park entrance.

Route to the summit

From the park entrance to the refuge is clearly signposted. It's a hard but interesting walk through lush vegetation. It is steep in parts and muddy underfoot. Horses can be hired to take gear up to the refuge; ask the truck driver. From the refuge to the summit takes 4-5 hrs, a tough but rewarding climb. Most parties set out around 0300. At first the path is easy to follow, as far as the antenna and hut, then it becomes a bit vague on fine scree up to the snowline, but still possible to follow. The last hour is on snow. There is no need for rope as there are no crevasses, though novices may need one as it is steep. Crampons and ice-axe are essential from July to around September. The views when the sun rises at 0600 are awesome. It takes 1½-2 hrs to descend to the refuge, then a further 1½ hrs to the park office.

Tungurahua can also be reached from Río Puela, on the Baños-Riobamba road, at about 2,000m. A guide is needed through the forest, then you camp at 3,800m where the forest ends. The snowline is at 4,600m, so the last 400m is through snow, requiring crampons and ice-axe. There are thermal pools at Río Puela, ask where. Don't leave anything of value here.

● **Accommodation** It is 3-4 hrs from the park entrance up to the Santos Ocaña *refugio* at 3,800m, US$3.50 pp, pay the warden at the refuge. Do not leave baggage unattended in the refuge, as theft has been reported. Take a sleeping bag and mat (a hammock can be slung), and food. There are cooking facilities at the *refugio*, but no eating utensils and rarely any lighting, so don't forget your torch. There is no heating and it can be cold.

AMBATO TO GUARANDA

To the W of Ambato, a winding road leads up the valley of the Río Ambato, over a high area of desert called the Gran Arenal, past Carihuairazo and Chimborazo, and down through the Chimbo valley to Guaranda. This spectacular journey on the highest paved road in Ecuador takes about 3 hrs. It reaches a height of 4,380m and vicuñas can be seen. (Following a heavy rainy season in 1995-96, the road had many pot-holes and was in need of repair.)

This route makes an interesting walk, crossing *páramo* and with hot thermal springs along the way. From Ambato, you pass the Plaza de Toros on the left and follow the winding road down to the *estación de bombeo*, where a road branches off to the left. This is the old road to Guaranda, alongside the Río Ambato, which is followed all the way. After 3 hrs' walk (or 1 hr by frequent bus, or truck) there is a small turn off on the right to Pasa, where the interesting part of the hike begins, as the river snakes through the narrow valley. 4 hrs later you reach the village of Llangahua, the last camping spot before entering the *páramo* with its scarce vegetation and harsh climate. About 3 hrs on from the village there is a large, church-like building on the opposite bank of the river. Cross here and go back along the small channel for about 15 mins as far as the hot pools, which are surrounded by large rocks. Continue to the new road, which is reached in 2-3 hrs, at the foot of Chimborazo. Frequent buses pass for Ambato or Guaranda.

GUARANDA

(*Pop* 15,730) This beautiful, clean, quiet town, capital of Bolívar Province, proudly calls itself 'the Rome of Ecuador' because it is built on seven hills. The town maintains its colonial flavour, and there are many fine, though fading, old houses along the cobbled streets with narrow sidewalks. There are fine views of the mountains all around, with Chimborazo towering above. The climate can be very pleasant with warm days and cool evenings, however the area is also subject to rain and fog.

Guaranda is connected by a paved road to Ambato and Babahoyo (see above), and a poor, narrow but spectacular road to Riobamba. This latter route is known as the Gallo Rumi, so named because of a rock that is not only said to resemble a rooster, but also sound like one in a high wind! It is the main centre for the wheat and maize-growing Chimbo valley, but has long stagnated since newer, faster routes replaced the old Guayaquil-Quito road through Babahoyo (see page 263) and Guaranda (which is still good and beautiful).

Places of interest

Locals traditionally take an evening stroll in the palm fringed main plaza, **Parque Libertador Simón Bolívar**. Around the park are the Municipal buildings with an attractive courtyard and a large stone **Cathedral** with a nice marble altar, wooden ceiling and stained glass windows. The **Iglesia de las Marianitas** is on 7 de Mayo y Manuela Cañizares.

Towering over the city, atop one of the hills, is an impressive statue of '**El Indio Guaranga**', a local Indian leader after whom the city may have been named. The site offers fine views of the city, the surrounding hills and the summit of Chimborazo. A cultural centre at the base of the sculpture includes a regional history museum (entry free), an art gallery and auditorium. To get there, take a taxi (US$0.80); or take a 'Guanujo' bus to the stadium, walk past the stadium to Av La Prensa and follow it till you reach the first turning on the right (5-10 mins' walk). Alternatively, you can walk from the centre, which takes about 45 mins. Climb the stairs at the S end of García Moreno to the cemetery, turn right up Abdón Calderón, climb another set of stairs and follow the paths through the fields, or take the car road, which is longer.

The **Casa de la Cultura**, Manuela Cañizares 511, has a very small museum with pottery and a library.

Market days are Fri and Sat (larger), when many indigenous people from the nearby communities can be seen trading at the Mercado Minorista (at the N end of Calle Azuay), by Plaza 15 de Mayo (9 de Abril y Maldonado) and at Plaza Roja (Av Gen Enriquez). These markets are colourful and interesting. A water-powered grist mill on the river welcomes visitors. Also along the river, on the road to Riobamba, is the Centro Recreacional Camilo Montenegro, a park with an artificial lake, swimming pool and sports fields.

Excursions

North of Guaranda, 1½ hrs by car along poor roads, is **Salinas de Guaranda** (*Pop* 5,000), in a picturesque setting. The town is noted for its geological formations, dairy cooperative (El Salinerito brand cheese) and sweaters, which are also sold in Quito. It is a good area for walking, horseback riding and fishing. The nearby villages, Santiago and San Simón are described as picturesque.

● **Accommodation & transport** **E** *Hotel Refugio Salinas*, T 758-778 (Salinas office: Gen Enríquez y Cándido Rada, Plaza Roja, T 980-703, F 982-140), run by the dairy cooperative, with bath, **F** with shared bath, **G** pp in dormitory, meals available. Transportes 10 de Noviembre buses pass through Guaranda on the way to Salinas, wait by Verbo Divino School, daily about 0600 and 1400, return 0530 and 1300; taxi US$16.50 (US$23 with wait included). Also enquire at the cooperative office or Salinerito Cheese shop (Plaza Roja) about their vehicles going to Salinas.

The bus ride to Babahoyo (see page 263) is beautiful. There is an interesting church museum in **Huayco** (Santuario de Nuestra Señora de la Natividad), constructed around a 'Vatican Square', with interesting pre-Spanish artefacts. The trip is worth the 30 mins' taxi ride (24 km) from Guaranda.

Local festivals

Carnival in Guaranda is among the best known in the country. People of all walks of life share the festivities; parades, masks, dances, guitars and poetry fill the streets. Taita Carnaval (Father Carnival), a landowner who sponsors the party, opens the celebrations when he makes his grand entrance into town. As in other parts of the country water throwing (and at times flour, ink, etc) is common. In the surrounding countryside the celebrations last for 8 days.

Local information
● **Accommodation**

B *La Colina*, high up on Av Guayaquil (No 117,

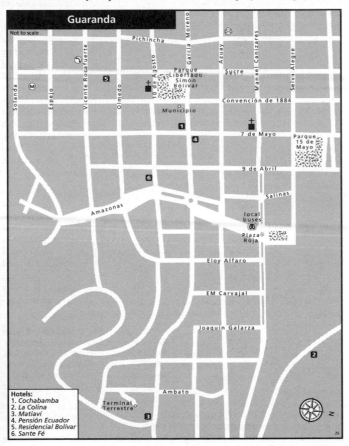

Hotels:
1. *Cochabamba*
2. *La Colina*
3. *Matiaví*
4. *Pensión Ecuador*
5. *Residencial Bolívar*
6. *Sante Fé*

T/F 980-666), with bath and TV, rooms bright and attractive, terraces give good view of town and surrounding mountains, restful, friendly, covered swimming pool open to non-residents US$2, restaurant mediocre.

D *Residencial Bolívar*, Sucre 704 y Rocafuerte, T 980-547, with bath, TV, intermittent hot showers, cheaper with shared bath, quiet inner court, restaurant not open for breakfast, motorbike parking; **D** *Cochabamba*, García Moreno y 7 de Mayo, T 981-958, F 982-125, PO Box 01-02-0095, with bath, TV, nice rooms, good service, cheaper with shared bath, very good restaurant.

E *Matiaví*, Av Eliza Mariño 314, T 980-295, next to the bus station, clean, motorbike parking; **E** *Residencial Acapulco*, 10 de Agosto y Amazonas, basic, small rooms, restaurant downstairs; next door is **E** *Santa Fé*, 10 de Agosto y 9 de Abril, T 981-526, with bath, electric shower, TV, cheaper with shared bath, very thin walls, noisy at times, friendly, restaurant.

F *Pensión Rosa Elvira*, Sucre 606, shared bath, basic; **F** *Pensión San José*, Sucre 607, shared bath, very basic; **F-G** *Residencial La Posada*, General Enríquez y 10 de Agosto, by Plaza Roja, T 980-867, shared bath, cold water, not very clean, basic, motorbike parking.

● **Places to eat**
The restaurant in the *Hotel Cochabamba* is arguably the best in town, but is not cheap, 4-course lunch *menú* is US$4 inc tax and service, closed Sun; *Marisquería El Conchal*, Plaza Roja, not open in the evening, open Sun, good *ceviche de pescado y camarones mixtos*, cheap, family-run; *Chifa Hong Kong*, Parque Simón Bolívar, very good and cheap; *Amazonas*, 9 de Abril y García Moreno, family run, good set meals for around US$3 and à la carte, closed Sun, rec; *Rumipamba*, General Enríquez, Plaza Roja, fresh fruit juices, set meals and à la carte; *Central*, Azuay y Mariana Ofir Carvajal, 2 blocks from Plaza Roja; *Coffee Burger*, 10 de Agosto y 7 de Mayo, for drinks and snacks; *Bolívar*, Sucre 706, has a nice musical instrument collection; *Santa Fé*, 10 de Agosto y 9 de Abril, set meals; next door is *Acapulco*, set meals. A popular meeting place in the evenings is *Heladería El Pingüiño*, next to *Chifa Hong Kong*.

● **Banks & money changers**
Filanbanco, on Av Kennedy, changes Amex and Visa TCs, 0900-1300 only. Delgado Travel, García Moreno y Sucre, by Parque Libertador Simón Bolívar, T 980-232, cash only,

Mon-Fri 0830-1800, Sat 0830-1700, Sun 0830-1500.

● **Post & telecommunications**
Post Office: Azuay y Pichincha, Mon-Fri 0800-1200 and 1400-1800; national and international fax service available. Emetel, Rocafuerte 508 y Sucre, 0800-2200 daily; and at bus terminal.

● **Shopping**
There are many well stocked shops in town. Mercado Municipal 10 de Noviembre, Sucre entre Espejo y Márquez de Solanda; *Salinerito* cheese, Gen Enríquez, Plaza Roja, good quality, also sell woollens knitted in Salinas.

● **Tour companies & travel agents**
Delgado Travel, on Parque Simón Bolívar at Moreno y Sucre, T 980-232, in addition to the usual services they buy dollars at current rates and operate an airmail service to the USA.

● **Transport**
Car rental: Delgado Travel, García Moreno y Sucre, T 980-232.

Buses The terminal is at Eliza Mariño Carvajal, on the way out of town towards Riobamba and Babahoyo; if you will be staying in town ask to be dropped off closer to the centre. Many daily buses to: **Ambato**, US$1.40, 2 hrs (beautiful views); **Riobamba**, US$1.40, 2 hrs; **Babahoyo**, US$1.65, 3 hrs; **Guayaquil**, US$2.30, 4½ hrs; **Quito**, 3 companies run almost 30 daily services, US$3.85, 4-5 hrs. Taxi to **Riobamba** 1½ hrs, US$11.50.

AMBATO TO RIOBAMBA

After Ambato, the Pan-American Highway and railway pass apple orchards and onion fields. Between Ambato and Riobamba is **Mocha**, where guinea-pigs (*cuy*) are raised for the table. You can sample roast *cuy* at stalls by the roadside. The valley's patchwork of fields gives an impression of greater fertility and prosperity than the Riobamba zone that follows. On the houses a small crucifix crowns the roof, where figurines of domestic animals are also found. The Quito-Guayaquil railway's highest point, Urbina (3,609m) is between Cevallos and Riobamba. At the pass there are fine views in the dry season of Chimborazo and its smaller sister mountain, Carihuairazo.

- **Accommodation** E *Posada de la Estación (Youth Hostel)*, PO Box 523, Riobamba, T/F 942-215, a converted station at Urbina on the Pan-American Highway at 3,618m, is a good place for acclimatization, clean, helpful, horses, trips and equipment arranged, tour to see the *hieleros* (who bring ice blocks down from the glacier, to be sold in the Riobamba market) Tues, Thur or Fri, US$18.

RIOBAMBA

Riobamba (*Pop* 95,505; *Alt* 2,750m) is the capital of Chimborazo Province. It is built in the wide **Tapi Valley** and has broad streets and many ageing but impressive buildings. Because of its central location Riobamba is known as the heartland of Ecuador. It also boasts the nickname 'La Sultana de Los Andes' in honour of its style and elegance.

Riobamba has many good churches and public buildings, and magnificent views of five of the great volcanic peaks, Chimborazo, Altar, Tungurahua, Carihuairazo and, on occasion, Sangay. The city is the commercial centre for the Province of Chimborazo and an important centre of highland culture, both because of the many indigenous communities which live in the province and because of the city's self-styled European aristocracy.

Places of interest

Riobamba has several nice plazas and parks. The main plaza is **Parque Maldonado** with a statue to the local scientist Pedro Vicente Maldonado and some interesting wrought-iron fountains. Around it are the **Santa Bárbara Cathedral**, the **Municipality** and several colonial buildings with arcades. Worth visiting is the house on the corner of Primera Constituyente and Espejo, restored in 1996; it now houses the Banco de Préstamos. **Parque Sucre** with a Neptune fountain is located nearby. Standing opposite, along Primera Constituyente, is the imposing building of Colegio Maldonado.

Four blocks NE of the railway station is the **Parque 21 de Abril**, named after the city's independence date. The Batalla de Tapi was fought in the Riobamba valley, on 21 April 1822. The Argentine General, Juan de Lavalle, and 97 patriots defeated 400 Spanish troops. The park, better known as **La Loma de Quito**, affords an unobstructed view of Riobamba and the peaks. It also has a colourful tile tableau of the history of Ecuador and is especially fine at sunset. **San Antonio de Padua** church, at the E corner of Parque 21 de Abril, tells bible stories in the windows.

At the intersection of Av Daniel L Borja and Av Miguel Angel León is the Vaca-Zebra (zebra-cow) an unusual sculpture by the local artist Guillermo Endara Crow. A stylized Simon Bolívar, donated by Venezuela, adorns the traffic circle at Av Daniel L Borja and Zambrano.

There is a new market building, but only a small part of the activity at the Sat market takes place there. Buying and selling go on all over town. The 'tourist' market in the small plaza S of the Convento de la Concepción museum (see below) is a good place to buy local handicrafts – *ikat* shawls (*macanas*), embroidered and finely woven belts (*fajas*), blankets, embroidered dresses and shirts, Otavalan weavings and sweaters, *shigras* and carvings of tagua, a nut that hardens and looks like ivory.

Indian women come to the plaza each week with sacks full of bead and coin necklaces, old belts and dresses, blanket pins (*tupus*), and much more. Since Indian-style clothing is also sold here, the plaza is full of colourful Indians from different parts of Chimborazo province, each group wearing its distinctive costume.

Two blocks E, there is a huge produce market in another plaza, also pottery, baskets, hats. All the streets in this area are filled with traders. There are also 2 markets on Wed, **Mercado La Condamine** and **Mercado San Alfonso**, which only sell local products. You

Andean dress pins

The dress of prehispanic women in the Andean region consisted basically of the *urku*, the *lliclla* and the *chumpi*, or belt. The *urku*, the principal vestment, was a large rectangular cloak which covered the woman from her shoulders to her feet in the manner of a tunic. It was fastened at shoulder level with a pair of metal *tupu* and at the waist with a belt.

This garb was widely used in rural areas up until about 100 years ago, and survives today though in a shortened and modified form. The *lliclla* was the outermost shawl, which covered the shoulders and was fastened at the chest with a single pin or a smaller clasp called a *ttipqui*. This garment is still worn today in the rural Andean world, although it is slowly being replaced by other western-style items of clothing.

Tupu and *ttipqui* are the ancient Quechua names for the two types of dress pins, but today all metal pins used by Indian women to fasten their clothing are known as *topos*, which is a Castellanization of the Quechua word *tupu*.

The use of the *tupu and ttipqui* is thought to have spread North from the Huari-Tiahuanuco empire throughout the entire Andean region. The first dress pins were simply cactus spines or carved from thin pieces of wood and of a strictly functional nature. However, the development of metallurgy allowed artisans to make the pins from metal, at first hammering gold and silver, and later through the smelting and moulding of copper.

should compare shop prices before buying from the markets.

Museums

The **Convento de la Concepción**, Orozco y España, entrance at Argentinos y J Larrea, has been carefully restored by the Banco Central and now functions as a religious art museum. It is a veritable treasure chest of 18th Century religious art; open Tues-Sat 0900-1200 and 1500-1800, admission, US$1 for Ecuadoreans, US$1.65 for others. The guides are friendly and knowledgeable (tip expected). The priceless gold monstrance, Custodia de Riobamba Antigua, is the museum's greatest treasure, one of the richest of its kind in South America. The museum is well worth a visit.

The Ateneo de Chimborazo, **Museo Particular Familiar Córdoba-Román**, Velasco 24-25 y Veloz, is a private museum which includes a photo collection, paintings, sculptures, furniture and documents; open Mon-Fri, 1000-1300 and 1500-1700.

Excursions

Guano is a sisal-working and carpet-making town of 6,000 inhabitants 10 km to the N, with prehistoric monoliths on a nearby hilltop. There are lovely views of El Altar from the plaza. A good handicraft shop is *Almacén Ciudad de las Fuentes*, in the plaza. Rugs have been produced here since colonial times when, under the encomiendas system, local Indian slaves were trained in this art. You can have rugs made to your own design. The town holds a Sun market and is very quiet other days.

• **Transport** There are frequent buses from NE Riobamba nr the road to Guano, US$0.15, or taxi, US$2.65.

After Guano you can take the bus on to Santa Teresita from where it is a 20-min walk downhill to **Balneario Los Helenes**, with 3 pools; 1 tepid, 2 cool. Camping is possible nearby. There are superb views of Altar and Tungurahua as you walk through the surrounding pasture land.

From Riobamba it is also possible to reach the fossil fields of the gorge of

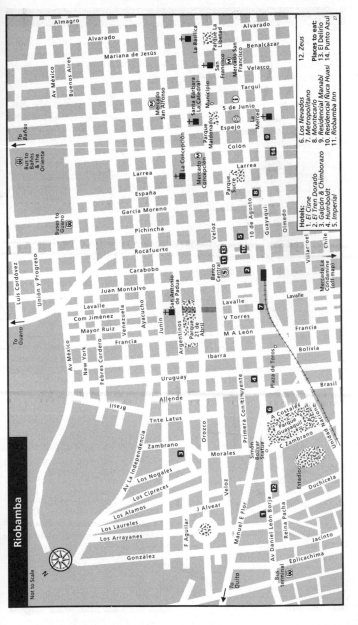

Riobamba

Not to Scale

Hotels:
1. El Cisne Dorado
2. Metro
3. Galpón & Chimborazo
4. Humboldt
5. Imperial
6. Los Nevados
7. Metropolitano
8. Montecarlo
9. Residencial Manabi
10. Residencial Ñuca Huasi
11. Riobamba Inn

Places to eat:
12. Zeus
13. El Delirio
14. Punto Azul

Chalán and the archaeological site of **Punín**.

In **Cacha**, a small Indian town nearby, the descendents of the indigenous ruling family still live. There have been many articles and books written about the 'Daquelmas'.

Local festivals

Fiesta de los Niños is on 2 Jan, with street parades, music and dancing. Riobamba's independence day is 21 April, celebrated for several days with lively parades, concerts, bullfights and drinking. Hotel prices rise and rooms may be difficult to find during this period. Festivals to celebrate the **Foundation of Riobamba**, 11 November.

Local information

Price guide

L1	over US$200	L2	US$151-200
L3	US$101-150	A1	US$81-100
A2	US$61-80	A3	US$46-60
B	US$31-45	C	US$21-30
D	US$12-20	E	US$7-11
F	US$4-6	G	up to US$3

● **Accommodation**

Slightly higher hotel prices can be expected in the height of the climbing season. In Jan, schools from the coast bring children here on vacation and many hotels are full. It is also difficult to find a room during the Nov basketball tournament.

B *Hostería Abraspungo*, Km 3½ on the road to Guano, T 940-820, F 940-819, beautiful house in country setting, with bath, TV, excellent restaurant, bar, pool, horse riding; **B** *Chimborazo Internacional*, Los Cipreces y Argentinos, T 963-475, F 963-473, attentive service, spacious rooms with fridge and cold drinks, fully carpeted, central heating, pool, sauna, Turkish bath, jacuzzi, noisy discotheque, restaurant overpriced; nearby is **B** *El Galpón*, Argentinos y Zambrano, T 960-981, pleasant location on a hill overlooking the city, but a bit run-down; **B** *El Cisne*, Av Daniel L Borja y Duchicela, T 964-573, F 941-982, with bath, TV, restaurant, sauna and Turkish bath, modern; **B** *Hostería La Andaluza*, 16 km from Riobamba along the Pan-American Highway to Ambato, T 904-223, with views of Tungurahua and Altar, good walking, friendly,

good restaurant; **B** *Hostería El Troje*, 4½ km on the road to Chambo, T 960-826, nice rooms, good views, tourist centre, camping, good restaurant.

C *Hostería El Toril*, Km 1 on the road to Baños, T 942-057, in country setting, with bath, TV, sports fields; **C** *Whymper*, Av Miguel Angel León 23-10 y Primera Constituyente, T 964-575, F 968-137, private bath, hot water, spacious rooms, safe parking, cafetería serves breakfast any time, but slow; **C** *Zeus*, Av Daniel L Borja 41-29, T 962-292, F 963-100, with bath, TV, modern, comfortable, nice, 24-hr cafetería, good restaurant, cash discounts.

D *El Altar*, Panamericana Norte Km 1, T 964-572, with bath, TV, restaurant, garage; **D** *Humboldt*, Borja 3548 y Uruguay, T 961-788, clean, with bath, TV, restaurant, parking; **D** *Los Alamos*, Av Lizarzaburo on the way N out of town, T 967-386, with bath, hot water, TV; **D** *Manabí*, Colón 19-58 y Olmedo, T 967-967/305, with bath, clean, hot water, safe, restaurant, parking; **D** *Montecarlo*, Av 10 de Agosto 25-41 entre García Moreno y España, in the same building as *Cambio Chimborazo* (see **Banks & money changers** below), T/F 960-554, clean, comfortable, **E** without window, hot water, restaurant, English spoken; **D** *Riobamba Inn*, Carabobo 23-20 y Primera Constituyente, T 961-696, parking, restaurant, basic but clean, group discounts; **D** *Tren Dorado*, Carabobo 22-35 y 10 de Agosto, T 964-890, with bath, modern, reliable hot water, clean, nice, parking.

E *Hostal Ñuca Huasi*, 10 de Agosto 2824 y Dávalos, T 966-669, with bath, **F** with shared bath, laundry facilities, noisy, poor beds, a bit dark and gloomy, hot water, friendly, safe parking, will arrange transport to the *refugio* on Chimborazo; **E** *Hostal Segovia*, Primera Constituyente 22-28 y Espejo, nr Parque Maldonado, T 961-259, with bath, cheaper with shared bath, clean, laundry service, good value, can arrange guides for Chimborazo; **E** *Imperial*, Rocafuerte 22-15 y 10 de Agosto, T 960-429, hot water 24 hrs, shared baths, expensive laundry facilities, stores luggage, good beds, clean, friendly and comfortable, good views from the roof, loud music from bar on Fri and Sat nights, tours to Chimborazo arranged, US$20-25/car but don't pay in advance as they may be cancelled, also check their equipment.

E *Los Nevados*, Luis Costales 24-37 y Av Daniel L Borja, across from Parque Guayaquil,

T 964-696, with bath, constant hot water, safe, clean, very good, laundry US$1.75/load, garage extra; **E** *Los Shyris*, 10 de Agosto y Rocafuerte 2160, T 960-323, F 967-934, nr the train station, with bath, hot water 0500-1000 and 1500-2200, good rooms and service, rooms at the back are quieter, cheaper rooms without bath on 4th floor, clean, nicely furnished, friendly, good value; **E** *Metropolitano*, Borja y Lavalle, T 961-714, nr the train station, with bath, central, traditional, large rooms, good beds, but noisy, insecure, water problems; **E** *Patricia*, Falconi y Brasil, T 961-525, quiet back street, family run, safe; **E** *Residencial Rocío*, Brazil 2168, y Av Daniel L Borja, T 961-848, bath, hot water (but water problems 1000 to 1800), towels and soap supplied, cheaper with shared bath, clean, friendly, quiet, parking.

F *Luzia Bärtsch de Noboa*, Espejo 27-28 y Junín, T 961-205, Ecuadorian-Swiss run, no sign, clean, hot water but supply reported as intermittent, very comfortable, secure, car parking, friendly and helpful; **F** *Monterrey*, Rey Cacha 44-29 y Eplicachima, across from the bus terminal, T 962-421, some with bath, hot water only in shared bath; **F** *Residencial Colonial*, Carabobo 21-62 y 10 de Agosto, across from the train station, T 966-543, shared bath, very basic, run-down colonial house; **F** *Residencial Las Colinas*, Av Daniel L Borja y Pasaje El Espectador, nr the bus terminal, T 968-708, with bath, electric shower, parking extra, basic; **F** *Residencial Marcelito*, Vargas Torres 22-64 y Primera Constituyente, shared bath, basic.

G *Guayaquil*, Montalvo y Unidad Nacional, by the train station, T 964-512, shared bath, basic; **G** *Venecia*, Dávalos 2221 y 10 de Agosto, T 961-809, hot water, short stay customers preferred, cannot stay more than 1 day.

● **Places to eat**
None is open after 2200. *El Delirio*, Primera Constituyente 2816 y Rocafuerte (Bolívar's house in Riobamba), T 960-029, closed Mon and Sun, excellent steaks for US$4, 2 courses US$8, patio garden, popular with tour groups, highly rec; *El Mesón de Inéz*, Orozco y Morales, excellent; *Cabaña Montecarlo*, 10 de Agosto 25-45, T 962-844, Viennese atmosphere, excellent food and service, main dishes US$3.50-5, large selection, good breakfasts for US$2.50-3.50, try the *jugo de babaco*, a local tropical fruit; *Tambo de Oro*, Zambrano y Junín, nr *Hotel El Galpón*, smart, expensive,

excellent cuisine, good wine list, one of the best places in town; *La Biblia*, Primera Constituyente s/n, nr V Torres intersection, *platos típicos*, good regional cooking, specialities on Sun, moderate prices; *Candilejas*, 10 de Agosto 27-33 y Pichincha, à la carte, set meals and pizzas, 20% tax and service is added to the bill; *El Faraón*, Av Daniel L Borja y la 44, meals and music; *Parrillada de Fausto*, Uruguay y Av Daniel L Borja, good meat.

Che Carlitos, Colón 22-44, between 10 de Agosto and Primera Constituyente, *parrilladas Argentinas* and *empanadas*, expensive but authentic, *peña* at weekend; *El Fogón del Chef*, Tarqui y Veloz, across from Emetel, chicken and grill; *Charlie's Pizzería*, García Moreno entre Guayaquil y 10 de Agosto, great pizza for US$5, vegetarian lasagne; *San Valentín Club Pizzería*, Torres y Borja, good pizzas, excellent chilli and lasagne, good coffee, cable TV, open 0800-1700 and Sun, rec.

Seafood: *Punto Azul*, Colón y Olmedo, excellent seafood, open 0800-1500, closed Sun; *La Fuente*, Primera Consituyente s/n y García Moreno, lower ground floor of building housing the *Ministerio de Obras Públicas*, very good *sopa marinera*, cebiches and fish, reasonably priced, open 0900-1300 and 1500-1900, rec; *El Portón Dorado*, Diego de Ibarra 22-50 y Av Daniel L Borja, set meals, à la carte, seafood, English and Italian spoken; *Cevichería Las Redes*, Primera Constituyente y Carabobo, set meals and seafood.

Chinese: *Chifa Joy Sing*, Guayaquil 29-27, behind the station, cheap, good; *Chifa China*, León Borja 43-49, good, cheap, *Chifa Internacional*, Veloz y Dávalos, Chinese, good.

Home cooking: *Don Bolo*, Veloz y Carabobo, good value set meals; *Los Alamos*, Juan de Lavalle 22-41, good à la carte and set meals; *El Paraíso*, Juan de Lavalle 22-23 y Av Daniel L Borja, good value.

Snacks and coffee: *Café Montecarlo*, Av 10 de Agosto 25-40 y Moreno, popular with tourists, good breakfast, meals for around US$2; *Gran Pan*, Moreno 22-46, nr Primera Constituyente, bakery and *cafetería*, fresh bread, tasty cakes, good coffee and breakfast, opens at 0800; also has a branch at Borjas s/n, nr V Torres; *Caffe Johnny*, Espejo 22-45 y Primera Constituyente, breakfast from 0700, good, closed Sun; *Bambario*, 10 de Agosto y Rocafuerte, coffee bar, friendly, helpful, rents mountain bikes and runs tours to Sangay National Park, very informative. There are also many snackbars along 10 de Agosto. Opposite the railway station, on 10 de Agosto is *Sandy's Pastelería*, good for cakes and coffee, friendly owner. For early departures, there are several small cafés at the back of the bus terminal, open early till late, serving breakfast and other meals.

● **Banks & money changers**
Banco Internacional, 10 de Agosto y García Moreno, cash only; Banco de Préstamos, Primera Constituyente y Espejo at Parque Maldonado, in a beautiful refurbished colonial building, cash and TCs, cash advances on Mastercard; Banco Popular, Primera Constituyente y Larrea, Parque Sucre; Banco del Pacífico, García Moreno 11-40, cash advance on Mastercard, also at Miguel A León y Veloz; Banco la Previsora, Colón 22-35 y 10 de Agosto, cash advance on Visa; Casa de Cambio Chimborazo, 10 de Agosto 25-33, will change TCs, major European and American currencies, fair rates, Mon-Fri 0900-1330 and 1500-1800, Sat 0900-1300; Delgado Travel, 10 de Agosto y Larrea, cash only, good rates; Coltur, 10 de Agosto 24-55 y España, cash only, good rates. Banks will not always exchange dollars even though the exchange rate is posted. Cash dollars are easy to change on the street and in shops showing *compra dolares* sign.

● **Entertainment**
Gens-Chop bar, León Borja 42-17 y Duchicela, good music, music and sport videos, open daily, US$3 for a jug of beer, popular, rec; *Peña* at *La Casa Vieja*, Orozco y Tarqui. The *Casa de la Cultura*, 10 de Agosto y Rocafuerte, has a good *peña* on Fri and Sat evenings. Disco, Thur-Sat at *La Bruja*, Km 1 on road to Quito; *Unicornio*, St Armand y Av Lizarzaburo, Vía Ambato Km 2, Piano Bar, Salsateca, cultural place, open Thur-Sat; *Pin Chop*, video bar at Borja 37-70; *Vieja Guardia* is a bar at Av Flor 40-43 y Av Zambrano; also *Juventus*, bardisco at 10 de Agosto 26-57.

● **Post & telecommunications**
Post Office: 10 de Agosto y Espejo, closed Sat; also fax service, national fax US$1.10/page, international fax US$7.90/page.

Telephone: Emetel at Tarqui entre Primera Constituyente y Veloz. National and international calls, 0800-2200; also at the bus terminal. Fax service also at the higher class hotels or travel agencies, but more expensive.

● **Shopping**
Nice tagua carvings and other crafts are on sale at *Alta Montaña* (see Tour companies). Porcelain masks and figurines at *Galerias Lys*, Argentinos y Juan Larrea, across from Convento de la Concepción Museum.

Supermarkets: *La Ibérica*, Av Daniel L Borja 37-62; *Su Comisariato*, Primera Constituyente 25-24 y España; *Tu Policentro*, Luis Costales y Av Daniel L Borja, next door to *Hotel Los Nevados*.

● **Sports**
Mountain biking: *Pro Bici*, at Primera Constituyente 23-51 y Larrea, T 960-189/961-877, F 961-923, run by guide and mechanic, Galo J Brito, bike trips and rental, guided tours with support vehicle, full equipment (use Cannondale ATBs), US$25-30 pp/day, excluding meals and overnight stays.

Cockfights: at Coliseo San Pedro, Alvarado 33-36 y Chimborazo, 2 blocks from the Baños bus terminal.

A variety of *pelota* games can be seen on Sun afternoons.

● **Tour companies & travel agents**
Metropolitan Touring, Av Daniel L Borja 37-64, T 969-600, F 969-601, tours, Western Union money transfers and airline tickets; *Coltur*, 10 de Agosto 24-55 y España, T/F 940-950, tickets, tours and exchange; *Alta Montaña*, Av Daniel L Borja 35-17 y Diego de Ibarra, T/F 942-215, PO Box 060123, trekking, climbing, cycling, running, bird watching, photography and horseback riding tours in mountains and jungle, logistical support for expeditions, transport, equipment rental, souvenirs, English spoken; *Andes Trek*, Colón 22-25 y 10 de Agosto, T 940-964, F 940-963, climbing, trekking and mountain biking tours, transport, equipment rental, good rates, English spoken; *Expediciones Andinas*, Argentinos 38-60 y Zambrano, T 964-915, climbing expeditions; *Delgado Travel*, 10 de Agosto y Larrea, T 961-152, F 963-914, also handles airmail and giros to USA and Europe.

● **Tourist offices**
Cetur, 10 de Agosto 20-72 y 5 de Junio, T/F 941-213, open Mon-Fri 0830-1700, the lady in charge is helpful, knowledgeable and speaks very good English.

● **Useful addresses**
Immigration: *Policia Nacional, Jefatura Provincial de Migración*, is at España 20-50, entre

Guayaquil y Olmedo, open Mon-Fri 0800-1200 and 1400-1800.

INEFAN: For information about Parque Nacional Sangay, Ministerio de Agricultura (MAG), Av 9 de Octubre y Quinta Macají, at the western edge of town, N of the roundabout at the end of Av Isabel de Godin, T 963-779; park people are only in the office in the early morning, be there before 0800. From town take city bus San Gerardo-El Batán.

● **Transport**
Trains Service to **Durán (Guayaquil)** daily except Tues and Thur at 0600, US$15 for foreigners; arrives Alausí 0930 (US$8), Bucay 1330 (US$12), get out at Bucay and change to bus to avoid arriving in Guayaquil in the dark. Interruptions to service occur. Tickets for the 0600 train to Durán go on sale at 0530 but get there at 0500. The station is closed on Sun. If time is limited, for the most spectacular section of the railway, take a bus before 0730 to Guayaquil and get out at Bucay (US$2.50), catch the train to Alausí, return to Riobamba by bus. Several buses wait for the train. Train to **Quito**, 0900 Fri, from Quito Sat 0800, US$10 for foreigners, 8 hrs; tickets sold on day of departure around 0800. Riding on the roof is recommended on both these trips, but you may be used for target practice by local farmers testing their apple-throwing skills. It's a good idea to sit as far back on the roof as possible to avoid getting covered in oil from the exhaust.

A privately-owned *autoferro* runs from Quito, details from Metropolitan Tours, Av República de El Salvador 970, Quito, T 464-780, rec, or other travel agencies. The railway administration office is on Espejo, next to the Post Office, reliable information available during office hours, T 960-115.

Buses There is a well-run Terminal Terrestre on Eplicachima y Av D L Borja for buses to Quito, Guayaquil, Ambato, etc, but buses to Baños and the Oriente leave from the Terminal Oriental, Espejo y Córdovez. Taxi from one terminal to the other, US$0.75. **Quito**, US$2.95, 3½ hrs, about every 30 mins; to **Guaranda**, US$1.40, 2 hrs, road, paved to San Juan, crosses a 4,000m pass, sit on the right, beautiful views; to **Ambato**, US$0.85, 1 hr, sit on the right; to **Babahoyo** via Guaranda, US$3, 5 hrs; to **Alausí**, US$1.15, 2 hrs; to **Huigra**, US$2.15, 3 hrs. To **Cuenca**, 6 a day via Alausí, 5½ hrs, US$4. This road is paved but landslides are a constant hazard and the road is often under repair. For a day trip to

Ingapirca (see page 201), take the 0530 bus to Cuenca, getting off at El Tambo at about 1000. Bus back to Riobamba passes through El Tambo at about 1600; last one about 1930. Bus to **Santo Domingo**, hourly, US$3.30, 5 hrs; to **Baños**, US$1, 1 hr; to **Puyo**, US$2, 3½ hrs direct. **NB** The Baños-Puyo road was under construction in 1996 and open to circulation only between Sun 1900 and Tues 0600, work is expected to continue into 1997. To **Huaquillas** at 2100 with Patria, avoiding Guayaquil, daily except Tues and Sat, US$5.45, 9 hrs. To **Guayaquil**, about 35 a day, first one leaves at 0600, US$4, 4½ hrs, the trip is really spectacular for the first 2 hrs. There are pirate buses which charge more than the regular lines and do not sell tickets in the bus station. They operate on a first come, first served basis, but they can be useful when all the others are full up.

CLIMBING AROUND RIOBAMBA

Riobamba is a good starting point for climbing and trekking expeditions. Chimborazo, Altar, Sangay, Tungurahua, and the Inca Trail to Ingapirca can all be accessed from here. Tour operators in Riobamba offer transport and trips to all the attractions, see **Tour companies & travel agents** above.

CHIMBORAZO

At 6,310m, this is a difficult climb owing to the altitude. No one without mountaineering experience should attempt the climb, and rope, ice-axe and crampons must be used. Dr Sverre Aarseth writes that in order to climb this mountain it is essential to have at least 1 week's acclimatization above 3,000m. The best season is Dec and June-September. Sr Héctor Vásquez at Colegio Nacional Bolívar, Ambato, has helped many expeditions with travel arrangements and information; he is a top-grade mountaineer.

● **Guides** There is a provincial association of mountain guides, Asociación de Andinismo de Chimborazo, which registers approved guides. Some guides who have been recommended are: **Enrique Veloz Coronado**, technical adviser of the Asociación de

AndinismodeChimborazo, Chile 33-21 y Francia, T 960-916, he is best reached after 1500 and is very helpful, his sons are also guides and now work with him. **Marcelo Puruncajas** of Andes Trek (see Agencies above), member of ASEGUIM, highly rec, speaks English, when not leading tours uses good guides, also offers trekking, 4WD transport and mountain biking. **Silvio Pesántez**, Argentinos 1140 y Darquea, PO Box 327, T 962-681, he is a member of ASEGUIM, an experienced climber and adventure-tour leader, speaks French, rec; **Marco Cruz** of Expediciones Andinas (see Tour companies & travel agents above), T 962-845 (house), recommended, he is a certified guide of the German Alpine Club and considered among the best and most expensive guides; **Rodrigo Donoso** of Alta Montaña (see Agencies above), for climbing and a variety of trekking and horseback riding trips, speaks English well. Trekking including guide, transport, equipment, shelter and food US$40-50 pp/day, min 2 persons; climbing with guides who belong to the Asociación de Andinismo about US$70 pp/day; overall cost for 2 between US$250-400.

The **Fiesta de las Nieves** is celebrated at the 4,800m shelter on the second or third Sun in December. There is much music and dancing, and the whole event is rather touristy with no folkloric roots, but at least buses from Riobamba go to the mountain. There are two routes up the mountain; the SW face and NW face.

The Southwest Face

● **Access** There are no direct buses so arrange with a travel agency, or for a similar price take a taxi from Riobamba; US$35 for 5-6 hrs, US$40 return next day or later, US$21 one way. There are usually several taxis and other vehicles at the car park in the early afternoon. A rec driver is Segundo López, Taxi 89, found at the taxi stand in Mercado Santa Rosa, Av Guayaquil y Rocafuerte, Riobamba; also Juan Fuenmayor, Veloz 25-31 y España, or arrange through Riobamba hotels, eg *Imperial*. You can also take a bus to San Juan village and hitch from there (better chance at the weekend). It is 56 km from Riobamba and takes about 1½ hrs. **NB** We have received reports of armed robberies on the way to the refuge by car. Check the situation with *Alta Montaña* in Riobamba, or with *Safari Tours* in Quito (see page 116).

● **Accommodation** The road ends at 4,800m, at a large white building, the Hermanos Carrel refuge. It has a guard, bunk beds with mattresses for 8, inc 1 private room for 2, dining area, cooking facilities, running water, toilet, electricity, bring food and warm gear, it gets very cold at night. In about 45 mins you can walk up to the Edward Whymper refuge, a pink building at 5,000m, which is at the foot of the Thielman glacier. The same facilities are available here, with capacity for 40, in 5 separate rooms. Both refuges are managed by Alta Montaña and a US$0.50 fee is charged for a day visit. Overnight stays are US$10 but card carrying members of a club or Youth Hostel Association pay less. Take padlock for the small lockers under the bunks, the guards also have a locked room for valuables, and you can leave your gear with them. If there are only a few people, you will be given the key to your room. Beware of thieves if you leave anything in the refuge or even in your car at 4,800m.

● **Climbing routes** From the Whymper refuge to the summit the climb is 8-9 hrs and the descent about 4 hrs. The path from the hut to the glacier is marked but difficult to follow at midnight, so it's best to check it out the day before. The route on the glacier is easy to follow as it is marked with flags, though it can be tricky in cloud or mist. There are several crevasses on the route, so you need to rope up. There are three routes depending on your experience and ability. It is recommended to go with a guide and start at 2400 or 0100. There are avalanche problems on the entire mountain.

The Northwest Face (Pogyos Route)

● **Access** Take the Guaranda bus from Ambato along the new paved road or a truck along the spectacular old road (50 km) to the valley of Pogyos. At Pogyos (4,000m) there is a house with a metal roof where you can hire mules for US$4 each to carry your luggage. Beware of pilfering from your bags on the ascent. Walk about 3 hrs to the Fabián Zurita refuge (4,900m) which is uninhabitable. From the refuge to the summit is an 8-hr climb and 3-4 hrs descent. It's advisable to start at 2330-2400 at the latest. Take tents and water (obtainable at Pogyos, containers in Ambato). (We are grateful to Enrique Veloz Coronado, page 195, for much of this information.)

From Riobamba to the NW face, a trip can be made by jeep via San Juan and a road to Arenal, which is W of Pogyos. This road also permits a round-trip Riobamba-Chimborazo-Ambato.

EL ALTAR

Guides and horses to El Altar can be hired; the approximate cost per day in 1996 was US$60 for a guide, US$5 per mule, US$5 per porter. Because of damage done to the track by mudslides the route is hazardous and you would be unwise to do it alone. Consult the National Park Office about conditions, they are in radio contact with the Guardería at Releche.

● **Access** Travel to Penipe by bus from Baños or Riobamba/Ambato, then to Candelaria by truck, or by bus which passes between 1200 and 1400. Walk out of the village, cross the bridge and go up about 2 km to the park station, a green building with a National Park sign, where you pay your entrance fee of US$7. In Penipe ask for Ernesto Haro, who will take you to the station in his jeep (US$8 one way) and pick you up from there at a pre-arranged time.

● **Routes** The track to El Altar leads on up a steep hill past the Hacienda Releche (muddy in the wet season), but it is best to ask someone to point out the faint track which branches to the left about 30-40 mins after the Hacienda and leads up a hill to a ridge where it joins a clear track. This goes S first and then turns E up the valley of the Río Collanes. It is about 8 hrs to the crater which is surrounded by magnificent snow-capped peaks. It is possible to camp in the crater, but better still, about 20 mins before you turn into the broad U-shaped valley leading up to the crater there is a good-sized cave, the floor of which is lined with dry reeds; there is a fire ring at the entrance.

● **Accommodation** You can stay in the park station overnight, although it is not a *refugio*; US$0.50, beds, warm water, shower, cooking facilities and friendly keeper. It is not always open, so it's a good idea to ask in Riobamba beforehand at the Ministry of Tourism or the Sangay National Park office (see above **Useful addresses**). *Hacienda Releche* rents horses and is building rooms.

● **Technical climbs** For experienced ice climbers the **Ruta Obispo** offers grade 4 and 5 mixed ice and rock. Cima El Obispo is the highest and most southerly of Altar's 9 summits, at 5,315m. Take the turn-off at Cruz de Chania (on the Riobamba-Baños road) to Puelazo. Walk or hire mules (in Puelazo or Inguisay) to the Cañon del Tiaco Chico and beyond to Machay del Negro Paccha (cave). You can camp at the Italian base camp beyond. Another technical route is to **Cima El Canónigo** (5,260m), the northernmost of the summits. It is mixed ice and rock climbing, grade 4 and 5. Altar's 7 other summits are, from N to S: Fraile Grande (5,180m); Fraile Central (5,070m); Fraile Oriental (5,060m); Fraile Beato (5,050m); Tabernáculo (5,100m); Monja Chica (5,080m); and Monja Grande (5,160m).

SANGAY

For **Sangay** (see page 318), take a taxi to Alao and hire guides or carriers of food, tents, etc there; ask for Tom Gillespie. Remember you have to pay for and organize the food for your porters separately, otherwise you have to pay them a lot more. Make sure the fee covers the return journey as well. For information go to the Inefan offices (see **Useful addresses** above). **NB** Sangay is one of the most active volcanoes in the world and can be dangerous even on quiet days.

CAJABAMBA

A small, rather poor town. In 1534 the original Riobamba was founded on this site, but in 1797 a disastrous earthquake caused a large section of the hill on the N side of the town to collapse in a great landslide, which can still be seen. It killed several thousand of the original inhabitants of Riobamba and the town was moved almost 20 km NE to its present site. The new Riobamba has prospered, but Cajabamba has stagnated. A colourful, Colta Indian market on Sun is small but uncommercialized and interesting.

● **Transport & places to eat** The town is easily reached by bus from Riobamba, 25 mins, US$0.15. There are few restaurants out of town on the Panamericana towards Cuenca.

ROUTES A fairly good dirt road leaves the Pan-American Highway 6 km N of Cajabamba, to the W. It is one of the oldest of the coast-Sierra routes and links Cajabamba with Guaranda and Babahoyo. 5 km S of Cajabamba, a paved highway branches SW to Pallatanga, Bucay, Milagro and Guayaquil.

CAJABAMBA TO GUAMOTE

Road and rail skirt the shores of **Laguna de Colta**, just after the fertile Cajabamba valley. The lake and surroundings are very beautiful and just a short bus trip from Riobamba. At the edge of the village along the main road on the shore of Laguna de Colta is a small chapel, **La Balbanera**, dating from 1534, making it the oldest church in Ecuador, although it has been restored several times because of earthquakes.

GUAMOTE

28 km S of Cajabamba is **Guamote** (3,056m). It has an interesting and colourful market on Thur with lots of animals and few tourists, and some good half day walks in the area. Work on a road to Macas had been halted because of environmental concerns, however at the end of 1996 it resumed (see page 315). Sit at the front of the bus for a splendid view of the volcanoes.

● **Accommodation & places to eat**
F *Hostal Turista*, at the railway station; F *Ramada Inn*, Vela y Riobamba, T 916-242, new. There are some places to eat nr the station.

● **Transport** Lots of buses from Riobamba, especially on Thur.

Palmira is a windswept village S of Guamote, close to the highest point on the Riobamba-Guayaquil railway. Between here and Guamote the newly-fixed dirt road to Osogoche, 32 km, is well-signed. A wild, cold, beautiful area of lakeland, it has good hiking and camping. Arrange pack animals and guides with the local community leader; take food and camping equipment.

Tixan has a beautifully restored church and many old houses. It is the home of many workers in the nearby sulphur mines. The *finados* on 2 Nov are very colourful.

The Southern Sierra

THE SOUTHERN SIERRA, comprising the provinces of Cañar, Azuay and Loja, may lack the dramatic volcanic peaks of the central and northern highlands, but compensates with its own unique attractions. Within its bounds are Ecuador's prime Inca site, one of its most spectacular National Parks, and one of the continent's top 'Gringo' destinations, while Cuenca, the focal point of the region, boasts some of the country's finest colonial architecture. The Cuenca basin, in the northern part of the region, is a major artesanía centre, producing ceramics, baskets, gold and silver jewellery, textiles and its famous *paja toquilla*, a straw hat made principally in Cuenca itself, Gualaceo and Girón.

In addition to the cultural attractions mentioned above, its pleasant climate and magnificent mountain scenery make the Southern Sierra ideal walking country, while undisturbed *páramo* and cloud forest are home to many birds and other wildlife.

History

Owing to its geographical location, this was among the first parts of what is now Ecuador to come under the domination of the Inca empire, which had expanded N. The Incas settled the area around Cuenca and called it Tomebamba, which roughly translates as 'River Valley of Knives'. The name survives as one of region's rivers. 70 km N of Cuenca, in an area known as *Hatun Cañar*, the Incas built the ceremonial

Southern Sierra

centre of Ingapirca, which remains the most important Inca archaeological site in the country.

After the Spanish conquest, Cuenca became an important and populous regional centre in the crown colony governed from Quito. The *conquistadores* and the settlers who followed them, were interested in the working of precious metals, for which the region's indigenous peoples had earned a well-deserved reputation. Following independence from Spain, Cuenca was capital of one of three provinces that made up the new republic, the others being Quito and Guayaquil.

ALAUSI

84 km S of Riobamba (*Pop* 5,500), Alausí is the station where many passengers join the train for the amazing descent to Bucay, via the famous Alausí loop and *Nariz del Diablo* (Devil's Nose). The town sits at the foot of Cerro Gampala, on a terrace overlooking the deep Chanchan gorge. The atmosphere is laid-back and friendly. Don't expect too much in the way of exciting diversions, though the Sun market, in the plaza by the church, just up the hill from the station, brings *campesinos* from the outlying villages and is colourful and interesting. The town celebrates its *fiesta*, *San Pedro de Alausí*, in late June. The area enjoys a temperate climate and was once a popular holiday destination for Guayaquileños wishing to escape their hottest season.

- **Accommodation** E *Americano*, García Moreno 159, T 930-159, modern, private bath, hot water, friendly, rec as the best in town; E *Gampala*, 5 de Junio 122, T 930-138, with bath, good; E *Residencial Alausí*, Orozco y 5 de Junio, T 930-361, nr the station, with bath, F without, clean, comfortable, restaurant, one of the best in town; E *Residencial Tequendama*, inc breakfast, clean, friendly, shared bath, hot water, erratic electric shower, and eccentric owners, quieter rooms upstairs, rec; opp is F *Europa*, check that the hot water is free, safe parking in courtyard; F *Panamericano*, nr the bus stop on the main street, T 930-156, has several nice rooms with bath, also with shared bath, quieter at the rear of the hotel, constant hot water, clean, food cheap and good value; G *Residencial Guayaquil*, C Eloy Alfaro 149, beside the rail tracks and behind the station, very noisy, basic, not too clean, friendly.

- **Places to eat** Alausí is not the culinary centre of Ecuador, but a few places serve decent meals: *Momentos Bar*, on 5 de Junio, at the far end away from the train station, good food; *San Juan*, nr the station, on main street, owner speaks English, helpful staff, good breakfast and other food; *Danielito*, opp Tequendama, good cheap food, will cook vegetarian meals, friendly; *El Flamingo*, behind the *Tequendama*, good set meals.

- **Transport Trains** Train at 0900-0930 daily except Tues and Thur (not Mon or Wed in other direction), 7-9 hrs to Durán, US$12; 4 hrs to Bucay, US$10; to Huigra, US$8. The train is unreliable, T 930-126 to check if it is running; tickets go on sale from 0730. If the train to Durán is delayed and you may miss the last ferry to Guayaquil (2200), get out at Bucay and take a bus to Guayaquil bus station. From Riobamba to Alausí, US$8. **Buses** By road from **Riobamba**, bus 1½ hrs, 84 km, all paved, through a windswept plain, pine forest and, after Km 72, steep hills and valleys. To **Quito**, buses from Cuenca pass through from 0600 onwards, about 20 a day, 5½ hrs, US$3.10; often have to change in Riobamba. To **Cuenca**, 4 hrs, US$3.20; to **Ambato** hourly, 3 hrs, US$1.35. Coop Patria has a small office where you can buy bus tickets to Guayaquil, Cuenca, or Riobamba. Other cooperatives have no office, but their buses pass through town, some at the highway and others outside the *Hotel Panamericano*.

Ecuador's most important Inca ruin lies 5½ km E of Cañar, at 3,160m.

A 10-min walk away from the site is the **Cara del Inca**, or 'face of the Inca', an immense natural formation in the rock looking over the landscape. Nearby is the a throne cut into the rock, the **Sillón de Inga** (Inca's Chair) and the **Ingachugana**, a large rock with carved channels. This may have been used for offerings and divination with water, *chicha* and or the blood of various sacrificial animals.

Entry to the site is US$4, including entry to the site museum. Open Mon-Sat 0900-1700; they sell a guide book, US$0.80, and will look after your belongings. An audio-visual guide in English is available, and there are guides at the site, as well as some photogenic llamas.

On Fri there is an interesting Indian market at Ingapirca. There is a good co-operative craft shop next to the church.

Local information

- **Accommodation & places to eat**
C *Posada Ingapirca*, 500m from the site,

Ingapirca: temple, fortress or tambo?

Though famed as a classic Inca site, Ingapirca, which translates as "Stone Wall", had already been occupied by the native Cañari people for 500 years.

The Inca Huayna Capac took over the site from the conquered Cañaris when his empire expanded North into Ecuador in the third quarter of the 15th century. Ingapirca was strategically placed on the Royal Highway that ran from Cusco to Quito and soldiers were stationed there to keep the troublesome Cañaris under control.

The site, first described by the Frenchman Charles-Marie de la Condamine in 1748, shows typical imperial Cusco-style architecture, such as tightly fitting stonework and trapezoidal doorways, which can be seen on the 'Castillo' and 'Governor's House'. The central structure is an *usnu* platform probably used as a solar observatory.

There is some debate as to Ingapirca's precise function. Though commonly known as a fortress complex, this is contradicted by some archaeologists. From what remains of the site, it probably consisted of storehouses, baths and dwellings for soldiers and other staff, suggesting it could have been a Royal *Tambo*, or Inn.

It could also have been used as a sun temple, judging by the beautiful ellipse, modelled on the *Qoricancha* in Cusco. Furthermore, John Hemming has noted that the length is exactly three times the diameter of the semicircular ends, which may have been connected with worship of the sun in its morning, midday and afternoon positions.

Perhaps then Ingapirca was actually all three: a fortress, a *Tambo* and a sun temple.

T (07) 838-508, F 832-340, run by Grupo Santa Ana, 8 luxurious rooms with bath, inc American breakfast, excellent restaurant and well-stocked bar in a converted farm, lunch around US$8, good wine list, good service, superb views, warmly rec; **F Inti Huasi**, in the village, clean, nice rooms, friendly, quiet, hot water, good restaurant, rec, there is a *refugio* at the site, with benches, table and a fireplace, but there are no beds or electricity, and water is intermittent, ask at the museum and for permission to stay overnight, the *refugio* is inc in the entry fee, camping at the site is possible, there is a small café opp the museum and in the village there's a *chifa* serving large portions.

In El Tambo: the nearest town to Ingapirca is El Tambo (for information on how to get there see **Transport** below): **F Pensión Ingapirca** on the main street, nr the service station at the N end of town, a red and yellow house, hot water, not too clean but friendly, very noisy can leave luggage for a small fee; *Restaurant El Turista*, good and cheap food but unfriendly; also good is *Restaurant El Gran Poder* and *Restaurant Jesus del Gran Poder*, at the truck stop on the hill 400m N of town. There are

several others; judge the quality by their popularity with truck drivers. There is a small Sat food market.

● **Transport**

A direct bus from the Terminal Terrestre in Cuenca leaves at 0900 and 1000, returning at 1300 and 1500, 2 hrs, US$1.60, with Transportes Cañar. There are also organized excursions and taxi tours from Cuenca (US$45 from bus terminal). Alternatively take any Guayaquil, Riobamba or Quito bus and get off at El Tambo, 2 hrs, US$1.30. Coop Cañar runs hourly buses Cañar-El Tambo from 0600, US$0.50. There is a daily 0600 bus from Cañar direct to Ingapirca (slower, rougher road than from El Tambo). From the plaza on the Panamericana in El Tambo, morning trucks and Transportes Juhuay buses pass the railway and continue to the ruins. Taxi El Tambo-Ingapirca US$5; camionetas US$1.30, beware of overcharging, especially at plaza. Taxis can also be caught at the railway station. Last colectivos leave Ingapirca at 1800 for El Tambo. It is a beautiful 2½-hr walk from Ingapirca to Cañar. The start of the road is clearly signposted, along the main street; take water.

INCA TRAIL TO INGAPIRCA

The 3-day hike to Ingapirca on an Inca trail starts at **Achupallas**, 25 km from Alausí. The IGM map (Juncal sheet, 1:50,000) is very useful; also a compass. The name Ingapirca does not appear on the Cañar 1:50,000 sheet and you may have to ask directions near the end. There are persistent beggars, especially children, the length of the hike. If you want to give them something, take pencils or something useful. Good camping equipment is essential. Take all food and drink with you as there is nothing along the way. A shop in Achupallas sells basic foodstuffs.

The route

Note that the numbers below correspond to the numbers on the route map.

1. Head for the arch with a cross at the top of the village. Follow the trail to the left of the arch and you'll soon pass the cemetery on the right.

2. The track then deteriorates into a stony footpath and crosses the first footbridge. Continue on the trail which follows alongside the river.

3. About 45 mins out of the village cross the river again on another footbridge and follow the left bank of the Río Cadrul. Head for a pass ahead between Cerro Mapahuiña to the left (4,365m) and Cerro Callana Pucará to the right.

4. At the pass there is an awkward climb over what looks like a huge rockfall. This involves squeezing through a very tight gap, too narrow for you and your backpack at the same time.

5. Soon after you need to cross the river to meet the trail on the other side. In the dry season it can be jumped.

6. A few hundred metres further on the trail starts to leave the river and climb diagonally up the mountain. There is enough flat ground near the river to pitch a tent for the night, if you're not up to the steep climb.

7. The trail climbs to 4,000m before following the contours of the W side of the valley.

8. Several km later the trail reaches Laguna Los Tres Cruces. From the previous camping spot it is about 4-6 hrs. There are places to camp here.

9. Follow the trail beyond the lake and across the pass. Beyond the pass the trail is not very clear. It crosses some worn rocks and then climbs steeply to the top

The Inca trail to Ingapirca

To Alausí — Achupallas

0   3
km

N

Cerro Callana Pucará

Cerro Mapahuiña

R Cadrul

Laguna las Tres Cruces

Quillalonna

Laguna Sansahuín

O Espíndola

Laguna Culebrillas

Paredones

Ingapirca Ruins

Ingapirca Village

R Cañar

Source: Bradt *Climbing and hiking in Ecuador*

34

Alpacas

of the left hand ridge. The views from here are stupendous and make the previous day's hard walking suddenly seem worthwhile.

10. Walk along the top of the ridge to the peak of Quilloloma. The trail becomes clear again and then descends sharply to the lush, marshy valley floor below. You can see the vestiges of the old Inca road running in a straight line across the valley floor to the remains of the foundations of an Inca bridge.

11. Follow the Inca road to the river which you have to cross. The best place is a little upstream from the bridge, where it may be narrow enough to jump.

12. There is a clear trail on the left hand side of the Quebrada Espíndola which leads past the southern shores of Laguna Culebrillas and to a ruined house.

13. It is a comfortable day's hike from Laguna Los Tres Cruces to the ruined house. This is a good place to camp but don't leave your rubbish to accumulate with the rest, especially as part of the house is still, surprisingly, inhabited. The name of the ruined house is Paredones de Culebrillas (or simply Paredones).

14. From the ruined house to the ruins of Ingapirca is a steady 5-6 hrs, leaving you enough time to explore the ruins and

then find a room for the night. Head SW on the Inca road, which is at its full width of about 6-7m. After a short while the trail turns S and continues across the marshy ground, through a landscape strewn with giant boulders.

15. After 2-3 hrs the trail fades out again. Walk in a southerly direction, keeping to the right and as high as possible above the river valley. Eventually you should see signs of cultivation and habitation.

16. Pick up the trail (not the Inca road) and follow it past fields and houses to a road which winds its way up to the ruins of Ingapirca.

Thanks to Rob Rachowiecki and Betsy Wagenhauser's *Climbing and Hiking in Ecuador* for the above route description (with a few amendments to allow for the Editor's physical condition).

● **Transport** A truck leaves Alausí almost every day, between 0900-1200 from outside *Residencia Tequendama*, US$0.40 to Achupallas. The trip takes a couple of hours and is spectacular in its own right.

SOUTH TO CUENCA

ROUTES The Pan-American Highway and railway S of Sibambe to Cuenca run through mountainous country and high above the valleys of the W-bound rivers.

The railway was damaged by floods in 1993 and the line was officially closed in Mar 1995. The countryside is poor, dry, chilly and wind-swept, and the Indians withdrawn and wrapped-up. Near Zhud and Cañar, more Indians, dressed in black, are seen. At Zhud a paved road runs to Cochancay and La Troncal in the coastal lowlands, from where there are paved roads to Guayaquil and Machala. Towards Cuenca the road loses height and the land is more intensively farmed. There are excellent roads linking Quito-Guayaquil and Guayaquil-Cuenca, which meet at El Triunfo on the coastal plain.

CHUNCHI

At 2,300m, 37 km S of Alausí along the Pan-American Highway and one stop from Sibambe on the line to Cuenca, it is a friendly village with a Sun market. On Tues, Thur, Fri, Sat or Sun, you can hike down the Huigra road to Chanchan and catch the afternoon train back up to Alausí via The Devil's Nose.

● **Accommodation & places to eat** F *Residencial Patricia* just off the main plaza, shared bath, basic, clean, beware of overcharging; also **G** *Residencial Carmita*, clean, basic, hot water, nr the station. There are many restaurants along the highway, better than those in Alausí.

● **Transport** Buses from the plaza, several daily, to Riobamba.

CAÑAR

(*Pop* approx 20,000; province 189,347) 67 km N of Cuenca, and 36 km N of Azogues, Cañar is very much the indigenous capital of the province. It's a lovely, friendly colonial town set in a good area for walking. The town is famous for double-faced weaving, although it is now difficult to find. The jail (Centro de Rehabilitación Social) is one place to find the backstrap weavings that the prisoners sell through the bars to supplement their income and pay for food.

You'll also find the **Nucanchi Huasi** (Our House), the Cañar Indian centre. It provides a home for students living in town during the week and is a place for conferences and meetings as well as being a discount store for bulk provisions and other services. The centre was badly damaged by fire during the strikes of 1994.

The market on Sun is very colourful and it is still relatively easy to find the Cañar hats for sale in several of the small stores in town. The rock work at the base of the church is supposed to be Inca or Cañari, but it has been faced and worked with cement and is difficult to see.

● **Accommodation** It's a better idea to stay here, rather than El Tambo, if possible. **F** *Residencial Mónica*, main plaza, T 235-486, often full, clean, shared bath, friendly, hot water, laundry facilities, owner's daughter offers tour service to Ingapirca, 2 hrs, US$2; **F** *Residencial Cañar*, T 235-682, small, friendly. Also *Ingapirca*, T 235-201.

● **Places to eat** *Los Maderos Restaurant*, nr the centre, friendly; *Chifa Florida*, on plaza, good and cheap food.

● **Transport** Buses every 30 mins to the Terminal Terrestre in Cuenca, US$0.80, 2 hrs; also to Quito and El Tambo (7 km).

Between Cañar and Azogues is **Biblián** with a sanctuary, La Virgen del Rocío, built into the rocks above the village. It's a pleasant walk up with impressive views of the river valley and surrounding countryside. 1 hr W of Azogues is Mount Cojitambo, which is good for rock climbing.

AZOGUES

(*Pop* 21,060) The administrative capital of the province, Azogues is a large, busy city, 31 km N of Cuenca and a centre of the panama hat industry. Hats are rarely for sale, even at the Sat morning market, but the *sombrerías* are very happy to show visitors their trade; eg *La Sin Ribal*, C Luis Cordero y 3 de Noviembre, or *Cahuzhun*, near the plaza, highly rec. The market is colourful and beautifully situated on the hill from the Panamericana to the city's huge church and convent San Francisco de la Virgen de las Nubes. Just off the main plaza beside the church is a

Panama Hat

small *artesanía* shop run by the nuns which sells some local knitting, embroidery and other handicrafts. Some of the older buildings around the plaza still have the lovely traditional colonial painted ceilings over the pavements.

- **Accommodation & transport E** *Charles 1*, Solano y Rivera, nr plaza, T 241-364, clean, simple; a new *Hotel Charles* is **No 2**, Serrano y Abad, T 241-883, 1 block E of the plaza, **E** pp with bath; *Chicago*, 3 de Noviembre y 24 de Mayo, T 241-040; **F** *Tropical*, Serrano y Sucre. 45 mins by bus to Cuenca.

CUENCA

Cuenca (*Pop* officially 194,981, more like 250,000; *Alt* 2,530m; *Phone code* 07), is capital of the province of Azuay and the third largest city in Ecuador. The city has preserved much of its colonial air, with many of its old buildings constructed of the marble quarried nearby and recently renovated. Most Ecuadoreans consider this their finest city and few would disagree. Its cobblestone streets, flowering plazas and whitewashed buildings with old wooden doors and ironwork balconies make it a pleasure to explore on foot.

As well as being the economic centre of the Southern Sierra, Cuenca is also an intellectual centre with a long tradition as the birthplace of notable artists, writers, poets and philosophers, earning it the title 'Athens of Ecuador'.

The city is bounded by the Río Machangara to the N. The Río Tomebamba separates the colonial heart from the stadium, universities and newer residential areas to the S. El Cajas recreational area can be seen to the W of the city. The climate is spring-like, but the nights are chilly.

History
Cuenca was originally a Cañari settlement, dating from AD 500 to around 1480, called Guapondeleg, which roughly translates as 'an area as large as heaven'. The suffix 'deleg' is still found in several local place names, a survival of the now extinct Cañari language. The city was founded by the Spaniard Gil Ramírez Davalos in 1557 on the site of the Inca settlement of Tomebamba and named Santa Ana de los Cuatro Ríos de Cuenca. French Jesuits came to Ecuador in the 1880s and architecturally there is still evidence of their presence, with many domes and mansard roofs.

Places of interest
On the main plaza, **Parque Abdón Calderón**, are both the Old Cathedral, also known as **El Sagrario**, begun in 1557 when modern Cuenca was founded, and the immense 'New' **Catedral de la Inmaculada**. The latter was started in 1885 and contains a famous crowned image of the Virgin. It was the work of the German architect Padre Johannes Baptista Stiehle, who also designed many other buildings in the Cuenca area. It was planned to be the largest cathedral in South America but the architect made some miscalculations with the foundations and the final domes on the front towers couldn't be built for fear that the whole thing would come down. Modern stained glass, a beautiful altar and an exceptional play of light and shade inside the cathedral make it worth a visit. The Sun evening worship is recommended.

El Sagrario was built on the foundations of an Inca structure and some of the Inca blocks are still visible facing the plaza. The French Geodesic Mission of

1736-1744 came to Ecuador to measure the Equator, and probably also to see what the Spanish were up to. They used El Sagrario as one of the fixed points for their measurements. The interior of the church was recently renovated.

Other churches which deserve a visit are **San Blas**, **San Francisco**, **El Cenáculo**, and **Santo Domingo**. Many churches are open at irregular hours only and for services, because of increasing problems with theft. The church of **El Carmen de la Asunción** is close to the SW corner of La Inmaculada and has a flower market in the tiny **Plazoleta El Carmen** in front. The church is open early in the morning and mid-afternoon, but the attached cloister of Carmen Alto is closed as the nuns inside live in total isolation.

South of city on Av Fray Vicente Solano, beyond the football stadium, is **Turi church and mirador**, a 40-min walk or take a bus. It's well worth a visit for the great views and a tiled panorama explains what you see. There is an orphanage attached to the church. There are good walks along attractive country lanes further S.

There is a colourful daily market in **Plaza Cívica** where pottery, clothes, guinea pigs and local produce, especially baskets, are sold. Thur is the busiest.

The suburb of **San Joaquín**, out W near the tennis club, is famous for its basketwork. There are many houses where you can see the different types of baskets being made. Some of the styles, especially the ones with a waist, are made only in the Cuenca and Azogues areas.

Museums

The **Banco Central 'Pumapungo'** museum, C Larga y Huayna Capac, on the edge of town is at the Tomebamba site where excavations are continuing. Open Sat 0900-1200, Tues-Fri 0900-1800, US$1.50; entrance is on the far left of the building. It contains all the pottery, bones, statues etc found at the site.

Padre Crespi used these artefacts to support his theory that the Phoenicians reached Cuenca via the Amazon. He died in June 1982 – his statue stands in Plaza María Auxiliadora. Although the Ingapirca ruins are more spectacular, it is believed that Tomebamba was the principal Inca administrative centre in Ecuador. There are book and music libraries and free cultural videos and music events. In the new Banco Central building (beside the old) there are museums of local and religious art, an ethnographical museum, and space for changing exhibitions.

About 300m from the Pumapungo site, at Larga 287, there are excavations at the Todos Los Santos site, which reveal traces of Inca and Cañari civilizations and show how the Spanish reused the stonework. The site is open Mon-Fri, 0800-1600.

The **Instituto Azuayo de Folklore**, is at Escalinata 303 y Larga, which is the extension of Hermano Miguel (the name change is rarely shown on maps), open Mon-Fri 0800-1200, 1400-1800. It has an exhibition of popular art, incorporating CIDAP (Centro Interamericano de Desarollo de Artes Populares), good exhibits, library, it also supports research and promotes sales for artesan workers, the craft shop is recommended, they offer good information and are helpful.

Museo de las Culturas Aborígenes, Av 10 de Agosto 4-70, between F Moscoso y J M Sánchez, T 811-706, a good private collection of precolumbian archaeology, in the house of Dr J Cordero López. There are guided tours in English, Spanish and French, a worthwhile visit, entry US$2, open Mon-Fri 0900-1230, 1530-1830, Sat 0900-1230, but phone in advance (taxi from centre US$1.50).

Museo del Monasterio de las Conceptas, Hermano Miguel 6-33 between Pdte Córdova and Juan Jaramillo, T 830-625, well-displayed collection of

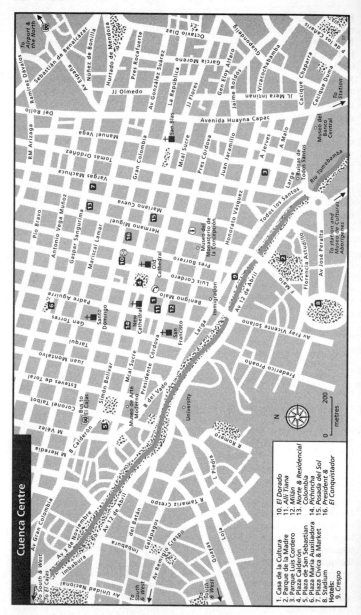

Cuenca Centre

1. Casa de la Cultura
2. Parque de la Madre
3. Parque Luis Cordero
4. Plaza Calderón
5. Plaza de San Sebastian
6. Plaza Maria Auxiliadora
7. Plaza Cívica & Market
8. Stadium

Hotels:
9. Crespo
10. El Dorado
11. Alli Tiana
12. Milán
13. Norte & Residencial Colombia
14. Pichincha
15. Posada del Sol
16. President & El Conquistador

religious and folk art, extensive collection of lithographs by Guayasamín housed in a cloistered convent founded in 1599. Open Tues-Fri 0900-1600, Sat 0900-1230, entrance US$2.

Modern Art Museum at Calles Sucre y Talbot, on the Plaza San Sebastián, often has shows of artists from around the world, which is worth seeing. There's a small museum, art gallery and bookshop in the **Casa de la Cultura**, Luis Cordero y Sucre (second floor). Look out for the wall of niches in the courtyard, each niche contains a statue of a saint. A lovely, restored colonial house is the **Casa Azul** on Gran Colombia y Pedro Aguirre, housing some small shops, restaurant and a little museum, cultural visits can also be arranged.

The **Casa de los Canónigos**, C Luis Cordero 888 opposite Parque Calderón, houses the **Galería del Portal**, T 833-492, original Latin American works of art for exhibition and sale. **Museo Remigio Crespo Toral Municipo**, C Larga 7-27 y Pres Borreo, open Mon-Fri 0930-1300 and 1500-1800, various collections housed in a beautifully-restored colonial mansion, free admission, nice café in basement.

Excursions

There are sulphur baths at **Baños**, with a domed, blue church in a delightful landscape, 5 km SW of Cuenca. These are the hottest commercial baths in Ecuador, so hot that there are steam baths at three of the complexes. Water temperatures at the source are measured at 76°C. There are many pools and four complexes altogether. Above *Hostería Durán* are two separate complexes of warm baths, *Marchan* and *Rodas*: the lower one is better, US$0.80 for private bathroom, US$0.40 for swimming pool; the upper one also costs US$0.40, neither is very clean. They are very crowded at weekends. The country lanes above the village offer some pleasant walks. (See also **Hot Springs**, page 41.)

- **Accommodation** At the baths is **B** *Hostería Durán*, Km 8 Vía Baños, T 892-485, F 892-488, with a restaurant, its own well-maintained, very clean pools, US$1.60 for non-residents, also tennis courts, steam bath US$3, camping is allowed. There are also four residencias, all **F**: *Residencial Baños*, *Rincón de Baños*, *Hostal Baños* and *Pensión Baños*.

- **Transport** Buses marked Baños go to and from Cuenca every 5-10 mins, 0600-2330, US$0.15; buses turn around at the airport, pass the front of the Terminal Terrestre, cross the city on Vega Muñoz and Cueva, then down Todos los Santos to the river, along 12 de Abril and onto Av Loja to the end where it joins Av de Las Américas. Taxis cost US$2.40, or walk 1½ hrs.

Local festivals

On the Sat before Christmas day there is an outstanding parade: **Pase del Niño Viajero**, probably the largest and finest Christmas parade in all Ecuador. Children and adults from all the *barrios* and surrounding villages decorate donkeys, horses, cars and trucks with symbols of abundance. Little children in colourful Indian costumes or dressed up as Biblical figures ride through the streets accompanied by Indian musicians. The parade starts at about 0800 at San Sebastián, proceeds along C Simón Bolívar, past the Plaza Calderón at about 1030 and ends at San Blas.

At New Year's Eve, as elsewhere in Ecuador, the festivities include the parading and burning at midnight of effigies called **Años Viejos** (some political, some fictional) which symbolize the old year. The festivities seem to go on until Lent and there are several smaller Pase del Niño parades between Christmas and Carnival.

On 6 Jan is the **Festival de Los Inocentes**, and 10-13 April is the **Foundation of Cuenca**. On **Good Friday** there is a fine procession through the town and up to the Mirador Turi. Cuenca hosts an internationally famous art competition every 2 years, which begins in April or May. Exhibitions occupy museums and galleries around the city for about 4 months. The whole event is coordinated by the Museo de Arte Moderno.

Septenario, the religious festival of Corpus Christi in June, lasts a week. On Plaza Calderón a decorated tower with fireworks attached, known as the 'vaca loca' or mad cow, is burnt every night after a mass and hundreds of hot air paper balloons are released. A spectacular sight which is not to be missed. There are also dozens of dessert sellers and games in the streets.

On 3 Nov is **Independence of Cuenca,** with street theatre, art exhibitions and night-time dances all over the city. One such venue is the **Puente Rota,** E of Escalinata.

Local information

Price guide

L1	over US$200	**L2**	US$151-200
L3	US$101-150	**A1**	US$81-100
A2	US$61-80	**A3**	US$46-60
B	US$31-45	**C**	US$21-30
D	US$12-20	**E**	US$7-11
F	US$4-6	**G**	up to US$3

● **Accommodation**

L3 *Oro Verde*, Ordóñez Lasso, on the road to Cajas, on a lake in the outskirts of town, T 831-200, F 832-849, completely refurbished, small pool, restaurant, cable TV.

A2 *El Dorado*, Gran Colombia 787 y Luis Cordero, T 831-390, F 831-663, nightclub, hot water in the mornings only, good restaurant, good view.

B *Crespo*, C Larga 793, T 842-571, F 839-473, friendly and comfortable, some lovely rooms, others dark or with no windows, restaurant overlooking river, a lovely building; **B** *Cuenca*, Borrero 10-69 y Gran Colombia, T 833-711, F 833-819, tourist and commercial area, bar, inc breakfast, restaurant, TV, modern, comfortable; **B** *El Conquistador*, Gran Colombia 665, T 831-788, F 831-291, inc breakfast, discounts for Youth Hostel members, disco, avoid back rooms Fri and Sat, very clean, good, friendly, good food and wine; **B** *Inca Real*, Torres 8-40 y Sucre, T 823-636, central, all rooms on courtyards, friendly, cafetería; **B** *Pinar del Lago*, next door to Oro

Verde, new in 1996, has received good reports; **B** *Prado Inn*, Presidente Rocafuerte 3-45 y Av Huayna Cápac, T 807-164, F 804-812, warm and comfortable rooms with private bathroom, TV, clean, friendly, inc breakfast, located in the colonial area; **B** *Presidente*, Gran Colombia 659, T 831-979, F 824-704, good value, comfortable, convenient, good restaurant.

C *Atahualpa*, Sucre 3-50 y Tomás Ordóñez, T 826-906/831-841, F 842-345, rec; **C** *Catedral*, Padre Aguirre 8-17 y Sucre, T 823-204, clean, cheerful, spacious, modern, but not very warm, English-speaking manager, safe, laundry service, good food, coffee shop opens 0700; **C** *Cuenca*, Borrero 1069 y Gran Colombia, T 833-711, new, clean, attractive; **C** *Internacional*, Benigno Malo 1015 y Gran Colombia, T 831-348, vaulted ceilings, a/c, TV, comfortable beds, hot water all day, pleasant but expensive restaurant, good bar, rec; **C** *Italia*, Av España y Av Huayna Capac, breakfast inc, very clean; **C** *La Orquídea*, Borrero 931 y Bolívar, T 824-511, new, pretty patio; **C** *Posada del Sol*, Bolívar 5-03 y Mariano Cueva, T 838-695, F 838-995, refurbished colonial building, owner Juan Diego also runs horse and bike treks into El Cajas, rec.

D *Alli-Tiana*, Córdova y Padre Aguirre, T 831-844, clean, inc breakfast; **D** *Cabañas Yanuncay*, 10-mins' drive from centre, C Cantón Gualaceo 21-49, between Av Loja y Las Américas (Yanuncay), T 883-716, rustic cabins with bath for 2-4 people, or room with bath, inc breakfast and dinner, fireplace in house, solarium, library, sauna, organic gardens, good home-cooked meals, run by Beto and Teresa Chico, Spanish and English spoken, helpful, friendly, transport to airport/bus terminal; rec; **D** *Chordeleg*, Gen Torres y Gran Colombia, T 824-611, charming, clean; **D** *Colonial*, Gran Colombia 1013 y Padre Aguirre, T 814-644; **D** *El Quijote*, H Miguel 958 y Gran Colombia, T 843-197, restored colonial house; **D** *Gran*, Torres 9-70 y Bolívar, T 831-934, with bath, clean, hot water, colour TV, phone, inc American breakfast, laundry service, good restaurant, beautiful patio, popular meeting place, good value, rec; **D** *Hostal Caribe Inn*, Gran Colombia 10-51 y Padre Aguirre, T/F 835-175, pleasant, comfortable, TV, phone, restaurant; **D** *Hostal Macondo*, Tarqui 11-64 y Lamar, T 840-697, restored colonial house, Youth Hostel, apartment available, mostly shared bathrooms, hot water, laundry, friendly, kitchen facilities, excellent breakfast, US run, Spanish classes, "a real treat", highly rec; **D** *Hostería El Molino*, Km 7.5 on road Azogues-Cuenca, T 800-150, pleasant position between road and river, Spanish run, typical Ecuadorean dishes, pool, rustic style, rec, advisable to book; **D** *Las Américas*, Mariano Cueva 13-59, T 831-160/835-753, clean, TV, ask for room with windows, friendly, parking, restaurant; **D** *Tomebamba*, Bolívar, between Torres and Tarqui, T 823-797, quiet, clean, hot water, laundry service, good breakfast.

E *El Cafecito*, Hermano Vásquez 7-36 y Luis Cordero, T 827-341, colonial house, discount for longer stay, good breakfast in restaurant with charming patio, rec; **E** *Hostal Paredes*, Luis Cordero 11-29 y Lamar, T 835-674, F 834-910, beautifully-refurbished colonial mansion, with bath, international phone and fax, laundry, luggage stored, money exchange, garage, highly rec; **E** *Milán*, Pres Córdova 989 y Padre Aguirre, T 831-104, with bath, cheaper without, rooms with balconies, good view over market, rooms variable but clean, reliable for storing luggage, laundry facilities, often full, best to reserve; **E** *Norte*, Mariano Cueva 11-63 y Sangurima, T 827-881, renovated, large rooms, clean, safe, hot showers, comfortable, not a nice area after dark, motorcycle parking, good restaurant downstairs, friendly, rec; **E** *Pichincha*, Gral Torres y Bolívar, T 823-868, spacious, helpful, clean, friendly, laundry facilities, hot water, luggage stored; **E** *Residencial Niza*, Mcal Lamar 41-51, T 823-284/838-005, clean, helpful; **E** *Residencial París*, Grl Torres 10-48, T 842-656, private bath, intermittent hot water, inc breakfast, clean, friendly, rec.

F *Residencial Astoria*, El Chorro 222 y Gil Ramírez Dávalos, T 809-252, cheaper without bath; **F** *Residencial Colombia*, Mariano Cueva 11-61, T 827-851, clean, basic, large rooms, noisy, friendly, helpful.

Near the bus terminal are: **D** *Hurtado de Mendoza*, Sangurima y Huayna Cápac, T 843-611, with bath, good, restaurant, parking; **D** *Residencial España*, Sangurima 1-17, T 831-351, F 831-291, with bath and TV, **E** without bath, clean, hot water, also communal showers and toilets, good restaurant, friendly, front upstairs rooms are best; **D** *Residencial Tito*, Sangurima 149, T 829-734, F 843-577, shared bath, safe, clean, hot water, restaurant very good value; **E** *Los Alamos*, Madrid y Av España, T 835-771, E without bath, TV, clean, will store luggage, opp a noisy

disco; **E** *Samay*, Tomás Ordóñez y Sangurima, T 831-119, with bath, cheaper without, clean, can be noisy, parking.

Furnished apartments are available: *El Jardín*, Av Pumapungo y Viracochabamba, cooking facilities and parking, T 804-103, or write to Casilla 298; **C** *Apartamentos Otorongo*, Av 12 de Abril y Guayas, T 811-184, 10-15-mins' walk from centre, fully-furnished flats for 4 with kitchenette, TV, phone, cleaning service inc, very friendly owners, discount for longer stay.

● **Places to eat**
International: *El Jardín*, Presidente Córdova 7-23, lovely, good food, closed Sun-Mon, very expensive; *El Puente*, Remigio Crespo 1-20 y Av Solano, very good international food, bar, nice atmosphere; *Villa Rosa*, Gran Colombia 12-22 y Tarqui, very elegant, excellent food, international and lcoal dishes; *Molinos de Ratan*, 12 de Abril y Puente El Vado, good setting by river, good food, expensive; *Rancho Chileno*, Av España, next to airport, good steak and seafood, slow service, pricey; *El Che Pibe*, Av Remigio Crespo 2-59, parrillada argentina, good, excellent service, also chicken, pizza, pasta, salads etc, open till late, expensive, 20% tax and service; also at Gran Colombia, 8-33 y Cordero, excellent pizzas, pleasant courtyard, friendly; *Fuente del Sabor*, Cueva 11-71, next to Hotel Norte, parrillada, also fish, chicken, ceviche, pasta, good, moderate prices, popular with market traders; *Atún*, Gran Colombia 8-80, pizzas and trout, popular; *La Napolitana*, C Solano nr Crespo, S of the river, nice atmosphere, good food; *NY Pizza*, Borrero 838 y Sucre, very good; *Los Pibes*, Gran Colombia 776 y Cordero, opp Hotel El Dorado, good pizzas and lasagne, moderately priced.

Los Capulíes, Córdova y Borrero, bar-restaurant, excellent Ecuadorean food, friendly, lovely setting, reasonable prices, Andean live music Thur-Sat 2030, reservations rec at the weekend, T 832-339; *Las Tres Caravelas*, part of hotel *El Conquistador*, good value Ecuadorean food, Andean live music at weekends; *Casa Grande*, San Joaquín-La Cruz Verde, local dishes, in picturesque San Joaquín district where flowers and vegetables are grown, T 839-992; *Los Sauces*, Bolívar 6-17, original dishes, reasonable prices; *Rumipamba*, Parque Calderón y Los Capulíes; *D'Bernardo*, Antonio Borrero 9-68 y Gran Colombia, opp the Post Office, T 829-967, breakfast, dinner, quiet music, coffee, excellent, open daily 0800-2300; *El Tequila*, Gran Colombia 20-59, good local food and more, good value and service; *El Túnel*, Gral Torres 8-60, T 823-109, reasonably priced, quick service, romantic atmosphere, good, cheap lunch menu; *Salad Bar*, Sucre y M Cueva, popular for lunch. There are two branches of *Pío Pío*, at the bus terminal and at Gran Colombia y Unidad Nacional, chicken, hamburgers, etc, open Sun.

The Zona Rosa, at the junction of Av Unidad Nacional and Gran Colombia has a variety of *pizzerías, heladerías*, burger and sandwich bars, steak houses, bars and discos, eg *Heladería Monte Bianco* y *Bar-Café Cambá* and a branch of *Balcón Quiteño*, with outdoor seating. The area is very popular with young people.

Vegetarian: *El Paraíso*, Hermano Vásquez 6-46, open Mon-Sat 0800-1600, good breakfast; *Govinda*, Aguirre 8-15, behind the Cathedral, limited menu; *Mañjaris*, Hermano Vázquez 6-46, English spoken, good, cheap; *Vegetariano Madre Tierra*, Gran Colombia 14-35, entre Talbot y Esteves de Toral, cheap, "imaginative cooking".

Oriental: *Chifa Pack How*, Presidente Córdova 772 y Cordero, not cheap, rec; *Chifa Asia*, Cueva 11 s/n, entre 34 y 68, medium price, large portions, rec; *La Gran Muralla*, Juan Jaramillo 8-38 y Luis Cordero; *Sol Oriental*, Gran Colombia y Vega, cheap, large portions.

Weekends and holidays and by arrangement: *Hacienda Sustag*, KM 17 via Joaquín-Soldados, T 830-834, F 832-340, located in the countryside, a farm with beautiful landscapes, camping and picnic area, delicious Ecuadorean food, reasonable; *Dos Chorreras*, via Cajas north road, excellent for fresh trout.

Snackbars and cafés: *Raymipampa*, Benigno Malo 8-59, on Plaza Calderón, open daily, very popular, especially at lunchtime, local dishes, good ceviche, crepes, good ice-cream, clean, reasonably priced, excellent value; *Wunderbar*, Hermano Miguel y C Larga, behind the Instituto Azuayo de Folklore, German-run, good atmosphere, good food and coffee, also vegetarian, expensive, book exchange, German magazines; *Café Chordeleg*, Gran Colombia 7-87, open 24 hrs, excellent breakfast for US$3.50-5, inc tax and service; *Pity's*, for sandwiches, hamburgers, rec, two branches, Av Remigio Crespo Toral y Alfonso Borrero, and Ordóñez Lazo y Circun-

valación; *Café Italia*, Pres Córdova 8-35, entre Luis Cordero y Benigno Malo, excellent cheap snacks; *Helados Honey*, Mcal Lamar 4-21, clean, rec milkshakes; *Café Capuchino*, Bolívar y Aguirre, open 0930, good hamburgers, real coffee and liqueur coffees; *Monte Bianco*, Bolívar 2-80 y Ordóñez, nr San Blas church, good cakes, ice cream, open Sun; *Café Austria*, Benigno Malo 5-99, good cakes, pies, sandwiches, coffee, fruit, ice cream, yoghurt, open Sun; *Heladería Holanda*, Benigno Malo 9-51, open 0930, yoghurt for breakfast, ice cream, fruit salads, great toilets; *MiPan*, Pres Córdova 824 between Cordero y Malo (also Bolívar y Aguirre), opens 0730, excellent bread, cakes, tarts, doughnuts, tea, coffee and chocolate.

● **Bars**

Picadilly Pub, Borrero 7-46 y Pres Córdova, upmarket, clean, relaxing; *Años 60*, Bolívar 5-69, bar and disco; *Saxon*, Av Ordóñez Lazo y Unidad Nacional (Zona Rosa), bar/disco; *La Morada del Cantor*, Av Ordóñez Lazo, 500m from *Hotel La Laguna*, T 837-197, bar, restaurant and *peña* with Latin American music, excellent atmosphere; *Eclipse Bar*, Bolívar 952 y P Aguirre, new, popular; *Chaos*, H Vásquez y H Miguel, popular; *UBR Bar*, Solano y Tres Puentes, also popular.

● **Airline offices**

TAME, Gran Colombia 6-61 y Hermano Miguel, in passage, T 827-609; **SAN**, Bolívar 5-33 y M Cueva, T 823-403; **Saeta**, Sucre 770 y Luis Cordero, T 831-548; **Aerogal**, L Cordero y Sangurima.

● **Banks & money changers**

Citibank, Gran Colombia 749, charges commission, no cheques; **Filanbanco**, several branches, no commission, quick service; **Banco del Pacífico**, Benigno Malo 9-75, advances money on Mastercard, good rates for TCs; **Banco del Austro**, Sucre y Borrero, T 842-492, changes cash and Citicorp TCs, cash on Visa on Sat; **Banco La Previsora** (main branch only) Gran Colombia y Benigno Malo, T 831-444, gives cash dollars on Visa; **Banco de Guayaquil**, Sucre entre Hermano Miguel y Borrero, also gives cash on Visa and changes TCs of all brands; **Banco del Pichincha**, Bolívar 9-74 y B Malo T 831-544, changes cash and TCs of all brands; **Granturs**, M Cueva y Gran Colombia, good rates, quick, usually open Sat afternoon; **Cambidex**, Luis Cordero 9-77, T 835-755, helpful, good rates; **Cambistral**,

Sucre 664 y Cordero, T 822-213, changes European currencies, TCs as well as cash; **Cambiosur**, Borrero 8-20 y Sucre, good rates for cheques and cash, no commission, fast, rec; **Cambiazuay**, Antonio Borrero 838 y Bolívar, T 823-536, cash and TCs; **Vaz Cambios**, Gran Colombia 7-98 y Cordero, T 833-434, open Sat morning, efficient. *Casas de Cambio* give the best rates but they are variable. No Peruvian currency is available.

● **Embassies & consulates**

Colombian Consulate, Cordero 9-55; **British Honorary Consul**, Sr Teodoro Jerves, Pasaje San Alfonso (same block as Iglesia San Alfonso), T 831-996; **Alliance Française**, Tadeo Torres 1-92, open Mon-Fri, 0830-1230, 1430-1830.

● **Entertainment**

Cinemas: there are four cinemas, the one opp the Casa de la Cultura shows interesting films at 1430 y 2100. Films also at the Casa de la Cultura itself, evenings. *Teatro Cuenca*, P Aguirre 10-50, also shows films.

Discos: at Hotels *Conquistador* and *Alli-Tiana*, and *Las Galaxias*, Núñez de Bonilla 239. *Fernández*, nr *Capulíes* restaurant, good disco music, reasonable dance floor, couples. See also **Bars** above.

● **Hospitals & medical services**

Health: *Clínica Santa Inés*, Dr Jaime Moreno Aguilar speaks English, Toral, T 817-888; *Clínica Los Andes*, Mariano Cueva 14-68 y Pío Bravo T 842-942/832-488, excellent care, clean, 24-hr service. *Farmacia Botica Internacional*, Gran Colombia 7-20 y Borrero, experienced staff, wide selection.

● **Language courses**

Centro de Estudios Interamericanos, Gran Colombia 11-02 y Gral Torres, Edif Assoc de Empleados, Casilla 597, T 839-003, F 833-593, classes in Spanish and Quechua, rec, accommodation, *Hostal Macondo* attached; *Centro Abraham Lincoln*, Borrero y Vásquez, T 830-373, small Spanish language section; *Lenguas y Culturas*, Galápagos 2-37 y Guayas, T 817-552; *Nexus Lenguas y Culturas*, Av 12 de Abril 2-75 y Paucarbamba, T 884-016, F 814-575, also teach English and German, short-term basis family stays, well-run, rec.

● **Laundry**

La Química, Borrero 734 y Córdova, same day service, expensive; *Lavamás*, Av España y Benalcázar, nr the Terminal Terrestre.

● **Post & telecommunications**

Post Office: on corner of Calles Gran Colombia and Borrero, helpful. **Emetel**: on Benigno Malo between Córdova and Sucre, deposit required, twice the price of the call, buy long distance *fichas* before contacting the international operator, collect calls.

● **Security**

There is a man who asks female travellers to write letters for him to non-existent friends, and then invites them out. He claims also to be a businessman planning to travel abroad, who asks women to answer questions and then go with him to meet his 'sister', or a 'woman friend', by way of thanks. Furthermore, he claims to be a homosexual businessman with good links abroad and invites couples to share a glass of wine with him on his 'birthday'. He is a known rapist and dangerous, but seems to have close relations with the police. Avoid him. **NB** Also take care around the market at night.

● **Shopping**

The Cuenca basin is noted for its *artesanía*. Good souvenirs are carvings, leather, basketwork, painted wood, onyx, woven stuffs (cheapest in Ecuador), embroidered shirts, etc. There are many craftware shops along Gran Colombia, in *El Dorado* hotel (good quality), and on Benigno Malo.

Arte Artesanías y Antigüedades at Borrero y Córdova has some lovely textiles, jewellery and antiques; *El Tucan*, Borrero 7-35, Ecuadorean *artesanía*, rec; *Bazaar Susanita*, Benigno Malo 1092, for good woollen sweaters at reasonable prices. Try *Torres* between Sucre y Córdova, or *Tarqui* between Córdova and the river for *polleras*, traditional Indian women's skirts. *Galería Claudio Maldonado*, Bolívar 7-75, has unique precolumbian designs in silver and precious stones; *Centro Cultural Jorge Moscoso*, Pdte Córdova 6-14 y Hermano Miguel, T 822-114, weaving exhibitions, ethnographic museum, antiques and handicrafts; *Galería Pulla*, Jaramillo 6-90, famous painter, sculpture and jewellery.

There are several good leather shops in the arcade off Bolívar between Benigno Malo and Luis Cordero, the quality and price are comparable with Cotacachi, nr Otavalo in Northern Ecuador. *Artesa*, Presidente Córdova 6-96 y Borrero, has several other branches around the city, sells modern Ecuadorean ceramics at good prices. *Joyería Turismo*, owned by Leonardo Crespo, at Gran Colombia 9-31, rec; he will let wholesale buyers tour his factory. *Unicornio*, L Cordero entre Gran Colombia y Lamar, good jewellery, ceramics and candelabra. Jewellery prices are reported as high, so shop around.

High quality Panama hats are made by *Homero Ortega P e Hijos*, Av Gil Ramírez Dávalos 3-86, T 823-429, F 834-045, he will show you his factory opp bus station, open 0900-1200, 1500-1800 for visits, they export all over the world. Panama hats also on Benigno Malo and *Exportadora Cuenca*, Mcal Lamar 3-80, Jaime Ortega Ramírez and his wife, Tania, highly rec, will make to order and won't apply bleach if so asked. Check the quality very carefully as some tend to unravel and shops are unwilling to replace or refund.

There's an interesting market behind the new cathedral. A *Centro Comercial* has opened in the industrial park, with interesting shops. There is a well-stocked supermarket behind *Residencial España*; *Supermaxi*, Colombia y Américas. Camping Gas is available at several locations; camping equipment can be found at *Bermeo Hnos*, Borrero 8-35 y Sucre, T 831-522, and *Créditos y Negocios*, Benigno Malo y Pdte Córdova, T 829-583.

Photography: *Foto Ortiz*, Gran Colombia y Aguirre, wide range of film, good same day developing, not rec for slides; *Asefot*, Gran Colombia 7-18, T/F 839-342, rec for colour prints; *Ecuacolor*, Gran Colombia 7-44 y Cordero, good service.

● **Sports**

Mountain biking: *Explor Bike*, Juan Jaramillo 5100 y Hermano Miguel, T 833-362, rental, cultural trips.

● **Tour companies & travel agents**

Santa Ana Tours, Presidente Córdova y Borrero, T 832-340, run day tours, to Cajas US$35 pp, bus to Ingapirca and return, US$50; *Metropolitan Touring*, Gran Colombia y Cordero, T 842-545/834-057; *Viajes Enmotur*, Borrero 7-51 y Sucre, excursions by bus to Ingapirca US$45, will buy US dollars on a Sat morning; *Ecotrek*, C Larga 7-108 y Luis Cordero, T 842-531, F 835-387, contact Juan Gabriel Carrasco, trips to new Kapawi Ecological Reserve, excellent, experienced guides who offer great adventure travel, monthly departures, specialize in Shaman trips; *Río Arriba Eco-Turismo*, Hno Miguel 7-14 y Córdova, T 840-031, rec; *Apullacta*, Gran Colombia y

G Torres, rent tents (no other equipment rental in Cuenca).

Rec guides: *José Rivera Baquero*, Pedro Carbo 1-48 y Guapondelig, has extensive knowledge of Cuenca and its surroundings; *Eduardo Quito*, T 823-018, F 834-202, has his own 4WD and offers special tours as a professionally-qualified guide, transports up to 10 people, speaks good English, highly rec; *Luis Astudillo*, C Azuay 1-48 entre Guayas y Tungurahua, T 815-234, tours to Ingapirca, US$30, good. **Club Andinismo Sangay**, T 806-615/844-313, for Sun treks, main one 2nd Sun of month, US$3; bus tickets from the camping shop at Gran Colombia y L Cordero.

● **Tourist offices**

Cetur, Hno Miguel 686 y Córdova, open Mon-Fri only, 0800-1200, 1430-1600 (1800 in July-Sept). Has maps of Cuenca. A map of the city is also available from major hotels. Local maps are not very accurate.

● **Useful addresses**

Immigration: Policía Nacional de Migración, Benigno Malo y Larga, T 831-020.

● **Transport**

Local Bus: city buses US$0.08. **Car rental**: *Budget Renta-Car*, Huayna Cápac 1018 y González Suárez, T 801-892/831-888, also at airport, T 804-063. *International*, Huayna Cápac y Suárez, T 801-892. **Taxis**: US$0.70-1 for short journey; US$1.80 to airport or bus station; US$3/hr; US$22/day.

Air The airport is 5-mins' walk from the Terminal Terrestre. No ticket reservations at airport. Local buses run along the road outside. To **Quito** and **Guayaquil**; with TAME. Reconfirm tickets and beware extra charges at check-in, arising from staff claiming incorrectly that your flight has not been confirmed. Arrive at least 1 hr before departure. Try getting a 'prechequeo' or advanced boarding pass.

Buses The Terminal Terrestre, well-organized and policed, is on Av España, a 20-min walk NW of the city centre, or take a minibus, US$0.10. The terminal for local or within-the-province buses is at the Feria Libre on Av Las Américas (destinations such as Gima, San Fernando, Deleg, etc); many city buses pass here too. To **Riobamba**, 5½-6 hrs, US$4, scenic, sit on the left. To **Ambato**, US$7, 7½ hrs (travel during day because scenery is magnificent, the road goes from 2,600m to under 200m and up again). To **Baños**, from 12 de Noviembre, Turismo Baños. To/from **Quito**,

9½-10½ hrs, US$6, US$8 by minibus, 8 hrs; Panamericana Internacional, Huayna Cápac y España, T 840-060; luxury coach service with Sucre Express, 8½ hrs, US$10. To **Loja**, 4½ hrs with San Luis, US$5, new road, lovely scenery, sit on the left, passport checks are likely. To **Machala**, 3-4 hrs, every 20 mins, US$3, sit on the left, wonderful scenery. To **Guayaquil**, 5 hrs, US$4, road now entirely paved – shop around for the most comfortable bus. Turismo Oriental (4 daily, better buses) and Coop Sucúa (3 nightly, one at 1000) go to **Sucúa** (10 hrs) and **Macas** (13 hrs, US$6), the day bus is rec for spectacular scenery (the left side is best overall although the right side is good for the last part with views of approach to tropical lowlands). To **Huaquillas**, 6 hrs, US$4, buses at 0530, 2000, 2300; the bus sometimes stops for 2 hrs in Machala, to avoid the wait get off at the large roundabout (well known to drivers) for the local bus to Huaquillas; evening bus arrives in Huaquillas at 0300, passengers sleep on the bus till daylight. Be prepared for frequent police checks on the way. To **Azogues**, US$0.35, leave every 30 mins. To **Saraguro**, US$2.65, 3½ hrs. Buses to **Gualaquiza**, 10 hrs. To **Alausí**, US$3.90, 4 hrs, all Quito-bound buses pass through, about 20 a day, from 0600 onwards.

EAST OF CUENCA

GUALACEO

Gualaceo is a thriving, modern town set in beautiful landscape, with a charming plaza and fine new church with splendid modern glass. Its Sun market doesn't cater to tourists. Woollen goods are sold on the main street near the bus station, while embroidered goods are sold from a private home above the general store on the main plaza. Inexpensive good shoes are made locally.

● **Accommodation** C *Parador Turístico*, T 255-110, outside town, chalets, rooms, modern, nice, swimming pool, good restaurant; **F** *Residencial Carlos Andrés*, T 255-379, new, clean; **F** *Residencial Gualaceo*, T 255-006, Gran Colombia, clean, friendly, camping possible, and **G** *Español*, T 255-158, very basic.

● **Transport** Buses from the corner of the Terminal Terrestre in Cuenca to Gualaceo,

US$0.65, 2 hrs.

From Gualaceo take a taxi to **Bulzhun** (10 mins) where backstrap weavers make *Macanas* (Ikat dyed shawls); from there walk back down to Bulcay, another weaving community, and catch a bus back to Cuenca.

ROUTES Since the 'disaster' in 1993, when heavy rains caused a huge landslide at La Josefina, the paved route from El Descanso (between Azogues and Cuenca) to Paute and Gualaceo and the train line have been totally wiped out. The connection between Azogues and Cuenca was repaired within a year, but nothing has been done about the train. The old riverside road was due to reopen after reconstruction in Oct 1996. To go to Paute you turn off to the E between Azogues and El Descanso, and to get to Gualaceo turn off S of El Descanso through the village of Jadan. The villages S of La Josefina and those to the N of the gorge are still connected in the E by some very small back lanes; follow the signs for *Hostería Huertas de Uzhpud*.

PAUTE

North of Gualaceo, on the Río Palma, is Paute, home to the largest hydroelectric plant in Ecuador. Improved access roads have converted much of the original farmland into weekend home developments and the farming has been pushed onto the higher slopes, contributing to deforestation. The rainwater runoff now carries much more mud and soil which is quickly silting up the Paute dam, which has to be continually dredged to function. All this contributes to the major dry season electricity cuts nationwide.

● **Accommodation** B *Hostería Huertas de Uzhpud*, set in the beautiful Paute valley, deluxe, good rooms, those at the back have best views, swimming pool, sports fields, small zoo, gardens, lots of orchids, highly rec, Casilla 01-01-1268, Uzhupud, Paute, T 250-339, T Cuenca 806-521 (taxi from Cuenca US$7, bargain hard); also **G** *Residencial Cutilcay*, T 250-133; *San Luis*, T 250-165; and *Las Tejas*, T 250-176.

CHORDELEG

South of Gualaceo, Chordeleg is a village famous for its crafts in wood, silver and gold filigree (though very little is available nowadays), pottery and panama hats. The village has been described as very touristy; watch out for fake jewellery. *Joyería Dorita* and *Joyería Puerto del Sol*, on Juan B Cobos y Eloy Alfaro, have been recommended. There are some good shops selling beautiful ceramics.

The church is interesting with some lovely modern stained glass. Chordeleg has a small Museo de Comunidad of fascinating local textiles, ceramics and straw work, some of which are on sale at reasonable prices. It's a good uphill walk from Gualaceo to Chordeleg, and a pleasant hour downhill in the other direction. With your own vehicle, you can drive back to Cuenca through San Juan and San Bartolomé. Two small mines after this village welcome visitors.

● **Place to eat** *Restaurante El Turista*.

● **Transport** Plenty of colectivos, or by local bus, US$0.15 from Gualaceo market, every 30 mins; direct bus from Cuenca, 1½ hrs, US$0.50.

South of Gualaceo, 83 km from Cuenca, **Sígsig**, with a Sun market and a few *sombrerías*, is worth a visit.

● **Accommodation & places to eat** G *Residencial*; *Restaurante Turista* is OK.

● **Transport** Buses, 1½ hrs, US$0.65, hourly bus also from Chordeleg.

From Sígsig take another bus S to Chiqüinda, 0900, 2½ hrs, buy tickets the night before. Stay overnight with Sr Fausto, the teacher.

A trail from Chiqüinda goes to **Aguacate** (4-5 hrs walking), a village of 70 people. After about 3 hrs the trail divides by a small school on the left. Take the left fork. There are shops and electricity at night only. The village hosts good *fiestas* at Christmas and New Year, and carnival in February.

● **Accommodation** Sr Jorge Guillermo

Vásquez has a *hospedaje*, **G**, very basic but friendly, coffee and popcorn for breakfast, horses can be hired for trekking to caves.

● **Transport** Buses to Cuenca, 2200 are often full, try going to Loja instead (2200, 9 hrs).

From Aguacate either walk 4 hrs or hire a horse to continue SE to Río Negro, a friendly village, from where daily buses or trucks at 1300 and 1600 go to Gualaquiza; 1-2 hrs on a dirt road, US$0.45 (see page 320). A road is being built between Sígsig and Gualaquiza, along a beautiful and unspoilt route. The trail can be hiked by the intrepid but is not yet passable by wheeled vehicles; take a minimum of luggage.

CAJAS NATIONAL PARK

Northwest of Cuenca, **Cajas** is a 28,000 ha national recreation area with over 230 lakes. Near the entrance is an altar and pilgrim area where a teenager saw 'Our Lady of the Faith' in 1988. Entrance to the park is US$6. There is a new visitors' centre and cafetería at Laguna Toreadora (3,810m), next to the old refuge.

The *páramo* vegetation, such as chuquiragua and lupin, is beautiful and contains interesting wildlife: Andean gull, black frogs, humming birds, even condors. On a clear morning the views are superb, even to Chimborazo, some 300 km away.

The valley of the Río Mazan was bought many years ago by the Cuenca water company to protect the water sources for the city. The Friends of Mazan have helped to set it up as a reserve with help from a group based in Norwich in England. It can be visited, but only with the permission of the water company in Cuenca.

Walking trails

Local maps are not always exact. It is better to get the IGM maps in Quito. It is easy to get lost as signs (if any) are of little help.

A trail around Laguna Toreadora takes

-4 hrs depending on your acclimatization to altitude. On the opposite side of the lake from the *refugio* is Cerro San Luis (4,200m) which may be climbed in a day, with excellent views. From the visitor's centre go anticlockwise around the lake, after crossing the outflow look for a sign 'Al San Luis', follow the yellow and black stakes to the summit, and beware of a side trail to dangerous edges.

A recommended 2-day walk is to take the bus to about 15 km past the park *refugio* into the Río Miguir valley. Hike through the Park and hitch back to Cuenca on the Soldados road. On Wed night or Thur morning it is possible to catch traffic going to Cuenca market; there are no buses. Take a tent, stove etc, t can be cold, a compass is useful if cloudy (often); parts of the walk are over 4,000m.

● **Walking conditions** The park offers ideal but strenuous walking, at 3,500-4,400m altitude, and the climate is rough. Deaths have occurred from exposure. The best time to visit is Aug-Jan, when you may expect clear days, strong winds, night-time temperatures to -8°C and occasional mist. From Feb-July temperatures are higher but there is much more fog, rain and snow. It is best to arrive in the early morning since it can get very cloudy, wet and cool after about 1300.

● **Access** It's a 2½-hr bus trip to the park; one daily with Occidental, except Thur and Sun, between 0600 and 0630 from the San Sebastián church, esq Simón Bolívar y Col Talbot. The bus back is between 1400 and 1600, US$1.35, daily except Wed or Sat; arrive early as the bus can get very full. Hitchhiking is difficult as there is little traffic. A taxi costs anything up to US$40, bargain hard.

● **Accommodation G** pp *Refugio*, cold, with four bunks and cooking facilities. There are also two primitive shelters by the shore of the lake, a 20 and 40-mins' walk from the refuge. Take food, fuel, candles, sleeping bags, warm clothes and strong sun cream.

● **Tours** There are organized tours to the lakes from Cuenca, fishing possible, but these tend to be up to US$34. Alternatively, hire a private truck, US$16 with driver. Jorge Moscoso, see under Cuenca **Shopping**, is knowledgeable and helpful about Cajas and says he has found an Inca road to the coast. A group of ramblers welcomes visitors for Sun walks in Aug and Sept, look for posters in Cuenca.

ROUTES The new road from Cuenca to Guayaquil via Molleturo is open and paved for much of its length. The road passes through Cajas National Park and continues over the mountains to the towns of Miguir, Molleturo and on to Naranjal on the coast. The scenery is spectacular and there are still a few places where there is undisturbed forest. There is nowhere to stay after the *refugio* at Laguna Toreadora (see above) until you reach the lowlands between Naranjal and La Troncal. Some buses are running on this road (eg San Luis and Semeria to Guayaquil). It is still prone to landslides during the rainy season (Feb-May).

CUENCA TO MACHALA

From Cuenca, the Pan-American Highway runs S to La Y, about 20 km away. Here the road divides into two: one continuing the Pan-American to Loja and the other, which is faster, running through sugar cane fields to Pasaje and Machala.

GIRON

1 hr from Cuenca is **Girón** whose beauty is spoiled only by a modern concrete church. After the battle on 27 February 1829 between the troops of Gran Colombia, led by Sucre, and those of Peru under Lamar, at nearby Portete de Tarqui, a treaty was signed in Girón. The building, **Casa de los Tratados**, is shown to visitors, as is the site of the Peruvians' capitulation (entry fee). Ask directions to El Chorro waterfall with cloudforest above.

From Girón trucks take passengers up a winding road to the hamlets of **San Fernando** (rooms at *La Posada*) and **Chumblín**. Friendly inhabitants will act as guides to three lakes high in the *páramo* where excellent trout-fishing is to be had. There is also rock-climbing on San Pablo, overlooking Lago Busa. Take camping gear. Return to the main road through Asunción: beautiful downhill stretch for bikers. The route goes through the Yungilla valley and **Santa Isabel** (**C** *La Molienda*, by Cataviña, just before Santa Isabel; **D** *Sol y Agua*, below the village, a weekend place for Cuencanos; **G** *Hostería al Durán*, basic, no water; many other small weekend farms), then descends through desert to the stark, rocky canyon of the Río Jubones. The next town is **Casacay** (**E** *Hostería San Luis*, attractive, good, pool, pleasant climate), after which lush banana plantations are entered. Before Casacay, at a military checkpoint, a road climbs S to **Chilla**, where crowds throng in annual pilgrimages during September. In the lowlands is **Pasaje** (*Pop* 27,000; **D** *San Martín*, clean, a/c, safe; many basic *pensiones*, F, and *Santa Isabel*.) Most buses travel NW to La Troncal and then S down the coast to Machala and Huaquillas for the Peruvian border (see page 252).

SOUTH OF CUENCA

The Pan-American Highway climbs S from La Y to the village of **Cumbe**, which has a small, colourful Wed market. The road then rises to the Tinajillas pass, 3,527m. Further S at La Ramada a branch road forks left to the delightful, sleepy colonial town of **Nabón**, with its weekend market. There is lovely hiking in the nearby valleys and several unexcavated ruins. A small *pensión* offers accommodation. With a rental car or bikes it is possible to do a loop rejoining the Pan-Amercian at Oña, though this trip is best done in the dry season (June-September).

The road descends sharply into the warm upper Jubones valley past cane fields and rises again after Río León (Km 95, 1,900m) to the small town of **Oña**, at Km 105, 2,300m (*Pop* 3,244). There is one hotel on the plaza and

several places to eat. The best place t eat is out of town on the old road S, ru by the Alvarez sisters; traditonal cook ing but not much choice. The sisters ar getting on a bit and it seems the daugh ters may soon take over. Another recom mended restaurant is *San Luis*.

From Oña the road weaves and climb through highland *páramo* pasture (3,040m) and then descends toward Saraguro (Km 144).

SARAGURO

(*Pop* 19,883) is a very cold town, fame for its weaving and distinctive indige nous population. Here the Indians, th most southerly Andean group in Ecua dor, dress all in black. They wear ver broad flat-brimmed hard felt hats. Th men are notable for their black shorts sometimes covered by a whitish kind o divided apron, and a particular kind o saddle bag, the *alforja*, and the women fo their pleated black skirts, necklaces o coloured beads and silver *topos*, ornat pins fastening their shawls. Many o them take cattle across the mountains to the tropical pastures above the Ama zonian jungle. The town has a pictur esque Sun market and interesting Mass

● **Accommodation & places to eat F** *Res dencial Armijos*, C Antonio Castro, col shower, clean, friendly, quiet, good; **F** *Res dencial Saraguro*, C Loja No 03-2 y Antoni Castro, shared bath, friendly, nice courtyard hot water, laundry facilities, rec. *Salón Crista* Azuay y Castro, lunch only, simple but goo food, clean; *Gruta Azul*, on plaza, OK. Chea food is available in the market.

● **Transport** Buses to Cuenca with Coo Viajeros, 4 daily, US$2.65, 4½ hrs; to Loja US$1.80, 1½ hrs.

From Saraguro a 3-4 day hike crosse the *páramo* to the jungle and takes yo to **Yacuambi** (called 24 de Mayo on map but not used) or **Tutupali**. You need t take a guide or lots of food and campin gear, as there is nowhere to eat or slee on the way. The locals know the bes camp sites on the route.

Saraguro Hats

West from Saraguro a road (passable from June to Sept) runs through **Celén, Selva Alegre, Manu, Guanazán** and **Chilla** down to the coast. It is very spectacular; a bus goes to Manu throughout the year and to Guanazan in the dry season. Chilla is famous for its Church of the Virgin and pilgrims flock here in Sept from all over the country. The only place to stay is the *Casa de Huéspedes* (Pilgrims' Guest House) which is empty the rest of the year.

South from Chilla mountain trails run over the mysterious **Cerro de Arcos** to **Zaruma** and **Piñas**.

ROUTES South from Saraguro there are two passes, at Km 150 and 156.5. Two further passes come after the village of San Lucas (Km 164), the highest of the two at Km 185, before a long descent towards Loja. The road between Cuenca and Loja is now paved and is one of the most beautiful and breathtaking in Ecuador. From San Lucas to Loja the old, unpaved, Panamericana runs alongside the river.

LOJA

This friendly, pleasant city (*Pop* 94,305; *Alt* 2,063m), lies near the Oriente. It was founded on its present site in 1548, having been moved from La Toma, and was rebuilt twice after earthquakes, the last of which occurred in the 1880s. Its first site, in the hotter, lower valley of Catamayo, had too high an incidence of malaria (documentation of this can be found in the Banco Central Museum, see below).

The city, encircled by hills, can be reached by air from Quito or Guayaquil to Catamayo (known locally as La Toma), and then 35 km by paved road. Loja has been a traditional gateway between the highlands and southern Amazonia. Tropical forest products such as chinchona (the natural base for quinine) first entered European pharmacopia through Loja. The town also has the distinction of being the first in the country to have electricity. A small hydroelectric plant was built close by at the end of the last century.

The city boasts two universities, with a well-known law school. The Universidad Técnica, on the hill to the NE of the centre, is the Open University for Ecuador, having correspondence students and testing centres scattered across the country. The Universidad Nacional has good murals on some of its buildings. There are also crude but original paintings on the patio walls of many of the old houses.

There is an expression in Loja which says that God crumpled the province like a piece of paper and if it were flattened out, it would cover the whole of Ecuador. In other words, this is quite a mountainous area. Much of the accessible land is deforested and it has a tendency to be rather dry. As in the province of Manabí, on the Pacific coast, Loja has a reputation for bad farming practices and high emigration into the newer areas which were opened to colonization by the now defunct IERAC (Instituto Ecuatoriana de Reforma Agraria y Colonización). For this reason the official name of Lago Agrio, capital of the province of Sucumbios, is Nueva Loja.

Places of interest

The **Cathedral** and **Santo Domingo** church, Bolívar y Rocafuerte, have painted interiors. **El Valle** church, on the S edge of the city is colonial, with a lovely interior. The **Banco Central museum** on the main plaza, 0900-1500, has exhibits of local folklore and history, and the **Casa de la Cultura**, Bolívar y Imbabura, sponsors cultural events. **Mercado Modelo**, 10 de Agosto y 18 de Noviembre, rebuilt in 1991, is worth a visit. It is clean and efficient, open 0800-1800 Mon to Sat, 0800-1500 Sun. There is a market on Sat, Sun and Mon, attended by many Saraguro Indians. There are souvenir and craft shops on 10 de Agosto between Iberoamérica and 18 de Noviembre.

Loja is famed for its musicians and has one of the few musical academies in the country. Musical evenings and concerts are often held around the town.

Excursions

Parque Educacional Ambiental y Recreacional de Argelia is superb, with trails through the forest to the *páramo*. It is 500m before the police checkpoint on road S to Vilcabamba. Take a city bus marked 'Argelia'; it is open 0830-1700 except Tues and Wed. Across the road and 100m S is the **Jardín Botánico Reynaldo Espinosa**, open Mon-Fri 0800-1700. It is nicely laid out and has several chinchona trees.

Local festivals

The **Fiesta de la Virgen del Cisne** (of the swan) is held 16-20 Aug, and the image of the Virgin remains in Loja until 1 November. The statue of the Virgen del Cisne spends a month each year travelling around the province and hundreds of the faithful walk in procession with it. The most important of these peregrinations is the 3-day 70 km walk from El Cisne to Loja cathedral, which begins on 17 August. Loja, Catamayo and El Cisne are crowded with religious pilgrims and Ecuadorean tourists during the last 2 weeks of Aug and the first week of September. It is very difficult to find a room and all prices rise during this period.

Local information

● **Accommodation**

C *Grand Hotel Loja*, Iberoamérica (also known as Av Manuel Agustín Aguirre) y Rocafuerte, T 575-200, F 575-202, bath, TV, phone; **C** *Hostal Aguilera Internacional*, Sucre 01-08 y Emiliano Ortega, T 563-189, F 572-894, with bath, nice rooms, TV, restaurant, sauna, parking; **C** *Libertador*, Colón 14-30 y Bolívar, T 570-344, F 572-119, Casilla 412, bath, TV, suites available, noisy, good restaurant *La Castellana*, parking.

D *Hostal La Riviera*, Universitaria y 10 de Agosto, T 572-863, carpet, TV, phone, good; **D** *Ramsés*, Colón 14-31 y Bolívar, T 960-868/961-402, bath, phone, TV, good restaurant; **D** *Vilcabamba*, Iberoamérica y Pasaje la FEUE, T 737-399 F 561-483, on river/sewer, clean.

E *Acapulco*, Sucre 749 y 10 de Agosto, T 570-651, clean, hot water, private bath, safe for leaving luggage, 1st floor rooms are quieter in the mornings, rec; **E** *Hostal Crystal*, Rocafuerte y 18 de Noviembre, clean, safe, large rooms; **E** *Hostal Orillas del Zamora*, 10 de Agosto y Sucre, with bath; **E** *Los Ejecutivos*, Universitaria 1076, T 560-004, good, also 'video club'; **E** *Metropolitano*, 18 de Noviembre 6-41 y Colón, T 570-007, with bath and TV, hot water, clean; **E** *Saraguro Internacional*, Universitaria 724 y 10 de Agosto, T 570-552, hot water, TV, parking, restaurant open Mon-Fri.

F *Alborada*, Sucre 1279 y Lourdes, with shower, clean; **F** *Caribe*, Rocafuerte 1552 y 18

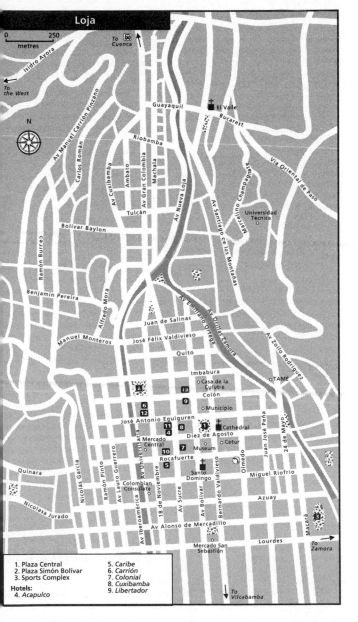

Loja

To Cuenca

To the West

N

Isidro Ayora

Av Manuel Carrión Pinzano

Carlos Román

Guayaquil

El Valle

Bucarest

Riobamba

Av Cuxibamba

Ambato

Av Gran Colombia

Machala

Av Nueva Loja

Tulcán

Bolívar Baylon

Ramón Burre?

Benjamín Pereira

Alfredo Mora

Manuel Monteros

Juan de Salinas

José Félix Valdivieso

Av Emiliano Ortega

Av Orillas Zamora

Marcelino Champagnate

Av Santiago de las Montañas

Via Oriental de pazo

Universidad Tecnica

Av Zoilo Rodríguez

Quito

Imbabura

Casa de la Cultura

Colón

Municipio

TAME

José Antonio Eguiguren

Mercado Central

Rocafuerte

Diez de Agosto

Museum

Cathedral

Cetur

Juan José Peña

24 de Mayo

Santo Domingo

Quinara

Nicolás García

Ramón Pinto

Lauro Guerrero

Av Universitaria

Av Iberoamérica

18 de Noviembre

Av Sucre

Colombian Consulate

Bernardo Valdivieso

Av Bolívar

Miguel Riofrio

Olmedo

Azuay

Nicolasa Jurado

Av Alonso de Mercadillo

Mercado San Sebastián

Lourdes

Macará

To Zamora

To Vilcabamba

1. Plaza Central
2. Plaza Simón Bolívar
3. Sports Complex

Hotels:
4. *Acapulco*
5. *Caribe*
6. *Carrión*
7. *Colonial*
8. *Cuxibamba*
9. *Libertador*

de Noviembre, T 572-902, shared bath, hot water, rec; **F** *Colonial*, Sucre 8-64, shared bath, basic; **F** *Cuxibamba*, 10 de Agosto y Sucre, basic, cheaper without bath; **F** *Hostal Carrión*, Colón 1630 y 18 de Noviembre, T 561-127, basic, hot water on request, friendly, safe; **F** *Hostal San Luis*, Sucre 4-56 e Imbabura, T 570-370, cheaper without bath, hot water, parking; **F** *Loja*, Rocafuerte 15-27, T 570-241, shared bath, intermittent hot water, nicely renovated, friendly; **F** *Londres*, Sucre 741 y 10 de Agosto, clean, friendly, nice big rooms, hot water.

G *Primavera*, Colón 1644, clean, cold shower; **G** pp *San Andrés*, Miguel Riofrío, friendly, more or less clean, very cheap. **Youth Hostel**, Av Miguel Riofrío 1661 y 18 de Noviembre, T 560-895. There are basic *residenciales* in our **G** range on Rocafuerte.

● **Places to eat**

José Antonio, Imbabura 15-30 entre Sucre y 18 de Noviembre, excellent *cebiche* and seafood, enthusiastic chef, highly rec; *La Cascada*, Sucre y Lourdes, very good food; *Don Quijote Pizzería*, Eguiguren, half a block W of El Río Malacatos, excellent food, wholewheat bread; *Trece*, Universitaria y Colón, also Eguiguren 1468, good; *México*, Eguiguren 1579 y Sucre, good set meals or à la carte, generous portions, popular, rec; *El Rincón de Francia*, Bolívar y Riofrío, good food; *La Tullpa*, 18 de Noviembre y Colón, cheap, good *churrasco*; *Parrillada Uruguaya*, Iberoamérica y Azuay, opens 1700, good grilled meat, owner helpful; *La Casona*, 18 de Noviembre nr Imbabura (the better of two branches), good; *El Paraíso*, Sucre 0435 y Quito, good vegetarian; *Salud y Vida*, Azuay nr Olmedo, vegetarian; *Marisquería Las Castañuelas*, 10 de Agosto 1167, clean, set meal US$1. In El Valle area the *Colonial* and *La Lolita* are rec, try their *cuy*. *Chifa El Arbol de Oro*, Eguiguren y 18 de Noviembre, good Chinese food. *Unicornio* is a piano bar on the main plaza.

Loja has many excellent bakeries. Good snacks, pastries and yoghurt at *Pastelería Persa* (2 locations – one at Rocafuerte 14-58). *Helados de Paila*, Av Iberoamérica, nr the market, good ice-cream and snacks; *Topoli*, Riofrío y Bolívar, best coffee and yoghurt in town, good for breakfast (not open for lunch); *Top Cream Ice Cream*, Iberoamérica y Colón, best ice cream in town.

One of the famous dishes from the Loja area is *repe*, a green banana soup made from a special type of banana which only grows in th S. Another local speciality is *cecina*, which i thinly cut meat, usually pork, often cooke over open flames.

● **Banks & money changers**

Filanbanco on the main plaza, changes Ame TCs, best rates; **Banco de Loja**, Rocafuerte Bolívar, good rates for TCs; **Banco del Azuay** on the main plaza, changes cash and TCs **Banco Mutualista Pichincha**, on plaza, cash advance on Mastercard. There are no *casas d cambio* but you can sell US dollars at a goo rate in the gift shop in front of *Hotel Acapulco* also *Loayza*, Riofrío 1450, helpful; *Librería Re ina del Cisne*, Bolívar y Riofrío; *Frankhitur* Centro Comercial Episcopal, Valdivieso y 10 d Agosto, T 573-378; *Joyería San Pablo*, Sucr 7-26 y 10 de Agosto, T 560-715, open Sat good rates; *Vilcatur Travel Agency*, Colón 14 30 y Bolívar, good rates for cash; also *Delgad Travel*, opp the Post Office on Colón y Sucre.

● **Embassies & consulates**

Colombia 18 de Noviembre y Azuay, T 960 573; **Peru** Lazo y Rodríguez, T 961-668.

● **Post & telecommunications**

Post Office: Colón y Sucre; no good for send ing parcels. **Emetel**: on Rocafuerte y Olmedo

● **Shopping**

The Mercado in the centre of town sells good cheap supplies. *Cer-Art Ceramics*, precolum bian designs on mostly high-gloss ceramics produced at the Universidad Técnica with a workshop and retail shop. Above the Univer sidad Técnica (see above) is the 'Ceramic Plaza', where you can buy directly from the crafts studio. The main shop sells high quality items but if you ask you will be shown the rooms where slightly imperfect ceramics are sold. A little higher on the same road is the Productos Lacteos, where you can buy excel lent cheeses and fresh butter, all produced by the university and contributing to its finances

● **Tourist offices**

Cetur, Valdivieso 08-22 y 10 de Agosto, T 572 964, F 570-485, open Mon-Fri, 0800-1300, 1500-1800. *Loja tradición, cultura y turismo* is a useful guidebook. *El Siglo* and *Crónica* give news of events.

● **Useful addresses**

Immigration: Venezuela y Argentina, T 960-500.

● **Transport**

Air TAME office is at Zamora y 24 de Mayo, 0830-1600. Reserve your seat in Cuenca if you want to leave from Loja the next day; or get an open ticket at the airport and push and shout to get on the plane. There are flights to Quito direct or via Guayaquil. On arrival at La Toma airport, shared taxis will be waiting to take you to Loja; 45 mins, US$3. They fill up quickly so choose a driver, give him your luggage claim ticket and he will collect your checked luggage. Bus to Loja US$0.80, or stay in Catamayo (see below). Flights are often cancelled due to strong winds and the airport is invariably closed by 1000.

Buses Terminal at Av Gran Colombia e Isidro Ayora, buses every 2 mins to/from centre, 10-mins' journey; left luggage, information desk, shops, Emetel office, pay US$0.15 terminal tax at information booth by main entrance. Taxi from centre, US$1. To **Cuenca**, 4½ hrs, 7 a day, US$4.50 with Trans Viajeros ('18 de Noviembre y Quito); **Machala**, 10 a day, 7 hrs, US$3. There are two routes from Loja to Machala, one goes through Piñas and is rather bumpy with hairpin bends but has the better views, the other is paved and generally quicker. **Quito**, with Cooperativa Loja (10 de Agosto y Guerrero), and Trans Santa, 4 a day, US$10-12, 13-14 hrs. **Guayaquil**, 5 a day, 8 hrs, US$5.85. Panamericana Internacional, office at *Grand Hotel Loja*, luxury coach service to Quito (US$15) and Guayaquil (US$10). To **Huaquillas** at 2030 and 2230, US$4.50, 6-8 hrs; get off at Machala crossroads, *La Avanzada*, and take a local bus from there. To **Macará**, 4 daily, 6-8 hrs, US$5; roadworks at El Limón, half way to Macará is paved, but the rest is terrible, numerous passport checkpoints. To **Saraguro**, 6 daily, 1½ hrs, US$1.80. To **Vilcabamba**, a spectacular 1½-hr bus ride, Sur Oriente hourly from Loja bus terminal, US$0.90. A taxi costs about US$7.50, 1 hr. To **Zamora**, 1½ hrs, with Coop Nambija.

PODOCARPUS NATIONAL PARK

UPPER PREMONTANE SECTION

The entrance to the upper premontane section of **Podocarpus National Park**, is about 15 km S of Loja on the Vilcabamba road at Cajanuma. The park contains spectacular walking country, lush tropical cloud forest and excellent bird-watch-

ing, but take waterproofs and warm clothing.

Permits (US$7) and an adequate map from Inefan, C Azuay entre Valdivieso y Olmedo, Loja (T 571-534), office open 0800; or at the entrance. There is a comfortable refuge at the information centre in the park; make bookings at office in Loja before going. Camping is possible but it can be very wet. Park guardian Miguel Angel is very knowledgeable and helpful. Additional information from conservation groups: Arco Iris, Olmedo y Riofrío, T 572-926, PO Box 860, Loja, or contact member Rodrigo Tapiz, T 560-895; Fundación Ecológica Podocarpus, Sucre 8-47 y 10 de Agosto, PO Box 11-01-436, Loja.

● **Access** Take a Vilcabamba bus, the park entrance is 20 mins from Loja, US$0.80, then it's a 8 km hike uphill to the guard station. It's possible to sleep here and there are cooking facilities. Direct transport by taxi only, US$10 round trip. You can arrange a pick up later from the guard station.

LOWER SUBTROPICAL SECTION

The lower subtropical section of Podocarpus Park can be reached from Zamora (see below). The scenic road to Zamora (65 km) has been rebuilt (1996). You can carry on from there into the Oriente. There are two entrances to the **Podocarpus National Park** here.

1: The lower altitude of the Zamora side of the Park makes wet weather less threatening but waterproof hiking boots are essential. Permission to enter the Park from Inefan, US$14 entrance, is essential. Inefan office at the town entrance, open Mon-Fri, 0830-1800. At weekends pay at the Park headquarters at the Bombuscara refuge. Camping is possible near the refuge. Park guardians can suggest walks. Incredible bird life: mountain tanagers flock around the refuge.

2: The other entrance is 2 hrs S by bus. This area is definitely off the beaten track but, for the virgin cloud forest and amazing quantity of flora and fauna, it is unmatched. It contains one of the last major habitats for the spectacled bear and many birds, such as the mountain toucan, Andean cock-of-the-rock, umbrella bird, green jay, etc. A 3- to 5-day hike is possible into this part of the park, but permission is not only needed from the Inefan office in Zamora but from the mining company. Inefan will get the permission for you after filling out a few papers; T 900-141 and let them know you are interested in entering the area. Ing Luis Cuenca is in charge of the Podocarpus Park. Most food supplies can be obtained in Zamora (but they are expensive), though all camping gear must be carried, as well as fuel for stoves.

● **Access 1**: Taxi US$2 to the entrance, 1 km walk to refuge. **2**: From the Zamora bus terminal, you can take a *ranchero*, or wooden, open-sided bus to Romerillos, which is a collection of a few houses and an Inefan office. Bus departs Zamora 0630 and 1415, return to Zamora at 0815 and 1600.

EAST FROM LOJA

ZAMORA

From Loja The road to the Oriente (see page 219) crosses a low pass and descends rapidly to **Zamora** (*Pop* 8,736), an old mission settlement about 65 km away at the confluence of the Ríos Zamora and Bombuscara. The road is beautiful as it wanders from *páramo* down to high jungle, crossing mountain ranges of spectacular cloud forest, weaving high above narrow gorges as it runs alongside the Río Zamora. The area has scarcely been affected by tourism yet. For the mission at Guadalupe, take a La Paz bus, which goes up the Yacuambi valley. The town itself is not very interesting, being a midway point for miners and gold prospectors heading further into the Oriente. The best month is Nov, but except for April-

June, when it rains almost constantly, other months are comfortable.

● **Accommodation D** *Internacional Torres*, new, best in town; **D** *Maguna*, Diego de Vaca, T 605-113, fridge, TV, bath, parking; **E** *Orillas del Zamora*, Diego de Vaca nr car bridge, **F** without bath, family run, friendly; **F** *Seyma*, 24 de Mayo y Amazonas, T 605-583, clean, friendly, rec; **F** *Zamora*, Sevilla de Oro y Pío Jaramillo, T 605-253, shared bath, clean; **F** *Residencial Venecia*, Sevilla de Oro, shared bathroom, basic.

● **Places to eat** Restaurants in *Hotel Maguna* (best), *GranRitz*, good, and *Comedor Don Pepe*; *Esmeraldas* in market area opp bus terminal, good, rec.

● **Useful addresses Immigration Office**: C José Luis Tamayo S of the park, visitors may be asked for documents, always carry your passport.

● **Transport** All buses leave from Terminal Terrestre. To **Loja**, 4 a day, 2½ hrs; to **Cuenca**, 1 daily via Loja, 6-7 hrs; to **Yantzaza** and **La Paz**, 6 a day.

Nambija is a gold mining town outside Zamora, a frontier town with its own, limited law and order. It is not entirely safe to visit, gold miners can be suspicious and trigger happy. North of Nambija is **Zumbi**, reached by 0800 bus from Zamora, last bus back 1500, a very scenic ride.

The road to the Southern Oriente passes through **Yantzaza**, with 4 hotels, including the new *Inca*, **F**, and several *comedores*, and **El Pangui** (**G** *Hotel Estrella del Oriente*) on its way N to Gualaquiza (see page 320).

VILCABAMBA

(*Pop* 3,894; *Alt* 1,520m; *Phone code* 07) Once an isolated village, Vilcabamba has become increasingly popular with foreign backpackers, a 'must' along the gringo trail from Ecuador to Peru or vice versa. There are many places to stay and several good restaurants. The whole area is beautiful and tranquil, with an agreeable climate (17°C min, 26°C max), wonderful for a few days relaxation. The local economy has benefitted from the influx of tourists, but there have also been negative effects; responsible tourism is especially important here.

There are many good walks in the Río Yambala valley (maps are available at *Cabañas Río Yambala*), and on the Mandango mountain trail (exposed and slippery in parts, directions obtainable at *Madre Tierra*). The Vilcagua factory here produces cartons of drinking water, which is transported around the country. Visits to the plant can be arranged. There is a Tourist Office on the main plaza next to Emetel, which is friendly and helpful, with good information and maps. There are no banks or cambios, but hotels and shops will change at a poor rate.

NB Vilcabamba is famous for its locally-produced hallucinogenic cactus juice called San Pedro. Though officially illegal, many travellers visit the town solely to experience its effects. Anyone tempted to try some should note that it is incredibly foul-tasting and it is difficult not to vomit within the first hour of taking it. You should also be discreet and find a quiet spot, away from the town. If you have any doubts, then err on the side of caution and abstain. The cactus juice has been known to affect people's psychological state.

Local information
● **Accommodation**

C *Hostería Vilcabamba*, T 580-271, F 580-273, excellent, comfortable, pool (may be used by non-residents for US$0.50), jacuzzi, bar, good Ecuadorean restaurant, massage, fitness instruction, language school, US$3/hr, minimum 4 hrs daily, classes in lounge area or poolside, run by Cortez family.

D *Parador Turístico*, also run by Cortez family, good rooms, with restaurant and bar, T 673-122, rec; **D** *Hostal La Posada Real*, C Agua del Hierro s/n, T 673-114, with bath, hot water, very clean, comfortable, excellent views, laundry facilities, relaxing atmosphere, rec.

E *Cabañas Paraíso*, 5 mins from town on the main road, cabins with bath, restaurant, good value; **E** *Hostal Madre Tierra*, a health farm set in idyllic surroundings about 2 km before village, T 580-269, coming from Loja, the farm is reached by a dirt track on the right-hand side of the road, just before the bridge, some cabins are dark and rather damp and insect-infested, but comfortable, shared bath, inc breakfast, dinner and free drinking water, reductions for long stay, excellent food, home made, vegetarian to order, non-residents welcome for meals but must reserve a day in advance, horses to rent (about US$15/day for 2 horses, food and gear), language school, small swimming pool, videos every night, massage, steam baths, English and French spoken, rec, very popular, often full, the Mendoza family make travellers very welcome, they have details of trails for walking, write in advance to Jaime Mendoza, PO Box 354, Loja, Ecuador; **E** *Pole House*, 10-mins' walk from town by the Río

Valley of the immortals

The tiny, isolated village of Vilcabamba gained a certain fame about 30 years ago when doctors announced that it was home to one of the oldest living populations in the world. It was said that people here often lived to well over 100 years old, some as old as 135. Fame, though, turned to infamy when it was revealed that many of these immortals were making claims based on their parents birth certificates. However, given that first children are often born to parents in the teenage years, this still means that there are some very old people kicking around in these parts.

There is also a high incidence of healthy, active elders. It's not unusual to find people in their seventies and eighties toiling in the fields and covering several miles a day to get there. Such longevity and vitality is not only down to the area's famously healthy climate. Other factors are also at play: physical exercise; strong family ties; a balanced diet low in animal fats; and a lack of stress.

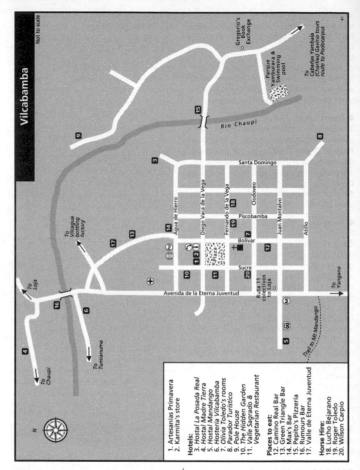

Vilcabamba

Not to scale

To Cabañas Yambala (Charlie) Gavino tours route to Podocarpus

Gregorio's Book Exchange

Parque Jamburara & Swimming pool

Río Chaupi

Santa Domingo

15

9

3

Diego Vaca de la Vega

Fernando de la Vega

Clodoveo

Piscobamba

Juan Montalvo

Atillo

To Vilcabamba bottling factory

17 13

14 Agua de Hierro

Plaza 1 2

10 11 Sucre

Bolívar

18

19

12

20

Ruta 11 colectivos to Loja

Avenida de la Eterna Juventud

16 6

To Loja

To Tumianuma

4

To Chaupi

N

To Yangana

Trail to Mt Mandango

5

8

Hotels:
1. Artesanías Primavera
2. Karmita's store
3. Hostal La Posada Real
4. Hostal Madre Tierra
5. Hostal Mandango
6. Hostería Vilcabamba
7. Olivia Toledo's rooms
8. Parador Turístico
9. Pole House
10. The Hidden Garden
11. Valle Sagrado & Vegetarian Restaurant

Places to eat:
12. Camino Real Bar
13. Green Triangle Bar
14. Max's Bar
15. Pepito's Pizzeria
16. Rumours Bar
17. Valle de Eterna Juventud

Horse Hire:
18. Lucho Bejarano
19. Roger Toledo
20. Wilson Carpio

Chamba, cabin built on stilts for 4 people for rent, with fully furnished kitchen, drinking water supplied, owned by Orlando and Alicia Falco, ask at their handicraft shop, *Prima Vera*, on the plaza, which will also double as the post office from 1997, Sr Falco also speaks English and runs excellent nature tours in and around the Podocarpus National Park, US$15 pp/day, inc boxed lunch; **E** *The Hidden Garden*, on Sucre, T/F (07) 580-281, new, quiet, clean, use of kitchen, lovely gardens, rec.

F *Hostal Mandango*, behind bus terminal, family run, with bath, inexpensive restaurant,

pretty quiet, good value; **F** *Hotel Valle Sagrado*, proprietor Abel Espinoza, on main plaza, shared baths not too clean, cold water, basic, friendly, noisy, good vegetarian restaurant, excellent breakfast of yoghurt, fresh fruit, homemade bread and coffee for only US$1, will store luggage, laundry facilities, use of kitchen; **F** *Sra Olivia Toledo*, Bolívar esq Clodoveo, 1 block from plaza, shared bath, hot water, family run, friendly. At the upper end of the Vilcabamba Valley, a beautiful 4 km walk from the village, are the highly rec **F** *Cabañas Río Yambala*, owned by Charlie and Sarah, different types of cabins for 3 to 6, or room, beautiful views in all directions, kitchen facilities if required, shopping done for you, vegetarian restaurant open all day, hot showers, laundry service, clean, helpful and very friendly, do not leave belongings on balcony or porch, horses for rent with or without guide, trekking arranged in the Podocarpus National Park with tents, sleeping bags, food etc provided.

● **Places to eat**

There are four restaurants on the plaza, inc an unnamed, good vegetarian place. Also *Café Pizzería Pepito's*, 5 mins from the plaza on the road to Cabañas Yambala, excellent pizzas and pasta, cheap, rec. Also: *Camino Real Bar*; *Green Triangle Bar*; *Max's Bar*; *Rumours Bar*; and *Valle de Eterna Juventud* (vegetarian) – see map.

● **Tours companies & travel agents**

New Zealander, Gavin Moore, runs *Caballos Gavilán*, offering 3-day horse treks to the cloud forest, days 1 and 3 are on horseback getting to and from his farmhouse at 2,500m, overlooking Vilcabamba, and day 2 is a trek in the forest; US$75 pp, inc food (vegetarian specialities), sleeping bags (if necessary), and basic lodging, highly rec. He lives a couple of km outside the town; contact him through the tourist office or F 573-186, or Casilla 1000, Loja, F (07) 571-025/673-186.

Horses can be hired from Roger Toledo (see map), he will organize 3-day trips into the mountains; also Wilson Carpio and Ernesto Avila, cost varies from US$4-8/half day. There's a campsite at the nature reserve, *Las Palmas*, on the edge of the Park, take taxi or pick-up, US$4, try Miguel Carpio who lives half a block from Tourist Office; for reservations call Comercial Karmita T 637-186, also fax service and tourist information.

SOUTH FROM VILCABAMBA

The dirt road S continues to **Yangana**, **Valledolid**, **Palanda** and **Zumba**. Although the locals occasionally cross into Peru by this route, there are no official border crossing facilities, and foreigners trying to enter or leave the country this way will be frowned upon.

The forests down here are still intact and the trail between **Amaluza** (Jimbura) and Zumba is passable, though only on foot. There are several areas between Yangana and Palanda where the locals will tell you that the old Inca trails are walkable. The trails are very beautiful but their archaeological authenticity may be in doubt. Treks into the ancient settlements of Vergel, Porvenir and Loyola can be arranged with the locals.

LOJA TO THE PERUVIAN BORDER

An alternative to the Huaquillas border crossing is the more scenic route via Macará. Leaving Loja on the main paved highway going W, the airport at **La Toma** (1,200m) is reached after 35 km.

CATAMAYO

If flying to or from La Toma, it's best to stay at **Catamayo**, nearby. There are several weekend resorts around Catamayo where you can go and relax by the pool in a warmer climate. To the NW of town is one of the largest *Ingenios*, sugar processing plants, in Ecuador.

High up in the mountains, to the NW of Catamayo, is the small village of **El Cisne**, dominated by its incongruous French-style Gothic church. There is a small museum housing all the sequined and jewelled clothes which have been donated to dress the statue of the Virgin for every conceivable occasion.

● **Accommodation & places to eat** In Catamayo: **D** *Hostería Bella Vista*, T 962-450, tropical gardens; pool; **F** *Hotel San Marcos*, on the plaza; **G** pp *Hotel El Turista*, Av Isidro Ayora, shared bath, basic, friendly, poor beds. Opposite is *Restaurant China*, good, cheap.

● **Transport** Taxi to airport US$1, or 20-mins' walk.

ROUTES At La Toma, where you can catch the Loja-Macará bus, the Pan-American Highway divides into two branches: one running W and the other S. The former, which is faster, runs via Velacruz and Catacocha, with 4 passport checks. The Loja to Catacocha section is paved, and Catacocha to Macará is paved halfway (early 1996).

CATACOCHA

West from La Toma, Catacocha is a spectacularly placed town built on a rock. The views from Shiriculapio, behind the hospital, are marvellous. Ask to walk through the hospital grounds. There are pre-Inca ruins around the town, which was once inhabited by the Palta Indians, a group which now only exists in history books.

● **Accommodation** There are four hotels in town: *Turismo*, behind the church; *Pensión Guayaquil*, between the plaza and the statue; and *Mirasol* and *Buena Esperanza*, down the hill from the statue, S of the town.

ROUTES From Catacocha, the road runs S to the border at Macará. A turn-off leads W at the military checkpoint at **Empalme** to **Alamor**, **Celica** and on to the petrified forest at **Puyango** (see page 251).

ZAPOTILLO

South from Celica a road heads SW to **Zapotillo** (*Pop* 5,000; *Alt* 325m), a charming riverside town on the Peruvian border, SW of Macará. It is said to be one of the best preserved towns in the S. Lots of locals cross to Peru here, but no tourists. Migración/police is in town. Canoes cross the river, then you walk to the bus to Sullana, which departs Tues, Thur and Sat at 0600 in the dry season. Alternatively, trucks leave in the morning to Lalamor and frequent trucks go to Sullana, 3 hrs.

● **Accommodation** G *Pensión Zapotillo* and F *Hotel Los Angeles*.

SOUTH FROM CATAMAYO

An alternative route to Macará is via Cariamanga. The road is paved to Cariamanga. Note that many of the roads shown on maps of this area are very inaccurate and are only passable with a 4WD, and then only in the dry season.

The road runs S to **Gonzanamá**, a pleasant, sleepy little town famed for the weaving of beautiful *alforjas* (multi-purpose saddlebags). Ask around and buy direct from the weavers as there are no

handicraft shops. Gonzanamá also produces a good soft cheese. Travellers should note that the town has a somewhat unusual reputation in the S for the high incidence of deafness. So don't be paranoid if everyone seems to be ignoring you!

● **Accommodation** F *Residencial Jiménez*, bath, cold shower.

From Gonzanamá there is an old and poorly maintained road to **Malacatos**, passing through the isolated village of **Purunuma**. There is almost no traffic but the views are great. It may be possible to get a ride in the morning up to the village, then it's a long hike down to the river and back up to Malacatos, which has a Sat market.

27.5 km SW from Gonzanamá is **Cariamanga**, whose main claim to fame is as the home town of Ecuador's most famous Drug Baron family, the Reyes. The town has several hotels and banks.

Beyond Cariamanga the two southern roads are unpaved. One heads SE to **Luzero** and **Amaluza**, both on the way to the most southerly parts of the country and the least visited. There are two small hotels in Amaluza, from where a daily bus runs to Quito, taking about 24 hrs.

The other road twists its way westwards to **Colaisaca** then follows a steep, rough descent, with a loss of about 2,000m in altitude to **Utuana** (not rec for cyclists in the other direction). From there the road heads NW to **Sozoranga**, 75 km from Gonzanamá. The town has one hotel (**G**, shared cold shower). The road then continues S for 36 km to Macará on the border.

MACARA

(*Pop* 14,296; *Alt* 600m) This dusty town on the border is in a rice-growing area. There are road connections to Sullana near the Peruvian coast. Several roads have been washed away by heavy rains.

• **Accommodation** E *Espiga de Oro*, opp the market, with bath, fan, TV, clean, rec; **E** *Parador Turístico*, the best in town, pool, restaurant may not be open, not far from the centre; **F** *Amazonas*, Rengel 418, clean, basic, friendly; **F** *Pensión Guayaquil*, with shower, not rec, fleas, large cell-like rooms; **F** *Residencial Paraíso*, Veintimilla 553, shared bath, clean, laundry facilities, noisy, unfriendly.

• **Places to eat** *Colonial Macará*, Rengel y Bolívar, helpful, but food not too good; *Dragón Dorado*, Calderón, seafood, popular; *Heladería Cream*, Veintimilla y Sucre, great ice cream; *Soda Bar Manolo* for breakfast.

FRONTIER WITH PERU

● Ecuadorean immigration

Open 0800-1800, closed 1200-1400, 7 days a week. Formalities last about 30 mins. It is reported as a much easier crossing than at Huaquillas.

A Peruvian tourist card can be obtained from the Peruvian Honorary Consul in Macará, if he is available, or at the border if not already obtained in Quito or Guayaquil.

● Exchange

The bank at Macará does not change money, so change sucres on the street to give you enough new soles to last you until you reach Sullana (Peru). You can change money at the market in the town centre, where the rates are better than at the border or in Loja. Better to change sucres in Ecuador, but beware of rip-offs changing sucres to soles.

● Transport

There is a 2½ km walk or taxi ride to the international bridge over the Río Macará; US$0.50 shared, up to US$2 in a pick-up from Macará market – less if more passengers. A truck can be caught from the plaza in Macará at 0745. Beware of overcharging coming from Peru. Coop Loja and Cariamanga, 13 buses a day Macará to Loja, 6 to 8 hrs, US$3.50. The whole journey can be done in a day if you arrive at the border at noon. The Loja-border journey

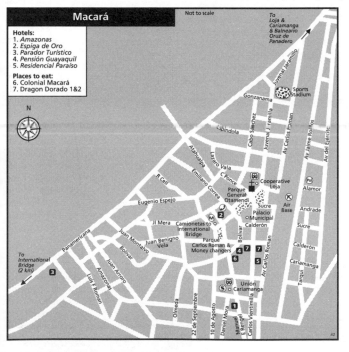

Macará

Not to scale

To Loja & Cariamanga & Balneario Cruz de Panadero

Hotels:
1. *Amazonas*
2. *Espiga de Oro*
3. *Parador Turístico*
4. *Pensión Guayaquil*
5. *Residencial Paraíso*

Places to eat:
6. *Colonial Macará*
7. *Dragon Dorado 1&2*

To International Bridge (2 km)

takes only 3½ hrs by car. On the Peruvian side, colectivos run to Sullana for US$2.25 pp, 3 hrs, 1 passport checkpoint. Colectivos take you to where camionetas leave for Piura, 30 mins, US$0.70.

INTO PERU

The border, on the Peruvian side, is known as **La Tina**. The first 16 km of road, to Suyo (one hotel), was due to be paved by the end of 1996. From there the road is paved via La Lomas (two hotels) to Sullana (136 km from the border). **Sullana** is a modern city with an immigration office, banks and *casas de cambio*, post and phone offices and a range of hotels. Buses can be taken to Piura, 38 km, which has good connections for Chiclayo, Trujillo and Lima. There are also direct Sullana-Lima buses.

Guayaquil and South to Peru

TO SAY that this part of Ecuador is not top of the list on many tourist itineraries would be a major understatement. Guayaquil is probably seen by most travellers as the departure point for a trip to the Gálapagos Islands and little else, while for most the southern coastlands merely provide the most convenient route South to Peru. Though this region may not see much in the way of tourist dollars, it remains the economic hub of the country.

The coastline south to Huaquillas, the main border crossing, gives the impression of being one giant banana plantation while increasing numbers of shrimp farmers battle it out with conservation groups over the future of the mangroves that line large parts of the Gulf of Guayaquil. Rice, sugar, coffee, mango and cacao are also produced in the hot and humid Guayas lowlands.

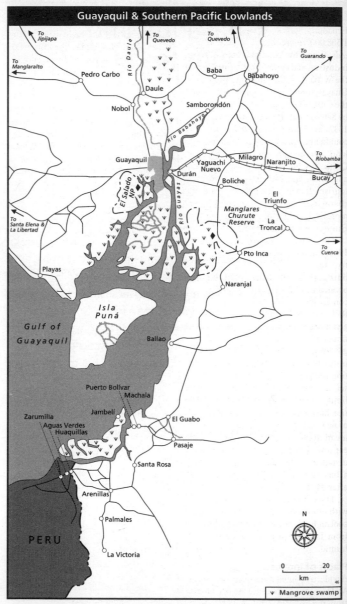

Guayaquil & Southern Pacific Lowlands

To Jipijapa

To Quevedo

To Quevedo

To Guarando

To Manglaralto

Río Daule

Pedro Carbo

Baba

Babahoyo

Daule

Nobol

Samborondón

Río Babahoyo

Guayaquil

Yaguachi Nuevo

Milagro

Naranjito

To Riobamba

El Salado NP

Durán

Boliche

Bucay

To Santa Elena & La Libertad

El Triunfo

Manglares Churute Reserve

La Troncal

To Cuenca

Playas

Río Guayas

Pto Inca

Isla Puná

Naranjal

Gulf of Guayaquil

Ballao

Puerto Bolívar

Machala

Jambelí

El Guabo

Zarumilla

Aguas Verdes

Huaquillas

Pasaje

Santa Rosa

Arenillas

Palmales

PERU

La Victoria

N

0   20
km

ᵛ Mangrove swamp

GUAYAQUIL

Ecuador's largest city (*Pop* officially 1,508,000, more like 2,400,000; *Phone code* 4) and the country's chief seaport, industrial and commercial centre lies on the W bank of the chocolate-brown Río Guayas, some 56 km from its outflow into the Gulf of Guayaquil. Founded in 1535 by Sebastián de Belalcázar, then again in 1537 by Francisco Orellana, the city couldn't be more different from its highland counterpart and political rival, Quito. It's hot, sticky, fast-paced, bold and brash and with few concessions to tourism. It may lack the capital's colonial charm, but Guayaquileños are certainly more lively, colourful and open than their Quito counterparts.

The Puerto Marítimo, opened in 1964, handles about 90% of the country's imports and 50% of its exports (a bulk grain and container extension was opened in 1979). It is a constant bone of contention between the 'costeños' and the 'serranos' that Guayaquil is not given better recognition of its economic importance in the form of more central government aid. Because of the huge influx of people caused by rural migration and population explosion, the city's services have been stretched beyond the limit. Water supply and rubbish collection have improved, but the installation of new water pipes and traffic schemes mean chaos for drivers (until 1997 at the earliest). It is often quicker to walk short distances in the centre, rather than take a bus or taxi. But you shouldn't walk after dark.

The climate from May to Dec is dry with often overcast days but pleasantly cool nights, whereas the hot rainy season from Jan to April can be oppressively humid.

Places of interest

A wide, tree-lined waterfront avenue, the Malecón, runs alongside the Río Guayas from the exclusive **Club de la Unión**, by the Moorish clock tower, past the imposing **Palacio Municipal** and **Government Palace** and the old Yacht Club to Las Peñas. Half way along, the Blvd 9 de Octubre, the city's main street, starts in front of La Rotonda, a statue to mark the famous yet mysterious meeting between Simón Bolívar and San Martín in 1822. There are 11 piers (*muelles*) running along the Malecón. From the most northerly public pier, near Las Peñas, ferries sail across the river to the train station at Durán (see page 245).

Don't look for ancient monuments in Guayaquil. Most of its history is confined to history books. There are several noteworthy churches but, because of sackings or fire, almost none of its wooden buildings remain. A notable exception is the old district of **Las Peñas**, a last picturesque, if ramshackle and small, vestige of colonial Guayaquil with its wooden houses and narrow cobbled street (Numa Pompilio Llona). The entrance is guarded by two cannon pointing riverward, a reminder of the days when pirates sailed up the Guayas to attack the city. Now occupied mostly by artists, there is a large open-air exhibition of paintings and sculpture held here

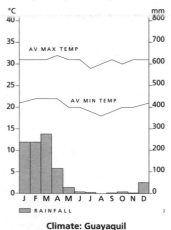

Climate: Guayaquil

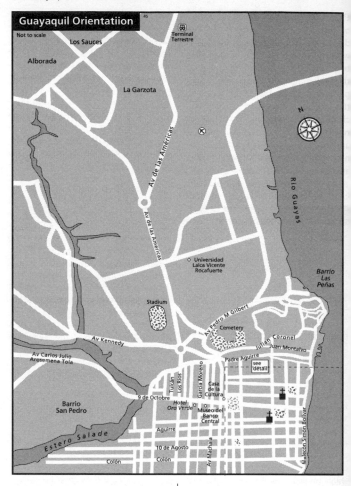

Guayaquil Orientatiion

Not to scale

Los Sauces

Alborada

La Garzota

Terminal Terrestre

Av de las Américas

Av de las Américas

Río Guayas

Universidad Laica Vicente Rocafuerte

Barrio Las Peñas

Stadium

Av Pedro M Gilbert

Cemetery

Julián Coronel

Juan Montalvo

Av Kennedy

Padre Aguirre

see detail

Av Carlos Julio Arosemena Tola

Tulcán

Los Ríos

García Moreno

Casa de la Cultura

Barrio San Pedro

9 de Octubre

Hotel Oro Verde

Museo del Banco Central

Aguirre

Av Machala

Malecón Simón Bolívar

10 de Agosto

Colón

Colón

Estero Salado

every year in July. It makes a pleasant walk, but this is a poor area and mugging is getting more common at night. You are strongly advised not to walk up the adjacent streets of the Cerro Santa Ana that overlook Las Peñas.

The main plaza half way up 9 Octubre is the **Plaza Centenario** with a towering monument to the liberation of the city erected in 1920. The pleasant, shady **Parque Bolívar** in front of the **Cathedral** is filled with tame iguanas which scuttle out of the trees for scraps.

There are several noteworthy churches. Santo Domingo, the city's first church founded by the Dominicans in 1548, stands just by Las Peñas. It was sacked and burned by pirates in 1624. Its present form was built in 1938, replacing the wooden structure with concrete in classical style.

Pirates also sacked the original church of **San Agustín**; the present building dates from 1931. The Cathedral's original wooden structure, built in 1695, survived both sackings and fire, but the years took their toll and a new building was completed in 1822. In 1924 construction on the present edifice was started, in the classical Gothic style, and it was inaugurated in the 1950s. Other notable churches are **San Francisco**, with its restored colonial interior, off 9 de Octubre and P Carbo, and the beautiful **La Merced**.

At the N end of the centre, below Cerro El Carmen, the huge, spreading **Cemetery** with its dazzling, high-rise tombs and the ostentatious mausolea of the rich is worth a visit. A flower market over the road sells the best selection of blooms in the city. It's best to go on a Sun when there are plenty of people about.

There are numerous sports clubs for golf, tennis, swimming, sailing and the horse race track of **El Buijo** is set in delightful surroundings some 5 km outside the city. There are two football stadia and the enclosed Coliseo Cerrado for boxing, basketball and other entertainments.

The **Centro Cívico**, heading S, finally

Feeling queer in Guayaquil

The much maligned seaport of Guayaquil gained even greater notoriety in the William Burrough's novel, *Queer*, which describes two men's search through Ecuador for a mind-altering drug. Burroughs, it seems, was not much taken with the place.

In *Queer*, the story opens in Mexico City, where the protagonist, Lee, is coping with the acute withdrawal symptoms from heroin addiction by drinking and smoking grass. His reawakened sexual desire leads him to the seduction of another ex-pat idler, Allerton, and together they plan a trip to Ecuador to try and get hold of an obscure drug called *Yage*. Lee is fascinated by stories he has read of various governments' experiments in mind-control with the drug.

They arrive in Quito, spending a few days there in search of a doctor who will give Lee a mild heroin substitute, after which he resolves to kick the habit once and for all. Next, they fly to Manta, where they lie around on the beach for a few days, before heading for Guayaquil. Here, Burroughs describes the city's parks full of tropical trees and shrubs, where the people "do a great deal of sitting". An undercurrent of sadness and apathy permeates Lee's impression of the city, and while his boyfriend sleeps at their hotel, he drifts around Guayaquil alone, wallowing in feelings of despair and withdrawal sickness.

From Guayaquil, Lee returns to Quito to get more information on the mysterious *Yage* plant. He is told to go to Puyo, where the plant grows in the high jungle on the Eastern flank of the Andes. The final part of their trip takes them by river to Babahoyo and from there up to Ambato and, finally, to Puyo.

Asking around in Puyo, Lee finds out that an American botanist in the area is experimenting with *Yage* and they pay him a visit. However, the botanist is not forthcoming. He has been conducting serious experiments with the plant for three years and is suspicious of Lee's junky talk and conspiracy theories. He does all he can to make the two men give up their search for *Yage*.

In his 1985 introduction, 35 years after writing *Queer*, Burroughs writes that the elusive drug that his character, ie Burroughs himself, was searching for was later bought and synthesized by chemical companies, and is now a standard component of many muscle-relaxing drugs.

Guayaquil Northern Suburbs

Not to scale

N

Av Jaime Roldós

Av Pablo Roldán

Av B Icaza

Av Egas

Av Ayora

La Rotonda

ALBORADA

SAUCES

OBEV

1

Roldós Statue

Plaza Mayor

2

Garzo Centro

Terminal Terrestre

Av Orellana

Av Freire

3

GARZOTA

Av Juan Tanca Marengo

K

Av Las Américas

CC Plaza Quil

To Urdesa

To City Centre

Hotels:	Places to eat:
1. *Youth Hostel*	2. Cangrejo Criollo
	3. Manantial del Marisco

47A

finished after 25 years in the making, provides an excellent theatre/concert facility and is home to the Guayaquil Symphony Orchestra which gives free concerts throughout the year. The new **Teatro Centro de Arte** on the road out to the coast is another first class theatre complex with a wide variety of presentations. The city is also well provided with museums, art galleries and cinemas, details of which are in *El Universo*. Colourful markets are held at the S end of the Malecón or along 6 de Marzo between 10 de Agosto and Ballén. The Mercado Sur, next to Club de la Unión, prefabricated by Eiffel (1905-07), is not safe to enter; it sells fruit, vegetables and illegal wild animals. See below under **Shopping** for the Bahía market.

Barrio Centenario to the S of the centre is the original residential sector, now a peaceful, tree-shaded haven. Newer residential areas are **Urdesa**, NW of the centre, in between two branches of the

Estero Salado (about 15 mins from downtown, traffic permitting). Near the international airport and bus terminal, which are conveniently close to each other, are the districts of **La Garzota**, **Sauces** and **Alborada**. Cleaner, less congested and safer than the centre, but with all services, entertainment and shops, these areas are 10-15 mins by taxi from downtown, and 5 mins from the airport and Terminal Terrestre.

Two long bridges span the Babahoyo and Daule rivers, as they merge into the Guayas. The road across the bridges leads to Durán and the rail terminal on the E bank. This is a vital link for the city since from Durán main highways continue to Quito, Milagro, Riobamba, Cuenca and Machala.

Museums

The **Museo Municipal** is housed in the Biblioteca Municipal, at Sucre y Pedro Carbo (near the *Hotel Continental*) where there are paintings, gold and archaeological collections, shrunken Shuar heads, a section on the history of Guayaquil and also a good newspaper library. Open Wed-Fri 0900-1600, Sat 1000-1500, Sun 1000-1300; US$0.15 for Ecuadoreans and US$0.40 for foreigners (free on Sat, but passport must be left at desk).

The Central Bank's **anthropological museum** is at Anteparra 900 y 9 de Octubre, it has excellent displays of ceramics, gold objects and paintings; entry US$1.20, open Mon to Fri 1000-1800, Sat 1000-1600, Sun 1000-1400. The Pinacoteca Manuel Rendoy Seminario is on the first floor of the same building. **Museo del Banco del Pacífico** (address under **Banks & money changers**) is a beautiful small museum mainly of archaeological exhibits, open Tues-Fri 1100-1800, Sat-Sun 1100-1300.

There is an impressive collection of prehistoric gold items at the museum of the **Casa de la Cultura**, together with an archaeological museum; at 9 de Octubre 1200 y Moncayo, open Tues-Fri 1000-

1700. **Religious Art Museum Nahim Isaias Barquet** is at Pichincha y Ballén, open Tues-Fri 0900-1700, Sat 1000-1300. There is a pinacoteca (art gallery) on the ground and first floors of the same building. There is a **small zoo**, open on Sun, at the Colegio Nacional.

Excursions

The **Botanical Gardens** with orchid house, are NW on Av Francisco de Orellana to Las Orquídeas housing estate, offering good views and a pleasant walk. Entrance US$2. There are over 3,000 plants, including 150 species of Ecuadorean and foreign orchids.

Cerro Blanco Forest Reserve This nature reserve is set in tropical dry forest with an impressive variety of birds (over 190 species listed so far), such as the Guayaquil green macaw, crane hawk, snail kite, etc, and with sightings of howler monkeys, ocelot, puma, jaguar, and peccaries among others. It is privately owned and managed by La Cemento Nacional: reservations and obligatory prepayment from Multicomercio, Oficina 91, p 1, Eloy Alfaro y Cuenca, or T 871-900, F 872-236; US$0.85 plus US$6.25 per group for guide, up to 8 in group. Defined trails are open Wed to Sun 0800-1600. The reserve is also open Sat and Sun without advance booking; pay for entrance and guide at the site office. Early morning visits are advisable as there is the possibility of seeing more wildlife. Mosquito repellent is a must. Camping can be arranged, US$2.50/night.

● **Access** The reserve is at Km 14.5 on the coast road to Salinas; entrance beyond the Club Rocafuerte. Taxi from Guayaquil US$10-20. The yellow and green 'Chongonera' buses leave every 30 mins from Parque Victoria and pass the park entrance on the way to Puerto Hondo.

On the other side of the road from Cerro Blanco is **Puerto Hondo**. Canoe trips through the mangroves can be made from here. They can be arranged on the spot at weekends from the Fundación Pro-Bosque kiosk for US$7 pp with guides, or through the week with La Cemento Nacional (see above).

Manglares Churute Ecological Reserve Heading E then S from Guayaquil, 22 km beyond the main crossroads at Km 26 on the road to Naranjal, lies the **Ecological Reserve of Manglares Churute**. Many waterbirds, animals and dolphins can be seen. Canoe trips into the mangroves with guides must be arranged through the Inefan office in Guayaquil, Dept Forestal, Av Quito 402 y P Solano, p 10, T 397-730. Reservations take 3-4 days to arrange a group visit. Trips can also be arranged through *Chasquitur* agency, Urdaneta 1418 y Av Del Ejército, T 281-085. Entrance fee of US$14 pp is charged on site just to walk self-guided nature trail over the hills. A boat trip costs an extra US$50/boat to cover the cost of fuel.

● **Transport** Buses leave the terminal nr the airport every 30 mins going to Naranjal or Machala. Ask to be let off at Churute information centre.

Local festivals

Public holiday, 9 and 12 October. 24 and 25 July, **Bolívar's birthday**, and **Foundation of the City**. **Carnival** is in the days before Lent; watch out for malicious throwing of water balloons, mud, ink and paint, women are prime targets. In contrast New Year's Eve is lots of fun. There is a large exhibition of tableaux, featuring **Años Viejos**, along the Malecón, children begging for alms for their life-size *viejos*, families with cars taking their *viejos* for rides through the centre of town, and a vast conflagration at midnight when all these figures are set on fire and explode.

Local information
● **Accommodation**

Hotel prices, which are higher than in Quito, are set by the Tourist Board, which stipulates their being posted inside hotels. It is common practice to have dual rates in the more upmarket establishments; one for nationals and a much higher one often only in dollars for foreigners. Always check the rate first; also whether the 20% service and taxes are included in the given price. Rooms in the better hotels can be in demand and booking is advised. Several new hotels were under construction in 1996, inc the *Hilton Colón*, Av Francisco Orellana, T 298-828, F 298-827, 280 rooms, luxury hotel, 4 restaurants, 2 pools, due open 1997. Most hotels are downtown, so take a taxi from the airport or bus station (about US$3). The cheap hotels are pretty basic, many cater to short stay customers, and singles seem hard to find. The following list

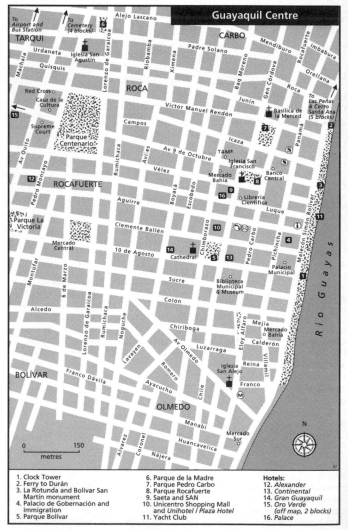

Guayaquil Centre

1. Clock Tower
2. Ferry to Durán
3. La Rotunda and Bolívar San Martín monument
4. Palacio de Gobernación and Immigration
5. Parque Bolívar
6. Parque de la Madre
7. Parque Pedro Carbo
8. Parque Rocafuerte
9. Saeta and SAN
10. Unicentro Shopping Mall and *Unihotel / Plaza Hotel*
11. Yacht Club

Hotels:
12. *Alexander*
13. *Continental*
14. *Gran Guayaquil*
15. *Oro Verde* (off map, 2 blocks)
16. *Palace*

includes 20% service and tax in the prices.

NB All of the downtown area is unsafe; caution is especially important at night. It is far to stay in the districts of La Garzota, Sauces and Alborada, nr the airport and bus terminal.

Price guide

L1	over US$200	**L2**	US$151-200
L3	US$101-150	**A1**	US$81-100
A2	US$61-80	**A3**	US$46-60
B	US$31-45	**C**	US$21-30
D	US$12-20	**E**	US$7-11
F	US$4-6	**G**	up to US$3

L1 *Oro Verde*, 9 de Octubre y García Moreno, T 327-999, F 329-350, PO Box 09-01-9636, restaurants, bar, disco, pool, rec.

L3 *Continental*, Chile y 10 de Agosto, T 329-270, F 325-454 (a KLM Golden Tulip hotel), 5-star, cable TV, good coffee shop, rec; **L3** *Gran Hotel Guayaquil*, Boyacá 1600 y 10 de Agosto, T 329-690, F 327-251, good restaurants, swimming pool, sauna, etc, non residents can use pool, US$2/day; **L3** *Presidente*, Chile 303 y Luque, T 531-300, F 531-354, luxury, suites more expensive; **L3** *Ramada*, Malecón y Orellana, T 565-555, pleasantly situated overlooking the river, with pool, mostly used by businessmen; **L3** *Unihotel*, Clemente Ballén 406 y Chile, T 327-100, F 328-352, good restaurant and breakfast.

A1 *Boulevard*, 9 de Octubre 432, T 566-700, F 560-076, very central, cable TV, casino, shows, rec.

A2 *Palace*, Chile 214 y Luque, T 321-080, excellent, good value for business travellers, TV, traffic noise on Av Chile side, restaurant, travel agency, fax service, highly rec, **A2** *Sol de Oriente*, Aguirre 603 y Escobedo, T 325-500, F 329-352, excellent value, rec.

A3 *Del Rey*, Aguirre y Marín, T 453-037, F 453-351, behind tennis club, inc breakfast, clean, friendly.

B *Doral*, Aguirre y Chile 402, T 328-490, F 327-088, good rooms and value, central, rec; **B** *Suite El Ejecutivo*, Escobedo 1403 y Luque, T 532-295, F 321-409, apart hotel, a/c, kitchenette, TV, parking; **B** *Tangara Guest House*, Ciudadela Bolivariana, Manuela Sáenz & O'Leary Block F, House 1, T 284-445, F 285-872, clean, safe and friendly, all rooms with private bathroom, located in a residential area between airport and town.

C *Los Andes*, Garaycoa 1233 y Ballén, T 329-741, a/c, bath; **C** *Majestic*, 9 de Octubre 709,

T 324-134, central, fan or a/c; **C** *Plaza*, Chile 414 y Clemente Ballén, T 324-006, some cheaper rooms, international newspapers; **C** *Ritz*, 9 de Octubre y Boyacá, T 324-134, F 322-151, with bath, a/c, hot water; **C** *Rizzo*, Clemente Ballén 319 y Chile, T 325-210, F 326-209, TV, bath, a/c, safe, central on Parque Bolívar, some rooms without windows, room service, *Café Jambelí* downstairs.

D *Acuario*, Luque 1204 y Quito, T 533-715, a/c, bath, fridge, TV, **E** with fan; **D** *Alexander*, Luque 1107 y Pedro Moncayo, T 532-000, F 514-161, with bath, a/c, comfortable, good value, some rooms without windows, noisy; **D** *Andy*, Rendón 819 y Riobamba, with bath, a/c, **E** with fan, some short stay customers; **D** *Capri*, Luque y Machala, T 326-341, with bath, a/c, cable TV, fridge, cafeteria, very clean and safe, busy at weekends; **D** *Luque*, Luque 1214 y Quito, T 523-900, with bath, a/c, TV, **E** with fan; **D** *Paseo Real*, Luque 1011 y 6 de Mayo, T 532-710, with bath, a/c, TV, **F** for inner rooms, cheaper with fan; **D** *Plaza Centenario*, Garaycoa 935, T 526-446, a/c, TV, inner rooms cheaper; **D** *Turista*, Baquerizo Moreno 903 y Junín, T 565-350, with bath, a/c or fan, TV; **D** *Venezia*, Quisquis y Rumichaca, with bath, clean, friendly.

E *Centenario*, Vélez 726 y Santa Elena, T 524-467, with bath, TV, a/c, cheaper with fan; **E** *Danubio*, P Icaza 604 y Escobedo, T 300-197, with bath, fan, some a/c; **E** *Ecuador*, Moncayo 1117 y Luque, T 321-460, with bath, fan; **E** *Galápagos*, Rendón 917 y Rumichaca, fan, basic, clean; **E** *Jitur*, Colón 804 y Rumichaca, T 523 073, with bath, TV, fan, clean; **E** *Nevada*, Garaycoa 710 y Rendón, T 311298, with bath, a/c, TV; **E** *Nuevo Sander*, Luque 1101 y Pedro Moncayo, T 320-030, with bath, a/c, cheaper with fan, central, nr a dangerous area; **E** *Primavera*, 6 de Marzo y Clemente Ballén, TV, fan, clean; **E** *Residencial Pauker*, Baquerizo Moreno 902 y Junín, T 565-385, shared bath, run down, old-time haunt for travellers, safe; **E** *Vélez*, Vélez 1021 y Quito, T 530-356, with bath, TV, a/c, cheaper without a/c and TV, clean, good value, rec.

F-G pp *Berlín*, Rumichaca 1503, T 524-648, with bath, fan, clean, front rooms noisy; **F** pp *Libertador*, Garaycoa 893, Parque Centenario, T 304-637, fan, bath.

G *Hostal Miami*, P Montúfar 534, T 519-667, fan, bath; **G** *Imperial*, Urdaneta 705, T 560-512, basic.

Youth Hostel: **E** pp *Ecuahogar*, Sauces I, Av

Isidro Ayora, opp Banco Ecuatoriana de La Vivienda, T 248-357, F 248-341, member of IYHA and Ecuadorean Hostelling Association, non-members welcome, inc breakfast, bunk rooms and rooms with bath, cooking and laundry facilities, tourist information, safe, will pick up from bus station and airport, or take buses 2 or 66, discount for longer stay, English and German spoken, set meals in restaurant US$2, very friendly and helpful, highly rec.

● **Places to eat**

The main areas for restaurants are the centre with many in the larger hotels, around Urdesa, or the newer residential and commercial centres of La Alborada and La Garzota, which have many good eating houses. 20% service and tax is added on in the smarter places.

International: *El Fortín* in *Hotel Continental* for good food and service; *1822* in the *Gran Hotel*, small but interesting menu, expensive, pleasant surroundings; *Le Gourmet* at the *Oro Verde*, expensive, good; *La Banca*, Icaza 115 y Pichincha, popular with business community; *Posada de las Garzas*, Urdesa Norte, Circunvalación Norte 536, also French style dishes; *El Parque*, top floor of Unicentro, for excellent popular buffet lunches at the weekends; *Juan Salvador Gaviota*, Kennedy Norte, Av Fco de Orellana, good seafood; *La Balandra*, C 5a 504 entre Monjas y Dátiles, Urdesa, for good fish, upmarket ambience, also has a crab house at Circunvalación 506 y Ficus, Urdesa.

Typical: *Canoa Bar* in *Hotel Continental* for traditional dishes rarely found these days, with different specials during the week; *Salón Melba*, Córdova 720 y Junín, old fashioned eating house/coffee shop; *Café Jambelí*, in *Rizzo Hotel* for coastal dishes and seafood; *El Pirata* floating restaurant on river opp VM Rendón, slow service; *Muelle 5*, Malecón y Urdaneta, on a pier, good seafood; *Pique Y Pase*, Lascano 16-17 y Carchi, popular with students, lively; *El Patio* in the *Oro Verde*, for reasonably priced food; *El Caribe*, VE Estrada 1017 y Jiguas, Urdesa, good value and service, cheap set lunches, rec, wonderful *chupes de pescado*; *El Manantial*, VE Estrada y Las Monjas, good; *La Guadalajara*, Av Kennedy, very good, cheap, open air café, *chuzos* (meat on sticks), popular with students from nearby University; *El Taller*, Quisquis y Esmeraldas, tiny place decked out with odd bits and pieces of old Guayaquil, live music in evenings. *Viejo Barrio*, over the bridge from the Policentro in Urdesa, lots of cafés offering a variety of dishes,

all in fake old Guayaquil style.

Italian: *La Trattoria da Enrico*, Bálsamos 504, expensive but fun surroundings, good antipasto. Pizzas: *Pizza Hut* on 9 de Octubre in Urdesa, La Garzota and Barrio Centenario; *El Hornero*, Estrada y Higuerilla, part of Quito chain; *Pizzería Del Ñato*, Estrada 1219, good value, sold by the metre.

Spanish: *Hostería Madrid*, Los Ríos y 9 Octubre, paellas; *Casa Basca*, Chile 406 y C Ballén, wonderful hole-in-the-wall place, expensive food, cash only, house wine good value, great atmosphere, gets very crowded; *Puerta de Alcalá*, Circulación y Ficus, upmarket.

French: *La Bastilla*, Bálsamos 606 y Ficus, Urdesa, upmarket, pretentious.

Mexican: *Noches Tapatías*, Primera y Dátiles, Urdesa, fun, good live music at weekends; *Mi Cielito Lindo*, Circunvalación 623 y Ficus, good.

Chinese: a wide variety in the city, most do take-away, good value. *Chifa Himalaya*, Sucre 309 y P Carbo, slow service but good for the price; *Gran Chifa*, P Carbo 1016, wide variety, good value; *Cantonés*, Av G Pareja y C 43, La Garzota, huge rather glaring emporium with authentic dishes and all-you-can-eat menu for US$9, karaoke. **Japanese**: *Tsuji*, Estrada 815, wonderful, authentic dishes, Teppan Yaki, expensive; *UniBar* in *Uni Hotel* complex, sushi.

Lebanese: *Beirut*, Urdesa C 4a 716.

Vegetarian: *Maranatá I*, Chile y Cuenca, and *II*, Quisquis y Rumichaca; *Super Nutrión I*, Chimborazo y 10 de Agosto, and *II* Chimborazo y Letamendi; *Girasol*, Chile y Colón; *Renacer*, G Avilés y Sucre; *Hare Krishna*, 1 de Mayo y 6 de Marzo; *Salud Solar*, Pedro Moncayo y Luque; *Bocado Natural*, Multicomercio, p 1; *Ollantay*, Tungurahua 508 y 9 de Octubre; *Paraíso*, Av Juan Tanca Marengo, Km 1.5; *Paxilandia*, Guayacanes 208 y C Primera in the Valmor Centre, Urdesa.

Steak Houses: *Donde el Ché*, F Boloña S21A, holds competition to see who can eat the biggest steak, winner doesn't pay, music, tango and shows; *Parillada Del Ñato*, Estrada 1219, huge variety and portions, excellent value; *La Selvita*, Av Olmos y Las Brisas, Las Lomas de Urdesa, good atmosphere and fine panoramic views, also at Calle D y Rosa Borja, Centenario; *El Torro*, Luque y Garaycoa, huge steaks, pay in advance, fast-food atmosphere.

Crab Houses: these are almost an institution

and great fun. *Manny's*, Av Miraflores y Segunda, not cheap but try the excellent *arroz con cangrejo*; *Casa del Cangrejo*, Av Plaza Dañín, Kennedy, for crab dishes of every kind; several others along the same street; *El Cangrejo Rojo*, Rumichaca 2901; *El Cangrejo Criollo*, Av Principal, Villa 9, La Garzota, excellent, varied seafood menu, rec.

Oyster Bars: cultivated oysters are all the rage and many menus carry them. *Oystercatcher*, Higueras y Mirtos, Urdesa, varied menu; *Bodegas del Mar*, Centro Comercial Plaza Quil opp the Policentro, a fish shop selling 12 fresh, opened oysters for US$2.25; bar next to *El Manantial* (see under *Typical*).

Brazilian: *Brasa Brasil*, opp the Albán Borja shopping centre.

Snacks: there are many places selling all sorts of snacks. Try *pan de yuca*, or *empanadas*, but beware of eating at street stalls. Excellent sandwiches at *Submarine*, 9 Octubre y Chile, *Miami Subs*, Chimborazo 425 y Ballén, and Estrada y Alborada, Urdesa, salads and sandwiches; *Uni Deli* in the Unicentro, good salami and cheese; *La Chivería*, Circunvalación y Ficus for good yoghurt and *pan de yuca*; *La Selecta*, Estrada y Laureles, good sandwiches.

Fast Food: *Kentucky Fried Chicken*, 9 Octubre y Escobedo and opp Policentro in Plaza Quil; *Italian Deli*, in Albán Borja and Policentro, good self-service meals, great salads; *Pollos Gus*, Maracaibo 530 y Quito, Plaza Triángulo in Urdesa, Terminal Terrestre, good chicken and typical dishes; *Burger King*, 9 Octubre 610 or Estrada y Las Lomas in Urdesa.

Ice-cream: *Top Cream*, the best, with many outlets throughout the city, try their local fruit sorbets.

All night: *La Canoa* at the *Hotel Continental*; *Sandry's* at the airport; *La Pepa de Oro* at the *Grand Hotel*; *El Patio* at the *Hotel Oro Verde*.

● **Airline offices**
TAME, 9 de Octubre 424, edif Gran Pasaje, T 561-751; **Saeta** and **SAN**, main admin office at Av Arosemena Km 2.5, sales office at 9 de Octubre 2002 y Los Ríos, T 200-600 (bilingual information line), 200-614; **Ecuatoriana de Aviación**, 9 de Octubre y Malecón, T 322-025, F 282-020; **Cedta**, T 301-165; **AELA**, T 288-580/228-110; **AeroPerú**, Icaza 451, T 563-600; **British Airways**, Velez 206 y Chile, T 325-080.

● **Banks & money changers**
Lloyds Bank, Pichincha 108-110, with Mercado Central and Urdesa agencies, high commission on TCs; **ABN-Amro**, P Icaza 454 y Baquerizo Moreno, T 312-900; **Citibank**, 9 de Octubre, Citicorp cheques only and before 1330; **Banco del Pacífico**, Icaza 200, p 4, no commission on TCs, advances money on Mastercard; **Filanbanco**, 9 de Octubre entre Pichincha y P Carbo, cash advance with Visa ATM, good rates, no commission; **American Express**, 9 de Octubre 1900 y Esmaraldas, for purchase of TCs. Queues are much longer in the afternoon. **Banco de Guayaquil**, ATMs advance cash with Visa (Sucres only). There is a Mastercard office on Rocafuerte, nr Parque Rocafuerte.

There are various **Casas de Cambio** on Av 9 de Octubre (eg **Cambio Paz**) and C Pichincha; also **Cambiosa**, in Albán Borja and **Cambitur** on Baquerizo Moreno 113 y Malecón, rec. Most open 0900-1900, closed Sat. **Wander Cambios** at airport (see below). It's difficult to change money at the bus station. When all the rest are closed (eg Sun) try *Hotel Oro Verde* and similar places, quite good exchange rate for cash, will change small TC amounts.

Street changers on 9 de Octubre y Pichincha, best rates for cash, very organized.

● **Embassies & consulates**
Argentina, Aguirre 104, T 323-574; **Bolivia**, P Ycaza 302 y Córdova, T 564-260; **Brazil**, Ciudadela Nueva Kennedy, C 9 Este A 208, T 393-979; **Colombia**, Gral Córdova 808 y VM Rendón, T 563-854; **Peru**, 9 de Octubre 411, p 6, T 322-730, 0900-1300, **Venezuela**, Chile 331, T 326-566.

Austria, 9 de Octubre 1312, T 282-303; **Belgium**, Lizardo García 310 y Vélez, T 364-429; **Denmark**, Gen Córdoba 604 y Mendiburu, T 308-020, open 0900-1200; **Finland**, Luis Urdaneta 212 y Córdova, T 304-381; **France**, Aguirre 503 y Chimborazo, p 6, T 328-159; **Germany**, 9 de Octubre 109, T 513-876; **Netherlands**, 9 de Octubre 2309, p 5, T 366-410; **Norway**, Blvd 9 de Octubre 109 y Malecón, T 329-661; **Switzerland**, 9 de Octubre 2105, T 453-6071; **UK**, Córdova 623 y P Solano, T 560-400.

Canada, Córdova 812 y Rendón, T 563-580; **USA**, 9 de Octubre 1571 y García Moreno, T 323-570.

● **Entertainment**
There are discos, bars and casinos in most of the major hotels: *Oro Verde, Unihotel, Boule-*

vard. Other discos at *Infinity*, Estrada 505; *Latin Palace*, Av J Tanca Marengo y Roldós; *El Corsario*, Los Ríos y Piedrahita; *Buccaneer* and *Flashdance* in centre. *Disco Gente*, Estrada 913, for café-theatre style comedy show with dancing afterwards; *Disco La Salsa*, Estrada for good salsa. *Reencuentros*, entrance to Urdesa Norte, C 6, music, bar, live show; *Cato's Pub*, Estrada 608 y Las Monjas; *Falls*, VE Estrada y Las Monjas, Urdesa, pool tables; *Aló*, VE Estrada y Dátiles, bar, disco, outdoor eating, cheap set lunches. For an unforgettable and alcoholic evening 'city tour' take *La Chiva* (open-sided bus) from *Infinity* on Fri at 2130, which provides en route as many rum punches as you can hold, stopping off occasionally for a ceviche, dancing, fireworks, crab sandwich before depositing you back at *Infinity* for US$14 pp. Usually for groups only, details available from *Viajes Horizontes*, T 281-260. Trips on the Río Guayas with the (fake) paddle boat *El Pedregal* to the Club Pedregal on E side; US$3.70, inc boat ride, use of pool, sauna, tennis courts, volleyball, children's amenities, the complex has restaurant and bar. Boat departs Muelle Pedregal Sat and Sun 1130 and 1330 returning 1630 and 1730. See *El Universo* for cinemas and other entertainments. Cinemas cost US$2.25, one double bill.

● **Hospitals & medical services**
Doctors: *Dr Angel Serrano Sáenz*, Boyacá 821, T 301-373, English speaking. *Dr Alfonso E León Guim*, Centro de Especialidades, Boyacá 1320 y Luque, T 517-793; also English speaking. *Clínica Santa Marianita*, Boyacá 1915 entre Colón y Av Olmedo, T 322-500, doctors speak English and Spanish, special rates for SAHB users.

Hospitals: the main hospital used by the foreign community is the *Clínica Kennedy*, Av del Periodista, T 286-963, which contains the consulting rooms of almost every kind of specialist doctor and diagnostic laboratory (Dr Roberto Morla speaks German); very competent emergency department.

● **Laundry**
Sistematic, F Segura y Av Quito, or C 6a y Las Lomas, Urdesa; *Martinizing* for dry cleaning, many outlets, don't rely on their 1-hr service; *Dryclean USA*, VE Estrada 1016, Urdesa.

● **Places of worship**
Anglican-Episcopalian Church, Calle D entre Bogotá y A Fuentes, T 443-050; Centro Cristiano de Guayaquil, Pastor John Jerry

Smith, Av Juan Tanca Marengo, Km 3, T 271-423; many other sects represented.

● **Post and telecommunications**
Emetel, the telephone company, and central post office are in the same block at Pedro Carbo y Aguirre. Buy long-distance *fichas* for telephone calls before contacting the international operator. Lots of small booths around the building selling stationery etc. Good *poste restante* service. Parcels to be sent abroad have to be sealed in front of postal assistant but is a surprisingly reliable service, p 1, ventanilla 12. Branch post offices in Urdesa, Estrada y Las Lomas by Mi Comisariato supermarket; 1st floor of Policentro; airport and Terminal Terrestre. The major hotels also sell stamps. Many courier services for reliable delivery of papers and packages, eg: *DHL*, C 8a Oeste 100 y San Jorge, Kennedy, T 287-044; *UPS*, Pedro Moncayo 700 y Quisquís, T 314-315; *AeroNet*, Plaza Quil, local 73, T 399-777, and others. *Urgentito*, Chile 126 y Vélez, or Carchi y 9 de Octubre, T 325-742, for interprovincial service.

● **Security**
Guayaquil is becoming increasingly insecure, especially around hotel or bank entrances, attackers usually working in pairs. The Malecón in early morning and from dusk onwards is bad for snatch thieves. Also near the toilets in the Terminal Terrestre bus station where thieves work in pairs. Street robbery also occurs in Durán. Do not walk anywhere with valuables and take taxis at night. Cholera, dengue and rabies are present.

● **Shopping**
Books: *Librería Científica*, Luque 223 y Chile and Plaza Triángulo on the Estrada in Urdesa, has English books and is good for field guides to flora and fauna and travel in general; *Librería Cervantes*, Aguirre 606-A y Escobedo; *Nuevos Horizontes*, 6 de Marzo 924 for book exchange. *Selecciones* in Albanborja has a choice of pricey novels and lots of magazines in English. Copyright laws are not applied anywhere and whole books can be copied and bound often cheaper than buying a new book, *Xerox* on 9 Octubre 1514 or Rendón y P Carbo, and *El Copión*, Quisquís 607 or Av Miraflores 206, among many others. For cheapest photocopies and stationery, try any of the copying shops on Av Delta by the State University.

Shopping malls: *Unicentro*, Aguirre y Chile; *Policentro* and *Plaza Quil*, both on Av San Jorge, N Kennedy; *Albán Borja*, Av Arosemena

Km 2.7; *Garzocentro 2000*, La Garzota, Av R Pareja; *La Rotonda*, entrance to La Garzota, US-style shopping; *Plaza Mayor*, La Alborada, Av R Pareja and, nearby, *Albocentro*. *Riocentro*, Av Samborondón, for expensive, US-style shopping. *Mall del Sol*, nr airport, to open 1997.

For handicrafts: good quality but expensive products are found at Madeleine Hollander's shop in the *Oro Verde*; *Manos* in Urdesa (Cedros 305 y Primera); *Artesanías del Ecuador*, 9 Octubre 104 y Malecón are good and reliable as is *Ocepa*, Rendón 405 y Córdova, where prices compare favourably with the towns where the goods are made. Good variety of *artesanías* in Albán Borja Mall at *El Telar*; *Ramayana* for good ceramics. *Vega*, VE Estrada 1200 y Laureles, Urdesa, Cuenca ceramics, full range, unfriendly service; *Centro de Artesanías Montecristi*, Juan Tanca Marengo Km 0.5 for straw and wicker goods and furniture.

Indian artefact

For bargains and variety try the *handicrafts market* between Loja y Montalvo and Córdova y Chimborazo, almost a whole block of permanent stalls; the Otavalan Indians sell their crafts along Chile between 9 Octubre y Vélez. Panama hats, good quality, authentic, from *Sombrero Barberán*, 1 de Mayo 112, N end of Parque Centenario; also in the handicraft market.

Photos: developed reliably at *Rapi-Color*, Boyacá 1418 y Luque, or *Photo Market*, VE Estrada 726 y Guayacanes, Urdesa, prints and slides. Camera repairs at *Cinefoto*, Luque 314 y Chimborazo, English spoken. Cheap film and instant ID photos from *Discount New York* in Albán Borja.

Camping equipment: (expensive) and camping gas are available from *Casa Maspons*, Ballén 517 y Boyacá, *Marathon*, 9 de Octubre y Escobedo, or in Policentro (also sells cheap T-shirts, choose your own motif). *Kao Policentro*, has fishing, camping and sports gear at good prices.

There are now lots of import shops in the centre and Urdesa selling American food and household products; however, the **Bahía**, or black market, on either side of Olmedo from Villamil to Chile, is still the most popular place for electrical appliances, clothing, shoes, food and drink. It was traditionally where contraband was sold from boats which put into the bay and is one of the city's oldest market places. Watch your valuables and be prepared to bargain. Throughout the city are very cheap, 'dump' stores selling below-market-price US clothing, tremendous bargains to be found, but also second-hand and shop-soiled goods.

● **Sports**

Horse racing: Hipódromos Buijo and Río Verde in Salinas. Parimutuel betting.

Swimming: pool at Malecón Simón Bolívar 116.

● **Tour companies & travel agents**
Wanderjahr, P Icaza 431, Edif Gran Pasaje, T 562-111, branches in Policentro, T 288-400, the *Hotel Oro Verde*, Albanborja, T 203-913; *Ecuadorean Tours*, 9 Octubre 1900 y Esmeraldas, T 287-111, is agent for Amex, branches Chile y 10 de Agosto and in Urdesa, Estrada 117, T 388-080; *Metropolitan Touring – Galapagos Cruises*, Antepara 915, T 330-300; *Ecoventura*, Av CJ Arosemena Km 2.5, T 206-748/9, F 202-990, see also under Quito **Tour companies** and under the Galápagos;

Machiavello Tours, Antepara 802 y 9 Octubre, T 282-902; *La Moneda Tours*, P Icaza 115 y Pichincha, PO Box 09-01-8908, T 563-950, F 320-374, Email travel@lamondea.com.ec, has branches in Riocentro Shopping Center T 831-201, F 831-214, Quito, Machala and in the USA (1390 Brickell Av, Miami, Florida 33131, T (305) 379-8110, F (305) 379-8112), specializes in coastal and archaeological tours; *Orbitur*, Malecón 1405 y Aguirre, T 325-777; *Galasam Cía Ltda*, Edif Gran Pasaje, 9 Octubre 424, p 11 of 1108, T 306-289, see Galápagos section (page 331) for their Economic Galapagos Tours programmes. *Canodros*, Luis Urdaneta, 1418 y Av del Ejército, T 285-711, F 287-651, PO Box 09-01-8442, e-mail: eco-tourism1@canodros.com.ec; run Galápagos cruises on their new MV *Renaissance*. They also operate the unique Kapawi Ecological Reserve, in conjunction with OINAE (Organization of Ecuadorean Achuar Nationalities), situated at the junctions of the Pastaza and Kapahuari rivers, in Morona Santiago province; 4 nights in a double cabin with bath costs US$700, plus US$200 return flight from Quito. This trip has been highly rec as very comfortable, educational, eco-friendly and sensitive to the needs of the Achuar people (see also page 317).

Whale watching is gaining in popularity; a rec company is *Whale Tours*, Vélez 911 y 6 de Marzo, El Forum, p 5, T 524-608, a day trip costs US$16 pp. Trips can also be arranged out of Puerto López.

Most agencies arrange city tours, 2½ hrs, US$8-10 pp with English-speaking guide, eg *Royal Tours Service*, T 326-688. Also Fernando Icaza, bilingual tourist services, T/F 200-925, has his own minibus.

● **Tourist offices**
Cetur, Aguirre 104 y Malecón, p 1, T 328-312; friendly but poorly informed about anything outside their area or other than standard tourist attractions, Spanish only, open 0900-1730, Mon-Fri. They sell a map of Ecuador. Maps also from **Instituto Geográfico Militar**, 9 de Octubre y Rumichaca. A Policía de Turismo man can be hired for a guided tour of Guayaquil. Cost will be about US$4/hr for taxi (2 hrs is enough) and US$3 to the Policía de Turismo.

● **Useful addresses**
Immigration: Av Pichincha y Aguirre (Gobernación), T 514-925/516-789, for visa extensions.

● **Transport**
Local Buses City buses are clean, modern and comfortable, US$0.25; also minibuses (*furgonetas*), US$0.20, which post up their routes in the windscreen. Buses are not allowed in the centre; almost all go along the Malecón. Bus No 15 will take you from the centre to Urdesa, 13 to Policentro, 14 to Albanborja, 74 to La Garzota and Sauces. **Car hire**: Budget T 288-510 (airport), 328-571 (by *Oro Verde*); **Ecuacars** T 283-247 (airport); **Avis** T 287-906 (airport); **Arrancar** T 284-454 (airport); **Delgado** T 287-768 (airport), 398-687 (centre); **Internacional** T 284-136 (airport). Cheapest rates US$26-30/day, inc 10% tax and insurance, mileage extra. All offer 3-day weekend rates (US$147-154, not inc tax and insurance, 600 km free, Group C-D) and weekly rates with 1,200 km free. **Taxis**: have no meters, so prices are very negotiable and overcharging is notorious (if you think Quito taxi drivers are difficult, you ain't seen nothing yet!). It should be approx US$3 from centre to Urdesa or Policentro, short runs US$1 (if you are very persistent). To Durán, across the bridge, see under **Trains**. *Taxi rutas* run a set route, charging US$0.40; they are yellow with contrasting bonnets, or stripes over the roof, eg ones with red bonnets run from the Bahía, Centro, Urdesa to Mapasingue and back.

Air Simón Bolívar International Airport is to the N about 10 mins by taxi (1 hr on foot) from the city centre. US$0.25 by bus; No 2 from Malecón, No 3 from Centro Cívico, No 69 from Plaza Victoria. If going straight on to another city, get the bus directly to bus station, which is close by; a taxi from the airport to the bus terminal is US$1.50. US$3-5 for a taxi from the centre or from airport, but if you are arriving in Guayaquil and need a taxi from the airport, walk half a block from the terminal out to Av Las Américas, where taxis and camionetas wait for passengers. The fare will be about half of what you will be charged for the same trip by one of the drivers who belong to the airport taxi cooperative. There are several car hire firms in booths outside the national section.

Other facilities at the airport are: an information desk; Cetur office (erratic hours); *Wander Cambio*, open 7 days a week, closed at night, rates lower than other *cambios* or banks, but better than hotels; several bank ATMs; a modern cafetería and a post office. Note that to get to the baggage reclaim area you must leave the airport and re-enter further down the building. Show your boarding pass to enter and baggage ticket to leave.

Air services: many flights daily to Quito, (TAME, Saeta, SAN; ensure seats are confirmed, not standby, though seats are usually available outside peak hours of early morning and evening). Sit on the right side for the best views. Also flights to **Cuenca**, **Loja**, **Machala**. Daily to **Galápagos** (see page 321). Commuter flights daily on small 5-17 seater planes from the Terminal de Avionetas on the city side of the international airport, on Cedta to Machala, or AELA, to Bahía de Caráquez, Manta, Portoviejo to **Pedernales** (reported unreliable). When passing through Guayaquil by air, do not put valuables into backpacks checked into the hold, things go missing.

Road There is a 3¼-km bridge from Guayaquil across the river to Durán. A good paved road from there (summit at 4,120m) connects with the Andean Highway at Cajabamba, nr Riobamba (see page 189). Also from Durán main roads go to Babahoyo, Quevedo and Santo Domingo, to Cuenca, and to the southern lowlands.

Buses The Terminal Terrestre is just N of the airport, just off the road to the Guayas bridge. The company offices are on the ground floor, departures on top floor. It can sometimes be confusing trying to find out where your bus leaves from. There is no left luggage depot and do not leave anything unattended. The terminal is chaotic and busy at weekends. There are some expensive restaurants, use of toilet US$0.10, bus tickets include terminal tax of US$0.05. A great many local buses go from the bus station to centre. Taxi to centre, US$3-5. Several companies to/from **Quito**, 8 hrs, from US$5 to US$13.35 for Rey Tours non-stop, a/c service (office in *Gran Hotel*). To **Cuenca**, 5½ hrs, US$6; **Riobamba**, 5 hrs, US$3.25; **Santo Domingo de los Colorados**, 4¾ hrs, US$4-5; **Manta**, 3 hrs, US$4; **Esmeraldas**, 7 hrs, US$5; **Portoviejo**, 3½ hrs, US$4, and to **Bahía de Caráquez**, 5½ hrs, US$4.45. To **Ambato**, 6½ hrs, US$6. To **Alausí**, 4 hrs, US$3.25. Regular and frequent buses to **Playas**, 2 hrs, US$1.35; and to **Salinas**, 2½ hrs, US$1.85. **Machala** (for Peru) 3½ hrs, US$2.65, frequent, or by minibus 2½ hrs, leave at 20-min intervals between 0600 and 1900, 10 kg baggage limit. For the **Peruvian border**, to **Huaquillas**, avoiding Machala, US$3.45, 4 hrs; via Machala, 6 hrs. Colectivos are not rec for journeys to the Sierra, they drive too fast and are dangerous. **Trucks**: carry

freight and passengers, slower, bumpy, cheaper than buses, and you see better. Enquire at Sucre 1104.

Sea Shipping agent: Luis Arteaga, Aguirre 324 y Chile, T 533-592/670/F 533-445, rec, fast, US$120 for arranging car entry.

RAILWAY TO THE SIERRA

The spectacular 464-km railway line (1.067m gauge), which was opened in 1908, passes through 87 km of delta lands and then, in 80 km, climbs to 3,238m. The highest point (3,609m) is reached at Urbina; it then rises and falls before reaching the Quito plateau at 2,857m. The line is a most interesting piece of railway engineering, with a maximum gradient of 5.5%. Its greatest achievements, the Alausí loop and the Devil's Nose double zigzag (including two V switchbacks), are between Sibambe and Alausí.

DURAN

The train station is in **Durán**, reached by ferry from Guayaquil, Malecón Bolívar y Montúfar about 10 blocks N of the Palacio de Gobernación (during temporary repairs – late 1996 – it will leave from the Mercado Sur behind the Club de la Unión for 6 months). The first ferry is at 0530, the last at 2200, every 15 mins, US$0.10. The buses run later; bus 17 goes to Durán, US$0.25, but drops you some blocks from station. Taxi to Durán from Guayaquil early is US$4.50 (beware 'special service' with prostitute as uninvited extra). Transport to Durán in the early morning is hard to find, eg no buses from the port area.

Durán is described as "a real good time town full of working men looking for action". There is an annual international fair which lasts 2 weeks, huge, exhibits, concerts, traffic jams till midnight.

● **Accommodation** Sparse and, in most cases, short-stay only. **E-F** *La Paz*, Esmeraldas 123 y Cuenca, main street, 2 blocks from and parallel to railway, T 803-465, with bath, fan, cheaper without, clean, light, early morning call for train passengers; **F-G** *Residencial Durán*, Esmeraldas 227, T 800342, with bath, with or without fan, basic, clean, noisy, ask for an outside room with a window; **F** *Residencial París*, Loja y Yaguachi, T 800-403, opp the market, with or without fan, filthy. *Residencial Sarmiento, Los Angeles, Hostal Shirley* all definitely hourly rate and are not rec.

● **Places to eat** Plenty of small restaurants on Esmeraldas and by the market. Good food, particularly fish, is available on the street.

● **Transport Trains** Durán-Riobamba, daily except Mon and Wed at 0625, 12 hrs (*autoferro* sometimes 0620, 8-10 hrs), fare US$15; to Alausí, US$12, 9 hrs. Tickets for Riobamba go on sale from 0600, they cannot be bought in advance; check details. It is rec to ride on the roof for the best views, but dress warmly and protect clothes from dirt on the roof. On the train, lock all luggage, even side pockets, as pilfering from luggage compartments is common. Popular, especially at weekends and public holidays; queue early or go midweek.

DURAN TO BUCAY

Leaving the river the train strikes out across the broad, fertile Guayas valley. It rolls through fields of sugar cane, or rice, past split cane houses built on high stilts, past sugar mills with their owners' fine homes. Everywhere there are waterways, with thousands of water-birds. The first station is **Yaguachi**. On 15 and 16 Aug more than 15,000 visitors pour into this little town to attend the feast day celebrations at the church of San Jacinto, who is honoured in the region for having put an end to many epidemics.

The first stop of importance is **Milagro**, a large but uninteresting town (*Pop* 93,637), centre of a pineapple growing region. Women swarm about the train selling sweet and juicy pineapples.

● **Accommodation & places to eat E-F** *Hotel Oasis*, nr the railway station, safe, clean; **F** *Hotel Viker*, no food, communal washing facilities; **G** *Hotel Azuay*, nr the station, dirty, unfriendly, fan, bath; *Restaurant Topo-Gigio*, nearby, good, cheap food.

● **Transport** Bus to Guayaquil US$0.40.

BUCAY

About 87 km from Durán the train stops for an hour or less at **Bucay** (proper name General Elizalde), at the base of the Andes. Not a particularly nice place to be stuck in and would-be adulterers beware, for this is the birthplace of the notorious Lorena Gallo, wife of John Wayne Bobbit (President Bucarám invited her to an elaborate lunch in Oct 1996). There's a market on Sun.

● **Accommodation E** *California*, clean, cold water, friendly; **F** *Florida*, across river, no nets, showers, small dark rooms, cheap restaurant; **G** *Central*, by station, should only be considered if all the others are full.

● **Transport Trains** Train leaves Bucay at 1045; arrives Alausí around 1530-1600, and Riobamba at 1830. Tickets may only be bought on the day of travel, trains very crowded; to Alausí, US$10, Riobamba US$10. The section to Alausí is stunning, rec to sit on roof for views, though it gets cold after Palmira in the late afternoon. **Buses** Buses run parallel to the train between Bucay and Guayaquil. Bus to Guayaquil 2 hrs, with Santa Marta agency in the town centre. To **Riobamba**, US$1.50, and **Ambato**, 3 hrs, US$3, change at either for Quito. Bus to **Cuenca**: go to El Triunfo, 50 mins, US$0.65, then change for Cuenca, US$2.65, 3½ hrs.

BUCAY TO THE ANDES

The train follows the gorge of the Río Chanchán until it reaches **Huigra**, a very pleasant little town. This offers a better option than Bucay for those who don't have time to do the full trip and wish to return to Riobamba by bus.

● **Accommodation C** *Hostería La Eterna Primavera*, T (04) 885-015/886-749, F (04) 885-015, inc tax and service, bath, hot water, restaurant, bar, pool, horse riding, trips by train to Nariz del Diablo, lovely place to relax for a few days in a pleasant climate. In the town itself are **G** *Huigra*, and *Residencial Paraíso*, nr the station.

● **Transport** Buses daily to Riobamba at 0530, 0600 and 1300; direct to Alausí at around 1000.

After leaving Huigra the train crosses

and recrosses the Río Chanchán, and then creeps along a narrow ledge between the mountain and the canyon. Here begins the most exciting part of the trip. The first mountain town reached is **Chanchán**, where the gorge is so narrow that the train has to pass through a series of tunnels and bridges in its zigzag course.

Next is **Sibambe**. There are no hotels here, but ask in the village for a room, or bring camping gear, but do not stay at the station. Shortly after leaving Sibambe the train starts climbing the famous Nariz del Diablo (Devil's Nose), a perpendicular ridge rising in the gorge of the Chanchán to a height of 305m. This almost insurmountable engineering obstacle was finally conquered when a series of switchbacks was built on a 5.5% grade.

Next comes **Alausí** (see page 201), popular with Guayaquileños wishing to escape the tropical heat and humidity. After crossing the 120m long Shucos bridge, the train pulls into **Palmira**, on the crest of the first range of the Andes crossed by the railway. One by one the great snow-capped volcanoes begin to appear: Chimborazo, Carihuairazo, Altar, Tungurahua, and the burning head of Sangay, all seeming very close because of the clear air.

ROUTES The road from Durán or Milagro heads S to Naranjal and on to Machala, a main crossroads and useful stopover before heading onto Huaquillas, Arenillas and Loja (216 km), or via Pasaje and Girón to Cuenca (188 km).

MACHALA

This booming agricultural town (*Pop* 144,197; *Phone code* 04) is in a major banana producing and exporting region with an annual banana fair in September. It is also a large pond shrimp producing area. The city is not very attractive, somewhat dirty, but definitely a prosperous area and a good stopping point on the way to Peru.

Excursions

Puerto Bolívar Built on the Estero Jambelí among mangroves, this is a major export outlet for over 1 million tonnes of bananas annually. There is a pleasant waterfront and from the old pier a motorized canoe service crosses to the beaches of **Jambelí** on the far side of the mangrove islands which shelter Puerto Bolívar from the Pacific. Lots of birdlife can be seen in the mangroves; rent a canoe for an hour and explore the narrow channels. The beaches of Jambelí are safe and long with a few straw beach umbrellas. Accommodation is moderately priced, but there is good, cheap food in the cafés along the beach. Canoes depart at 0700, 1000 and 1500, returning at 0800, 1200 and 1600 and costing U3$1.35.

Longer trips can be made to Playas Bravita, 30 mins away (no shade or facilities), or to Costa Rica, which is 2 hrs. Take your passport as a military post has to be crossed. Canoe hire to Costa Rica for the day is about US$70 for 15 people. It's cheaper to arrange a trip from Huaquillas.

The beach at Puerto Bolívar is pleasant but waves and currents can be dangerous. The trip through mangrove channels is interesting especially for bird watchers. Take repellent against mosquitoes and other biting insects.

● **Accommodation In Puerto Bolívar**: **F** *Jambelí*, basic, fan, bath; better value is **G** pp *Pacífico*, Gral Páez 244. **At Jambelí**: *Cabañas del Pescador*, and *María Inez*, both **E**, clean, OK.

● **Places to eat Puerto Bolívar**: *El Acuario* one block back from pier for good seafood, also *Restaurant Sarita* nearby; *Miramar* for a toasted sandwich and beer at the pierhead. There are lots of seafood kiosks between the old and new piers. Food here is better and cheaper than in Machala.

Santa Rosa 30 km S on the main road to the Peruvian border lies Santa Rosa, an agricultural market town. Just by the air strip at Santa Rosa is a turnoff for

Puerto Jelí, a tiny fishing village 4 km at the road's end, right in the mangroves on a branch of the main *estero*. Good eating at *Picantería Jambelí* and *Riberas del Pacífico*. Canoe trips can be arranged through the mangroves with Segundo Oyola (ask for him opposite the dock) to the beach of Las Casitas, or fishing or clam collecting. Price varies according to group size and bargaining is recommended.

● **Accommodation & places to eat In Santa Rosa**: **D** *América*, El Oro y Colón T 943-130, new with a/c, TV, private bath; **E** *Santa Rosa*, one block from plaza, good with a/c, private bath. Cheap *residencias* on Av Colón; **G** *Residencia Santa Rosa*, dirty, noisy. Several *chifas* serve good food.

Local information
● **Accommodation**
In Machala: **L3** *Oro Verde*, Circunvalación Norte, Urb Unioro, T (07) 933-140, F 933-150, luxury, nice pool (US$9 for non-residents) and grounds, tennis courts, restaurant.

B *Rizzo*, Guayas y Bolívar, T 921-906, F 921-502, a/c, TV, suites available, recently refurbished, pool (US$2 for non-residents), casino, cafetería, restaurant, noisy late disco.

C *Montecarlo*, Guayas y Olmedo, T 931-901, F 933-104, a/c, TV, hot water, clean, modern, restaurant; **C** *Oro*, Olmedo y Juan Montalvo, T 930-783, F 937-569, refurbished, with bath, a/c, TV, good, friendly, helpful, expensive restaurant but good, cheaper café downstairs.

D *Araujo*, 9 de Mayo y Boyacá, T 935-257, with bath, hot water, a/c, TV, parking, cheaper with fan, clean, some rooms are small, restaurant, parking, good value, rec; **D** *Edison*, Boyacá y Colón, T 938-120, with bath, a/c, TV, cheaper with fan, modern, clean, nice large rooms, restaurant, rec; **D** *Ejecutivo*, Sucre y 9 de Mayo, T 933-992, F 933-987, with bath, a/c, TV, hot water, modern, in the market area; **D** *Gran Hotel Machala*, Juan Montalvo 835 y Rocafuerte, T 920-159, re-opened in 1996, undergoing renovations, with bath, fan, some a/c, **E** with shared bath; **D** *Inés*, Montalvo 1509 y Pasaje, T 922-301, F 931-473, a/c, TV, parking, good restaurant; **D** *Mosquera*, Olmedo entre Guayas y Ayacucho, T 931-752, F 930-390, cheaper with fan, TV, hot water, restaurant, rec; **D** *Perla del Pacífico*, Sucre 603 y Páez, T 930-915, TV, a/c, no hot water; **D** *San Francisco*, Montalvo entro Sucre y 9 de Octubre, T 930-441, with a/c, parking, cheaper with fan.

E *Ecuatoriano*, 9 de Octubre y Colón, T 930-197, unfriendly, overpriced, bath, a/c, TV, cheaper with fan and shared bath; **E** *Julio César*, 9 de Mayo 1319 y Boyacá, T 937-978, with bath, fan, TV; **E** *Residencial Internacional*, Guayas y Sucre, T 930-244, water shortages, friendly.

F *Hostal La Bahía*, Olmedo y Junín, T 920-581, with bath, fan, cheaper with shared bath, by market, good value, basic; **F** *Residencial Patty*, Boyacá 619, T 931-759, with bath, fan, basic, cheaper with shared bath, some short stay customers; **F** *Residencial Pichincha*, Sucre 516, shared bath, very basic; **F** *Residencial Almache*, Sucre y Juan Montalvo, very basic, dirty; **F** *Residencial Pesantes*, 9 de Mayo y Pasaje, T 920-154, with bath, fan, basic; **F** *Residencial San Antonio*, 9 de Mayo y Pasaje, with bath, basic. A mosquito net may be needed for sleeping.

● **Places to eat**
The best food is found in the better hotels. *Cafetería San Francisco*, Sucre block 6, good filling breakfast; *Parrillada Sabor Latina*, Sucre y Guayas, good steaks and grills; *Don Angelo*, 9 de Mayo just off main plaza, open 24 hrs, elaborate set meals and à la carte, good for breakfast; *Copa Cabana*, on main plaza, good clean snack bar; *Chifa Central*, Tarqui y 9 de Octubre, good Chinese; *Palacio Real*, 9 de Octubre y Ayacucho, good set meal; *Las Redes*, 9 de Mayo 18-23 y Bolívar, à la carte seafood and choice of cheap set meals; *Palacio Real 2*, 9 de Octubre y Ayacucho, good set meal; *Melba*, Junín y Bolívar; *Aquí es Correita*, Av Arízaga y 9 de Mayo, popular for seafood, closed Sun; two branches of *La Fogata*, Av Las Palmeras nr the telephone office, for good chicken. For ice cream: *Zanzibar*, Rocafuerte y Tarqui; and *Pingüino*, Juan Montalvo y Rocafuerte.

● **Banks & money changers**
Banco del Pacífico, Rocafuerte y Tarqui, changes TCs and cash; **Banco Machala**, advances cash against Visa, friendly and efficient; **Filanbanco**, Rocafuerte y Guayas, does Visa cash advances; **Banco Continental**, 9 de Octubre y Juan Montalvo, cash and TCs, good rates. **Casa de Cambio Ullauri**, Páez y 9 de Octubre, T 931-349, cash only, poor rates; **Comercial Quezada**, Rocafuerte entre Páez

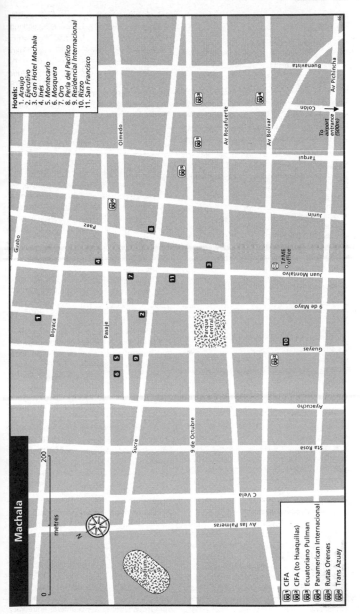

Machala

Hotels:
1. Araujo
2. Ejecutivo
3. Gran Hotel Machala
4. Inés
5. Montecarlo
6. Mosquera
7. Oro
8. Perla del Pacífico
9. Residencial Internacional
10. Rizzo
11. San Francisco

CIFA
CIFA (to Huaquillas)
Ecuatoriano Pullman
Panamerican Internacional
Rutas Orenses
Trans Azuay

metres

Stadium

Av las Palmeras

C Vela

Sucre

9 de Octubre

Sta Rosa

Ayacucho

Guayas

9 de Mayo

Juan Montalvo

TAME office

Junín

Tarqui

Parque Central

Boyacá

Pasaje

Páez

Gabo

Olmedo

Av Rocafuerte

Av Bolívar

Buenavista

Colón

Av Pichincha

To airport entrance (500m)

y Junín, cash only, poor rates, open longer hours than others.

● **Embassies & consulates**
Peruvian Consulate, at the NW corner of Colón y Bolívar, p 1, T 930-680.

● **Entertainment**
Cinemas: there are several, of which *El Tauro* is the best, a/c, cushioned seats, good sound.

Post & telecommunications
Post Office: Bolívar y Montalvo; telephone and cable office, **Emetel**, 9 de Octubre nr the stadium.

● **Sports**
A development just outside Machala on the Pasaje road has two large outdoor swimming pools.

● **Shopping**
Supermarkets: *Unico*, Bolívar y 9 de Mayo; *Mi Comisiarato* at Unioro Shopping Centre, Circunvalación Norte. *UNO service station*, 9 de Octubre y Tarqui, 24-hr gasoline, inc unleaded.

● **Tour companies & travel agents**
Ecuadorean Tours, Bolívar y Guayas, T 922-670; *Orotour*, Bolívar 603, T 931-557; *Glendatur*, Bolívar 613 y Guayas, T/F 921-855, helpful, sells Faucett air tickets for Peru; *Delgado*, 9 de Mayo 1820 y Bolívar, T 923-154. *La Moneda Tours*, Rocafuerte 518 entre Junín y Tarqui, T 562-230, has offices in Quito and Guayaquil, specializes in coastal and archaeological tours.

● **Tourist offices**
Cetur, 9 de Mayo y Pichincha, little information.

● **Transport**
Air Daily flights from Guayaquil with CEDTA (light aircraft), Mon-Fri, depart Guayaquil from the Terminal de Avionetas 0715, 1130, 1400, 1615 returning from Machala 1 hr later, US$16 each way; also with TAME, Juan Montalvo y Bolívar, T 930-139.
Buses To **Quito**, with Occidental (Buenavista entre Sucre y Olmedo), 12 hrs, US$6, 8 daily between 0700 and 2230; with Panamericana (Colón y Bolívar), 9 daily, luxury service, 9 hrs, US$10 a/c, US$8 without a/c. To **Guayaquil**, 4 hrs, US$3.80, hourly with Ecuatoriano Pullman (Colón y 9 de Octubre), CIFA (9 de Octubre y Tarqui) and Rutas Orenses (9 de Octubre y Tarqui). To **Esmeraldas**, 11 hrs, US$7.40, with Occidental at 2200. To **Loja**, 7 hrs, US$4,

several daily with Transportes Loja (Tarqui y Bolívar). To **Cuenca**, hourly with Trans Azuay (Sucre y Junín), 3½ hrs, US$3.80. To **Huaquillas**, with CIFA (Bolívar y Guayas) and Ecuatoriano Pullman (Colón y 9 de Octubre), direct, 1 hr, US$1.40, every 30 mins; via Arenillas and Santa Rosa, 2 hrs, US$1.15, every 10 mins. There are passport checks on this route. **Warning** Do not take night buses into or out of Machala, they are not safe. **Taxis**: to **Guayaquil**, Orotaxis run a scheduled taxi service between the *Hotel Rizzo*, Machala and *Hotel Rizzo*, Guayaquil, every 30 mins or so for US$7 pp.

For the route Machala-Cuenca, see page 217.

ZARUMA

Southeast from Machala is the gold-mining town of **Zaruma** (118 km; *Alt* 1,170m). It is reached either by paved road via Piñas (military check point at Saracay), or via Pasaje and Paccha on a scenic, dirt road.

Founded in 1549 on orders of Felipe II to try to control the gold extraction, Zaruma is a delightful town perched on a hilltop, with steep, twisting streets and painted wooden buildings. The beautiful main plaza has, unfortunately, been marred by the tasteless cement monstrosity put up by the municipality and facing one of Ecuador's loveliest wooden churches. A preservation order now protects the centre of town from similar acts of architectural vandalism.

Beside the plaza is a lovely little museum showing the history of gold mining in the area. Gold mining is still a major employer here among the noticeably white-skinned, blue-eyed inhabitants of direct Spanish stock. Near Busa is a large *Chancadora*, a primitive rock-crushing operation. Many of the local mines bring their gold-bearing rocks here to be crushed then passed through sluices to wash off the mud. It is possible to visit some of the small roadside mining operations and watch the whole process.

Agricultural production in this area is almost zero, as no one has time, though some coffee is harvested. One small store in Zaruma roasts its own for sale and sends weekly shipments to Quito. On top of the small hill beyond the market is a public swimming pool, from where there are amazing views over the hot, dry valleys.

● **Accommodation** D *Rosales de Machay*, up the Busa valley between Zaruma and Piñas, access is difficult without a car or taxi, it's a long, hot walk upstream then down the other side, pool, restaurant, tennis, popular at weekends, clean, comfortable cabins; **E** *Roland*, new, outside town; **F** *Municipal*, dilapidated, good views; **F** *Colombia*, on the main plaza, very basic; *Pedregal*, on the Malvas road, has 2-3 rooms.

● **Transport** Transportes Paccha departs Machala nr the market, or Trans TAC, Sucre y Colón departs every hour from 0500 to 1700 via Piñas, last bus back at 1800, US$1.70, 3 hrs to Zaruma, US$0.80, 3½ hrs to Piñas.

Beyond the *Hotel Rosales de Machay* (see above) is the lovely, wooden colonial town of **Piñas**. Two orchid specialists will show their collections if you ask around. One is a local school teacher and has a museum-like collection of memorabilia in his house. There are three *residencias*, one in town and the others on the hill on the way out of town to Zaruma. There are buses to **Paccha** up in the hills to the N (**F** *Residencial Reina del Cisne*, clean, pleasant), and to **Ayapamba** and many other old gold mining villages.

PORTOVELO

South of Zaruma, Portovelo was once the HQ of the Vanderbilt mining company, down in the valley. The huge gold mine took many hundreds of tonnes of gold out of the country but allegedly never paid any taxes. When quizzed by the government, the company pointed to the fact that they had built a new road and not charged them for it. The fact that most of these roads rather conveniently went to new areas ready to be exploited for gold deposits seems to have been ignored.

Portovelo was deemed too hot and unhealthy so the miners' families were moved to the top of the neighbouring hill and the beautiful wooden town of Zaruma was built. There are numerous tiny chapels scattered across the surrounding hills and, in the times when the mines were functioning, it was fashionable to take a trip in the horse and carriage to these outlying chapels for the Sunday services. Many of the roads built by Vanderbilt end at these chapels.

There are hot thermal springs at **Aguas Calientes**, 6 km from Portovelo, but no facilities. A nice walk is 5 km on the Loja road to Río Pindo or Río Luis.

● **Accommodation & transport** There are a couple of small *residencias*. There are lots of buses from Machala, and a local bus runs up and down to Zaruma.

PUYANGO

The petrified forest of **Puyango**, due S of Machala, is supposedly the most extensive outside Arizona. Over 120 species of birds can be seen. There is no accommodation in the village but ask around for floor space or try at the on-site information centre. If not, basic accommodation is available in Alamor. Campsites are also provided. For further information, contact Comisión Administradora de Los Bosques Petrificados de Puyango, Ciudadcla Las Brisas, Manzana B-6, Villa 2, Apto No 05, Machala, T 930-021, F 924-655.

● **Transport** Bus for Alamor 0830 and 1400, 3 hrs, US$2.50, ask to be dropped off at Puyango. Several military checkpoints between Puyango and Machala.

CROSSING INTO PERU

HUAQUILLAS

The most commonly used route overland to Peru is via Machala. Many buses (see **Transport** above) go to **Huaquillas**, the Ecuadorean border town, which is something of a shopping arcade for Peruvians, though all shops close about 1730. It has grown into a small city with a reasonable selection of hotels and other services.

Local information
● Accommodation

D *Lima*, Portovelo y Machala, T 907-794, bath, a/c, TV, phone, **E** with fan, mosquito net; **D** *Vanessa*, 1 de Mayo 323, T/F 907-263, bath, a/c, TV, phone.

E *Alameda*, Tnte Córdovez y José Mendoza, bath, fan, TV, mosquito net, basic; **E** *Guayaquil*, Remigio Gómez 125, behind Immigration, with bath, **F** without, fan, clean, mosquito net, limited water supply, noisy; **E** *Internacional*, Machala y 9 de Octubre, T 907-963, bath, fan, small rooms, basic, cheaper with shared bath; **E** *Rodey*, Tnte Córdovez y 10 de Agosto, T 907-736, bath, fan, TV, fridge, clean, basic.

F *Gabeli*, Tnte Córdovez 311 y Portovelo, T 907-149, bath, fan, mosquito net, cheaper without bath, parking; **F** *Mini*, Tnte Córdovez y Rocafuerte, bath, fan, mosquito net, restaurant, poor water supply; **F** *Residencial Fabiolita*, Tnte Córdovez y Santa Rosa, shared bath, mosquito net, basic; **F** *Residencial Loja*, Portovelo y Machala, very basic, mosquito net, dirty; **F** *Residencial San Martín*, Av la República opp the church, 1 block from immigration, T 907-083, shared bath, fan, basic, noisy, mosquito nets, convenient; **F** *Rivieras*, Tnte Córdovez y El Oro, bath, fan, mosquito net, OK, disco downstairs at weekends.

G *Quito*, Portovelo y Remigio Gómez, behind immigration, shared bath, mosquito net, basic. **NB** A number of the cheaper hotels in Huaquillas are primarily for short stay customers.

● Places to eat

Acuario, Portovelo y José Mendoza, a/c, good set meal and à la carte, rec; *Guayaquil*, Remigio Gómez, behind immigration, basic; *Chic*, behind *Hotel Guayaquil*, set meal US$1; *Flamingo*, Tnte Córdovez y 10 de Agosto; *Mini*, opp Transportes Loja, good set lunch

US$2. Excellent patisseries on main street sell delicious pain-au-chocolat and cheese empanadas. Expect bananas with everything here (except your change).

● Banks & money changers

Verify rates of exchange with travellers leaving Peru. Fair rates are available for soles, sucres and dollars cash on both sides of the border but you will always be offered a low rate when you first enquire. Ask around before changing, do your own arithmetic and don't be rushed into any transaction. Avoid those changers who chase after you. Be sure to count your change carefully. The money changers (recognized by their black briefcases) are very clever, particularly with calculators, and often dishonest. It is difficult to change TCs.

● Post & telecommunications

Post Office: Av la República, in the same building as Immigration. **Emetel**: Av la República, opp Immigration.

● Tourist offices

An information centre is just by the international bridge. It is staffed by tourism students and is friendly and helpful, but has limited information.

● Transport

Buses There are three checkpoints (Transit Police, Customs and military) along the road N from Huaquillas, keep your passport to hand. To **Machala**, with CIFA (Santa Rosa y Machala) and Ecuatoriano Pullman (Av la República y 9 de Octubre), direct, 1 hr, US$1.40, every hour between 0400 and 2000; via Arenillas and Santa Rosa, 2 hrs, US$1.15, every 10 mins. To **Quito**, with Occidental (Remigio Gómez 129), 3 daily, 12 hrs, US$7; with Panamericana (Remigio Gómez, behind Immigration), luxury service, 11½ hrs, 6 daily via Santo Domingo, US$10 a/c, US$8.30 without a/c; 2 daily via **Riobamba** and **Ambato**, 12 hrs, US$10 (you may see all the great volcanoes). To **Guayaquil**, frequent service with CIFA and Ecuatoriano Pullman, about 5 hrs, US$3.70. If in a hurry to reach Quito or Guayaquil, Cuenca or Loja, it may be advisable to change buses in Machala.

To **Cuenca**, several daily, 6 hrs, US$4. To **Loja**, with Transportes Loja (Tnte Córdovez y Arenillas) daily at 1330 and 1800, 7 hrs, US$4. To **Tulcán** for the Colombian border, with Panamericana, at 1630, 16 hrs, US$12. The main roads to Guayaquil, Quito and Cuenca are all paved.

FRONTIER WITH PERU

● Ecuadorean Immigration

Complete Ecuadorean formalities at customs (several hundred metres before the border) and immigration, Av de la República y Portovelo, in Huaquillas.

The border is officially open 0800-1800, but long lunches are common (Ecuadorean lunch 1200-1400). On Sun facilities may close at 1600. It is always best to cross before 1700. Allow up to 1-2 hrs to complete formalities, although it can sometimes be much quicker.

Then walk along the main street and across the bridge. Tricycle porters operate between customs and the border, US$1, never let go of your bags. Arrange the price in advance and the currency in which it is to be paid to avoid rip-offs. At the bridge, the police check passports. Immigration formalities are, generally, straightforward.

● Crossing by Private Vehicle

If there is a problem entering with a car, contact Tulio Campoverde Armijos, Agencia Aficionado de Aduanas, Gómez 123 y Portovelo.

● Peruvian immigration

The main Peruvian immigration and customs complex is outside Zarumilla, about 3 km past

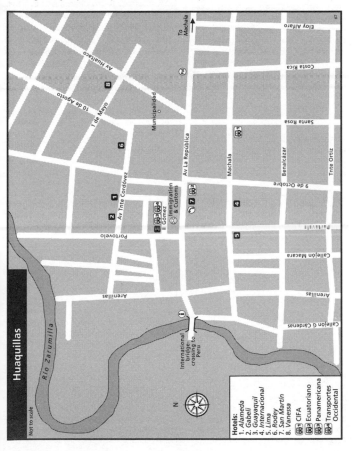

Huaquillas

Hotels:
1. Alameda
2. Gabeli
3. Guayaquil
4. Internacional
5. Lima
6. Rodey
7. San Martín
8. Vanessa
CIFA
Ecuatoriano
Panamericana
Transportes Occidental

the international bridge, however there is also a small immigration office in Aguas Verdes, just past the bridge on the right hand side, as you go into Peru. As of March 1996, visitors entering Peru received their entry stamps in Aguas Verdes, while visitors leaving Peru got their exit stamp at Zarumilla. These procedures are frequently changing so enquire locally.

● **Exchange**

Coming from Peru, you can buy sucres at the official rate with the money changers outside Peruvian immigration, but you also need to be careful here.

● **Transport**

There are three forms of transport between the frontier and Tumbes. Some colectivos leave from near the bridge; they charge higher prices, especially for foreigners. Other, cheaper ones leave 2 blocks down along the main street by a small plaza opp the church; US$1 pp, or US$6/car. Colectivos should stop and wait at the immigration complex on the Peruvian side. Buses and minivans leave from an esplanade 3 blocks E from the colectivo stop and go to the market in Tumbes, US$0.50 (they don't wait at immigration). There are also mototaxis from the bridge to the Zarumilla immigration complex, US$0.90 for up to 2 people. Taxi to Tumbes, including the wait at immigration, US$6.

Coming from Peru into Ecuador; take a bus to Tumbes and a colectivo from there to the border. A ticket out of Ecuador is not usually asked for at this border.

INTO PERU

Both the *Peruvian Handbook* and the *South American Handbook* give details on the services and excursions at **Tumbes**. There are national parks and beaches to visit, a fair range of hotels and places to eat and good transport links S down the coast as far as Lima.

Pacific Lowlands

THOUGH popular with Quiteños and Guayaquileños, who come here in their droves for weekends and holidays, the Pacific Lowlands receive relatively few foreign visitors, which is surprising given the natural beauty, diversity and rich cultural heritage of the coast. This vast tract covers everything west of the Andes and north of the Guayas delta and comprises the provinces of Esmeraldas, Manabí, Los Ríos, the western part of Guayas and the lowland corner of Pichincha.

You can surf, watch whales at play, visit ancient archaeological sites, or just relax and enjoy the best food that this country has to offer. The jewel in the coastal crown, Machalilla National Park, protects an important area of primary tropical dry forest, precolumbian ruins, coral reef and a wide varity of wildlife.

Even if your time is limited, the coast is easily accessible from Quito, making it the ideal short break from the Andean chill. The water is warm for bathing and the beaches, many of them deserted, are generally attractive, thanks to a number of successful clean-up programmes.

THE LAND

Compared with the mountains, Galápagos and Oriente, the Ecuadorean coast has been relatively overlooked by travellers although it covers a third of the country's total area. This region is a mosaic of landscapes full of abrupt contrasts and paradox. Topography, local climate and vegetation vary remarkably both along the coast and from the shore inland towards the highlands. If it were possible to travel N from Machala to the Colombian border in a single day, you would see the sun rise over endless banana plants, eat lunch shivering in a cold, grey drizzle amid parched cactus scrub, and arrive at sundown in tropical heat under the tall, dense canopy of one of the world's wettest rainforests.

Climate

The reason for this dramatic difference in climate and vegetation between the N and S coasts is the effects of the opposing and seasonal ocean currents offshore. The cold Humboldt comes N as far as the level of Portoviejo in mid Manabí, which accounts for the semi-arid conditions in the southern coast, particularly in the Santa Elena peninsula. Nevertheless, lush forest grows on hills above about 700m and in the sheltered Gulf of Guayaquil and humid Guayas delta. Though the overall picture for the coast is of decreasing average temperatures and rainfall from N to S, there is striking local variability, generally resulting from topographical features but also from human impact upon the native vegetation.

Development of infrastructure

Roads, cashcrops and population all exploded on the coast of Ecuador during the latter half of the 20th century, particularly in the 1960s after this previously overlooked Latin American country joined the world market for oil exploration. Major banks began encouraging Ecuador's military government to borrow money for construction, followed by the fast growth of its coastal towns, road system, land cultivated for export products and foreign debt. The towering forests, previously inaccessible except near the well-populated bays and along navigable rivers, began to recede swiftly.

The extent of deforestation

For some years Western Ecuador has been cited in various expert publications as one of the world's blackspots for deforestation. Nevertheless, it came as a shock when two leading field scientists, Calaway Dodson and Alwyn Gentry, studied the full picture and presented it in 1991. *Biological Extinction in Western Ecuador* is a thorough and disturbing report on the "then and now" of the coastal forests, and reveals how rapidly and completely unique ecosystems are vanishing.

The botanists' chilling findings indicated not only a staggering loss of forest cover, but also distressingly high rates at which endemic species are being wiped out.

This pioneering study drew attention to the semi-arid life-zone, whereas previous conservation research in Ecuador outside the Galápagos had emphasized the Amazon rainforests and Andean cloudforests, at the expense of the apparently quite barren Tropical Dry Forest (TDF). Dodson and Gentry, comparing diversity and endemism in all the life-zones, found that the Dry Forest equalled the Wet in having an astounding 21% of endemic species, unique to each and ever more restricted geographically into their shrinking habitats. Countless plants and animals have already been lost.

According to this paper, no more than 4% of all the coast's original forests survive intact now compared to early this century. The five major forest types (including mangrove) have fared more or less badly depending on their accessibility and the successful establishment of conservation areas. In the least affected, the northernmost Pluvial Tropical Forest, which contains valuable hardwoods, close to a quarter has survived, thanks only to the steepness of the hills and constant downpours discouraging the use of machinery on its unpaved tracks. This remaining portion must be a very important "sponge" in the hydrological cycle, and a rich source of nutrients to the adjacent ocean. But recently it has come under serious threat from the construction of an all-weather highway from Colombia, designed to promote the flow of tourists from the wealthier northern nation to the safer beaches of Ecuador. The road, now underway, cuts through virgin rainforest containing the world's highest biodiversity, and thus puts this forest type in a similar plight to the others on the coast.

Tropical Wet Forest

Hardest hit at present is the Tropical Wet Forest, with only one known fragment of 90 km protected in Jaunache, a University Reserve. This cloudforest is rich in endemic species and pertains to the Premontane formations of the western skirts of the Andes. The Wet Forest once formed a narrow, almost continuous swathe from N to S, 20 km at its widest point, but has been replaced by cocoa, coffee, bananas and other tree crops. These still provide some soil protection, but are far less effective than cloudforest in trapping moisture and regulating streams. They are also comparatively low in biodiversity. Severe lowland flooding is one result of this change.

At the foot of these slopes, the extensive northern plains were once covered in Tropical Moist Forest, but only about 4.5% remains, a sample of which is protected in the private Río Palenque Reserve. With its deep fertile soils and 4-month dry season, this area N of Portoviejo provides prime conditions for various cash crops and dairy cattle. Here, where farming is sustainable and sustaining, the native forest has still fared better than in the dryer S.

Tropical Dry Forest

Where Tropical Dry Forest once grew all over the semi-arid plains from Portoviejo to Peru, including southern Manabí, northern Guayas and the Santa Elena Peninsula and much of El Oro and Loja, less than 1% survives today. A vital buffer against the creeping Atacama Desert in this area of very low rainfall and prolonged dry season, it has been cut for its hardwoods and charcoal-making, and degraded by overabundant goats.

Mangroves

As for the mangrove, once present with 30m tall trees in every sheltered bay and estuary, its destruction became systematic in the 1980s with the shrimp farm boom, and is ongoing, despite legal protection everywhere. Such widespread clearing has had severe repercussions upon the marine life dependent for food and shelter upon these immensely productive ecosystems.

Obstacles to conservation

In the light of the critical situation presented by the Dodson and Gentry report, a Rapid Assessment was carried out in the early 1990s by a team of four key field researchers, which confirmed the alarming rate of destruction of unique forest habitats. In some spots there was not time for them to carry out detailed studies before the relevant patch of forest was felled.

Worse still, scientific knowledge of native forests and their protection was set back in Aug 1993 by a disastrous accident. Alwyn Gentry, along with ornithologist Theodore Parker and Eduardo Aspiazu Estrada, a leading Ecuadorean conservationist were killed when their small plane crashed into a high peak on the dry coast while surveying the Dry Forest of the Cordillera Chongon Colonche.

Even without such a disheartening tragedy, conservation efforts on the dry coast are constantly beset by difficulties such as prolonged droughts, torrential rains brought by El Niño, disruptive political decrees and inadequate resources for grass-roots work which undermines progress with the local communities.

A brighter future

Despite all these problems, the efforts of a few committed individuals are bearing fruit in encouraging the locals to value, protect and restore the flora and fauna. Increasingly, communities well aware of the drying up of rivers welcome any input that combines advice with practical support for dire needs. This can take the form of environmental awareness- raising backed with incentives to reforest the stripped hillsides and watersheds, assistance in marketing traditional renewable forest resources, and the promotion of other income-providing activities that appear environmentally sound. One of the latter which is currently being tried is ecotourism, but it is too early to say whether development and dependence on tourism will prove desirable or not in the long term for both locals and land.

WESTERN LOWLANDS

QUITO TO SANTO DOMINGO

Roads from the highlands to the coast may be cut off because of landslides during the rainy season, enquire ahead. The main route from Quito goes down the valley of the Ríos Naranjal/Pilatón/Blanco, turning off the Panamericana at Alóag and continuing past Tandapi (the official name M Cornejo Astorga is never used), 45 km from Alóag. There are two hotels, **F**, with shared bath and many road side restaurants and *fritada* stands.

Then comes Alluriquín, with accommodation in **E** *Florida* at Km 104, T in Quito 560-948, with bath, rooms a bit run down, swimming pool, restaurant, horse riding, busy at weekends.

Sit on right for views going down, but on the left look for El Poder Brutal, a devil's face, complete with horns and fangs, carved in the rock face, 2.5 km W of Tandapi. This road is very busy, gets much heavy truck traffic and it can be dangerous owing to careless drivers passing on the many curves, especially when foggy and at night. An alternative route from Quito is via Calacalí, San Miguel de los Bancos, Puerto Quito and La Independencia.

SANTO DOMINGO DE LOS COLORADOS

The main route to the coast from Quito goes through **Santo Domingo de los Colorados**, in the hills above the western lowlands (*Pop* 114,442). It's a scenic bus trip of 129 km, but visibility is best in the morning.

The city became Ecuador's main transport hub in the mid 1960s when the road from Quito through Alóag was completed. Since that time it has experienced very rapid growth and any immigrants from Colombia have settled here. The name de los Colorados is a reference to the traditional red hair dye, made with achiote (annatto), worn by the native Tsáchila men. Today the Tsáchila only wear their native dress on special occasions and they can no longer be seen in traditional garb in the city, except for the Monumento al Colorado statue, at the W end of the city centre where the roads to Quevedo, Chone, and Esmeraldas meet.

Santo Domingo is an important commercial centre for the surrounding palm oil and banana producing areas. The city itself is noisy, streets are prone to flooding after heavy rains and it has little to offer the tourist. However, it is a good access point for visits to the Tsáchila communities and the nearby subtropical forest, a bird and butterfly watchers paradise. Sun is market day and therefore many shops in town are only open from Tues to Sun. The main plaza is Parque Joaquín Zaracay. There is a cinema in town.

Excursions

The Tsáchila nation are known locally as the Indios Colorados because of their custom of coating their hair with red vegetable dye, although they do not approve of this name. There were approximately 1900 Tsáchilas in 1996, living in eight communities off the roads leading from Santo Domingo to Quevedo, Chone and Quinindé. Their lands make up a reserve of some 8000 hectares.

Visitors interested in their culture are welcome at the **Complejo Turístico Huapilú**, in the Chihuilpe Commune, where there is a small but interesting museum (contributions expected) run by Augusto Calazacón; also a snack bar, dance floor with disk jockey and swimming in the river. It gets busy at weekends, but camping is possible. Previous arrangements are necessary for a complete tour, including a demonstration of body and hair paint, folk music and dancing, natural medicine, weaving, fishing techniques, sugar cane pressing and traditional cooking. Such a tour will give you the opportunity to photograph the natives in traditional dress, otherwise you will have to make arrangements with a family and pay; this is discouraged.

● **Access** Via the turnoff E at Km 7 on the road to Quevedo, from where it is 4 km. Tours are available from travel agencies in town. A taxi is US$5-10, or take a city bus Centro-Vía Quevedo-Km 7 and walk. Guides sometimes wait at the turnoff and offer their services, but are not indispensable.

There are several options for fishing and bird/butterfly watching excursions in the Santo Domingo area, see out of town **Accommodation** below. With an all-terrain vehicle, the old road to Quito, via Chiriboga and San Juan, offers access to a forested area on the E bank of the Río Toachi. The turnoff is just E of La Unión del Toachi, between Alluriquín and Tandapi. Tours can be arranged through travel agencies (see below).

Local information
● **Accommodation**
NB Many hotels are along Av 29 de Mayo, a noisy street, so request a room away from the road. Several of the cheaper establishments also cater to short stay customers.

In town: C *Diana Real*, 29 de Mayo y Loja, T 751-380, F 754-091, modern spacious rooms, with bath, hot water, fan, TV (local DHL Courier and Western Union representatives).

D *Aracelly*, Vía Quevedo y Galápagos, T 750-334, F 754-144, large rooms, with bath, electric shower, restaurant, parking; **D** *Caleta*, Ibarra 141, T 750-277, good restaurant, private bath, **E** without TV, friendly, good; **D** *Ejecutivo*, 29 de Mayo entre Ambato y Cuenca, T 752-893, with bath, TV, cafeteria, **E** without TV, OK; **D** *Genova*, 29 de Mayo e Ibarra, T 759-694, clean, comfortable, electric shower, **E** without TV, parking, good value, rec; **D** *La Siesta*, Av Quito 606 y Yambo, T 751-013, with bath, hot water, **E** with shared bath, restaurant, parking, ageing but nice; **D** *Unicornio*, 29 de Mayo y Ambato, T 760-147, with bath, cold water, **E** without TV, restaurant, parking, nice.

E *Amambay*, 29 de Mayo y Ambato, T 750-696, quite good, water on demand; **E** *El Colorado*, 29 de Mayo y Esmeraldas, T 750-226, with bath, a bit noisy, restaurant, parking; **E** *Galápagos*, Galápagos e Ibarra, quiet; **E** *Hostal Lucy*, Av Quito y Guayaquil, T 756-292, with bath, cold water, fan, basic; **E** *Hostal*

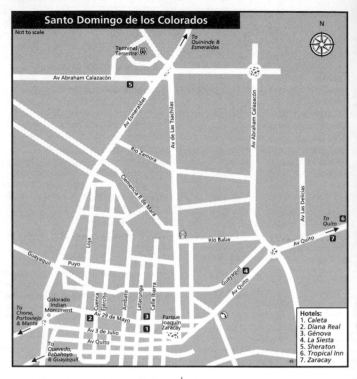

Santo Domingo de los Colorados

Not to scale

To Quininde & Esmeraldas

Terminal Terrestre

Av Abraham Calazacón **5**

Av Esmeraldas

Río Zamora

Clemencia R de Mara

Av de Las Tsáchilas

Av Abraham Calazacón

Av Las Delicias

Loja

Guayaquil

Puyo

Río Baba

To Quito **6**

Av Quito **7**

Guayaquil

Av Quito

Colorado Indian Monument

To Chone, Portoviejo & Manta

Cuenca

Ejercito

Ambato

Latacunga

Calle Ibarra

2 Av 29 de Mayo **3**

1

Av 3 de Julio

Av Quito

Parque Joaquin Zaracay

4

To Quevedo, Babahoyo & Guayaquil

Hotels:
1. *Caleta*
2. *Diana Real*
3. *Génova*
4. *La Siesta*
5. *Sheraton*
6. *Tropical Inn*
7. *Zaracay*

Maracaibo, Cocaniguas y Río Pilatón, T 750-031, with bath, TV, **F** with shared bath; **E** *Jennifer*, 29 de Mayo y Latacunga, T 750-577, with bath, some with hot water, rooms away from the street are quieter, parking, restaurant, good value; **E** *Las Brisas #2*, Cocaniguas y Río Pilatón, T 753-283, with bath, clean, modern, parking extra; under the same management is **E** *Las Brisas #1*, Av Quito y Cocaniguas, T 750-560, with bath, basic, **F** with shared bath; **E** *Príncipe*, Ambato 410 y Portoviejo, opp the Municipal Market, T 750-492, with bath, parking; **E** *San Fernando*, 2 blocks from the bus terminal, T 753-402, with bath, clean, modern, comfortable, cheaper with shared bath, parking; **E** *Hostal Santo Domingo*, Quito y Cuenca, T 754-078.

On Av Abraham Calazacón, opp the bus terminal are: **E** *Sheraton*, T 751-988, modern, clean, with bath, hot water, parking, new in 1996, good value, rec; **E** *Hostal Patricia*, T 761-

906, with bath, cold water, parking.

F *Hostal Ejecutivo*, 29 de Mayo y Ambato, T 751-943, with bath, basic, cheaper with shared bath; **F** *Hostal Ontaneda*, Av de los Tsáchilas 226 y 29 de Mayo, with bath, basic, cheaper with shared bath, not clean. There are 3 *Hostales Turistas*; **G** *No 1* at 3 de Julio y Latacunga, T 751-759, very basic, **F** *No 2* at Ambato y 29 de Mayo, with bath, hot water, basic, noisy, no windows and **F** *No 3* at 3 de Julio y Latacunga, with bath, basic. **F** *Pensión Bolívar*, 3 de Julio y Cuenca, and *Pensión La Perla*, 3 de Julio y Loja, both at lower end of pedestrian street; **F** *Pensión San José*, T 751-062, beside *Turista No 1*; **F** *Residencial Ambato*, Av de los Tsáchilas 127 y 29 de Mayo, shared bath, cold water, very basic, not clean; **F** *Residencial El Paraíso*, Las Provincias y 29 de Mayo, T 754-178, some rooms with bath, basic; **F** *Residencial El Viajero*, 29 de Mayo y Latacunga, with bath, cold water, basic, cheaper with shared bath; **F** *Residencial España*, on

Av Abraham Calazacón, opp the bus terminal, entrance on the side street, with bath, clean, basic; **F** *Residencial Groenlandia*, 29 de Mayo y Ambato, T 752-877, shared bath, cold water, basic; **F** *Residencial Madrid*, 3 de Julio 438 y Riobamba, shared bath, basic; **F** *Residencial Noroña*, 29 de Mayo 185 y Av de los Tsáchilas, small rooms, shared bath, cold water, not clean, very basic.

G *Aldita* and *Pichincha* (T 751-052), both on Tulcán y Quito, both basic.

Out of town: 20 km from Santo Domingo, on the road to Quito, is **A2** *Tinalandia*, pleasant and small, chalets with bathrooms, including meals, with its own golf course overlooking the Toachi valley, and excellent food, many species of birds, flowers and butterflies in the woods behind (and many biting insects in the evening), lunch with right to use facilities US$10 for non-residents. It is poorly signposted, take small road between Km 16 and 17 from Santo Domingo on the right; Casilla 8, Santo Domingo de los Colorados, or T 09-494-727, in Quito T 449-028, F 442-638. For cheaper accommodation nr *Tinalandia*, see Alluriquín above.

A3 *Zaracay*, Av Quito 1639, T 750-316, F 754-535, 1½ km from the centre on the road to Quito, restaurant, casino, noisy disco, gardens and a swimming pool, good rooms and service, breakfast inc, best available, advisable to book, especially at weekend; **A3-B** *Tropical Inn*, Av Quito next to the fairground, opp *Zaracay*, T 761-771, F 761-775, modern, with bath, TV, fridge.

B-C *Hostería Rancho Mi Cuchito*, Vía a Chone Km 2, T 750 030, F 755 003, with bath, hot water, TV, pool, restaurant; *La Hacienda*, Km 13 Vía a Chone, T 754-118; **B** *Hostería Valle Hermoso*, Km 25 on the road to Esmeraldas, S of La Concordia, T/F 759-095, office in Santo Domingo: Cocaniguas 289, T/F 759-095, **A3** full-board, with bath, hot showers, fan, TV, restaurant, pool, sauna, horse riding, fishing, 120 forested hectares on the shores of the Río Blanco, lakes, waterfalls.

C *El Marqués*, Vía Quevedo Km 3½, T 750-950, with bath, TV, pool, restaurant; **C** *Hostería Los Colorados*, 12 km from Santo Domingo on the road to Quito, just W of the toll booth and police control, T/F 753-449, nice cabins with fridge, TV, pool, artificial lake with fish, restaurants, good cafetería; **C** *Hotel del Toachi*, Vía a Quito, Km 1, just W of Zaracay, T/F 754-688, spacious rooms, with bath, good showers, TV, swimming pool, parking.

D *Complejo Campestre Santa Rosa*, Vía Quevedo Km 16, T 754-145, F 754-144, office in Santo Domingo at *Hotel Aracelly*, on the shores of the Río Baba, rooms with bath, restaurant, swimming, water sports, fishing, salsoteca; **D** *Don Kleber*, Vía Esmeraldas Km 2, T/F 761-243, with bath, hot water, TV, pool, sauna.

E *Hostal Descanso del Conductor*, Vía Quevedo Km 4½, T 754-418, with bath, hot water, TV, restaurant, parking; **E** *Hostal Rey*, Av Chone Km 1, with bath, TV, cheaper with shared bath, cafeteria.

● **Places to eat**
Parrilladas Argentinas, on Quevedo road Km 5, for good barbecues; *Mocambo*, Tulcán y Machala, good; *La Fuente*, Ibarra y 3 de Julio, good. There are several chicken places in the Cinco Esquinas area where Avs Quito and 29 de Mayo meet, inc *Rico Pollo*, Quito y Río Pove; *Tacos Mexicanos*, Quito, a super deli, highly rec; two *chifas*, *Tay Happy* and *Central*, on Calle Tulcán by the Parque Zaracay.

For seafood: *Juan El Marino*, 1.5 km from Monument Circle on road to Quevedo, reasonably priced, huge portions, good seafood, rec; also several *marisquerías* along Av 29 de Mayo. Several restaurants on Av Abraham Calazacón across from the bus terminal, inc *Sheraton*, popular. For ice cream: *Heladería* at Edificio San Francisco, Av Quito entre Río Blanco y Río Toachi, good, made on the premises, also sell fresh cheese; opp is *Pingüino*.

● **Banks & money changers**
Banco Internacional, Av Quito y Río Blanco, US$ cash and TCs (4% commission); Banco Bolivariano, Av Quito y Napo, cash only, 0900-1500; Filanbanco, Av Quito y Av de los Tsáchilas, by Parque Zaracay, cash and TCs, 0900-1400; Delgado Travel, Av Quito 148 y Cocaniguas, cash only, Mon-Fri 0900-1700, Sat 0900-1300; Turismo Zaracay, 29 de Mayo y Cocaniguas, cash only, Mon-Fri 0830-1900, Sat 0830-1630; Western Union money transfers at Hotel Diana Real.

● **Entertainment**
Aruba's Disco, Av de los Tsáchilas y 29 de Mayo; *Cervecería-Salsoteca The Jungle*, Av Quito across from *Hotel La Siesta*. Discos in the peripheral neighbourhoods are not considered safe.

● **Post & telecommunications**
Post Office: Av de los Tsáchilas y Río Baba, 0800-1830; fax service 0800-1630, national US$1/page, Andean countries US$4.65,

Americas US$7.15, Europe US$8.90, other continents US$10.60. **Emetel**, Edificio San Francisco, Av Quito entre Río Blanco y Río Toachi, p 2, and at bus terminal, 0800-2200 daily.

● **Security**
Santo Domingo is not safe late at night, caution is recommended at all times in the market areas, including the pedestrian walkway along 3 de Julio and in peripheral neighbourhoods.

● **Tour companies & travel agents**
Turismo Zaracay, 29 de Mayo y Cocaniguas, T 750-546, F 750-873, runs tours to Tsáchila commune US$12 pp, minimum 5 persons; fishing trips US$24 pp, 8 hrs, bird/butterfly watching tours. *Cayapatours*, 29 de Mayo y Tulcán, T/F 762-933, tickets and tours. *Delgado Travel*, Av Quito 148 y Cocaniguas, T 760-036, F 759-967, tickets, money transfers, courier service, car rentals,

● **Useful addresses**
Immigration: Subjefatura de Migración, Av de los Tsáchilas, across from the cemetery, just S of the bus terminal, T 750-225.

● **Transport**
If passing through Santo Domingo, it is not necessary to drive through the congested centre of the city, as there is a bypass road around it. The bus terminal is on Av Abraham Calazacón, at the N end of town, along the city's bypass road; long-distance buses do not enter the city. Taxi downtown, US$1, bus US$0.09.

As it is a very important transportation centre, you can get buses going everywhere in the country. To **Quito** via Alóag US$2, 3 hrs, via San Miguel de los Bancos US$3,50, 5 hrs; to **Guayaquil** US$3.25, 4 hrs; to **Machala**, US$4.55, 6 hrs; to **Huaquillas** US$5.20, 7½ hrs; to **Esmeraldas** US$1.95, 3 hrs; to **Ambato** US$2.60, 4 hrs; to **Loja** US$9.70, 12 hrs; to **Manta** US$4.40, 6 hrs; to **Bahía de Caráquez** US$3.60, 4 hrs; to **Pedernales** US$2.60, 3 hrs.

ROUTES TO THE COAST

A busy paved highway connects Santo Domingo de los Colorados with Esmeraldas, 185 km to the N (see page 288). On this road are La Concordia (**D** *Hotel Atos*, new, very good), just before which is the private La Perla Forest Reserve, 40 km from Santo Domingo (you can hike in for free), La Independencia (junction with road from San Miguel de Los Bancos and

the Sierra) and **Quininé** (**Rosa Zárate**). The road deteriorates after Quininé.

● **Accommodation & places to eat in Quinindé**: **D** *Sanz*, on main street, with bath, clean, parking; *Residencial Paraíso*, clean, quite good, with water 24 hrs a day; **E** *Turista*, 8 blocks S of town, on main road, quieter than central hotels, parking; *Restaurant Jean*, T 736-831, at bottom of hill 3 blocks S of town on the main road, excellent steaks and seafood, huge portions, good salads, reasonable prices, probably the best restaurant for miles.

A paved road runs W to **El Carmen**, with a cattle market on the outskirts (several basic hotels on the noisy main street, some quieter ones near the Emetel office behind the central plaza). From El Carmen a paved road goes to **Pedernales** (see page 284). Continuing SW of El Carmen is Chone where the road divides, either to Bahía de Caráquez (207 km from Santo Domingo, 340 km from Quito, see page 281), or to Portoviejo and Manta (257 km from Santo Domingo, 390 km from Quito).

SOUTH FROM SANTO DOMINGO

QUEVEDO

Another highway goes S to **Quevedo** (*Pop* 86,910) 1½ hrs by bus. Set in fertile banana lands and often flooded in the rainy season, Quevedo is known as the Chinatown of Ecuador, with a fair-sized Chinese colony. It is a dusty, noisy, crowded town which has grown exceptionally rapidly over the last 25 years.

● **Accommodation** At Km 47 from Santo Domingo on the Quevedo road is **B** *Río Palenque*, lodge with capacity for 20, cooking facilities, US$5 for day visit. Set in a biological field station, good bird watching, T 561-646 or 232-468 in Quito for information and reservations. In town, all are noisy: **C** *Quevedo*, Av 7 de Octubre y C 12, modern rooms with fridge, TV, good restaurant; **D** *Olímpico*, Bolívar y 19a, restaurant best in town, nr stadium; **E** *Ejecutivo Internacional*, 7 de Octubre y C Cuarta, modern, large rooms, a/c, private bath, good value, the least noisy; on or nr Av 7 de Octubre and the plaza are **E** *El*

Cóndor, with a/c, **F** with fan; **E** *Rancho Vinicio*, out of town on road to La Maná, quiet cabins, pool; **F** *Continental*, basic.

● **Places to eat** On 7 de Octubre: *Rincón Caleño*, No 1103, Colombian; *chifas* at Nos 806, 809 and 707; *Tungurahua*, No 711, good breakfast US$1; *Hong Kong*, C Ambato, rec.

● **Transport Buses** Quevedo is an important route centre. To **Quito**, US$4, 7 hrs; to **Portoviejo**, from 7 de Octubre and C 8, 5 hrs, US$1.85, uncomfortable, watch your possessions; to **Guayaquil**, 3 hrs, US$1.65. Portoviejo, Tosagua and several coastal towns can be reached via Velasco Ibarra, Pichincha, Rocafuerte and Calceta.

LATACUNGA TO QUEVEDO

The old highway from Latacunga in the highlands to Quevedo carries very little traffic; it is extremely twisty in parts but it is one of the most beautiful of the routes connecting the highlands with Portoviejo, Manta and the coast. Between Zumbahua and La Maná are the pretty little towns of **Pilaló** (2 restaurants and petrol pumps) and **El Tingo** (one restaurant and lodging at *Carmita's*). The road is paved to 10 km past Pujilí and from just after Pilaló, through **La Maná** to Quevedo. Paving of the road continues, making it quicker and even more pleasant. This is a great downhill bike route.

● **Accommodation** 2½ km beyond La Maná on the road to Quevedo is **E** *Rancho Hostería Inmisahu*, T 688-003/281, new, with pool, clean, restaurant.

BABAHOYO

Quevedo is connected with Guayaquil by two paved highways, one through Balzar and Daule, one through **Babahoyo** (*Pop* 50,250).

● **Accommodation** *Hotel Emperador*, Gral Barona, T 730-535, bath, a/c, TV, restaurant; *Hotel Cachari*, Bolívar 120, T 731-205, acceptable, restaurant nearby; also *Nuevo Hotel Cachari* at No 107; *Residencial San Martín* provides an en suite bucket of water and entertainment from the rats running along the redundant plumbing.

Improvements on the road from Guayaquil to Santa Elena and N to Manabí has made for faster access and brought about a noticeable increase of national tourism along this stretch of coast. Little new accommodation has been provided but several new major projects are in the pipeline, mostly in the shape of highrise club-style complexes, with casinos, swimming pools, discos, restaurants etc.

The popular beach resorts of the Guayas coast can be reached along a paved toll highway from Guayaquil. The road divides after 63 km at El Progreso (Gómez Rendón).

PLAYAS

One branch leads to General Villamil, normally known as **Playas**, the nearest seaside resort to Guayaquil. Look out for the bottle-shaped ceibo (kapok) trees between Guayaquil and Playas as the landscape becomes drier, turning into tropical thorn scrub where 2-5m cacti prevail.

Fishing is still important in Playas and a few single-sailed balsa rafts can still be seen among the motor launches returning laden with fish. These rafts are unique, highly ingenious and very simple. The same rafts without sails are used to spread nets close offshore, then two gangs of men take 2-3 hrs to haul them in. The beach shelves gently, and is 200-400m wide, lined with singular, square canvas tents hired out for the day.

As the closest resort to Guayaquil, Playas is popular with local city dwellers, especially during the high season, *temporada*, when there are frequent promotional beach parties. The authorities are trying to keep the packed beaches cleaner at the western end as well as by the beach cafés and generally they are less dirty and safer than before. The Malecón has been improved with new grass and trees. Out of season, when it is

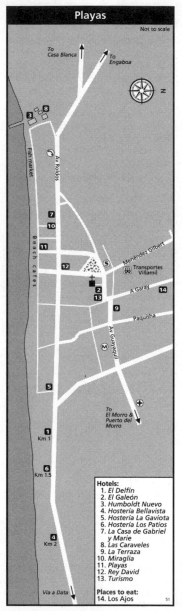

Playas

cloudier, or midweek the beaches are almost empty especially for anyone who walks N up the beach to Punta Pelado (5 km), although the new Club Casa Blanca, 20 mins up the beach, will intrude on the isolation. Other changes that are afoot are the construction of three high-rise condominiums known as *Las Caraveles*, and a new *Hotel Humboldt*, due for completion in 1997/98. Playas is also a popular surfing resort with six good surf points.

NB Thieving is rampant during busy times – do not leave **anything** unattended on the beach.

Excursions

An interesting walk, or short drive, is to the village of **El Morro**, with a disproportionately large wooden church with impressive façade (under 'permanent' repair) and the nearby mysterious rock formation of the Virgen de la Roca, where there are a small shrine and marble stations of the cross. There is a regular camioneta service from the crossroads of Av Guayaquil y Av Paquisha.

Some 3 km further down the road is **Puerto del Morro**, up a scenic mangrove estuary, where there are several working wooden trawlers and other traditional boats. It is possible to rent a canoe for 3 hrs to visit the mangroves and probably see dolphins (about US$25). There's no accommodation, but a few basic eating places.

Northwest up the coast is **Engabao**, a small settlement where you can find deserted beaches and wooden fishing boats along the coast. There's no food or lodging here, but there are some surfing points. A camioneta goes here from the crossroads, a 30-min bumpy ride down sandy tracks.

Local information
● **Accommodation**

C *Hostería Bellavista*, Km 2 Data Highway, T 760-600, rooms or suites in bungalows on beach, booking necessary, Swiss-run, friendly, clean, camping at the S end of beach; **C** *El*

Hotels:
1. *El Delfín*
2. *El Galeón*
3. *Humboldt Nuevo*
4. *Hostería Bellavista*
5. *Hostería La Gaviota*
6. *Hostería Los Patios*
7. *La Casa de Gabriel y Marie*
8. *Las Caraveles*
9. *La Terraza*
10. *Miraglia*
11. *Playas*
12. *Rey David*
13. *Turismo*

Places to eat:
14. Los Ajos

Tucán, Km 1.5 Vía Data, pool, restaurant, parking.

D *Cattan*, on the Malecón, safe; **D** *Hostería La Gaviota*, 500m out on Data road, T 760-133, colour TV, a/c, friendly, good clean restaurant; **D** *Hostería Los Patios*, Km 1½ Data Highway, T 760-327, well-equipped suites, restaurant; **D-E** *Playas*, T 760-121, on Malecón, accepts credit cards, beach hotel, plain rooms with fans, clean, safe, restaurant, parking, rec.

E *El Delfín*, Km 1.5, T 760-125, old fashioned, big rooms, on beach, hacienda type building, nice but sporadic water supply, electric showers, restaurant sometimes closed at night; **E** *El Galeón*, T 760-270, beside the church, friendly, clean, mosquito nets or netting over the windows, water all day, cheap restaurant with seafood (closes 1800 Sun), good breakfast, cheaper for long stay; **E** *Hostería Costa Verde*, T 760-645, Lebanese management, excellent meals, cheaper rates for longer stays; **E** *La Casa de Gabriel y Marie*, Av Roldós, 1 block in from Malecón, T 760-047, family atmosphere, basic suites with bath, cooking and laundry facilities, French, English spoken, long-term rates; **E** *La Terraza*, Paquisa y Guayaquil, T 760-430, centre of town, dingy but clean rooms, substantial good value meals; **E** *Parasoles*, Principal y Alfonso Jurado, T 760-532, clean, helpful; **E** *Rey David*, T 760-024, characterless concrete building, clean rooms, sea view.

F *Miraglia*, T 760-154, popular with surfers, run-down but clean, sea view, showers, fresh drinking water, parking for motorcycles, cheaper rates for longer stays; **F** *Turismo*, next door to *El Galeón*, noisy.

Most hotels are 5 mins' walk from the Transportes Villamil bus station. Some are connected to Guayaquil's mains water supply, but many have wells which take water from the sea which is slightly brackish. Downmarket places have buckets for washing, if you're lucky.

● **Places to eat**
Excellent seafood and typical dishes from over 50 beach cafés (all numbered and named). Rec are *Cecilia's* at No 7 or *Barzola* at No 9. Good food at *Cabaña Típica* next to *Rey David*, good, closed Mon. *Mario's*, central plaza opp Banco de Guayaquil, big hamburgers, good yoghurt; *Los Ajos*, at end of street leading from plaza, good soups, varied menu but variable quality. Giant oysters and 'mule foot' black conchs are opened and served from stalls in a side road down from *La Costa Verde*; worth a look if nothing else.

● **Banks & money changers**
Banco de Guayaquil, they can be fussy about the quality of US$ notes.

● **Entertainment**
Discos: *Motivos*, S end of Malecón; *Mr Frog*, diagonally opp *Miraglia*; *Peña de Arturo*, opp Transportes Villamil bus terminus.

● **Post & telecommunications**
Emetel: on Av Jaime Roldós Aguilera, service good, open Sun.

Post Office: reliable; mail for collection at Post Office may be listed under first or last name.

● **Useful services**
There are showers, toilets and changing rooms along the beach, with fresh water, for a fee.

● **Transport**
Buses to **Guayaquil**, 2 hrs by frequent bus, US$1.35; US$40 by taxi.

WEST TO SANTA ELENA

West of El Progreso (Gomez Rendón) a good quality road runs to **Santa Elena** where the road forks W for Salinas or N for the northern coastal towns (*Hostal El Cisne* on the plaza; restaurant *Echeverría*). Near Santa Elena is the **Museo de los Amantes de Sumpa**, opened May 1996, which has a very interesting display on the Las Vegas culture. Beyond Zapotal, by the old race course (now stables), is the turnoff for **Chanduy**, a tiny, picturesque port (accommodation at restaurant on E side of the bay), where 12 km along is the Real Alto Museum. It offers a well laid-out explanation of the peoples, archaeology and customs of the area; open daily 1000-1700, US$0.70.

7 km before Santa Elena, a well-signed turnoff leads 8 km to **Baños San Vicente**, Cetur-run hot thermal baths, which consist of a swimming pool and a big mudhole which claim to cure assorted ailments. US$0.30 entrance, massages extra, open from 0600-1800. It's best to go early or late to avoid the crowds (see also **Hot Springs**, page 42).

● **Accommodation F** *Hotel Florida*, basic, clean, next to baths.

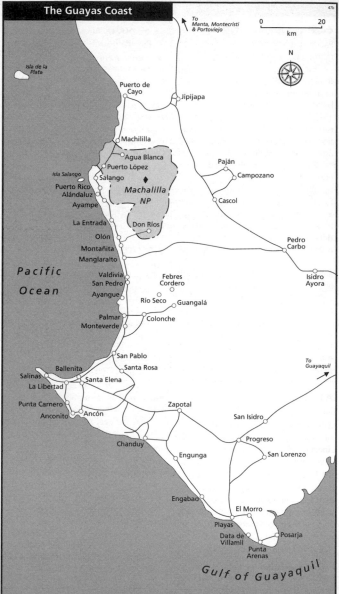

The Guayas Coast

To Manta, Montecristi & Portoviejo

0   20

km

N

Isla de la Plata

Puerto de Cayo

Jipijapa

Machilila

Agua Blanca

Puerto López

Salango

Paján

Campozano

Isla Salango

Puerto Rico
Alándaluz

Machalilla NP

Ayampe

Cascol

La Entrada

Olón

Don Ríos

Montañita

Pedro Carbo

Manglaralto

Pacific Ocean

Valdivia
San Pedro

Febres Cordero

Isidro Ayora

Ayangue

Río Seco

Guangalá

Palmar
Monteverde

Colonche

San Pablo

Santa Rosa

Ballenita

Salinas

Santa Elena

La Libertad

Punta Carnero

Ancón

Anconito

Zapotal

San Isidro

To Guayaquil

Progreso

Chanduy

Engunga

San Lorenzo

Engabao

El Morro

Playas

Posarja

Data de Villamil

Punta Arenas

Gulf of Guayaquil

47b

A brief history of the humpback

🐾 Whale watching has taken off as a major tourist attraction in the tropical Pacific waters off the coast of Ecuador. One of the prime sites to see these massive mammals is around Isla La Plata.

Every year, between June and Sept, the acrobatic humpback whale makes the long 8,000 km trip from the Antarctic to visit the Ecuadorean coast in search of a partner. The whales spend the northern summer in Antarctica feeding and by the time they leave the icy polar seas on their migration north their blubber is 15-20 cm thick. Unfortunately for the slow-moving humpbacks, this made them extremely vulnerable to whalers' harpoon guns. Although humpback oil was at first less valuable than sperm whale oil, demand rose suddenly in the 20th century after it became one of the main ingredients in margarine.

By the time whaling nations began to introduce controls in the 1960s, the humpback population had been reduced to less than one-tenth of its original number. The humpback population appears to be recovering, though very slowly, thanks to a ban on commercial hunting since 1966 in all but a few places. Ironically, the same behaviour that once allowed them to be harpooned so easily makes the humpbacks particularly appealing to whale watchers today. The difference now is that each sighting is greeted with the shooting of film and not lethal harpoons.

Humpbacks got there name from the humped dorsal fins and the way they arch when diving. Their scientific name, *Megaptera novaeangliae*, which translates roughly as "large-winged New Englanders", comes from the fact they were first identified off the coast of New England. Also when a 30-ton humpback leaps out of the water with its huge white flippers flapping, it does appear large-winged.

Aside from the acrobatic antics, the whale-watcher may even be treated to a song or two from the multi-talented humpbacks, who are also renowned for their vocal performances. Chirrups, snores, purrs and haunting moans are all emitted by solitary males eager to use their chat-up techniques on a prospective mating partner. And who can blame them after travelling all that way?

LA LIBERTAD

To the W of Santa Elena the road passes a petroleum refinery and enters the busy port and regional market centre of **La Libertad**. It's not the most appealing of towns, and you'll be eager to jump on the first bus out. Thankfully, these are frequent, so there's no need to spend the night here, unless you're incredibly unlucky, or perhaps doing it for a bet. Car racing takes place at the Autódromo half way between La Libertad and Santa Elena. **Warning** Muggings are frequent.

• **Accommodation & places to eat** **B** *Samarina*, Av 9 de Octubre, Cetur-run, some bungalows, swimming pool, restaurant, coffee shop, bar, with views of the oil refinery and tankers; **E** *Hostal Viña del Mar*, in town centre, T 785979, clean, fan, bath; **F** pp *Turis Palm*, Av 9 de Octubre, opp CLP bus terminal, fan, bath, **G** pp without, bit run down; next door and similar is **G** pp *Reina del Pacífico*; **G** *Seven Seas*, on Malecón, T 786-858, very basic. **Restaurant**: *Mar y Tierra*, N end of main street.

• **Transport** Buses to Guayaquil, with Coop Libertad Peninsular (opp *Hotel Turis Palm* and CICA across the street), US$2.50, 2½ hrs, every 15 mins (the two companies alternate departures); rec; get off at Progreso for **Playas**, 1 hr, US$1.15. Buses every hour, until 1715 to **Manglaralto** (US$1.25), **Puerto López**, **Jipi-japa** (US$3.65) and **Manta** (US$4.35) from the terminal nr the market. To **Quito** with Trans Esmeraldas (opp Coop Libertad Peninsular), 2 nightly, 9½ hrs, US$8.50.

SALINAS

A few kilometres further on, surrounded by miles of salt flats, is **Salinas** *(Pop* 19,298), Ecuador's answer to Miami Beach. There is safe swimming in the bay and high rise blocks of holiday flats and hotels line the sea front. The town is dominated by the Choclatera hill on the southern point of the bay overlooking the well-equipped and very exclusive Salinas Yacht Club.

There are increasing complaints that during *temporada* (Jan to April/May) it is overcrowded, with traffic jams, rubbish-strewn beaches and food and water shortages. At this time the highway from Guayaquil becomes one-way, depending on the time of day, and is said to resemble a Grand Prix racetrack, especially on Sun. Obviously not a good time to hitch a lift. During off season it is quieter, but still not for 'getting away from it all'.

● **Accommodation**   **A3-B** *Miramar*, Malecón, T 772-576, a/c, cheaper with fan, with casino, bath and telephone; **A3** *El Carruaje*, Malecón 517, T 774-282, a/c, TV, hot water, good restaurant; **C** *Salinas*, Gral Henríquez Gallo y 27, T 774-267, modern, off Malecón, good restaurant; **C** *Yulee*, Diagonal Iglesia Central, T 772-028, with bath, TV, **D** without, clean, excellent food, friendly, nr the beach; **D** *Residencial Rachel*, C 17 y Av Quinta, T 772-501, with bath, TV, fans, looks OK from the outside (the Editor doesn't like Dobermans); **E** *Florida*, Malecón y C 2, Chipipe, T 772-780, with bath, cheaper inside rooms.

● **Places to eat** *Mar y Tierra*, close to *Hotel Miramar*, excellent seafood, especially lobster; also nr the *Miramar* is *Flipper*, cheap, simple, clean and friendly. Good freshly-cooked seafood in the market, 2 blocks in from the Malecón and *Hotel Yulee*, *La Lojanita*, excellent *cebiches*. *Oystercatcher*, Malecón y 32, rec, safe oysters, friendly, bird and whale watchers ask here for local expert, Ben Haase.

● **Banks & money changers** Banco del Pacífico changes cash and TCs and gives good rates on Mastercard; also Filanbanco opp the market. You can change cash at the supermarket and the *Hotel Salinas*, at poor rates.

● **Post & telecommunications** Emetel: at Radio Internacional, good service.

● **Tour companies & travel agents** Tours, hire of sailing boats, water skis, fishing trips arranged through *Pesca Tours*, on the Malecón, T (04) 772-391, or *Salitour*, T 772-800, F 772-789.

● **Transport** Buses to Guayaquil, US$2.50, 2½ hrs; for the return journey, go to La Libertad by bus or colectivo (US$0.25, 15 mins, they pass by the market) and take a bus from there (see above).

SOUTH FROM LA LIBERTAD

On the southern shore of the Santa Elena peninsula, 8 km S of La Libertad, is **Punta Carnero**, a magnificent 15-km beach with wild surf and heavy undertow, which is virtually empty during the week. In July, Aug and Sept there is great whale watching.

● **Accommodation** **A2** *Punta Carnero*, T 775-450, all rooms with sea view, restaurant, swimming pool; **A3-C** *Hostería del Mar*, T 775-370, with or without a/c, restaurant, swimming pool, family suites to let on weekly basis.

A few kilometres to the E of Punta Carnero, along the coast, lies **Anconcito**, a fishing port at the foot of steep cliffs. Pelicans and frigate birds gather round the colourful boats when the catch is brought in. There's nowhere in town to stay. Further on is Ancón, centre of the declining local oilfield.

NORTH FROM SANTA ELENA

The northern fork of the road at Santa Elena leads past **Ballenita** which has a pleasant beach.

● **Accommodation & places to eat** **B** *Hostería Farallón Dillon*, Lomas de Ballenita, T 786-643, F 785-611, restaurant, museum; **C** *Ballenita Inn*, T 785-008, at the fork, cottages to rent. Good food at *La Cabaña*, at the fork, where the filling station has good bathrooms.

Most of this coastal road is paved as far as Puerto Cayo but beyond, when it turns inland for Jipijapa and Manta, some sections are bad. The vegetation is tropical desert scrub as far as **La Entrada** with very little rainfall, giving onto a lusher landscape as far as Ayampe, with the hills of the Colonche range falling to the coast. Most of the numerous small fishing villages have good beaches, though beware of rip currents and undertow.

Before **Punta Blanca** are several seafood stands on a wild beach. Look for the *semilleros* all along the coast trudging through wave breaks to collect larvae which is then sold via middle men to the shrimp farms. There is basic accommodation in Punta Blanca at *La Cabaña*.

Further N is **B** *Hostería Las Olas*, T 887-987, Km 18 Vía Santa Elena, before San Pablo, a bleak new complex, but clean and spacious.

The road hugs the coast, passing **Mon-** **teverde**, and then **Palmar**, with popular beaches and beach cafes, but no accommodation. Continuing N is **Ayangue**, in a horseshoe bay, just off the main highway. It gets very crowded and dirty at peak weekends/holidays.

● **Accommodation In Ayangue**: *Cumbres de Ayangue*, T 366-301, on the S point of the bay, expensive, new complex of cabins, restaurant, impressive views; **E** *Hostal Un Millón De Amigos*, with fan and bath, T 916-975, in town; **G** *Los Hermanos*, T 916-029, basic, clean.

VALDIVIA

San Pedro and Valdivia are two unattractive villages which merge together. There are many fish stalls; *Cevichería Playa Linda* is reported as reliable. This is the

Culture shock

The village of Valdivia gave its name to one of the earliest of Ecuador's cultures, dating back to 3,300 BC, and famed for its ceramics.

In the 1950s and 1960s these were the earliest ceramics known in the Americas. The superficial similarities between Valdivia ceramics and those of the Jomon Culture of Japan led many archaeologists to the conclusion that the Valdivia ceramics were first introduced to the Americas by Japanese fishermen.

However, discoveries over the past 35 years show that ceramic manufacture in the Americas has its own long path of development and that the idea of a Japanese contribution to pre-European cultures in South America should be discarded.

A much more compelling notion is that ceramic production in Ecuador had its origins in the non Ecuadorean eastern Amazon basin. Now claims from Brazilian sites place early pottery there at between 6,000-5,000 BC. It is possible that ceramic technology was transmitted from the Amazon basin through commerce or movement of people. The third alternative is that the development of pottery occurred locally and may have accompanied the development of a more sedentary lifestyle on the Colombian, Venezuelan and Ecuadorean coasts.

The impressive Valdivia figurines are, in general, female representations and are nude and display breasts and a prominent pubic area. Some show pregnancy and in the womb of these are placed one or more seeds or small stones. There are others with infants in their hands and some have two heads.

These figurines fill museum cases throughout the country (notably the excellent museums of the Banco Central in Guayaquil, Quito and Cuenca). They are still being produced by artisans in the fishing village of Valdivia today and can be purchased here or at the site museum in Salango, further N near Puerto López. In fact, according to several Ecuadorean archaeologists, many of the figurines housed in the museum collections were made in the 1950s and 1960s because the archaeologists working at that time would pay for any figurines that were found. (Jonathan D Kent, PhD, Associate Professor, Metropolitan State College of Denver).

site of the 5,000 year-old Valdivia culture. Many houses offer 'genuine' artefacts and one resident at N end of the village will show you the skeletons and burial urns dug up in his back garden.

It is illegal to export precolumbian artefacts from Ecuador. The replicas are made in exactly the same manner as their predecessors, copied from genuine designs, and whilst sacrificing historic authenticity, their purchase prevents the trafficking of originals and provides income for the locals. Ask for Juan Orrala, who makes excellent copies, and lives up the hill from the museum. Most artefacts discovered at the site are in museums in Quito and Guayaquil.

MANGLARALTO

(*Pop* 18,510) The main centre of the region N of Santa Elena. As cantonal capital it has a hospital and Emetel office, though most villages along the coast have a house where the Emetel public phone is available. A tagua nursery has been started; ask to see examples of worked 'ivory' nuts. It is a nice place, with a good, quiet, clean beach, good surf but little shelter. Take plenty of sun tan lotion.

Pro-pueblo is an organization promoting ecotourism with many of the local communities. It encourages tourists to go on trips with locals and stay in the villages (a string of community *posadas* is planned and many interesting routes into the interior have been set up). *Pro-pueblo's* projects include reforestation, organic gardening, recycling, health, and tagua-nut carving. There is a volunteer programme and all profits go to the community. Their office is beside *Las Tangas*, T (04) 901-195.

- **Accommodation D** *Sr Ramón's house*, S of main plaza, orange/beige building, with bath, hot water, clean, safe, fan, mosquito net; **F** *Alegre Calamar*, at the N end of town, big, open-walled room, shared bath, mosquito nets, dirty, basic, poor seafood restaurant; **F** *Posada del Emperador*, T 901-172, basic rooms and a cabin, long stays arranged, Doña Lupita will cook vegetarian meals; **F** rooms in house beside church, on Av 24 de Mayo, new, clean, good value.

- **Places to eat** *Restaurante Las Tangas*, on beach, seafood, slow service; *Comedor Familiar* has meals weekends only; also *Comedor Florencia*, moderately cheap and friendly.

- **Transport** Buses to **La Libertad**, US$1; to **Jipijapa**, US$2, 3½ hrs, 100 km via Salango; to **Puerto López**, 1 hr, US$1.50.

MONTAÑITA

3 km N of Manglaralto, has a good beach but watch out for stingrays close to the water's edge. If stung, the small hospital in Manglaralto will treat you quickly. Here you'll find the best surfing in Ecuador. Various competitions are held during the year and at weekends the town is full of Guayaquileños. Major development has taken place at the surfing end of the beach. It's a good place to hang out in, with a relaxed atmosphere.

- **Accommodation & places to eat A3-C** *Baja Montañita*, T 901-218, F 287-873, a/c, cabins and rooms, pool, jacuzzi etc, 2 restaurants, bars, loud beach parties during the high season; **E** *Rincón de Amigos*, T 02-225-907, with bath, cheaper without, cold water, cabins or rooms, relaxed, vegetarian food, expensive breakfast, beach bar, snorkelling trips offered; **F** *Vito's Cabañas*, T 241-975, next door, clean and friendly, good cheap food, camping facilities, mixed reports but generally rec; **F** *El Puente*, by bridge on main road, basic. *Camping Los Delfines* has tents for hire, restaurant; several other rooms for rent nr the surfing beach. *Pelícano*, good pizzas, open till 2200. It's cheaper to eat in the village S of the surf beach. There's also an Emetel phone here, T 901-190.

OLON

A few kilometres N, **Olón** has a spectacular long beach.

- **Accommodation & places to eat A3** *Hotel Al Risco*, at Las Nuñez beyond Olón, T 09-410-022 (cellular), rustic, cabins and restaurant, horse riding; **G** *Hostería Olón Beach*, clean, basic, with Emetel. Fanny Tomalá rents rooms in the village.

Restaurant Puertolón, expensive, indifferent food, plans to build 16 cabins. *Veronica*, just off the beach, scruffy, good seafood, Emetel phone.

● **Transport Buses** Transportes Manglaralto from Montañita to La Libertad, 1 hr, US$1. CLP 3 direct buses a day to Guayaquil, 0500, 1300, 1430 (return 0600, 1300, 1430).

Further N, by **La Entrada**, the road winds up and inland through lush forest. Just before Ayampe is the new **A3** *Hotel Atamari*, T 02-226-072, it consists of beautiful, expensive cabins in spectacular surroundings, wonderful food, no public transport.

ALANDALUZ ECOLOGICAL CENTRE

5 km beyond Ayampe, just before Puerto Rico, is **Alándaluz**, an ecologically and socially sound hotel of bamboo cabins with palm-leaf thatched roofs and fresh flowers. It is a very peaceful place, with a clean beach and stunning organic vegetable and flower gardens in the middle of a desert. They give working demonstrations of recycling of rubbish and water and composting toilets, eco-friendly practices which are increasingly being taken up along the coast. The owners also work in organic agriculture with local communities. They have developed various workshops and courses in ecological architecture, garbage recycling, nutritional food etc and worked in cooperation with the nearby community of Puerto Rico to create the first community garbage recycling patio in the country. Alándaluz has thus become a model for other self-sufficient projects in Ecuador.

It is a good base for exploring the nearby area and Machalilla National Park. The hotel will arrange excursions to Isla de la Plata if there are enough people, though tours are expensive.

● **Accommodation & places to eat** Prices range from **F** pp camping, to **D** pp in cabins. There are student and youth hostel discounts, and 10% discount if you pay in sucres cash. The hotel offers good home-made food, vegetarian or seafood, breakfast costs US$2.80, other meals

US$5.15, and there's a bar. You can cook your own if you take a stove. Cheaper meals can be ordered in **Puerto Rico**, on the main road, ask for Don Julio Mero, at the first house by the road that branches off to left, also rents cabins for longer stays. Reservations are necessary as it is so popular, friendly and highly rec. More information and reservations T 604-173 in Puerto López, or in Quito, *Pacarina*, Baquedano 330 y Reina Victoria, T 543-042/505-084, or write to Casilla 17-15-006-C, the same office also offers tours to the Oriente. **D** *Piqueros Patas Azules*, N on Río Chico beach, nice setting, has a museum, not as eco-aware as Alándaluz; **D** *Hostería Río Chico*, by the road at Río Chico, new, clean, also **F** bunk rooms in Albergue, T (05) 604-181.

● **Transport Buses** Trans Manglaralto from La Libertad, US$2, or from Jipijapa if coming from Manta and the N. Ask to get off at Puerto Rico, though the centre is easily seen from the road. The last bus from the S passes at 1930, from the N at 1730, hitching is difficult. It's 20 mins from Puerto López. A pick up from Portoviejo costs US$7.

PUERTO LOPEZ

This pleasant little fishing town (*Pop* 10,212) is beautifully set in a horseshoe bay, with a broad sweep of beach enclosed by headlands to the N and S. The beach is fairly clean at the northern end, away from the fleet of boats moored offshore. It's interesting to watch the arrival of the fishermen in the morning and evening. The town is becoming increasingly visited by foreign tourists. Since a visit to the Galápagos is now beyond the means of most low-budget visitors, many are heading to this area for the attractions of Parque Nacional Machalilla and Isla de la Plata (see below). Though there are several decent restaurants, Puerto López is not yet well placed to accommodate the increase in visitors. Scooter rental is US$3/hr, with daily and weekly rates available.

Excursions

The Presley Norton archaeological museum in the nearby village of **Salango** is worth visiting; entry US$1. Artefacts

Treasure Island

The precise location of Robert Louis Stevenson's *Treasure Island* has been the subject of some debate. One contender for the mythical island is Isla La Plata, off the Manabí coast.

This classic tale of mutiny and buried treasure begins in the West of England, where young Jim Hawkins and his mother take a sealed parchment from the trunk of a dead sea captain in part-payment of his overdue bill at their inn. On showing the parchment to the local squire, it is discovered to be a treasure map of an island situated somewhere off the coast of South America. Jim and the squire, Dr Livesey, set off for the nearest seaport where they charter a ship, the Hispaniola, and crew for the long voyage.

However, the ship has barely reached its destination when Jim overhears plans for mutiny, spearheaded by the cook, Long John Silver, who seems to have most of the crew on his side. Jim informs Dr Livesey, who lets the crew ashore to keep them away from the ship. Jim also goes ashore, where he meets Ben Gunn, a seaman who has been marooned on the island for 3 years. Keen to leave the island, he agrees to help Jim and the Doctor in their confrontation with the mutineers.

So, along with a handful of crew members still loyal to their captain, Jim, the Doctor and Ben Gunn take refuge in an abandoned log fortress on the island's main beach. The mutineers lay siege and a long battle ensues, during which most of Long John's band are either killed or abandon their ringleader. After more killing and desertions, Long John Silver hands himself over to Doctor Livesey and Ben Gunn, who have found the buried treasure. Along with Jim, they all set sail for England to become rich, but not before the infamous Long John flees at the first opportunity with a bagful of coins.

from the excavations in the local fish meal factory's yard are housed in a beautiful museum on the plaza.

- **Places to eat In Salango**: excellent eating but slow service at *El Delfín Mágico* (order meal before visiting museum), try the *spondilus* (spiny oyster) in fresh coriander and peanut sauce with garlic coated *patacones*.

- **Transport** Buses to and from Puerto López every 20 mins; US$0.40, 10 mins.

Local information
● Accommodation

In Puerto López: **C** *Hotel Pacífico*, nr the Malecón, T 604-133, with bath, hot showers, friendly, safe, comfortable, a/c, cheaper with fan, need mosquito net, **D** in cabañas with shared bath, good breakfast, rec.

D-E *Hotel Buenos Aires*, at least a 15-min walk from the highway, away from the beach, with bath, clean, comfortable, fan; **D** *La Terraza*, on the hill behind the clinic, new, fresh breeze, great views.

E hotels: *Los Cerezos*, 1.5 km inland from bus stop, and *Tuzco*, 500m inland.

F *Residencial Isla de la Plata*, on the main street running from the highway, T 604-114, one block from beach, basic but clean, shared bath, mosquito nets, friendly, good restaurant downstairs; **F** *Soraya*, one street back from park office; **F** *Viña del Mar*, restaurant on seafront, rents rooms next door, friendly but no running water, dirty bathrooms downstairs, good food, breakfast from 0700; nearby is **F** *Residencial Cristian*, basic.

G rooms on the S Malecón, very basic.

● Places to eat

Carmita on the Malecón, seafood, rec for freshness, try *pescado al vapor*, rents rooms for longer stays, **G** pp; next door is *Mayflower*, good but not cheap; *Spondylus*, on seafront, also video-bar and disco, good cheap breakfast, friendly, good juices; *Acapulco*, nr the bus stop, on corner, good value, friendly; *Flipper*, next to bus stop, cheap, friendly, rec; *Diana's Pizzería*, originally in Playas, due open

1997. Try the local avocado *licuados* and *chuzos*, rec. Excellent banana bread from the *panadería* behind church.

● **Tour companies & travel agents**
Machalilla Tours, on Malecón, T 604-206; *Pacarina*, behind *Carmita's* restaurant; *Mantaraya*, on Malecón. All these companies run tours to Isla de la Plata, Agua Blanca, San Sebastián and Los Frailes, as well as diving trips. Whale watching trips can be arranged out of Puerto López with *Pacarina*, or with *Whale Tours* in Guayaquil (see page 244). The best boat is the 20-person sports fisherman *Manta Raya*, which is more comfortable and spacious and has a toilet. *Sercapez*, T 604-130, arranges tours in the area, as does *Machalilla Tours*, T 604-206. Cheaper trips are available in open fishing boats, which are smaller and faster and can get closer, but have no toilet. American Kevin Gulash runs cheaper, alternative trips and is found next door to Alándaluz (see above).

● **Transport**
Buses every 30 mins to **Jipijapa**, 1½ hrs, US$1.30; **La Libertad**, 2 hrs; and **Manglaralto**, 1 hr, US$1.35. To **Portoviejo**, 1 hr, good road, 68 km. To **Manta** direct, every 2 hrs.

MACHALILLA NATIONAL PARK

The Park extends over 55,000 has, including Isla de la Plata, Isla Salango offshore, and the magnificent beach of Los Frailes and is concerned with preserving marine ecosystems as well as the dry tropical forest and archaeological sites on shore. The continental portion of the park is divided into three sections which are separated by private land, including the

town of Machalilla. Entrance is US$14 (ask for 5-6 days), and is payable at the Park Office next to the market in Puerto López (open 0700-1800), or directly to the park rangers (insist on a receipt). The park is recommended for bird watching, and there are also several species of mammals and reptiles.

Los Frailes

Take a bus towards Jipijapa and alight at the turnoff just S of the town of **Machalilla**, then walk for 30 mins. Show your national park ticket on arrival. There is no transport back to Puerto López after 1630.

● **Accommodation & places to eat** On the main road through Machalilla is **D** *Hotel Internacional Machalilla*, T 345-905, conspicuous cement building, clean, fan, overpriced, talk to the manager about cheaper rates for longer stays. Next door is *Comedor La Gaviota*. *Bar Restaurant Cabaña Tropical* at S end of town. Also a few shops with basic supplies.

Agua Blanca

About 5 km N of Puerto López, at Buena Vista, on the road to Machalilla there is a dirt road to the right marked to Agua Blanca. Here, 5 km from the main road, in the National Park, amid hot, arid scrub, is a small village and a fine, small archaeological museum containing some fascinating ceramics from the Manteño civilization found at the site. Entry is US$1.15; open 0800-1800. It is cheaper to find a guide for Agua Blanca in the village

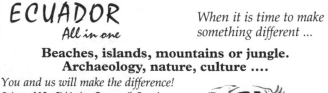

itself for a visit to the pre-Inca ruins; US$1.50 pp for a 2-3-hr tour for 2 people. It's a 45-min walk to the ruins, or hire horses for US$7.50 pp/day.

● **Accommodation & transport** Camping and one very basic room for rent above the museum at Agua Blanca; US$1.50 pp, minimal facilities. Public transport to Agua Blanca leaves Sat only from *Carmita's* in Puerto López at 0630 and 1200, returning 0700 and 1300.

San Sebastián

A recommended trip is to San Sebastián, 9 km from Agua Blanca up in tropical moist forest (800m) for sightings of orchids and possibly howler monkeys. Although part of the national park, this area is administered by the *Comuna* of Agua Blanca, which charges its own fees in addition to the park entrance (as above).

A tour to the forest costs US$15 per day for the guide (fixed rate), US$1.50 pp to stay overnight at guide's house, US$5 for meals, US$15 per horse. Transportation to Agua Blanca is an extra US$5 pp. 5 hrs on foot or by horse. Camping is possible at San Sebastián, US$1.50.

Isla de la Plata

Trips to the island, about 24 km offshore, have become popular because of the similarities with the Galápagos. Wildlife includes nesting colonies of waved albatross, frigates and three different booby species. Whales maybe seen in July, Aug and September. It is also a precolumbian site with substantial pottery finds, and there is good diving and snorkelling.

The island can be visited in a day trip. There are two walks, of 3 and 5 hrs; take water. Reservations can be arranged at most nearby hotels in Puerto López, Puerto Cayo or Machalilla and there are touts only too willing to organize a trip. Cheapest trips are with *Machalilla Tours*, US$20 pp for a full day, including guide and snack, 6-8 people. The park wardens in Puerto López will arrange trips which don't use pirate operators. Take dry clothes, water, precautions against sun and seasickness and snorkelling equipment.

PUERTO CAYO

North from Machalilla is **Puerto Cayo**, where the road turns inland for Jipijapa. The beach is not particularly clean here, but improves as you walk away from town.

● **Accommodation** B-D *Puerto Cayo*, pleasant situation at the S end of beach and good food, but overpriced rooms; **D** *Hostal Jipijapa*, clean, TV, fridge, restaurant; **E** *Mar del Plata*, basic, with bath, new cabins nearby **C**; **E** *Residencial Zavala's*, on the Malecón, with bath, clean, ask for sea view, meals available; ask at *Picantería Avelina* for houses to rent.

● **Places to eat** *La Cabaña* just back from the beach for good seafood; *D'Comer*, next to *Zavala's*, good cheap seafood.

JIPIJAPA

The paved road climbs over humid hills to descend to the dry scrub around **Jipijapa** (*Pop* 32,225), an unattractive town but an important centre for the region's trade in cotton, cocoa, coffee and kapok.

● **Accommodation** **D** *Hostal Jipijapa*, T 600-522, 2 blocks S of the cemetery, clean, overpriced; **G** pp *Pensión Mejía*, 2 blocks from the plaza, no fan, unfriendly, bug-ridden.

● **Transport** Buses to Manglaralto, 2 hrs, US$2; to Puerto López, 1½ hrs, US$1.10; to Manta, 1 hr. Buses leave from the plaza.

At **La Pila**, due N of Jipijapa, the road turns E for Portoviejo. The village's main industry is fake precolumbian pottery, with a thriving by-line in erotic ceramics.

MONTECRISTI

A few kilometres further W from La Pila is the quiet, dusty town of **Montecristi** (*Pop* 37,660), set on the lower slopes of an imposing hill, high enough to be watered by low cloud which gives the region its only source of drinking water. The town is one of the main centres of Panama hat production and is renowned for the high

The last straw hat

🐾 Where does the Panama hat come from? Ecuador, of course! The confusion over the origin of this natty piece of headwear dates back over 100 years.

The major trading post for South American goods in the 19th and early 20th centuries was at the Isthmus of Panama, the quickest and safest seafaring route to Europe and North America. Sugar, fruit, minerals, cloth and dozens of other products, including the Ecuadorean straw hats, passed through the Isthmus.

In the mid-1800s gold seekers from the East coast of the US heading for the California gold rush picked up the straw hats on their way West. 50 years later, workers on the Panama Canal found these hats ideal for protection against the tropical sun and, like the forty-niners before them, named the hats after their point of purchase, rather than their place of origin. The name stuck.

The source of Ecuador's most famous export is the *Carludovica Palmata*, named after the King of Spain and his wife, Luisa, by a pair of Spanish botanists in the 18th century. The plant grows best in the low hills West of Guayaquil, owing to the unique climate. The hats are woven from the very fine fronds of the plant, which are boiled, then dried in the sun before being taken to the weaving centres – Montecristi and Jipijapa in Manabí, and Azogues, Biblián and Sigsíg in Azuay. Montecristi, though, enjoys the reputation of producing the best *superfinos*. These are Panama hats of the highest quality, requiring up to 3 months' work. They are tightly woven, using the thinnest, lightest straw. When turned upside down they should hold water as surely as a glass, and when rolled up, should be able to pass through a wedding ring.

From the weaver, the hat passes to a middleman, who then sells it on to the factory. The loose ends are trimmed, the hat is bleached and the brim ironed into shape and then softened with a mallet. The hat is then rolled into a cone and wrapped in paper in a balsawood box ready for exporting. The main export centre, and site of most of the factories, is Cuenca, where countless shops also sell them direct to tourists.

Given the amount of time taken to make each Panama hat, or *paja toquilla* as they are known locally, the final retail price in the US and Europe, around US$50 and upwards, seems reasonable. But the most important person in the whole process, the weaver, receives the miserly sum of 50 cents or less per hat. This is not exactly an example of fair trading.

Perhaps then few tears should be shed for the decline of this industry. Once the height of fashion and the hallmark of confidence and achievement, demand for the Panama hat has fallen steadily. At its peak, in 1946, the industry constituted 20% of the country's export earnings and every household in the little town of Montecristi produced top quality hats. Now, though, only a handful of families in the region are engaged in making the *superfinos*.

This lack of demand has pushed up retail prices dramatically, but the weaver's wage has barely risen in 25 years, with the result that many are turning to more profitable occupations such as farming and ranching, or even weaving baskets, bags and plantpot holders. The future for the famous hat with the identity crisis looks bleak.

Manabí Province

Cojimies

Pacific Ocean

0   20
km

Pedernales

El Carmen

To Santo Domingo

Palmar
Tabuga

Jama

El Matal

Flavio Alfaro

San Isidro   Eloy Alfaro

Canoa
B Briceño
Napo
San Vicente

Chone

Bahía de Caráquez

Tosagua

Pichincha

San Clemente
San Jacinto

Calceta

Crucita

Junín

Rocafuerte

Manta

Portoviejo

Cerro de Hoja

Montecristi   La Pila

San Lorenzo

Jipijapa

Puerto Cayo

Paján

Machalilla

Puerto López

Salango
I Salango

Puerto Rico   Alándaluz

Ayampe

N

50

---

quality of its output. Varied straw and basketware is also produced here (much cheaper than in Quito), and wooden barrels which are strapped to donkeys for carrying water. Ask for José Chávez Franco, Rocafuerte 203, T/F 606-343, where you can see Panama hats being made; he also sells wholesale and retail. Montecristi is also famous as the birthplace of the statesman Eloy Alfaro.

MANTA

(*Pop* 125,505; *Phone Code* 04) Ecuador's second port after Guayaquil is an important commercial centre, with a large fishing fleet and port. It is a busy, lively town that sweeps round a bay filled with all sorts of boats. The western section comprises steep, narrow streets and the Malecón that fills in the evenings with impromptu parties and cars cruising with blaring music. The constant breeze makes it pleasant to walk along the front or stop for a drink at one of the many small bars. Playa Murciélago at the W end of the Malecón is very wide but not protected. You can walk further W towards the point for spotless beaches and isolation. The town's fine wooden church was burnt down when a Boeing 707 cargo plane flew into it in Oct 1996. Miraculously, the statue of the Virgin survived.

A bridge joins the main town with **Tarqui** on the E side of the Río Manta. The Tarqui beach is more popular, especially at weekends and holidays, but dirtier. Part of it is even used as a makeshift carpark at low tide. The seafront, and the streets leading off behind it, has a decaying, dilapidated look and does not inspire a feeling of security. Do not leave **anything** unattended anywhere (in Tarqui or Manta).

Museums

The Banco Central museum, Av 6 y C4, has a small but excellent collection of ceramics of the Huancavilca-Manteño culture (AD 800-1550). It is open 0830-1630, and the curator speaks English and French.

Local information

Water shortages are very common. All streets have numbers; those above 100 are in Tarqui (those above C110 are not safe). Most offices, shops and the bus station are in Manta. There is a wider selection of hotels in Tarqui.

● Accommodation

In Manta: A3 *Cabañas Balandra*, Av 8 y C20, Barrio Córdova, T 620-316, F 620-545, cabins with a/c, TV, bathroom, 3- and 2-bedded rooms in each, breakfast inc, secure; **B** *Manta Imperial*, Malecón by Playa Murciélago, on beach, T 621-955, F 623-016, inc taxes, a/c, pool, parking, disco and dancing, plenty of insect life.

Manta

1. Club Ejecutivo &
   Banca Pichincha
2. El Inca
3. Haddad Manabi
4. Hostal Manta Mar
5. Hostal Miami
6. Las Gaviotas
7. Las Rocas
8. Lun Fun
9. Manta Imperial
10. Pacífico
11. Panorama Inn
12. Playita Mía
13. Residencial Monte Carlo

In Tarqui: B *Las Gaviotas*, Malecón 1109 y C
106, T 620-140, F 611-840, the best in Tarqui
by some length, a/c, poor restaurant, tennis
court; **B-C** *Las Rocas*, C 101 y Av 105, T 610-
856, a/c, TV, cheaper with fan, pool, private
parking, restaurant poor; **B-C** *Lun-Fun*, nr the
bridge, 3 blocks from the bus terminal, a/c,
with bath, TV, restaurant, expensive.

C *El Inca*, C 105 y Malecón, T 610-986, bath,
TV, phone, fan or a/c, good and reasonably
priced restaurant, friendly, OK.

D *Pacífico*, Av 106 y C 102, T 622-475, with
bath, a/c, discount for longer stay; **D** *Panorama Inn*, C 103 y Av 105, T 611-552, a/c,
bath, TV, pool, restaurant, parking, helpful, rec.

E *Boulevard*, Av 105 y C 103, T 625-333, with
bath, TV, garage; **E** *Hostal Miami*, C 108 y
Malecón, T 611-743, hot showers, fan, basic,
clean, friendly; **E-F** *Residencial Viña del Mar*,
Av 106 y C 104, T 610-854, with bath and fan.

F *Residencial Monte Carlo*, C 105 y Av 105,
with bath, no fan, friendly, dirty and basic;
F *Playita Mía*, Malecón y C 103, restaurant,
shared bath, very basic.

● **Places to eat**
Club Ejecutivo, Av 2 y C 12, top of Banco de
Pichincha building, first class food and service,
great view; *Paraná*, C 17 y Malecón, nr the
port, local seafood and grill, cheap, highly rec;
Shamu, C 11 No 1-12, downtown, good set
meals and à la carte; *Mima*, C 104 y Malecón,
Tarqui, good fish and seafood, US$3-4. There
are many good, cheap *comedores* on Tarqui
beach which are open at weekends; *El Marino*, specializes in *sopa marinera*.

● **Banks & money changers**
Banco de Pichincha and Banco del Pacífico
change TCs. Filanbanco accepts Visa. *Casa de
Cambio Zanchi*, Av 2 No 11-28, T 613-857,
Cambicruz, Av 2 No 11-22, T 622-235; *Del-
gado Travel* (see below).

● **Post & telecommunications**
Post Office: above Banco de Pichincha.

Telephone: Emetel, Malecón nr C 11.

● **Tour companies & travel agents**
Ecuadorean Tours, at Av 2 y C 13; *Metropolitan Touring* at Av 3 No 11-49; *Delgado
Travel*, C 12 y Av 2, T 624-614, F 621-497, also
changes dollars.

● **Tourist offices**
Cetur, Pasaje José María Egas, Av 3 y C 11,
T 622-944, helpful, Spanish only.

● **Useful addresses**
Immigration: Av 4 de Noviembre y J-1 (police
station).

● **Transport**
Air Eloy Alfaro airport is nearby. TAME fly to
Quito daily.

Buses To **Quito**, 9 hrs, US$6.60, hourly 0400-
2300; **Guayaquil**, 4 hrs, US$4, hourly; **Esmer-
aldas**, 0630, 0800 and 2000, 8 hrs, US$6.80;
Santo Domingo, 4½ hrs, US$5.65; **Por-
toviejo**, 45 mins, US$0.70, every 10 mins;
Jipijapa, 1 hr, US$1, every 20 mins; **Bahía de
Caráquez**, 3 hrs, US$2.20, hourly. All buses
leave from the terminal behind the new central
bank building.

PORTOVIEJO

40 km inland from Manta and 65 km NE
from Jipijapa, Portoviejo is capital of
Manabí province and a major commercial centre (*Pop* 132,937). It is the only
provincial capital in the country without
an immigration office, the nearest one
being Manta. It was once a port on the
Río Rocafuerte, but as a result of severe
deforestation the river has silted and almost completely dried up. In the rainy
season, however, it floods badly, often
breaking its banks.

The cathedral, overlooking Parque
Eloy Alfaro, has recently been restored.
You can see sloths taking it easy in the
plaza's trees and you may be tempted to
do the same in this, Ecuador's hottest
city. Portoviejo is one of the main places
where kapok mattresses and pillows are
made from the fluffy fibre of the seed
capsule of the ceibo. In Calle Alajuela
you can buy *montubio* hammocks, bags,
hats etc made by the coastal farmers, or
montubios (see page 60).

Local information
● **Accommodation**
B *Casa Blanca*, Vía a Rocafuerte, T 639-600,
new 1996; **B** *Ejecutivo*, 18 de Octubre y 10
de Agosto, T 632-105, F 630-876, very good,
expensive, extra charge for the guard, but
unfriendly, does not accept Visa despite sign
outside; **B** *Hostería California*, Ciudadela
California, T 634-415, a/c, very good.

C *Cabrera Internacional*, García Moreno y Pedro Gual, T 633-201, a/c, clean, noisy; C *Conquistador*, 18 de Octubre y 10 de Agosto, T 651-472, friendly; C *New York*, Fco de P Moreira y Olmedo, T 632-037/051, F 632-044, a/c and fridge, D with fan, clean, nice, restaurant downstairs.

D *El Gato*, Pedro Gual y 9 de Octubre, T 636-908; D *Madrid*, Pedro Gual, T 631-326.

E *Apartamento Mendoza*, Vicente Marcos y 29 de Julio, T 637-377, cheap, basic, dangerous area; E *Pacheco*, 9 de Octubre 1512 y Morales, T 631-788, with or without bath, fan; E *París*, Plaza Central, T 652-727, one of the oldest hotels, classic.

F *San Marco*, Olmedo y 9 de Octubre, T 630-651.

● Places to eat

Zavalito, Primera Transversal entre Duarte y Alajuela, lunch only, popular; *Los Geranios*,

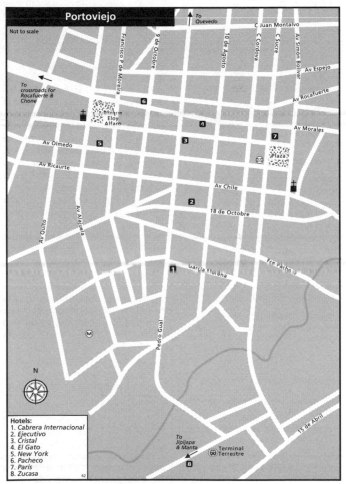

Portoviejo

Not to scale

To Quevedo

C Juan Montalvo

To crossroads for Rocafuerte & Chone

Parque Eloy Alfaro

Av Olmedo

Av Ricaurte

Av Chile

18 de Octubre

García Molina

Francisco P de Moreira

9 de Octubre

10 de Agosto

C Córdova

C Sucre

Av Simón Bolívar

Av Espejo

Av Rocafuerte

Av Morales

Plaza

Av Quito

Av Alajuela

Pedro Gual

Fco Pacheco

15 de Abril

To Jipijapa & Manta

Terminal Terrestre

N

Hotels:
1. Cabrera Internacional
2. Ejecutivo
3. Cristal
4. El Gato
5. New York
6. Pacheco
7. París
8. Zucasa

62

Chile 508 nr Quito, good set lunch; on same street *La Esquina* and *El Gaucho*; *Mariano Internacional*, Córdova y García Moreno, good food. There's a good Chinese restaurant at the bus terminal. *El Palatino*, off main plaza, good coffee and cheap local specialities; *Peña Gol Bar*, late drinking.

● **Tourist offices**
Cetur, Morales 613 y Sucre.

● **Transport**
Air Flights to Quito.

Buses To Quito, 8 hrs; routes are either E via Quevedo (147 km), or, at Calderón, branch NE for Calceta, Chone and on to Santo Domingo de los Colorados. Services also to Guayaquil. Bus station is on the edge of town, taxi US$0.90.

CRUCITA

(Pop 8,300) A rapidly growing beach resort, 45 mins by road from Portoviejo, Crucita is popular with bathers on Sun. It can be crowded and dangerous during carnival, but is relaxed and friendly at other times. Hang gliding and parasailing are practised from the dry cliffs S of town. The beach and ocean are lovely but it's advisable not to go barefoot as there are many pigs roaming loose and *nigua* (a type of burrowing flea which likes to nest under toenails – *Sarcopsylla penetrans*) are common. Much cleaner beaches are to be found on either side of town. There is an abundance of sea birds in the area, including brown pelicans, frigates, gulls and sandpipers among others.

● **Accommodation** From N to S along the beach: **E** *Hipocampo*, the oldest in town, private bath, simple, friendly, good value; **E** *Residencial San José*, shared bath, intermittent water supply, basic; **D** *Hostería Zucasa*, T 634-908 (Portoviejo), 244-713/320-271 (Quito) fully equipped cabins for up to 6, the best accommodation in town; **D** *Fernando's*, some rooms with bath, friendly; **D** *Hostería Las Cabañitas*, T 931-037, cabins for 4-5 people, basic, friendly.

● **Places to eat** Many simple restaurants and kiosks serving mainly fish and seafood line the beach.

● **Post & telecommunications** Emetel: for long distance phone calls (no international service), 2 blocks back from beach on main highway.

● **Transport** Buses and open sided trucks with slatted seats, called *chivas* or *rancheros*, leave from the beach and plaza for **Portoviejo**, US$ 0.45, 45 mins.

2 km N along a paved road running parallel to the beach is the fishing village of **Las Gilces**, which has been less influenced by tourism. Accommodation is available in the *Hotel Centro Turístico Las Amazonas*.

SAN CLEMENTE AND SAN JACINTO

About 60 km N of Portoviejo (60 km NE of Manta, 30 km S of Bahía de Caráquez) are **San Clemente** and, 3 km S, **San Jacinto**, in an area known for its salt production. Both get crowded during the holiday season but are not as nice as they once were owing to the large rocks placed along the beach for protection. The ocean is magnificent but be wary of the strong undertow. Also, do not go bare foot because of the risk of *nigua*, especially in the towns.

● **Accommodation** In San Clemente: **C** *Hostería San Clemente*, T 420-076, modern clean cabins for 6 to 10 persons, swimming pool, restaurant, book ahead in season, closed in low season; **E** *Las Acacias*, 150m from the beach, 800m N of San Clemente, clean, T 541-706 (Quito), bath, nice 3-storey wooden building with huge verandas, prices go up in high season, good seafood, rec; **E** *Hostal El Edén*, 1 block from beach along the main street, some rooms have bath, some have sea views, clean, basic; **E** *Cabañas Espumas del Mar*, on the beach, good restaurant, family run. **San Jacinto**: **D** *Hostal San Jacinto*, on the beach, with bath; **D** *Cabañas del Pacífico*, T 523-862 (Quito), private bath, fan, fridge; **E** *Cabañas Los Almendros*, T 533-493 (Quito), private bath, basic, cramped. **Between San Clemente and San Jacinto**: **E** *Cabañas Tío Gerard*, T 459-613, F 442-954 (Quito), with bath and kitchenette, small rooms, clean, fan; **F** *Residencial Virgen de Lajas*, opp *San Jacinto*, very basic; **F** *Amarilus*, at the S end of town, very basic.

● **Places to eat** In San Clemente: *Tiburón*, on the beach, cheap and good; *El Paraíso del Sabor*, on beach, good, cheap.

• **Buses**   Most Guayaquil-Portoviejo-Bahía de Caráquez buses pass San Clemente. To Jipijapa, 1 hr, US$1.50.

BAHIA DE CARAQUEZ

Set on the southern shore at the seaward end of the Chone estuary (*Pop* 15,308; *Phone code* 05), Bahía is a friendly, relaxed town and a pleasant place in which to spend a few days or more. The river front is attractively laid out with parks on the Malecón Alberto Santos, which becomes Circunvalación Dr Virgilio Ratti and goes right around the point. The beach follows the road around the point and is quite clean. While there are still some buildings with wooden windows and balconies, and some arcaded shops in the centre, the point is built up with smart houses and blocks of flats. Indeed, from San Vicente across the estuary, it resembles a mini Miami beach, but don't let that put you off. The town has become popular as a beach resort, hence the increasing number of high-rise holiday apartments, but it manages to retain its small-town feel. The busiest times are from July to Sept and at Christmas and Easter. The town is also a centre of the shrimp farming industry, which has boosted the local economy but also destroyed much of the estuary's precious mangroves.

Museums

The archaeological museum of the Central Bank is in Casa de la Cultura next door. Admission is free, it's open 1500-1700, it has a collection of precolumbian pottery.

Excursions

Guacamayo Adventures (see below) has the concession for visiting the **Isla de Fragatas**, 15 mins by boat in the middle of the Bahía de Caráquez estuary, which has a stunning number of bird species, including a higher concentration of frigate birds than on the Galápagos. This is an excellent trip for photographers because you can get really close, even under the mangrove trees where they nest. The

frigate birds can be seen displaying their inflated red sacks as part of the mating ritual; best from Aug to January. The 3-hr trip costs US$12 for 4 (less for larger groups). Dolphins can also be seen in the estuary.

The **Chirije** archaeological site can be visited with Bahía Dolphin Tours (see below). This site was a seaport of the Bahía Culture and is an important archaeological discovery. There is a museum on site.

Local information
● **Accommodation**

Only hotels with their own supply do not suffer water shortages.

A3 *La Piedra*, Circunvalación nr Bolívar, T 690-780, F 690-154, inc taxes, pool, good restaurant but expensive, laundry, modern, good service, access to beach, lovely views; **A3** *Herradura*, Bolívar y Hidalgo, T 690-446, F 690-265, inc taxes, a/c, cheaper with fan, friendly, comfortable, restaurant, very pretty; **A3** *Casa Grande*, T 692-097, F 692-088, located in an exclusive residential on the Pacific Ocean, deluxe guest rooms, private bath, outdoor swimming pool and terrace.

C *Hostería Quinta W*, on the road to Chone, 6 km beyond Bahía, motel-style, a/c, refrigerator, TV, warm showers, pool, tennis, guarded, clean, rec; **C** *Italia*, Bolívar y Checa, T 691-137, F 691-092, private bath, fan, hot water, TV, restaurant.

D *Americano*, Ascázubi 222, 690-594, with bath, a/c, TV, some rooms are nice, others not so good; **D** *Bahía*, on Malecón nr Banco Central, rooms at the back are nicer, fan, TV, clean, occasional water shortages; **D** *Bahía Bed & Breakfast Inn*, Ascázubi 322 y Morales, T 690-146, with bath, clean, quite good value; **D** *Hostal Querencia*, Malecón 1800 by main road out of town, T 690-009, some rooms with bath, clean, friendly, may be full, rec.

E *Palma*, Bolívar 914 y Riofrío, T 690-467, with bath, clean, basic, restaurant below, good set meals, excellent value breakfast.

F pp *Residencial Los Andes*, Ascázubi 318, T 690-587, with bath, very basic.

G *Hostal San José*, Ascázubi y Juan de Velasco, clean, safe, big rooms and friendly; **G** pp *Pensión Miriam*, Montúfar, entre Ascázubi y Riofrío, shared bath, basic but clean, friendly, rooms at front have windows, has its own water supply; **G** *Residencial Vera*, Montúfar y Ante, T 691581, rec.

● **Places to eat**

Brisas del Mar, Hidalgo y Circunvalación, good fish, cheap; nearby is *Albatros*, good, friendly; *Los Helechos*, Montúfar y Muñoz Dávila, by Circunvalación, good and clean; *Chifa China*, Bolívar y Ascázubi, cheap, good; *Pablo's*, on Malecón entre Ascázubi y Río Frío; *La Chozita*, on the Malecón nr the San Vicente ferry station, barbecue style food, good; nearby is *Genesis*, popular, good seafood; *Donatella's*, 1 block from Reina del Camino bus terminal, good, cheap pizza.

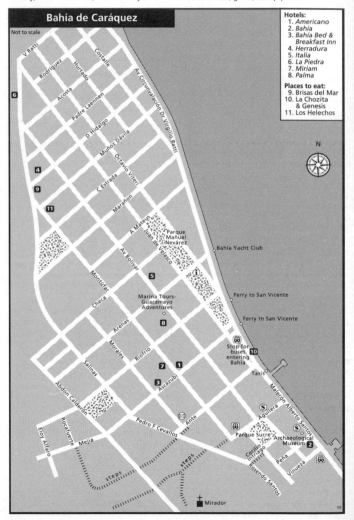

Bahía de Caráquez

Not to scale

Hotels:
1. *Americano*
2. *Bahía*
3. *Bahía Bed & Breakfast Inn*
4. *Herradura*
5. *Italia*
6. *La Piedra*
7. *Miriam*
8. *Palma*

Places to eat:
9. Brisas del Mar
10. La Chozita & Genesis
11. Los Helechos

● **Banks & money changers**
Banco Comercial de Manabí, Malecón y Ante; nearby, heading out of town is **Banco Central**, changes dollars cash; **Filanbanco**, Aguilera, nr Malecón, cash advance on Visa.

● **Tour companies & travel agents**
Marina Tours – Guacamayo Adventures, Av Bolívar y Arenas, T 691-412, F 691-280, excursions to Isla de Fragatas (see above), coastal caves N of Canoa (see below), to see the shrimp ponds, mangroves and the great migratory bird watching of the wetlands of the estuary (including fishing for ugly, black *chame*, which can live 72 hrs out of water – boys sell them in Bahía and Chone in the morning) and into the fascinating tropical dry forest at Punta Bellaca. On this trip you will have excellent views of Bahía and the coast; also, you avoid paying the US$14 entrance fee that you must pay to enter the dry forest of Machalilla National Park. Also offered are 3-day trips on horseback to an organic farm at Río Muchacho, accommodation is with a family in a bamboo house or tree house, traditional food, 'an eye opener to rural coastal culture', US$70-86 depending on numbers, highly rec, reservation necessary. Río Muchacho is promoting agro-ecology and reforestation in the area and Guacamayo Tours designates 10% of all tour fees to its environmental primary school as well as to other conservation work.

Bahía Dolphin Tours, C Salinas, Edif Dos Hemisferios, PO Box 25, T 692-097/086, F 692-088, Email archtour@srv1.telconet.et, home page http//www.qni.com/~mj/bahia/bahia.html; owners of Chirije, for tours there and to other local and national destinations

● **Tourist offices**
Cetur, Malecón y Arenas, T 691-124, Mon-Fri 0830-1800.

● **Transport**
Air Airport at San Vicente. Direct flights from Quito twice weekly. At present (mid 1996) it is being extended to make it international.

Buses Coactur and Reina del Camino offices are on the Malecón 1600 block. All buses coming into Bahía stop by the monument at the Malecón end of Ascázubi before returning to the bus office. Departing buses do not go to the centre. To **Quito**, 8 hrs, US$6.60; **Santo Domingo de los Colorados**, 4-4½ hrs, US$4.10; **Esmeraldas**, at 1515, 8 hrs, US$6.90; **Portoviejo**, 2 hrs, US$1.55, hourly; **Puerto López** or **Manta**, go to Portoviejo or Jipijapa and change; to **Guayaquil**, 6 hrs,

US$5.50, hourly; to **Manta**, 3 hrs, US$2.20, hourly. Open-sided *rancheros* leave from the park on Aguilera to Chone (US$1.05) and other nearby destinations.

ROUTES From Bahía de Caráquez to the highlands there are two main roads. The first one is via Chone and **El Carmen** to Santo Domingo. This road, which has many potholes, climbs quickly over the coastal range, with views of the estuary, the remaining mangroves and the shrimp ponds that destroyed them. In the following wetlands, with more shrimp ponds, are cattle fincas and bamboo houses on stilts. The second road is via San Clemente and Rocafuerte to Pichincha, Velasco Ibarra and on to Quevedo. Alternatively you can go via Calceta, then on an unpaved dry season road directly to Pichincha. This road is very scenic but rarely passable. There are two rivers without bridges, which are not deep. 4WD is recommended.

CHONE

Chone (*Pop* 41,437), is 1½ hrs E from Bahía. At the Santo Domingo exit is a strange sculpture of 4 people suspending a car on wires across a gorge. It represents the difficulty faced in the first ever trip to Quito by car. One of the figures is the famous explorer, Carlos Alberto Aray, who formed one of the first bus companies in Manabí, which still exists. There is a new bus terminal just out of town; catch a bus from the centre. The Emetel office is opposite the post office at Bolívar y Atahualpa.

● **Accommodation C** *Atahualpa de Oro*, Av Atahualpa y Páez, T 696-627, with bath, TV, restaurant, garage, clean, very good; **D** *Chone*, Pichincha y Páez, T 695-014, TV, garage, restaurant; **D** *Hostal Los Chonanas*, T 695-236, shared bath, poor service. The following are all **F** category, with shared bath and poor service: *Brazil*, Av Atahualpa; *Colón*, C Vargas Torres y Alajuela, T 695-510; *Los Naranjos*, Washington y Pichincha; *Manabí*, Vargas Torres y Washington.

● **Places to eat** *Maikito*, Av Atahualpa, cheap, typical food, clean; *Rico Pollo*, Bolívar y Colón, friendly, fast food, clean, cheap.

NORTH TO ESMERALDAS

SAN VICENTE

San Vicente, on the N side of the Río Chone, can be reached by taking the ferry from Bahía de Caráquez, or the road W from Chone. It is being transformed from a dusty, noisy market centre into a pleasant coastal town thanks to the injection of government money. This is because the stretch of coast between San Vicente and Canoa (see below) is said to have the most tourist potential in the country. As well as the upgrading of the airport, a new market has been built on the road to San Isidro. The Santa Rosa church, 100m to the left of the wharf, is worth checking out for the excellent mosaic and glass work by José María Peli Romeratigui (better known as Peli). There are examples of his work in town.

● **Accommodation** On the road to Canoa, across the road from the beach: **A3** *Cabañas Alcatraz*, T 674-179, cabins for 5, nice, a/c, pool; **A3-B** *Monte Mar*, Malecón s/n, T 674-197, excellent food, pool, views, various rooms for rent; **B** *El Velero*, cabañas and suites, pool, restaurant, good; **C** *Las Hamacas*, T 674-134, rooms or cabañas, restaurant, bar, disco, pool, tours; **D** *El Montés*, T 674-201, with bath, bar, no restaurant, friendly; **D** *Restaurant Las Gaviotas*, 3 rooms with bath, nice. **In town**: **C-D** *Vacaciones*, T 674-116/8, nr the old market, bath, a/c, pool, tennis court, restaurant, TV in rooms; **E** *San Vicente*, Av Primera y C 1, opp the old market, T 674-182, cheaper with shared bath, basic, clean, mosquito nets; next door is *Chifa Chunking 2*.

● **Transport Buses** Coactur, opp *panga* dock, to Portoviejo, Manta, Guayaquil. Reina del Camino (nr *Hotel Vacaciones*), to **Portoviejo**, 4 daily, US$1.55; **Chone**, 7 daily, US$1, 45 mins; **Guayaquil**, 4 daily, 6 hrs, US$5.70; **Quito**, at 0630 and 2215, 7½ hrs, US$6.60; **Esmeraldas**, US$5.65; **Santo Domingo**, US$3.70; **Quininldé**, US$4.50. Several companies run along the route to **Pedernales**, US$4, 3 hrs, and **Cojimíes**. The road is paved as far as Pedernales. **Boats** *Pangas* cross to Bahía continually until 2200, 10 mins, US$0.20; car ferry every 20 mins or so, free for foot passengers, very steep ramps very difficult for low clearance cars.

CANOA

The beautiful 17 km beach between San Vicente and **Canoa** is a good walk or bike ride. You will see many people harvesting shrimp larvae, especially at full and new moon. Just N along the beach are nine natural caves at the cliff base. You can walk there at low tide but allow time to return. Canoa is a quiet fishing town. Its clean beach is 800m wide, the widest in Ecuador, relatively isolated and great for surf.

● **Accommodation & places to eat** **D** *Posada de Daniel*, at the back of the village, T 691-201, an attractive renovated homestead, with or without bath, friendly, cheaper if booked through Guacamayo Tours in Bahía; **D** *Bambu*, by the beach, T 753-696, nice cabins, with bath, **E** shared bath, restaurant; *Pensión Canoa*, basic; *Comedor Dixie* has rooms. *Costa Azul*, has good food; *El Torbellino*, good for typical dishes, cheap, large servings; *Arena Bar* on the beach, snacks, beer, T-shirts.

Inland, cutting across Cabo Pasado through the more humid pasture-lands, is the small market centre of **Jama**, 2½ hrs from San Vicente; accommodation in *Pensión Jamaica*.

PEDERNALES

From Jama the road runs parallel to the beach past coconut groves and shrimp hatcheries, inland across some low hills and across the Equator to **Pedernales**, an undeveloped small market town on the coast with nice beaches. The town is being touted as a major future beach resort but as yet is mainly bypassed by foreign visitors. There are enough decent hotels and restaurants, however, if you're stuck here. A mosaic mural on the church overlooking the plaza is one of the best pieces of work by Peli (see above); exquisite examples of his stained glass can be seen inside the church. About 50 more examples of his work can be seen throughout the country.

● **Accommodation** C *América*, García Moreno, on the road to the beach, T 681-174, TV, fans, balcony, very comfortable, expensive restaurant; **D** *Playas*, Juan Pereira y Manabí, nr the airport, T 681-125, with bath, TV, fans, nets, clean, comfortable; **E** *Pedernales*, on Av Eloy Alfaro, 2 blocks from plaza, basic but clean, rooms at front have windows, fans, nets, good value.

● **Places to eat** *El Rocío*, on Eloy Alfaro, good cheap food; *La Fontana*, just off main plaza, good vegetarian food; *Habana Club*, next to *Hotel Playas*, good seafood, cheap. There are several good soda bars on Eloy Alfaro.

● **Transport** Buses to **Santo Domingo**, via El Carmen, 6 daily, 2½ hrs, US$3, and on to **Quito**, 6 hrs, US$5.70; to **Esmeraldas**, at 0515 and 1630, US$5.30, and on to **Muisne**, US$7.15.

COJIMIES

A real one-horse town, with unpaved streets. It is continually being eroded by the sea and has been moved about three times in as many decades.

● **Accommodation & places to eat** **F** *Costa Azul*, shared bath, very basic; **F** *Mi Descanso*, with bath, slightly better looking; *Cabañas* for rent, **E**, ask at *Mi Descanso*. 14 km before Cojimíes on the beach is **C** *Cocosolo*, cabins with bath, set among palm trees, French, English and Italian spoken, clean, restaurant, breakfast US$2.25, lunch US$4.50, also rooms without bath, **E** pp, camping **E**/tent, horses for hire, US$7.50/hr; reservations through Guacamayo Tours in Bahía, T (05) 691-412 or Safari Tours in Quito, T (02) 552-505. *Restaurant Flavio Alfaro*, is by the beach where boats leave for Muisne, friendly, cheap.

● **Transport Buses** To Pedernales by a rough, unpaved road, 1½ hrs, US$1.90, last one departs at 1500, minibuses depart more frequently; pickups also ply back and forth along the beach at low tide, they leave from the beach where the boats land, it's an exhilarating 30-mins' ride, US$1.90, last one leaves around 1500. **Boat** Horacio Gostalle sails to Bahía twice a week. Daily canoes to Chamanga and Muisne, 2 hrs, US$5.70 pp, not for the faint-hearted, those prone to sea-sickness or weak swimmers; the entry into Cojimíes and Muisne is treacherous and many boats have been thrown into the shallows by the swell.

The town, on an island across a narrow stretch of water, is a bit run down but lively and friendly. 15 mins' walk from town (or a tricycle ride for US$0.35), is a long expanse of beach, which makes for a pleasant walk at low tide but practically disappears at high tide. The beach end of town is a great place in which to kick back and relax for a few days. The atmosphere is friendly and peaceful and it's cheaper than either Atacames or Bahía de Caráquez, with some very good food on offer.

Some 50,000 stems of bananas a month are exported through Muisne via Esmeraldas, though the main trade is now shrimps. On the Río Sucio, inland from Muisne and Cojimíes, is an isolated group of Cayapa Indians, some of whom visit the town on Sun. There are no banks, instead you can change TCs at a slightly lower rate at Marco Velasco's store, near the dock. Marcelo Cotera and Nisvaldo Ortiz arrange boat trips to see the mangrove forests which are being replanted by the Fundación Ecológica Muisne, donations welcome, contact them through the tourist office.

Las Manchas, a small island S of Muisne, once the starting point for the beach hike to Cojimíes, was sold for a private hotel development, due open in 1997/98. All the inhabitants of the village were bought out and removed.

Local information
● **Accommodation**

E *Galápagos*, 200m from beach, with bath, modern, clean, fans, mosquito nets, restaurant, rec; **E** *Oasis*, nearby, clean, fans, nets, friendly, secure, rec.

F *Cabañas Ipanema*, 100m from beach, cabins with bath, basic, mosquito nets, secure; **F** *Cabañas San Cristóbal*, wooden cabins on the beach to the right coming from town, no sign, very basic, toilet, fetch water from well nearby, friendly, cheaper for long stay; **F** pp

Calade, 150m away at the S end of the beach, clean, comfortable, negotiable for longer stays, excellent meals; **F** *Playa Paraíso*, clean, basic, mosquito nets.

A new hotel is being built on the beach: planned opening date Christmas 1996, price **C**.

In town are: **F** *Residencial Isla*, and **F** *Sarita*, both very basic. Insist on a mosquito net.

● **Places to eat**
Mi Delfín, in a palm hut on the beach, clean, good food, very friendly, rooms to let **G**, rec; *El Tiburón*, good, cheap, rec; *Las Palmeiras*, excellent seafood, try *camarones a la plancha*; nr the beach is *Restaurante Suizo-Italiano*, good pizza and pasta, breakfast, good atmosphere, the owner is quite a character; *Habana Club*, good rum and reggae. Several other excellent kiosks on the beach; try *encocada de cangrejo*, crab in coconut.

● **Security**
Avoid a man named Lionel, or Zapato, as he is reportedly dangerous.

● **Transport**
Canoes ply the narrow stretch of water between the island and mainland (El Relleno); US$0.10. Buses to **Esmeraldas** US$1.50, 3 hrs; to **Quito** once a night, direct. Boats to **Cojimíes** at 0930 and 1300, US$5.70, 2 hrs, buy your ticket at the dock, take waterproofs and be prepared to wait until the boat is full. Also cargo boats to **Manta**. A new road is being built between Muisne and Bolívar, inland, behind the beaches.

Tonchigüe is a quiet little fishing village, 2 hrs N from Muisne.

● **Accommodation & transport** New expensive *cabañas* and two small, cheap hotels. Bus to Atacames, US$0.50; to Esmeraldas, US$1, 1 hr.

PLAYA ESCONDIDA

2 km S of Tonchigüe is the turn-off for **Playa Escondida**, at Km 14 via Tonchigüe-Punta Galera. This charming beach hideaway, run by Canadian Judith Barrett on an ecologically sound basis, is set in 100 ha stretching back to secondary tropical dry forest. Accommodation is in rustic cabins overlooking a lovely little bay; **E** pp, and camping, **F** pp, 3 meals US$10-15. The food is excellent, swimming is safe, and you can walk along the beach at low tide. The place is completely isolated and wonderfully relaxing. For reservations, T (09) 733-368.

● **Access** To get there take a *ranchera* or bus from Esmeraldas for Punta Galera; El Pacífico departs at 1330 and La Costañita at 1630, 2 hrs. From Quito take a Trans Occidental bus at 2300, arriving in Tonchigüe at 0530-0600, then wait till 0730 for the *ranchera* to Punta Galera.

SAME

Beyond Tonchigüe is Playa de **Same**, with a beautiful, long, clean, grey sandy beach lined with palms. It's safe for swimming and there's good birdwatching in the lagoon behind the beach. There is no cheap accommodation here, mostly high-rise apartment blocks for rich Quiteños.

● **Accommodation** **A3** *Club Casablanca*, restaurant, tennis courts, swimming pool, luxurious (reservations through Metropolitan Touring in Quito); **D** *La Terraza*, on beach, T 544-507 (Quito), 5 cabins for 3-4, with bath, fan, hammocks, Spanish and Italian owners, good restaurant; **D** *Seaflower*, T/F 861-789, reasonable value, restaurant. On the hill by the sea, S of Same is **C** *El Acantilado*, 14 rooms for 2-3 people, 30 cabins up to 5 people, T 235-034 in Quito, excellent food. Booking is advisable at holiday times and weekends. In the low season good deals can be negotiated.

● **Transport** Buses every 30 mins to and from Atacames via, La Costeñita, 15 mins, 18 km, US$0.35, make sure it drops you at Same and not at *La Casablanca*; to Muisne, US$0.60.

SUA

Súa is another beach resort, a 15-min bus ride S of Atacames. It is a quiet and friendly little place, set in a beautiful bay with pelicans and frigate birds wheeling overhead when the fishing boats land their catches. Hotel prices are lower out of season.

● **Accommodation & places to eat** **D** *Chagra Ramos*, on the beach, T 731-070, with bath, clean, fans, good restaurant, good value;

D-E *Buganvillas*, on the beach, T 731-008, with bath, very nice; D *Pensión del Súa*, in the village, with bath, good, clean, restaurant; D *Súa*, on the beach, 6 rooms, hot water, fans, clean, comfortable; **G** pp *Malibu*, on the beach, basic. *La Plage*, on the beach, French-run restaurant, excellent seafood, friendly, rec.

ATACAMES

25 km S of Esmeraldas (*Phone Code* 06), Atacames is one of the main resorts on the Ecuadorean coast. It's a real 24-hr party town during the high season (April-Oct), at weekends and local holiday times. Those who enjoy peace and isolation and who like to sleep at night should avoid the place. The palm trees on the beach, washed away in 1983, are growing again. **NB** The sale of black coral jewellery has led to the destruction of much of the offshore reef. Consider the environmental implications before buying.

Local information
● Accommodation

Prices quoted are for the high season; discounts are available in the low season. Hotels are, generally, expensive for Ecuador. Most accommodation has salt water in the bathrooms; fresh water is not always available and not very good. It's best to bring a mosquito net as few hotels supply them.

A3 *Complejo Turístico Piriapolis*, at the S end of the beach, T 731-238, T/F 713-500, a/c, TV, pool.

B *Le Marimba*, S end of beach, cabins, pool; **B** *Lé Castell*, T 731-542, F 731-442, cabins with bath, TV, phone, pool, garage, restaurant, comfortable; **B** *Villas Arco Iris*, at the N end of the beach, T 525-544 (Quito), or T 731-069, F 731-437, with bath, fridge, clean, charming, English, German and French spoken, rec.

C *Cabañas Caída del Sol*, 150m from the beach, T/T 731 479, with bath, fan, clean, spacious, quiet, good value, Swiss-run.

D *La Casa del Manglar*, 150m from the beach beside the footbridge, T 731-464,

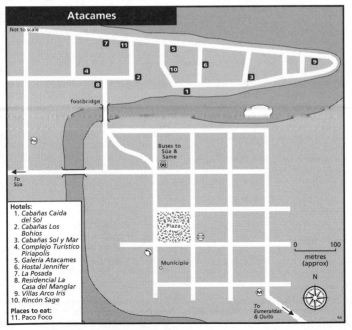

shared bath, clean, friendly, rec; **D** *Cabañas Los Bohíos*, T 731-094, bungalows with fresh water showers, clean, comfortable, quite good value; **D** *Galería Atacames*, T 731-149, on the beach, with bath, fresh water, clean, good restaurant, money exchange, cash and TCs, book exchange, safe deposit.

E *Tahiti*, with bath, TV, pool, fan, nets, friendly, breakfast, good restaurant, also cabins, **F** pp; **E** *Cabañas Rincón del Mar*, on the beach, T 731-064, new, with bath, clean, friendly, fresh water, secure, cosy, English, French and German spoken, highly rec; **E** *Rincón Sage*, 120m from beach,T 731-246, with bath, quiet, money exchange, clean, comfortable; **E** pp *Rodelú*, T 731-033, with bath, fridge, fan, clean, OK; **E-F** *Cabañas de Rogers*, at the S end of the beach, T 751-011, quiet, constant water supply, restaurant, bar, rec.

G pp *Residencial Rebecca*, round corner from *Galerías Atacames*, clean, friendly, noisy at night.

● **Places to eat**
The beach is packed with bars and restaurants, too numerous to list; most offer seafood at similar prices. The best and cheapest *ceviche* is found at the stands at the S end of the beach and at the market, but avoid *concha*. Many restaurants on the beach rent rooms. *La Galería*, on Malecón, rec; *Comedor Pelícanos*, only open weekends and holidays, fresh fish, chicken, *ceviche*, occasionally music, rec; also *Cafetería Pelícanos*, good, menu includes vegetarian dishes and salads; *Marco's*, good steak and fish, rec; *El Tiburón*, on the beach, good seafood, cheap; *Comedor Popular*, good Italian and criollo cooking, order special requests in advance; *Paco Foco*, great seafood, very popular. *Cocada*, a sweet made from coconut, peanut and brown sugar, is sold in the main plaza.

● **Security**
Many assaults on campers and beach strollers were reported in 1995. Walkers along the beach from Atacames to Súa regularly get assaulted at knife point where there is a small tunnel. Gangs seem to work daily. Note also that the sea can be very dangerous, there is a powerful undertow and many people have been drowned.

● **Transport**
Buses to/from Esmeraldas, every 15 mins, US$0.70, 40 mins; to/from Muisne, hourly; to Guayaquil, US$7.

ESMERALDAS

(*Pop* 98,558) The city has little to recommend it. It is hot, sticky, not too friendly and it suffers from water shortages. There are gold mines in the vicinity, tobacco and cacao grown inland, cattle ranching along the coast, timber exports, and an oil pipeline from the Oriente to an ocean terminal at nearby Balao. An oil refinery has been built nearby. The development of shrimp farms has destroyed much of the surrounding mangrove forest. A road bridge over the river at San Mateo upstream from Esmeraldas gives a direct road link to the General Rivadeneira airport.

NB Mosquitoes and malaria are a serious problem throughout the province of Esmeraldas in the rainy season. All the beaches have mosquitoes that come out in hordes at night and bite through clothing. Take plenty of insect repellent because the Detán sold locally does not work well. Most *residencias* provide mosquito nets (*toldos* or *mosquiteros*). It's best to visit in the June-Dec dry season. Use sun tan lotion or cover up, even when it's cloudy.

Excursions
Las Palmas, just N of Esmeraldas, is being developed as a resort. Several hotels have been built and restaurants opened. There is a broad sandy beach but it is reported unsafe (theft), filthy and used as a speedway. Even the water is muddy. Outsiders, especially single women, are advised to avoid the shantytown on the Malecón and to take care everywhere.

● **Accommodation** The best hotels in Las Palmas are along Av Kennedy: **D** *Cayapas*, T 711-022, a/c, showers and hot water in all rooms, overpriced, good restaurant; **D** *Colonial*, Plata y Barrizoty; **E-D** *Del Mar*, on the sea front, modern, mixed quality and size of rooms but all a/c and mosquito-proofed, restaurant closed at 1400, not cheap; good breakfast. Camping at *El Edén* S of town nr the beach. *Artrang*, main plaza, good food, good value.

• **Transport** Buses to Las Palmas, US$0.18, taxi US$1.50; leave regularly from the main plaza in Esmeraldas.

Local information

● **Accommodation**

Generally, hotels in the centre of **Esmeraldas** are not up to much and you are advised to stay in the outskirts.

D *Apart Hotel Casino*, Libertad 407 y Ramón Tello, T 728-700, F 728-704, excellent, good restaurant, casino.

E *Galeón*, Piedrahita 330 y Olmedo, T 713-116, bath, a/c; **E** *Miraflores*, on plaza, shared bath, clean, fans, basic, good; **E** *Diana*, Cañizares y Sucre, showers, safe.

F *Asia*, 9 de Octubre 116, T 711-852, nr the bus station, basic but clean.

G *Hostal Domínguez*, on Sucre nr the Plaza Central, noisy, hot water, open all night; **G** *Turismo*, Bolívar 843, basic, with bath and fan, clean and friendly; **G** *Valparaíso I*, Libertad y Pichincha, very basic but good value, cheap restaurant.

● **Places to eat**

Chifa Restaurante Asiático, Cañizares y Bolívar, Chinese, excellent; *La Marimba Internacional*, Libertad y Lavallén, rec; *Las Redes*, main plaza, good fish, cheap. *Budapest*, Cañizares 214 y Bolívar, Hungarian-run, clean, pleasant; *Balcón del Pacífico*, Bolívar y 10 de Agosto, nice atmosphere, good view overlooking city, cheap drinks; *Los Alamos*, 9 de Octubre, nr the plaza, good, popular. There are numerous typical restaurants and bars by the beach selling *ceviches*, fried fish and *patacones*.

● **Banks & money changers**

Banco Popular, Bolívar entre Cañizares y Piedrahita; and **Filanbanco**, upstairs at both until 1200; *Botica Koch*, Sucre y 9 de Octubre, good rates.

● **Entertainment**

El Portón peña and discotheque, Colón y Piedrahita; *El Guadal de Ña Mencha*, 6 de Diciembre y Quito, peña upstairs, marimba school at weekends; good *Bar Asia* on Bolívar by central Parque.

Cockfights: Eloy Alfaro y 9 de Octubre, at weekends.

Cinema: *Ciné Bolívar*, Bolívar y 9 de Octubre, with a/c and upholstered seating. *Cine Esmeraldas* shows newer movies.

● **Shopping**

There is a Cayapa basket market across from

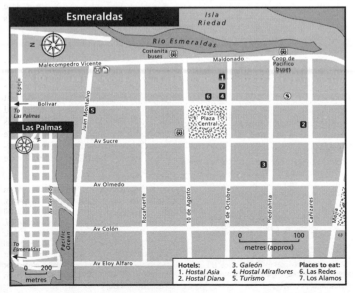

Hotels:
1. *Hostal Asia*
2. *Hostal Diana*
3. *Galeón*
4. *Hostal Miraflores*
5. *Turismo*

Places to eat:
6. *Las Redes*
7. *Los Alamos*

the Post Office, behind the vegetables. Also three doors down, Tolita artefacts and basketry. The market nr the bus station is good for buying mosquito nets. *Más por Menos* supermarket has a good selection of imported goods.

● **Useful addresses**
Immigration: Av Olmedo y Rocafuerte, T 720-256.

● **Transport**
Air Gen Rivadeneira Airport is on the road to La Tola; taxi to centre, 30 km, about US$5; buses to the Terminal Terrestre from the road outside the airport pass about every 30 mins. There are several buses to La Tola and Borbón, so it's not necessary to go into Esmeraldas if you want to go on to San Lorenzo or other places. Daily flights to Quito with TAME, 30 mins. Check in early, planes may leave 30 mins before scheduled time. Intercontinental flies to Cali twice weekly.

Buses To **Quito**, US$6, 5-6 hrs, 30 a day, good paved road (or 7 hrs via Mindo, San Miguel de los Bancos and La Independencia), with Trans-Esmeraldas (best buses, Av Piedrahita 200), Occidental and Trans Ibarra; also with Pan Americana (at *Hotel Casino*) twice daily, slow but luxurious, US$10; by Aerotaxi (small bus), 5 hrs, 12 passengers, reserved seats, their office is nr the main plaza. To **Santo Domingo**, US$2.25, 4 hrs; to **Ambato**, 5 times a day with Coop Sudamericana, 8 hrs, US$6.50; to **Guayaquil**, hourly, US$7, 7 hrs; to **Bahía de Caráquez**, via Santo Domingo de los Colorados, US$7; to **Portoviejo**, US$2.75; **Manta**, US$7; to **Quevedo**, 6 hrs. La Costeñita buses go to: **La Tola** (the road is good to Río Verde), every 2 hrs, between 0600 and 1500, US$2.85, 3½ hrs; to **Muisne**, hourly, US$1.50, 3½ hrs; to **Súa**, **Same** and **Atacames**, every 15 mins from 0630 to 2030; to **Borbón**, every 2 hrs, US$3, 4 hrs.

Boat To Limones and San Lorenzo: the service is irregular; ask at the Port Captain's office at Las Palmas. A combined boat/bus service leaves for San Lorenzo at 1330.

ESMERALDAS TO THE COLOMBIAN BORDER

There are no good beaches for swimming N of Esmeraldas. **Río Verde**, where the paved road ends, has a dirty beach. It was the setting for Moritz Thompson's books

on Peace Corps life, *Living Poor* and *Farm on the River of Emeralds*.

● **Accommodation** F *Paz y Bueno*, on the N side of river, basic.

Beyond Río Verde is **Rocafuerte**, recommended as having the best seafood in the province.

At **La Tola**, where you catch the boat for Limones and San Lorenzo, the shoreline changes from sandy beaches to mangrove swamp. The wildlife is varied and spectacular, especially the birds. Try to avoid staying overnight in La Tola; women especially are harassed.

● **Transport** The road to Esmeraldas is dusty and uncomfortable; buses often get stuck in the wet season. Boats between La Tola and San Lorenzo connect with buses to/from Esmeraldas; 2 hrs La Tola-San Lorenzo, US$4.25, via Limones and Tambillo. Boats can rather overcrowded at times.

LIMONES

The town is the focus of traffic down-river from much of northern Esmeraldas Province where bananas from the Río Santiago are sent to Esmeraldas for export. The Cayapa Indians live up the Río Cayapa and can sometimes be seen in Limones, especially during the crowded weekend market, but they are more frequently seen at Borbón.

Nancy Alexander, of Chicago, writes that about 75% of the population of Limones, Borbón and San Lorenzo has come from Colombia in the last 50 years. The people are mostly black and many are illegal immigrants. Smuggling between Limones and Tumaco in Colombia is big business (hammocks, manufactured goods, drugs) and there are occasional drug searches along the N coastal road.

Limones has two good shops selling the very attractive Cayapa basketry, including items from Colombia. The first is opposite *Restaurant El Bongó* and the second by the dock opposite Banco de Fomento. There are two hotels, both barely habitable. Limones is 'the mosquito and rat capital of Ecuador', a title disputed by Borbón which has the highest rate of malaria in the country. It's a much better idea to stay at San Lorenzo.

- **Transport** A hired launch provides a fascinating trip through mangrove islands, passing hundreds of hunting pelicans; 6 people US$1.75 pp, 1½ hrs. Information on boat journeys from the Capitanía del Puerto, Las Palmas, reached by bus No 1 from the main plaza in Esmeraldas. From Limones you can also get a canoe or boat to Borbón.

BORBON

On the Río Cayapas past mangrove swamps, Borbón is a dirty, unattractive, busy, dangerous place and best avoided. It is developing as a centre of the timber industry. Ask for Papá Roncón, the King of Marimba, who, for a beer or two, will put on a one-man show. Across from his house are the offices of *Subir*, the NGO working in the Cotacachi-Cayapas reserve, they have information on entering the reserve and guide services. Inefan can also provide information.

- **Accommodation** E *Tolita Pampa de Oro*, T Quito 525-753, bath, clean, mosquito nets, helpful; **F** *Residencial Capri*; **G** *Panama City*, mosquito nets, noisy.

- **Places to eat** *Comedor*, where the *ranchera* buses stop, excellent fish.

- **Transport** Buses to/from Esmeraldas, US$3 with El Pacífico, 4 hrs, 0600-1700, beware of theft or sit on the roof; by boat to Limones and San Lorenzo 3 hrs, US$5.20, at 0730 and 1100.

UPRIVER FROM BORBON

Upstream are Cayapa Indian villages. From Borbón hire a motor launch or go as a passenger on launches running daily around 1100-1200 to the mouth of the Río Onzole; US$5 pp, 3½ hrs.

Santa María is just beyond the confluence of the Cayapas and Onzole rivers.

- **Accommodation** Board and lodging with Sra Pastora at the missionary station, F, basic, mosquito nets, meals US$2, unfriendly, her

brother offers river trips; or at the **G** *Residencial*, basic, will prepare food but fix price beforehand, owner offers 5 hrs' jungle trips to visit Cayapa villages (beware deadly red and black river snakes); or camp in front of school free. At the confluence of the Cayapas and Onzole rivers, there is a fine lodge built by a Hungarian (for advance bookings write to Stephan Tarjany, Casilla 187, Esmeraldas), **C** with full board, good value, clean, warm showers. Jungle walk with guide and small canoes at no extra charge. Water skiing available, US$12/hr. Steve organizes special tours to visit remote areas and a trip to the Ecological Reserve, US$250 for 3 days including transport and food.

Zapallo Grande, further upriver, is a friendly village with many gardens, where the American missionary Dr Meisenheimer has established a hospital, pharmacy, church and school; there is an expensive shop. You will see the Cayapa Indians passing in their canoes and in their open long houses on the shore.

San Miguel has a church, a shop (but supplies are cheaper in Borbón) and a few houses beautifully situated on a hill at the confluence of two rivers.

Trips from San Miguel into the **Cotacachi-Cayapas National Park** (entry US$14) cost US$22.50 for a group with a guide, US$5 for boat rental, US$5/meal. Ask for an official guide, eg Don Cristóbal.

- **Accommodation** You can sleep in the rangers' hut, **F**, basic (no running water, no electricity, shared dormitory, cooking facilities), or camp alongside, but beware of chiggers in the grass; also **F** *residencial*.

- **Transport** Borbón to San Miguel, US$8 pp, 5 hrs, none too comfortable but interesting jungle trip.

SAN LORENZO

The hot, humid town of San Lorenzo stands on the Bahía del Pailón, which is characterized by a maze of canals. The area around San Lorenzo is rich in timber and other plants, but unrestricted logging is putting the forests under threat.

The prehistoric La Tolita culture thrived in the region.

The town was once notable as the disembarkation point on the thrilling train journey from Ibarra, high up in the sierra. The train has now been replaced by the bus, but San Lorenzo is still worth visiting. There's a very different feel to the place, owing to the large number of Colombian immigrants, and the people are open and friendly. The culture is distinct and there are opportunities for trips into virgin rainforest.

Excursions

It is possible to take a trip to **Playa de Oro**, on the Río Santiago up in the Cotacachi-Cayapas Reserve. For information ask for Victor Grueso, who has a store in town and also works for the Insituto Permacultura Madre Selva, on the outskirts, near the football field (T 780-257). Basic accommodation is available on the trip, but bring your own food and water; meals are cooked on request. Trips can also be made upriver from Playa de Oro into unspoiled rainforest where you can see howler and spider monkeys and jaguar prints; an unforgettable experience. Contact Mauro Caicedo in San Lorenzo. For information on how to contact Mauro, T 529-727 (Quito), or contact Jean Brown at Safari Tours in Quito (see page 120). It is possible to stay at Madre Selva, F pp including breakfast; you can find out about permaculture and do various trips in the area.

At the seaward end of the bay is a sandy beach at San Pedro, with fishing huts but no facilities. It can be reached by canoe on Sat and Sun at 0700 and 1500, 1 hr; contact Arturo or Doris, who will cook meals.

Local information

When arriving in San Lorenzo, expect to be hassled by children wanting a tip to show you to a hotel or restaurant. Insect repellent is a 'must'.

● **Accommodation**

E *Carondelet*, on the plaza, with or without bath, some rooms are small, fans, mosquito nets, friendly, reliable; **E** *Continental*, C Imbabura, T 780-125, F 780-127, with bath, TV, mosquito nets, clean, family-run, breakfast on request; **E** *Pampa de Oro*, C 26 de Agosto, T 780-214, clean, friendly, with bath, cheaper without; **E** *San Carlos*, C Imbabura, nr the train station, T 780-240, F 780-284, with bath, clean, friendly, fans, nets, rec; **E** *Residencial Patricia*, with bath, cheaper without, good, clean, friendly, fans, noisy from nearby disco.

F *Residencial Imbabura*, nr the station, fan, nets, very basic; **F** pp *Residencial Imperial*, cheaper without bath, clean, friendly, nets, fans; **F** *Yeaniny*, 3 large rooms, fan, clean, mosquito nets, 1 private bath, 2 shared, rec; **F-G** *Vilma*, nr train station, basic, ask for rooms 15 or 16, they are newer and bigger.

San Lorenzo

Hotels:
1. *Carondelet*
2. *Continental*
3. *Ecuador*
4. *Imbabura*
5. *Imperial*
6. *Pampa de Oro*
7. *Residencial Ibarra*
8. *Residencial Patricia*
9. *San Carlos*
10. *Vilma*
11. *Yeaniny*

Places to eat:
12. El Pentagulo
13. La Conchita
14. La Estancia
15. La Red

● Places to eat

La Red, Imbabura y Ayora, good seafood; *La Conchita*, 10 de Agosto, excellent fish, rec; *La Estancia*, next to *Hotel San Carlos*, good food and service, rec. Great juices at *El Pentagulo*, Women's co-op restaurant, just off the plaza.

● Entertainment

Marimba can be seen during the local fiesta on 30 September. Groups practice Thur-Sat; one on C Eloy Alfaro, another nr the train workshops; ask the kids at the train station (for a price). Two discos nr *Hotels Ecuador* and *Patricia*.

● Transport

Buses To Ibarra, depart 0700 and 1500 (and others), 5-6 hrs, US$5.70; they leave from the train station or nr *Hotel San Carlos*.

Trains The train journey to Ibarra, which gives an excellent transect of Ecuador, has been almost completely superseded by buses (see under **Ibarra**).

Sea Launches to **La Tola**; 2 companies with sailings hourly between 0530 and 1430, 2½ hrs, US$4.25; to **Borbón**, at 0700 and 1300, 3 hrs, US$5.20, stops at Tambilla and Limones en route.

CROSSING TO COLOMBIA

From San Lorenzo there are boats to **Tumaco** in Colombia every other day at 0700 and 1400. It's 1½ hrs to the frontier at **Palmarreal**, US$3.20, from there take another canoe to **Monte Alto** and then a *ranchero* to **Puerto Palmas**, cross the Río Mira, then take a Land Rover taxi to Tumaco; 6-7 hrs in total.

Entry stamps in Colombia must be obtained by crossing the border at Ipiales and returning again. When arriving in San Lorenzo from Tumaco, the customs office run by navy personnel is in the harbour, but you have to get your passport stamped at the immigration office in Ibarra or Esmeraldas. Problems may arise if you delay more than a day or 2 before getting an entry stamp, as the immigration police in Ibarra are less easy going.

NB If taking an unscheduled boat from Colombia, be prepared for anti-narcotics searches (at least). This can be a dangerous trip, try to seek advice before taking a boat. Gringos are not normally welcome as passengers because contraband is being carried.

The Oriente

EAST of the Andes the hills fall away to tropical lowlands, sparsely populated with indigenous settlements along the tributaries of the Amazon. Agricultural colonists have cleared parts of the forest for cattle rearing, while even more isolated areas are major oil producers, leading to the gradual encroachment of towns into the jungle.

The vast majority of this beautiful green wilderness, comprising the provinces of Sucumbíos and Napo in the N, Pastaza in the centre, Morona Santiago and Zamora Chinchipe in the S, remains unspoiled and unexplored. A large proportion of the Northern Oriente is taken up by the protected areas of Yasuni National Park, the Cuyabeno Wildlife Reserve and most of the Cayambe-Coca Ecological Reserve. The Ecuadorean jungle has the advantage of being relatively accessible and the tourist infrastructure is well developed, with the emphasis strongly on environmental and cultural awareness and conservation.

NB Anti-malaria tablets are recommended and be sure to take a mosquito net and an effective repellent, especially below 600m. A yellow fever vaccination is also recommended for travel into the Oriente.

Communications

Ecuador's Eastern tropical lowlands can now be reached by four different road routes, from Quito, Ambato, Cuenca or Loja. These roads are narrow and tortuous and subject to landslides in the rainy season, but all have regular, if poor bus services and all can be attempted in a jeep or in an ordinary car with good ground clearance. Their construction has led to considerable colonization by highlanders in the lowland areas. Several of the towns and villages on the roads can be reached by air services from Quito and places further into the immense Amazonian forests are generally accessible by river canoe or small aircraft from Shell or Macas.

The Oriente also has an unpredictable air service provided by army planes. Fares are low and the flights save a lot of time. There are frequent military checks, so always have your passport handy. You may be required to register at Shell-Mera, Coca, Misahuallí, Puerto Napo and Lago Agrio.

NORTHERN ORIENTE

TYPES OF ECOTOURISM

The Northern Oriente offers an extensive variety of ecotourism services and programmes. These can be divided into four basic types: lodges; guided tours; indigenous ecotourism; and independent travel without a guide.

Jungle lodges

These cabaña complexes are normally located in natural settings away from towns and villages and are in most cases built to blend into the environment through the use of local materials and elements of indigenous design. They are generally owned by urban-based nationals or foreigners, have offices in Quito and often deal with national or international travel agencies. When staying at a jungle lodge, you will need to take a torch, insect repellent, protection against the sun and a rain poncho that will keep you dry when walking and when sitting in a canoe. Rubber boots can be hired.

Experiencing the jungle in this way usually involves the purchase of an all-inclusive package in Quito or abroad, quick and convenient transport to the lodge, a comfortable stay at the lodge and a leisurely programme of activities suited to special interests. Getting to the lodge may involve a long canoe ride, with a longer return journey upstream to the

The origin of the Amazon

The legends of the Incas only served to fuel the greed and ambition of the Spanish invaders, who dreamed of untold riches buried deep in the Amazon jungle. The most famous and enduring of these was the legend of El Dorado which inspired a spate of ill-fated expeditions deep into this mysterious and inhospitable world.

Francisco Pizarro, conqueror of the Incas, sent his younger brother, Gonzalo, to seek out this fantastic empire of gold. In 1542, an expedition under the command of Gonzalo Pizarro left what is now Quito with 200 Spanish soldiers, 4,000 Indian slaves, horses, llamas and livestock. They headed across the Andes and down through the cloud forest until they reached the Coca river.

After following the Coca for some distance, the expedition began to run out of food. Rumours that they would find food once they reached the Napo river led one of the conquistadores, Francisco de Orellana, to set out with his men to look for this river and bring back provisions. But the jungle natives fled their small farms as soon as they saw the Spanish approach and Orellana and his party found nothing.

Without food and not being able to cross the river against the current, there was no point in returning. Orellana sent 3 messengers on foot to inform Gonzalo Pizarro of their decision to continue down river. After a few weeks they reached the Amazon river – so called by Orellana because he claimed to have been attacked by the legendary women warriors of the same name.

A few months later, Orellana arrived at the mouth of the Amazon, then began the long trip back to Ecuador, via Panama. 18 months after first setting out, Francisco Orellana and a ragged band of 80 men staggered back into Quito, having become the first Europeans to travel the 3,500 km of the mighty Amazon river.

airport, perhaps with a pre-dawn start. Standards of services are generally high and most lodges show a relatively high degree of environmental awareness, have standardized arrangements with neighbouring indigenous communities and rely on well-qualified personnel. Their contribution to local employment and the local economy varies.

Guided tours

Guided tours of varying length are offered by tour operators, river cruise companies and independent guides. These should be licenced by the Ecuadorean Tourism Corporation (CETUR). Tour companies and guides are mainly concentrated in Quito, Tena, Coca and Misahuallí, where backpackers tend to congregate to form or join groups and arrange a jungle tour, usually of between 1-7 days. Tena also has become a popular base recently. In these towns there is always a sufficient number of guides offering a range of tours to suit most needs, but there may be a shortage of tourists for group travel outside of months of July and August.

Since the cost of a tour largely depends on group size, the more budget-conscious travellers may find that in the off-season it will take several days to assemble a reasonably sized group. In order to avoid such delays, it may be easier to form a group in Quito or Baños, before heading for the Oriente. Conversely, the lack of tourists in the off-season can give you more bargaining power in negotiating a price.

When shopping around for a guided tour ensure that the guide or agency specifies the details of the programme, the services to be provided and whether park fees and payments to indigenous communities are involved. Breaches of contract can be reported to CETUR and to the South American Explorers Club in Quito. Most guided tours involve sleeping in simple cabañas or camping shelters (open-sided with raised platforms) which the guides own or rent. On trips to more remote areas, camping in tents or sleeping under plastic sheets is common.

Indigenous ecotourism

In recent years a number of indigenous communities and families have started to offer ecotourism programmes on their properties. These are either community-controlled and operated, or organized as joint ventures between the indigenous community or family and a non-indigenous partner. These programmes usually involve guides who are licensed by CETUR as *guías nativos* with the right to guide within their communities.

Accommodation typically is in simple cabañas of varying, but generally adequate, quality, and safe food. A growing number of independent indigenous guides are working out of Coca and Misahuallí, offering tours to their home communities.

Tours without a guide

Though attractive from a financial point of view, this is not to be encouraged, for several reasons. From an ecotourist perspective, it does not contribute adequately to the local economy and to intercultural understanding and it may be environmentally damaging. Furthermore, it involves a greater risk of accident or injury.

While unguided trekking is possible in some settled areas, such as around Baeza, and in cleared areas, particularly in the Tena region, travellers should definitely avoid unguided river travel, unguided hiking in remote forested areas and unguided entry into indigenous community lands.

QUITO TO BAEZA

From Quito, through Pifo, to Baeza, the road is paved to a point 9 km beyond the top of the Papallacta pass (4,064m), 5 km before the turn to the Papallacta hotsprings. Thereafter it worsens. It crosses

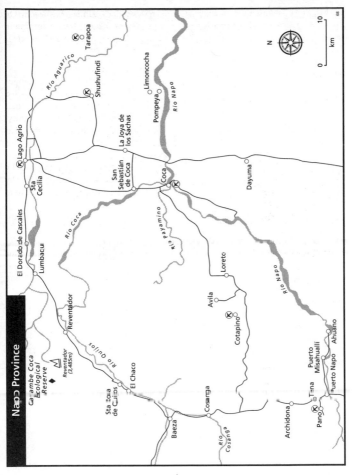

the Eastern Cordillera at the pass, just N of the extinct volcano **Antisana** (5,705m), and then descends via the small villages of Papallacta (see page 131) and Cuyuja to the old mission settlements of Baeza and Borja. The trip between the pass and Baeza has beautiful views of Antisana (clouds permitting), high waterfalls, tropical mountain jungle, *páramo* and a lake contained by an old lava flow.

Antisana gets vast quantities of snow and has huge glaciers. It is very difficult to climb, experience is essential. There are two accesses: one is from Pintag to Hacienda Pinantura, then to Hacienda El Hato from where it is 4-5 hrs on foot (1 hr by 4WD) to Crespo Norte (morraine); the second access is from Hacienda El Tambo above Papallacta Lake to Laguna del Volcán (NW of Antisana). Permission may be required to go beyond Hacienda Pinantura. It can be obtained from *Fundación Antisana*, Av Mariana de Jesús y La Isla, T 433-851, in Quito.

BAEZA

This is a colonist dairy-farming region with little indigenous presence, surrounded by the Cayambe-Coca, Antisana and Sumaco-Galeras Biological Reserves. Its mountainous landscape and high rainfall have created many spectacular waterfalls, pristine rivers and dense vegetation. Because of the climate, *ceja de montaña*, orchids (in flower June/July) and bromeliads abound. The numerous hiking trails make this ideal territory for trekkers, and for fishing enthusiasts, the rivers are full of trout.

At the heart of this region is the small town of Baeza, in the beautiful setting of the Quijos pass. The town is about 1 km from main junction of the Lago Agrio and Tena roads. You need to get off the Lago Agrio bus at the police checkpoint and walk up the hill, but the Tena bus goes through the town. The town of Baeza is divided in two: Baeza Colonial (Old Baeza) and Andalucía (New Baeza). The old settlement, however, is dying as people have moved to a new town, 1 km down the road towards Tena, where the post office and Emetel are located.

● **Accommodation** F *Samay*, in the new town, shared bath, basic, clean, friendly; F pp *Hostal San Rafael*, in the new town, shared bath, clean, friendly, spacious, cheaper cabins at rear, parking, restaurant, rec; **G** pp *Jumandí*, in old town, basic, full of character, very friendly (walls have holes). 30 mins S of Baeza, in the Cosanga Valley, **A3** *Cabañas San Isidro*, comfortable cabins, excellent birding, good exploring in the surrounding primary cloudforest, reservations only, T (Quito) 228-902.

● **Places to eat** The best restaurants are in the old town. *El Fogón*, the best; *Gina*, in old town, very good, cheap, friendly; *Guaña*, breakfasts US$1, friendly, TV. Everything closes by 2030.

● **Transport** Many buses to Tena can be caught outside the *Hostal San Rafael*, 2 hrs.

HIKES AROUND BAEZA

There are many hiking trails in this region which generally can be done without a guide. A recommended source for maps and route descriptions is *The Ecotourist's Guide to the Ecuadorian Amazon*, by Rolf Wesche, which is available in Quito, or in the *Hostal San Rafael*.

Camino de la Antena

This is a 3-4 hr round trip, with a moderate climb and beautiful views along a mountain road which passes through pasture and, at the top, dense cloudforest. The trail is straightforward and easily accessible, with lots of birdlife to be seen. In the rainy season parts can be difficult due to deep mud.

The climb starts in Old Baeza, beside the church. Pass the cemetery and head up the antenna maintenance road. After about 500m, you cross a wooden bridge and turn left. Then there's a steep uphill climb to the top (accessible with 4WD) but on a clear day the views of the Quijos Valley are fantastic.

BAEZA TO LAGO AGRIO

At Baeza the road divides. One branch heads S to Tena, with a newly constructed branch road going directly via Loreto to Coca (7 hrs). The other goes NE to Lago Agrio, following the Río Quijos past the villages of **Borja**, a few kilometres from Baeza, and **El Chaco** (cabins on the edge of town and excellent food at the restaurant on the road in) to the slopes of the still active volcano **Reventador**, 3,485m. The route to the top follows a difficult trail of non-technical climbing, requiring 2-4 days, depending on your experience and physical condition.

● **Accommodation** At the village of Reventador there is *Pensión de los Andes*, basic, clean, and a restaurant.

SAN RAFAEL FALLS

The road winds along the N side of the river, past the impressive 145m San Rafael Falls, the highest in Ecuador. To get to the falls take a Quito-Baeza-Lago Agrio bus. About 2-3 hrs past Baeza (500m km before the bridge crossing the Río Reventador), look for a covered bus stop and an INECEL sign on the right-hand side of the road. From here, walk about 5 mins on a gravel road to the guard's hut, just beyond a small bridge, where you must pay the US$3.75 entry fee. Near the guard's hut is accommodation in some functional cabins (the former INECEL complex).

The path to the falls begins behind the INECEL complex. It's an easy 1½ hr round trip through cloudforest. After about 5 mins, you will come to an intersection; take the right-hand path, then cross the river and it's a further 30-min walk to falls. At the ridge overlooking the falls is a small cross commemorating the death of a Canadian photographer who got too close to the edge. Camping is possible, but take all equipment and food. An extremely steep, slippery trail leads down to the bottom of the falls and should only be attempted by the most experienced of trekkers, preferably with a guide.

Many birds can be spotted along the trail, including the Andean cock-of-the-rock, and there are swimming holes and waterfalls near the INECEL complex, making this a worthwhile stopover on the way to or from Coca or Lago Agrio.

ROUTES From San Rafael the road crosses the watershed between the Coca and Aguarico rivers and runs along the N bank of the river to the developing oil towns of Santa Cecilia and Lago Agrio.

LAGO AGRIO

Lago Agrio (*Pop* 13,165), capital of Ecuador's newest province of Sucumbíos (*Pop* 77,500), is first and foremost an oil town, full of hard drinking oilmen and prostitutes. It was once a rough, primitive frontier town, but the infrastructure has improved and most of the streets in the centre have been paved or adoquined, making it a much cleaner place. Virtually everything in the town is along the main road, Av Quito.

Lago Agrio takes its name from Sour Lake, the US headquarters of Texaco, the first oil company to exploit the Ecuadorean Amazon. They built the road and the pipeline to Quito. The pipeline passes through southern Quito and follows the Chiriboga road to the coastal lowlands at Santo Domingo, then via Quinindé to the Japanese-built refinery at Esmeraldas. The pipeline is the smoothest footpath in the jungle and is used as such. It's also good for drying clothes as the pressurized oil produces enough heat to dry people's washing. People even ride their bicycles along the top. The town's official name is Nueva Loja, owing to the fact that the majority of the first colonizers were from the province of Loja. They left in droves because their lands and soils were so denuded from poor farming practices.

The Cofan, Siona and Secoya Indians all have villages not far from Lago Agrio and they still come into town at the weekend, though you'll rarely see them in traditional dress. Some of these indigenous groups have recently become more aware of tourism as a way of earning a living. Traditionally, most of these groups were at least partially nomadic, but with the arrival of oil drilling, they have been forced to stay in one place and alter their lifestyles accordingly.

Cattle have been introduced to the region to feed the hamburger industry in the USA. However, these are unsuitable animals for grazing on the poor or non-existent soils of the rainforest and now there are desert-like areas where only poor, useless grasses cover the land. For more information, see *Amazon Crude*, by Judith Kimerling.

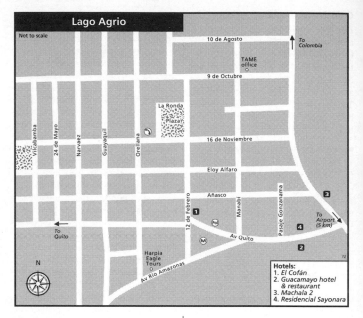

Lago Agrio

Not to scale

10 de Agosto

To Colombia

TAME office

9 de Octubre

La Ronda Plaza

16 de Noviembre

Vilcabamba

24 de Mayo

Narvaez

Guayaquil

Orellana

Eloy Alfaro

Añasco

12 de Febrero

Manabí

Pasaje Gonzanama

3

To Quito

Pol

Av Quito

To Airport (5 km)

4

2

N

Harpia Eagle Tours

Av Río Amazonas

Hotels:
1. *El Cofán*
2. *Guacamayo* hotel & restaurant
3. *Machala 2*
4. *Residencial Sayonara*

Excursions

20 years ago this town was set deep in the jungle and a favourite of entomologists who came here to collect the vast array of insects attracted by the night light of the oil camps. Today, there is no virgin jungle anywhere close. It is, however, the best access for the Cuyabeno and Yasuní Reserves (see below).

From Lago Agrio it is possible to take a bus to **Chiritza** and then a 2-hr boat ride to **San Pablo de Kantesiya**, a small village on stilts with one hut where visitors can stay. For permission to go downriver on the Aguarico go to the Brigada (military post); the store owner there will give you permission to go anywhere as long as you buy something from his shop.

Local information
● **Accommodation & places to eat**
C *El Cofán*, 12 de Febrero y Av Quito, T 830-009, inc taxes, a/c, best in town, but overpriced, no hot water, TV, fridge, clean, restaurant mediocre and expensive.

E *Cabaña*, next to *Hotel Willigram*, clean, rec; **E** *Machala 2*, with bath, TV, fan, clean, safe, friendly, restaurant, sometimes water shortages.

F *Guacamayo*, inexpensive, good meeting place, good restaurant; **F** *La Mexicana*, reasonable, mosquito nets; **F** *San Carlos*, clean, safe, a/c, cheaper with fan; **F** *Residencial Sayonara*, with bath, good, sometimes water shortages; **F** *Willigram*, with bath, doors unlockable, noisy, above bar. *Comercial Calvopeña* is the best place to buy groceries and supplies. *Mi Cuchita* beside *El Cofán*, cheap, good chicken.

● **Banks & money changers**
Several *casas de cambio* on Av Quito, good rates for notes, impossible to change TCs or use credit cards.

● **Tour companies & travel agents**
Harpia Eagle Tours, Cuyabeno, Robin Torres arranges tours, rec only if Robin is the guide.

● **Transport**
Air TAME flight to **Quito** (not Sun), book 1-2 days in advance. **Buses to Quito**, US$7.50, 10-11 hrs; **Baeza**, 7 hrs; **Coca**, 3 hrs; also many *ranchero* buses which leave when full; to **Tena**, US$8.30, 9 hrs.

CUYABENO WILDLIFE RESERVE

Down the Aguarico from Lago Agrio is an extensive jungle river area on the Río Cuyabeno, which drains eventually into the Aguarico 150 km to the E. In the National Park there are many lagoons and abundant wildlife (entry US$14). Transport is mainly by canoe and motorboat, except for one road to Río Cuyabeno, 3 hrs by truck from Lago Agrio.

● **Tour companies & travel agents** To visit Cuyabeno contact *Jungletur*, Amazonas 854 y Veintimilla, Quito, who have 6 day tours of the area. An experienced guide is Alejandro Quezada, T 571-098, Quito. *Neotropic Tours*, Rik Pennartz, PO Box 09-01-4690, Guayaquil, F (593-4) 374-078, takes trips to the Cuyabeno National Park, lodges, everything provided. *Pacarina*, in the same Quito office as *Hostería Alándaluz*, runs 5 day tours to a Secoya community down the Río Aguarico. *Transturi* of Quito (Orellana 1810 y 10 de Agosto, T 544-963) do trips into the jungle on a floating hotel, *Flotel Orellana*, US$567 (4 nights, 3 days) in double cabin with fan, inc all meals, guides, etc. Services and food are good, although wine is very expensive. Flights extra (US$125): bus to Chiritza on the Río Aguarico, then launch to the *Flotel*. Different itineraries for different interests are available on the *Flotel*. Prices are quoted by Metropolitan Touring. Metropolitan Touring run their own excursions (3/4, 4/5, 5 night/6 day) to the **Imuya** and **Iripari** camps. Depending on length, tours involve stops at the Aguarico Base Camp and the **Flotel**; **Imuya** (220 km from Lago Agrio) involves a speedboat trip to get there, earplugs provided; it is very unspoilt, with good birdlife. **Iripari**, on Lake Zancudo, involves a 5 km walk, plus a paddle across the largest lake in Ecuador's Oriente; the camp itself is basic but adequate. Prices do not include US$106 air fare from Quito: low season, 4-day US$375, 5-day US$450, 6-day US$510; high season (1 Jan-15 Mar, 15 June-31 Aug, 1 Nov-31 Dec) 4-day US$470, 5-day US$560, 6-day US$635 (all pp, double occupancy).

FRONTIER WITH COLOMBIA

The road to the N connects Lago Agrio with Colombia, but goes through an area which has suffered some terrorist and kidnapping problems. There is regular transport to the frontier on the Río San Miguel. Crossing here is possible but not easy.

Get an exit stamp from Migración in Lago Agrio (Quito 111 – police station, T 125) before taking a bus N to **La Punta** (US$0.50, 1¼ hrs), where you hand in your Tourist Card to the military and get a boat across the Río San Miguel to the village of **San Miguel** in Colombia (La Punta-San Miguel, 1 hr, US$2.65). From there you can catch a jeep or bus (5 hrs) to **Puerto Asís** and on to **Hormiga** (1 hr, hotels and restaurants), then a bus to Mocoa and on to Pasto. There are DAS office and border formalities at Mocoa. A Colombian entry stamp can be obtained at the Consulate in Lago Agrio.

ROUTES At Lago Agrio, a temporary ferry crosses the Río Aguarico (bridge washed away), then the road heads S to Coca. The route from Tena via Loreto also involves a ferry crossing a few kilometres before Coca, US$2/car.

COCA

Officially named Puerto Francisco de Orellana, Coca is a hot, dusty, noisy, sprawling oil town at the junction of the Ríos Coca and Napo (*Pop* 15,199). As a tourist centre it offers few attractions other than being closer to undisturbed primary rainforest than any other town in Napo province. Hotel and restaurant provision is adequate and there are plenty of bars and discos.

All foreigners going beyond town into the jungle must register with the police, and all guides who accompany foreigners have to be licensed. If going alone beyond the bridge at Coca into the jungle, you must get permission from the Ministerio de Defensa, Av Maldonado, Quito (full details from South American Explorers Club). Considering its relative isolation, food and supplies are not that much more expensive than other, more accessible parts of the country. The town's power supply is erratic; there is usually no electricity after midnight.

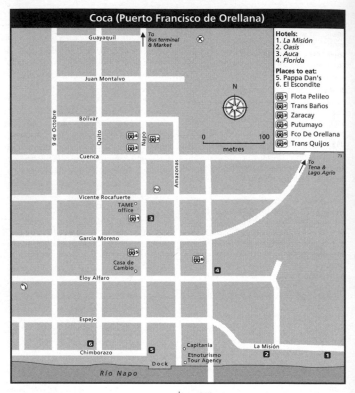

Coca (Puerto Francisco de Orellana)

Hotels:
1. La Misión
2. Oasis
3. Auca
4. Florida

Places to eat:
5. Pappa Dan's
6. El Escondite

1. Flota Pelileo
2. Trans Baños
3. Zaracay
4. Putumayo
5. Fco De Orellana
6. Trans Quijos

Local information

● Accommodation

C *La Misión*, T 553-674, F 564-675 (Quito), in Coca 880-260/1, a/c, very smart, English spoken, restaurant, arranges tours.

D *Auca*, cabins with bath, cold water, comfortable, big garden with monkeys roaming free, small rooms without bath **F** pp, manager speaks English, friendly, good meeting place to make up tour party, restaurant.

E *Oasis*, nr the bridge at the end of town, clean, comfortable, hot water and fans, rec; **E** *Florida*, on main road from airport, with fan, basic, dark rooms, clean.

G pp *Residencial Tungurahua*, basic but OK, showers clean. Other hotels and *residencias* are populated by oil workers and range from basic to barely inhabitable.

● Places to eat

Los Cedros, down by the river, 2 blocks from Capitanería, good fish, *patacones*, *yuca*, fairly expensive; *Doña Erma's* set meal is cheap and filling; *Escondito*, by river, good, cheap, filling, friendly, popular with locals; *Pappa Dan's*, Napo y Chimborazo, by river, hamburgers, chilli, tacos etc, good; *Mama Carmen*, good for early breakfast; *El Buho*, good food, jungle specialities, capibara etc, reasonably priced.

● Banks & money changers

Banks won't change TCs; reasonable rate for cash and TCs at Napo y Eloy Alfaro.

● Post & Telecommunications

Emetel on Eloy Alfaro; 0800-110 and 1300-1700.

● Transport

Air Flights to **Quito** with TAME, reserve 48

hrs in advance, planes are small and flights can be very bumpy, flights in and out of Coca are heavily booked, military and oil workers have priority on standby; also flights to **Tena** and **Shell-Mera** from Coca on Mon, Wed and Fri. TAME office at Napo y Rocafuerte, T 881-078, always reconfirm.

Buses The bus terminal is a 20-min walk from *Hotel Auca*, away from river. To **Quito**, 10 hrs, US$10.50, several daily 1030-2200, Trans Baños and Putumayo, depart from their offices on Napo y Cuenca; to **Lago Agrio**, 3 hrs, US$3.40; to **Tena**, 6 hrs, US$6; to **Misahuallí**, 14 hrs; to **Baeza**, 8 hrs.

River For passenger boats out of Coca, ask the Capitanía at the dock; to Misahuallí, US$20 pp; Nueva Rocafuerte, US$28; canoes go if there are 8 or more passengers, taking about 14 hrs, if it is not reached before nightfall, the party will camp beside the river. For a price, of course, the willing traveller can hire a canoe with owner and outboard motor to take him anywhere along the Napo. (To Misahuallí the charge is about US$115. Take a cushion and waterproofs for yourself and luggage.)

JUNGLE TOURS FROM COCA

Most of the Coca region is taken up by the Yasuní National Park and Huaorani Reserve. This uninterrupted lowland rainforest offers excellent opportunities for a true jungle experience, but wildlife in this area is under threat and visitors should insist that guides and all members of their party take all litter back and ban all hunting and shooting; it really can make a difference.

This area is unsuited to tours of less than 3 days owing to the remoteness of its main attractions. Most tours, including visits to lodges, require extended periods of canoe travel there and back. Shorter visits of 3-4 days are worthwhile in the Coca-Yuturi segment of the Río Napo, where the lodges are concentrated. Tours to the Huaorani Reserve and Yasuní Park really need a minimum of 5 days. Trips which do not go beyond the Río Napo itself are not worth taking since you will see nothing. To see animals you should go downstream from Coca to the Río Tiputini, or to the Cuy-

abeno Wildlife Reserve (see above under Lago Agrio).

NB If a guide offers a tour to visit Indians, ask to see his/her permission to do so. The only guides permitted to take tourists into Huaorani territory are Samuel Padilla, Juan Enomenga, Moi Enomenga (with Tropic Tours), Expediciones Jarrín and Amazon Jungle Adventures. If any other guide offers a trip into their territory, do not accept, it would be in contravention of an authorization of Feb 1992. Some guides also kill animals found en route.

All guides out of Coca charge about US$30-50 pp per day, but you may have to bargain down to this. At popular times it may be difficult to find a choice of worthwhile tours or English-speaking guides. You are strongly advised to check what precisely is being offered, and that the price includes equipment such as rubber boots, tents, mosquito nets, cooking equipment and food, and transport. The South American Explorers Club in Quito can provide updated information about jungle tours, recommended guides and how to arrange your trip.

● **Agencies**
Amazon Jungle Adventures (PO Box 17-21-841, Quito), Pappa Dan and Mike Buzzo have a contract with the Huaorani of Ñonaeno for educational adventure trips up the Shiripuno. The Huaorani benefit from the tourism and are employed as guides, cooks etc. 4-day trip US$280 all inclusive except rubber boots, sleep in tents, T 880-606, F 880-451, Coca. Among other guides are Luis Alberto García, *Emerald Forest Expeditions*, Amazonas 1023 y Pinto, Quito, T 526-403, ext 13, operates out of Coca, speaks English, knowledgeable, rec; *Yuturi Jungle Adventure*, Amazonas entre Pres Wilson y Pinto, Quito, T 233-685, good rates for groups, a typical trip is 4 days staying at *Cabaña Yuturi* downriver towards Nuevo Rocafuerte (see below), US$390 pp, rec; *Jumandy Explorers*, Wilson 718 y J L Mera, T 220-518/551-205, Quito, guide Isaias Cerda is an indigenous Quichua, very knowledgeable, speaks some English, does trips on the Río Arajuno. The Vasco brothers, Wilson, Daniel, Jonas and Walter, of *Vasco Tour Travel*

The Huaorani people

👣 South of Coca is the homeland of the Huaorani, a forest people who traditionally lived a simple, nomadic life in the jungle as hunters and subsistence farmers. They refer to anyone living outside their communities as *cohuode*, meaning either "those that cut everything to pieces" or "people from other places/not living in the territory", and, until recently, lived in complete isolation. There are presently 18 Huaorani communities spread over a large area reaching S into Pastaza province.

Since the 1970s the Huaorani have been greatly affected by the activities of the petroleum industry and have suffered at the hands of an uncontrolled tourist trade. Both have dramatically changed their culture and disturbed their traditional village life. The Huaorani have responded to the tourist invasion by imposing tolls for the use of their rivers and entrance fees to their communities as well as demanding gifts. This latter practice has been encouraged by oil companies who have used it to their advantage when bargaining with Huaorani communities. There has even been some conflict between the indigenous people and tour guides, with violent confrontation in the past. Overall, though, tourism has had a negative effect on the Huaorani people.

Randy Smith, author of *Crisis Under the Canopy*, who has worked with the indigenous peoples of Ecuador on the development of ecotourism projects, states that tourism has taken a major toll in the deculturation process of the Huaorani as the guides offer gifts or cash for the use of their lands or services. He continues that the tourist dollar offers the Huaorani a chance to join the cash economy. The Huaorani visit the various centres outside their territory for food, staples and clothes and therefore require money to sustain this new way of life that many of them have chosen.

For some time, ONHAE (the Huaorani Indigenous organization) opposed tourism, but revised its position in 1992, allowing a number of ONHAE-approved guides to operate in their territory. Lately a number of communities have shown greater interest in getting involved in ecotourism, as the Huaorani have become more integrated into the money economy and are now aware of the amount of money that outside guides receive for taking tourists through their land. They would like to have more control over the tourism that comes through their area and derive more benefits from it.

Agency, can be contacted only in Baños, T (03) 740-017, rec, no litter, no killing of animals, no intrusion of Indians' privacy, their guide, Juan Medina, is frequently rec. Also in Baños, *Tsantsa Expeditions*, T 740-957.

● **Guides in Coca**

Ejarsytur, opposite *Hotel Oasis*, T 887-142, in Quito at Santa Prisca 260 y 10 de Agosto, T 583-120, run by the Jarrín family, German and English spoken, US$40 pp/day, rec. Canoes and guides for jungle trips can be hired from *Fernando Silva*, who lives at the end of the riverside lane next to the bridge, his nephew Ricardo Silva has been described as an enthusiastic guide and a good cook. *Etno-*

turismo Amasanga Supay, run by indigenous co-operative to help local communities, opposite Capitanía, or contact César Andi at *Hotel Oasis*. Other rec guides are *Klever* and *Braulio Llori*, T 880-487/141; *Wimper Torres*, T 880-336, or through *Hotel Auca*.

● **Jungle lodges**

Hacienda Primavera is 2 hrs downstream from Coca. There are clean, basic rooms (**F** pp), or you can camp (US$0.50). Meals cost US$2.50, breakfast US$1.50, bring bread. There is a generator but candles are used for after-generator hours. Excursions are not cheap (eg US$13 to Monkey Island, US$30 to Monkey Island and Pompeya Catholic Mission,

US\$45 to the above and Limón Cocha, divide prices by the number of people (1-10) and add 10% service) and there is not much wildlife to see apart from birds, but it is supposed to be possible to hire canoes from the *hacienda* to visit other places along the Napo. Independent travellers to *Primavera* should check carefully prices quoted on transport back to Quito, and to/from Coca.

La Selva, a jungle centre 3 hrs down the Napo from Coca, has been frequently rec for the quality of its accommodation (built of natural materials) and food. It holds the highest award in ecotourism. It offers interesting excursions into the jungle, 140 ft observation tower, a butterfly farm for breeding and observation: one entomologist has told us he believes this to be one of the richest forest wildlife areas anywhere. The birdlife is arguably the best in the world (over 550 birds have been listed, including some virtually unknown species) and the calibre of guiding is described as unequalled. *La Selva* runs the Neotropical Field Biology Institute, a field studies programme in conjunction with Harvard University and other institutions; genuine field biologists may apply to work at *La Selva* (subject to approval, discounts may be awarded). Guests often meet biologists in the field. 4-night packages from Quito including all transport, lodging, and food, not cheap, but worth it. There is a laundry service. Also available 6-night, 7-day 'Amazon Light Brigade' adventure expedition, with 8 guests, 15 staff and a free bar, the height of luxury. Best to book directly at *La Selva*, 6 de Diciembre 2816 y James Orton, PO Box 635/Suc 12 de Octubre, Quito, T 550-995/554-686, Tx 2-2653 JOLEZ ED, F 567-297 (extra Fax 563-814), alternatively through most travel agencies in Quito.

Sacha Lodge, 2½ hrs by motor boat from Coca, owned by Swiss Benny, comfortable, hot water, excellent food, good jungle trips, prices lower than *La Selva*, rec. Has a good tree tower for canopy observations and uses biologist guides. Bookable through *Explorer Tours*, Lizardo García 613 y Reina Victoria, Quito, T 522-220.

Yuturi, 5 hrs downriver from Coca, on a tributary river, good value, prices lower than *Sacha*, uses local guides with a translator into English, very good birdwatching, sandflies may be a problem.

COCA TO NUEVO ROCAFUERTE

An irregular canoe service (best to hire your own) passes Coca carrying passengers and cargo down-river to Limoncocha, the Capuchin mission at Pompeya with a school and museum of Napo culture, Pañacocha and on to Nuevo Rocafuerte, on the border with Peru. Canoes from Nuevo Rocafuerte return to Coca.

Limoncocha

The Laguna de Limoncocha is an excellent spot for birding. The area was once used by Metropolitan Touring, until 1991, but they moved on and left the cabaña complex to the local villagers, who have created a Biological Reserve. The facilities are beautifully situated, overlooking the lagoon.

Nearby is the Pompeya Capuchin mission, on the left bank of the river, about 2 hrs down-river from Coca. Upriver from Pompeya is Monkey Island. You can rent a canoe to visit the small island with free-roaming monkeys.

Pañacocha

Halfway between Coca and Nuevo Rocafuerte is Pañacocha, near which is the magnificent lagoon of Pañacocha on the Río Panayacu. This was recently declared a protected forest region. Canadian Randy Smith is working on a management plan for the area in order to ensure that the local Quichua community get the best out of tourism.

- **Accommodation G** *Pensión*, in Pañacocha, friendly, but watch out for chiggers in the mattresses.

Nuevo Rocafuerte

The end of the line is Nuevo Rocafuerte, where the missionaries and Sra Jesús let rooms; there are no restaurants. It is possible to hire a boat and guide in Nuevo Rocafuerte, but it would be unwise to add tourism to the pressures to which the Huaorani Indians are already subjected; eg oil exploration on their land.

- **Transport** There is a boat from Coca to

Nuevo Rocafuerte but you must get a military permit to enter the area. The officer has to write exactly the area you wish to visit and you have to leave your passport. The boat takes 8 hrs (hammocks provided). There is a cargo boat back on Mon, but it doesn't always run and you may have to wait until Fri. To Coca it is a 2½-day ferry ride (US$9) with an overnight stop at Sinchichieta and a meal stop at Pañacocha. It is not possible to cross from Nuevo Rocafuerte into Peru.

ARCHIDONA

Roads from both Baeza and Coca go S to **Archidona**, 65 km from Baeza. Founded in 1560, at the same time as Tena, 10 km to the S, this was an important mission and trading centre. The small painted church is striking and said to be a replica of one in Italy (possibly in Sienna). The plaza, once planted with tall, shady trees, has been "renovated", leaving a rather boring and shade-free replacement. The gas station to the N of town rarely has petrol. Next door is the only handicrafts store in town, which sells feathered stuff, as well as some interesting local medicines, spears, shigras, basket work and endangered animal skins (which it is illegal to take out of the country).

● **Accommodation & places to eat E** *Residencial Regina*, Rocafuerte 446, T 889-144, modern, clean, rec, cheaper without bath, pleasant and friendly; *Hostal Archidona*, hidden down a back street, 5 blocks S of the plaza. There are few decent places to eat, though *Restaurant Los Pinos*, nr *Residencial Regina*, is good.

EXCURSIONS FROM ARCHIDONA

The road leaving the plaza to the E goes 10 km to an old bridge over the Río Hollin and on to the access for the **Galeras Reserve**. To enter the Reserve you must have a guide and permission.

Tours can be arranged by special arrangement to the **Izu Mangallpa Urcu (IMU) Foundation**, 3 km E of town off a side turning down the road to Galeras, set up by the Mamallacta family to protect territory on Galeras mountain. They

---

Mud, glorious mud

Archidona came to prominence when American engineers came to town to try and build a road in the rainforest. They didn't so much come, see and conquer as come, get stuck in the mud and give up.

After the 1986 earthquake, the US offered to build a much-needed road to Coca, as the one through Lago Agrio had been destroyed. The Ecuadorean Ministry of Public works (MOP) had already begun a road from Naulpa, near Cotundo, but work was going very slowly. Lack of money was one reason, as was the very difficult terrain; they were cutting through virgin forest on steep hillsides.

Enter the US Army reserves who, in their infinite wisdom, decided to take the shortest route and not cut into the hills. After all, they were the experts who would practise building rainforest roads for future battle readiness. Archidona thus became a base for the US servicemen, with lots of equipment and lots of money. Hotels were opened and restaurants sprung up to cope with the invasion.

It didn't last, however. The US Army soon packed their bags and left defeated and disgusted. They had never encountered mud quite like this. They lost huge roadbuilding machines in the mud, and the soldiers spent most of their time wading around waist deep in the stuff. There are tales of digging equipment and trucks still there, buried up to their roofs. Who knows what happened to some of the personnel.

In the 6 months they were there, the army reserves had managed to complete 3 km of road. Meanwhile, the MOP soldiered on and joined the Cotundo road to the Coca-Loreto road.

have started work on a women's healing centre, for which they have received some foreign aid, to work with local women on traditional medicines. They charge US$35/day for accommodation and day trips, taking groups of 8-10; US$65/day, 5 days trekking, groups of 2 minimum. It's tough going but the forest is wonderful. Ask around or book through *Safari Tours* in Quito, T 552-505, PO Box 17-11-6060.

Just outside Archidona, to the S, a small turning leads to the river. About 200m along there is a large rock with many petroglyphs carved on its surface. There are quite a few others within a 30 km radius of Archidona, but most are very difficult to find. These precolumbian petroglyphs are unique to this area. The symbols depict mysterious stories and messages whose meanings are no longer known by the local Quichua people.

TENA

10 km further S, Tena is the capital of Napo Province (*Pop* 13,790). Once one of the important early colonial missionary and trading posts of the Amazon, it is now a commercial centre with an attractive plaza overlooking the confluence of the Ríos Tena and Pano. Along the rivers are several popular sand and pebble beaches. There is a beautiful riverside walk starting down the steps between two houses, near the Emetel office.

Tena has a large lowland Quichua Indian population living in the vicinity, many of whom are panning for gold in the rivers. These Indians are unlike the Indian groups further into the Oriente forests, they are Quijos, of Chibcha stock. Despite external pressure from the ever-encroaching modern world, many of these communities have maintained their distinct ethnicity, mythologies and customs.

Compared to Coca and Misahuallí, Tena tends to be overlooked by tourists, but for travellers who want to get off the beaten track, the region has much to offer in the way of culture, history and traditional lifestyles.

Excursions

The numerous limestone caves of the Tena area are of special significance to the Quichua. Caves are generally feared and respected and are seldom entered by local people. The intrepid tourist who dares to defy local beliefs can visit the famous **Jumandí caves**, 5-6 km N of Archidona. Take a taxi, or bus from Archidona, 30 mins. It is necessary to go with a guide; take good boots and a strong torch. It is very muddy (sometimes full of water) so it can be useful to take spare clothes. The side ducts of the caves are extremely narrow and claustrophobic. There are several colonies of vampire bat (*Desmodus rotundus*) in the caves. A tourist complex has been built with swimming pool, waterslide and restaurant. The pool and the caves are always open but the other facilities usually only at weekends and holidays.

The cave complex is large and several of the entrances are on private land. In an attempt to preserve some of the caves from stalagtite thieves and graffiti artists, some of the landowners have denied access to the caves on their land. The caves are subject to flash flooding in the rainy season and care should be taken when entering beyond the first chamber. Before going, make full enquiries about routes and conditions.

Sumaco Volcano can be climbed from Tena. It is an extremely long, difficult excursion because of the steepness and dense vegetation. But the trek allows you to enjoy stunning views of the surrounding rainforest. Expect to take 5-6 days. Contact Don Francisco in Huamaní on the new Tena-Coca road.

Local information
● **Accommodation**

The water supply in most cheaper hotels is poor.

C *Los Yutzos*, at the S end of town overlook-

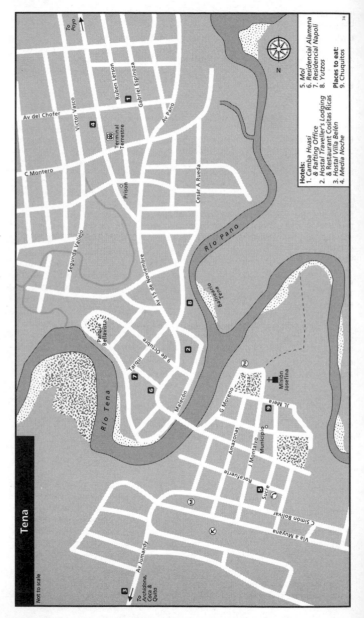

Tena

Not to scale

To Puyo

N

Av del Chofer

C Montero

Ruben Larson

Gabriel Espinoza

Victor Vasco

Av Pano

Terminal Terrestre

Prison

Cesar A Rueda

Segunda Vallejo

Río Pano

Av 15 de Noviembre

Balneario B Tena

Parque Bellavista

Tiraqui

9 de Octubre

Río Tena

Malecon

Mision Josefina

Plaza

JL Mera

G Moreno

Amazonas

Montalvo

Municipio

Rocafuerte

To Archidona, Coca & Quito

Av Jumandy

Sucre

Simón Bolívar

Via a Muyuna

Hotels:
1. Camba Huasi
2. Hostal Traveller's Lodging & Restaurant Costas Ricas
3. Hostal Villa Belén
4. Media Noche
5. Mol
6. Residencial Alamena
7. Residencial Napoli
8. Yutzos

Places to eat:
9. Chuquitos

ing the Río Pano, superior, clean, comfortable, beautiful grounds, family-run.

D *Mol*, Sucre 432, T 886-215, with bath, clean, garage, rec; **D** *Hostal Turismo Amazónico*, Av Amazonas y Abdón Calderón, T 886-487, with bath, TV, fan, fridge, parking.

E *Auca*, on the river out of town, 1½ km on road to Archidona, T 886-461, modern resort-style hotel, Cetur-owned, restaurant and bar, nice grounds, discotheque, casino, swimming in river, electricity and water unreliable; **E** *Hostal Traveler's Lodging*, 15 de Noviembre by pedestrian bridge, T 886-372, F 886-015, modern, cheaper with cold shower, friendly, run by *Amarongachi Tours*; **E** *Hostal Villa Belén*, on Baeza road (Av Jumandy), T 886-228 N of town, new, friendly, clean, cold shower, quiet, rec; **E** *Media Noche*, 15 de Noviembre 1125, T 886-490, nr the bus station, with bath, cheaper without, good, clean, inexpensive restaurant; **E** *Residencial Alemana*, Díaz de Pineda 210 y Av 15 de Noviembre, T 886-409, good and fairly clean, **D** for cabin.

F *Residencial Nápoli*, Díaz de Pineda 147, T 886-194, fan, shared bath, parking, friendly; **F** *Residencial Laurita*, opp the bus terminal, shared bath, basic; **F** *Jumandy*, clean, friendly, balcony, breakfast from 0600, the Fausto Cerda family arrange jungle tours, US$20 pp/day.

G *Enmita*, Bolívar y Montalvo, T 886-253, nr the footbridge; **G** *Hostal Baños*, nr the bus station, basic, clean, restaurant; **G** *Hostal Cambahuasi*, nr the bus terminal, basic but clean accommodation.

● **Places to eat**
Cositas Ricas, Av 15 de Noviembre 432, tasty meals, vegetarian available, good fruit juices, run by Patricia Corral of *Amarongachi Tours*; *Chuquitos*, Montalvo y Calderón, popular; *El Toro*, on the left arriving from Archidona, good *almuerzo*. There are also *chifas* in town. *Tatus* is a riverside bar, built of river mangrove and thatched, attractive and popular.

● **Tour companies & travel agents**
Ríos Ecuador, 12 de Noviembre, opp *Cositas Ricas*, run 1-day trips on remote rivers in the area; specialize in white water rafting and guided kayak excursions; also 5-day kayak school. Contact Gynner Coronel at the *Hostal Cambahuasi*, T 887-438, or T (Quito) 553-727.

● **Tourist offices**
Near the market at the N end of town.

● **Transport**
Air To Shell-Mera (see below). Short flights over the canopy in superlight plane, one person at a time, contact Jorge through *Ríos Ecuador*.

Buses Quito, via Baeza, 11 daily 0200-2345, US$4.50, 5 hrs, book in advance; **Baeza**, 2 hrs; **Ambato**, via Baños, 10 daily, US$5, 5 hrs; **Baños**, 4 hrs; **Riobamba**, via Puyo and Baños, 6 daily from 0200, 5 hrs, US$4.50; **Archidona** every 20 mins, US$0.20, 15 mins; **Misahuallí**, hourly, US$0.70, 45 mins, buses leave from the local bus station not the long distance terminal; to **Coca**, 6 hrs, US$6, 8 daily 0600-2200; to **Lago Agrio**, with Jumandy at 1830, 9 hrs, US$8.30; **Puyo**, 3 hrs; to **Ahuano** 0600 and 1100, return 0800, 1400.

JUNGLE TOURS FROM TENA

Trips are organized to **Amarongachi** by Patricia Corral and Jesús Uribe; *Amarongachi Tours*, 15 de Noviembre 422, PO Box 278, T 886-372, F 886-015, highly recommended. They have a cooperative travel agency, hotel and restaurant, and *Shangri-La* cabins S of Río Jatunyacu.

Comunidad Capirona is 1 hr by bus, then 3 on foot from Tena. It is run by FOIN, Federación de Organizaciones Indígenas de Napo. Information is available from Sr Tarquino Tapuy, C Augusto Rueda, Casilla Postal 217, Tena, T 886 288. FOIN represents areas of health, education, environment and the marketing of local products; they will accept volunteers. Fees per day are from US$30-40 pp depending on the number in the party. (Ricancie in Quito, c/o Aguda en Acción, T 529-934, also take reservations.)

Alternatively contact the Cerda family, who act as guides for tour agencies, only US$20 pp/day. Nelli (daughter) lives at C 9 de Octubre 356, Barrio Bella Vista Baja, a 10-min walk from the bus station. If she is not at home, catch a bus to Talag from the bridge upstream (6 daily, 30 mins), walk 2 km to the Río Napo and ask for Olmedo Cerda (father) or Escuela Pedro Carbo (Comunidad Sirena), cross the river on the ferry and walk 25 mins upstream. Both Olmedo and Oswaldo (son) are recommended guides. You can also contact them through *Hotel Jumandy*.

Sr Delfín Pauchi, T 886-434, Casilla 245, Tena, has built *Cabañas Pimpilala*, 45 mins by taxi from Tena, where for 2-5 days you can live with a Quichua family, US$30 pp/day, including lodging, meals, transport and guide. Trails for hiking have been made on his 30 ha of undeveloped land, but emphasis is on culture rather than animals. Delfín speaks only Quichua and Spanish. He knows about plants and their medicinal uses, legends and music. Also, *Hacienda Jatún Yacu*, a family farm in the rainforest, is excellent. Contact through *Ríos Ecuador* (see above) or *Safari Tours* in Quito.

TENA TO MISAHUALLI

From Tena the main highway (unpaved) runs S to Puyo.

Puerto Napo, a few kilometres S of Tena, has a bridge across the Río Napo. Pato García, a guide, has a nice room to rent, G, full board. He will also take independent tours, but works mostly for Quito agencies.

On the N bank a road runs E to Misahuallí, about 17 km downstream. From the **Napo bridge** you can get a ride in a truck, US$0.50, or colectivos. If you're travelling N from Puyo, avoid going into Tena by getting off the bus here.

MISAHUALLI

This small port (*Pop* 3,579) at the junction of the Napo and Misahuallí rivers, was once the Río Napo access point and very important because of the lack of roads. Its decline as a port began with the opening of the Loreto road after the earthquake of 1986. Fortunately for Misahuallí the tourist trade was already established, and as commerce declined,

tourism replaced it. Now, the town is almost totally devoted to tourism.

Despite the fact that there is almost no extensive primary forest anywhere near Misahuallí, other than Jatun Sacha (see below), it still attracts many visitors. The area provides many possibilities for visiting the jungle, being one of the easiest places to get to. It is only 7-8 hrs from Quito and 5 hrs from Baños, though the latter road is only open on Mon at present. There is not a great deal of wildlife around Misahuallí, but plants, butterflies and birds are plentiful and there is good hiking. For wildlife you are advised to go to Coca or to take an excursion lasting several days. Oil exploration in the area is also diminishing chances of seeing wildlife. There is a fine, sandy beach on the Río Misahuallí, but don't camp on it as the river can rise unexpectedly.

Excursions

A nice walk is along the **Río Latas**, 7 km W of Misahuallí, where there are some small waterfalls. You walk through dense vegetation for about 1½ hrs, often through water to get to the largest fall and pass quite a few pools where you can swim. To get there catch the bus towards the Napo bridge and ask to be set down by the river. The bridge is the third one out of Misahuallí. The path leads from the road by the bridge to a rock bench beside a small pool that is a popular swimming-hole with local schoolchildren. Continue hiking up the river, past a series of chutes and natural slides that have been carved out of the bedrock, until you reach a small waterfall to your left. From here, if you wish to continue to the larger waterfall at the end of the canyon, be prepared to get wet and for some difficult terrain. It's best to hike in the water, as the exposed rocks are very slippery.

A strenuous day trip can be made to **Palmeras**. Take the road N and cross the bridge over the Río Misahuallí, a muddy road (rubber boots essential) goes through fields skirting the jungle. There are many birds in this area. Palmeras, a friendly village with no food or safe water, is reached after about 3 hrs. Continue to a patch of primary forest where there are side trails. If you are lucky, and quiet, you may see monkeys.

Local information
● Accommodation

C *Misahuallí Jungle Hotel*, across the river from town, cabins for up to 6, nice setting, friendly, restaurant operates sporadically, US$165 for 3 days/2 nights inc full board and excursions: in Quito, Ramírez Dávalos 251, T 520-043, F 454-146.

D *El Albergue Español*, PO Box 254, Tena, Quito T/F 584-912, owned by Dr José Ramón Edesa, meals US$3, some vegetarian, all rooms with bath, clean and screened with balconies overlooking Napo, family room sleep 6, highly rec, they also run jungle tours to Coca; **D** *Txalaparta*, just before Misahuallí, T 584-964, peaceful cabins.

E *Dayuma Hotel* (see also **Restaurants** and **Guides** below), T (Tena) 584-964, 2 and 3-bedded rooms with bath, fan, balcony, clean, often fully booked with tour groups, same owners as *Dayuma Camp* (see below); **E** *El Paisano*, good meeting place, intermittent water supply, clean, cheaper without bath, washing facilities, hammocks, nice garden, rec, 8 rooms behind restaurant, good breakfast, information on guides (Alfredo, who hangs around, is not an official guide); **E** *Milca Isca*, on the main plaza, friendly, clean, cheap, good restaurant, English spoken; **E** *Residencial Pepe*, on the main plaza, basic rooms with fan, safe to leave luggage, information on jungle tours; **E** *Sacha*, very basic, bamboo walls, noisy bar, at the point where the rivers meet, monkeys in the garden, path to hotel floods when rains are heavy, buy souvenirs of the Oriente here, cheaper than in Baños or Quito.

F *Balcón del Napo*, basic, central, meals available, clean, friendly, noisy from disco at weekends, safe motorcycle parking, may change currency; **F** *Etsa*, with or without bath, very simple, owner is guide Carlos Cordero; **F** *Fifty*, on the main plaza, communal baths, safe, friendly, family run (familia Vasco), vegetarian restaurant.

● Places to eat
The best is *El Albergue Español*; Douglas Clarke's *Restaurant Dayuma* is reasonably good and cheap; as is *El Paisano*, mostly good vegetarian food (but meat should be treated with caution), popular meeting place for gringos, hence its nickname *Restaurant Paleface*, closes 2100 sharp; *La Abuela Pizzería*, on plaza, good breakfast, pizza, friendly, cheap, good music, rooms for rent; *Jenifer*, cheap, good restaurant on plaza; *Cactus*, on the road to *El Paisano*, drinks, Mexican, breakfast. *Peña/Disco* on same street. The bars down by the river have a frontier feel to them, as do the handful of general stores.

● Transport
Buses From Quito via Baños and Tena, about 8 hrs, several daily; also from Quito via Baeza and Tena, about 5 hrs. Since the Baños road is closed, except Mon, at least until mid 1997, there are many more buses on the Tena-Baeza-Quito route, and the road has been improved.

River There are still twice weekly canoes scheduled to Coca, leaving Wed and Sun, returning Thurs and Mon, or if you are in a group you can charter a canoe; 6 hrs to Coca, 9-14 back. If going downstream, you must register with the port captain's office, where there is a list of approved prices to various destinations. Bartering may get you a slight reduction. The office will want to keep your passport after stamping it. If you are returning the same way, it's a safe place to leave it. However, if you want to keep it, or are not returning to Misahuallí, tell them you are returning via Coca or Ahuano, if they ask where you are leaving from. Tickets are available across the street from the port captain's office.

During and after heavy rainfall there are obviously no services, nor are there any services during a long dry period. You can rent a boat to Coca, US$115 for up to 20 people, it leaves only in the morning. Take something to sit on.

JUNGLE TOURS FROM MISAHUALLÍ

There are many guides available to take parties into the jungle for trips of 1 to 10 days, all involving canoeing and varying amounts of hiking. Travellers should ask to see a guide's licence (we have frequent reports of unlicenced guides cheating tourists). It is advisable to insist on paying part of the cost on completion of the trip (for tour agencies based in Quito, see page 117). The going rate is between US$30 and US$50 pp per day, depending on the season, size of group and length of trip. This should include food and rubber boots, which are absolutely essential. Overnight tours are recommended only for the hardy.

Some guides visit zoos of hotels where animals are kept in unsatisfactory conditions; make sure beforehand that zoos are not on the itinerary. Travellers into the Oriente must have their passports stamped at the naval office, which is clearly marked at the canoe embarkation point. If a guide offers to take a trip into Indian villages (eg of the Huaorani), ask to see written permission from the Indian leaders and insist that no wildlife will be purchased on the trip. Fees for chartering a canoe are open to bargaining; fares on excursions are fixed. Every canoe pilot is supposed to have his passenger list checked before going downstream but this is not always done. For your own safety ensure that the authorities have a record. Essential items for a trip of any length are rubber boots (or, if you prefer, two pairs of suitable light shoes – keep one pair dry), sleeping bag, rain jacket, trousers (not shorts), binoculars, insect repellent, sunscreen lotions, mosquito net, water-purifying tablets, sticking plasters. Wrap everything in several small plastic bags.

● **Guides**
We list only those guides who have been

recommended to us: *Héctor Fiallos*, of Fluvial River Tours (information in Quito T 239-044, or write PO Box 225, Tena-Misahuallí, T 740-002), arranges outings from 1-15 days. A 6-day tour takes in the Cuyabeno National Park (special permit needed, US$14, passport must be left at the naval office) and the Río Aguarico. A 10-day tour goes down the Napo to Nuevo Rocafuerte and up the Aguarico to the Cuyabeno National Park. There are also other tour operators using Hector's name.

Viajes y Aventuras Amazónicas, on the plaza, friendly, good food, ask for Celso; *Julio Angeles*, at *Crucero Fluvial Cononaco*, will arrange anything you wish to do; a 4-day tour on Río Tiputini is the minimum time to see animals.

Douglas, Wilfred Clarke and *Albin Caicedo* (speak English), from the *Hotel Dayuma*, Casilla 291, Tena, T 584-964, F 584-965, or Av 10 de Agosto 3815 y Mariana de Jesús, edif Villacis Pazos, of 301, T/F 564-924, Quito, arrange trips with other guides. Their 1-and 2-day walks are rec. Also trips to Coca, to smaller rivers and lagoons, Limón Cocha, and longer ones into the jungle of up to 10 days, similar to those organized by Héctor Fiallos. They also have *Dayuma Camp* at the junction of the Arajuno and Puni rivers (15 mins by canoe plus a 4-hr walk from Misahuallí).

At *Hotel Balcón del Napo* contact *Carlos Sevilla*, whose tours up to 18 days are well rec. (Carlos Sevilla can also be contacted via his sister in Quito, T 241-981.) *Marcos Estrada* of *Crucero Fluvial Yasuni* is knowledgeable, honest and offers tours of different lengths. *Jaime Recalde* and *Eugenio Martínez*, good meals, contact them at *Balcón del Napo*, interesting on fauna and flora.

Sócrates Nevárez, PO Box 239, Tena, runs 1-10

day tours including trips further down the Río Napo, well-organized. *Carlos Herbert Licuy Licuy*, locally born, is good on history, legends and culture of the area. *John Cordero*, at *Etsa*. *Alfredo Andrade*, T 584-965, or PO Box 268, Tena, English spoken, money exchanged. *Pepe Tapia González* of *El Oriente*, PO Box 252, Tena, speaks English, knowledgeable, 1 to 10 day tours, good cook (Gary), can pay by TCs. *Luis García* at *Emerald Forest Expeditions* is rec.

● **Jungle lodges**

B *Anaconda*, on Anaconda Island in the Río Napo, about 1 hr by canoe, US$1.20 down-stream from Puerto Misahuallí, reservations required. It consists of 10 bungalows of bamboo and thatch, with space for about 48 guests, no electric lights, but flush toilets and cold showers, with water available most of the time. There is a zoo with animals in small, unsatisfactory cages. Watch out for thieving monkeys. The meals are good. Canoe and hiking trips arranged, US$50 for 4 days, meals and guides included, guides only speak Spanish.

Opposite, on the river bank at **Ahuano**, is **A3** *Casa del Suizo*, Swiss, Ecuadorean-owned, price pp full board, but little scope for vegetarians, cheaper with shared bath, highly rec for hospitality and location, electricity till 2200, pool, animal sanctuary, trips arranged. For further information contact Giulliano Bonello, Koescherruetistr 143, 8052 Zurich, Switzerland, T 01-302-37-27, or *Explorer Tours*, Reina Victoria y Lizardo García, Quito, T 522-220, F 508-872.

There are no public canoes from Misahuallí on Sun afternoon, only private hire, US$30 but there are buses Tena-Ahuano, 2 hrs, US$1.50, ask to be dropped at the ferry point.

C *Hotel Jaguar*, 1½ hrs downstream from Misahuallí, congenial atmosphere, price pp with full board, vegetarians catered for, good value, a full tour (3 days) including meals and good excursions into the jungle costs US$70 from Misahuallí with an extra charge of US$32 for each additional day. Avoid paying in US$ as they give you a very bad rate (independent canoe journey there costs US$30, except by public canoe at 1100); in Quito reservations at Luis Cordero 1313, T 230-552.

2 hrs downstream is *Yachana Lodge*, part of the Funedesin Project, based in the indigenous village of Mondaña; US$50/day including 3 meals, hiking, bird watching, river trips, etc. Reservations at Funedesin, Francisco Andrade Marín 188 y Diego de Almagro, Quito, PO Box

17-17-92, T 543-851, F 220-362.

Jatun Sacha

8 km downriver is **Jatun Sacha** Biological Station (quichua meaning 'big forest'), a reserve set aside for environmental education, field research, community extension and ecotourism. The biological station and the adjacent Aliñahui project together conserve 1,300 ha of tropical wet forest. So far, 507 birds, 2,500 plants and 765 butterfly species have been identified at Jatun Sacha. They offer excursions with good views and walking on a well-developed trail system.

● **Access** 25-mins by boat, US$2.50; but also reached by road on the S bank of the Río Napo, 25 km from the bridge in Puerto Napo, bus to La Punta or Campacocha from Tena passes, but it has to ford the river, can be difficult if the level is high.

● **Accommodation** Lodging at *Cabañas Aliñahui*; 8 cabins with 2 bedrooms and bathroom, lush tropical garden, rainforest and nature trails; US$44/day, including three delicious meals in dining hall, or US$6 for entrance only; profits contribute to conservation of the area's rainforest. Reservations are necessary and can be made by writing to Fundación Jatun Sacha, Av Río Coca 1734, Casilla 17-12-867, Quito, T 253-267/441-592, F 253-266.

CENTRAL AND SOUTHERN ORIENTE

In terms of tourist infrastructure, the Central and Southern Oriente lags far behind its northern neighbour. It comprises the provinces of Morona Santiago and the vast, largely unexplored Pastaza.

PUYO

This is the most important centre in the whole Oriente (*Pop* 15,563); the junction for road travel into the Southern Oriente and for traffic heading to or from **Ambato** via Baños (see page 178). The Policia Nacional in Puyo handles visa extensions. The Sangay and Altar volcanoes can be seen.

Excursions

Parque Pedagogico Etno-Botánico is 2 km from Puyo and offers guided tours with indigenous experts, also basic accommodation in traditional housing, close to the Río Puyo, good swimming, interesting plant collections; T 883-001.

22 km from Puyo is the 40 ha **Reserva de Bosque Tropical**, a private nature reserve with forest paths and a beautiful waterfall administered by *Fundación*

Hola Vida, US$1 per day, there is a basic shelter for 10 people, bring camping gear, tent not necessary. Access is 16 km S on the road to Macas then turnoff W 6 km to the reserve.

Local information
● Accommodation

D *El Araucano*, Celso Marín 576, T 885-227, **F** without bath, Chilean owned, rooms on the road side best, family atmosphere, clean, hot water, video club, restaurant, stores luggage; **D** *Hostería Turingia*, Orellana y Villamil, T 885-180, small huts with bath, in tropical garden, comfortable but noisy, restaurant quite expensive but good.

E *Europa Internacional*, 9 de Octubre y Orellana, T 885-407, with bath, shower, bright, pleasant, good restaurant; **E** *Hostería Safari*, Km 5.5 on the road to Puerto Napo outside town, T 885-465, peaceful.

F *California*, 9 de Octubre 1354, T 885-189, noisy.

G *Grenada*, C 27 de Febrero y Orellana, dirty.

● Places to eat

Mesón Europeo, Mons Alberto Zambrano, nr the bus station, the fanciest in town; *Europa*, next to *Hotel Europa*, 9 de Octubre y Marín, good; *Rincón Ambateño*, on the river front, follow 29 de Julio, restaurant and pool complex; *Viña del Mar* and *El Delfín* (both seafood), on Marín; *Chifa China*, 9 de Octubre y

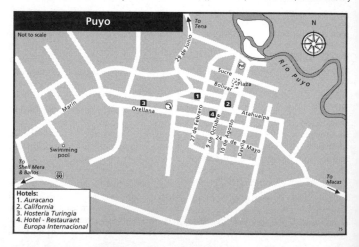

Puyo

Not to scale

Hotels:
1. Auracano
2. California
3. Hostería Turingia
4. Hotel - Restaurant Europa Internacional

24 de Mayo, clean; *Mistral*, Atahualpa y 9 de Octubre, good for breakfast; *Pan Selecto*, Marín y 9 de Octubre, good, fresh bread; *Vitapán*, also Marín y 9 de Octubre, good breakfast with eggs and fresh bread, US$0.75; *El Chileno*, fuente de soda run by owner of *El Araucano*, rec.

● **Banks & money changers**

Cambios Puyo, 9 de Octubre y Atahualpa, T/F 883-064, good rates.

● **Tour companies & travel agents**

Enlsa Tours, PO Box 16 01 856, T 885-500, rec for tours into the jungle, Mentor Marino helpful and knowledgeable; *Amazonia Touring*, 9 de Octubre y Atahualpa, T 883-219, F 883-064, land based and fly-in trips for 1-10 people.

● **Transport**

Air Military flights to Tena; Macas via Taisha, good views; Shell-Mera (see below) can be reached from Quito, 30 mins; also flights from Shell-Mera to Montalvo and Tiputini. Military passenger flights only go if there are 16 people.

Buses To Baños, US$1.50, Mon only, many delays, 4 hrs at least (roadworks); **Ambato**, US$2.60, 3 hrs; **Quito**, US$2.75, 7 hrs (9 hrs via Baeza, US$3.50); **Tena**, US$1.25, 3½ hrs, fight for a seat, rough road; **Riobamba**, US$1.60, 3½ hrs. Most buses leave from the new Terminal Terrestre on the outskirts of town, 10-15-mins' walk. Those for **Macas** leave from the old terminal, before going to the new terminal nr the market at far end of Atahualpa, past Amazonas (sign says Transportes Amazónicas), they leave daily 0600, 0900, 1100 and 1500, US$3.70, 3 hrs.

PUYO TO BANOS

The road from Puyo to Baños is a dramatic journey with superb views of the Pastaza valley and a plethora of waterfalls. **NB** Road is closed until 1997 at least, except Sun 1800 to Tues 0600.

Shell-Mera is 8 km W of Puyo, 50 km from Baños, 1½ hrs. It has an airfield and an army checkpoint where foreigners must register (passport required) if coming from Baños or Ambato. The Brigada in Shell will give permission for visiting the jungle.

● **Accommodation** D *Hostal Germania*, new, quiet; F *Hostal Cordillera*, with bath,

restaurant; **G** *Hotel Esmeraldita*, basic, restaurant.

● **Transport** Servicio Aereo Regional/Edgar Rosero, T (Quito) 592-032; (Shell) 795-175, charges US$125/hr for 3 passengers/400 kgs.

PUYO TO MACAS

The first leg of the Puyo-Macas bus journey goes as far as **Chuiguaza**, a small settlement at the junction of the Chiguaza and Pastaza rivers (accommodation at indigenous house a short distance downstream on the N bank). There is a bridge suitable only for cars and small *busetas*. On the opposite shore, a bus carries passengers the rest of the way to Macas (this bus is rather smaller than the first). It stops often at small settlements, mostly inhabited by Shuar descendants. The ride is slow and rough, the road hard packed dirt, full of potholes. The jungle which borders this road is rapidly being removed.

MACAS

(*Pop* 9,720; *Alt* 1,000m approx) capital of Morona-Santiago province, situated high above the broad Río Upano valley, is developing rapidly thanks to nearby oil deposits. It is a clean-looking town, established by the missionaries over 400 years ago. The immense snow-capped Sangay volcano can be seen on clear mornings from the plaza, creating an amazing backdrop to the tropical jungle surrounding the town. Puffs of smoke can often be seen and a red glow at night from the crater of this still very active volcano.

The modern cathedral, completed in 1992, with beautiful stained-glass windows houses the much venerated image of La Purísima de Macas. Several blocks to the N of the cathedral, in the park which also affords great views of the Upano Valley, is an excellent orchid collection. Several blocks S of the cathedral there is a public swimming pool, which is open at weekends and holidays. There is good birdwatching down the hill from

Macas into the Upano Valley and alongside the tributary streams. The whole area has been developed for beef production. The climate is not too hot and the nights are even cool.

Excursions

You can cross the Río Upano by bridge or take a bus (30 mins) to the Salesian Sevilla-Don Bosco mission. The modern archaeological museum, Don Bosco y Montalba, is a good place to rest and see views of the river, and there is a recreation area nearby.

On the road to the mission there is a small stream in which you can swim or wash clothes. Tres Marías is a base for visiting *tolas* and an archaeological site, 1 hrs' walk (4 buses a day from Macas).

In Taisha, a village E of Macas, the *Casa Morocho* rents a few basic rooms, G.

Local information
● Accommodation

D *Hostal Esmeralda*, Cuenca 6-12 y Soasti, T 700-160, modern, clean, hot water, cheaper with cold, good value, rec.

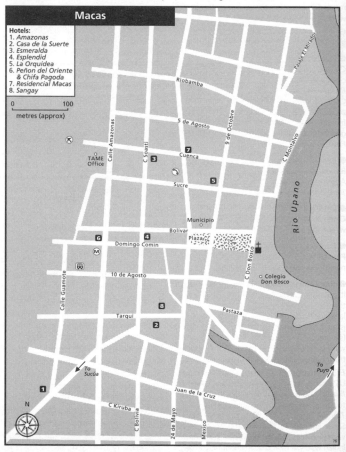

Macas

Hotels:
1. *Amazonas*
2. *Casa de la Suerte*
3. *Esmeralda*
4. *Esplendid*
5. *La Orquídea*
6. *Peñon del Oriente & Chifa Pagoda*
7. *Residencial Macas*
8. *Sangay*

0   100
metres (approx)

Río Upano

Riobamba
5 de Agosto
Cuenca
Sucre
Municipio
Bolivar
Plaza
Domingo Comín
10 de Agosto
Tarqui
Pastaza
Juan de la Cruz

Calle Amazonas
C Soasti
9 de Octubre
C Montalvo
C Don Bosco
Calle Guamote
C Kiruba
C Bolivia
24 de Mayo
Mexico

TAME Office
Colegio Don Bosco
Pasaje El Mirador

To Sucúa
To Puyo

N

E *Amazonas*, Guamote, at the S end of town; **F** without bath, parking; **E** *Esplendid*, Soasti 15-18, with bath, clean, modern, rooms without bath F, basic; **E** *La Orquídea*, 9 de Octubre 13-05 y Sucre, T 700-970, with bath, hot water, cheaper with cold, clean and bright, beds comfortable; **E** *Peñón del Oriente*, Domingo Comín 837 y Amazonas, T 700-124, F 700-450, modern, clean, secure, hot water, good views from roof, rec.

F *Hostal Casa de La Suerte*, Tarqui 6-30, basic; **F** pp *Hostería del Valle*, 5 km out on the Sucúa road, self-contained cabins. Also **F**: *Mayflower*, one tiny bathroom but clean rooms, *Residencial Macas*, clean, cheaper without bath.

G *Sangay*, Tarqui 6-05, very basic, dirty toilets, friendly.

● **Places to eat**
Chifa Pagoda China, Amazonas 15-05, delicious, generous portions, good value, rec; *Rincón del Miguel*, Soasti y 10 de Agosto, Chifa menu, wide variety, rec; *Eros Café*, Amazonas y Tarqui, good for snacks, breakfast, friendly owners; *Café El Jardín*, Amazonas, good breakfast, US$1.50; *Pan Selecto Francesa*, good bakery.

● **Banks & money changers**
Banco del Austro, 24 de Mayo y 10 de Agosto, will change cash or TCs; *Delgado Travel*, Domingo Comín nr the plaza, cash only.

● **Entertainment**
Cinema: next to Emetel, 24 de Mayo y Sucre, weekends only.

● **Post & telecommunications**
Post Office: 9 de Octubre y Domingo Comín, next to the park.

● **Tours companies & travel agents**
It is possible to visit the jungle from Macas and there are agencies specializing in tours to villages inc flight, for US$30-50 pp. However, it is advisable to contact the Shuar Federation (see below, Sucúa) before taking a tour and verify what is involved before signing any contract. Malaria precautions are recommended.

ETSA, Amazonas y 10 de Agosto, T 700-550, US$160 for 4 day flying tour to Shuar villages; *Ikiaam*, Domingo Comín 5-16, T 700-457, tours to jungle and Sangay National Park; *Tuntiak Tours*, T 700-185, Carlos Arcos is half Shuar and speaks the language, he offers a variety of trips; *Marcelo Cajecui* is a Shuar Indian who will fly you deep into jungle to live with a Shuar family, contact through *Hotel Peñon del Oriente*.

ROW, a US company from Idaho is offering whitewater rafting on the Upano (River Odysseys West, PO Box 579, Coeur d'Alene, Idaho, 83816-0579, T (208) 765-0841). Ecuador contact: Juan, Quito, T 458-339. Seasons are limited owing to the extreme unpredictability of the Upano river.

Kapawi Ecological Reserve: run by *Canodros*, Luis Urdaneta 1418 y Av del Ejército, Guayaquil, T (04) 285-711/280-173, F 287-651, e-mail eco-tourism1@canodros.com.ec, PO Box 09-01-8442: this project is being developed jointly by the tour company in Achuar Territory with the full participation of the local people. It is also built according to the Achuar concept of architecture. It is in a zone rich in biodiversity, with a lodge and many opportunities for seeing the forest and its inhabitants. From Quito you go either to Shell-Mera or Macas, then a plane takes you to Sharamentza; from here canoes go 1½ hrs down the Río Pastaza to the confluence with the Kapawari; 4 nights in a double cabin costs US$700, plus

anawi is a state of the art eco lodge, with 20 double rooms, each one with private bathroom. Powered by solar energy we offer the best service you will find in the Amazon Basin were you can customize your own itinerary. Kapawi is a unique project in partnership with the Achuar culture, a place where you can see giant otters and pink dolphins, and 490 species of birds have been registered.

Canodros S.A.

tel: (543-4) 285 711 Fax: (593-4) 287 651
e-mail: eco-tourism1@canodros.com.ec
web:http://mia.lac.net/canodros

US$200 for transport to and from Quito. The location, quality of service, cabin accommodation and food have all been highly rec.

● **Transport**

Air Flight to Quito, TAME, Mon, Wed, Fri, sit on left for best views of Sangay. The air force flies Shell, Taisha, Macas, Morona and vice versa Tues, Thur and Fri.

The paved runway at Macas is the main access for the southern jungle, but DAC (Dirección de Aviación Civil) occasionally tightens up the regulations making it almost impossible for tourists to fly with local airlines, who, they claim, are only licensed to transport missionaries, volunteers, Indians and people needing medical attention. Tour operators have tried to change this policy as it restricts the development of tourism in the area. The only way round this is to charter a plane from a licensed company in Shell or Quito, which is obviously much more expensive. It may sometimes be possible to get a flight from Sucúa's grass strip, a 40-min taxi ride to the S (see below).

Buses To Cuenca, 11 hrs, US$7, 4 a day with Turismo Oriental; Transportes Sucúa, 1700, spectacular views, 0530 bus to see it in daylight; hourly to Sucúa, 1 hr, no regular service on Thur. Two bus companies Macas-Puyo: Coop San Francisco 5 a day, 3 continue to Ambato and Quito, 0300, 2000 and 2300, US$4.50 to Puyo, 6 hrs, US$7 to Quito; Coop Macas almost hourly from 0600-1500.

ROUTES A new road from Macas to Riobamba has reached 9 de Octubre, N of Macas, and from the mountains was being built out of Guamote (see page 198). If travelling by public transport on this route enquire at the bus stations in Macas and Puyo about the condition of the roads.

SANGAY NATIONAL PARK

The surrounding hills give excellent views of the volcano **Sangay**, 5,230m, within the Sangay National Park, entrance US$20, information from Inefan in Macas, Juan de la Cruz y 29 de Mayo. Sangay is an active volcano; the South American Explorers Club has information on organizing a trip, equipment, helmet, etc, and guide essential. The trek takes 7 days and is only for those who can endure long, hard days of walking and severe weather. Protection against falling

stones is vital. Mecánica Acosta, Plaza Arenas, Quito (near the prominent basilica), will make shields, arm loops welded to an oil drum top, for US$2-3. Dec/Jan is a good time to climb Sangay. Construction on the Guamote-Macas road which was supposed to traverse the park has been stalled because of environmental considerations.

● **Access** The park may be reached by bus 1½ hrs to village of 9 de Octubre, Wed, Fri and Sun 0730 and 1600, then walk.

SUCÚA

23 km from Macas, is of particular interest as the centre of a branch of the ex-head-hunting Shuar (Jívaro) Indians. Their crafts can be seen and bought but it is tactless to ask them about head-hunting and shrinking (a practice designed to punish those who bewitched others and to deter anyone wishing to cause sickness or disaster in future). Outside the schools, scenes from Shuar mythology are displayed in painted tableaux. You can contact the **Shuar Federation** at Domingo Comín 17-38 (C Tarqui 809), T/F 740-108, about visiting traditional villages. This is possible with an Indian guide, but takes time as the application must be considered by a council of seven and then you will be interviewed and told how you should behave. Allow at least 1½ days. There is a small craft shop across the street from the Shuar Federation. There is an interesting bookshop and, 10 mins' walk from the town centre, a small museum and zoo (very few animals) run by Shuar Indians, in the Centro de Formación.

Nearby is the Río Upano, a 1½-hr walk, with plenty of Morpho butterflies. A cablecar crosses the river. Also close by is the Río Namangoza, a 15-min walk, with rapids and good swimming, but be careful after rain.

● **Accommodation** F *Hostería Orellana*, at the S end of town, T 740-193, one room with bath, others without; **F** *Hostal Alborada*, cheap, restaurant; **F** *Rincón Oriental*, shared bath, clean, parking, rec; **G** *Sangay*, very basic; **G** *Cuenca*, small rooms, basic, toilets filthy. *Hostal Karina* is new, just off the plaza, parallel to the main street, and is clean and light.

● **Places to eat** *Restaurant La Fuente*, Domingo Comín nr the plaza, good; bar/restaurant *Sangay*, opp *Rincón Oriental*; *Paolita*, Domingo Comín S of centre. *Jefralisavi*, N of the plaza, snacks and drinks, open till midnight, changes US$ cash and TCs.

SUCUA TO MORONA

From Sucúa, the road heads S for 1 hr to Logroño. A short walk out of town are extensive limestone caves; take a torch, rope, etc. They are subject to flash floods during rainstorms. There is a gate; obtain the key before walking out of the village. A guide is useful. Another 1 hr S is (Santiago de) **Méndez**, a nice town with a modern church. In 1994 work was begun on a long promised road to Cuenca via Paute, following an ancient trade route.

● **Accommodation** 4 basic *residenciales* on C Cuenca, all **G**: *Pensión Miranda, Pensión Amazonas, Residencial Vanesa, Residencial Anita*.

Near Méndez a road (1 bus daily) goes

The family of Achuar

The Achuar is one of the four groups of the linguistic family Jívaro; Achuar, Shuar (or Shiwiar), Aguaruna and Huambisa. This is by far the most important remaining indigenous culture in the Amazon Basin, with a population of around 80,000, and occupying huge tracts of Ecuador and Peru's rainforest. They get their name from the Shuar word *achu* meaning *morete*, a kind of palm that grows in flooded areas, and *shuar*, meaning people.

Though known in the past for their internal wars, the Achuar live today in peace, mostly in small villages. They hunt, fish and forage in the forests and also tend small plots (*chacras*) where they practice slash-and-burn cultivation. This is a necessary practice given that the rainforest soils are particularly infertile. Each *chacra* covers an area of roughly 4,000 sq metres, generally near a river, and is used for an average of 3 years before being left in favour of a new plot of land.

The Achuar believe in multiple spirits that give them guidance for a harmonious relationship with the rainforest and its wildlife. Magic and healing powers are used by the shaman (*uwishin*), who gets his force by means of hallucinogenic plants like *natem*. They maintain a very intimate relationship with nature and its processes. Primarily based in astronomical calculations and biological cycles, the Achuar have created a model of respresentation of annual cycles in the rainforest much more precise than any developed by modern biologists or meteorologists. Since they did not have a written language before the arrival of missionaries, the use of myths has been very important in keeping the traditions alive.

Until the end of the 18th century, the region occupied by the Shuar was only occasionally visited by the most determined of missionaries. The region was not affected by the rubber boom, which converted thousands of Indians into slaves during the 19th century. Although from the end of the 19th century to the 1950s this area was visited by some explorers and naturalists, it was, for the most part, considered *terra incognita* until the late 1960s. Between 1968 and 1970 Catholics and Evangelists established the first contacts with the group in order to convert them to Christianity, a process that drastically altered their way of living. Since 1991 the majority of the Achuar belong to OINAE (Organization of Ecuadorean Achuar Nationalities). Today OINAE is divided into 3 groups, each one with its own centre.

E into the jungle to **Morona**. Along the road is the junction of the Zamora-Coangos rivers. East of the confluence, at the village of Santiago, a canoe can be hired (about US$30) to a point from where you can walk in 2½ hrs to the **Cueva de Los Tayos**, a huge cave, 85m in depth. The trail is obscure, and a guide is necessary. Mario Cruz, in conjunction with Metropolitan Touring in Quito, organizes treks from the capital.

It is 9 hrs to the village of **Morona**, located on the Río Morona just at the (disputed) Peruvian border. There is no accommodation but camping is possible, and there is a house where you can get meals and drinks. No border crossing is permitted. Following the Jan-Feb 1995 border conflict with Peru, visitors should make extensive local inquiries before attempting to visit border areas.

LIMON

2 hrs, 50 km S of Méndez is **Limón**, official name Gen Leónidas Plaza, a mission town founded in 1935, now a busy, friendly place, surrounded by high jungle.

● **Accommodation & places to eat** 3 residenciales on C Quito, all **F**: *Residencial Limón*, T 770-114, modern, basic, clean and friendly, front rooms noisy; *Residencial Domínguez*, friendly; *Residencial Santo Domingo*, basic. *Chifa Rincón de Taiwán*, C Quito.

● **Transport** Buses, all from C Quito, go to Cuenca, Macas and Gualaquiza.

LIMON TO CUENCA

From Limón, the road to Cuenca (132 km) passes through Gualaceo, via Jadán. It is a longer route (Macas-Cuenca) than from Quito, but just as spectacular. From Limón the road rises steeply with many breathtaking turns and the vegetation changes frequently, partly through cloud

forest and then, at 4,000m, through the *páramo*, before dropping very fast down to the valley of Gualaceo. There is a police checkpoint at Plan de Milagro, where foreigners have to register. There is nowhere to stay along the Limón-Gualaceo road. A trip by car Cuenca-Gualaceo-Limón-Sucúa-Macas-Mera and onwards to Quito is possible with the opening of the Río Pastaza bridge.

GUALAQUIZA

Continuing S from Limón the road passes **Indanza** (very basic *residencial* and *comedor*), before reaching **Gualaquiza**, a pioneer town off the tourist track. It is surrounded by densely forested mountains, in which are interesting side trips. If you intend to explore the area, bring a tent and sleeping bag.

Among the excursions are the caves near Nuevo Tarqui, the Salesian mission at Bomboisa and Tutusa Gorge. It's a 3-hr walk, 2 hrs by boat, take a guide, eg Sr José Castillo.

Also Aguacate, a 6-hr walk, near which are precolumbian ruins; food and bed at Sr Jorge Guillermo Vázquez. Yumaza is a 40-min walk, for more precolumbian ruins (2 sites).

● **Accommodation F** *Amazonas*, Domingo Comín 08-65, basic, friendly; **E** *Turismo*, Gonzalo Pesantes 08-16, **F** without bath, good value, restaurant; **F** *Guaquiz*, Orellana 08-52, shared bath, friendly. *Cabaña los Helechos*, opp the bus station, rec.

● **Post & telecommunications Emetel**: García Moreno y Ciudad de Cuenca, Mon-Sat 0800-1100, 1400-1700, 1900-2100.

● **Transport** Buses to Cuenca, 1900, 2000 and 2100, 6 hrs; **Loja**, 0300 and 2200; **Macas**, 1800, 10 hrs. *Rancheros* leave for Yantzaza in the morning, from where a bus reaches Zamora before dark. (See **Southern Sierra**).

Galápagos Islands

*T*AKE FIVE-AND-TWENTY *heaps of cinders dumped here and there in an outside city lot; imagine some of them magnified into mountains, and the vacant lot the sea; and you will have a fit idea of the general aspect of the* Encantadas, *or Enchanted Isles. A group rather of extinct volcanoes than of isles, looking much as the world at large might, after a penal conflagration.* Herman Melville, author of *Moby Dick*, was obviously not too enamoured of the Galápagos when he visited in 1841.

These islands, claimed by Ecuador in 1832, gained world recognition thanks to the observations of an English naturalist named Charles Darwin. Now they are the country's prime tourist destination, attracting so much interest that the number of visitors has to be strictly limited in order to protect their unique assets.

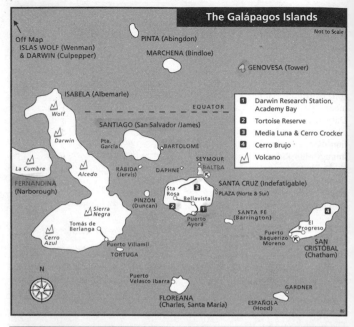

The Galápagos Islands

Not to Scale

Off Map
ISLAS WOLF (Wenman)
& DARWIN (Culpepper)

PINTA (Abingdon)

MARCHENA (Bindloe)

GENOVESA (Tower)

ISABELA (Albemarle)

Wolf

EQUATOR

SANTIAGO (San Salvador /James)

Darwin

Pta. García

BARTOLOMÉ

La Cumbre

Alcedo

RÁBIDA (Jervis)

DAPHNE

SEYMOUR
BALTRA

FERNANDINA (Narborough)

PINZON (Duncan)

Sta Rosa

SANTA CRUZ (Indefatigable)

Bellavista

PLAZA (Norte & Sur)

Sierra Negra

Tomás de Berlanga

2

Puerto Ayorá

1

SANTA FE (Barrington)

4

Cerro Azul

El Progreso

Puerto Villamil

TORTUGA

Puerto Baquerizo Moreno

SAN CRISTÓBAL (Chatham)

N

Puerto Velasco Ibarra

GARDNER

FLOREANA (Charles, Santa María)

ESPAÑOLA (Hood)

1 Darwin Research Station, Academy Bay
2 Tortoise Reserve
3 Media Luna & Cerro Crocker
4 Cerro Brujo
⛰ Volcano

Albatross, Hood Island

Lying on the Equator, 970 km W of the Ecuadorean coast, the Galápagos consist of 6 main islands (San Cristóbal, Santa Cruz, Isabela, Floreana, Santiago and Fernandina – the last two uninhabited); 12 smaller islands (Baltra and the uninhabited islands of Santa Fe, Pinzón, Española, Rábida, Daphne, Seymour, Genovesa, Marchena, Pinta, Darwin and Wolf) and over 40 small islets. The islands have a total population of nearly 10,000 and because of immigration the annual growth rate is about 12%. The largest island, Isabela (formerly Albemarle), is 120 km long and forms half the total land area of the archipelago. Its notorious convict colony was closed in 1958; some 1,000 people live there now, mostly in and around Puerto Villamil, on the S coast. San Cristóbal (Chatham) has a population of 3,000 with the capital of the archipelago, Puerto Baquerizo Moreno. Santa Cruz (Indefatigable) has 7,000, with Puerto Ayora, the main tourist centre; and Floreana (Charles) fewer than 50. The group is quite widely scattered; by boat, Puerto Baquerizo Moreno and Puerto Ayora are 6 hrs apart.

GEOLOGY

The islands are the peaks of gigantic volcanoes, composed almost exclusively of basalt. Most of them rise from 2,000 to 3,000m above the seabed. Eruptions have taken place in historical times on Fernandina, Isabela, Pinta, Marchena, Santiago and Floreana. The most active today are Fernandina, Isabela, Pinta and Marchena, and fumarolic activity may be seen intermittently on each of these islands.

EARLY DISCOVERY

The islands were discovered accidentally by Tomás de Berlanga, the Bishop of Panama, in 1535. He was on his way to Peru when his ship was becalmed and swept 800 km off course by the currents.

In a letter to the King of Spain, the bishop was less than enthusiastic about the islands: "I do not think that there is a place where one might sow a bushel of corn, because most of it is full of very big stones and the earth there is much like dross, worthless, because it has not the power of raising a little grass". Like most of the early arrivals, Bishop Tomás and his crew arrived thirsty and disappointed at the dryness of the place. He did not even give the islands a name.

The islands first appeared on a map in 1574, as 'Islands of Galápagos', which has remained in common use ever since. The individual islands, though, have had several names, both Spanish and English. The latter names come from a visit in 1680 by English buccaneers who, with the blessing of the English king, attacked Spanish ships carrying gold and relieved them of their heavy load. The pirates used the Galápagos as a hide-out, in particular a spot North of James Bay on Santiago island, still known as Buccaneers' Cove. The pirates were the first to visit many of the islands and they named them after English Kings and aristocracy, or famous captains of the day.

The Spanish also called the islands 'enchanted', or 'bewitched', owing to the fact that for much of the year they are surrounded by mists giving the impression that they appear and disappear as if by magic. Also, the tides and currents were so confusing that they thought the islands were floating and not real islands.

(From *Galápagos: the Enchanted Isles*, by David Horwell).

FLORA AND FAUNA

The Galápagos have never been connected with the continent. Gradually, over many hundreds of thousands of years, animals and plants from over the sea developed there and as time went by they adapted themselves to Galápagos conditions and came to differ more and more from their continental ancestors. Thus many of them are unique: a quarter of the species of shore fish, half of the plants and almost all the reptiles are found nowhere else. In many cases different forms have evolved on the different islands. Charles Darwin recognized this speciation within the archipelago when he visited the Galápagos on the *Beagle* in 1835 and his observations played a substantial part in his formulation of the theory of evolution. Since no large land mammals reached the islands, reptiles were dominant just as they had been all over the world in the very distant past. Another of the extraordinary features of the islands is the tameness of the animals. The islands were uninhabited when they were discovered in 1535 and the animals still have little instinctive fear of man.

The most spectacular species to be seen by the visitor are the giant tortoise (species still survive in 6 or 7 of the islands, but mostly on Isabela); marine iguana (the only seagoing lizard in the world and found throughout most of the archipelago; it eats seaweed); land iguana (on Fernandina, Santa Cruz, Santa Fe, Isabela, Seymour and Plaza); Galápagos albatross (which nests only on the island of Española – apart from 2 pairs on Isla de la Plata; it leaves in December and returns in late March-early April); Galápagos hawk, red-footed, blue-footed and masked boobies, red-billed tropic-bird, frigate birds, swallow-tailed gulls, dusky lava gulls, flightless cormorants (on Isabela and Fernandina), mockingbirds, 13 species of Darwin's finches (all endemic and the classic examples of speciation quoted by Darwin); Galápagos sea-lion (common in many areas) and the Galápagos fur-seal (on the more remote and rocky coasts).

The most-visited islands from Puerto Ayora are Plaza Sur (an estimated 1,000 sea-lions living on 1 ha, land and sea iguana, many birds flying close to the cliff top), Santa Fe (land and sea iguanas, cactus forest, swimming with sea-lions), Seymour Norte (sea-lions, marine iguanas, swallow-tailed gulls, magnificent frigate birds, blue-footed boobies – the latter not close to the tourist trail), Rábida (sea-lions, flamingoes, pelican rookery), and Santiago (James Bay for fur seals, snorkelling with sea-lions, migratory coastal birds; Sullivan Bay and Bartolomé Island for fantastic lava fields on the climb to the summit, fine views, snorkelling around Pinnacle Rock and maybe a few penguins). On a tour of these islands it may be possible to go also to Punto García on Isabela to see flightless cormorants (it takes at least a full day to climb up Sierra Negra volcano to see the tortoises – it can be climbed on foot, horseback or by pickup). Daphne Island with very rich birdlife may be visited by each boat only once a month (a permit is required).

More distant islands from Puerto Ayora, but visited from there or from Puerto Baquerizo Moreno are Española (blue-footed boobies, masked boobies, waved albatross, many other birds, brightly-coloured marine iguanas, sea-lions, snorkelling at Tortuga Islet), Genovesa (red-footed boobies – brown and white phase, masked boobies, swallow-tailed and lava gulls, frigate birds and many others, marine iguanas, snorkelling) and Floreana (flamingoes, sea-lions, endemic plants,

Frigate birds

Charles Darwin and the Galapagos

In September 1835, a small, three-masted brig sailed into Galápagos waters. She was called HMS *Beagle* and was captained by the aristocratic FitzRoy, a descendent of King Charles II, whose job was to chart lesser-known parts of the world. FitzRoy wanted on board a naturalist, to study the strange new animals and plants they would find en route. He chose Charles Darwin.

Darwin was only 23 years old and it would be 5 years before he saw home again. They were to sail around the world, giving Darwin the chance to explore the entire continent of South America. The visit to the Galápagos had been planned as a short stop on the return journey, by which time Darwin had become an experienced observer. It was a stroke of luck that he had been picked for this unique cruise.

During the 5 weeks that the *Beagle* spent in the Galápagos, Darwin went ashore to collect plants, rocks, insects and birds. The unusual life forms and their adaptations to the harsh surroundings made a deep impression on him and eventually inspired his revolutionary theory on the evolution of life. The Galápagos provided a kind of model of the world in miniature. Darwin realized that these recently created volcanoes were young in comparison with the age of the Earth, and that life on the islands showed special adaptations. Yet the plants and animals also showed similarities to those from the South American mainland, where he guessed they had originally come from.

Darwin concluded that the life on the islands had probably arrived there by chance drifting, swimming or flying from the mainland and had not been created on the spot. Once the plants and animals had arrived, they evolved into forms better suited to the strange environment in which they found themselves. Darwin also noted that the animals were ex-

tremely tame, because of the lack of predatory mammals. The islands' isolation also meant that the giant tortoises did not face competition from more agile mammals and could survive. Today, they can be found only on remote islands where land mammals never arrived.

On his return to England, Darwin spent the rest of his life developing his ideas. It was only when another scientist, named Wallace, arrived at a similar conclusion to his own that he dared to publish a paper on his theory of evolution. Then followed his all-embracing *The Origin of the Species by means of Natural Selection*, in 1859. It was to cause a major storm of controversy and to earn Darwin recognition as the man who "provided a foundation for the entire structure of modern biology".

(From *Galápagos: the Enchanted Isles*, by David Horwell).

Black Iguana

snorkelling at Corona del Diablo). There is a custom for visitors to Post Office Bay on the N side of Floreana since 1793 to place unstamped letters and cards in a barrel, and deliver, free of charge, any addressed to their own destinations. Fernandina is best visited on longer cruises which include Isabela. For more details on Santa Cruz, San Cristóbal and Isabela, see below. Never miss the opportunity to go snorkelling, there is plenty of underwater life to see, including rays, sharks (not all dangerous) and many fish. All the other islands are closed to tourists.

Do not touch any of the animals, birds or plants. Do not transfer sand or soil from one island to another. Do not leave litter anywhere; it is highly undesirable in a National Park and is a safety and health hazard for wildlife. Do not take raw food on to the islands. The number of tourists to the island is controlled by the authorities to protect the environment but critics claim that the ecology is seriously threatened by current levels. Limits were increased from 12,000 in 1974 to 60,000 in 1990, but tourism infrastructure remains fairly basic. There are reports that galapagueños often charge foreigners more than locals. Understand that they feel overrun by people who must be rich; be courteous but firm. Avoid visiting in July and especially August (high season).

CLIMATE

The Galápagos Climate can be divided into a hot season (Dec to May), when there is a possibility of heavy showers, and the cool or *garúa* season (June to Nov), when the days generally are more cloudy and there is often rain or drizzle. July and Aug can be windy, force 4 or 5. Daytime clothing should be lightweight. (Clothing generally, even on 'luxury cruises' should be casual and comfortable.) At night, however, particularly at sea and at higher altitudes, temperatures fall below 15°C and warm clothing is required. Boots and shoes soon wear out on the lava terrain. The sea is cold July-Oct; underwater visibility is best Jan-March. Sept is the low point in the meteorological year.

TRAVEL TO THE ISLANDS

● **By Air**
There are 2 **airports**, one at Baltra (South Seymour), across a narrow strait from Santa Cruz, the other at Puerto Baquerizo Moreno, on San Cristóbal. The two islands are 96 km apart; regular boat services between them with Ingala (see page 331). When booking make sure your flight goes to the island of your choice. Cruises leave from both islands so itineraries depend on which port of departure is used, the capability of the boat and the length of the cruise. From either port prearranged tours can be paid for in advance. In Puerto Ayora, Santa Cruz, cruises can be arranged on the spot and can be arranged to finish at Baltra for the airport. It is more difficult in very high or low season to arrange tours. There are few opportunities to do this in Puerto Baquerizo Moreno.

All flights originate in Quito and make a long stopover in Guayaquil. Normal return fare in 1996, US$378 from Quito, US$333 from Guayaquil; 21-day excursion low season fare

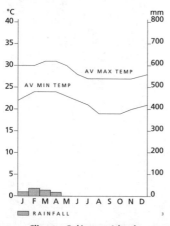

Climate: Galápagos Islands

US$290 with TAME to Baltra (16 Jan-14 June; 1 Sept-30 Nov), valid for 21 days from date of purchase. Independent travellers must reconfirm outward and return flights 2 days before departure and see their name written on the Manifest, not the 'Lista de Espera'. This is especially critical during high season.

TAME flies daily (not Sun out of the high season) **to Baltra**, and offers 15% reductions on flights originating in Quito to holders of International Student Identity Cards with evidence of home student status (details from office at Edif Pichincha, p 6, Amazonas y Colón, Quito, two photocopies of ID required, allow at least 4 hrs for documents to be endorsed); return to Guayaquil is permitted. TAME office in Puerto Ayora opens 0800 and closes Sat pm and all day Sun.

Boat owners make block bookings with the airlines in the hope of filling their boat. Visitors may buy tickets where they like, but in the busy season will have to take the ticket to the tour operator for the reservation. Tickets are the same price everywhere, except for student discounts on TAME.

SAN flies to **Puerto Baquerizo Moreno** (daily, except Sun). One-way tickets are available and it is now possible to buy an open-ended ticket (valid one year). SAN will change dates for return to mainland. SAN offers 20% discount to holders of International Student Identity Cards; your home college ID card, 3 copies of each and the originals plus a passport and US$ cash (not credit cards) required. Go to the office in Av Cristóbal Colón y 6 de Diciembre. Saeta has excellent 30-day excursion packages Miami-Quito/Guayaquil-Galápagos (SAN to San Cristóbal)-Guayaquil/Quito-Miami (US$584), usually the cheapest deal, but you land in a more difficult place for arranging tours, rec if you have 10 days available.

The **Air Force flights**, known as *logísticos*, may be booked at the military airport, Colegio Técnico y Escuela 1, Av de la Prensa 3212, T 445-043, just past the civil airport; single fare US$140, payable only in dollars. Reservations can only be made in advance for the Wed or Sat flight you want to take; the office is open 0800-1200. For those who succeed, a Lockheed C-130 Hercules departs Quito for Guayaquil, San Cristóbal and Baltra at 0700, be there at 0500. This can be very time consuming and there is no guarantee. The flights are not reliable and flying for 2 hrs in a cargo aircraft with no windows and no facilities is not much fun. To return, make reservation at the Marine Station by the harbour (if they say 'no' for foreigners, show the used ticket from Quito), pay the exact fare in dollars at the airport, no change given. *Café Booby* in Puerto Ayora sells tickets at 0715 before 0800 bus to the airport.

● **Airport transfer**
From the airport on Baltra, one takes a combination of bus (US$1), ferry (US$0.50) and bus (US$2.50) to Puerto Ayora, Santa Cruz. The whole process takes 1½ hrs. Airport buses leave Puerto Ayora (supermarket at the pier) at 0730, 0745 and 0800 for Baltra (best buy a ticket the night before – not possible for Sat bus though). Hotels may make prior arrangements. The airport in Puerto Baquerizo Moreno is within walking distance of town, but those on prearranged tours will be met at the airport.

● **By Sea**
The supply vessel (tramp steamer) *Piquero* takes 10 passengers between Guayaquil and the Galápagos, US$200 pp in a double cabin, 3½ days inc food (US$150 without food). The ship leaves Guayaquil on the 25th (usually) of each month. You can return after 5-7 days or next month. To stay on board during its sailing round the islands costs US$40 plus US$7/day for food. Information from Johnny Franco, *Acotramar*, T 04-401-711/004 (04-360-779 in evening), or go on board and speak to the purser or captain, it docks on the Malecón in Guayaquil. Take care of the cranes, etc, and be very alert to theft at all times (report of very basic facilities, inadequate food, accommodation and guides): "an experience, but not a way to see the Galápagos". The park entry tax must be paid on arrival.

● **Entry tax**
Every visitor has to pay a National Park Tax of US$80, payable only in sucres or US$ cash. It is paid on arrival, or at Quito or Guayaquil airports on request. On San Cristóbal there is a municipal tax of US$30; on Santa Cruz or on Baltra the tax is US$12. In each case it is paid by arriving plane passengers. Do not lose your park tax receipt; boat captains need to record it. A 50% reduction on the national park fee is available to children under 12 and students with a student identity card from their home university who are under 26.

What to expect on a boat

It is not possible to generalize about exactly what you will find on the boat in which you cruise around the Galápagos Islands. The standard of facilities varies from one craft to another. The following is based on a cruise in a boat at the upper end of the market, but is not untypical of a day's activities. On shore, no matter what price you have paid, each visitor is shown the same things because of the strict Park rules on limited access.

Each day starts early and schedules are usually full (if they aren't you are not getting your money's worth). If you are sailing overnight, your boat will probably have reached its destination before breakfast. After eating, you disembark for a morning on the island. The usual time for snorkelling is between the morning excursion and lunch. The midday meal is taken on board because no food is allowed on the islands. If the island requires two visits (eg Genovesa/Tower, or Española/Hood), you will return to shore after lunch, otherwise part of the afternoon may be taken up with a sea voyage. After the day's activities, there is time to clean up, have a drink and relax before the briefing for the next day and supper. Some boats have videos and, if you haven't already retired, you can fall asleep in front of the screen.

A possible day: The boat has anchored in James Bay/Puerto Egas on the W side of Santiago/James. At the landing point there are several birds to be seen: brown noddy terns, storm petrels and Audubon sheerwaters fishing. In the bay there are turtles. Sealions, as everywhere, lie around on the sand and clamber in and out of the surf. On the short walk along the coast you see migratory coastal birds and, on the rocks, marine iguanas and bright Sally Lightfoot crabs. The landscape includes good examples of pahoyhoy and tuff (types of lava). The main place of interest is a fur seal colony at a series of inlets, where the crystal clear sea washes into the gullies in the lava rock. One set of holes through which the sea flushes is delightfully known as Darwin's Toilets. With luck you will have been advised to bring snorkel gear as the swimming with the sealions (and seals if you are fortunate) is fabulous. Other birds of which you may catch sight include the Galápagos martin, finches, yellow warbler and the Galápagos hawk.

Sally lightfoot crab

During lunch the boat sails E, past Buccaneer's Cove which was used by 18th and 19th century pirates. The afternoon's destination is Bartolomé, a small island off the E coast of Santiago. This island has the famous, much-photographed Pinnacle Rock. Snorkelling at its base you may be accompanied by Galápagos penguins, in addition to the ubiquitous sealions. On shore, a walk across the neck of the island leads to a bay where white-tip reef sharks come close to the beach. Then it's a 350-step climb over reddish volcanic cinders to the summit. On a clear day 19 islands can be seen. Finally, you return to the boat for the next stage of the cruise.

ISLAND CRUISES

There are two ways to travel around the islands: a 'tour navegable', where you sleep on the boat, or less expensive tours where you sleep ashore at night and travel during the day. On the former you travel at night, arriving at a new landing site each day, with more time ashore. On the latter you spend less time ashore and the boats are smaller with a tendency to overcrowding in high season. Prices are no longer significantly cheaper in the low season (Feb-May, Sept-Nov).

Itineraries are controlled by the National Park to distribute tourism evenly throughout the islands. Boats are expected to be on certain islands on certain days. They can cut landings, but have to get special permission to add to a planned itinerary. An itinerary change may be made if time would be better spent elsewhere. A good guide will explain this and you can trust their advice. Altering an itinerary to spend more time in Puerto Ayora or San Cristóbal is unacceptable (except in extreme bad weather). This sometimes occurs because not all passengers are on the same length of tours and boats come into port to change passengers.

Legitimate complaints should be made to Edgar Vargas, the Jefe de Turismo at the park in Puerto Ayora, or to Jimena Larrea, the head of Cetur, who is helpful. Any 'tour navegable' will include the days of arrival and departure as full days. Insist on a written itinerary or contract prior to departure as any effort not to provide this probably indicates problems later. The South American Explorers Club (Jorge Washington 311 y L Plaza, T 225-228 – Apdo 21-431, Quito; Av Rep de Portugal 146, Breña, T 250142 – Casilla 3714, Lima 100; USA: 126 Indian Creek Rd, Ithaca, NY 14850, T 607-277-0488) has produced a useful, brief guide to the Galápagos which includes a specimen contract for itinerary and living conditions.

Choosing a tour

The less expensive boats are normally smaller and less powerful so you see less and spend more time travelling, also the guiding is likely to be in Spanish only (there are some exceptions to this). The more expensive boats will probably have 110 volts, a/c and private baths, all of which can be nice, but not critically important. All boats have to conform to certain minimum safety standards (check that there are enough liferafts) and have VHF radio, but the rules tend to be quite arbitrary (eg windows and portholes may have domestic, rather than safety glass). A watermaker can make quite a difference as the town water from Puerto Ayora or Puerto Baquerizo Moreno should not be drunk. Note that boats with over 18 passengers take quite a time to disembark and re-embark people, while the smaller boats have a more lively motion, which is important if you are prone to seasickness.

The least expensive tours, about US$300-450 tend to travel during the day, with nights spent ashore. For US$450-800 for 8 days you will be on a smaller boat but travelling at night, with more time ashore in daylight. US$800-1,400 is the price of the majority of the best boats, most with English guiding. Over US$1,400 is entering the luxury bracket, with English guiding the norm, more comfortable cabins and better cuisine. No boat may sail without a park-trained guide: Naturalists II have little or no English and only basic knowledge; Naturalists III are English-speaking naturalist guides.

Booking a cruise

If wishing to plan everything ahead of time, there are many good tour operators. In Britain, David Horwell, naturalist and author of *Galápagos, the Enchanted Isles*, London, Dryad Press, 1988 (£9.95 through his agency), arranges tailor-made tours to Ecuador and the Galápagos islands. For further details write to him at Galapagos Adventure Tours, 37-39 Great Guildford St, London SE1 0ES, T 0171 261 9890, F 0171 289 3266. Also rec is Penelope Kellie, T 01962-779317 who is the UK agent for Quasar Nautica. *Galapagos Classic Cruises*, 6 Keyes Road, London NW2 3XA, T 0181 933 0613, F 0181 452 5248, specialise in tailor-made cruises and diving holidays to the islands with additional land tours to Ecuador and Peru available on request. In the USA, *Wilderness Travel* (801 Allston Way, Berkeley, CA 94710, T 1-800-368-2704) and *Inca Floats* (Bill Robertson, 1311 63rd St, Emeryville, CA 94608) have been rec.

Shopping around the agencies in Quito is a good way of securing a value-for-money cruise, but only if you can deal with the boat owner, or his/her representative, rather than someone operating on commission. It is worth asking if the owner has 1-3 spaces to fill on a cruise; you can often get them at a discount. A much simpler way is to fax from home to an agency which acts as a broker for the cruise ships. The broker can recommend a vessel which suits your requirements. Allow about 2 months for arrangements to be made. Rec are *Safari Tours*, F (593-2) 220-426, e-mail admin@safariec.ecx.ec, and *Angermeyer's Enchanted Excursions*, F (593-2) 569-956, full addresses under Quito **Tourist Agencies**.

Arranging a tour from the islands

If you wish to wait until you reach the islands, Puerto Ayora, Santa Cruz, is the only practical place for arranging a cruise. Here you can hire boats (lists available from National Park Service) and a 2-week sojourn will allow you to see most of the Islands. Reservations are strongly recommended for June-Aug, Dec-Jan and Easter Week. Out of season boats do not run unless they are full, so either book in advance or be prepared to wait until a group forms.

For cheaper tours it is generally recommended that you form a group once you reach the Islands, talk to people about the boats they may have used and then visit the office of the small boat owners (*armadores*). Negotiate the route (don't include the Darwin Research Station or Tortuga Bay as these are easy from Puerto Ayora) and the price, and get a firm commitment from the owner on dates and itinerary, leave a deposit 'to buy food' and get a receipt. To arrange last-minute tours, contact Jenny Devine, *Moonrise* travel agency, opp Banco de Pacífico, Puerto Ayora, T 05-526-348, F 05-526-403.

Prices are fixed by the *armadores*; if you believe you have been misled see the Port Captain who is usually honest, but changes annually. A small boat taking 8 or 12 people costs US$55 pp/day (low season) – US$80 (high season) for a full load, often excluding food, drinks and

US$2 harbour exit tax. Prices are set according to the 8, 12 or 16 capacity of the boats; parties of other sizes may upset calculations. Check that the small boats can carry enough food and supplies for the length of journey so you do not waste a day restocking. Many boats require you to provide your own drinking water: check this when you make arrangements.

NB If not booking a cruise in advance, it can take several days to arrange a tour, so allow yourself plenty of time (a week, maybe more). If you do get stuck, the Tourist Office in Puerto Ayora offers 1-day tours (US$36 pp with lunch; departure 0600-0800) to Seymour Norte, Plaza Sur or Santa Fe. These smaller islands have a good sample of animal species (although fewer in numbers) and, together with sightseeing on Santa Cruz, can be a worthwhile experience for the tourist with only limited time.

Ingala sails from Puerto Ayora to Puerto Baquerizo Moreno Tues 1000, returning Wed 1000, and Sat 0800, returning Mon 1000, US$9 for locals, US$18 for Ecuadoreans, US$42 for foreigners; at 0800 on Thur it sails Puerto Ayora-Isabela (US$36), returning Fri via Floreana. Buy all tickets the day before sailing. The Ingala office in Puerto Ayora is on Padre Herrera, near the petrol station on the outskirts; in Puerto Baquerizo Moreno it is up the hill on the road leading inland, on the edge of town.

Agencies and boats

With over 100 boats operating in the islands, we cannot give them all. We list those for which we have received positive recommendations. Exclusion does not imply poor service.

In Guayaquil, *Galasam* (Economic Galapagos Tours), Av 9 de Octubre 424, Edif Gran Pasaje, p 11 (T 306-289/313-724, F 313-351/562-033) sell flights as well as their own tours. If you book the SAN flight to San Cristóbal with them, they throw in the Ingala boat trip to Santa Cruz free. In Quito, Galasam is at Pinto 523 y Av Amazonas, T 507-080/507-079, F 567-662. The Galasam 7-night tours depart Tues, Wed and Sat, depending on the boat,

Sea Lion

frequently rec. In 1995 they were operating with three 16-passenger boats in superior tourist class (*Dorado, Cruz del Sur* and *Estrella*), three 12-passenger craft (*Yolita, Darwin* and *Islas Plazas*) and two 10-passenger boats (*Moby Dick*, the newest, and *Antártida*). As an example of 1996 fares, a 7-night cruise on the *Moby Dick* was US$660, 4 nights US$480, 3 nights US$380. A 7-night trip on *Darwin* was US$740. The more luxurious boats have specially trained bilingual guides. The guides on all boats are English-speaking.

Metropolitan Touring, Av República de El Salvador 970, PO Box 17-12-310, Quito, T (593-2) 464-780, F 464-702 (represented in the USA by Adventure Associates, 13150 Coit Rd, Suite 110, Dallas, Texas 75240, T 214-907-0414, F 783-1286) offers 7-night cruises on the MV *Santa Cruz* (90 passengers), said to be the best boat, very professional service, with multilingual guides, also the *Isabella II*. They also use *Yate Encantada* and *Delfín II*, and have yachts for private charters (eg Ecuacruceros' *Rachel III* and *Diamante*) and can arrange tours on a number of boats of all types, from 8 to 34 passengers. Metropolitan can also arrange scuba diving trips. Bookings can also be made for the *Reina Silvia*, owned by Rolf Siebers, who also owns the *Delfín Hotel* in Puerto Ayora. This vessel makes daily sailings, returning to the hotel each night, but its speed means that the day trips are worthwhile and comfortable, rec.

Ecoventura, Av CJ Arosemena, Km 2.5, Guayaquil, T 593-4-203-080/205-293, F 202-990 (in Quito Av Colón 535 y 6 de Diciembre, T 593-2-507-408, F 507-409) is another agency with Galápagos cruises, operating in conjunction with *Galapagos Network*, 7200 Corporate Center Drive, Suite 309, Miami, FL 33126, T (805) 592-2294, F 592-6394, e-mail gpsnet@ao1.com: 3 motor yachts, *Eric, Flamingo* and *Letty* (good guides, atmosphere and food, highly rec); 1 motor vessel, *Corinthian*; and *M/S Sea Cloud*; 3, 4 and 7-night cruises available out of Puerto Baquerizo Moreno. 7-night fares start at US$1,375 on *Corinthian* to US$1,600 on *Eric*.

Angermeyer's Enchanted Expeditions, Foch 726 y Amazonas, Quito, T 593-2-569-960, F 569-956, have been rec for their professional, well-organized cruise on the *Beluga*, good English-speaking guide, lots of good food, worth the expense. They also operate the *Cachalote*, which is also rec.

Quasar Nautica, Av Los Shyris 2447, Edif Autocom, Quito, T 441-550, F 436-625 (USA T 305-599-9008, F 305-592-7060, UK representative, Penelope Kellie, T 01962-779-317, F 01962-779-458), sail and power yachts, multilingual guides, naturalist and diving cruises offered. Also arrange mainland tours.

Canodros SA, Luis Urdaneta 14-18, Guayaquil, T 280-164, F 287-651. Other rec agencies with tours to/in the Galápagos are given under Quito and Guayaquil **Tourist Agencies**.

Two boats with consistently high recommendations are the sailing brigantine *Andando* and the motor trawler *Samba*, both owned by Jane and Fiddi Angermeyer; book through *Andando Tours*, T/F (593-5) 526-308, Puerto Ayora, or PO Box 17-21-0088, T (593-2) 465-113, F 443-188, Quito; personal service always given.

Other recommendations: Pepe Salcedo's *Sulidae*, an old Norwegian fishing boat; Pepe is very experienced (Sulidae Charters, PO Box 09-01-0260, Guayaquil, T 593-4-201-376, F 323-478). Georgina and Agustín Cruz' *Beagle III*, friendly, good cooking (bookable through Metropolitan Touring). The motor yacht *Orca* (Etnotours, J L Mera y Cordero, Quito, T 593-2-230-552) and *Angelique* (owner Franklin Angermeyer), the latter has lots of character, good food.

Rolf Wittmer, son of Margaret Wittmer of the famous 1930s Galápagos Affair, owns and runs *Tiptop III*, no snorkelling equipment. His son has the sailing yacht *Symbol*, a converted ship's lifeboat, very basic, but a good way to drift between the islands (Wittmer Turismo, T 593-2-449-337, F 448-173). *Seaman*, run by Galápagos Travel, has good tours but cramped lower cabins (Amazonas 519 y Roca, Quito, T 593-2-500-064, F 505-772). The sailing catamaran *Pulsar* is rec, US$580/8 days, but best when the owner Patric is on board; some cabins are very small indeed (Ecuagal, Amazonas 1113 y Pinto, T 593-2-229-579, F 550-988).

Good service on the *Golondrina, Frigata*, Golondrina Turismo, J L Mera 639 y Carrión, Quito, T 593-2-528-570, F 528-570. *Isla Galápagos* is rec; the guide is Peter Freire, good, but fair English. *Elizabeth II*, good crew and food; *Angelito* of Hugo Andrade, with a new *Angelito* in service; *Española* (8 passengers, good food); *Lobo del Mar* (12 passengers); *Daphne* (8 – good cook); and *San Antonio* (12 – good food, nice crew).

Day tours can be arranged on *North Star*, small but fast, contact David Asencio at *Hotel*

Darwin; Santa Fe II, owned by Byron Rueda, T (05) 526-593; *Esmeraldas*, owned by Ninfa Tours.

It must be stressed that a boat is only as good as its crew and when the staff change, so will these recommendations. The South American Explorers Club in Quito has an extensive file of trip reports for members to consult and David, at *Safari Tours*, Quito, tries to keep abreast of all new developments.

PUERTO AYORA

Places of interest

In 1959, the centenary of the publication of Darwin's *Origin of Species*, the Government of Ecuador and the International Charles Darwin Foundation established, with the support of Unesco, the Charles Darwin Research Station at Academy Bay 1½ km from Puerto Ayora, Santa Cruz, the most central of the Galápagos islands, open Mon-Fri 0700-1300, 1400-1600, Sat 0700-1300. A visit to the station is a good introduction to the islands as it provides a lot of information. Collections of several of the rare sub-species of giant tortoise are maintained on the station as breeding nuclei, together with a tortoise-rearing house incorporating incubators and pens for the young. The Darwin Foundation staff will help bona fide students of the fauna to plan an itinerary if they stay some time and hire a boat.

Excursions on Santa Cruz

Ask at *Neptuno Tours* in Puerto Ayora for tours of the interior. Walk to **Tortuga Bay** on a marked path for excellent sunsets and nice beach (very strong undertow), 5 km. Take drinking water and do not go alone (armed robbery reported). Overnight camping is possible with permission from the Park offices in Puerto Ayora. There are several beaches by the Darwin Station, very crowded at weekends.

Hike to the higher parts of the island called Media Luna, Puntudo and Mt Crocker. The trail starts at Bellavista, 7 km from Puerto Ayora. A round trip from Bellavista is 4 to 8 hrs, depending on the distance hiked, 10-18 km (permit and guide not required, but a guide is advisable). Take water, sun block and long-sleeved shirt and long trousers to protect against razor grass.

To see giant tortoises in the wild, go to Steve Devine's Butterfly ranch beyond Bellavista on the road to Santa Rosa (the bus passes the turn-off), only in the dry season; in the wet season the tortoises are breeding in the arid zone Vermillion flycatchers can be seen here also. Entry US$2, inc free cup of *hierba luisa* tea, or juice. Steve Devine is a guide on the island, highly rec (ask for him or Jack Nelson at *Hotel Galápagos*).

There are several natural tunnels (lava tubes): one 3 km from Puerto Ayora on the road to Bellavista, unsigned on the left, look for the black-and-white posts (tread carefully); barn owls may be seen here. Two more are 1 km from Bellavista; on private land, US$1.50 to enter, bring torch or pay for one – it takes about 30 mins to walk through the tunnels. Ask for Bolívar at *Pensión Gloria*, his ex-wife's family have lands with lava caves, a *mirador* and other attractions.

Hike to the **Chato Tortoise Reserve**, 7 km; the trail starts at Santa Rosa, 22 km from Puerto Ayora. Horses can be hired at Santa Rosa, US$6 each, guide compulsory, US$6.50 (again ask Bolívar at *Pensión Gloria*). A round trip takes 1 day. The Puerto Ayora-Bellavista bus stops at the turnoff for the track for the reserve (US$0.95). It's a hot walk; take food and drink. From Santa Rosa, distance to different sites within the reserve is 6-8 km (permit and guide not required). To walk to the Reserve from Santa Rosa, turn left past the school, follow the track at the edge of fields for 40 mins, turn right at the memorial to the Israeli, 20 mins later turn left down a track to Chato Trucha.

Two sinkholes, **Los Gemelos**, straddle the road to Baltra, beyond Santa Rosa; if you are lucky, take a *camioneta*

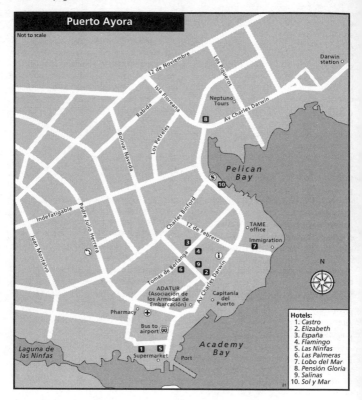

Puerto Ayora
Not to scale

Darwin station

12 de Noviembre

Los Piqueros

Isla Floreana

Rabida

Neptuno Tours

Av Charles Darwin

Bolívar Naveda

Los Petreles

🟦8

Pelican Bay

Indefatigable

Padre Julio Herrera

Charles Binford

🟦⑤ 🟦10

Juan Montalvo

12 de Febrero

TAME office

Immigration

🟦3
🟦4
🟦9 ⓘ
🟦2 🟦7

Tomás de Berlanga

Av Charles Darwin

N

ADATUR
(Asociación de los Armadas de Embarcación) ○

Capitanía del Puerto

Pharmacy ✚

Bus to airport 🚌

🟦1 🟦5
Supermarket

Laguna de las Ninfas

Academy Bay

Port

Hotels:
1. *Castro*
2. *Elizabeth*
3. *España*
4. *Flamingo*
5. *Las Ninfas*
6. *Las Palmeras*
7. *Lobo del Mar*
8. *Pensión Gloria*
9. *Salinas*
10. *Sol y Mar*

all the way, otherwise to Santa Rosa, then walk. A good place to see the Galápagos hawk and barn owl.

The highlands and settlement area of Santa Cruz are worth seeing for the contrast of the vegetation with the arid coastal zones. Ask for Tim Grey and Anita Salcedo at *Garapata* in Puerto Ayora, they have a *finca* for arranging barbecues.

● **Transport To Santa Rosa and Bellavista** From San Francisco school in Puerto Ayora buses leave for Santa Rosa and Bellavista at 0630, 1230 and 1630, 30-min trip, return immediately; fare for all destinations US$1. There are also trucks (cheaper). On roads to the main sites hitching is easy but expect to pay a small fee.

Local information – Puerto Ayora
Electricity is off between midnight and 0600 and INECEL cuts power to a different section of town from 1900-2200 every night. Most hotels have a portable generator. Carry a passport at all times.

● **Accommodation**
Hotel space is limited and reservations are strongly rec in high season.

L3 *Delfín*, on the far side of Academy Bay, with lovely beach (local class 1), expensive, accessible only by boat, write to Mrs Sievers.

A3 *Galápagos*, bungalows with private bathroom, hot water, ocean-view, laundry service, generator, restaurant with fixed menu, fruit and meat from hotel farm, nr Darwin Research centre, reservations can be made through Ecuadorean travel agencies, day excursions can be made from hotel in Pedro and Sally García's own dinghy for 10, the *Fernandina*, also *Scuba Iguana* with fast launch for diving; **A3** *Red Mangrove Inn* (in Guayaquil T 880-618, F 880-617), 4 rooms oceanfront, hot showers, jacuzzi, deck bar, restaurant, warmly rec, owner Polo Navaro offers tours inc sea kayaking, highland farm, cruises in *Azul* and diving (*Nauti Diving*, has a fast launch).

C *Castro*, with private bath, owned by Sr Miguel Castro, he arranges 7-day inclusive tours, includes Fri TAME flight, rec. He is an authority on wildlife and his tour includes 1 or 2 nights away visiting the islands of Plazas and Santiago, and a day-trip to Santa Fe, with visits to the tortoise reserve and the Darwin Institute.

B *Las Ninfas*, very close to harbour, basic, cold showers, good restaurant, has its own boat at reasonable price for day trips and Fernando Jiménez is helpful with arrangements.

D *Salinas*, opp Lirio del Mar, 20 beds, with bath and fan, clean, good value; **D** *Sol y Mar*, next to bank, 20 beds (double, triples and quadruples) in cabins, with 3 meals, C without meals, 10% discount for stays of 2 weeks or more; reservations can be made by writing to the owner (Sr Jimmy Pérez), or Transgalapagos Inc, PO Box 11227, T 562-151, F (593) 4-382-444, Guayaquil; **D** *Las Palmeras*, good.

E *Elizabeth*, with bath, reasonable, now re-modelled, owner very helpful, reported noisy; **E** pp *Lirio del Mar*, private bath, cafetería, laundry facilities, pleasant, clean; **E** pp *Lobo de Mar* with bath, 30 beds, modern, clean, can do laundry on roof, noisy on occasions.

F *Darwin*, with bath, restaurant (order meals in advance), rec but don't leave valuables in your room; **F** *España*, clean, good beds, hot water, very friendly, excellent value, rec; **F** *Flamingo*, opp, with private bath, fan, decent, clean; **F** *Pensión Gloria*, 12 beds, simple, you can cook your own food over a wood fire, mosquito repellent needed, new rooms with unusual decor, laundry facilities, very friendly; **F** *Los Amigos*, Av Darwin in front of TAME office, without bath, run by Sra Rosa Rosera, cool, reasonable, friendly, airy rooms (upstairs best), laundry facilities, clean, rec; **F** pp *Peregrino*, on main street behind *Restaurante Pippo*, inc good breakfast, highly rec.

● **Places to eat**
Expect slow service and shortages of items such as flour which will reduce menu availability. *Rincón del Alma*, nr the plaza, best, good

food, reasonable prices; *La Garrapata*, open air, on road to research station, popular meeting place for travellers, morning and evening but not Sun, drinks expensive, check the bill; *Viña del Mar*, on main street, good value, popular with locals, OK; *Sol y Mar*, good but expensive breakfast on terrace full of marine iguanas; *4 Linternas*, pizza and Italian; *Trattoria de Pippo*, Italian; *Salvavida*, on the docks, good breakfast, almuerzo, seafood; *Media Luna Pizza*, also sandwiches, good; *Moon Rise Café*, good breakfast, friendly, highly rec.

● **Banks & money changers**
Banco del Pacífico, Av Charles Darwin, 0800-1700, good rates for TCs, but no cash advance. In emergency offers international telephone service, T 17390, via Guayaquil, by Telex, Fax and satellite. Most boats accept US$ cash and TCs. The Hotel Sol y Mar and Bodega Blanca and Ninfa restaurants will change notes and cheques, but at a poor rate. Several shops change US$ notes.

● **Embassies & consulates**
British Consul, David Balfour, c/o Etica, Barrio Estrada, Puerto Ayora.

● **Entertainment**
Cinema: there is a cinema at Puerto Ayora – each evening at 2015.

Music: Disco La Panga; 5 Fingers disco and bar, popular.

● **Shopping**
For boat charters and camping trips most basic foodstuffs generally can be purchased on the islands, eg Proinsular supermarket opp the pier. The mercado municipal is on Padre Herrera, beyond the telephone office, on the way out of town to Santa Rosa. Fresh milk available in Puerto Ayora from Christine Aldaze, 0930, on main road (24 hrs notice appreciated). Medicines, sun lotions, mosquito coils, film, and other useful items are either not available or cost a lot more than on the mainland. *Galapaguito* can meet most tourists' needs, the owners are both naturalists, very helpful. There is a wide variety of T-shirt and souvenir shops, eg Galápagos Souvenirs; Artesanías Bambú, nr Hotel Galápagos. Do not buy items made of black coral; it is an endangered species.

● **Hospitals & medical services**
Hospitals: there is a hospital in Puerto Ayora; consultations US$10, medicines reasonably-

priced, but they can not perform operations.

● **Laundry**
Ask at the *farmacia* nr *Hotel Santa Cruz*, good service. *Lavagal*, by football stadium, machine wash and dry US$0.80/lb, good, reliable, US$1 taxi ride from town.

● **Post & telecommunications**
Post Office: the Post Office sometimes runs out of stamps (never leave money and letters), ask in the 'red boat' (*Galería Jahanna*) or *Artesanías Bambú*.

Telecommunications: telephone office on Padre Herrera.

● **Sports**
Diving: *Galapagos Sub-Aqua*, Av Charles Darwin, the owner Fernando Zambrano provides courses for beginners and trips for the experienced, all equipment for hire, inc for snorkellers, T/F 526-350 (Dátiles 506 entre Quinta y Sexta, Guayaquil, T 304-132, F (593-4) 314-510), safe, rec. Day tours US$75 to US$100, inc boat, gear, instructor, 2 dives (mainly drift diving). Multi day tours inc meals, accommodation from US$130 pp/day. Introductory courses US$75/day. *Scuba Iguana*, Jack Nelson and Mateaus at *Hotel Galápagos*, experienced on the islands, knowledgeable about different sites; *Nauti Diving*, Polo Navaro at *Red Mangrove Inn*. Also Alvaro Solorzano,

Rosa Borja de Icazay, El Oro, Barrio Centenario, US$80 for certification course.

For snorkelling, masks and snorkels can be rented from dive shops, US$4-5 a day, US$60 deposit. 1-day snorkelling tours US$15-20, 3 locations, rec, ask for Marcello through Marcos Martínez at *Bar/Restaurant Five Fingers*. **NB** Please help to maintain or in some cases improve standards by not disturbing or touching underwater wildlife.

● **Tourist offices**
Cetur, on main road, open Mon-Fri 0800-1200, 1500-1600, T 328-312, 324-471. Information also available at the boat owners' cooperative office nearby.

● **Tour companies & travel agents**
Tierra del Sol, Amazonas 338 y Jorge Washington, T/F 228-655, rafting, climbing and adventure tours.

● **Useful services**
Immigration: the immigration police will extend visas with a little persuasion for those who overstay their visa or tourist card.

Lost property: information and retrieval of lost property from Radio Santa Cruz, next to Catholic Church.

WARNING Valuables should be watched.

Galápagos penguin

PUERTO BAQUERIZO MORENO

(*Pop* 3,023) on San Cristóbal island to the
E, is the capital of the archipelago. The
island is being developed as a second
tourist centre.

Places of interest

In town, the cathedral, 2 blocks up from
the post office, has interesting, mixed-
media relief pictures on the walls and
altar. Next door is the municipal museum of natural history; 0830-1200, 1530-
1730, US$1, stuffed exhibits, old photos,
a tortoise called Pepe.

Excursions on San Cristóbal

Bus (shuttle) to **El Progreso**, then 2½-hr
walk to El Junco lake, tortoises may be seen
on the way. The road continues to a school,
above which is a shrine, a deserted restau
rant and a *mirador* overlooking the different
types of vegetation stretching to the coast.
From El Progreso (tree house *El Tarzan* for
rent; eating places), a trail crosses the high
lands to **Cerro Brujo** and **Hobbs Bay**; also
to **Stephens Bay**, past lakes.

A 3-hr hike to **Galapaguera** in the NE
allows you to see tortoises in the wild. **At
La Lobería**, beyond the airport, is a bay
with shore birds, sea-lions and huge marine iguanas. You can continue along the
cliff, but do not leave the trail, to see
tortoises and rays.

Boats go to **Punta Pitt** in the far N
where you can see all three boobies. Off
the NW coast is **Kicker Rock** (León
Dormido), the basalt remains of a crater;
many seabirds, including masked and
blue-footed boobies, can be seen around
its cliffs. Up the coast is **Cerro Brujo**
beach with sea-lions, birds, crabs (none
in any abundance). Raul Sánchez offers
short trips on his boat *Ana Mercedes*,
ending in Puerto Ayora, much time
spent travelling, T 163. Española
(Hood) is within day trip reach.

Local information
● Accommodation
C *Orca*, OK, good food, has its own boat for
cruises.

D *Hostal Galápagos*, E end of town, a/c cabins, fridge; **D** *Chatham*, on road to airport,
with bath; **D** *Mar Azul*, on road to airport,
with bath, hot showers, clean, nice gardens,
rec, restaurant.

E *Res San Francisco*, with bath, good, clean,
friendly; **E** *Res Northia*, with bath.

F pp *Cabañas Don Jorge*, close to beach,
clean, friendly, 'not luxurious', member of
Ecuadorean and International Youth Hostal
Associations; **F** *Res Miramar*, good value,
clean restaurant, good; **F** *Res Flamingo*, basic, clean, friendly.

● Places to eat
Rosita, best in town; *Nathaly*, good food,
open late; *Chatham*; *Laurita*, fair; *La Terraza*,
disco, on beach; *Fragata*, on road to airport.
Cafetería Tagu, cheap.

● Banks & money changers
Banco del Pacífico, 0800-1700, 0800-1300
Sat, changes cash, cheques and gives cash
against Mastercard. SAN office on Darwin,
Mon, Tues, Wed, Fri 0800-1600, Thur and Sat
0800-1200.

● Hospitals & medical services
There is a hospital but if you need an operation
you have to go yourself to the pharmacy to
buy everything they need.

● Post & telecommunications
Post Office: next to Banco Central on Av
Charles Darwin (main street).
Telephone office: on Av Quito.

● Shopping
There are a few souvenir shops (poorer quality
than Puerto Ayora); best is *Edliz* for T-shirts, in
Moorish-style house opp the jetty with the
whale. Do not buy black coral.

● Transport
See **Travel Between the Islands**, above, for
boat connections to Puerto Ayora. Be warned
that it can take several days to find room on a
boat to Puerto Ayora.

ISABELA ISLAND

Isabela is not highly developed for tourism but if you have a few days to spare it
is worthwhile spending time there.

Excursions

Good walks in the highlands (eg to Cerro
Negro volcano) and beautiful beaches;

also to the 'walking wall' left from the penal colony. Tours to the volcanoes can be made with two guides, compare prices. Horses can be hired. A 3-5 day trip can be arranged in Puerto Ayora at Darwin 606, 10 people required. Also ask Marcos Martínez in Puerto Ayora about 4-day tours, inc riding, accommodation and food, US$100 excluding board and lodging. The climb up the volcanoes takes 3 days, 1 for the ascent, 1 at the top and 1 to come down.

● **Accommodation E** *Alexandra*, nice site on the beach; **E** *Loja*, on the road to the highland, clean, sometimes water shortages, patio, friendly staff, cheap and very good restaurant; *El Rincón del Bucanero*, on the beach, more expensive; **F** *Isabela del Mar*, T 125, friendly, good food, water supplied, rec; **F** *El Capitán*, pleasant, friendly; **E-F** pp *Ballena Azul*, T (593-5) 529-125 or through *Safari Tours*, Quito, safe, clean, family atmosphere, rooms or cabins, meals available, rec, run by Dora Gruber, Swiss; **G** *Antonio Gil*, rents 2 rooms with shower, friendly, helpful, tours arranged with horses. There are a few *comedores* but food is seldom available unless you order in advance.

● **Transport**
An airport is being built at Villamil and a light aircraft shuttle is operating from San Cristóbal. Besides Ingala on Thur (see above), *Estrella del Mar* sails from Puerto Ayora on Wed, or contact fishermen, US$20-30; ask for Don Vicente at Proinsular office.

GENERAL ADVICE

● **Tipping**
On a cruise, it will be suggested to you that you tip US$50-100/passenger for the crew and the same for the guide. As elsewhere, tips should always reflect service, and should be given according to the service in relation to what you requested. On first and second-hand evidence, it appears that US$25-30/cabin is the top limit, and that for outstanding service.

● **If you have problems**
See above for complaints regarding itineraries. If a crew member comes on strong with a woman passenger, the matter should first be raised with the guide or captain. If this does not yield results, a formal complaint, in

Giant Galápagos tortoise

Spanish, giving the crew member's full name, the boat's name and the date of the cruise, should be sent to Sr Capitán del Puerto, Base Militar de Armada Ecuatoriana, Puerto Ayora, Santa Cruz, Galápagos. Failure to report such behaviour will mean it will continue. To avoid pilfering, never leave belongings unattended on a beach when another boat is in the bay.

● **What to take**

A remedy for seasickness is rec; the waters S of Santa Cruz are particularly choppy. A good supply of sun block and skin cream to prevent windburn and chapped lips is essential. A hat and sunglasses are also rec. You should be prepared for dry and wet landings, the latter involving wading ashore.

Take plenty of film with you; the birds are so tame that you will see far more than you expected; a telephoto lens is not essential, but if you have one, bring it. Also take filters suitable for strong sunlight. Snorkelling equipment is particularly useful as much of the sea-life is only visible under water. Most of the cheaper boats do not provide equipment and those that do may not have good snorkelling gear. If in doubt, bring your own, rent in Puerto Ayora, or buy it in Quito. It is possible to sell it afterwards either on the islands or try the *Gran Casino* travel agency in Quito.

● **The cost of living**

The cost of living in the Galápagos is high, particularly in the peak season (Dec, July and Aug). Most food has to be imported although certain meats, fish, vegetables and fruit are available locally in the Puerto Ayora market. Bottled drinks are expensive, beer US$1.50.

● **Recommended reading**

The *Galápagos Guide* by Alan White and Bruce White Epler, with photographs by Charles Gilbert, is published in several languages; it can be bought in Guayaquil in Librería Científica and the airport, Libri Mundi (US$5) in Quito, or at the Charles Darwin station. The South American Explorers Club in Quito sells a useful brief guide, *Galapagos Package*, US$4.

Galápagos: the Enchanted Isles by David Horwell (London: Dryad Press, 1988, available through his agency).

The Enchanted Isles. The Galápagos Discovered, John Hickman (Anthony Nelson, 1985).

The Galápagos Affair, John Treherne (Jonathan Cape, 1983).

Journal of the Voyage of HMS Beagle, by Charles Darwin, first published in 1845. Penguin Books of the UK have published Darwin's account of the Galápagos in their Penguin 60s Classics series.

The Galápagos Islands, 1:500,000 map by Kevin Healey and Hilary Bradt (Bradt Publications, 1985).

Galápagos: A Natural History Guide, Michael H Jackson (University of Calgary Press, 1985).

Reef Fish Identification, Paul Humann (Libri Mundi, 1993).

A Field Guide to the Fishes of Galápagos, Godfrey Merlen (Libri Mundi, 1988).

Plants of the Galápagos Islands, Eileen Schofield (New York: Universe Books, 1984).

A Guide to the Birds of the Galápagos Islands, Isabel Castro and Antonia Phillips (Christopher Helm, 1996).

The Galápagos Conservation Trust (18 Curzon Street, London W1Y 7AD, T 0171 626 5049, F 0171 629 4149, publishes a quarterly Newsletter for its members.

Noticias de Galápagos is a twice-yearly publication about science and conservation in the Islands. It is the official publication of the Charles Darwin Foundation. 'Friends of the Galápagos' (US$25/year membership) receive the journal as a part of their membership.

Brown pelican

The Charles Darwin Research Station can be reached via the Internet: http://fcdarwin.org.ec/welcome.html.

The Galápagos Coalition web pages are also worth visiting: http://www.law.emory.edu/PI/GALAPAGOS.

THE GALAPAGOS ISLANDS: SOME POLITICAL CONSIDERATIONS

Human settlement on the Galápagos is limited to about 3% of the islands' land area and is concentrated in eight settlements. Two are on San Cristóbal, Puerto Baquerizo Moreno, the capital, and a village inland called El Progreso. There are three settlements on Santa Cruz, Puerto Ayora, the largest town and the main tourist centre, Bellavista and Santa Rosa, two farming communities inland. On Floreana, the longest inhabited island, there is a permanent settlement at Black Beach and on Isabela there is a small, thriving community at Puerto Villamil and a village inland at Santo Tomás. Additionally, there is a navy base on South Seymour at the site of an old US Airforce camp.

AN EVOLUTIONARY HISTORY

The continuing volcanic formation of the islands in the W of the archipelago has not only created a unique marine environment, but the drift eastwards of the whole island group at the nexus of several major marine currents has created laboratory-type conditions where only certain species have been allowed access. Others, most significantly, practically the whole of the terrestrial kingdom of mammals, have been excluded. The resulting ecology has evolved in a unique direction, with many of the ecological niches being filled from some unexpected angles. A highly-evolved sunflower, for instance, has taken over the niche left vacant by the absence of trees. Within the islands, evolutionary pressures are so intense that there is a very high level of endemism (species confined to a particular area). For example, not only have the tortoises evolved differently from those in the rest of the world, but each of the five main volcanoes on Isabela has evolved its own subspecies of giant tortoise. This natural experiment has been under threat ever

Sea iguanas

The nature cruise of the century

🐟 *Galápagos*, Kurt Vonnegut's blend of satire, environmental politics, Darwinism and morality tale, is set on the imaginary, lava-encrusted Galápagos island of Santa Rosalia. The "Nature Cruise of the Century", aboard the luxury liner, the *Bahía de Darwin*, is to sail to the islands from Guayaquil. Travel companies all over the world have been building up the passenger list for a year into a roll-call of the richest and most powerful people on Earth.

However, not long before the ship is to set sail, dramatic world events lead to most of the luminaries cancelling their trip. The passenger list shrinks to only six seemingly ordinary members of the public.

The novel is narrated a million years hence by the ghost of a North American named Leon Trout, who had a hand in the construction of the *Bahía de Darwin*. Vonnegut uses this viewpoint as a means to observe the drastic effects that the ship's journey has on the evolution of mankind. When World War Three breaks out, the passengers on the cruise ship are to be the only human survivors on the planet. They will be forced to cohabit and reproduce in order to propagate the species, once they realize they are stranded on Santa Rosalia for ever. Darwin's theory of natural selection figures throughout the novel, with particular reference to the strange animals which have evolved on the remote Galápagos islands.

Vonnegut's narrative viewpoint is a clever literary device which enables him continually to refer to the long-term consequences of the events of the novel. At an early stage the reader is told, for example, who is going to die, who will father the future children on the island and, most importantly, what kind of creature the human race will evolve into over the next million years. He constantly refers to the 'big-brained' humans of the 20th century and the problems those big brains have wrought on the world. The future Vonnegut maps out for humankind will have to be discovered by those who wish to read this fascinating book. (*Galápagos*, Kurt Vonnegut, first published in USA 1985, UK 1987.)

since the arrival of the first whaling ships and their acceleration with the first permanent human settlement. Despite the authorities' best efforts, 'new' species are being introduced at an increasing rate. Species that had evolved to fill the ecological niches in the Galápagos are now being evicted and destroyed by the more recent introductions.

THE HUMAN EFFECT

The most devastating of the newly-introduced species are human beings, both visitors and settlers. To a large degree, the two groups are connected, one supporting the other economically, but there is also a sizable proportion, over half of the islands' permanent residents, who make an income from working the land or at

sea. While no great wealth has accumulated to those who farm, fortunes have been made by fishermen in a series of destructive fisheries: black coral, lobster, shark fin and sea cucumber (see below). Sharks were caught by setting gill nets across a bay. These nets took a wide range of marine animals and birds as a by-catch, including pelicans, boobies, seals, turtles and dolphins. As none have any commercial value, they were dumped. Each successive fishery was encouraged by foreign demand involving large amounts of money. Even sea lion penis bone, known as baculum, is being exported to Asia.

It is, however, farmers who are responsible for the largest number of introduced species. Recent introductions

Lava heron

(since the formation of the National Park) include elephant grass to provide pastures, the ani to eat parasites living on cattle (although in the Galápagos it prefers baby finches when it can get them) and walnut trees planted on Isabela in the last few years.

THE TOURIST INDUSTRY

Each of the colonizing groups on the islands, scientific, the tourist industry, settlers, farmers and fishermen, have all become powerful pressure groups. Each has its own agenda, with different expectations of the islands. The most sophisticated pressure groups are probably those involved in tourism, divided between boat owners and guides. Being mostly Ecuadorean, the boat owners are easily identified and, as they are looking for long-term stability and profit, they can be monitored through a system of licences and permits issued by both the Ministry of Agriculture and the Navy. Of all the commercial groups, the boat owners are the most likely to support any aggressive attempts by the Park authorities to clean up the islands. The guides,

though, have other priorities. They fall roughly into two groups: the more established guides, including the multilingual and the specialists, often foreigners, and the local and national, Spanish-speaking guides. The former are not as politically active as the latter, who have been involved in a number of civil incidents during the last six years. Among the demands of the Association of Guides, formed by the Galápagos and Ecuadorean guides, have been the exclusion of foreigners (not always defined in consistent terms) from guiding, the reform of the guides' licensing system, stopping all immigration to the islands, the repatriation of settlers and the creation of an independent Galápagos state. The former leader of the Association, Eduardo Veliz, is now a congressman for the islands, and a keen promoter of laws which aim to change many aspects of the way the islands are governed. The most recent, in mid-1996, proposes, among other things, the transfer of most political and economic power to a local government body. Although it has received congressional approval, the president has not passed the law. Since a Special Commission for the Galápagos is drafting a special law for the islands, it is also seen as hasty and with too little regard for conservation issues.

THE PARK AUTHORITY

The National Park authority is responsible for the 95% of the archipeligo that is National Park. It represents Inefan (Ecuadorean National Institute for Forestry, Natural Areas and Wildlife), a government agency that is nominally under the auspices of the Ministry of Agriculture (although a new Ministry of the Environment has just been created – 1996), but is understood to be heavily financed from outside Ecuador and to have a great deal of autonomy. The principal policies pursued by Inefan, since taking control of the National Parks system in 1992, do not appear to have benefited the parks, with little evidence that the high entry fees are being reinvested in the parks themselves (the fees collected by park personnel are transferred to a general fund at the Ministry of Finance). At park level, however, leadership has been well-intentioned. Operating within the Galápagos National Park, the Charles Darwin Research Station has tried to remain outside the main political flow, concentrating on scientific support to the Park authority, funding its own research and assisting visiting scientists with their work. While the Research Station has a great deal of influence at an international level, it has no direct say in the management of the Park itself.

WHAT IS THE PROBLEM?

Because tourism is so easily controlled and involves relatively large amounts of money, it is this area which has been debated more than any other. Tourists and their guides form the vast majority of the visitors to the 90% land area that is Park, but it is equally true that, from the point of view of the islands as a whole, it is settlers who are responsible for the largest amount of damage. The remains of abandoned habitations can be seen on Floreana, at Post Office Bay, at Puerto Egas (an abandoned salt works), near Puerto

Land iguana, South Plaza Island

Villamil and most extensively on Baltra. There is no will to remove them. What is taken to the islands by modern settlers will presumably also be left behind.

The impact of tourism in the Park can best be seen at places like the Plaza islands on the E side of Santa Cruz and a photostudy being undertaken by the Darwin Station shows many of the changes. Tourists are limited to some 40 landing sites throughout the entire island group and each has a clearly defined trail from which visitors are not allowed to deviate. The impact that a farmer can have, importing just one species from outside the islands, or one family of settlers, is therefore far greater than that of tourism. Nevertheless, the successfully controlled impact of tourism has led to an over-concentration on this area as the source of all evils in the Galápagos and has permitted the national government gratefully to ignore some of the other pressing problems that have accumulated over the past two decades. Top of the list is uncontrolled immigration.

THE IMPACT OF IMMIGRATION

For some Ecuadoreans, the Galápagos Islands are an El Dorado, with strong economic growth, plenty of work opportunities and salaries about 50% higher than on the mainland. Population growth has been astronomic and land prices have soared. Proposals in 1995 to categorize and limit immigration were shelved after a referendum indicated, predictably, that the majority of Ecuadoreans did not want to be excluded from living on the islands. Economic growth has been concentrated in Puerto Ayora. The airports on San Cristóbal and Isabela have been built in an attempt to spread the benefits from tourism throughout the islands, but government policy is not going to change the fact that centrally-located Santa Cruz is the ideal base for the tourist industry. Similarly it is the obvious home port for the fishing

fleet, made up mostly of vessels capable only of coastal navigation. There has been strong reaction in other communities to the flow of wealth into Puerto Ayora. Fishermen in Puerto Villamil, for example, threatened to kill the giant tortoises in 1995 after they had lost their livelihood catching sea cucumbers off Fernandina. They were evicted from Fernandina because the island is in the National Park and has a highly sensitive ecology with no introduced species. Sea cucumber fishing elsewhere has led to mass extinctions and the eventual effect on the unique penguin and flightless cormorant populations which feed on the cucumbers remains to be seen.

THE FUTURE OF THE ISLANDS

The successful, long-term future of the islands depends on discouraging immigration and removing pollution and introduced feral species from the environment. The policies needed to curtail immigration would have profound political consequences. It is therefore unlikely that they will be adopted by any but the most environmentally-conscious of governments. There is opportunity for a more aggressive stance on the removal of waste products from the islands: they could be shipped back to the mainland. This should include used engine oils (eg from tourist yachts), thousands of gallons of which are being imported monthly into each island's tidal water table. The existing rubbish tips, in which rats breed, could also be shipped out and cleaned up. Abandoned housing could be taken down. The money from park entry fees could be put towards this, once the question of whose responsibility the task is (Inefan may argue that the problem stems from the settlement areas which are outside its control). Similarly, the feral species, dogs and cats in the settlements, pigs on Santiago/James, could be removed.

Ecuador is not a rich country and it has many pressing social problems. The economy needs the foreign currency generated in the Galápagos Islands. So while it is conceivable that a government may find the political will to take a stronger line on pollution, no government is likely to try to reduce vigorous settlement. There is an additional reason for this. The islands are contiguous with Antarctica, giving Ecuador a legitimate claim to the mineral riches expected to be forthcoming when commercial exploitation of Antarctica becomes internationally acceptable. In fact, Ecuador already has its own base on Antarctica and is the only country with territorial claims on both the equator and the South Pole. Ecuador is also a signatory of the Permanent Commission of the Southern Pacific, under which it has proclaimed a 200-nautical-mile territorial limit from its coasts (the wider the territorial area, the greater the claim on Antarctica). This was taken into consideration in the formation of the Galápagos Marine Resources Reserve in 1986, the second largest marine protected area in the world (after the Great Barrier Reef). In 1995, the president suggested that the reserve's 15-nautical-mile limit be extended to 40, which would vastly increase the difficulties currently experienced in its management. Having gained international support for its efforts to conserve the land-based ecology of the Galápagos, Ecuador also needs international support for marine conservation. It therefore faces a difficult task in balancing domestic political opinion, the nation's strategic needs and international credibility when drawing up policies for the benefit of the islands.

Blue-footed booby

Notes

Notes

Notes

Notes

Information for travellers

BEFORE TRAVELLING

ENTRY REQUIREMENTS

● Documents

A passport (valid for at least 6 months required on arrival at Quito airport), and a tourist card valid for 90 days obtainable on arrival. Tourists are now allowed only 90 days on entry in any 365-day period; you can leave the country and return within that 90 days, but if your 90 days end on 31 Dec, you cannot return in Jan, you have to wait 12 months for another 90-day entitlement. You are required to say how many days you intend to stay and the card and your passport will be stamped accordingly; most travellers are given 15 or 30-day stamps irrespective of their requests (at Huaquillas, Macará and Tulcán), and travellers arriving by air may be given a stamp valid for only 10 days (transit pass) unless they request otherwise. It is therefore better to overestimate as you can be fined on leaving the country for staying too long.

Extensions can be routinely obtained at the Policía Nacional de Migración in Quito, or at the Jefatura Provincial de Migración in any provincial capital (except Portoviejo, go to Manta instead); 30 days are given for each extension, which cost appox US$10 (payable in sucres), up to a maximum of 90 additional days (180 days total); make sure the extension is given an official stamp. If you are late in applying there is a US$3.25 fine. Evidence of sufficient funds (see below) is sometimes required.

French citizens need a **visa**; US$30, 4 photos, a return ticket and at least 6 months validity on passport required. A visa is also required for those from China, Taiwan, N and S Korea, Vietnam and Cuba and for business people and students who stay longer than 90 days (3 photos required), application to be made in home country, and they must get an exit permit (*permiso de salida*, once obtained this is valid for multiple trips out of Ecuador during one year) with both tax and police clearance. It costs US$17 for renewing a visa after its expiry date; extending a 90-day consular visa is not easy. If travelling on anything other than a 90-day tourist card, check if you need to register upon arrival with the Extranjería and Policía Nacional de Migración as well as obtaining an exit permit.

The procedure for obtaining a **student visa** involves taking a letter from the school at which you will be studying to the Ecuadorean consulate, a letter from your bank and a ticket out of Ecuador (or

Simon Bolívar on the 100 sucre note (currently being phased out)

South America), plus a fee of US$30 in cash (only dollars, wherever paid): it is illegal to study on a tourist visa. There are many other essential procedures, for which at least 6 passport photos will be required (4 face, 2 profile). You are also required to remit US$1000 to a Quito bank to open an account in your name on arrival. There is considerable further paperwork in Ecuador after you get there. A student visa is given for 6 months. Holders of student visas do not have to pay the Cuota de Compensación Militar on leaving, although business visa holders do. Verify all details at the Consulate before departure.

NB Students visiting the Galápagos, and in other cases, are entitled to discounts. Because of local, counterfeit international student cards, they do not accept Ecuadorean-issued student cards. ISICs are sometimes honoured, but proof of home student status is essential. See page 117 on purchasing student ID in Quito.

If you are in full-time education you will be entitled to an International Student Identity Card, which is distributed by student travel offices and travel agencies in 77 countries. The ISIC gives you special prices on all forms of transport (air, sea, rail etc), and access to a variety of other concessions and services. If you need to find the location of your nearest ISIC office contact: The ISIC Association, Box 9048, 1000 Copenhagen, Denmark T (+45) 33 93 93 03.

Tourists crossing from Colombia or Peru may be asked for evidence that they possess US$20 pp for each day they pro-

pose to spend in Ecuador. Theoretically you must have an onward ticket out of Ecuador, but this is almost never enforced if you are travelling overland. However, travellers arriving from Miami by plane have been refused entry without a ticket and an MCO may not be sufficient.

Warning Always carry your passport with you, or a photocopy with the immigration visa date, except when travelling in the Oriente or border areas when the real thing is required. Failure to produce this as identification could result in imprisonment. Remember that it is your responsibility to ensure that your passport is stamped in and out when you cross frontiers. The absence of entry and exit stamps can cause serious difficulties: seek out the proper migration offices if the stamping process is not carried out as you cross.

You should always carry your passport in a safe place about your person, or if not going far, leave it in the hotel safe. Do not lose your entry card; replacing one causes a lot of trouble, and possibly expense. Some embassies recommend you register with them details of your passport and accommodation in case of emergency. Tourists are not permitted to work under any circumstances.

● **Tourist information**
Corporación Ecuatoriana de Turismo (Cetur), Eloy Alfaro 1214 y Carlos Tobar, Quito, T 507-559/560, F 507-564. The addresses of tourist offices are given in the main text, in the **Local information** sections. See under Rounding up (page 383)

for a list of specialist tour operators operating from outside of Ecuador.

MONEY

● Currency

The sucre is the unit of currency. Bank notes of the Banco Central de Ecuador are for 100, 500 (both being phased out), 1,000, 5,000, 10,000, 20,000 and 50,000 sucres; there are nickel coins of 50, 100 and 500 sucres. (A 100,000 sucre note and a 1,000 sucre coin were expected by end-1996.)

There is no restriction on the amount of foreign money or sucres you can take into or out of Ecuador. It is very easy to change US$ cheques into US$ notes at the *cambios*; the commission varies so it is worth shopping around and *cambios* sometimes run out of US$ notes; you can try to bargain for a better rate than shown on the blackboard. Most banks charge no commission on US$ cheques into sucres. Note that although many hotels and restaurants have signs indicating acceptance of credit cards, this is often not the case; always check first. ATMs in the Mastercard/Cirrus network can be found in branches of Banco del Pacífico, Banco General de Crédito, Banco de Préstamos and Banco Holandés Unido. Visa ATMs are at Banco de Guayaquil and Filanbanco branches. Note that difficulties have been reported with Amex cards, an alternative credit card may be more useful. It is quite difficult to change TCs outside the main towns, especially in the Oriente. US$ money orders cannot be exchanged anywhere in Ecuador. For Western Union money transfers, T (2) 565-059 in Quito.

● General tips

Low-value US dollar bills should be carried for changing into local currency if arriving in the country when banks or *casas de cambio* are closed. They are also useful for shopping. If you are travelling on the cheap it is essential to keep in funds; watch weekends and public holidays carefully and never run out of local currency. Take plenty of sucres, in small denominations, when making trips into the interior.

It is a good idea to take 2 kinds of travellers' cheque: if large numbers of one kind have recently been forged or stolen, making people suspicious, it is unlikely to have happened simultaneously with the other kind.

There are two international **ATM** (automatic telling machine) acceptance systems, Plus and Cirrus. Many issuers of debit and credit cards are linked to one, or both (eg Visa is Plus, Mastercard is Cirrus). Look for the relevant symbol on an ATM and draw cash using your PIN. Frequently, the rates of exchange on ATM withdrawals are the best available. Find out before you leave what ATM coverage there is in Ecuador and what international 'functionality' your card has. Check if your bank or credit card company imposes handling charges. Obviously you must ensure that the account to which your debit card refers contains sufficient funds. With a credit card, obtain a credit limit sufficient for your needs, or pay money in to put the account in credit. If travelling for a long time, consider a direct debit to clear your account regularly. Do not rely on one card, in case of loss. If you do lose a card, immediately contact the 24-hr helpline of the issuer in your home country (keep this number in a safe place).

Money can be transferred between banks. A recommended method is, before leaving, to find out which local bank is correspondent to your bank at home, then when you need funds, telex your own bank and ask them to telex the money to the local bank (confirming by fax). Give exact information to your bank of the routing number of the receiving bank. Funds can be received within 48 banking hours.

GETTING THERE

AIR

● **From Europe**

Air France three times from Paris to Quito. Iberia flies from Madrid to Quito via Santo Domingo, Dominican Republic, twice

weekly. KLM flies weekly from Amsterdam to Guayaquil via Curaçao and Quito. Lufthansa flies from Frankfurt to Quito three times weekly via Bogotá. Viasa flies from Caracas with connecting flights to several European destinations.

● **From North America**

There are flights from New York to Quito and Guayaquil with Saeta, which also flies from Miami. Ecuatoriana flies from New York to Quito and from Miami to Quito and Guayaquil. American Airlines fly daily from Miami to Quito and Guayaquil. Continental flies from Houston to Quito and Guayaquil. LanChile flies Miami-Guayaquil. From other US cities make connections in Miami.

● **From Latin American cities**

Bogotá (Lufthansa, Air France, Continental, Saeta, Avianca, Servivensa, Viasa and AeroPerú to Quito; Saeta to Guayaquil); Cali to Esmeraldas with TAME; Lima (LAB, Saeta, Servivensa, Avianca and Aeroperú to Quito, Copa, Saeta and AeroPerú to Guayaquil); Caracas (Saeta to Quito and Guayaquil,

Avianca, Servivensa and Viasa to Quito only, LanChile to Guayaquil only); Panama (to Quito and Guayaquil Saeta, Tame, Continental and Copa); Santiago de Chile (Lan-Chile to Guayaquil, Tame to Quito and Guayaquil, Saeta to Quito). From Brazil Lacsa and Ecuatoriana to Guayaquil and Quito from São Paulo, Lacsa also to both cities from Rio de Janeiro; Lacsa also flies to San José. Connections with other Central American capitals in San José or Panama City; Copa's Lima-Guayaquil-Panama routes continues to Santo Domingo and San Juan, 4 times a week.

● **General tips**

Airlines will only allow a certain weight of luggage without a surcharge; this is normally 30 kg for first class and 20 kg for business and economy classes, but these limits are often not strictly enforced when it is known that the plane is not going to be full. On some flights from the UK via Paris special outbound concessions are offered (by Iberia, Viasa, Air France, Avianca) of a 2-piece allowance up to 32 kg, but you

may need to request this. Passengers seeking a larger baggage allowance can route via USA, but with certain exceptions, the fares are slightly higher using this route. On the other hand, weight limits for internal flights are often lower; best to enquire beforehand.

● **Prices and discounts**

1. It is generally cheaper to fly from London rather than a point in Europe to Latin American destinations; fares vary from airline to airline, destination to destination and according to time of year. Check with an agency for the best deal for when you wish to travel.

2. Most airlines offer discounted fares of one sort or another on scheduled flights. These are not offered by the airlines direct to the public, but through agencies who specialize in this type of fare. In UK, these include Journey Latin America, 16 Devonshire Rd, Chiswick, London W4 2HD (T 0181-747 3108); Trailfinders, 48 Earl's Court Rd, London W8 6EJ (T 0171-938 3366); South American Experience, 47 Causton St, Pimlico, London SW1P 4AT (T 0171-976 5511); Last Frontiers, Swan House, High St, Long Crendon, Buckinghamshire, HP18 9AF (T 01844 208405); Passage to South America, Fovant Mews, 12 Noyna Road, London. SW17 7PH (T 0181 767 8989); STA Travel, Priory House, 6 Wrights Lane, London W8 6TA (T 0171-938 4711), Cox & Kings Travel, St James Court, 45 Buckingham Gate, London (T 0171-873 5001).

The very busy seasons are 7 Dec – 15 Jan and 10 July – 10 Sept. If you intend travelling during those times, book as far ahead as possible. Between Feb-May and Sept-Nov special offers may be available.

3. Other fares fall into three groups, and are all on scheduled services:

● **Excursion (return) fares** with restricted validity eg 5-90 days. Carriers are introducing flexibility into these tickets, permitting a change of dates on payment of a fee.

● **Yearly fares**: these may be bought on a one-way or return basis. Some airlines require a specified return date, changeable upon payment of a fee. To leave the return completely open is possible for an extra fee. You must, fix the route (some of the cheapest flexible fares now have 6 months validity).

● **Student (or Under 26) fares**. (Do not assume that student tickets are the cheapest; though they are often very flexible, they are usually more expensive than A or B above). Some airlines are flexible on the age limit, others strict. One way and returns available, or 'Open Jaws' (see below). **NB** If you foresee returning home at a busy time (eg Christmas, Aug), a booking is advisable on any type of open-return ticket.

4. For people intending to travel a linear route and return from a different point from that which they entered, there are 'Open Jaws' fares, which are available on student, yearly, or excursion fares.

5. Many of these fares require a change of plane at an intermediate point, and a stopover may be permitted, or even obligatory, depending on schedules. Simply because a flight stops at a given airport does not mean you can break your journey there – the airline must have traffic rights to pick up or set down passengers between points A and B before it will be permitted. This is where dealing with a specialized agency (like Journey Latin America!) will really pay dividends. On multi-stop itineraries, the specialized agencies can often save clients hundreds of pounds.

6. Although it's a little more complicated, it's possible to sell tickets in London for travel originating in Latin America at substantially cheaper fares than those available locally. This is useful for the traveller who doesn't know where he will end up, or who plans to travel for more than a year. Because of high local taxes a one-way ticket from Latin America is more expensive than a one-way in the other direction, so it's always best to buy a return. Taxes are calculated as a percentage of the full IATA fare; on a discounted fare the tax can therefore make up as much as 30-50% of the price.

7. Travellers starting their journey in continental Europe may try: Uniclam-Voyages, 63 rue Monsieur-le Prince, 75006 Paris for charters. The Swiss company, Balair (owned by Swissair) has regular charter flights to South America. For cheap flights in Switzerland, Globetrotter Travel Service, Renweg, 8001 Zürich, has been recommended. Also try Nouvelles Frontières, Paris, T (1) 41-41-58-58; Hajo Siewer Jet Tours, Martinstr 39, 57462 Olpe, Germany, T (02761) 924120. The German magazine *Reisefieber* is useful.

8. If you buy discounted air tickets *always* check the reservation with the airline concerned to make sure the flight still exists. Also remember the IATA airlines' schedules change in March and October each year, so if you're going to be away a long time it's best to leave return flight coupons open.

In addition, check whether you are entitled to any refund or re-issued ticket if you lose, or have stolen, a discounted air ticket. Some airlines require the repurchase of a ticket before you can apply for a refund, which will not be given until after the validity of the original ticket has expired. The Iberia group and Air France, for example, operate this costly system. Travel insurance in some cases covers lost tickets.

9. Note that some South American carriers change departure times of short-haul or domestic flights at short notice and, in some instances, schedules shown in the computers of transatlantic carriers differ from those actually flown by smaller, local carriers. If you book, and reconfirm, both your transatlantic and onward sectors through your transatlantic carrier you may find that your travel plans have been based on out of date information. The surest solution is to reconfirm your outward flight in an office of the onward carrier itself.

SEA

Enquiries regarding passages should be made through agencies in your own country, or through John Alton of Strand Cruise and Travel Centre, Charing Cross Shopping Concourse, The Strand, London WC2N 4HZ, T 0171-836 6363, F 0171-497 0078. In Switzerland, contact Wagner Frachtschiffreisen, Stadlerstrasse 48, CH-8404 Winterthur, T (052) 242 14 42, F 242 14 87. In the USA, contact Freighter World Cruises, 180 South Lake Ave, Pasadena, CA 91101, T (818) 449-3106, or Travltips Cruise and

Freighter Travel Association, 163-07 Depot Rd, PO Box 188, Flushing, NY 11358, T (800) 872-8584. The *Nordwoge* Shipping Company carries 7 passengers on a 70-day round trip Felixstowe, Bilbao, Panama Canal, Buenaventura, Guayaquil, Callao, Arica (or Iquique), San Antonio, Valparaíso, Talcahuano, Antofagasta, Guayaquil, Buenaventura, Panama Canal, Bilbao, various N European ports, Felixstowe, £5,300 pp. Chilean Line's *Laja* and *Lircay*, New Orleans, Houston, Tampico, Cristóbal, Panama Canal, Guayaquil, Callao, Antofagasta, San Antonio, Arica, Callao, Buenaventura, Panama Canal, Cristóbal, New Orleans, 48-day round trip, US$4,800-5,280 pp.

CUSTOMS

Personal effects, a litre of spirits and a reasonable amount of perfume are admitted free of duty.

ON ARRIVAL

● **Clothing**
Spring clothing for Quito (mornings and evenings are cold). In Guayaquil tropical or light-weight clothes. Most Latin Americans, if they can afford it, devote great care to their clothes and appearance; it is appreciated if visitors do likewise. An unkempt look is said to attract a 'gringo tax' and reduce friendliness. Buying clothing locally can help you to look less like a tourist. A medium weight shawl with some wool content is recommended for women: it can double as pillow, light blanket, bathrobe or sunscreen as required. For men, a smart jacket can be very useful. Laundering is excellent.

● **Courtesy**
Remember that politeness – even a little ceremoniousness – is much appreciated. In this connection professional or business cards are useful. Men should always remove any headgear and say "con permiso" when entering offices, and be prepared to shake hands; always say "Buenos días" (until midday) or "Buenas tardes" and wait for a reply before proceeding further. Always remember that the traveller from abroad has enjoyed greater advantages in life than most

Latin American minor officials, and should be friendly and courteous in consequence. Never be impatient; do not criticize situations in public: the officials may know more English than you think and they can certainly interpret gestures and facial expressions. Politeness can be a liability, however, in some situations; most Latin Americans are disorderly queuers. In commercial transactions (buying a meal, goods in a shop, etc) politeness should be accompanied by firmness, and always ask the price first.

Politeness should also be extended to street traders; saying "No, gracias" with a smile is better than an arrogant dismissal. Whether you give money to beggars is a personal matter, but your decision should be influenced by whether a person is begging out of need or trying to cash in on the tourist trail. In the former case, local people giving may provide an indication. Giving money to children is a separate issue, upon which most agree: don't do it. There are occasions where giving food in a restaurant may be appropriate, but first inform yourself of local practice.

● **Official time**
Local time is 5 hrs behind GMT (Galápagos, 6 hrs behind.)

● **Photography**
Pre-paid Kodak slide film cannot be developed in South America; it is also very hard to find. Kodachrome is almost impossible to buy. Some travellers (but not all) have advised against mailing exposed films home; either take them with you, or have them developed, but not printed, once you have checked the laboratory's quality. Note that postal authorities may use less sensitive equipment for X-ray screening than the airports do. Modern controlled X-ray machines are supposed to be safe for any speed of film, but it is worth trying to avoid X-ray as the doses are cumulative. Many airport officials will allow film to be passed outside X-ray arches; they may also hand-check a suitcase with a large quantity of film if asked politely.

Developing black and white film is a problem. Often it is shoddily machine-proc-essed and the negatives are ruined. Ask the store if you can see an example of their laboratory's work and if they hand-develop.

Exposed film can be protected in humid areas by putting it in a balloon and tying a knot. Similarly keeping your camera in a plastic bag may reduce the effects of humidity.

● **Police**
Whereas in Europe and North America we are accustomed to law enforcement on a systematic basis, in general, enforcement in Latin America is achieved by periodic campaigns. The most typical is a round-up of criminals in the cities just before Christmas. In December, therefore, you may well be asked for identification at any time, and if you cannot produce it, you will be jailed. If a visitor is jailed his/her friends should provide food every day. This is especially important for people on a diet, such as diabetics. In the event of a vehicle accident in which anyone is injured, all drivers involved are automatically detained until blame has been established, and this does not usually take less than 2 weeks.

Never offer a bribe unless you are fully conversant with the customs of the country. Wait until the official makes the suggestion, or offer money in some form which is apparently not bribery, eg 'In our country we have a system of on-the-spot fines (*multas de inmediato*). Is there a similar system here?' Do not assume that an official who accepts a bribe is prepared to do anything else that is illegal. You bribe him to persuade him to do his job, or to persuade him not to do it, or to do it more quickly, or more slowly. You do not bribe him to do something which is against the law. The mere suggestion would make him very upset. If an official suggests that a bribe must be paid before you can proceed on your way, be patient (assuming you have the time) and he may relent.

● **Safety**
Although Ecuador has been generally one of the safer countries in the region, there have been reports of increased crime and violence: police searches are now more frequent. If your luggage is searched, make

sure that you are present during the search: women travelling alone, especially in Otavalo, should beware of police officers who ask to look at their passport and then insist on taking them to a police station. Do not leave valuables strewn about your hotel room. Theft and mugging are on the increase throughout Quito, particularly in the old city, climbing Panecillo, the Antenna Loma on Pichincha; also Tungurahua and on the beaches at Manta and near Atacames. Guayaquil has long been plagued with gang violence, which is also present in the city of Esmeraldas, caution is also advised at nearby beaches. Robberies on city buses, even in the morning, and intercity bus holdups are now more common. Beware of pickpockets wherever there are crowds, but especially in markets and at bus stations. Also beware of theft of luggage stored on interprovincial bus roofs. There have been guerrilla incursions from Colombia and drug related violence in the northern jungle province of Sucumbios, but many of the public safety problems are worst in the big cities while the countryside has remained generally safer and more tranquil. See *Latin American Travel Advisor* above for safety information.

● **General tips**
Keep all documents secure; hide your main cash supply in different places or under your clothes: extra pockets sewn inside shirts and trousers, pockets closed with a zip or safety pin, moneybelts (best worn below the waist rather than outside or at it or around the neck), neck or leg pouches, a thin chain for attaching a purse to your bag or under your clothes and elasticated support bandages for keeping money and cheques above the elbow or below the knee have been repeatedly recommended (the last by John Hatt in *The Tropical Traveller*). Keep cameras in bags (preferably with a chain or wire in the strap to defeat the slasher) or briefcases; take spare spectacles (eyeglasses); don't wear wrist-watches or jewellery. If you wear a shoulder-bag in a market, carry it in front of you. Backpacks are vulnerable to slashers: a good idea is to cover the pack with a sack (a plastic one will also keep out rain and dust) with maybe a layer of wire netting

between, or make an inner frame of chicken wire. Use a pack which is lockable at its base.

Be wary of 'plainclothes policemen'; insist on seeing identification and on going to the police station by main roads. Do not hand over your identification (or money – which he should not need to be anyway) until you are at the station. On no account take them directly back to your lodgings. Be even more suspicious if he seeks confirmation of his status from a passer-by. If someone tries to bribe you, insist on a receipt. If attacked, remember your assailants may well be armed, and try not to resist.

It is best, if you can trust your hotel, to leave any valuables you don't need in safe-deposit there, when sightseeing locally. Always keep an inventory of what you have deposited. If you don't trust the hotel, lock everything in your pack and secure that in your room (some people take eyelet-screws for padlocking cupboards or drawers). If you lose valuables, always report to the police and note details of the report – for insurance purposes.

Never accept food, drink, sweets or cigarettes from unknown fellow-travellers on buses or trains. They may be drugged, and you would wake up hours later without your belongings.

● **Tipping**
In restaurants, 10% usually in the bill (in cheaper restaurants, tipping is uncommon – but obviously welcome!). Taxi, nil. Airport and railway porters, US$0.10-0.20, according to number of suitcases; cloakroom attendants, US$0.05, hairdressers, 20%.

● **Travelling alone**
First time exposure to a country where sections of the population live in extreme poverty or squalor and may even be starving can cause odd psychological reactions in visitors. So can the exceptional curiosity extended to visitors, especially women. Simply be prepared for this and try not to over-react. The following hints have mainly been supplied by women, but most apply to any single traveller. When you set out, err on the side of caution until your instincts have adjusted to the customs of a new

culture. If, as a single woman, you can befriend a local woman, you will learn much more about the country you are visiting. Unless actively avoiding foreigners like yourself, don't go too far from the beaten track; there is a very definite 'gringo trail' which you can join, or follow, if seeking company.

This can be helpful when looking for safe accommodation, especially if arriving after dark (which is best avoided). Remember that for a single woman a taxi at night can be as dangerous as wandering around on her own. At borders dress as smartly as possible. Travelling by train is a good way

Insurance tips

Insurance companies have tightened up considerably over recent years and it is now almost impossible to claim successfully if you have not followed procedures closely. The problem is that these often involve dealing with the country's red tape which can lead to some inconvenience at best and to some quite long delays at worst. There is no substitute for suitable precautions against petty crime.

The level of insurance that you carry is often dictated by the sums of medical insurance which you carry. It is inevitably the highest if you go through the USA. Also don't forget to obtain sports extensions if you are going to go diving, rafting, climbing etc. Most policies do not cover very high levels of baggage/cash. Don't forget to check whether you can claim on your household insurance. They often have worldwide all risks extensions. Most policies exclude manual work whilst away although working in bars or restaurants is usually alright.

Here are our tips: they apply to most types of policies but always check the details of your own policy before you leave.
1. Take the policy with you (a photocopy will do but make sure it is a complete one)
2. Do not travel against medical advice. It will invalidate the medical insurance part of the cover.
3. There is a 24 hour medical emergency service helpline associated with your insurance. You need to contact them if you require in-patient hospital treatment or you need to return home early. The telephone number is printed on the policy. Make sure you note the time of the call, the person you were talking to and get a reference number. Even better get a receipt from the telephone company showing the number you called. Should you need to be airlifted home, this is always arranged through the insurance company's representative and the hospital authorities. Ironically this can lead to quite intense discussions which you will not be aware of: the local hospital is often quite keen to keep you!
4. If you have to cancel your trip for whatever reason, contact your travel agent, tour operator or airline without delay.
5. If your property is damage by an airline, report it immediately and always within 3 days and get a "property irregularity report" from them.
6. Claims for baggage left unattended are very rarely settled unless they were left in a securely locked hotel room, apartment etc; locked in the boot of a car and there is evidence of a forced entry; cash is carried on your person or is in a locked safe or security box.
7. All loss must be reported to the police and/or hotel authorities within 24 hours of discovery and a written report obtained.
8. If medical attention is received for injury or sickness, a medical certificate showing its nature must be obtained. Keep all receipts as they will be needed to substantiate the claim.

to meet locals, but buses are much easier for a person alone; on major routes your seat is often reserved and your luggage can usually be locked in the hold. It is easier for men to take the friendliness of locals at face value; women may be subject to much unwanted attention. To help minimize this, do not wear suggestive clothing and, advises Alex Rossi of Jawa Timur, Indonesia, do not flirt. By wearing a wedding ring, carrying a photograph of your 'husband' and 'children', and saying that your 'husband' is close at hand, you may dissuade an aspiring suitor. If politeness fails, do not feel bad about showing offence and departing. When accepting a social invitation, make sure that someone knows the address and the time you left. Ask if you can bring a friend (even if you do not intend to do so). A good rule is always to act with confidence, as though you know where you are going, even if you do not. Someone who looks lost is more likely to attract unwanted attention.

● **Voltage**
110 volts, 60 cycles, AC throughout Ecuador. Very low wattage bulbs in many hotel rooms, keen readers are advised to carry a bright bulb.

● **Weights and measures**
The metric system is generally used in foreign trade and must be used in legal documents. English measures are understood in the hardware and textile trades. Spanish measures are often used in the retail trade.

● **What to take**
Everybody has his/her own list, but those most often mentioned include air cushions for slatted seats, inflatable travel pillow for neck support, strong shoes (and remember that footwear over 9½ English size, or 42 European size, is difficult to obtain); a small first-aid kit and handbook, fully waterproof

Writing to the editor

Many people write to us - with corrections, new information, or simply comments. If you want to let us know something, we would be delighted to hear from you. Please give us as precise information as possible, quoting the edition and page number of the Handbook you are using and send as early in the year as you can. Your help will be greatly appreciated, especially by other travellers. In return we will send you details about our special guidebook offer.

For hotels and restaurants, please let us know:

- each establishment's name, address, phone and fax number
- number of rooms, whether a/c or air-cooled, attached (clean?) bathroom
- location - how far from the station or bus stand, or distance (walking time) from a prominent landmark
- if it's not already on one of our maps, can you place it?
- your comments - either good or bad - as to why it is distinctive
- tariff cards
- local transport used

For places of interest:

- location
- entry, camera charge
- access - by whatever means of transport is most appropriate, eg time of main buses or trains to and from the site, journey time, fare
- facilities - nearby drinks stalls, restaurants, for the disabled
- any problems, eg steep climb, wildlife, unofficial guides
- opening hours
- site guides

368 Information for travellers

top clothing, waterproof treatment for leather footwear, wax earplugs (which are almost impossible to find outside large cities) and airline-type eye mask to help you sleep in noisy and poorly curtained hotel rooms, sandals (rubber-thong Japanese-type or other – can be worn in showers to avoid athlete's foot), a polyethylene sheet 2m x 1m to cover possibly infested beds and shelter your luggage, polyethylene bags of varying sizes (up to heavy duty rubbish bag size) with ties, a toilet bag you can tie round your waist, if you use an electric shaver, take a rechargeable type, a sheet sleeping-bag and pillow-case or separate pillow-case – in some countries they are not changed often in cheap hotels; a 1½-2m piece of 100% cotton can be used as a towel, a bedsheet, beach towel, makeshift curtain and wrap; a mosquito net (or a hammock with a fitted net), a straw hat which can be rolled or flattened and reconstituted after 15 mins soaking in water, a clothes line, a nailbrush (useful for scrubbing dirt off clothes as well as off oneself), a vacuum flask, a water bottle, a small dual-voltage immersion heater, a small dual-voltage (or battery-driven) electric fan, a light nylon waterproof shopping bag, a universal bath- and basin-plug of the flanged type that will fit any waste-pipe (or improvise one from a sheet of thick rubber), string, velcro, electrical insulating tape, large penknife preferably with tin and bottle openers, scissors and corkscrew – the famous Swiss Army range has been repeatedly recommended (for knife sharpening, go to a butcher's shop), alarm clock or watch, candle, torch (flashlight) – especially one that will clip on to a pocket or belt, pocket mirror, pocket calculator, an adaptor and flex to enable you to take power from an electric-light socket (the Edison screw type is the most commonly used). Remember not to throw away spent batteries containing mercury or cadmium; take them home to be disposed of, or recycled properly.

Useful medicaments are given in the Health section (page 390); to these might be added some lip salve with sun protection, and pre-moistened wipes (such as 'Wet Ones'). Always carry toilet paper. Natural fabric sticking plasters, as well as being long-lasting, are much appreciated as gifts. Dental floss can be used for backpack repairs, in addition to its original purpose. **Never** carry firearms. Their possession could land you in serious trouble.

A note for **contact lens wearers**: lens solution can be difficult to find, especially outside major cities. Ask for it in a chemist/pharmacy, rather than an optician's.

ON DEPARTURE

● **Airport tax**
There is a 10% tax on international air tickets for flights originating in Ecuador, regardless of where bought, and 12% on domestic tickets, and a tax of US$25 on all passengers departing on international flights (except those who stay under 24 hrs in the country).

WHERE TO STAY

● **Hotels**
Outside the main towns; almost standard prices are charged of US$2.50-4 pp (without bath) in a *pensión*, *residencial*, or hotel (where this is the minimum charge). One can bargain at cheaper *pensiones* and *residenciales*. Outside the provincial capitals and the resorts of Salinas and Playas, there are few higher-class hotels. Service of 10% and tax of 10% are added to 1st and 2nd class hotel and restaurant bills. The cheaper hotels charge at most 5%, if anything. Hotel owners tend to try and let their less attractive rooms first, but they are not insulted if you ask for a bigger room, better beds or a quieter area. The difference is often marked.

Note that in the text "with bath" usually means 'with shower and toilet', not 'with bath tub'. Remember, cheaper hotels don't always supply soap, towels and toilet paper; in colder (higher) regions they may not supply enough blankets, so take your own or a sleeping bag.

NB The electric showers used in innumerable hotels should be checked for obvious flaws in the wiring; try not to touch the rose while it is producing hot water.

● **Cockroaches**
These are ubiquitous and unpleasant, but

not dangerous. Take some insecticide powder if staying in cheap hotels; Baygon (Bayer) has been recommended. Stuff toilet paper in any holes in walls that you may suspect of being parts of cockroach runs.

● **Toilets**
Many hotels, restaurants and bars have inadequate water supplies. **Almost without exception used toilet paper should not be flushed down the pan, but placed in the receptacle provided**. This applies even in quite expensive hotels. Failing to observe this custom will block the pan or drain, a considerable health risk. It is quite common for people to stand on the toilet seat (facing the wall – easier to balance), as they do in Asia. If you are concerned about the hygiene of the facility, put paper on the seat.

● **Camping**
White gas, like US Coleman fuel, is not available. Campers should be sure that their stove will either burn Camping Gas, a compressed gas which comes in a non-refillable cylinder, kerosene, or unleaded car gas/petrol (generally an acceptable substitute for white gas). For stoves, kerosene is known as 'kerex' and is available at many rural petrol stations and in outdoor markets in towns and cities outside Quito; it is, however, very impure. Gasoline is better. Pure alcohol fuel is sold in hardware stores, *ferreterías*, take your own bottle or ask for it 'en bolsa' (in a plastic bag). See also page 116.

Obey the following rules for 'wild' camping: (1) arrive in daylight and pitch your tent as it gets dark; (2) ask permission to camp from the parish priest, or the fire chief, or the police, or a farmer regarding his own property; (3) never ask a group of people – especially young people; (4) never camp on a beach (because of sandflies and thieves). If you can't get information from anyone, camp in a spot where you can't be seen from the nearest inhabited place, or road, and make sure no one saw you go there.

FOOD AND DRINK

FOOD
The cuisine varies extensively with region. The following are some typical dishes worth trying. **In the highlands**: *locro de papas* (potato and cheese soup), *mote* (corn burst with alkali, a staple in the region around Cuenca, but used in a variety of dishes in the Sierra), *caldo de patas* (cowheel soup with *mote*), *llapingachos* (fried potato and cheese patties), *empanadas de morocho* (fried snacks: a ground corn shell filled with meat), *morocho* is a drink made from *mote*, milk, sugar and cinnamon, *sancocho de yuca* (vegetable soup with manioc root), roast *cuy* (guinea pig), *fritada* (fried pork), *hornado* (roast pork), *humitas* (tender ground corn steamed in corn leaves), and *quimbolitos* (similar to *humitas* but prepared with corn flour and steamed in banana leaves). *Humitas* and *quimbolitos* come in both sweet and savoury varieties.

On the coast: *empanadas de verde* (fried snacks: a ground plantain shell filled with cheese, meat or shrimp), *sopa de bola de verde* (plantain dumpling soup),

Hotel prices

Our hotel price ranges, including taxes and service charges but without meals unless stated, are as follows:

L1	Over US$200	L2	US$151-200	L3	US$101-150
A1	US$81-100	A2	US$61-80	A3	US$46-60
B	US$31-45	C	US$21-30	D	US$12-20
E	US$7-11	F	US$4-6	G	Up to US$3

NB Prices are for double rooms, except in **F** and **G** ranges where the price is almost always per person.

Other abbreviations used in the book (apart from pp = per person; a/c = air conditioned; rec = recommended; T = telephone; TCs = travellers' cheques; s/n = "sin número", no street number; p = piso – floor, in Spanish-speaking countries) should be self-explanatory.

ceviche (marinaded fish or seafood, popular everywhere, see below), *encocadas* (dishes prepared with coconut milk, may be shrimp, fish, etc, very popular in the province of Esmeraldas), *cocadas* (sweets made with coconut), *viche* (fish or seafood soup made with ground peanuts), and *patacones* (thick fried plantain chips served as a side dish).

In Oriente: dishes prepared with yuca (manioc or cassava root) and a wide variety of river fish.

Throughout the country, if economizing ask for the set meal in restaurants, *almuerzo* at lunch time, *merienda* in the evening – very cheap and wholesome; it costs US$1-2. *Fanesca*, a fish soup with beans, many grains, ground peanuts and more, sold in Easter Week, is very filling. *Ceviche*, marinated fish or seafood which is usually served with popcorn and roasted maize, is very popular throughout Ecuador but has acquired a sinister reputation among visitors as a possible means of transmission of cholera. In fact, only *ceviche de pescado* (fish) and *ceviche de concha* (clams) which are marinated raw, potentially pose this hazard. The other varieties of *ceviche* such as *camarón* (shrimp/prawn) and *langostino* (jumbo shrimp/king prawn) all of which are cooked before being marinated, are generally safe delicacies (check the cleanliness of the establishment). *Langosta* (lobster) is an increasingly endangered species but continues to be illegally fished. It is out of season until the year 2000, please be conscientious. Ecuadorean food is not particularly spicy. However, in most homes and restaurants, the meal is accompanied by a small bowl of *aji* (hot pepper sauce) which may vary greatly in potency. Those unfamiliar with this condiment are advised to exercise caution at first. *Colada* is a generic name which can refer to cream soups or sweet beverages. In addition to the prepared foods mentioned above, Ecuador offers large variety of delicious temperate and tropical fruits, some of which are unique to South America. Chocolate lovers can try the Superior and Rico bars, good quality, excellent value.

Vegetarians should be able to list all the foods they cannot eat; saying "Soy vegetariano/a" (I'm a vegetarian) or "no como carne" (I don't eat meat) is often not enough.

DRINK

Argentine and Chilean wines are available in the larger cities and cheaper than European or US ones. The best fruit drinks are *naranjilla*, *maracuyá*, *taxo* and *mora* (blackberries), but note that fruit juices are often made with unboiled water. Main beers available are Pilsener and Club. Good *aguardiente* (unmatured rum, Cristal is rec), *paico* and *trago de caña*. The usual soft drinks, known as *colas*, are available. Instant coffee or liquid concentrate is common, so ask for *café puro* if you want real coffee.

GETTING AROUND

AIR TRANSPORT

The local airlines Saeta, SAN, TAME and Aerogal operate internal flights between the main cities. TAME and SAN fly to the Galápagos; both have received favourable reports on reliability and baggage control. Also local airline Cedta operating Santa Rosa, near Machala-Guayaquil. Ecuavia and Icaro operate charter flights. There are air taxis (Cessnas or Bonanzas) to anywhere you want to go, also helicopters. On internal flights passengers may have to disembark at intermediate stops and check in, even though they have booked all the way to the final destination of the plane. Seats are not assigned on internal flights, except to the Galápagos. *Pre-chequeo* procedures speed up boarding as passes are issued up to 8 days in advance. If you miss the plane you need half a day and US$5 to revalidate your ticket for another flight. Your space on the plane is held until loading.

LAND TRANSPORT

● **Trains**
Although the Quito-Riobamba-Guayaquil and Ibarra-San Lorenzo stretches were used for passenger services in 1996, the future of all trains was under debate (a combination of severely decaying infrastructure, a lack of money and possible privatization). In 1995 the Sibambe-Cuenca line was per-

manently closed, a 2-tier price system was introduced for Ecuadoreans and foreigners, and a steam locomotive service for tourists started between Quito and Cotopaxi National Park. Rail services are often unreliable, depending on weather.

● Bus

Bus travel has improved greatly and is generally more convenient, and cheaper, than in other Andean countries. Since most buses are small they fill up and leave at frequent intervals. A modernization of the intercity bus fleet started in 1994, when several companies acquired luxury a/c units for use on their longer routes. Many new luxury buses are in service; all are called Volvo, even if they are other makes. Fares for these are higher and some companies are again setting up their own stations, away from the main bus terminals, exclusively for the new buses. The length of paved highway is developing rapidly, inc Quito-Guayaquil, Quito-Riobamba, Quito-Tulcán, Quito-Cuenca, Guayaquil-Cuenca, Guayaquil-Riobamba, Riobamba-Baños and the lowland (Costa) road Huaquillas-Machala-Guayaquil-Babahoyo-Santo Domingo-Esmeraldas. New tolls are due to be introduced on main highways.

● Motoring

Driving in Ecuador has been described as 'an experience', partly because of unexpected potholes and other obstructions and the lack of road signs, partly because of local drivers' tendency to use the middle of the road. Some surfaces at high altitude are slippery and some, that appear paved, are crude oil sprayed onto compacted gravel. Beware the bus drivers, who often drive very fast and rather recklessly (passengers also please note). Driving at night is not rec, especially in rural areas where speed humps to reduce speed in villages have become places for robbers to lurk.

'Extra' gasoline, 82 octane, costs US$1.20/US gallon, Eco 85 (85 octane unleaded, also known as *gasolina verde*, although it is coloured red rather than green), US$1.25, Super SP (92 octane unleaded), US$1.40, diesel US$1.20. Unleaded gasoline is becoming increasingly common

throughout the country although it may still be unavailable in the more remote rural areas and in parts of Oriente. Super is only available in the main cities.

The road maps published by Nelson Gómez are probably the most useful (see under **Maps** below).

Preparation Preparing your own car for the journey is largely a matter of common sense: obviously any part that is not in first class condition should be replaced. It's well worth installing extra heavy-duty shock-absorbers (such as Spax or Koni) before starting out, because a long trip on rough roads in a heavily laden car will give heavy wear. Fit tubes on 'tubeless' tyres, since air plugs for tubeless tyres are hard to find, and if you bend the rim on a pothole, the tyre will not hold air. Take spare tubes, and an extra spare tyre. Also take spare plugs, fan-belts, radiator hoses and headlamp bulbs; even though local equivalents can easily be found in cities, it is wise to take spares for those occasions late at night or in remote areas when you might need them. You can also change the fanbelt after a stretch of long, hot driving to prevent wear (eg after 15,000 km/10,000 miles). If your vehicle has more than one fanbelt, always replace them all at the same time (make sure you have the necessary tools if doing it yourself). If your car has sophisticated electrics, spare 'black boxes' for the ignition and fuel injection are advisable, plus a spare voltage regulator or the appropriate diodes for the alternator, and elements for the fuel, air and oil filters if these are not a common type. (Some drivers take a spare alternator of the correct amperage, especially if the regulator is incorporated into the alternator.) Dirty fuel is a frequent problem, so be prepared to change filters more often than you would at home: in a diesel car you will need to check the sediment bowl often, too. An extra in-line fuel filter is a good idea if feasible (although harder to find, metal canister type is preferable to plastic), and for travel on dusty roads an oil bath air filter is best for a diesel car. It is wise to carry a spade, jumper cables, tow rope and an air pump. Fit tow hooks to both sides of the vehicle frame. A 12 volt neon light for camping and repairs will be invaluable.

Spare fuel containers should be steel and not plastic, and a siphon pipe is essential for those places where fuel is sold out of the drum. Take a 10 litre water container for self and vehicle.

Security Apart from the mechanical aspects, spare no ingenuity in making your car secure. Use heavy chain and padlocks to chain doors shut, fit security catches on windows, remove interior window winders (so that a hand reaching in from a forced vent cannot open the window). All these will help, but none is foolproof. Anything on the outside – wing mirrors, spot lamps, motifs etc – is likely to be stolen too. So are wheels if not secured by locking nuts. Try never to leave the car unattended except in a locked garage or guarded parking space. Remove all belongings and leave the empty glove compartment open when the car is unattended. Also lock the clutch or accelerator to the steering wheel with a heavy, obvious chain or lock. Street children will generally protect your car fiercely in exchange for a tip. Be sure to note down key numbers and carry spares of the most important ones (but don't keep all spares inside the vehicle).

Documents Always carry your passport and driving licence. You also need the registration document in the name of the driver, or, in the case of a car registered in someone else's name, a notarized letter of authorization.

There are police checks on all the roads leading out of main towns and you can be in serious trouble if you are unable to present your documents. A *carnet de passage* (or *libreta de pasaje*, known locally as a *tríptico*) is no longer required to enter Ecuador with a car or motorcycle, but many have found their passage eased by being able to present one.

According to the RAC in the UK there are three recognized documents for taking a vehicle into South America: a *carnet de passages* issued by the Fedération Internationale de l'Automobile (FIA – Paris), a *carnet de passages* issued by the Alliance Internationale de Tourisme (AIT-Geneva), and the *Libreta de Pasos por Aduana* issued by the Federación Interamericana de Tour-

ing y Automóvil Clubs (FITAC). The *libreta*, a 10-page book of three-part passes for customs, should be available from any South American automobile club member of FITAC; cost seems to be US$200, half refundable. The *carnet de passages* is issued only in the country where the vehicle is registered (in the UK it costs £65 for 25 pages, £55 for 10 pages, valid 12 months, either bank indemnity or insurance indemnity, half of the premium refundable value of the vehicle and countries to be visited required), available from the RAC or the AA. In the USA the AAA seems not to issue the *carnet*, although the HQ in Washington DC may give advice. It is available from the Canadian Automobile Association (1775 Courtwood Crescent, Ottawa, K2C 3JZ, T 613-226-7631, F 613-225-7383) for Canadian and US citizens, cost C$450; full details obtainable from the CAA.

Insurance for the vehicle against accident, damage or theft is best arranged in the country of origin, but it is getting increasingly difficult to find agencies who offer this service. It is very expensive to insure against accident and theft, especially as you should take into account the value of the car increased by duties calculated in real (ie non devaluing) terms. If the car is stolen or written off you will be required to pay very high import duty on its value. Get the legally required minimum cover, not expensive, as soon as you can, because if you should be involved in an accident and are uninsured, your car could be confiscated. If anyone is hurt, do not pick them up (you may become liable). Seek assistance from the nearest police station or hospital if you are able to do so.

If intending to buy a car or motorcycle, you must have an international drivers licence (bring one from home, costs US$70 in Ecuador). Use a lawyer to help sort out ownership documentation. **NB** Vehicles imported from Peru cannot be sold in Ecuador.

Shipping Shipping in a vehicle through Guayaquil is also hazardous; you will be charged by customs for every day the car is left there and will need assistance from an agent. Spare cash may be needed. Manta is a smaller, more relaxed and efficient alternative port. If bringing in a motorcycle by air it can take over a week to get it out of customs. You need a customs agent, who can be found around the main customs building near the airport, fix the price in advance. Best to accompany the agent all the time and a letter from the Ecuadorean Automobile Club (ANETA) can be helpful. If you need boxes/cartons to send bicycles home, *Global Transportes*, Veintimilla 878 y Av Amazonas, p 3, might be able to help you (German-run).

● **Car hire**

Hire rates are given under Quito. Be sure to check the car's condition, not forgetting things like wheelnuts. Also make sure it has good ground clearance. Always make sure the car is securely garaged at night.

Car hire insurance Some car hire firms do not have adequate insurance policies and you will have to pay heavily in the event of an accident. Check exactly what the hirer's insurance policy covers. In many cases it will only protect you against minor bumps and scrapes, not major accidents, nor 'natural' damage (eg flooding). Ask if extra cover is available. Also find out, if using a credit card, whether the card automatically includes insurance. Beware of being billed for scratches which were on the vehicle before you hired it.

● **Motorcycling**

People are generally very amicable to motorcyclists and you can make many friends by returning friendship to those who show an interest in you.

The machine It should be off road capable: a good choice would be the BMW R80/100/GS for its rugged and simple design and reliable shaft drive, but a Kawasaki KLR 650s, Honda Transalp/Dominator, or the ubiquitous Yamaha XT600 Tenere would also be suitable. A road bike can go most places an off road bike can go at the cost of greater effort.

Preparations Fit heavy duty front fork springs and the best quality rebuildable shock absorber you can afford (Ohlins, White Power). Fit lockable luggage such as Krausers (reinforce luggage frames) or make some detachable aluminium pan-

niers. Fit a tank bag and tank panniers for better weight distribution. A large capacity fuel tank (Acerbis), +300 mile/480 km range is essential if going off the beaten track. A washable air filter is a good idea (K&N), also fuel filters, fueltap rubber seals and smaller jets for high altitude Andean motoring. A good set of trails-type tyres as well as a high mudguard are useful. Get to know the bike before you go, ask the dealers in your country what goes wrong with it and arrange a link whereby you can get parts flown out to you. If riding a chain driven bike, a fully enclosed chaincase is useful. A hefty bash plate/sump guard is invaluable.

Spares Reduce service intervals by half if driving in severe conditions. Take oil filters, fork and shock seals, tubes, a good manual, spare cables (taped into position), a plug cap and spare plug lead. A spare electronic ignition is a good idea, try and buy a second hand one and make arrangements to have parts sent out to you. A first class tool kit is a must and if riding a bike with a chain then a spare set of sprockets and an 'o' ring chain should be carried. Spare brake and clutch levers should also be taken as these break easily in a fall. Parts are few and far between, but mechanics are skilled at making do and can usually repair things. Castrol oil can be bought everywhere and relied upon.

Take a puncture repair kit and tyre levers. Find out about any weak spots on the bike and improve them. Get the book for international dealer coverage from your manufacturer, but don't rely on it. They frequently have few or no parts for modern, large machinery.

Clothes and equipment A tough waterproof jacket, comfortable strong boots, gloves and a helmet with which you can use glass goggles (Halycon) which will not scratch and wear out like a plastic visor. The best quality tent and camping gear that you can afford and a petrol stove which runs on bike fuel is helpful.

Security Try not to leave a fully laden bike on its own. An Abus D or chain will keep the bike secure. A cheap alarm gives you peace of mind if you leave the bike outside a hotel at night. Most hotels will allow you to bring the bike inside. Look for hotels that have a courtyard or more secure parking and never leave luggage on the bike overnight or whilst unattended.

Documents Passport, International Driving Licence, bike registration document are necessary. Riders fare much better with a *carnet de passages* than without it.

● Cycling

At first glance a bicycle may not appear to be the most obvious vehicle for a major journey, but given ample time and reasonable energy it most certainly is the best. It can be ridden, carried by almost every form of transport from an aeroplane to a canoe, and can even be lifted across one's shoulders over short distances. Cyclists can be the envy of travellers using more orthodox transport, since they can travel at their own pace, explore more remote regions and meet people who are not normally in contact with tourists.

Choosing a bicycle The choice of bicycle depends on the type and length of expedition being undertaken and on the terrain and road surfaces likely to be encountered. Unless you are planning a journey almost exclusively on paved roads – when a high quality touring bike such as a Dawes Super Galaxy would probably suffice – a mountain bike is strongly recommended. The good quality ones (and the cast iron rule is **never** to skimp on quality) are incredibly tough and rugged, with low gear ratios for difficult terrain, wide tyres with plenty of tread for good road-holding, cantilever brakes, and a low centre of gravity for improved stability. Although touring bikes, and to a lesser extent mountain bikes, and spares are available in the larger cities, remember that most indigenous manufactured goods are shoddy and rarely last. Buy everything you possibly can before you leave home.

Bicycle equipment A small but comprehensive tool kit (to include chain rivet and crank removers, a spoke key and possibly a block remover), a spare tyre and inner tubes, a puncture repair kit with plenty of extra patches and glue, a set of brake blocks, brake and gear cables and all types of nuts and bolts, at least 12 spokes (best taped to the chain stay), a light oil for the chain (eg Finish-Line Teflon Dry-Lube), tube of waterproof grease, a pump secured by a pump lock, a Blackburn parking block (a most invaluable accessory, cheap and virtually weightless), a cyclometer, a loud bell, and a secure lock and chain. *Richard's Bicycle Book* makes useful reading for even the most mechanically minded.

Luggage and equipment Strong and waterproof front and back panniers are a must. When packed these are likely to be heavy and should be carried on the strongest racks available. Poor quality racks have ruined many a journey for they take incredible strain on unpaved roads. A top bag cum rucksack (eg Carradice) makes a good addition for use on and off the bike. A Cannondale front bag is good for maps, camera, compass, altimeter, notebook and small tape-recorder. (Other rec panniers are Ortlieb – front and back – which is waterpoof and almost 'sandproof', Mac-Pac, Madden and Karimoor.) 'Gaffa' tape is excellent for protecting vulnerable parts of panniers and for carrying out all manner of repairs.

All equipment and clothes should be packed in plastic bags to give extra protection against dust and rain. (Also protect all documents, etc carried close to the body from sweat.) Always take the minimum clothing. It's better to buy extra items en route when you find you need them. Generally it is best to carry several layers of thin light clothes than fewer heavy, bulky ones. Always keep one set of dry clothes, including long trousers, to put on at the end of the day. The incredibly light, strong, waterproof and wind resistant goretex jacket and overtrousers are invaluable. Training shoes can be used for both cycling and walking.

Useful tips Wind, not hills is the enemy of the cyclist. Try to make the best use of the times of day when there is little; mornings tend to be best but there is no steadfast rule. Take care to avoid dehydration, by drinking regularly. In hot, dry areas with limited supplies of water, be sure to carry an ample supply. For food, carry the staples (sugar, salt, dried milk, tea, coffee, porridge oats, raisins, dried soups, etc) and supplemented these with whatever local foods can be found in the markets. Give your bicycle a thorough daily check for loose nuts or bolts or bearings. See that all parts run smoothly. A good chain should last 2,000 miles, 3,200 km or more but be sure to keep it as clean as possible – an old toothbrush is good for this – and to oil it lightly from time to time. Remember that thieves are attracted to towns and cities, so when sight-seeing, try to leave your bicycle with someone such as a café owner or a priest. Country people tend to be more honest and are usually friendly and very inquisitive. However, don't take unnecessary risks; always see that your bicycle is secure (most hotels will allow bikes to be kept in rooms). In more remote regions dogs can be vicious; carry a stick or some small stones to frighten them off. Traffic on main roads can be a nightmare; it is usually far more rewarding to keep to the smaller roads or to paths if they exist. Most towns have a bicycle shop of some description, but it is best to do your own repairs and adjustments whenever possible.

The Expedition Advisory Centre, administered by the Royal Geographical Society, 1, Kensington Gore, London SW7 2AR has published a useful monograph entitled *Bicycle Expeditions*, by Paul Vickers. Published in March 1990, it is available direct from the Centre, price £6.50 (postage extra if outside the UK). (In the UK there is also the Cyclist's Touring Club, CTC, Cotterell House, 69 Meadrow, Godalming, Surrey, GU7 3HS, T 01483-417217, e-mail cycling@ctc.org.uk, for touring, and technical information.)

Most cyclists agree that the main danger comes from other traffic. A rearview mirror has been frequently recommended to forewarn you of vehicles which are too close behind. You also need to watch out for oncoming, overtaking vehicles, unstable loads on trucks, protruding loads etc. Make yourself conspicuous by wearing bright clothing and a helmet.

● Hitchhiking
Hitchhiking on the main roads is reported to be easy in the N, but nearly impossible S of Riobamba, and it can be very cold in the mountains in the back of a truck (when hitching, it is common to pay a small sum). In the arid S the unpaved roads are dusty; use a wet cotton handkerchief to filter the air you breathe. Whether hitching or driving always take plenty of drinking water. Be judicious when accepting a ride or picking up hitchhikers, armed car robberies by the latter are increasingly common.

COMMUNICATIONS

● Language
The official language is Spanish. English and other European languages are spoken in many establishments catering for tourists in Quito and popular tourist destinations. Away from these places, knowledge of Spanish is essential.

● Newspapers
The main newspapers are *El Comercio*, *Hoy*, *Tiempo*, and *Ultimas Noticias*, in Quito; *Expreso*, *El Telégrafo*, *El Universo* (with good international news), *La Prensa*, *La Razón* and *Extra* (an afternoon paper), in Guayaquil; *El Mercurio*, in Cuenca; *La Opinión del Sur*, in Loja; and *El Espectador*, in Riobamba. *City* is a free weekly magazine in Quito, with tourist information and details of what's on; a similar magazine is *The Explorer*.

● Postal services
Many post offices away from Quito may not know the foreign rates (20g airmail to the Americas US$0.65, Europe and rest of world US$0.84) and give incorrect ones. For US$1.15 you can certify your letters and parcels; ask for 'con certificado' when you buy stamps, so that they are stamped separately. The only post office (probably in all Ecuador) which deals in International Reply Coupons is in Quito, at Eloy Alfaro 354 y 9 de Octubre (new city). **For sending parcels**: up to 20 kg maximum dimensions permitted is 70 x 30 x 30 cms. Take contents and packaging (unpacked) to the Correo Marítimo Aduana, Ulloa 273 y Ramírez Dávalos (next to the Santa Clara Market – not a safe area), for customs inspection. Ask for SAL/APR (surface-air-lifted, reduced priority) rates for the cheapest tariffs. Parcels under 20 kg can also be sent from the post office at Reina Victoria y Colón. The Post

Office at the airport is more helpful and the smaller quantity of packages being handled should mean less chance of them going astray. Rates vary according to weight and destination. Packages under 2 kg can be sent 'certificado' (US$5.50 for 1 kg to the Americas, US$16 to rest of world; 2 kg US$9.15 within the Americas, US$30 other continents; for 3-5 kg US$33 within Americas, US$76 other continents) from the post offices at Espejo, entre Guayaquil y Venezuela, and at Eloy Alfaro. Rates quoted are for airmail: SAL/APR, surface-air-lifted rates are US$23 (3-5 kg) and US$32 (5-10 kg) to USA, US$28 and 43 elsewhere. Transpak (also called STAIR), Amazonas y Veintimilla, will ship out packages for about US$4/kg to USA, minimum charge about US$50. Letters for Europe bearing the correct Ecuadorean postage can be dropped off at the Lufthansa office, 6 de Diciembre 955 y 18 de Setiembre, to be sent in the next international bag; by 1200 on the day before the flight. Packages coming in to Ecuador should be less than 2 kg and of no stated value to avoid hefty import duty.

NB Some correspondents report that parcels and letters sent 'certificado' are more vulnerable to theft and that packages should be marked as 'used clothing' and the value declared as US$0.00. Even if not certifying your mail, watch to see that the stamps are franked (then they cannot be stolen). For cardboard boxes and large, strong, plastic-lined envelopes, try Japon Color Film Lab on Amazonas, Quito.

To receive mail, letters can be sent to Poste Restante/General Delivery (*lista de correos*), your embassy, or, for cardholders, American Express offices. Remember that there is no W in Spanish; look under V, or ask. For the smallest risk of misunderstanding, use title, initial and surname only. If having items sent to you by courier (eg DHL), do not use poste restante, but an address such as a hotel: a signature is required on receipt.

● **World Band Radio**

South America has more local and community radio stations than practically anywhere else in the world; a shortwave (world band) radio offers a practical means to brush up on the language, sample popular culture and absorb some of the richly varied regional music. International broadcasters such as the BBC World Service, the Voice of America, Boston (Mass)-based Monitor Radio International (operated by *Christian Science Monitor*) and the Quito-based Evangelical station, HCJB, keep the traveller abreast of news and events, in both English and Spanish.

Compact or miniature portables are recommended, with digital tuning and a full range of shortwave bands, as well as FM, long and medium wave. Detailed advice on radio models (£150 for a decent one) and wavelengths can be found in the annual publication, *Passport to World Band Radio* (Box 300, Penn's Park, PA 18943, USA). Details of local stations is listed in *World TV and Radio Handbook* (WTRH), PO Box 9027, 1006 AA Amsterdam, The Netherlands, US$19.95. Both of these, free wavelength guides and selected radio sets are available from the BBC World Service Bookshop, Bush House Arcade, Bush House, Strand, London WC2B 4PH, UK, T 0171-257 2576.

● **Telephone services**

All the principal towns have long-distance telephone facilities. Interprovincial phone calls must be prefixed by the following codes: Pichincha 02; Bolívar, Cotopaxi, Chimborazo, Pastaza, Tungurahua 03; Guayas 04; Galápagos, Los Ríos, Manabí 05; Carchi, Esmeraldas, Imbabura, Napo, Sucumbios 06; Azuay, Cañar, El Oro, Loja, Morona, Zamora 07. Discount period 1900-0700 and all day Sat-Sun: 3 mins to USA US$11 person to person (regular), US$9 (discount); to Europe US$13.60 person to person (regular), US$11 (discount). For international operator dial 116, normally only 5-20 mins wait for call to UK. There is an acute shortage of lines, expect long waits from outlying areas. Direct lines to foreign countries for collect or credit cards are available: dial 999 then for Brazil 177, Canada 175, Chile 179, Italy 174, Spain 176, Switzerland 160, UK 178, USA 119, 170, 171, 172. Collect calls can be made from Ecuador to some countries (not Australia, Denmark, Germany or Belgium). A charge is made for person-to-person calls even when the person is not there. Fax to Europe from US$7.10/page; to USA US$5.80/page; US$8.40 Asia and Oceania; US$3.70 Andean countries. Telegrams, ordinary US$4.30 first 7 words and US$0.57/word thereafter, nightletter US$0.20/word. There are public telex booths in the best hotels in Quito and Guayaquil (US$13.50 for 3 mins), and at Cuenca.

SPORT

The Sierra country is excellent for riding, and good horses can be hired. Quito, Guayaquil and Riobamba have polo clubs. There are golf clubs at Guayaquil and Quito and on the Santa Elena Peninsula. There is excellent big-game fishing for bonito and marlin off Playas, Salinas and Manta. Bull fighting is rarely seen at Guayaquil, but there is a well-known bullfight festival during the week preceding 6 Dec at Quito. A favourite sport is cock fighting; every town has its pits, but association football is fast taking over as the national sport. Volleyball and basketball are also popular. There is Sun horse-racing at Guayaquil.

For adventure sports in which visitors can participate, see the **Adventure Tourism** section at the beginning of the book.

HOLIDAYS AND FESTIVALS

1 Jan	New Year's Day
6 Jan	Reyes Magos y Día de los Inocentes
27 Feb	Día del Civismo
Lent	Mon and Tues before Lent (Carnival)
Easter	Holy Thursday; Good Friday; Holy Saturday
1 May	Labour Day
24 May	Battle of Pichincha
early June	Corpus Christi
24 July	Birthday of Bolívar
10 Aug	first attempt to gain the Independence of Quito, Opening of Congress
9 Oct	Independence of Guayaquil
12 Oct	Columbus' arrival in America
1 Nov	All Saints' Day
2 Nov	All Souls' Day
3 Nov	Independence of Cuenca and Manta
4 Nov	Independence of Azóguez and Bahía
6 Dec	Foundation of Quito
25 Dec	Christmas Day

Rounding up

ACKNOWLEDGEMENTS

The editor would like to thank: Robert and Daisy Kunstaetter and family, Quito, for their kind hospitality and their contributions; Jean Brown and David Gayton of Safari Tours, Quito; Damaris Carlisle and Melanie Ebertz, and other members of the South American Explorers Club, Quito; Darío Proaño-Leroux and Nicola Mears of Guacamayo Adventures-Marinatours, Bahía de Caráquez; Vicky Longland and Mike Powel, Guayaquil, David Horwell; Gavin Clark for his contributions on William Burroughs, Kurt Vonnegut and Robert Louis Stevenson; Simon Harvey and Mark Duffy; Geoffrey Taylor, Quito; Gavin Tinning, San Lorenzo; Judith Jane Barrett, Playa Escondida, Esmeraldas; Norma and Cleopatra of Albatros restaurant, Bahía de Caráquez; Camila and Jorge Velasco of Hotel Cocosolo, Cojimíes; Patricia and staff at the Youth Hostel, Guayaquil; Andy Hammerman and Michelle Kirby of The Black Sheep Inn at Chugchilán; all those travellers who wrote to the South American Handbook and whose letters have helped in the preparation of this Handbook; Katie Box for her help with the illustrations; Ben Box for his patience, knowledge, experience and invaluable help in putting together the finished product.

FURTHER READING

The History, Literature, Adventure Tourism, and The Galápagos Islands sections all contain suggestions for further reading as well as those for birdwatching, mountaineering and literature below. More general are: *The Ecotourist's Guide to the Ecuadorean Amazon*, by Rolf Wesche, 1995. *The Discovery of the Amazon*, edited by José Toribio Medina, translated by Bertram T Lee, edited by H C Heaton (New York: Dover, 1988). *Return of the Indian: Conquest and Revival in the Americas*, by Phillip Wearne (London: Cassell/Latin America Bureau, 1996). *El poder político en el Ecuador*, by Osvaldo Hurtado (Barcelona: Ariel, 1981). *5000 años de ocupación: Parque Nacional Machalilla*, edited by Presley Norton and Marco Vinicio García (Quito: Centro cultural Artes y Ediciones Abya-Yala, 1992), especially 'Las culturas cerámicas prehispánicas del Sur de Manabí', by Presley Norton, pages 9-40. *Living Poor*, by Moritz Thomsen (London: Eland). Also *Farm on the River of Emeralds. The Panama Hat Trail*, by Tom Miller (Abacus, 1986); Ecuador (Ediciones Libri Mundi); *Ecuador Island of the Andes*, by Kevin Kling and Nadia Christianson (London: Thames & Hudson, 1988).

380

Birdwatching

Dunning, JS *South American Land Birds – A photographic aid to identification*. Harrowood Books, USA, 1982; Fjeldsa, J and Krabbe, N: *Birds of the High Andes*, Apollow Books, Svendborg, Denmark, 1990; Heijnen, T *Birdwatching in Mainland Ecuador*, a guide to 75 Birding Sites, Eersel, The Netherlands, 1995; Hilty, S and Brown, W *A guide to the Birds of Colombia*, Princetown University Press, USA, 1986; Ortiz Crespo, F, Greenfield, PJ and Matheus JC *Birds of Ecuador*, locational checklist with English and Spanish common names, FEPROTUR, Quito, Ecuador, 1990; Taylor, K *A Birders Guide to Ecuador*, Victoria, B.C. Canada, 1995.

Literature

Jorge Enrique Adoum, *La gran literatura ecuatoriana del 30* (Quito: El Conejo, 1984); Benjamín Carrión, *El pensamiento vivo de Montalvo* (Buenos Aires: Losada, 1961); Jean Franco, *Spanish American Literature since Independence* (London, New York:Benn, 1973); Karl H Heise, *El Grupo de Guayaquil* (Madrid: Nova Scholar, 1975); Gerald Martin, *Journeys through the Labyrinth* (London, New York: Verso, 1989); Antonio Sacoto, *Catorce novelas claves de la literatura ecuatoriana* (Cuenca: 1990) and *The Indian in the Ecuadorian Novel* (New York: Las Americas, 1967); Darío Villanueva y José María Viña Liste, *Trayectoria de la novela hispanoamericana actual* (Madrid: Austral, 1991); Jason Wilson, *Traveller's Literary Companion: South and Central America* (Brighton: In Print, 1993). Thanks are also due to Anja Louis of Grant and Cutler, London, and Libri Mundi, Quito.

Mountaineering

Mountaineering journals include: *Campo Abierto* (not produced by the Travel Agency of the same name), an annual magazine on expeditions, access to mountains etc, US$1; *Montaña* is the annual magazine of the Colegio San Gabriel mountaineering club, US$1.50.

Recommended books are: *Montañas del Sol*, by Marcos Serrano, Iván Rojar and Freddy Landazuri, Ediciones Campo Abierto, 1994; it covers 20 main mountains and is an excellent introduction, it costs US$5; *Cotopaxi: Mountain of Light*, by Freddy Landazuri, Ediciones Campo Abierto, 1994, in English and Spanish, is a thorough history of the mountain. *The High Andes, A Guide for climbers*, by John Biggar (Castle Douglas, Kirkcudbrightshire, Scotland: Andes, 1996), has a chapter on Ecuador.

Maps and guide books

The Instituto Geográfico Militar in Quito (see page 122), produces a 1:1,000,000 map of Ecuador which is quite good, but large. 1:50,000 is good for hiking but 1:25,000 is too detailed to be accurate. A comprehensive road map (1989 edition) is also available as well as various other maps; e-mail igm2@igm.mil.ec. ITMB's 1:1,000,000 map of Ecu0ador, by Kevin Healey, 1994-96 edition, is available from ITMB Publishing Ltd, 345 West Broadway, Vancouver, BC, Canada, 5Y 1P8. A good series of pocket maps and city guides by Nélson Gómez, published by Ediguias in Quito, inc: *The Pocket Guide to Ecuador* (English), *Guía Turística del Ecuador* (Spanish), *Guía Vial del Ecuador* (road atlas), *Guía Informativa de Quito* (city guide), *Quito:*

Guía de Bolsillo (pocket map), *Guía del Area Metropolitana de Quito* (road atlas of the areas surrounding Quito), *Guía Informativa de Guayaquil* (city guide), and *Guía Informativa de Cuenca* (city guide). These are available in book shops throughout the country and by mail order from *Latin American Travel Consultants*, PO Box 17-17-908, Quito, Ecuador, F (593-2) 562-566, Internet: LATA@pi.pro.ec. Tourist maps and information are available from *Ecuatorial Publicaciones*, Av 10 de Agosto 4111 y Av Atahualpa, T 439-281, F 443-844, Casilla 17-16-1832 CEQ, Quito. See also **South American Explorers Club**, page 122. Stanfords, Long Acre, London, stock good road maps.

Information for business travellers is given (1) in 'Hints to Exporters: Ecuador', available from DTI Export Publications, PO Box 55, Stratford-upon-Avon, Warwickshire, CV37 9GE; (2) *Ecuadorean News Digest*, published by the Ecuadorean American Association, 150 Nassau St, New York, NY 10038. Telephone directories in Ecuador have 'green pages' giving useful tourist information, sometimes in English.

A recommended guide to climbing is *Climbing and Hiking in Ecuador*, by Rob Rachowiecki and Betsy Wagenhauser (published by Bradt Publications, 3rd edition 1994). Edward Whymper's, *Travels among the Great Andes of the Equator* (published by Gibbs M Smith, Salt Lake City) is available from Libri Mundi. Jorge Anhalzer publishes a series of five mountain guides, for each of Ecuador's most frequently climbed peaks, with updated information on routes to the summits. Available from book and camping shops, and by mail order from Latin American Travel Consultants, PO Box 17-17-908, Quito, F 593-2-562-566, Internet: LATA@pi.pro.ec. *Die Schneeberge Ecuador* by Marco Cruz, a German translation from Spanish is excellent, as is *Iberetur*, although it is difficult to find. See also under **Adventure Tourism**, **Mountaineering**, for the book *Montañas del Sol* and other details.

The **Latin American Travel Advisor** is a quarterly news bulletin with up-to-date detailed and reliable information on countries throughout South and Central America. The publication focuses on public safety, health, weather and natural phenomena, travel costs, the economy and politics in each country. Annual airmail subscriptions US$39, a single current issue US$15, information transmitted by fax or e-mail $10 per country. Payment by US$ cheque, MC or VISA (no money orders, credit card payments by mail or fax with card #,, expiry date, cardholder's name and signature). Contact PO Box 17-17-908, Quito, Ecuador, F +593-2-562-566, internet LATA@pi. pro.ec, World Wide Web http://www. amerispan.com/latc or http://www.greenarrow. com/latc.htm.

Useful addresses

Australia
388 George St, Suite 1702 A, American Express Tower NSW 2000, Sydney, 223-3266, 223-0041.

Belgium
Chaussée de Charleroi No 70, 1060 Brussels, T 0 537-9193, F 0 537-9066.

Canada
50 O'Connor Str #,1311, Ottawa, ON K1P 6L2, T 613 563-8206, F 613 235-5776, 151 Bloor St West, Suite 470 Toronto, Ontario M5S 1S4, T 416 968-2077, F 416 968-3348, 1010 Sainte Catherine W #,440, Montreal, QC H3B 3R3, T 514 874-4071, F 514 874-9078.

France
34 Ave de Messine, 75008 Paris, T 1 456 11021, F 1 425 60664

Germany
Koblenzer Strasse 37, 5300 Bonn 2, T 0 288 352544, F 0 228 361765.

New Zealand
Ferry Bldg, 2 Floor, Quai St, Auckland, T 09 309-0229, F 09 303-2931.

Sweden
Engelbrektsgatan 13, Box 260 95, S-100 41 Stockholm, T 0 679-6043, F 0 611-5593.

Switzerland
Helvetiastrasse 19-A, 3005 Berne, T 031 351-1755, F 031 351-2771.

UK
Flat 3B, 3 Hans Crescent, Knightsbridge, London, SW1X 0LS, T 0171 584-1367.

It does not seem to be very straightforward to obtain tourist information outside of Ecuador. The most reliable seems to be to contact Corporación Ecuatoriana de Turismo (Cetur), Eloy Alfaro 1214 y Carlos Tobar, Quito, T 507-559/560, F 507-564. Alternatively consult the Ecuadorian embassy or consulate in your own country who may be able to advise (see above). Cetur has now constructed an internet site http//mia.lac.net/mintur/ingles. Limited at the moment, Cetur are promising great things in the future. Details of tour operators, hotels etc can also be obtained from the Cetur site on EcuaNet's Tourism Page.

Details of Cetur offices within Ecuador are given under local information under the respective towns and cities.

Journey Latin America
16 Devonshire Road, Chiswick, London W4 2HD, T 0181-747 3108. Long established company running escorted tours throughout the region. They also offer a wide range of flight options.

Trailfinders
48 Earl's Court Road, London W8 6EJ, T 0171-938 3366.

South American Experience
47 Causton Street, Pimlico, London SW1P 4AT, T 0171 976 5511, F 0171 986 6908. Apart from booking flights and accommodation, also offer tailor-made trips.

Last Frontiers
Swan House, High Street, Long Crendon, Buckinghamshire, HP18 9AF, T 01844 208405. Offer a whole range of tours to

Ecuador including the Galápagos as well as other countries on the continent.

Passage to South America
Fovant Mews, 12 Nonya Road, London SW17 7PH, T 0181-767 8989. Wide range of tailor-made packages throughout the region including the lost kingdom of the Incas.

STA Travel
Priory House, 6 Wrights Lane, London W8 6TA, T 0171-938 4711

Cox & Kings Travel
St James Court, 45 Buckingham Gate, London, T 0171-873 5001

Ladatco Tours
Based in Miami, run "themed" explorer tours based around the Incas, mysticism etc. T USA (305) 854-8422 or F (305) 285-0504.

Hayes & Jarvis
152 King Street, London W6, T 0171 222 7844. Long established operator. Offers tailor-made itineraries as well as packages.

Adventure Travel Centre
131-135 Earls Court Road, London, SW5 9RH.

Galapagos Classic Cruises
6 Keyes Road, London NW2 3XA, T 0181 933 0613, F 0181 452 5248. Specialise in tailor-made cruises and diving holidays. Will also organise land tours to mainland Ecuador and Peru.

Galapagos Adventure Tours
37-39 Great Guldford Street, London SE1 0ES, T 0171 261 9890, F 0181 239 3266. Run by David Horwell who has an abundant knowledge of the Galapagos. Escorted tours to the islands as well as the Andes and rainforest.

Explore Worldwide
1 Frederick Street, Aldershot, Hants GU11 1LQ, T 01252 344161, F 01252 343170. Highly respected operator with offices in Eire, Australia,New Zealand, USA and Canada who run 2-5 week tours in more than 90 countries worldwide including Peru.

Useful words and phrases

N O AMOUNT of dictionaries, phrase books or word lists will provide the same enjoyment as being able to communicate directly with the people of the country you are visiting. Learning Spanish is an important part of the preparation for any trip to Ecuador and you are encouraged to make an effort to grasp the basics before you go. As you travel you will pick up more of the language and the more you know, the more you will benefit from your stay. The following section is designed to be a simple point of departure.

General pronunciation

The stress in a Spanish word conforms to one of three rules: 1) if the word ends in a vowel, or in **n** or **s**, the accent falls on the penultimate syllable (*ventana, ventanas*); 2) if the word ends in a consonant other than **n** or **s**, the accent falls on the last syllable (*hablar*); 3) if the word is to be stressed on a syllable contrary to either of the above rules, the acute accent on the relevant vowel indicates where the stress is to be placed (*pantalón, metáfora*). Note that adverbs such as *cuando*, 'when', take an accent when used interrogatively: *¿cuándo?*, 'when?'

Vowels

a not quite as short as in English 'cat'

e as in English 'pay', but shorter in a syllable ending in a consonant

i as in English 'seek'

o as in English 'shop', but more like 'pope' when the vowel ends a syllable

u as in English 'food'; after 'q' and in 'gue',

'gui', **u** is unpronounced; in 'güe' and 'güi' it is pronounced

y when a vowel, pronounced like 'i'; when a semiconsonant or consonant, it is pronounced like English 'yes'

ai, ay as in English 'ride'

ei, ey as in English 'they'

oi, oy as in English 'toy'

Unless listed below **consonants** can be pronounced in Spanish as they are in English.

b, v their sound is interchangeable and is a cross between the English 'b' and 'v', except at the beginning of a word or after 'm' or 'n' when it is like English 'b'

c like English 'k', except before 'e' or 'i' when it is as the 's' in English 'sip'

g before 'e' and 'i' it is the same as **j**

h when on its own, never pronounced

j as the 'ch' in the Scottish 'loch'

ll as the 'g' in English 'beige'; sometimes

as the 'lli' in 'million'

ñ as the 'ni' in English 'onion'

rr trilled much more strongly than in English

x depending on its location, pronounced as in English 'fox', or 'sip', or like 'gs'

z as the 's' in English 'sip'

GREETINGS, COURTESIES
hello
  hola
good morning
  buenos días
good afternoon/evening/night
  buenas tardes/noches
goodbye
  adiós/chao
see you later
  hasta luego
how are you?
  ¿cómo está?/¿cómo estás?
pleased to meet you
  mucho gusto/encantado/encantada
please
  por favor
thank you (very much)
  (muchas) gracias
yes
  sí
no
  no
excuse me/I beg your pardon
  permiso
I do not understand
  no entiendo
please speak slowly
  hable despacio por favor
what is your name
  ¿cómo se llama?
Go away!
  ¡Váyase!

BASIC QUESTIONS
where is_?
  ¿dónde está_?
how much does it cost?
  ¿cuánto cuesta?
how much is it?
  ¿cuánto es?
when?
  ¿cuándo?
when does the bus leave?

¿a qué hora sale el autobus?
  - arrive?
  - llega -
why?
  ¿por qué?
what for?
  ¿para qué?
what time is it?
  ¿qué hora es?
how do I get to_?
  ¿cómo llegar a_?
is this the way to the church?
  ¿la iglesia está por aquí?

BASICS
bathroom/toilet
  el baño
police (policeman)
  la policía (el policía)
hotel
  el hotel (la pensión,el residencial, el alojamiento)
restaurant
  el restaurante
post office
  el correo
telephone office
  el centro de llamadas
supermarket
  el supermercado
bank
  el banco
exchange house
  la casa de cambio
exchange rate
  la tasa de cambio
notes/coins
  los billetes/las monedas
travellers' cheques
  los travelers/los cheques de viajero
cash
  el efectivo
breakfast
  el desayuno
lunch
  el almuerzo
dinner/supper
  la cena
meal
  la comida
drink
  la bebida
mineral water

el agua mineral
soft fizzy drink
la gaseosa/cola
beer
la cerveza
without sugar
sin azúcar
without meat
sin carne

Getting around
on the left/right
a la izquierda/derecha
straight on
derecho
second street on the left
la segunda calle a la izquierda
to walk
caminar
bus station
la terminal (terrestre)
train station
la estación (de tren/ferrocarril)
bus
el bus/el autobus/ la flota/el colectivo/ el micro etc
train
el tren
airport
el aeropuerto
aeroplane/airplane
el avión
first/second class
primera/segunda clase
ticket
el boleto
ticket office
la taquilla
bus stop
la parada

ACCOMMODATION

room
el cuarto/la habitación
single/double
sencillo/doble
with two beds
con dos camas
with private bathroom
con baño
hot/cold water
agua caliente/fría
noisy
ruidoso

to make up/clean
limpiar
sheets
las sábanas
blankets
las mantas
pillows
las almohadas
clean/dirty towels
toallas limpias/sucias
toilet paper
el papel higiénico
Chemist
farmacia
(for) pain
(para) dolor
stomach
el estómago
head
la cabeza
fever/sweat
la fiebre/el sudor
diarrhoea
la diarrea
blood
la sangre
altitude sickness
el soroche
doctor
el médico
condoms
los preservativos
contraceptive (pill)
anticonceptivo (la píldora anticonceptiva)
period/towels
la regla/las toallas
contact lenses
las lentes de contacto
aspirin
la aspirina

TIME

at one o'clock
a la una
at half past two/ two thirty
a las dos y media
at a quarter to three
a cuarto para las tres
or a las tres menos quince
it's one o'clock
es la una
it's seven o'clock
son las siete

it's twenty past six/
six twenty
  son las seis y veinte
it's five to nine
  son cinco para las nueve/
  son las nueve menos cinco
in ten minutes
  en diez minutos
five hours
  cinco horas
does it take long?
  ¿tarda mucho?
Monday lunes
Tuesday martes
Wednesday miercoles
Thursday jueves
Friday viernes
Saturday sábado
Sunday domingo
January enero
February febrero
March marzo
April abril
May mayo
June junio
July julio
August agosto
September septiembre
October octubre
November noviembre
December diciembre

NUMBERS

one uno/una
two dos
three tres
four cuatro
five cinco
six seis
seven siete
eight ocho
nine nueve
ten diez
eleven once
twelve doce
thirteen trece
fourteen catorce
fifteen quince
sixteen dieciseis

seventeen diecisiete
eighteen dieciocho
nineteen diecinueve
twenty veinte
twenty one, two veintiuno, veintidos etc
thirty treinta
forty cuarenta
fifty cincuenta
sixty sesenta
seventy setenta
eighty ochenta
ninety noventa
hundred cien or ciento
thousand mil

KEY VERBS

To Go
  ir
I go voy; you go (familiar singular) vas; he, she, it goes, you (unfamiliar singular) go va; we go vamos; they, you (plural) go van.

To Have (possess)
  tener
tengo; tienes; tiene; tenemos; tienen (also used as To Be, as in 'I am hungry' tengo hambre)
(**NB** haber also means to have, but is used with other verbs, as in 'he has gone' ha ido. he; has; ha; hemos; han.
Hay means 'there is'; perhaps more common is No hay meaning 'there isn't any')

To Be (in a permanent state)
  ser
soy (profesor - I am a teacher); eres; es; somos; son.
To Be (positional or temporary state)
  estar
estoy (en Londres - I am in London); estás; está (contenta - she is happy); estamos; están.

This section has been compiled on the basis of glossaries compiled by André de Mendonça and David Gilmour of South American Experience, London, and the Latin American Travel Advisor, No 9, March 1996.

Health in Latin America

WITH the following advice and precautions you should keep as healthy as you do at home. Most visitors return home having experienced no problems at all apart from some travellers' diarrhoea. In Latin America the health risks, especially in the lowland tropical areas, are different from those encountered in Europe or the USA. It also depends on where and how you travel. There are clear health differences between the countries of Latin America and in risks for the business traveller, who stays in international class hotels in large cities, the backpacker trekking from country to country and the tourist who heads for the beach. There is huge variation in climate, vegetation and wildlife from the deserts of Chile to the rain forests of Amazonia and from the icy remoteness of Andean peaks, to the teeming capital cities. There are no hard and fast rules to follow; you will often have to make your own judgment on the healthiness or otherwise of your surroundings. There are English (or other foreign language) speaking doctors in most major cities who have particular experience in dealing with locally-occurring diseases. Your Embassy representative will often be able to give you the name of local reputable doctors and most of the better hotels have a doctor on standby. If you do fall ill and cannot find a recommended doctor, try the Outpatient Department of a hospital – private hospitals are usually less crowded and offer a more acceptable standard of care to foreigners.

BEFORE TRAVELLING

Take out medical insurance. Make sure it covers all eventualities especially evacuation to your home country by a medically equipped plane, if necessary. You should have a dental check up, obtain a spare glasses prescription, a spare oral contraceptive prescription (or enought pills to last) and, if you suffer from a chronic illness (such as diabetes, high blood pressure, ear or sinus troubles, cardio-pulmonary disease or nervous disorder) arrange for a check up with your doctor, who can at the same time provide you with a letter explaining the details of your disability in English and if possible Spanish and/or Portuguese. Check the current practice in countries you are visiting for malaria prophylaxis (prevention). If you are on regular medication, make sure you have enough to cover the period of your travel.

Children

More preparation is probably necessary for babies and children than for an adult and perhaps a little more care should be taken when travelling to remote areas where health services are primitive. This is because children can be become more rapidly ill than adults (on the other hand they often recover more quickly). Diarrhoea and vomiting are the most common problems, so take the usual precautions, but more intensively. Breastfeeding is best and most convenient for babies, but powdered milk is generally available and so are baby foods in most countries. Papaya, bananas and avocados are all nutritious and can be cleanly prepared. The treatment of diarrhoea is the same for adults, except that it should start earlier and be continued with more persistence. Children get dehydrated very quickly in hot countries and can become drowsy and uncooperative unless cajoled to drink water or juice plus salts. Upper respiratory infections, such as colds, catarrh and middle ear infections are also common and if your child suffers from these normally take some antibiotics against the possibility. Outer ear infections after swimming are also common and antibiotic eardrops will help. Wet wipes are always useful and sometimes difficult to find in South America, as, in some places are disposable nappies.

MEDICINES AND WHAT TO TAKE

There is very little control on the sale of drugs and medicines in South America. You can buy any and every drug in pharmacies without a prescription. Be wary of this because pharmacists can be poorly trained and might sell you drugs that are unsuitable, dangerous or old. Many drugs and medicines are manufactured under licence from American or European companies, so the trade names may be familiar to you. This means you do not have to carry a whole chest of medicines with you, but remember that the shelf life of some items, especially vaccines and antibiotics, is markedly reduced in hot conditions. Buy your supplies at the better outlets where there are refrigerators, even though they are more expensive and check the expiry date of all preparations you buy. Immigration officials occasionally confiscate scheduled drugs (Lomotil is an example) if they are not accompanied by a doctor's prescription.

Self-medication may be forced on you by circumstances so the following text contains the names of drugs and medicines which you may find useful in an emergency or in out-of-the-way places. You may like to take some of the following items with you from home:

Sunglasses
ones designed for intense sunlight

Earplugs
for sleeping on aeroplanes and in noisy hotels

Suntan cream
with a high protection factor

Insect repellent
containing DET for preference

Mosquito net
lightweight, permethrin-impregnated for choice

Tablets
for travel sickness

Tampons
can be expensive in some countries in Latin America

Condoms

Contraceptives

Water sterilising tablets

Antimalarial tablets

Anti-infective ointment eg Cetrimide

Dusting powder for feet etc
containing fungicide

Antacid tablets
for indigestion

Sachets of rehydration salts
plus anti-diarrhoea preparations

Painkillers
such as Paracetamol or Aspirin

Antibiotics
for diarrhoea etc

First Aid kit
Small pack containing a few sterile syringes
and needles and disposable gloves. The risk
of catching hepatitis etc from a dirty needle
used for injection is now negligible in Latin
America, but some may be reassured by
carrying their own supplies – available from
camping shops and airport shops.

Vaccination and immunisation
Smallpox vaccination is no longer required
anywhere in the world. Neither is cholera
vaccination recognised as necessary for international travel by the World Health Or-
ganisation – it is not very effective either.
Nevertheless, some immigration officials
are demanding proof of vaccination against
cholera in Latin America and in some countries outside Latin America, following the
outbreak of the disease which originated in
Peru in 1990-91 and subsequently affected
most surrounding countries. Although very
unlikely to affect visitors to Latin America,
the cholera epidemic continues making its
greatest impact in poor areas where water
supplies are polluted and food hygiene
practices are insanitary.

Vaccination against the following diseases
are recommended:

Yellow Fever
This is a live vaccination not to be given to
children under 9 months of age or persons
allergic to eggs. Immunity lasts for 10 years,
an International Certificate of Yellow Fever
Vaccination will be given and should be kept
because it is sometimes asked for. Yellow
fever is very rare in Latin America, but the
vaccination is practically without side effects and almost totally protective.

Typhoid

A disease spread by the insanitary preparation of food. A number of new vaccines
against this condition are now available; the
older TAB and monovalent typhoid vaccines
are being phased out. The newer, eg Typhim
Vi, cause less side effects, but are more
expensive. For those who do not like injections, there are now oral vaccines.

Poliomyelitis
Despite its decline in the world this remains
a serious disease if caught and is easy to
protect against. There are live oral vaccines
and in some countries injected vaccines.
Whichever one you choose it is a good idea
to have booster every 3-5 years if visiting
developing countries regularly.

Tetanus
One dose should be given with a booster
at 6 weeks and another at 6 months and
10 yearly boosters thereafter are recommended. Children should already be properly protected against diphtheria,
poliomyelitis and pertussis (whooping
cough), measles and HIB all of which can
be more serious infections in Latin America
than at home. Measles, mumps and rubella
vaccine is also given to children throughout
the world, but those teenage girls who have
not had rubella (german measles) should be
tested and vaccinated. Hepatitis B vaccination for babies is now routine in some
countries. Consult your doctor for advice on
tuberculosis inoculation: the disease is still
widespread in Latin America.

Infectious Hepatitis
Is less of a problem for travellers than it used
to be because of the development of two
extremely effective vaccines against the A
and B form of the disease. It remains common, however, in Latin America. A combined hepatitis A & B vaccine is now licensed
and will be available in 1997 – one jab
covers both diseases.

Other vaccinations:
Might be considered in the case of epidemics eg meningitis. There is an effective vaccination against rabies which should be
considered by all travellers, especially those
going through remote areas or if there is a
particular occupational risk, eg for zoolo-
gists or veterinarians.

FURTHER INFORMATION

Further information on health risks abroad, vaccinations etc may be available from a local travel clinic. If you wish to take specific drugs with you such as antibiotics these are best prescribed by your own doctor. Beware, however, that not all doctors can be experts on the health problems of remote countries. More detailed or more up-to-date information than local doctors can provide are available from various sources. In the UK there are hospital departments specialising in tropical diseases in London, Liverpool, Birmingham and Glasgow and the Malaria Reference Laboratory at the London School of Hygiene and Tropical Medicine provides free advice about malaria, T 0891 600350. In the USA the local Public Health Services can give such information and information is available centrally from the Centre for Disease Control (CDC) in Atlanta, T (404) 3324559.

There are additional computerised databases which can be assessed for destination-specific up-to-the-minute information. In the UK there is MASTA (Medical Advisory Service to Travellers Abroad), T 0171 631 4408, F 0171 436 5389, Tx 8953473 and Travax (Glasgow, T 0141 946 7120, ext 247). Other information on medical problems overseas can be obtained from the book by Dawood, Richard (Editor) (1992) *Travellers' Health: How to stay healthy abroad*, Oxford University Press 1992, £7.99. We strongly recommend this revised and updated edition, especially to the intrepid traveller heading for the more out of the way places. General advice is also available in the UK in *Health Information for Overseas Travel* published by the Department of Health and available from HMSO, and *International Travel and Health* published by WHO, Geneva.

STAYING HEALTHY

INTESTINAL UPSETS

The thought of catching a stomach bug worries visitors to Latin America but there have been great improvements in food hygiene and most such infections are preventable. Travellers' diarrhoea and vomiting is due, most of the time, to food poisoning,

usually passed on by the insanitary habits of food handlers. As a general rule the cleaner your surroundings and the smarter the restaurant, the less likely you are to suffer.

Foods to avoid: uncooked, undercooked, partially cooked or reheated meat, fish, eggs, raw vegetables and salads, especially when they have been left out exposed to flies. Stick to fresh food that has been cooked from raw just before eating and make sure you peel fruit yourself. Wash and dry your hands before eating – disposable wet-wipe tissues are useful for this.

Shellfish eaten raw are risky and at certain times of the year some fish and shellfish concentrate toxins from their environment and cause various kinds of food poisoning. The local authorities notify the public not to eat these foods. Do not ignore the warning. **Heat treated milk** (UHT) pasteurised or sterilised is becoming more available in Latin America as is pasteurised cheese. On the whole matured or processed cheeses are safer than the fresh varieties and fresh unpasteurised milk from whatever animal can be a source of food poisoning germs, tuberculosis and brucellosis. This applies equally to icecream, yoghurt and cheese made from unpasteurised milk, so avoid these homemade products – the factory made ones are probably safer.

Tap water is rarely safe outside the major cities, especially in the rainy season. Stream water, if you are in the countryside, is often contaminated by communities living surprisingly high in the mountains. Filtered or bottled water is usually available and safe, although you must make sure that somebody is not filling bottles from the tap and hammering on a new crown cap. If your hotel has a central hot water supply this water is safe to drink after cooling. Ice for drinks should be made from boiled water, but rarely is so stand your glass on the ice cubes, rather than putting them in the drink. The better hotels have water purifying systems.

TRAVELLERS' DIARRHOEA

This is usually caused by eating food which has been contaminated by food poisoning germs. Drinking water is rarely the culprit.

Water purification

There are a number of ways of purifying water in order to make it safe to drink. Dirty water should first be strained through a filter bag (camping shops) and then boiled or treated. Bringing water to a rolling boil at sea level is sufficient to make the water safe for drinking, but at higher altitudes you have to boil the water for longer to ensure that all the microbes are killed.

There are sterilising methods that can be used and there are proprietary preparations containing chlorine (eg Puritabs) or iodine (eg Pota Aqua) compounds. Chlorine compounds generally do not kill protozoa (eg giardia).

There are a number of water filters now on the market available in personal and expedition size. They work either on mechanical or chemical principles, or may do both. Make sure you take the spare parts or spare chemicals with you and do not believe *everything* the manufacturers say.

Sea water or river water is more likely to be contaminated by sewage and so swimming in such dilute effluent can also be a cause.

Infection with various organisms can give rise to travellers' diarrhoea. They may be viruses, bacteria, eg Escherichia coli (probably the most common cause worldwide), protozoal (such as amoebas and giardia), salmonella and cholera. The diarrhoea may come on suddenly or rather slowly. It may or may not be accompanied by vomiting or by severe abdominal pain and the passage of blood or mucus when it is called dysentery.

How do you know which type you have caught and how to treat it?

If you can time the onset of the diarrhoea to the minute ("acute") then it is probably due to a virus or a bacterium and/or the onset of dysentery. The treatment in addition to rehydration is Ciprofloxacin 500 mg every 12 hrs; the drug is now widely available and there are many similar ones.

If the diarrhoea comes on slowly or intermittently ("sub-acute") then it is more likely to be protozoal, ie caused by an amoeba or giardia. Antibiotics such a Ciprofloxacin will have little effect. These cases are best treated by a doctor as is any outbreak of diarrhoea continuing for more than 3 days. Sometimes blood is passed in ameobic dysentery and for this you should certainly seek medical help. If this is not available then the best treatment is probably Tinidazole (Fasigyn) 1 tablet four times a day for 3 days. If there are severe stomach cramps, the following drugs may help but

are not very useful in the management of acute diarrhoea: Loperamide (Imodium) and Diphenoxylate with Atropine (Lomotil) They should not be given to children.

Any kind of diarrhoea, whether or not accompanied by vomiting, responds well to the replacement of water and salts, taken as frequent small sips, of some kind of rehydration solution. There are proprietary preparations consisting of sachets of powder which you dissolve in boiled water or you can make your own by adding half a teaspoonful of salt (3.5 gms) and 4 tablespoonsful of sugar (40 gms) to a litre of boiled water.

Thus the lynch pins of treatment for diarrhoea are rest, fluid and salt replacement, antibiotics such as Ciprofloxacin for the bacterial types and special diagnostic tests and medical treatment for the amoeba and giardia infections. Salmonella infections and cholera, although rare, can be devastating diseases and it would be wise to get to a hospital as soon as possible if these were suspected.

Fasting, peculiar diets and the consumption of large quantities of yoghurt have not been found useful in calming travellers' diarrhoea or in rehabilitating inflamed bowels. Oral rehydration has on the other hand, especially in children, been a life saving technique and should always be practised, whatever other treatment you use. As there is some evidence that alcohol and milk might prolong diarrhoea they should be avoided during and immediately after an attack.

Diarrhoea occurring day after day for long periods of time (chronic diarrhoea) is notoriously resistent to amateur attempts at treatment and again warrants proper diagnostic tests (most towns with reasonable sized hospitals have laboratories for stool samples). There are ways of preventing travellers' diarrhoea for short periods of time by taking antibiotics, but this is not a foolproof technique and should not be used other than in exceptional circumstances. Doxycycline is possibly the best drug. Some preventatives such as Enterovioform can have serious side effects if taken for long periods.

Paradoxically **constipation** is also common, probably induced by dietary change, inadequate fluid intake in hot places and long bus journeys. Simple laxatives are useful in the short-term and bulky foods such as maize, beans and plenty of fruit are also useful.

HIGH ALTITUDE

Spending time at high altitude in South America, especially in the tropics, is usually a pleasure – it is not so hot, there are no insects and the air is clear and spring like. Travelling to high altitudes, however, can cause medical problems, all of which can be prevented if care is taken.

On reaching heights above about 3,000m, heart pounding and shortness of breath, especially on exertion are a normal response to the lack of oxygen in the air. A condition called acute mountain sickness (*Soroche* in South America) can also affect visitors. It is more likely to affect those who ascend rapidly, eg by plane and those who over-exert themselves (teenagers for example). Soroche takes a few hours or days to come on and presents with a bad headache, extreme tiredness, sometimes dizziness, loss of appetite and frequently nausea and vomiting. Insomnia is common and is often associated with a suffocating feeling when lying in bed. Keen observers may note their breathing tends to wax and wane at night and their face tends to be puffy in the mornings – this is all part of the syndrome. Anyone can get this condition and past experience is not always a good guide: the author, having spent years in Peru travelling

constantly between sea level and very high altitude never suffered symptoms, then was severely affected whilst climbing Kilimanjaro in Tanzania.

The treatment of acute mountain sickness is simple – rest, painkillers, (preferably not aspirin based) for the headache and anti sickness pills for vomiting. Oxygen is actually not much help, except at very high altitude. Various local panaceas – Coramina glucosada, Effortil, Micoren are popular in Latin America and mate de coca (an infusion of coca leaves widely available and perfectly legal) will alleviate some of the symptoms.

To **prevent** the condition: on arrival at places over 3,000m have a few hours rest in a chair and avoid alcohol, cigarettes and heavy food. If the symptoms are severe and prolonged, it is best to descend to a lower altitude and to reascend slowly or in stages. If this is impossible because of shortage of time or if you are going so high that acute mountain sickness is very likely, then the drug Acetazolamide (Diamox) can be used as a preventative and continued during the ascent. There is good evidence of the value of this drug in the prevention of soroche, but some people do experience peculiar side effects. The usual dose is 500 mg of the slow release preparation each night, starting the night before ascending above 3,000m.

Watch out for **sunburn** at high altitude. The ultraviolet rays are extremely powerful. The air is also excessively dry at high altitude and you might find that your skin dries out and the inside of your nose becomes crusted. Use a moisturiser for the skin and some vaseline wiped into the nostrils. Some people find contact lenses irritate because of the dry air. It is unwise to ascend to high altitude if you are pregnant, especially in the first 3 months, or if you have a history of heart, lung or blood disease, including sickle cell.

A more unusual condition can affect mountaineers who ascend rapidly to high altitude – **acute pulmonary oedema**. Residents at altitude sometimes experience this when returning to the mountains from time spent at the coast. This condition is often preceded by acute mountain sickness and comes on quite rapidly with severe breathlessness, noisy breathing, cough, blueness of the lips and frothing at the mouth. Anybody who develops this must be brought down as soon as possible, given oxygen and taken to hospital.

A rapid descent from high places will make sinus problems and middle ear infections worse and might make your teeth ache. Lastly, don't fly to altitude within 24 hrs of Scuba diving. You might suffer from 'the bends'.

HEAT AND COLD

Full acclimatisation to high temperatures takes about 2 weeks. During this period it is normal to feel a bit apathetic, especially if the relative humidity is high. Drink plenty of water (up to 15 litres a day are required when working physically hard in the tropics), use salt on your food and avoid extreme exertion. Tepid showers are more cooling than hot or cold ones. Large hats do not cool you down, but do prevent sunburn. Remember that, especially in the highlands, there can be a large and sudden drop in temperature between sun and shade and between night and day, so dress accordingly. Warm jackets or woollens are essential after dark at high altitude. Loose cotton is still the best material when the weather is hot.

INSECTS

These are mostly more of a nuisance than a serious hazard and if you try, you can prevent yourself entirely from being bitten. Some, such as mosquitos are, of course, carriers of potentially serious diseases, so it is sensible to avoid being bitten as much as possible. Sleep off the ground and use a mosquito net or some kind of insecticide. Preparations containing Pyrethrum or synthetic pyrethroids are safe. They are available as aerosols or pumps and the best way to use these is to spray the room thoroughly in all areas (follow the instructions rather than the insects) and then shut the door for a while, re-entering when the smell has dispersed. Mosquito coils release insecticide as they burn slowly. They are widely available and useful out of doors. Tablets of insecticide which are placed on a heated mat plugged into a wall socket are probably the most effective. They fill the room with insecticidal fumes in the same way as aerosols or coils.

You can also use insect repellents, most of which are effective against a wide range of pests. The most common and effective is diethyl metatoluamide (DET). DET liquid is best for arms and face (care around eyes and with spectacles – DET dissolves plastic). Aerosol spray is good for clothes and ankles and liquid DET can be dissolved in water and used to impregnate cotton clothes and mosquito nets. Some repellents now contain DET and Permethrin, insecticide. Impregnated wrist and ankle bands can also be useful.

If you are bitten or stung, itching may be relieved by cool baths, antihistamine tablets (care with alcohol or driving) or mild corticosteroid creams, eg. hydrocortisone (great care: never use if any hint of infection). Careful scratching of all your bites once a day can be surprisingly effective. Calamine lotion and cream have limited effectiveness and antihistamine creams are not recommended – they can cause allergies themselves.

Bites which become infected should be treated with a local antiseptic or antibiotic cream such as Cetrimide, as should any infected sores or scratches.

When living rough, skin infestations with body lice (crabs) and scabies are easy to pick up. Use whatever local commercial preparation is recommended for lice and scabies. Crotamiton cream (Eurax) alleviates itching and also kills a number of skin parasites. Malathion lotion 5% (Prioderm) kills lice effectively, but avoid the use of the toxic agricultural preparation of Malathion, more often used to commit suicide.

TICKS

They attach themselves usually to the lower parts of the body often after walking in areas where cattle have grazed. They take a while to attach themselves strongly, but swell up as they start to suck blood. The important thing is to remove them gently, so that they do not leave their head parts in your skin because this can cause a nasty allergic reaction some days later. Do not use petrol, vaseline, lighted cigarettes etc to remove the tick, but, with a pair of tweezers remove the beast gently by gripping it at the attached (head) end and rock it out in very much the same way that a tooth is extracted. Certain tropical flies which lay their eggs under the skin of sheep and cattle also occasionally do the same thing to humans with the unpleasant result that a maggot grows under the skin and pops up as a boil or pimple. The best way to remove these is to cover the boil with oil, vaseline or nail varnish so as to stop the maggot breathing, then to squeeze it out gently the next day.

SUNBURN

The burning power of the tropical sun, especially at high altitude, is phenomenal.

Always wear a wide brimmed hat and use some form of suncream lotion on untanned skin. Normal temperate zone suntan lotions (protection factor up to 7) are not much good; you need to use the types designed specifically for the tropics or for mountaineers or skiers with protection factors up to 15 or above. These are often not available in Latin America. Glare from the sun can cause conjunctivitis, so wear sunglasses especially on tropical beaches, where high protection factor sunscreen should also be used.

PRICKLY HEAT

A very common intensely itchy rash is avoided by frequent washing and by wearing loose clothing. Cured by allowing skin to dry off through use of powder and spending two nights in an airconditioned hotel!

ATHLETES FOOT

This and other fungal skin infections are best treated with Tolnaftate or Clotrimazole.

OTHER RISKS AND MORE SERIOUS DISEASES

Remember that rabies is endemic throughout Latin America, so avoid dogs that are behaving strangely and cover your toes at night from the vampire bats, which also carry the disease. If you are bitten by a domestic or wild animal, do not leave things to chance: scrub the wound with soap and water and/or disinfectant, try to have the animal captured (within limits) or at least determine its ownership, where possible, and seek medical assistance at once. The course of treatment depends on whether you have already been satisfactorily vaccinated against rabies. If you have (this is worthwile if you are spending lengths of time in developing countries) then some further doses of vaccine are all that is required. Human diploid vaccine is the best, but expensive: other, older kinds of vaccine, such as that derived from duck embryos may be the only types available. These are effective, much cheaper and interchangeable generally with the human derived types. If not already vaccinated then anti rabies serum (immunoglobulin) may be required in addition. It is important to finish the course of treatment whether the animal survives or not.

AIDS

In South America AIDS is increasing but is not wholly confined to the well known high risk sections of the population, ie homosexual men, intravenous drug abusers and children of infected mothers. Heterosexual transmission is now the dominant mode and so the main risk to travellers is from casual sex. The same precautions should be taken as with any sexually transmitted disease. The Aids virus (HIV) can be passed by unsterilised needles which have been previously used to inject an HIV positive patient, but the risk of this is negligible. It would, however, be sensible to check that needles have been properly sterilised or disposable needles have been used. If you wish to take your own disposable needles, be prepared to explain what they are for. The risk of receiving a blood transfusion with blood infected with the HIV virus is greater than from dirty needles because of the amount of fluid exchanged. Supplies of blood for transfusion should now be screened for HIV in all reputable hospitals, so again the risk is very small indeed. Catching the AIDS virus does not always produce an illness in itself (although it may do). The only way to be sure if you feel you have been put at risk is to have a blood test for HIV antibodies on your return to a place where there are reliable laboratory facilities. The test does not become positive for some weeks.

MALARIA

In South America malaria is theoretically confined to coastal and jungle zones, but is now on the increase again. Mosquitos do not thrive above 2,500m, so you are safe at altitude. There are different varieties of malaria, some resistant to the normal drugs. Make local enquiries if you intend to visit possibly infected zones and use a prophylactic regime. Start taking the tablets a few days before exposure and continue to take them for 6 weeks after leaving the malarial zone. Remember to give the drugs to babies and children also. Opinion varies on the precise drugs and dosage to be used for protection. All the drugs may have some side effects and it is important to balance the risk of catching the disease against the albeit rare side effects. The increasing complexity of the subject is such that as the malarial parasite becomes immune to the new generation of drugs it has made concentration on the physical prevention from being bitten by mosquitos more important. This involves the use of long sleeved shirts or blouses and long trousers, repellants and nets. Clothes are now available impregnated with the insecticide Permethrin or Deltamethrin or it is possible to impregnate the clothes yourself. Wide meshed nets impregnated with Permethrin are also available, are lighter to carry and less.claustrophobic to sleep in.

Prophylaxis and treatment

If your itinerary takes you into a malarial area, seek expert advice before you go on a suitable prophylactic regime. This is especially true for pregnant women who are particularly prone to catch malaria. You can still catch the disease even when sticking to a proper regime, although it is unlikely. If you do develop symptoms (high fever, shivering, headache, sometimes diarrhoea), seek medical advice immediately. If this is not possible and there is a great likelihood of malaria, the treatment is:

Chloroquine, a single dose of 4 tablets (600 mg) followed by 2 tablets (300 mg) in 6 hrs

and 300 mg each day following.

Falciparum type of malaria or type in doubt: take local advice. Various combinations of drugs are being used such as Quinine, Tetracycline or Halofantrine. If falciparum type malaria is definitely diagnosed, it is wise to get to a good hospital as treatment can be complex and the illness very serious.

INFECTIOUS HEPATITIS (JAUNDICE)

The main symptoms are pains in the stomach, lack of appetite, lassitude and yellowness of the eyes and skin. Medically speaking there are two main types. The less serious, but more common is Hepatitis A for which the best protection is the careful preparation of food, the avoidance of contaminated drinking water and scrupulous attention to toilet hygiene. The other, more serious, version is Hepatitis B which is acquired usually as a sexually transmitted disease or by blood transfusions. It can less commonly be transmitted by injections with unclean needles and possibly by insect bites. The symptoms are the same as for Hepatitis A. The incubation period is much longer (up to 6 months compared with 6 weeks) and there are more likely to be complications.

Hepatitis A can be protected against with gamma globulin. It should be obtained from a reputable source and is certainly useful for travellers who intend to live rough. You should have a shot before leaving and have it repeated every 6 months. The dose of gamma globulin depends on the concentration of the particular preparation used, so the manufacturer's advice should be taken. The injection should be given as close as possible to your departure and as the dose depends on the likely time you are to spend in potentially affected areas, the manufacturer's instructions should be followed. Gamma globulin has really been superceded now by a proper vaccination against Hepatitis A (Havrix) which gives immunity lasting up to 10 years. After that boosters are required. Havrix monodose is now widely available as is Junior Havrix. The vaccination has negligible side effects and is extremely effective. Gamma globulin injections can be a bit painful, but it is much cheaper than Havrix and may be more available in some places.

Hepatitis B can be effectively prevented by a specific vaccine (Engerix) – 3 shots over 6 months before travelling. If you have had jaundice in the past it would be worthwhile having a blood test to see if you are immune to either of these two types, because this might avoid the necessity and costs of vaccination or gamma globulin. There are other kinds of viral hepatitis (C, E etc) which are fairly similar to A and B, but vaccines are not available as yet.

TYPHUS

Can still occur carried by ticks. There is usually a reaction at the site of the bite and a fever. Seek medical advice.

INTESTINAL WORMS

These are common and the more serious ones such as hookworm can be contracted from walking barefoot on infested earth or beaches.

Various other tropical diseases can be caught in jungle areas, usually transmitted by biting insects. They are often related to African diseases and were probably introduced by the slave labour trade. Onchocerciasis (river blindness) carried by black flies is found in parts of Mexico and Venezuela. Leishmaniasis (Espundia) is carried by sandflies and causes a sore that will not heal or a severe nasal infection. Wearing long trousers and a long sleeved shirt in infected areas protects against these flies. DET is also effective. Epidemics of meningitis occur from time-to-time. Be careful about swimmimg in piranha or caribe infested rivers. It is a good idea not to swim naked: the Candiru fish can follow urine currents and become lodged in body orifices. Swimwear offers some protection.

LEPTOSPIROSIS

Various forms of leptospirosis occur throughout Latin America, transmitted by a bacterium which is excreted in rodent urine. Fresh water and moist soil harbour the organisms which enter the body through cuts and scratches. If you suffer from any form of prolonged fever consult a doctor.

SNAKE BITE

This is a very rare event indeed for travellers. If you are unlucky (or careless) enough to be bitten by a venomous snake, spider, scorpion or sea creature, try to identify the creature, but do not put yourself in further danger. Snake bites in particular are very frightening, but in fact rarely poisonous – even venomous snakes bite without injecting venom. What you might expect if bitten are: fright, swelling, pain and bruising around the bite and soreness of the regional lymph glands, perhaps nausea, vomiting and a fever. Signs of serious poisoning would be the following symptoms: numbness and tingling of the face, muscular spasms, convulsions, shortness of breath and bleeding. Victims should be got to a hospital or a doctor without delay. Commercial snake bite and scorpion kits are available, but usually only useful for the specific type of snake or scorpion for which they are designed. Most serum has to be given intravenously so it is not much good equipping yourself with it unless you are used to making injections into veins. It is best to rely on local practice in these cases, because the particular creatures will be known about locally and appropriate treatment can be given.

Treatment of snake bite Reassure and comfort the victim frequently. Immobilise the limb by a bandage or a splint or by getting the person to lie still. Do not slash the bite area and try to suck out the poison because this sort of heroism does more harm than good. If you know how to use a tourniquet in these circumstances, you will not need this advice. If you are not experienced do not apply a tourniquet.

Precautions

Avoid walking in snake territory in bare feet or sandals – wear proper shoes or boots. If you encounter a snake stay put until it slithers away, and do not investigate a wounded snake. Spiders and scorpions may be found in the more basic hotels, especially in the Andean countries. If stung, rest and take plenty of fluids and call a doctor. The best precaution is to keep beds away from the walls and look inside your shoes and under the toilet seat every morning. Certain tropical sea fish when trodden upon inject venom into bathers' feet. This can be exceptionally painful. Wear plastic shoes when you go bathing if such creatures are reported. The pain can be relieved by immersing the foot in extremely hot water for as long as the pain persists.

DENGUE FEVER

This is increasing worldwide including in South and Central American countries and the Caribbean. It can be completely prevented by avoiding mosquito bites in the same way as malaria. No vaccine is available. Dengue is an unpleasant and painful disease, presenting with a high temperature and body pains, but at least visitors are spared the more serious forms (haemorrhagic types) which are more of a problem for local people who have been exposed to the disease more than once. There is no specific treatment for dengue – just pain killers and rest.

CHAGAS' DISEASE (SOUTH AMERICAN TRYPANOSOMIASIS)

This is a chronic disease, very rarely caught by travellers and difficult to treat. It is transmitted by the simultaneous biting and excreting of the Reduvid bug, also known as the Vinchuca or Barbeiro. Somewhat resembling a small cockroach, this nocturnal bug lives in poor adobe houses with dirt floors often frequented by opossums. If you cannot avoid such accommodation, sleep off the floor with a candle lit, use a mosquito net, keep as much of your skin covered as possible, use DET repellent or a spray insecticide. If you are bitten overnight (the bites are painless) do not scratch them, but wash thoroughly with soap and water.

DANGEROUS ANIMALS

Apart from mosquitos the most dangerous animals are men, be they bandits or behind steering wheels. Think carefully about violent confrontations and wear a seat belt if you are lucky enough to have one available to you.

WHEN YOU RETURN HOME

Remember to take your antimalarial tablets for 6 weeks after leaving the malarial area. If you have had attacks of diarrhoea it is worth having a stool specimen tested in case you have picked up amoebas. If you have been living rough, blood tests may be worthwhile to detect worms and other parasites. If you have been exposed to bilharzia (*schistosomiasis*) by swimming in lakes etc, check by means of a blood test when you get home, but leave it for 6 weeks because the test is slow to become positive. Report any untowards symptoms to your doctor and tell the doctor exactly where you have been and, if you know, what the likelihood of disease is to which you were exposed.

The above information has been compiled for us by Dr David Snashall, who is presently Senior Lecturer in Occupational Health at the United Medical Schools of Guy's and St Thomas' Hospitals in London and Chief Medical Adviser to the British Foreign and Commonwealth Office. He has travelled extensively in Central and South America, worked in Peru and in East Africa and keeps in close touch with developments in preventative and tropical medicine.

Travelling with children

People contemplating overland travel in South America with children should remember that a lot of time can be spent waiting for buses, trains, and especially for aeroplanes. On bus journeys, if the children are good at amusing themselves, or can readily sleep while travelling, the problems can be considerably lessened. If your child is of an early reading age, take reading material with you as it is difficult, and expensive to find. A bag of, say 30 pieces, of Duplo or Lego can keep young children occupied for hours. Travel on trains, while not as fast or at times as comfortable as buses, allows more scope for moving about. Some trains provide tables between seats, so that games can be played. Beware of doors left open for ventilation especially if air-conditioning is not working.

Food

Food can be a problem. It is easier to take biscuits, drinks, bread etc with you on longer trips than to rely on meal stops where the food may not be to taste. Avocados are safe, easy to eat and nutritious; they can be fed to babies as young as 6 months and most older children like them. A small immersion heater and jug for making hot drinks is invaluable, but remember that electric current varies. Try and get a dual-voltage one (110v and 220v). Agua Linda is a good and safe bottled water for young children.

Nappies Luggis are the best disposable nappies/diapers, other makes are useless.

Fares

On all long-distance buses you pay for each seat, and there are no half-fares if the children occupy a seat each. For shorter trips it is cheaper, if less comfortable, to seat small children on your knee. Often there are spare seats which children can occupy after tickets have been collected. In city and local excursion buses, small children generally do not pay a fare, but are not entitled to a seat when paying customers are standing. On sightseeing tours you should *always* bargain for a family rate – often children can go free. (In trains, reductions for children are general, but not universal.)

All civil airlines charge half for children under 12, but some military services don't have half-fares, or have younger age limits. Note that a child travelling free on a long excursion is not always covered by the operator's travel insurance; it is adviseable to pay a small premium to arrange cover.

Hotels

In all hotels, try to negotiate family rates. If charges are per person, always insist that two children will occupy one bed only, therefore counting as one tariff. If rates are per bed, the same applies. In either case you can almost always get a reduced rate at cheaper hotels. Occasionally when travelling with a child you will be refused a room in a hotel that is 'unsuitable'. On river boat trips, unless you have very large hammocks, it may be more comfortable and cost effective to hire a 2-berth cabin for 2 adults and a child. (In restaurants, you can normally buy children's helpings, or divide one full-size helping between two children.)

Travel with children can bring you into closer contact with Latin American families and, generally, presents no special problems – in fact the path is often smoother for family groups. Officials tend to be more amenable and they are pleased if your child knows a little Spanish. Moreover, even thieves and pickpockets seem to have some of the traditional respect for families, and may leave you alone because of it!

Year planner

1997

J	F	M	A	M	J	J	A	S	O	N	D
								1			1
			1			1		2			2
1			2			2		3	1		3
2		1	3	1		3		4	2		4
3		2	4	2		4	1	5	3		5
4	1	1	5	3		5	2	6	4	1	6
5	2	2	6	4	1	6	3	7	5	2	7
6	3	3	7	5	2	7	4	8	6	3	8
7	4	4	8	6	3	8	5	9	7	4	9
8	5	5	9	7	4	9	6	10	8	5	10
9	6	6	10	8	5	10	7	11	9	6	11
10	7	7	11	9	6	11	8	12	10	7	12
11	8	8	12	10	7	12	9	13	11	8	13
12	9	9	13	11	8	13	10	14	12	9	14
13	10	10	14	12	9	14	11	15	13	10	15
14	11	11	15	13	10	15	12	16	14	11	16
15	12	12	16	14	11	16	13	17	15	12	17
16	13	13	17	15	12	17	14	18	16	13	18
17	14	14	18	16	13	18	15	19	17	14	19
18	15	15	19	17	14	19	16	20	18	15	20
19	16	16	20	18	15	20	17	21	19	16	21
20	17	17	21	19	16	21	18	22	20	17	22
21	18	18	22	20	17	22	19	23	21	18	23
22	19	19	23	21	18	23	20	24	22	19	24
23	20	20	24	22	19	24	21	25	23	20	25
24	21	21	25	23	20	25	22	26	24	21	26
25	22	22	26	24	21	26	23	27	25	22	27
26	23	23	27	25	22	27	24	28	26	23	28
27	24	24	28	26	23	28	25	29	27	24	29
28	25	25	29	27	24	29	26	30	28	25	30
29	26	26	30	28	25	30	27		29	26	31
30	27	27		29	26	31	28		30	27	
31	28	28		30	27		29		31	28	
		29		31	28		30			29	
		30			29		31			30	
		31			30						

Year planner

1998

J	F	M	A	M	J	J	A	S	OO	NN	DD
					1						
					2			1			1
			1		3	1		2			2
1			2		4	2		3	1		3
2			3	1	5	3		4	2		4
3			4	2	6	4	1	5	3		5
4	1	1	5	3	7	5	2	6	4	1	6
5	2	2	6	4	8	6	3	7	5	2	7
6	3	3	7	5	9	7	4	8	6	3	8
7	4	4	8	6	10	8	5	9	7	4	9
8	5	5	9	7	11	9	6	10	8	5	10
9	6	6	10	8	12	10	7	11	9	6	11
10	7	7	11	9	13	11	8	12	10	7	12
11	8	8	12	10	14	12	9	13	11	8	13
12	9	9	13	11	15	13	10	14	12	9	14
13	10	10	14	12	16	14	11	15	13	10	15
14	11	11	15	13	17	15	12	16	14	11	16
15	12	12	16	14	18	16	13	17	15	12	17
16	13	13	17	15	19	17	14	18	16	13	18
17	14	14	18	16	20	18	15	19	17	14	19
18	15	15	19	17	21	19	16	20	18	15	20
19	16	16	20	18	22	20	17	21	19	16	21
20	17	17	21	19	23	21	18	22	20	17	22
21	18	18	22	20	24	22	19	23	21	18	23
22	19	19	23	21	25	23	20	24	22	19	24
23	20	20	24	22	26	24	21	25	23	20	25
24	21	21	25	23	27	25	22	26	24	21	26
25	22	22	26	24	28	26	23	27	25	22	27
26	23	23	27	25	29	27	24	28	26	23	28
27	24	24	28	26	30	28	25	29	27	24	29
28	25	25	29	27		29	26	30	28	25	30
29	26	26	30	28		30	27		29	26	31
30	27	27		29		31	28		30	27	
31	28	28		30			29		31	28	
		29		31			30			29	
		30					31			30	
		31									

Year planner

1999

J	F	M	A	M	J	J	A	S	OO	NN	DD
										1	
					1					2	
					2			1		3	1
			1		3	1		2		4	2
1			2		4	2		3	1	5	3
2			3	1	5	3		4	2	6	4
3			4	2	6	4	1	5	3	7	5
4	1	1	5	3	7	5	2	6	4	8	6
5	2	2	6	4	8	6	3	7	5	9	7
6	3	3	7	5	9	7	4	8	6	10	8
7	4	4	8	6	10	8	5	9	7	11	9
8	5	5	9	7	11	9	6	10	8	12	10
9	6	6	10	8	12	10	7	11	9	13	11
10	7	7	11	9	13	11	8	12	10	14	12
11	8	8	12	10	14	12	9	13	11	15	13
12	9	9	13	11	15	13	10	14	12	16	14
13	10	10	14	12	16	14	11	15	13	17	15
14	11	11	15	13	17	15	12	16	14	18	16
15	12	12	16	14	18	16	13	17	15	19	17
16	13	13	17	15	19	17	14	18	16	20	18
17	14	14	18	16	20	18	15	19	17	21	19
18	15	15	19	17	21	19	16	20	18	22	20
19	16	16	20	18	22	20	17	21	19	23	21
20	17	17	21	19	23	21	18	22	20	24	22
21	18	18	22	20	24	22	19	23	21	25	23
22	19	19	23	21	25	23	20	24	22	26	24
23	20	20	24	22	26	24	21	25	23	27	25
24	21	21	25	23	27	25	22	26	24	28	26
25	22	22	26	24	28	26	23	27	25	29	27
26	23	23	27	25	29	27	24	28	26	30	28
27	24	24	28	26	30	28	25	29	27		29
28	25	25	29	27		29	26	30	28		30
29	26	26	30	28		30	27		29		31
30	27	27		29		31	28		30		
31	28	28		30			29		31		
		29		31			30				
		30					31				
		31									

TEMPERATURE CONVERSION TABLE

°C	°F	°C	°F
1	34	26	79
2	36	27	81
3	38	28	82
4	39	29	84
5	41	30	86
6	43	31	88
7	45	32	90
8	46	33	92
9	48	34	93
10	50	35	95
11	52	36	97
12	54	37	99
13	56	38	100
14	57	39	102
15	59	40	104
16	61	41	106
17	63	42	108
18	64	43	109
19	66	44	111
20	68	45	113
21	70	46	115
22	72	47	117
23	74	48	118
24	75	49	120
25	77	50	122

The formula for converting °C to °F is:
$$°C \times 9 \div 5 + 32 = °F$$

WEIGHTS AND MEASURES

Metric

Weight
1 Kilogram (Kg) = 2.205 pounds
1 metric ton = 1.102 short tons

Length
1 millimetre (mm)= 0.03937 inch
1 metre = 3.281 feet
1 kilometre (km) = 0.621 mile

Area
1 heactare = 2.471 acres
1 square km = 0.386 sq mile

Capacity
1 litre = 0.220 imperial gallon
 = 0.264 US gallon

Volume
1 cubic metre (m³) = 35.31 cubic feet
 = 1.31 cubic yards

British and US

Weight
1 pound (lb) = 454 grams
1 short ton (2,000lbs) = 0.907 m ton
1 long ton (2,240lbs) = 1.016 m tons

Length
1 inch = 25.417 millimetres
1 foot (ft) = 0.305 metre
1 mile = 1.609 kilometres

Area
1 acre = 0.405 hectare
1 sq mile = 2.590 sq kilometre

Capacity
1 imperial gallon = 4.546 litres
1 US gallon = 3.785 litres

Volume
1 cubic foot (cu ft) = 0.028 m³
1 cubic yard (cu yd) = 0.765 m³

NB 5 imperial gallons are approximately equal to 6 US gallons

Tinted boxes

Advertisers

Illustrations

Index

Maps

Map Symbols

Administration

International Border

State / Province Border

Cease Fire Line

Neighbouring country

Neighbouring state

State Capitals

Other Towns

Roads and travel

Main Roads
(National Highways)

Other Roads

Jeepable Roads, Tracks

Railways with station

Water features

River   *Amazon*

Lakes, Reservoirs, Tanks

Seasonal Marshlands

Sand Banks, Beaches

Ocean

Waterfall

Ferry

Topographical features

Contours (approx),
Rock Outcrops

Mountains

Mountain Pass

Gorge

Escarpment

Palm trees

Cities and towns

Built Up Areas

One Way Street

National Parks, Gardens, Stadiums

Fortified Walls

Airport

Banks

Bus Stations (named in key)

Hospitals

Market

Police station

Post Office

Telegraphic Office

Tourist Office

Key Numbers

Bridges

Cathedral, church

Guided routes

National parks, trekking areas

National Parks and
Bird Sanctuaries

Hide

Camp site

Refuge

Motorable track

Walking track

Other symbols

Archaeological Sites

Places of Interest

Viewing point

Footprint Handbooks

All of us at Footprint Handbooks hope you have enjoyed reading and travelling with this Handbook, one of the first published in the new Footprint series. Many of you will be familiar with us as Trade & Travel, a name that has served us well for years. For you and for those who have only just discovered the Handbooks, we thought it would be interesting to chronicle the story of our development from the early 1920's.

It all started 75 years ago in 1921, with the publication of the Anglo-South American Handbook. In 1924 the South American Handbook was created. This has been published each year for the last 73 years and is the longest running guidebook in the English language, immortalised by Graham Greene as "the best travel guide in existence".

One of the key strengths of the South American Handbook over the years, has been the extraordinary contact we have had with our readers through their hundreds of letters to us in Bath. From these letters we learnt that you wanted more Handbooks of the same quality to other parts of the world.

In 1989 my brother Patrick and I set about developing a series modelled on the South American Handbook. Our aim was to create the ultimate practical guidebook series for all travellers, providing expert knowledge of far flung places, explaining culture, places and people in a balanced, lively and clear way. The whole idea hinged, of course, on finding writers who were in tune with our thinking. Serendipity stepped in at exactly the right moment: we were able to bring together a talented group of people who know the countries we cover inside out and whose enthusiasm for travelling in them needed to be communicated.

The series started to grow. We felt that the time was right to look again at the identity that had brought us all this way. After much searching we commissioned London designers Newell & Sorrell to look at all the issues. Their solution was a new identity for the Handbooks representing the books in all their aspects, looking after all the good things already achieved and taking us into the new millennium.

The result is Footprint Handbooks: a new name and mark, simple yet assertive, bold, stylish and instantly recognisable. The images we use conjure up the essence of real travel and communicate the qualities of the Handbooks in a straightforward and evocative way.

For us here in Bath, it has been an exciting exercise working through this dramatic change. Already the 'new us' fits like our favourite travelling clothes and we cannot wait to get more and more Footprint Handbooks onto the book shelves and out onto the road.

The Footprint list

Andalucía Handbook
Cambodia Handbook
Caribbean Islands Handbook
Chile Handbook
East Africa Handbook
Ecuador Handbook
  with the Galápagos
Egypt Handbook
India Handbook
Indonesia Handbook
Laos Handbook
Malaysia & Singapore Handbook
Mexico & Central America
  Handbook
Morocco Handbook
  with Mauritania
Myanmar (Burma) Handbook
Namibia Handbook
Pakistan Handbook
Peru Handbook
South Africa Handbook
South American Handbook
Sri Lanka Handbook
Thailand Handbook
Tibet Handbook
Tunisia Handbook with Libya
Vietnam Handbook
Zimbabwe & Malawi Handbook
  with Botswana, Moçambique &
  Zambia

New in Autumn 1997
Israel Handbook
Nepal Handbook

In the pipeline
Argentina Handbook
Brazil Handbook
Colombia Handbook
Cuba Handbook
Jordan, Syria & Lebanon Handbook
Venezuela Handbook

Footprint T-shirt

The Footprint T-shirt is available in 100% cotton in various colours.

Mail Order

Footprint Handbooks are available worldwide in good bookstores. They can also be ordered directly from us in Bath (see below for address). Please contact us if you have difficulty finding a title.

The Footprint Handbook website will be coming to keep you up to date with all the latest news from us (http://www.footprint-handbooks.co.uk). For the most up-to-date information and to join our mailing list please contact us at:

Footprint Handbooks
6 Riverside Court
Lower Bristol Road
Bath BA2 3DZ, England
T +44(0)1225 469141
F +44(0)1225 469461
E Mail handbooks@footprint.cix.co.uk